Neerihiinjìk

We Traveled From Place To Place

Johnny Sarah Hàa Googwandak
The Gwich'in Stories of Johnny and Sarah Frank

Third Edition

Edited with introductory essays by Craig Mishler
With Kenneth Drizhuu Frank and Crystal Frank Welker

Transcribed and translated by Judy Erick, Lillian Garnett, and Mary Rose Roberts, with assistance from Ron Frank and Kenneth Drizhuu Frank

Copy editing and tone marking by Katherine Peter and Jeff Leer

Song transcriptions by Tony Scott Pearce

Family tree compiled by Kenneth Frank, Craig Mishler, and Crystal Frank Welker

Alaska Native Language Center
2026

Copublished by the Alaska Native Language Center and University Press of Colorado

Alaska Native Language Center
PO Box 757680
Fairbanks, AK 99775-7680

University Press of Colorado
1580 North Logan Street, Suite 660
PMB 39883
Denver, Colorado 80203-1942

Library of Congress Control Number: 2026930976
ISBN 978-1-55500-142-1

Cover photo: Johnny and Sarah Frank, Gold Camp, 1974 by Mike Holloway, courtesy of Margie Gibson
Back cover photo: Johnny and Sarah Frank, Arctic Village, 1927 by John. B. Mertie, Jr., courtesy of U.S. Geological Survey photo archives, Denver
Layout and editing: Lillian Maassen, Alaska Native Language Center

First Edition, 1995
Second Edition, 2001
Third Edition, 2026

This book was made possible through funding provided by the National Endowment for the Humanities, the Yukon Flats School District, and the Alaska Humanities Forum.

The University Press of Colorado is a proud member of the Association of University Presses.

The University Press of Colorado is a cooperative publishing enterprise supported, in part, by Adams State University, Colorado School of Mines, Colorado State University, Fort Lewis College, Metropolitan State University of Denver, Regis University, University of Colorado, University of Northern Colorado, University of Wyoming, Utah State University, and Western Colorado University.

Let us honor the sacred languages of the Indigenous peoples of Alaska, whose words, stories, prayers, and guidance are respectfully recorded in these few pages. The origins of these languages are unknown, but they have been treasured, spoken, and lived by the first peoples of Alaska. As we read and learn, let us respect both the speakers who brought these languages to us and the ones who learned the written form to share with our peoples and our friends throughout the world.

Neerihiinjìk

We Traveled From Place To Place

Johnny Sarah Hàa Googwandak
The Gwich'in Stories of Johnny and Sarah Frank

Third Edition

Contents

Illustrations

Preface

The passing of Johnny and Sarah Frank of Venetie and Gold Camp, in the upland boreal forest of northeastern Alaska, draws attention to two individuals who figured prominently in the history of 20th century Gwich'in Athabaskan Indians. The Gwich'in are an Indigenous nation of tribes whose wilderness homeland extends well above the Arctic Circle for thousands of square miles, from the Mackenzie River delta of Canada's Northwest Territories westward through the northern Yukon Territory to the Chandalar River in northeast Alaska. Theirs is a land of extreme winter cold and summer heat. Their population is small in comparison with the size of their territory. About three thousand people occupy a dozen small villages, most of them well off the road system.

Johnny and Sarah lived most of their lives in remote areas far from these villages, yet their extraordinary ability to touch and shape the lives of their children, grandchildren, community, and tribal group was due to their abundant social warmth, manifest intelligence, clean living, and great physical health. Master storytellers, Johnny and Sarah both lived well into their nineties and transmitted their traditional Indian lifeways and language to several younger generations. Both individually and together, they offer us a portal to western Gwich'in history and prehistory.

The Franks' great reputation as rugged people steeped in subsistence methods and versed in the old ways attracted scholars and folklore enthusiasts who sensed the importance of their vanishing way of life. Starting in 1933 with Robert McKennan, one of the first professional anthropologists to work with the Gwich' in, a number of individuals have felt inspired to document Johnny and Sarah's stories, songs, beliefs, and reflections in field notes and on tape. I am lucky to be among them.

Johnny's stories are dramatically focused on the days of long ago — the adventures of Indian warriors such as Tł'eevì Tì', Ool Tì' Kǫ̀'ehdan, and Gogwhaii, and the feats and songs of powerful medicine men such as Dak Neehaa and Khagoohoonjik Tì'. Johnny himself was a medicine man and a singer who greatly enjoyed performing for an audience. Sarah, on the other hand, was gentle and soft-spoken. Her stories are shaped around her own daily life experiences and her practical knowledge of how to live off the country in times of adversity and hardship. Together, their repertoires complement and balance each other beautifully — not only the masculine and and the feminine, the hunter and the gatherer, but also the idealist and the realist, the visionary dreamer and the meticulous sewer of waterproof pants, the singing shaman and the vigilant nurse. Although they lived lives of great hardship and suffering, their loving partnership gave them the strength and balance to survive times of famine, extreme cold, isolation, and the deaths of ten of their fourteen children.

From this perspective, the humor, songs, games, and narrative arts of Johnny and Sarah Frank add individually and collectively to our understanding of the creative human spirit and the human condition. How the Franks survived as a family is a microcosm of how the Gwich' in survived as a nation, often moving camp every day to locate game, sharing food with others less fortunate even when it added to their own hardship, providing leadership to the villages of Venetie and Arctic Village, and living with strength and dignity in one of the world's harshest, most unforgiving environments. This book is a special treasure box of their own words and the words of their ancestors. *Neerihiinjìk* has become a touchstone and a reference point for Indigenous language performance.

Fig. 1. Aerial view of the K'aii'eechų'njik at Gold Camp, where the Frank family lived for more than forty years. Photo by Ron Kent, BIA ANCSA, 1983.

Notes on the Third Edition

Background

Since the 2nd edition of *Neerihiinjìk* went out of print in early 2020, demand for copies has continued, and we were invited by Siri Tuttle, former ANLC Director, to work on a 3rd edition. Unfortunately, we were unable to locate the digital files used for the 2nd edition, released 24 years ago. Craig found copies of the files on 3½" floppy disks, but these proved to be unreadable on today's software and operating systems. We sent the floppies off to a lab specializing in retrieving and restoring lost files, but even they were unable to retrieve the original Gwich'in.

Without the master files, there were only two options: completely retype the book from scratch or scan in all the pages from the second edition. We chose the latter. This was a fairly slow and tedious process, since the OCR scanning software available to us did not recognize specialized Gwich'in characters such the barred-l (ł) or nasalized vowels such as ąįį or tonal diacritics such as à, ě, ù, and ô.

All of these characters had to be hand-edited. It really gets complicated when there's a vowel with both a low tone and a nasal, in a word like dą̀į'. Most of these marks had to be inserted by hand, one at a time, after the file was scanned and converted from a PDF to a Microsoft Word document. Whenever possible, we speeded up the restoration process using Word's search and replace function, but even this required dozens of search-and-replacements for each story.

Since 2020, only used copies of the 2nd edition have been available and have recently commanded a price of anywhere from $500 to $928 — certainly not affordable to anyone except wealthy collectors. By releasing this 3rd edition, we hope that this collective Gwich'in classic is now accessible to all Gwich'in language learners and scholars, as well as to casual readers who wish to discover the exciting and beautiful world that Johnny and Sarah knew.

Orthography and Errata

Since the appearance of the 2nd edition in 2001, some speakers and writers of the language have started calling it Dinjii Zhuh K'yaa instead of Gwich'in. While we respect this shift, we have retained Gwich'in as the name of the language and of the tribal group who speak it. This is due to what was accepted as the standard linguonym and ethnonym during the time when this book was first conceived in the early 1990s. For us, Gwich'in is not a pejorative term and is certainly an improvement over Kutchin in terms of phonetic accuracy. On the other hand, we've changed the translation of Ch'eekwaii from "Eskimo" to "Inuit" to acknowledge a less pejorative term (see especially Part III).

In the first two editions, the four Gwich'in sequences (*chy', tły', try', ky'*) were so spelled out of respect for the wishes of the Frank family. Following a change of mind by family members in recent years, they are now shown here according to the standard practiced at the Alaska Native Language Center *(ch'y*, *tł'y, tr'y,* and *k'y)*. We also decided to standardize certain word combinations as implemented in other recent publications (see for example Mishler and Frank, 2020). Most notably, we now write the common conjunction *aii ts'ą̀'* as *aiits'ą̀'*, while *aii tł'ee* is now *aiitł'ee.*

During our review of the 2nd edition, Kenneth Frank and I noticed there were numerous gaps and mistakes in the original translation that required close attention. Due to time constraints that prevented us from re-transcribing and re-translating all of the recordings, Kenneth and I decided to identify and fix the problematic areas in each story by focusing on selected passages and pages. Here and there we also added extra punctuation to both the Gwich'in and the English texts to define lines and eliminate long run-on sentences.

-Nyaa, Gwich'in Verbs of Saying

In many Native American languages, verbs of saying are part and parcel of narration. Who says what is important, so direct reported speech and indirect reported speech are both carefully marked by the accompanying reporting speech. For example, "'Look out!' he said": The words "Look out!" are the reported or quoted speech, and the words "he said" are the reporting speech.

When I was a graduate student, I published a paper in the European folklore journal *Fabula* called "'He Said, They Say': the Uses of Reporting Speech in Native American Folk Narrative" (Mishler 1981). In this essay I essentially collected together verb stems equivalent to the English verb "they say" or "it is said" for eighteen Native American languages based on their recurrence in a wide variety of published scholarly texts. Since then I've added stems from four additional languages (Mishler and Frank 2023:161-174).

A comparison of hundreds of texts showed that Indigenous language verbs for "say" provide a common if not universal common denominator for understanding the artistic voices of storytellers, particularly when the texts are traditional in the generic sense that they were not based on the storyteller's personal experience or life history, but passed down instead from many generations of elders.

In my 50 years of fieldwork with Gwich'in speakers in northeastern Alaska and the Yukon, I've learned Gwich'in storytellers are especially conscious of distinguishing between their own words and those of their ancestors, so they are very careful not to claim traditional story ownership or appropriate their ancestors' vernacular speech. Doing so would be both disrespectful and plagiaristic. My continued fascination lies with discovering just how many forms of saying there are in Gwich'in, and how verbs of saying are cleverly doubled or tripled up to establish the quotative. In Gwich'in, the verb stem for the English "say" or "tell" is *-nyaa*, pronounced *-nuu* in Canadian Gwich'in dialects.

-Nyaa is especially fascinating because of its large inflectional paradigm. I've been collecting these for many years from both oral and written sources and have discovered that even fluent speakers get them confused. One reason for this confusion is that there are so many variants and they are used almost unconsciously and unreflexively in narration. They are so common, in fact, that they often go by almost unnoticed when Gwich'in speakers are translating texts into English. To date, Kenneth and I have identified and listed well over a hundred inflections, with little doubt that there are still many, many others in print or in oral circulation that we may have missed (see Mishler and Frank, 2023 Chapters 8, 9, and

Appendix B). This huge list illustrates the richness and complexity of the language.

In Gwich'in storytelling these inflections are often tacked on at the end of sentences to tell us who said what. In oral traditions, of course, there are no quotation marks. Even in English the only way to signify quotation marks orally is to say "Quote" and "Unquote," or to hold up both hands with the two index and middle fingers extended. In Gwich'in, many variants of *-nyaa* may be understood as aural quotation marks. And their presence in texts tells us much more than who said what.

When we edited the first two editions of *Neerihiinjìk*, we were not fully conscious of the full paradigm of *-nyaa*, and so some of our fluent translators did not translate them all. These omissions largely escaped us. When we came back to the texts again in 2023, we realized that these verbs were probably left out because they are highly repetitive. In English, they might even be perceived as slightly annoying. However, we now see these verbs of saying as poetic constructs which greatly amplify the rhythm and voices of the stories, especially when they get doubled up, as in *jyaa nyaa, varahnyaa* ('that's what he said, they say'). Consequently, we have gone to great lengths to restore them in the new 3rd edition translations, trusting that readers will grasp their power and significance in Gwich'in oral tradition. Instances of reporting speech such as *nyaa*, *gwinyaa*, and *varahnyaa* are just the most common overt manifestations of an underlying ethnopoetic sensibility. But they are only the tip of the iceberg. You may now find them and enjoy them in both Johnny's and Sarah's stories.

Ch'iteehàakwąįį

Over the summer of 2020, Kenneth and I worked online for a long time on a new line-by-line translation for the Ch'iteehàakwąįį story cycle. Due to time and funding constraints, Ch'iteehàakwąįį is now the only story in the book with a new fully revised translation, although we also targeted isolated "trouble spots" in the transcription and translation of many other stories. The vast majority of the texts have now been significantly sharpened, both in Gwich'in and in English.

With the story of Ch'iteehàkwąįį, Kenneth and I went back and started largely from scratch, re-listening to the original tape recordings and correcting much of the Gwich'in transcript as well as the English translation.

What we discovered in Ch'iteehàakwąįį is something new and surprising about the storytellers' point of view, a kind of breakthrough. In both Johnny's and Sarah's variants of the story, there are a number of pronoun shifts from "he" and "him" and "his" to "we" and "us" and "our." This shift to the second person plural point of view has the rhetorical effect of inviting the listener in to be a part of the story. It's also something that our original translator either largely overlooked or perhaps felt was awkward to read in English. Yet pronoun shifts clearly have a strong literary effect and deepen our understanding of Gwich'in oral tradition. For additional detailed insights and contexts please see our essay, "They Haven't Found Us Yet": Pronoun Shifts in Gwich'in Conversation (Mishler and Frank, 2023:209-216).

Here's an example from the episode of "Ch'iteehàakwąįį and Frog" told by Sarah. Compare this new translation below with the old one found in the second edition of *Neerihiinjìk*:

6.30 Aiitł'ee chan hee, chan hee yeetèedhakwąįį izhìk it'ee
t'inyąą, vàràhnyàa (adlaa).
Diinaah'in gwiizhik,
"Dèiinch'yaa shijiindèe khìdhįį'aii ch'yaa gwįįch'in?"
danàhnyą̀ą.

Original translation:

On his way back, he canoed back to shore where the frog
was, and they say the frog looked at him and said
(laughs),
"Aren't you the one who has my hook?"

New translation:

Once again, he paddled right up to the frog on the shore
and told him right there, they say (laughs).
While he [*Frog*] was looking at **us**,
"Don't you look just like the one who took my hook?"
he told **us**.

Here's another example, told by Johnny, when Wolverine is pestering Ch'iteehàakwąįį after catching him in his trap. Compare the granularity of this with the original translation:

15.10 Aii gwiizhik ch'aghwarh thah t'àa'ą̀įį, nàhtryàa aii.
"Ah! Nadhalzhòo," nyaa.
Ts'ą̀' t'ee reh **dii**nanh gwahjòk tthak chan gwahjòk vàràhnyàa.

Original translation:

On his waist *Wolverine* had a wood hammer which he used as a weapon.
"Ah! I'm going to tickle you!" he said.
He even tickled *Ch'iteehàakwąįį* to make sure he was dead.

New translation:

On his waist band *Wolverine* had a stone axe.
"Ah! Nadhalzhòo," he said.
So he's tickling **us** all over, tickling **us** again and again, they say.

Here, we would expect that Wolverine was in fact tickling **him**, Ch'iteehàakwąįį, all over **his** body. But Kenneth's insight into a new and more accurate translation helps readers more fully appreciate the depth and richness of Johnny and Sarah's verbal art, their dynamic authorial voices and narrative presence. These subtle pronoun shifts, displayed in prefixes, are numerous in the Ch'iteehàakwąįį story and open our eyes and ears, adding another humorous and personal dimension to Gwich'in expressive culture.

With these and other pronoun shifts we, the listeners and readers of the story, begin to represent Ch'iteehàakwąįį and thus magically become characters *in* the story. Such tropes, many of which are identified in the story's footnotes, are not commonly found in English, except perhaps in experimental fiction or in the "we" found in newspaper editorials.

Illustrations

We've used virtually all of the photos and maps from previous editions, but we are happy to announce that one important new photo is that of the Ch'atthanh or Ice Bear, taken near Dawson City by Peter Mather. This photo proves that such bears still exist and still pose a threat to people living in the wilderness during the winter. We have also added a new cover photo, taken of Johnny and Sarah by the late Dr. Mike Holloway and provided to us by his wife, Margie Ann Gibson.

Frank Family Tree

Finally, Crystal Frank Welker, Kenneth's daughter and Johnny and Sarah's great granddaughter, has worked actively and admirably on an update of the Frank family tree in Appendix A, contacting many of her relatives for information about all the children born since the second edition appeared in 2001. If you figure that a generation amounts to 20-30 years, Crystal has now added a whole new eighth generation to the tree. She has also added a Foreword to this new edition that shares her moving personal perspective.

— Craig Mishler, November, 2025

Foreword

by Crystal Frank-Welker

I am the great-granddaughter to Johnny and Sarah Frank. All my life I've always believed I had a spiritual connection to my great-grandfather. He passed before I was born, but he has been with me in my life. I often feel him guiding me and watching over me. I notice when I'm having a rough time, mentally, spiritually, and physically, my mind always goes to my great-grandfather. I think of him often, and imagine my life with him, teaching me, loving me, and inspiring me. I often wonder what he would say to me. He would probably just laugh and tell me to take it easy. No use to worry. I imagine his warm, welcoming cabin smelling like his tobacco pipe. I would sit with him and try to beat him at checkers. Listen to his stories until I fall asleep. Eat bannock, drink tea with him. I wonder and I daydream, then I feel better because I know what he would probably say to me. I have to continue to live a healthy life. Pray all the time. Protect my happiness. Live simply. Take it easy.

I still remember my great-grandmother Sarah. She was very kind, loving, and precious. Almost immediately she treated people with such kindness, as if they were her own grandchildren. I imagine her cooking and feeding visitors and telling stories along with my great-grandfather. My great-grandfather Johnny was successful because of her. She knew how to hold others up. She took care of old women, children, and many others. As you read you will see she was a very hard worker. She worked even with a child on her back.

Her love was instant and made you feel right at home. As my grandfather told stories, she sat nearby with her eyes closed and listened, often laughing and imagining his stories. Well into their nineties, the two of them lived alone at Gold Camp, over twenty miles away by trail from Venetie, the nearest village. They took care of each other. I strive to be like my great-grandmother, to be strong and fierce like her. To be kind and loving towards others. I often imagine her hands on my head, praying for me and blessing me. I believe her prayers are still felt through the generations.

I know my great-grandfather's spirit is always with me. I live my life by listening to my elders, protecting our way of life and my faith in K'eegwaadhat. My great-grandfather said, "Look out on the land, look at all the trees and animals. They were created by God." I know my great-grandfather's spirit guides me in times of challenges and in times of peace.

A big *mahsi'choo* to Dr. Craig Mishler for gathering and studying my great-grandparents' stories and for publishing them so that those like me can listen to their stories and read their exact words. The work that Craig has done has been instrumental to my identity and my knowledge of our history. I also get to be closer to my great-grandfather because of Craig's work. This book is very special to me, that I can be a part of it and hear my great-grandparents speaking. I live my life knowing these stories have been passed down for many generations. And I know who I am because of it. I understand my language and the values that come from turning these pages.

In these stories, there are many names of my ancestors mentioned, such as Kǫ̀'ehdan, Òol Tì', Drizhuu, Drit, and Mil Vahan. Stories of hardship and survival, but also stories of humor and teachings. It's a part of our history. Our way of life as Gwich'in people. Knowing these stories gives me an understanding that we came from strong people, people who survived in one of the harshest environments in North America.

The stories are translated from Gwich'in to English. The meaning can be distorted and at times can be confusing. But by learning and understanding the language, the meaning is a lot deeper and is filled with more information than what's on the surface. However delicate the translation is, it takes so much work and time to get the translations as good as they can be. This book is a masterpiece of all those who helped with it. Their legacy lives on through the many hours they worked on transcriptions and translations.

My great-grandparents' spirits are within these pages. They will make you laugh and cry, and they will also tell you the history of our Gwich'in people. I have wished so much to see my great-grandfather, and to have been old enough to sit and talk with my great-grandmother, but I have seen them in my dreams, and I hold them close to my heart. I know my great-grandfather Johnny and I know my great-grandmother Sarah. I am very grateful that our Gwich'in language is preserved in this work. I hope that for generations to come we still hold our language close and precious, that we hold our ancestors close, and that we never stray too far from our ancestors' trail.

Fig. 2. K'aii'eechų'njik (The East Fork of the Chandalar River) and Gold Camp. Photo by Ron Kent, BIA ANCSA, 1983.

Acknowledgments

In addition to those individuals mentioned on the title page, Helen Howard, administrative assistant at the Alaska Native Language Center, helped write and monitor the project budget and kept everyone in close communication. Tom Alton copy-edited the English text, did the original book design and facing page layouts, and drafted the regional map of Gwich'in place names (Figure 7). Michael Krauss, Director of the ANLC, helped shape the initial research design, coordinated staffing needs, and provided important technical advice on matters of orthography. Special thanks go to Katherine Peter and Jeff Leer for providing the Gwich'in tone marking.

Other people who helped substantially in seeing this book to completion are Dick Mueller of Fairbanks, who read and commented on some preliminary texts. William Schneider and Richard Nelson reviewed the finished manuscript and made numerous suggestions for its improvement. Lawrence Roberts supplied personal recollections of how Johnny and Sarah raised him as their grandson and, with Kenneth Frank, made useful corrections to the place names map. Eddie Frank, First Chief of Venetie and another grandson, wrote valuable letters of support for our grant applications. Tony Scott Pearce transcribed the sixteen Johnny Frank songs into musical notation, and Judy Erick transcribed the lyrics. Leif Thompson typeset the songs using Finale software. John Ritter of the Yukon Native Language Centre and Ruth Carroll of Whitehorse provided much encouragement and welcome advice, reminding us that Gwich'in is indeed an international language.

Lincoln Tritt of Arctic Village and Fairbanks deserves much credit for writing letters of support and helping us locate additional tapes in Arctic Village. Ron Kent of the Bureau of Indian Affairs also led us to tapes of Sarah Frank and aerial photographs of Gold Camp in the BIA Anchorage office that had previously escaped our attention, and David Libbey supplied a glossy print of the photo he took of Sarah and her many friends at Old John's cabin. Pat Aubin, the daughter of Gerald Fitzgerald, generously furnished us with a copy of her father's unpublished diary, which offers one of the first-ever glimpses into the life of the Franks when they were staying in Arctic Village in 1927. Bill Schneider, director of the oral history archives at the University of Alaska Fairbanks, dutifully made copies of all of the Frank tapes in the University's oral history collection, some of which he had personally recorded. Dr. Mike Holloway, a close friend of the Franks since the early 1960s, freely shared his wealth of memories, copies of his personal tapes, and many fine photographs of the Franks. Mike's wife, Margie Ann Gibson, has kindly shared several of Mike's photos of Johnny and Sarah after his passing. This book would not have been possible in its present form without the abundant warmth and good will of all of these people. For readers wanting to learn more about the Franks, I strongly recommend Mike's engaging memoir, *Dreaming Bears* (2014).

Our greatest thanks go to these four children of Johnny and Sarah: Nathaniel Frank, Hamel Frank, Dan Frank, and Maggie Roberts. They strongly supported all our efforts and not only offered sage advice on how to interpret difficult words and passages in the texts but clarified and elaborated many key events in their childhood and family history. I recorded a lengthy interview with the four of them at Dan Frank's house in Venetie on October 5, 1989, and again with three of them on June 19, 1990. The 1989 interviews were taped in Gwich'in and later transcribed and translated by Judy Erick but for lack of space could not be included here.

On June 19, 1990, Nathaniel was not feeling well, but I again gathered Hamel, Dan, and Maggie together with Kenneth and Caroline Frank for an interview that suddenly turned into a wonderful performance of Vasaagihdzak tales by Hamel and Dan. These Frank Family tapes are also being archived, and the transcripts from the 1989 interview have provided important supplemental information on Johnny and Sarah's lives, summarized below in the Life History Notes preceding Part II. Dan Frank has been especially generous in sharing old family photos from his personal collection, and Hamel and Mary Frank deserve special mention for providing me with their endless warm hospitality, good Indian cooking, and kind friendship for many, many years.

As this book was nearing completion in September, 1994, Nathaniel Frank passed away at the age of 83 and regrettably never saw more than a few pages of the finished manuscript. He was kind and good to all of us and will be greatly missed by everyone who worked on this project.

As we were about to go to press with the first edition in 1995 we received the good news that Maggie Roberts had been elected First Chief of Venetie, carrying on in the grand tradition of her mother Sarah, who was elected women's chief in the late 1930s, and her father Johnny, who was elected First Chief. We're now sorry to report that Maggie, the youngest of Johnny and Sarah's twelve children, left us in December, 2013. Her door was always open and her kitchen was the center of Venetie.

As we went to press with the 2nd edition of this volume, we were sad to announce the deaths of several of its key contributors. Nathaniel Frank passed away in September, 1994, Hamel Frank in April, 1998, Ron Frank in June, 1998, and Judy Erick, our brilliant transcriber and translator, in November, 1999. From 1997 to 1999 Judy interviewed many additional elders and transcribed and translated their tapes relating to historic sites around the Venetie Reserve. Since then we also lost Lillian Garnett, another talented transcriber and translator and a gifted teacher of the Gwich'in language, in 2021. For many years Lillian taught Gwich'in as a member of the faculty at the Alaska Native Language Center. As a group they were kind and good to all of us and will be greatly missed by everyone who has read the book and has donated time and energy to this project. Their collective hard work and love of the Gwich'in language live on beautifully in this book.

Finally, we offer a tip of the hat to Sam Alexander, department chair of the Alaska Native Language Center and Associate Professor of Gwich'in for encouraging and facilitating this revised 3rd edition. And many kudos to Lillian Maassen, ANLC's Editor, for her endless patience, meticulous eye, and graceful book design.

Introduction: A Personal Recollection

On Tuesday, November 15, 1972, I set out on a toboggan towed by a snowmachine to visit Johnny and Sarah, who were reported by their son Dan to be alive and well at Gold Camp, a small place located at the mouth of the North Fork of the East Fork of the Chandalar River. I had met Dan Frank because he lived near the house my wife and daughter and I had rented in Fort Yukon the previous summer. As a young folklorist and anthropologist just beginning to visit rural Alaskan villages, I was eager to meet them for several reasons, but my primary interest was to learn and document their Native language.

I was truly excited about recording Johnny, whose reputation as a wonderful storyteller had been established by Robert McKennan in 1933. But I was amazed that this old-fashioned couple was still rugged enough to be living independently in such a remote and isolated mountainous area. By this time both Johnny and Sarah were in their eighties, and they were probably the last Gwich'in couple in Alaska to carry on the traditional ways of living alone off the country. By the time of my first visit, virtually everyone else on the Venetie Reservation and elsewhere in the Alaskan Gwich'in homeland had already moved into the villages.

The easy way to get to Gold Camp in the summer is to take a flat-bottomed riverboat up the Chandalar or simply charter a small plane out of Fort Yukon and land on the gravel bar in front of the cabins. Ski planes can land there in the winter, but from mid-September to mid-April the most practical way to get to Gold Camp is to fly to Venetie and then traverse the fifty-mile trail by dog sled or snowmachine.

On this cold overcast day in 1972, 1 was fortunate to link up with Stanley Frank, one of Johnny and Sarah's grandsons, who covered the distance every two weeks or so, transporting mail and supplies from Venetie. Our small party consisted of Stanley Frank, Edward Tritt, Christopher Johnson, and me. Stanley drove one snowmachine while Edward Tritt rode behind him on a *dachan vał* (wooden toboggan with upright handles). Christopher drove the other snowmachine, pulling me along on another *dachan vał.*

Our start was delayed while Chris made a steel claw anchor brake, which I was instructed to use whenever I wanted to slow down the toboggan. As I quickly learned, this brake must be used on every turn and every downhill stretch. If it isn't, the toboggan fishtails into the brush and rolls over or bumps up and down so hard it becomes nearly impossible to hold on to.

The trail from Venetie to Gold Camp is rough and often so narrow that the toboggan rider's hands collide violently with abutting spruce trees. Several times when I fell off into the deep snow, the toboggan remained upright, and I was left far behind, walking a quarter mile or so to catch up.

We climbed the mountain for several hours before reaching the camp at Neet'ak Van, where an 8-by-10 white canvas tent was occupied by Robert and Amos Frank and Albert Williams, who had arrived just ahead of us to check their traplines. Inside the tent a fire was started in a small homemade stove fabricated from two Blazo cans, and the floor was covered with spruce boughs. While tea was made and moose meat was fried, the seven of us hunched around the stove, relaxing and conversing as we hung up our hats and gloves to dry.

When I asked if Johnny Frank could speak English very well, Robert said, "Well, yes. You know he even has a degree. He's a professor, and he flies 747s. Everybody comes to see Johnny Frank. Even President Nixon comes to visit him." I was cheerfully warned that Johnny Frank sometimes talked for four or five hours at a time. Often, they said, they would go to sleep at night while he was talking and when they got up in the morning, he would still be talking.

After we ate, we packed up the toboggans again and moved on. Past Neet'ak Van, the trail comes out of the woods and winds through high open country where it is easy to see game from a great distance. As we traversed this section of the trail, however, the daylight began to fade, and Stanley began to have trouble with the headlight on his snowmachine. We were delayed for nearly half an hour until the wiring was repaired, and by then it was dark. Dry snow had drifted over the trail until it was all but impossible to follow under the starlight.

The two snowmachines bogged down on the uphill stretches, and the only way we made any progress was by taking turns breaking trail. At last, we approached the crest of a large watershed, and I was told that for the next four miles I would have to ride the brake all the way down to the river to prevent the toboggan from crashing into the snowmachine.

On the right side of the trail near the bottom of this long descent, I saw an old cabin that appeared to be abandoned. I learned later that this is where Johnny and Sarah had lived until a few years before, when some people helped them build a new cabin across the river on the opposite bank. But just when the trail came out onto a small slough, Christopher's engine ran out of gas. By the time we refilled the tank, crossed the Chandalar River, and saw the lighted windows of Gold Camp on the far bank, Johnny Frank and his son-in-law Ambrose William were waiting outside in the cold night air to greet us.

Once we were inside the single-room cabin lit by Coleman white gas lanterns, Sarah served us a roasting pan full of boiled moose meat, a plate of hot biscuits, and a pot of hot tea. Chris had brought along a half case of Black Bull chewing tobacco, which pleased Sarah to no end. While we ate our supper, Johnny smoked his pipe and put on his glasses to read a large stack of mail. I was exhausted, but that evening we talked for several hours, until at last I crawled into my big blue down sleeping bag on the floor.

At that time, Gold Camp consisted of two log cabins, two elevated cabin caches, a platform for whipsawing lumber, and several white canvas tents and doghouses. The cabins sit on a flat bench above the riverbank facing east and overlooking the shallow braided channels of the East Fork. Over the next two days, in addition to making cassette tape recordings of Johnny, I observed and participated in their daily routine. At 6 a.m. Johnny would get up to build a fire in the wood stove, and by 7:30 everyone else would rise. Stanley would turn on his battery-powered radio, and to the sound of American country music, the men would slip on a pair of boot rubbers over their socks, step outside to pee, and then come in and wash up with soap and water in a basin by the door.

Breakfast was prepared by 8 o'clock, but hot tea was always ready before that. The hearty morning meal consisted of pancakes eaten with butter or ketchup, oatmeal with canned milk, and a slice of "fry meat," either moose or caribou. After breakfast the men cut and split wood and packed water from the river with a yoke and two buckets made from Blazo cans. While Sarah did the dishes, the men would work on toboggans, chain saws, and snowmachines.

One morning I asked Johnny to show me the inside of one of his elevated log caches, thinking it would be full of dry moose and caribou meat or dry fish. When he climbed the ladder and unlocked the door, I looked in and discovered it was chock full of nothing but toilet tissue! The noon meal was quite large, consisting of brown beans and bacon, roasted lynx or moose meat, pilot bread, tea or coffee, and boiled prunes. Although her grandchildren had brought her a brand new four-burner propane cookstove, Sarah never used it, preferring instead the flattened top of her wood-burning barrel stove. This stove would overheat the cabin until someone finally pulled open the front door, and then it would suddenly get too cold. The cabin always seemed too hot or too cold.

Afternoons were less active than the mornings. The men would go out to check their traps and snares, or heat up a big pot of meat scraps and cornmeal mush over an outdoor fire to make dog feed, but after a while they would come in, and Stanley would play his fiddle, backed up by Edward chording on the guitar.

One of their tunes was *Goodbye Sheenyaa,* a Gwich'in love song composed by Annie Cadzow in the 1940s when she left her husband for another man. I soon discovered that fiddling and square dancing are at the very core of 20th century Gwich'in expressive culture (Mishler 1974, 1993), and that Johnny himself had once been a noted dance fiddler.

It was common for Johnny to challenge someone to a game of checkers, at which he was a master, or perhaps take out a deck of cards and start up a round of Mizhur on the corner of the bed. Mizhur is a Gwich'in card game similar to Euchre, with one suit being trump, and is played in foursomes (Mishler 1983b). Those not playing Mizhur might relax on one of the wooden beds and read comic books or dismantle a chain saw or a Coleman lantern.

Suppers were fairly informal. Coming about 6 or 7 o'clock, they were mostly self-serve and consisted of leftovers from the noon meal. In the evening everyone ate whenever they were hungry, and sometimes Sarah would make "fry bread" *(khwaii łuch'yaa)*. The final event of the day was listening to "Tundra Topics," a five-minute program of personal messages for people living in the bush and broadcast from Fairbanks every night at 9:15 on radio station KFAR. Shortly after "Tundra Topics" was over, Sarah and Johnny would retire for the night after Sarah pulled the white cloth curtain around their bed.

Fig. 3. Johnny and Sarah Frank at Gold Camp, November 17, 1972. Photo by Craig Mishler.

Johnny explained that the reason he and Sarah stayed in Gold Camp was to avoid the drinking and trouble that went on in the villages. "Tea and sugar," he said with a chuckle, "that's my wine." On the morning of November 18, I took some photos of Johnny and Sarah, put a 20-dollar bill in Johnny's hand, jumped back on the toboggan, and returned to Venetie with the boys. For a couple of days, I stayed at the Mission house with a young Episcopal lay worker named Joe Wagner and met other members of the Frank family, including Hamel and Mary Frank. Little did I know that this was the first and last time I would ever see Johnny, who died December 27, 1977, while I was a student in Austin, Texas.

I visited Sarah in Venetie at least twice after that, and the last time I saw her was July 11, 1988, just before her death on July 15. She was staying with her daughter Maggie in Venetie while we were first planning this book, and I was looking for Nathaniel Frank to talk to him about it. He wasn't home, and when someone directed me to Maggie's house, I softly approached the open door. Looking in, I saw Sarah propped up in bed in the middle of the living room, resting in Maggie's arms with her long silver hair flowing down her shoulder.

It was a warm day and the sun was shining brightly, flooding the room and the bed with an intensity that was reflected off the white sheets covering the bed. Most of the family had gathered for these final days and hours, and Nathaniel, along with many others, was seated on the floor, watching his mother in reverence. The whole house was very silent, and I left without saying a word, but this loving scene of the family watching and waiting together will always be with me.

— Craig Mishler

Recording History

My first recording session with Johnny took place at Gold Camp on November 16, 1972, the morning after my arrival there by toboggan. Although I slept and ate in Johnny and Sarah's cabin, we decided to record next door in the cabin occupied by their son-in-law Ambrose William because it was quieter and less subject to interruptions. Both log cabins were open one-room structures with unpainted, heavily scarred wooden plank floors and rough-hewn wooden beds in the back corners. Both had barrel stoves on the right as you entered the door and small six-paned glass windows on the front wall and left side walls. Recycled cardboard boxes were tacked to the inside walls for insulation.

While I set up the Sony cassette recorder, Johnny went back to the other cabin to get his tobacco pouch, which was filled with Granger brand tobacco. When he came in, he sat on a chair handmade out of a log stump. He was wearing two pairs of long gray woolen socks inside his black rubber galoshes, which were cut down so there were only two buckles left. He also wore a pair of button-up long johns under his dark gray cotton pants and long-sleeved cotton shirt, and a quilted black cap with a soft brown button-like object fastened on the bill. He had a handsome gold wedding band on his left hand, a *Takkudh* Gwich'in hymnal in his right back pocket, and was smoking his pipe. As his trademark, this pipe went with Johnny wherever he went.

When he began to perform his stories and songs, Johnny laid his pipe and tobacco pouch aside on a Blazo box, closed his eyes to concentrate, and tuned out everything else in the room. The cadence of his Gwich'in began very slowly, filled with long pauses at first, but then little by little became more rapid and continuous as he recalled the distant past with increasing clarity. From time to time, he would scratch his head or twiddle his thumbs or take off his cap and twirl it in his hands. Ambrose listened carefully and hardly said a word, but I was glad to have him there for an audience since at that time I understood only a little Gwich'in.

Around noon Sarah came to the door and announced lunch with the word *"Lidii"* (tea), which I understood. However, not until many years later did I get a full translation of her announcement: "I'm making tea for everybody, but the meat we have up on the cache is being eaten by the puppies." After lunch and tea, I turned the tape recorder back on to capture Johnny singing a few songs I had heard him humming to himself. One of them, which has not been musically transcribed, has the comical cowboy-like lyrics, "Money, liquor nąįį-ąįį-ąįį. Money, liquor, money, nąįį-ąįį-ąįį. Aai-yai yai yippi yee! Aai-yai yippi yee!"

In his own cabin, with Sarah and the other men present, Johnny was much more dynamic with his gestures. Sarah sat on the bed behind him, listening carefully and laughing occasionally. Their German shepherd puppy *Draanduu* 'No Good' was wandering around the cabin still making a nuisance of himself, but this did not hinder the performance. Stanley Frank sat and stared at the fire, and Edward Tritt was sound asleep, but Johnny found an attentive listener in Chris Johnson, who was kneeling on the floor fixing a chain saw. The next day I took some preliminary written notes for the Frank family genealogy, which appears at the end of this volume, and taped some additional stories and songs. On the morning of the third day, I left with Stanley, Christopher, and Edward to return back over the trail to Venetie.

After I visited Johnny, two other people also made the long trip to Gold Camp to record him. Most notably, Kathy Alexander (now Kathy Carroll of Fort Yukon) visited Gold Camp several times beginning in April 1973, and made six excellent tapes of Johnny's Gwich'in stories. In September 1976, Mike Holloway, a medical doctor with the Indian Health Service and the Franks' personal physician, recorded nine additional hours of Johnny's stories, told almost entirely in English, and that is virtually all we have. Johnny died a little over a year later.

After Johnny's passing, everyone's attention began to focus on Sarah, who until that time had remained quietly in the background. She had been overlooked for several reasons. First, Johnny was such a compelling storyteller that he usually insisted on the total attention of his guests, and second, he spoke English much more freely than

Sarah did. Sarah was modest, but her mind was extremely clear, and she was able to recall much from the distant past that we had forgotten to ask Johnny about.

In 1979, after returning from graduate school in Texas, I made another trip to Venetie and found Sarah living with her grandson, Lawrence Roberts and his wife, Mary Rose. Sarah remembered me

Fig. 4. Johnny Frank at Gold Camp, November 16,1972. Photo by Craig Mishler.

and greeted me warmly, and I persuaded her to tell me a couple of her favorite old-time stories in Gwich'in on the afternoon of May 14. I was her sole listener. Quite fittingly for a widowed woman of her age, she told me stories of an old woman who lived alone and skillfully fought off a grizzly bear and another old woman who defended herself courageously against a stalking brush man.

In July of that same summer, while Sarah was visiting in Arctic Village, staff members from the Bureau of Indian Affairs interviewed her at length on tape about historic and cemetery sites in the Arctic Village area where she was born and raised. A team of oral historians and archaeologists flew Sarah by helicopter to Old John Lake with several other Gwich'in elders to document historic and cemetery sites. Two tapes were made there by David Libbey, with assistance from Caroline Tritt-Frank, who served as Sarah's interpreter. A field site report on Old John's cabin, occupied by Sarah and her parents from 1904 until about 1910 was also written (Bureau of Indian Affairs 1980).

In 1980, Dr. Holloway, who had been visiting Gold Camp since about 1965, teamed up in Venetie with William Schneider, then curator of oral history at the University of Alaska's Rasmuson Library, and made a wonderful systematic week-long series of eight tape recordings of Sarah, assisted by Maggie, who acted as their interpreter.

Starting in 1983, family members and friends began showing a stronger interest in preserving Sarah's knowledge. In that year, Sarah's grandson, Ron Frank, made an important two-hour tape recording of her personal life history and religious beliefs, and on August 3, 1983, Alice Lynch of the Bureau of Indian Affairs did an interview with her about Chief Peter, whose cabin was built just downriver from Gold Camp. Then, in June 1984, while Sarah was visiting Arctic Village and staying with her friend Martha James, the mother of Lillian Garnett, Lillian interviewed Sarah and made two tapes.

In the fall of 1985, Kenneth and Caroline Frank also made three tapes of Sarah while she was living by herself in Venetie, but one of those got lost. In June, 1986, during a visit Sarah made to Fort Yukon, Virginia Alexander taped some brief comments from Sarah on the traditional Gwich'in use of plants for folk medicine. And finally, Joe Wagner, an Episcopal lay worker, had the fine presence of mind to videotape Sarah being interviewed by Sarah John and Maggie Frank in Venetie in June, 1987. A list of all the original cassette tape recordings of Johnny and Sarah can be found in Appendix B.

Fig. 5. Kenneth Frank in Venetie, September, 1994. Photo by Craig Mishler.

Project History: Transcription and Translation

In June, 1988, with much personal encouragement from Will Schneider and Mike Holloway to do something with all of the dispersed Frank tape collections, Ron Frank (Sarah and Johnny's grandson) and I applied for and received a small planning grant from the Alaska Humanities Forum. This grant allowed us to make a preliminary inventory of the location and contents of all the Frank tapes and decide what the scope of work would be in a larger study. This seed money also gave me an opportunity to consult with the Franks' four surviving children – Nathaniel, Hamel, Dan, and Maggie – and the Venetie Tribal Council to insure not only their backing for the project but also their full participation in its planning and implementation. At the kind invitation of Mike Holloway, I was able to meet with the family at the first modern gathering of the Gwich'in nation, *Gwich'in Niin Tsyaa,* which was held in Arctic Village in August, 1988. All four were interested in seeing their mother's and father's knowledge and life achievements recognized for the benefit of coming generations.

By the fall of 1988, shortly after Sarah's death, I had located copies of nearly all of the Frank tapes known to be in public and private collections. This helped me determine the scope of work when I wrote a proposal to the National Endowment for the Humanities to obtain funding for transcribing and translating major portions of the tape-recorded corpus. The Alaska Native Language Center at the University of Alaska Fairbanks agreed to sponsor the proposal, and at this time I also recruited the assistance of several of the accomplished Gwich'in writers who had been involved in Gwich'in bilingual teaching projects in Venetie and Arctic Village. Expressing interest in the work were Judy Erick and Mary Rose Gamboa in Venetie, and Lillian Garnett and Katherine Peter in Fairbanks. Ron Frank, living in Gulkana, expressed the desire to become literate in his Native tongue by learning from the others.

In June, 1989, NEH awarded project funds to begin this work, and in the spring of 1990 the Yukon Flats School District provided additional matching grant funds. At a two-day training workshop at the University of Alaska Fairbanks in early October, 1989, I gave each transcriber copies of several of Johnny's or Sarah's audiocassette tapes and a Sony BM-75 transcribing machine to begin their work. Their first task was to compile tape indexes summarizing in English what stories, songs, and topics of discussion were found on each tape. The beginning and end of each text or topic were identified with time markings from the transcribing machine, measured in minutes and seconds. These indexes were mailed directly to me for a quick scan of the contents of each tape.

The indexes were almost like outlines of the tape contents, and, based on my own intuitive and subjective sense of what was important and complete, I identified which segments of the tapes should be transcribed and which ones should be skipped over. Transcribers were frequently consulted about these segments. We decided, for example, that variation in performance was of considerable interest and that we would transcribe variants of the same story told by Johnny and Sarah to different interviewers on different occasions. Since different transcribers were sometimes involved in processing these variants, however, readers should be cautioned that on stylistic grounds the variants may not be strictly comparable.

While most of the tapes have great value and generate a high level of interest, many sections were partly inaudible or were simply lacking in substance. When the taped discourse turned exclusively to English or alternated heavily between Gwich'in and English, as in translating questions back and forth, the transcribers were asked to transcribe only the Gwich'in parts of the discourse. Isolated words and phrases in English, however, are preserved in their original places and shown in italics. Although many taped segments were passed over for this printed collection, scholars with special research interests or Gwich'in speakers wishing to review the entire contents of each tape may consult the indexes and then listen to the digitized tapes in the Rasmuson Library Oral History Archives and the Alaska Native Language Archives at the University of Alaska Fairbanks.

Members of the team were asked to transcribe the Gwich'in first, marking the minutes and seconds of the texts at frequent intervals on the tape, just as they had done with the indexes. Then they were to write translations of the texts in such a way that identical time markings would be used, leading to a close correspondence between the Gwich'in originals and the English translations. These time markings have been preserved in the 3rd edition and serve as reference points for anyone wishing to listen to the tapes as they follow along in the printed texts. Each time there is a change of speaker, the speaker is identified by his or her initials. A listing of the speakers' initials is given in Appendix B.

When the cursive transcriptions for a complete tape were finished, they were sealed in manila envelopes and mailed to me for making backup copies. I then forwarded them to Katherine Peter, our senior Gwich'in scholar, who reviewed them for spelling and grammatical accuracy. Although four Gwich'in transcribers and translators began working on this project, family commitments forced Ron and Mary Rose to withdraw from the project shortly after it began. As a result, Judy Erick and Lillian Garnett did nearly all of the important

Fig. 6. The original project team which transcribed and translated the Johnny and Sarah Frank texts. Left to right are Ron Frank, Judy Erick, Lillian Garnett, and Mary Rose Gamboa in Fairbanks, September, 1989. Photo by Craig Mishler.

transcription and translation work. Both patiently spent hundreds of hours listening and relistening to the tapes.

Readers of the texts and listeners of the tapes will notice a distinct difference in the Gwich'in transcribing styles adopted by Judy and Lillian. Judy's transcriptions are fairly literal and detailed, preserving incomplete sentences along with many repetitions and false starts. By contrast, Lillian's are more literary, preserving only the essential words, eliminating false starts and many quotative redundancies such as *gwinyaa* (they say) or *varahnyaa* (they say, it is said) that often appear at the ends of sentences. See my discussion of this ethnopoetic feature in Mishler and Frank (2023:161-174). Such a stylistic difference between two skilled writers of the language illustrates that the complex process of transcribing and translating, moving from the oral to the written, is not a simple mechanical reproduction of what can be heard on the tapes, but an expressive and critical interpretation which benefits from a close collaboration (Mishler and Frank 2021).

Katherine Peter then gave the corrected transcriptions to her daughter, Adeline Raboff, who typed them onto a Macintosh computer. The Macintosh, with Microsoft Word and the Super French font, allowed us to put tone marks above the vowels and nasalization marks below the vowels. When the texts were all typed, they were reviewed again by Jeff Leer, linguist with the Alaska Native Language Center, who worked closely with Katherine to edit the Gwich'in texts, mark them for tones, and standardize spellings, a process that spanned the better part of two years.

In October, 1990, I returned to Venetie with the indexes and most of the draft transcriptions in hand and called the Frank family – Nathaniel, Hamel, Dan, and Maggie – together to review what was on the tapes and decide what portions of the transcriptions should go into the book. Kenneth Frank and Caroline Tritt-Frank also participated. In a few select cases, affecting less than half a dozen passages, they asked me to delete certain portions of the transcripts and omit the names of certain individuals. This was done only to reduce potential personal harm or embarrassment to these individuals and their descendants. Also, because many of Johnny Frank's songs are medicine songs, the family felt that the power of these songs might be misunderstood or misused by non-Gwich'in readers. Accordingly, they asked that no direct translations be provided.

The typed texts, with tones added, were then recirculated to Lillian and Judy for proofreading and annotation. Katherine and I also added annotations. These proofs were then returned to Adeline for typing and for some additional annotations. Finally, I reviewed the texts side by side to identify gaps and inconsistencies between the Gwich'in and English versions. In some passages, there was a lot more Gwich'in than there was English, and I consulted again with the transcribers to iron these out. These passages had to be expanded and reworked to obtain good facing-page translations. Still, in many instances it became clear that English sentences could combine several Gwich'in sentences in a compressed form that was more fluent and less stiff than exact sentence-for-sentence translation. In many cases direct quoted speech that had been transcribed passively needed to be restored to the active dramatic voice. "He told them to pretend to be caribou" was revised to read: "'Pretend to be caribou,' he told them."

Following the advances in folkloristics made during the 1970s and 1980s by scholars such as Dennis Tedlock (1972) and Dell Hymes (1981), I became persuaded that the poetic-dramatic model is a more faithful representation of Gwich'in verbal art than the conventional short story model. Consequently, Johnny's and Sarah's formal narratives are interpreted with lines, rather than sentences, as the basic unit of measure. These lines are generally defined by independent or dependent clauses (Hymes) and occasionally by punctuated breath units (Tedlock). We have used prose paragraphs, nevertheless, for those texts that are essentially free-flowing conversations or informal question-and-answer sessions.

When it was reasonably clear that the English translations matched the Gwich'in originals as closely as possible, I passed the texts on to Tom Alton, ANLC's book editor, who reformatted the texts in Aldus PageMaker, the desktop publishing program. A few sample texts were also sent to the Frank family for their review and suggestions, and this process resulted in some additional formatting changes. Motivated in part by seeing early drafts of the book,

Kenneth Frank became literate in Gwich'in and took a greater and greater interest in the way it was being shaped. Kenneth carefully proofread many parts of the Gwich'in manuscript, raising lots of good questions and snaring many little errors. He also suggested the book's title, from a word used by his grandmother in "The First School." The English translations were edited by Judy Erick and Craig Mishler, with some additional assistance from Katherine Peter. Final copy-editing of the English was done by Tom Alton.

In May, 1995, we applied for and were awarded a modest publication grant from the Alaska Humanities Forum. Funds from this grant were dedicated to the final technical production and printing of the book. In the 2nd edition, a Gwich'in language CD was included, allowing readers to follow selected texts as they listen to the voices of Johnny and Sarah.

For the 3rd edition, the same ten CD audio tracks may be accessed digitally online via the Alaska Native Language Archive [https://www.uaf.edu/anla] using Identifier KU995FMi2026. Copy this Identifier number into the Identifier box, then click on Search. Now click on the Identifier hyperlink that appears below. At the "Resource Details" page, scroll down till you find the ten .wav files. Click on these to hear Johnny and Sarah's original recordings and follow along in the book.

The Johnny and Sarah Frank Scholarship Fund

This endowed fund was first created in 1993 by Craig Mishler and Dr. Mike Holloway and has since been supported by many individuals. The fund is managed by the University of Alaska Foundation and is designed to honor the memory of Johnny and Sarah by providing financial support to Alaskan and Canadian undergraduate students attending any branch of the University of Alaska. Interested applicants and prospective donors should contact the University of Alaska Foundation in Fairbanks and the UAF Financial Aid website.

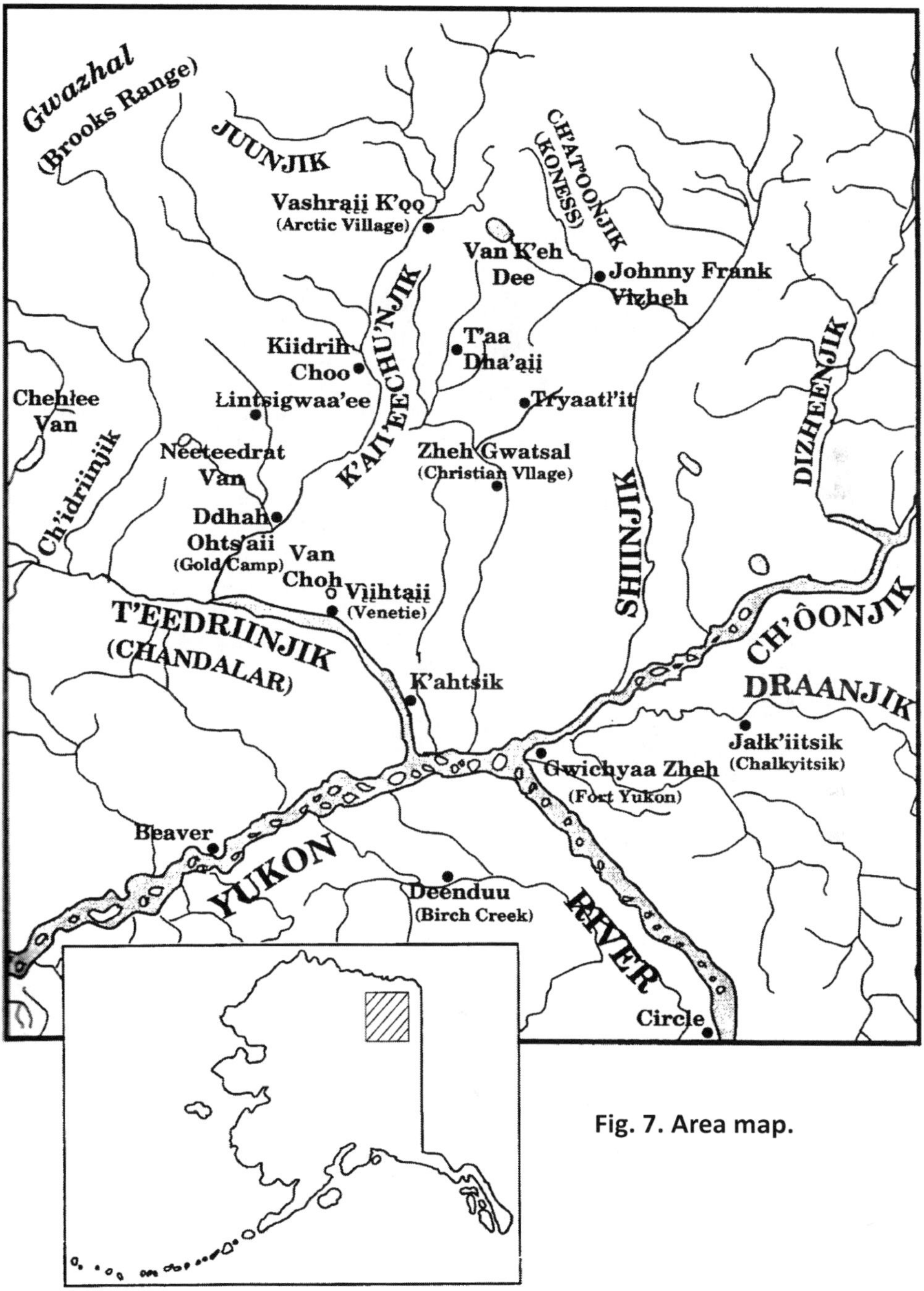

Fig. 7. Area map.

Fig. 8. Johnny and Sarah Frank in dress parkas, March, 1974. Photo by Mike Holloway, courtesy of Margie Gibson.

Part I
Traditional Stories and Songs

Unfortunately, none of the folktales in Johnny Frank's vast repertoire has been carried through to publication except for the thirty-three Robert McKennan published in English in his seminal ethnography, *The Chandalar Kutchin* in 1965, and none of Sarah's stories has previously appeared anywhere. Only two of Johnny's songs have been published as sound recordings, and only three additional ones, all included here, have previously been transcribed into musical notation (Mishler, 1974; 1981a).

As tradition bearers, Johnny and Sarah inherited an ancient system of storytelling, and they learned much of what they knew from their elders. Johnny's principal mentor seems to have been Shyaaghan Ndik, his father's mother, who was probably born in the 1820s or 1830s and was one of the wives of the Di'hąįį Gwich'in leader, Diitsii Giitł'uu. While reminiscing about his childhood, Johnny talks about her penchant for sitting by the fire and telling stories all day long.

Sarah, on the other hand, repeatedly acknowledges her debt to Mil Vahan, her great-grandmother. Both Shyaaghan Ndik and Mil Vahan were crippled and had to be carried on other people's backs, especially in the summer months. This was a considerable burden for their children and grandchildren, but such women were considered living libraries and were highly valued for their knowledge. Sarah mentions that Mil Vahan also stayed for a while with Maggie Gilbert, another great Arctic Village storyteller (see one of her texts in Mishler 2013).

Johnny Frank was enamored of two traditional Gwich'in story cycles, the adventures of Ch'iteehàakwąįį (literally, 'he paddles amongst them') and Vasagìhdzak. In 1933, Robert McKennan (1965:98-126) heard and recorded some of the same episodes included here but identified the protagonists as Jateaquoint and Savitha respectively. McKennan also recorded a number of

Ch'iteehàakwąįį stories from Johnny's mother, Old Lucy Frank, suggesting that Johnny may have learned some of these from his mother, although he undoubtedly heard them elsewhere as well.

For readers familiar with northern Dene folklore, Ch'iteehàakwąįį is the Gwich'in version of The Traveler, the heroic person who travels down river in his canoe killing or 'fixing' hostile animals and bad men who prey on humans. Thanks to Ch'iteehàakwąįį the world is now safe to live in.

Sarah was familiar with at least some episodes of both cycles, and her contribution nicely supplements those told by Johnny. Comic in tone and certain to provoke laughter when told in Gwich'in, the stories of Vasagìhdzak and Ch'iteehàakwąįį seem distantly related and some people today think the two protagonists are really the same person. However, Sarah Frank believed they were different. She carefully distinguished the two, noting that "Vasaagìhdzak's stories are more comical" while "Ch'iteehawąįį is the one who took care of everything that was bad." Episodes from the two cycles are often told at one sitting, but in both cases the syntax of episodes is fairly loose and disconnected, and they are performed in many different orders.

It is curious that Vasagìhdzak is not a well-known character among other Northern Dene, with the single notable exception of the Chipewyan. Upriver from the Alaskan Gwich'in, for example, the Han and Upper Tanana tell a distinctly different cycle about a man named Tsae'oh Shae or Tsa-o-sha (McKennan 1959), while the Tanacross people have the adventures of Yaamaagh Telcheegh (Thomas 2005), and the Koyukon downriver are fond of a completely unrelated cycle of stories about another canoe paddler named K'etetaalkkaanee (Attla 1990).

Johnny and Sarah's texts do not represent the complete story cycles. At least two other diverse collections of Vasagìhdzak stories have been previously published in Gwich'in (see Williams 1976; Peter and Pope 1981). Henry Williams' version incorporates some of the same episodes told by Johnny and Sarah as well as numerous additional ones. Perhaps the most surprising episode in the Williams collection is the story of "The Blind Man and the Loon," a tale type which is very old and traditional but which is usually told separately by other Gwich'in and other Native American performers (see Mishler 2013). Williams says the blind man in this story was the father of Vasagìhdzak. By contrast, Katherine Peter and Mary Pope's collection contains quite a different series of episodes about "Vasagìhdzak and the Giant," "Vasagìhdzak and the Lynx," and "Vasagìhdzak and the Eagles." In Katherine's stories, Vasagìhdzak "fixes" the animals who are hostile toward humans so that they no longer prey on humans.

Both Vasaagìhdzak and Ch'iteehàakwąįį are peripatetic, paddling alone up and down rivers and hiking across the country, where they encounter various talking animals, some of whom are friendly to them and some of whom are not. An underlying theme of Johnny and Sarah's versions is that these animals are just as smart if not smarter than humans, and for that reason they need to be respected. Vasaagìhdzak is a sly trickster who pays the price for his homocentric air of superiority and repeatedly ends up playing the dupe.

The last episode in Johnny's Vasaagìhdzak repertoire is the unusual and unique one of "Vasaagìhdzak and the King," which seems to have been influenced by European folklore. When I played the tape of this story for the four surviving children in the Frank family in 1989, they said they had never heard it, even though they knew all the rest of their father's stories in the cycle. Of all the Johnny Frank stories then, this one seems closest to his own invention, an invention within the tradition.

Vasaagìhdzak (or in Canada sometimes pronounced Vasaagihjik) is probably the Gwich'in pronunciation of *Wasagatchak*, the protagonist of a similar story cycle well known among the Woods Cree and Plains Cree of central and eastern Canada (see Russell 1898; Bloomfield 1934). Although no one knows which cycle came first, the Cree or the Gwich'in, or which way the stories traveled, or historically (or prehistorically) when they were transmitted, certain episodes such as "Vasagìhdzak and the Dancing Ducks," "Vasagìhdzak and Fox," and Vasagìhdzak juggling his eyes have diffused all across the North American subarctic and are told in several Indian languages. The names Vasagìhdzak and Wasagatchak are related to the English words "whiskey jack," which became the common nickname for the camp robber or gray jay, a bird that hangs around Indian camps looking for scraps of food to steal.

For Gwich'in storytellers living on the Canadian side, Ch'iteehàakwąįį is usually pronounced *Ataachookaii* ("he paddled the wrong way"). In a prefatory remark to his telling of "Ch'iteehàakwąįį and the Big Man," however, Johnny says that some Inuits he knew insisted Ch'iteehàakwąįį was really one of their own, but to my knowledge none of the episodes in the Ch'iteehàakwąįį cycle has ever been recorded from the Iñupiat on Alaska's North Slope.

Formally, Gwich'in storytellers do not classify their stories by genre. In Gwich'in, the word *gwandak* applies to all kinds of stories, whether or not they contain supernatural characters and events, talking animals, historical or legendary material, autobiographical recollections, or the latest news. The Euro-American concept of myth does not apply to the repertoires of the Gwich'in or other Native American tribes and may actually distort their nature and scope (see Mishler 1983a; Petrone 1990).

In the present collection, readers will take particular delight in the stunning descriptive images and tropes of Johnny's tales. In the story of the death of Òol Ti', for example, we are introduced to a wonderfully mysterious man coming across the lake: "The sun was sparkling on his muskrat skin jacket, they say." In another story, the merciless warrior Goghwaii and his younger brother escaped "on the moving ice like young otters," and later on when they attacked the Inuit, "Goghwaii's people came down the ridge like an avalanche." On a much smaller scale, Johnny's stories of the wars between the Gwich'in and the Inuit are graphically reminiscent of the clash between the Achaeans and the Trojans in Homer's *The Iliad.* Our imagination soars when we read that "the arrows fell toward each other like snowflakes until there was nobody left alive," or that "Tł'èevì' Tì's wife was shot in her breast with an arrow," and that after the battle "the arrows were stacked up like piles of porcupine quills." These are all literary gems.

One group of stories that holds a special fascination for Alaska women's studies is the little old woman trilogy, two of them told by Sarah and one by Johnny. These three texts — "The Old Woman and the Grizzly Bear," "The Old Woman and the Brush Man," and "The Little Old Woman and the Big Fish" — show the tremendous resilience and resourcefulness of elderly women left to survive on their own in a hostile world. The tremendous appeal of Velma Wallis's bestseller, *Two Old Women* (1993), is based on a similar Gwich'in folktale told to her by her mother, Mae Wallis of Fort Yukon. We discover that for these women, fish, rabbits, and ground squirrels are much more important to everyday survival than moose and caribou. Sarah Frank's recollection of the four old women she looked after (see Part II) also frames these stories and grounds them in the real world, for not every little old woman was independent and self-sufficient. Many of them depended heavily on younger friends and relatives like Sarah to take care of them.

Another group of texts could be called the Iñupiat wars trilogy — the stories of Kǫ̀'ehdan, told by Sarah, and Goghwaii and Tł'èevì' Tì', told by Johnny. These are historical tales which chronicle the struggle over territory between the Gwich'in and Iñupiat on the Arctic slope and in the central Brooks Range. It is interesting that Goghwaii, even though he is Gwich'in and prevails over the Iñupiat in battle, is not portrayed as a hero but as a ruthless "bad man" without heart or feeling.

We have supplied some annotations which illuminate the texture of the stories, both in English and Gwich'in, but the texts must by necessity remain somewhat distant from the non-Gwich'in reader, even in translation. Fortunately, much of the missing context is supplied by ethnographies of the Gwich'in written by Cornelius Osgood (1936) and Robert McKennan (1965), whose work is highly recommended. Although still available in many public and university libraries, McKennan's book, which contains a fine photograph of Johnny Frank, has long been out of print and is now a collector's item. When I visited John Fredson High School in Venetie in early June, 1995, I was saddened to learn that the school library had not even one reference copy of this important monograph available for teachers and students.

The life histories of Johnny and Sarah which follow in Part II and the ethnographic and historical information in Part III provide the context for the traditional stories in Part I. The distant past is framed by the recent past. Américo Paredes, one of my mentors in folklore at the University of Texas, always said that one of the great sins of American folklore scholarship has been the separation of the folk from the lore. Certainly Alaska already has more than its share of published collections of stories that tell us nothing at all about the storytellers. Luckily, here we are able to join the two.

In the Frank stories included here and in McKennan's (1965) collection, as well as in those told by other Gwich'in storytellers, the animals that have human attributes are usually not those used for food, and most of these are either predators or scavengers. The wolverine, wolf, eagle, raven or crow, fox, marten, mouse, loon, camp robber, brown bear, and frog, for example, all have speaking parts in traditional tales and are all considered inedible except in times of great starvation. A second smaller group consists of largely inedible species such as the owl and the dog who seldom play any role at all in traditional stories.

By contrast, Dall sheep, ground squirrel, lynx, and most kinds of fish, which are depended upon by the Gwich'in for food, often appear in traditional stories but usually remain objectified. A fourth group, however, including caribou, moose, muskrat, beaver, porcupine, hare, and a few species of ducks, provide food for humans and also have speaking parts in some of the stories. They are anthropomorphic fixtures.

This taxonomic separation of roles by species actually has a lot to do with the Gwich'in world view and belief system, and it only becomes apparent by looking at the entire corpus of published Gwich'in stories. It is no accident that those listed in the first and second groups seem to be the animals used most often by Gwich'in shamans for medicine power when they dream.

The assembled corpus of Johnny and Sarah Frank's stories provides many opportunities for students of folklore to do additional scholarly research and add breadth and depth to the texts. Tracking down tale types and variants in other collections is one of these opportunities. Looking at the historical evolution and shaping of the Vasagìhdzak and Ch'iteehàakwąįį cycles is another, and writing informed explications of the stories by drawing upon ethnographic knowledge is a third. From the very beginning of the project, we made a special effort to transcribe and preserve Johnny's and Sarah's multiple tellings of the same tales, and a close reading will reveal subtle differences between these tellings depending on the audience and the persons who made the recordings. It is intriguing, for example, to compare Johnny's telling of the story of Dak Neehaa to me in 1972 with the version McKennan recorded from him thirty-nine years earlier (McKennan 1965:82-83).

Gwich'in Folklore Scholarship in Retrospect

Most printed collections of Gwich'in folklore include only loose English translations of the Gwich'in, but sometimes these translations can be useful for understanding the geographic distribution and changes in the motifs and sequencing of individual tales. The earliest collections were made by the Anglican missionary Robert McDonald (1876) at La Pierre's House and by the Oblate missionary Émile Petitot (1886; 1970). In comparison with contemporary texts and translations, Petitot's now seem fairly unreliable. In the early part of the 20th century small collections of stories from Fort McPherson, NWT, were published in English in the *Journal of American Folklore* by Frank Russell (1900) and Charles Camsell (1915).

In 1923 the linguist Edward Sapir met and worked with John Fredson, who later taught school in Venetie, and Sapir recorded a large number of Fredson's traditional stories and personal experience narratives in Gwich'in. Sapir's transcriptions, which were made with the International Phonetic Alphabet, were later retranscribed by Katherine Peter and published by the Alaska Native Language Center (McGary 1982) in the new Gwich'in orthography developed by Dick Mueller. In the early 1930s Robert McKennan (1965) and Cornelius Osgood (1936) both collected Gwich'in stories, and both men used John Fredson as their principal translator. Then in the early 1950s Douglas Leechman (1950; 1952) published two small collections of Gwich'in stories from Old Crow, and Charles Keim (1964) also collected a few from the same community.

After this, very little documentation was done with Gwich'in oral tradition until John Ritter began collecting stories from a large number of elderly and middle-aged speakers in Fort McPherson in the late 1960s and early 1970s. Ritter's collection is now archived in the Yukon Native Language Centre in Whitehorse, with security copies deposited in the Canadian National Museum Ethnology Division Archives in Ottawa. Other Canadian Gwich'in tape collections are housed in Inuvik and Fort McPherson.

In the mid-1960s the Canadian National Museum published a unique collection of Gwich'in stories written in nonstandard English by Paul Voudrach (1965), an elder born in the Gwich' in village of Tsiigehtchic but who ended up spending most of his life at Fort Good Hope among the Hare.

In 1972, Kathy Alexander, a Gwich'in speaker herself, made systematic taped collections in Alaskan Gwich'in villages for the Alaska Library Association. That year also, I began work in many of these same communities under a fellowship from the National Endowment for the Humanities, recording Gwich'in stories, songs, riddles, card games, personal names, and fiddle tunes from elders in Venetie, Arctic Village, Fort Yukon, Circle, Birch Creek, and Chalkyitsik (Mishler 1973, 1974, 1981a, 1983b, 1984, 1993, 2013). Most of these recordings are now deposited with the Alaska Native Language Archive in Fairbanks. While the large Alaska Library Association Songs and Legends collection has been archived at the University of Alaska in Fairbanks and copies of the tapes are still readily available, only six Gwich'in stories from this vast collection were ever transcribed, translated, and published. These appeared as poster-size broadsides (Alaska Library Association 1977).

During the early-1970s, Katherine Peter, the senior Gwich' in editor for this volume, began working at the Alaska Native Language Center as a literacy specialist. In the course of her work at the Center she produced four books of Gwich'in folktales over a two-year period. One of these volumes, *Deenaadai' Gwich'in Gwandak: Traditional Gwich'in Stories* (1975a) was based on collections from an elder whom I also have recorded, the late Natalie Erick of Fort Yukon (see Mishler 1981a). The others, including *Vasagìhdzak, Shoh Deetry'a haa Gwandak, Tr'injaa* (Peter 1975b), *Olti' Daga'at Dik Haa: Olti' and His Wife Dik* (Peter 1975c), and *Alaskan Folktales: Dinjii Zhuu Gwandak/Gwich'in Stories* (Peter 1976), were transcribed from the way Katherine Peter herself had heard them circulating in Gwich'in oral tradition. Together, these stories constitute an important body of work from a noted Gwich'in tradition bearer and scholar.

Fig. 9. Katherine Peter in Fairbanks, May, 1995. Photo by Craig Mishler.

Canadian anthropologist Richard Slobodin (1975), a specialist on Gwich'in culture, has published one of the few interpretive studies of a single Gwich'in tale, that of Kwanetun (Kǫ̀'ehdan), which he collected from William Iitza at a hunting camp forty miles northwest of Fort McPherson in 1947. Slobodin's discussion of aboriginal raiding and wife-stealing is helpful in understanding Sarah Frank's two versions of the same story in this volume. The earliest recorded version of the Kǫ̀'ehdan story was written down by Émile Petitot at Fort Good Hope in 1870 as told to him by Sylvain Vitoedh. The Petitot version broadly resembles these modem variants but seems hopelessly corrupt in many details. Apparently Petitot had an inadequate grasp of the language or relied upon an interpreter who only summarized the material.

Another interpretive study which sheds light on Johnny Frank's story "Ch'iteehàakwąįį and the Wolverines" (which appears in Part I of the present volume) is Anna Birgitta Rooth's essay, "The Wolverine's Trap" (Rooth 1980). Rooth, a Swedish folklorist, collected a variety of Athabaskan and Inuit folktales performed in English from various tribal groups in Alaska's Interior in 1966 and later published her extensive collection (Rooth 1971). Rooth did a five-part structural analysis of motifs and catchwords (key words) in "The Wolverine Trap" tale type based upon her own collections and upon previously published versions, including the one told by Johnny Frank to Robert McKennan in 1933 (McKennan 1965:116-120). A portion of Rooth's analysis is also focused on the comic aspects of the story, noting that "the Indians often laughed when a monologue or a dialogue was retold" (Rooth 1980:36). By observing first-hand the reaction of Indian audiences when the story was performed in front of her, Rooth was able to identify which motifs have the highest entertainment value.

Fig. 10. Sarah Frank, June, 1984. Photo by Alice Lynch, BIA ANCSA. Alaska and Polar Regions Collections and Archives, Rasmuson Library, University of Alaska Fairbanks.

Fig. 11. Hamel Frank and Craig Mishler in Venetie, July, 1994. Photo by Susanna Mishler.

The motif of the wolverine children telling their father that the apparently dead Ch'iteehàakwąįį moved or opened his eye is one of these comic moments and helps explain its appearance in more than one tale type. However, when we look at the transcription of Johnny Frank's Gwich'in version included herein, it's clear that what made Johnny himself laugh was not retelling the monologue or dialogue per se, but his descriptions and asides following the dialogue. Johnny's own laughter is indicated in the texts by the word *adlaa* in parentheses.

The exploratory work of Slobodin and Rooth is suggestive of what can be done to situate Gwich'in stories ethnohistorically within longstanding Gwich'in cultural traditions and ethnographically within contemporary Gwich'in performance settings. Between the present volume and other published and unpublished collections, there's now a rich abundance of texts and contexts waiting to be interpreted by students of Gwich'in language, history, and folk culture.

Johnny Frank

Deenaa Dą̀į' Dinjii Zhuu

<jfcm1a>

JF11.10 Aiits'ą' dinjii datthak, nihłi'izhii gwich'in datthak nihkheenjit[1] naajàt.

Łąąjat ts'ą' reh, nihts'ą' nįįzhìt kwaa nagadàl gwats'an dinjii nèekwąįį oo'àn nà'òo, nihłanjii ts'ą' geegwaandak tł'ęę t'ee nihts'ą' nigiidàl.

11.33 "Niłiriheeghàa jì' shrǫ̀'," ginyaa ts'ą' reh.

Aiits'ą' gwinzįį ts'ą' t'ee nihts'ą' nagadàl ts'ą' ginjih trak[2] hàa nihłàa *meeting* gahtsìi.

Łì'hàa dinjii chì' nizįį, izhìk gwànaa.

Dinjii datthak nankat gwandàii tthak *Alaska* gwandàii datthak ch'ihee'àa geegwitr'it'agwah'ìn.

12.08 Kwàt dinjii gwinzįį gwiheendàii gwizhrįh geenjit khàihłak gogwą̀h'įį.

Nàgaazhrìi dą̀į' dinjii *two hundred* ch'ihłòk naazhrìi.

Nankat gwintsìi *line up* ginlįį ts'ą' jyàa diginjìk, ts'ą' jidìi gwandàii datthak gaahkhòk ts'ą' shree nanh nèekwąįį.

That's two months, three months gwigwich'įį jyàhts'ą' gwizhrįh khaii neegiidàl.

Kwàt shin hee chan.

Łuk, jidìi nankat łuk jidii nintsal datthak shin hee keegii'ìn.

Geeghaih chan gwitr'it t'agagwah'in kwàa, ch'igihee'àa gwizhrįh.

13.09 Izhìk gwànaa nankat ch'atthą̀įį gwintł'òo gǫ̀ǫlįį kwaa, dinjii tr'ikhit gǫ̀ǫlįį.

Chandalar maybe four thousand jyàa dinjii dą̀ąych'yą̀ą.

Old Crow chan *five thousand people.*

Gwichyaa nahkat agàa datthak, *Fort Yukon.*

13.43 Kwàt Ch'eekwaii naii chan łi'hàa gwandaa ginlę̀įį.

---

1. In our contemporary dialect *nihkheenjit* becomes *nihłeenjit*. —KP

2. *Ginjih trak* means a speech so loud that people around the camp can hear it in their tents. —KP

Johnny Frank

The Early Days Indians

<jfcm1a>

JF11.10 Bands of Indians were always scared of each other.

When they got near each other, they usually sent out two people from each band to meet each other before the whole bands met.

11.33 "We shouldn't fight," they said.

And so when they met, they held a meeting using loud speeches.

People those days were very smart.

Every person living in Alaska worked for what he would eat.

12.08 People thought only about having better lives.

When they hunted, two hundred of them would hunt together.

They would all line up side by side and move forward killing any animals in their path.

They lived there for up to two or three months and that's the only way they made it through the winter.

In the summertime too.

They fished for all kinds of fish and hunted for all kinds of small animals.

Nobody did anything except work for their next meal.

13.09 In those days, there were hardly any big animals because there were too many people.

The population at *Chandalar* was maybe four thousand.

At *Old Crow* also there were five thousand people.

Even at *Fort Yukon* too.

13.43 But the population of the Inuit was even higher.

Some place Point Barrow, Hudson Island,[3] *Hudson* aii datthak *four thousand people.*

14.05 Àkwàt aiits'ą̀' jidìi datthak shik nitsyą' ilìk dą̀į' dinjii lę̨įį ihdàndhàgą̀įį.

Ch'atthą̀įį chan nitsyą̀' neelìk dą̀į' dinjii lę̨įį ti'ìdlį̀'.

Łì'hàa gògwàntrii ch'iinaa tr'iniinjìl.

14.35 Kwàt shįį shitsųh reh lyâa tthak gànaandàii.

Aiits'ą̀' ti'yąą hàa gwich'įį ts'ą̀' reh vàn khàchii'ak, ts'ą̀' drin t'ąhthee datthak gwaandak, deenaa dą̀į'gogwandàk.

Adan t'ee tr'iinin nilįį gwànaa gwandak aii datthak łì'hàa gwinzįį tthak gànaandàii.

Jyàa dinch'yaa ts'ą̀' jyàanch'yąą ts'ą̀' nihzhyąą neegidiijìi.

Kwàt ch'izhii nihzhyąą needijii naii chan akòodìginyaa kwaa ts'ą̀' reh gwandak gii'įį kwaa ts'ą̀' nihzhyąą neegidiijìi.

Aii naii t'ee giveh'an gwìizų̀ų.

Nankat datthak gòo'ą̀įį.

15.35 Aiits'ą̀' shitsii *Ditsii Gìitł'ųų,*[4] aii chan Di'hąįį Gwich'in nilįį ts'ą̀' łyâa khàihkwaii nitsìi nilįį.[5]

Aii vyuu Dèets'è', aii chan gwik'ìt t'iinch'yà'.

16.03 Aiits'ą̀' *Neets'ąįį*[6] ch'adą̀į' łyâa dinjii gǫ̀ǫlįį.

Łì'hàa tthał gǫ̀ǫlįį.

Aii k'ìighai' dinjii gwandàii.

Aiits'ą̀' oo'àt dachan ehdan gwà'àn googàa *Dinjii Zhuh* gǫ̀ǫlįį.

16.38 Aii naii k'ìighai' gwinzįį ts'ą̀' gogwąąhtł'òo gòo'ą̀įį.

---

3. *Hudson Island* seems to be Johnny Frank's way of pronouncing *Herschel Island.* —CM

4. Diits'ii Giitł'uu was Johnny's father's father — see the Frank Family Tree in Appendix A. —CM

5. The Di'hąįį Gwich'in were a separate band from the Neets'it Gwich'in around *Arctic Village*, and Johnny belonged to the Di'hąįį. Diitsii Giitł'uu was the common ancestor from whom all of the Franks, Tritts, and Roberts families trace their lineage. Much has been written about this historic lost tribe (see esp. McKennan, 1935 and 1965; Hadleigh-West, 1959; and Burch and Mishler, 1995). —CM

6. *Neets'ąįį* is a nickname for *Arctic Village*. —JE

There were four thousand people at *Point Barrow* and at *Hudson Island* and all around there.

14.05 When the food ran out, lots of people starved.

And when big game animals were scarce, lots of people froze to death.

So we've come a long way through a really hard life.

14.35 My grandmother remembered it all.

When she was living with my father, she got up in the morning and told stories all day long about the days of long ago.

She really remembered well all the stories about the time when she was a child.

That was her generation, but there were some people her age who didn't tell stories at all.

It was no good because of them.

They were all over the country.

15.35 My grandfather *Ditsii Giitł'uu* was *Di'hąįį Gwich'in* and was a big chief.

His younger sister's son *Dèets'è'* was the same way too.

16.03 So there used to be lots of people at *Arctic Village*.

There were lots of caribou fences too.

And that's how people lived.

There were also lots of Indians living on the tundra.

16.38 It was because of them that there was power to go on living.

Oonjìt *Old Crow,* izhìk chan *Òol Tì'*, dagoondee hàa chan łyâa dinjii gwintsii veegòo'ą̀įį ginlì'.

16.54 Łyâa zhyą̀ą *President* k'ìt t'iginch'yàa.

Aii datthak t'ee *Demòcrat* naii.[7]

Aiits'ą̀' oonjìt *Teetł'it Zheh* [8] chan izhìk chan dinjii jyàa dìnch'yàa.

Aii chan t'ee *K'i'naats'ų̀'* òozhìi.

Lyâa dinjii gǫ̀ǫzhįį.

17.33 Aii vaghàih dinjii łanaadàl gwànaa łì'hàa dinjii gǫ̀ǫlįį gwinyàa.

Dinjii kak ànàa'ąį' gwi'ìt deehiindak gwinyàa.

18.05 Aii gehnaa nįįzhìt jyàa dìgwii'in ts'ą̀' gehnaa nįįzhìt gwanaa hee reh nankat dinjii datthak nihiłą̌ąjat, nihłigidìitth'ak kwaa ts'ą̀' łyâa chan gą̌ąjàt.

18.28 Kwàt izhìk gwànaa *Gwichyaa* Gwich'in naii łyâa neeshreegâahch'yaa.

Aii *chief* gòodlit gwats'an, aii gwats'ą̀' nąhjyàa łyâa dinjii neeshrâahch'yaa *Gwichyaa* nąhkak.[9]

K'ì' googàa gii'įį kwaa gooràhnyàa.

18.57 Aiits'ą̀' geetèe hee dinjii ìizųų naii k'ìighai' geetèe chan nihłiriighàk nàgwàatth'ak.

19.17 Aii shitsųh *Ndìk* aii vijùu vàh ch'izhii tr'ìnjyàa nèekwąįį haa geetèe hee *April* nan zhyą̀ą ch'ii'àn gahadàl.

19.35 Yeendee zhat gwich'in naii teetł'an ts'ą̀' tr'inghan ts'ą̀', zhyą̀ą ch'ii'àn gahadàl ts'ą̀' tthaa khàh'òo, dagǫǫ chan ghadi'giintł'įį.

19.50 Aii gwik'ìighai' gwinzįį gogwandàii, ts'ą̀' gavàa gwahgǫ̀' ts'ą̀' shin datthak chan tthaa gyàh, chii khyą̀h hàa, aii kee gii'in ts'ą̀' gogwandàii geetèe hee.

20.05 Tł'ęę khaiits'ą̀' hee neegooràą'ìk.

---

7. Johnny is referring to Gwich'in clans, which he likens to political parties such as Democrats and Republicans. —CM

8. *Teetł'it Zheh* is the name for *Fort McPherson, N.W.T.*, a major Gwich'in community on the *Peel River*. —CM

9. *Gwichyaa* is the shortened form of *Gwichyaa Zhee* (literally 'Flatlands House'), the traditional name for *Fort Yukon*. —JE and CM

Over at *Old Crow*, there were *Òol Tì’* and his older brother, who were rich and powerful men.

16.54 They were like Presidents.

They were all Democrats.

And so was everybody over at *Fort McPherson.*

There was also a man named *K’i’naats’ų̀’.*

He was really a smart man.

17.33 Whenever there was a gathering, they say there were lots of people.

Way before all this happened though, they say people were afraid of each other.

18.05 They didn’t understand each other’s languages, and that’s why they were afraid of each other.

18.28 People on the *Yukon Flats* were very poor in those days.

People there were poor before the first chief was made chief at *Fort Yukon.*

They didn’t even have bows and arrows, that’s what they said about them.

18.57 Sometimes a war started because of some bad people.

19.17 My grandmother *Ndik’s* younger sister and two other women sometimes took off in April to parts unknown.

19.35 Half of those people in *Arctic Village* were killed at one time.

Some took off to live on the ground squirrels and also whatever ptarmigan they could snare.

19.50 They lived well that way, and they made it through the winter until spring.

All summer long, they lived by snaring and trapping ground squirrels.

20.05 Later on we would finally see them again in the fall.

Khanjii *one year* tthak, tr'ìnjàa nèekwąįį googàa zhik ch'ii'àn.

Geetèe *two year* tł'ęę googàa ch'ii'ęę tr'eegii'òo.

20.24 Łì'hàa gògwàntrii, dinjii haa t'igehee ch'yaa geenjit chan gooveegògwàntrii.

Ch'ii'àn than chan ch'ànjaa naii than hee, geetee hèe goolat naii zhat gwats'ą' gookwàa, angilik.

20.44 Łì'hàa gògǫǫntrii yeenaa gwinìindhàt.

Aii googàa dinjii gwats'an gwandàii tr'aadlìt.

Anihłik kwaiik'ìt hee.

21.25 Kwàt izhìk gwànaa K'eegwaadhat[10] hàa gwiindàii kwaa.

Aii googàa łyâa tsingwąhch'yaa t'iginyaa ts'ą' reh.

Zhyąą yeedàk gwęętak kwàa ginyąą.

Kwàt jii geeghaih chan jidii Ch'ank'yàa Tr'aanduu[11] gwiheenjyàa łii, aii chan reh dee'ęę t'įįnch'ii jyàa googàhnyàa.

21.54 Tr'ąh'in kwaa gwiizhìk vik'ìighai' gwìizųų.

Jyàa nyaa t'iginyàa.

Ginjih vàgwàntrii reh.

Kwàt shįį zhrįh dìhtth'ak, gàh duuyeh tr'îitth'àk.

22.07 Kwàt aii shitsųh vik'ìighai' datthak gàashandàii.

Googàa geetàk hee chan dinjii łyâa gògwàntrii, dinjii goodhaii năadhàk zhyąą *one place,* zhyąą jyàa dòonch'yaa dài', gwik'ìighai' gwiheezyàa geenjit gwitr'it t'ideegogwąąh'in dąį', dinjii lęįį geeginkhii.

Dinjii dazhan aii naii chan gwintsìi t'eegwąąhch'yà'.

22.59 Dzaa jùk gweendàa aii *Russiàn* tr'oochìt Dinjii Zhuh.

Ts'ą' tr'iinjìk aiitł'ęę chan *English* naii.

Oonjùk hee nankat deegaajil gwinyaa gàa łi'hàa, gwinzįį goot'èegwąąhch'yą kwàa.

Giveh'àn chan dinjii, *Alaskà* Dinjii Zhuh khaiinjii datthak ts'ik ìizųų tthak hàa nĭinjìk.

---

10. *K'eegwaadhat* is the Lord or God. —KP

11. Johnny and Sarah had a puppy dog named *Tr'aanduu* ('The Bad One') when I visited them at *Gold Camp* in November, 1972. He was jokingly referred to as 'The Devil.' —CM

Sometimes two women stayed out for almost a whole year.
Two old women went out like that for one or two years, but they still came back.

20.24 Life was hard for them when they stayed together, so even the old people went out.
Sometimes they didn't make it and died.

20.44 Life was really hard in the past.
We are here today somehow due to those people in almost all the villages.

21.25 In those days, we didn't know anything about God.
Still, they say something really odd happened.
People still say there is no secret about us up in heaven.
But besides this they also talked about the Devil.

21.54 What they meant about the Devil back then was that you can't see him when he causes trouble.
That's what they said.
They used difficult words to explain these situations.
I was the only one who could understand it.

22.07 I know all of this from my grandmother.
During the hard times when people were in trouble, they stayed in one place, and that's when they talked about all of these things.
They also used medicine men for help.

22.59 The Russians were the first to help the Indians around here.
We also heard that after them the English people landed somewhere down that way.
But they say we didn't get any help from them.
Because of them many Alaskan Indians died off from all the diseases they brought over.

23.38 Kwàt izhìk gwànaa dinjii chan nį̀įzhìt kwàa, dinjii chan iłts'ik kwàa, dinjii chan igwîinjii kwàa.

23.53 Aiits'ą̀' łyâa dinjii lęįį, aii k'ìighai' gwizhrįh dinjii gwinzįį gwandàii.

24.22 Kwàt aii dą̀hthee dąį' gwats'an jii nankak dinjii gwahą̀hdàii, dinjii ch'ìhłęę gàa gàadandàii kwàa.

Jidii nankat gwandàii tsal datthak chan dinjii nilįį gwànaa gwinyàa.

24.44 Ną̀htryàa, zhoh, shih, aii datthak dinjii.

Neegǫǫ tthak dinjii nilįį.

Oozhòk chee łuk googàa datthak reh dinjii nilįį gwinyàa.

Aii tthak chan googwandàk gǫ̀ǫlį̀į.

25.21 Izhìk gwànaa dinjik googàa kwàa.

Kwàt deenaa dąį' nank'atą̂ąhąįį gwinyaa.

Izhìk dąį' hee vakwàa ts'ą̀' valàt van zhìt, tąįh zhìt hàa gwandàii łii, aii van chųų zhìt.

Aii reh van ts'an khą̀h'oo k'ìighai' nankak, dinjik gòodlit łyâa gwinzįį gàagwiindàii.

AW26.00 Gàashandàii kwaa gik'yàhaldal łii.

JF26.06 Ą̀ahą'.

Kwàt izhìk gwànaa aii gwandàii łuk *or* nankat nintsal, ch'atthàii hàa dinjii nilįį gwànaa.

Aii googàa chan ginjih ch'ìhłak zhrįh t'eegwąąhch'yaa gwinyaa gavăihnyàa.

Łuk dinjii nilįį dąį' vàariginkhii eedan t'eh danàaginkhìi.

Zhik gwà'àn nintsal oo'òk neehiniidàl, dzii tsal agàa.

Aii googàa chan vàa riginkhii danàaginkhii.

26.44 Lyâa zhyą̀ą ginjih ìhłak zhrįh t'eegwąąhch'yaa gwinyaa tr'oochìt dąį'.

23.38 But before that, our people didn't die from diseases, and people didn't get hurt.

23.53 And it was really because of lots of people that they lived so well.

24.22 Nobody knows how long there have been men on this earth.

Even the small animals that were alive back then were people, they say.

24.44 The wolverines, the wolves, and the brown bears were all people.

Even the foxes were people.

All the fish in the water were people, they say.

Lots of their stories are like that too.

25.21 But there were no moose in those days.

They say all the animals died from the great flood long, long ago. Some animals lived underground and some lived under water.

And we all know that the moose came from the lakes to the land.

AW26.00 I'm listening to stories I didn't even know about before.

JF26.06 Yes.

In those days all the fish and all the small animals and large game animals were human.

And yet they all spoke one language, they say.

A human could talk back and forth to the fishes and to the birds.

And they in turn could talk to humans.

26.44 In the beginning, they say, there was really only one language.

Sarah Frank

Ch'iteehàakwąįį

<sfwsl05fa>

SF5.09 Aiits'ą̀' yaaghà' *Ch'iteehàakwąįį* giyàhnyąą chan.
Aii chan reh *Jesus* aii veeragwaandak t'aràhnyą̀ą gwìch'in reh gwinyaa.
Aii chan reh jidii nin ìizųų, nàhąą?
Nin ìizųų kwaii reh tthak àn iłtsąįį k'ìt reh t'igiyàhnyą̀ą.
5.45 Aiitł'ęę neeghaii (adlaa).
Neeghaii chan eetèedhakwąįį izhìk.
It'ee, izhìk it'ee gwats'ą̀' dą̀i' yeetèeheekwaa gwats'ą̀', it'ee oondòk tr'ih hàa yeendòk jyàa dìi'in.
6.05 Akhài' jidìi dinjii vàhtr'įįzhraa di'įį łee aii. Aii t'ee oondàa chiitthaii ts'ą̀' t'ee yitr'ìi hàa t'ee yiihiłshrą̀ą dǫ̀hłį̀į.
Akhài'aii yazhràa dik'yàatł'įį t'inch'yaa. Kwàt aii reh, aii reh òonjik reh giyàhnyą̀ą, Aiits'ą̀' t'ee zhyą̀ą reh yehgǫǫ dhakwąįį dǫ̀hłį̀į.
6.30 Aiitł'ee chan hee, chan hee yeetèedhakwąįį izhìk it'ee t'inyąą, vàràhnyàa (adlaa).
Diinaah'in[1] gwiizhìk, "Dèiinch'yaa shijiindèe khìdhįį'aii ch'yaa gwį̀įch'in?" danàhnyą̀ą.
DF6.54 Aii łuk yeenjit idîiltsąįį vàràhnyàa oiihnyąą łii?
SF6.59 Tr'ih reh giyàhnyą̀ą.
7.09 Aiits'ą̀' aii jidìi yats'an oonjik, aii t'ee zhik tr'ih, tr'ih chì'[2] khat gwà'àn k'iindàa gwit'eh yį̀į'ąįį.
Aiits'ą̀' t'ee jyàa dìyìinlìk, ts'ą̀' t'ee yàagaandàii eenjit t'ee.
"Łyâa vàhshatr'ôołchį'," yàhnyàa.
7.31 "Àkwàt aii jì' dhinchįį," nyàa.
Aii gwiizhìk aii diitsįh t'ee aii tr'ih na'at łee vàràhnyàa.
Na'at łee, ts'ą̀' oondàa jidii yats'àn oonjik nǐin'ą̀įį gwats'ą̀'.

1. In Gwich'in it's often the case that alternating point of view is used humorously. So "Dii'naah'in" here literally means "he [Frog] was looking at us," but figuratively it means "he was looking at him, i.e. Ch'iteehàakwąįį." This pronoun shift is further amplified by the quotative "danàhnyą̀ą" which glosses as 'he told us.' —KF and CM

2. The little *tr'ih tsal* canoes Gwich'in make aren't open all the way. The front part, which is covered on top, is called *tr'ih ki'*, or in Sarah's dialect, *tr'ih chi'*. —KP

Sarah Frank

Ch’iteehàakwąįį: He Paddled Among Them

<sfwsl05fa>

SF5.09 And then there’s also this person they call *Ch’iteehàakwąįį*.
We all think maybe he’s the same as the one they call *Jesus*, so they say.
Also you see all those bad wild animals?
It seems like he got rid of all those bad wild animals.
After that there’s the frog (laughs).
He [*Ch’iteehàakwąįį*] paddled ashore to the frog.
Now, before he came ashore to him, he was out canoeing.

6.05 The frog had a hook which he used to hook people with. He dove in and must have hooked it up to *Ch’iteehàakwąįį*’s canoe, where the hook was attached to the end of a pole.
They say *Ch’iteehàakwąįį* grabbed the hook, and so he just paddled right past the frog.

6.30 Once again, he paddled right up to the frog on the shore and told him right there, they say (laughs).
While he [*Frog*] was looking at us,
“Don’t you look just like the one who took my hook?” he told us.

DF6.54 I thought they said *Ch’iteehàakwąįį* turned himself into a fish for him?

SF6.59 They said it was a canoe.

7.09 So what he took from him, then he put it inside the bow of the canoe.
So *Ch’iteehàakwąįį* did that, and he knew.
“I’m really sleepy,” he told him.

7.31 “Then go to sleep,” the frog said.
While he was sleeping, they say the frog was unstitching the canoe.
He was unstitching it towards where *Ch’iteehàakwąįį* hid the hook.

It'ee tthak neeya'at łee gwiizhìk it'ee yats'ą̀' tr'ineeriidhat, izhìk t'ee t'iyàhnyąą dǫ̀hłį̀į.

7.58 "Ijìi aii tr'ih shrigwindit neera'at łee chan."

Aii chan na'at vàràhnyàa.

8.11 Izhìk t'ee t'inyąą vàràhnyàa.

"Shineedoolk'àt neehąąl'yàa ghat t'ishi'ìn,"[3] nyaa vàràhnyàa.

Aiits'ą̀', "Aii jì' chan hee gwintsàl neenichį̀į," nyą̀ą.

Aiits'ą̀' chan hee gineechirii'aii gwiizhìk, hee t'ee aii tr'ih neeya'at ch'yąą tthak nizįį niłtsąįį.

Jyàa reh giyàhnyąą.

8.36 Aii t'ee nįįzhit dą̀į' hee yaaghà' Shitsųų *Mil Vahan* aii,[4] aii ti'yąą chįh dą̀į' gwats'an vagǫ̀ǫlii į'.

DF8.50 Hmm.

SF8.52 Aii naįį shandàh geegogwaandak hee t'iginyąą t'agwaihnyą̀ą.

Aii Shitsųų *Mil Vahan*, aiit'ee łyâa *old* nilįį.

<sfkf2b>

CF45.23 Shitsųų aii *Ch'iteehàakwąįį* giyàhnyaa ijìi?

SF Ą̀ąhą'.

CF45.28 Aii *Vasaagìhdzak* lèe t'agàhnyàa?

SF45.32 Ch'izhįį t'agàhnyàa.

Vasaagìhdzak aii chan thòk.

Aiits'ą̀' yaaghà' *Ch'iteehàakwąįį* ginyaa aii chan thòk.[5]

CF45.43 Aii gwandak dagantł'oo łyâa zhyą̀ą nihtee gwigwiinlii łii.

Aiits'ą̀' shįį aii jyàhts'ą̀' gwîihtth'ak kwaa gwiizhìk t'iginyaa t'agavăihnyàa.

Izhìk geh'àn noaałkat t'iihnyàa.

SF45.58 *Vasaagìhdzak* chat thòk aiits'ą̀' zhik *Ch'iteehàakwąįį* chan ginyaa aii chan thòk.

---

3. I heard from my grandmother Maggie Roberts that the expression "I will see my own eyebrow," was an old saying that meant "Excuse me." —KF

4. *Shitsuu* Mil Vahan, *Sarah Frank vitsuu aii vahan*. Sarah is referring here to her grandmother Mil's mother, her own great-grandmother. —JE

5. They changed Vasaagìhdzak's name to Ch'iteehàakwąįį when he floated down the river. He's the same person. —KP

Just when he was near it (the hook), *Ch'iteehàakwąįį* was suddenly startled.

This is what he told the frog:

7.58 "It's a bad omen that you're taking the canoe apart."

They say he was unstitching the canoe.

8.11 That's when they say the frog told him,

"I will see my own eyebrow," he said, they say.

So the frog told him, "Take another short nap," which he did.

And while he was napping, the frog stitched his canoe back together again.

This is what they say about it.

8.36 A long time ago, my grandmother *Mil Vahan* was born way before my father.

DF8.50 Hmm.

SF8.52 I'm saying that they're the ones who were telling each other this story.

My grandmother *Mil Vahan* was really old.

<sfkf2b>

CF45.23 Grandma, you know that one they talk about, *Ch'iteehàakwąįį?*

SF Yes.

CF45.28 Do you mean *Vasaagìhdzak?*

SF45.32 He's a different one.

So *Vasaagìhdzak* is one, and *Ch'iteehàakwąįį* is another one too.

CF45.43 The stories written about him are all mixed up.

They all say it happened that way, but I didn't hear about it that way.

That's why I'm asking you about it.

SF45.58 They say that *Ch'iteehàakwąįį* is the same person as *Vasaagìhdzak.*

Vasaagìhdzak aii zhik nankat dinjii ìizųų chan gwinyąą, nàhąą.

CF Ą̀ąhà’.

SF46.50 Aii it’ee *Ch’iteehàakwąįį* chan gwinyąą.

Àkwàt jii *Vasaagìhdzak* aii ree vagwandàk łyâa tsyąąhch’yaa roh.

Àkwàt jii *Ch’iteehàakwąįį* aii, aii jùk nankat jidii shrigwirilii, nàhąą?

CF Ą̀ąhà’.

SF46.56 Oondùk diihit nąįį jyàa dìgìi’ìn.

Aii łì’hàa *Jesus* nankat indì’.

Aii zhyą̀ą gogwandàk k’it t’avăihnyàa, *Ch’iteehàakwąįį*.

Johnny Frank

Ch’iteehàakwąįį Dinjii Choh Hàa

<jfka404>

JF5.36 *Ch’iteehàakwąįį* aii reh Ch’eekwaii t’aràhnyaa łee į’.

Aii Ch’eekwaii ch’ìhłak aii, *Ch’iteehàakwąįį* eegavàagwaldak, akhài’ Ch’eekwaii t’aràhnyaa shàgàhnyàa (adlaa).

5.48 Aiits’ą̀’ nankat dinjii gwintł’òo gòolįį kwaa, nàhąą?

Aiits’ą̀’ yee’àt gwà’àn nangwinjirh zhyą̀ą oondùk ddhah zhìt k’aii tsal izhìk hèe Ch’eekwaii gwich’įį, vigii ch’ìhłak gòodlit.

6.12 Łyâa nįįzhùk zhik gwigwih’įį gàa vigii ihłak gòodlit aii łyâa, chan goonzhįį ts’ą̀’ chan dinjii niint’aii nilį̀į, *lucky* chan nilį̀į.

6.19 Aiits’ą̀’ zhyą̀ą giits’ą̀’ giinkhii kwàa.

Dink’indhat gwats’an giits’a’ giinkhii kwaa gàa reh.

Naazhrii datthak jidii eenjit naazhrii, oo’ęę naazhik.

6.32 Haahchii kwaa ts’ą̀’ reh.

Gwiizhìk łąįį tik reh gii’ii.

Aii chan łyaa łąįį nizii.

Aiits’ą̀’ reh, giits’a’ giinkhii kwaa akwàt t’ǫ̀ǫhłįį dinjii ji’ gàa reh gàandaii kwàa.

Although I myself did not hear it that way, that’s what they say, you see.

CF Yes.

SF46.50 They talk about *Ch’iteehàakwąįį* too.
But *Vasaagìhdzak* stories are really more comical.
Ch’iteehàakwąįį is the one who took care of everything that was bad, you know?

CF Yes.

SF46.56 You see how they traveled around up here.
Truly, *Jesus* was on this earth.
I’m saying *Ch’iteehàkwąįį* is just the same story.

Johnny Frank

Ch’iteehàakwąįį and the Big Man

<jfka404>

JF5.36 *Ch’iteehàakwąįį* was actually an Inuit.
I was telling the Inuit about *Ch’iteehàakwąįį* once, and they told me he was an Inuit guy (laughs).

5.48 So you see?
There were hardly any people around that area.
There was this Inuit guy who lived on a mountain
Somewhere up that way. He had one child born.

6.12 They lived there a long time, but he had only one child.
He was smart, strong, and lucky too.

6.19 Nobody talked to him all the time he was growing up.
But each time he hunted he brought back whatever he hunted for.

6.32 He was always quiet.
They had three dogs.
They were really good dogs too.
Nobody talked to him, so he didn’t know if there were people living anywhere around.

6.58 Aiits'ą̀' adan aii it'ee goonzhį̀į dhidlìt ts'ą̀' ginìnjih'ahthat akhài' reh, ts'ą̀' łyâa ninzhùk gweedhaa gwideezhak reh.

Ch'anjàa dhidlìt gwiizhìk reh, t'ǫ̂ǫhłįį dinjii aii ts'an yuu, ti'yąą, ni'ęę hàa t'iginch'yaa gwìch'in nindhan reh.

Giyàagwaandak kwàa.

7.13 Zhik nankat gwinzįį gwigwih'įį izhìk geegintsą̀į' ts'ą̀' reh giyàagwaandak kwàa.

T'ǫ̂ǫhłįį dinjii ts'ą̀' rohoojyàa heenjyàa giyàandaii, nàhąą?

7.29 Aiits'ą̀' reh, gohch'it reh, łyâa gwintł'òo nìnjich'adhat.

Aiits'ą̀' t'ee reh shin tthak, shih kee'in.

Shìh oo'ęę naazhik, aii chan yahgąįį, kwàt jidìi khwaii tr'ahahtsyàa tthak chan.

7.50 Jidìi ch'atthą̀įį daazhyaa datthak — divii, vadzaih, shih.

Aiits'ą̀' aii zhik zheh chan giveegwìłtsą̀įį.

Zhyą̀ą nyą̀' kwành, chii gwakwaiitł'ęę gwats'ą̀' nèelzhii nantį̀į.

8.07 Nyą' shril jeiinch'yaa ts'ą̀' k'àii hàa zhyą̀ą gwizhìt khaihłak ginch'yaa gwìłtsąįį roh.

Zheh gwaghoo gwachoh reh.

8.21 Aiits'ą̀' t'ee chan traa nihk'yàa łyâa niinzhìk gwà'àn łąįį tik hàa traa t'ah'in.

K'il chan taih gwìch'in zhik gwà'àn dhidlii.

Kwàt shìh chan gwik'ìt t'iyinlìk.

8.48 Łyâa gwinlęįį neegwadadhat.

Giit'èehaahch'yàa aii goveenjit tthak shriìnlik tł'ęę.

Khaiits'ą̀' gǫ̀ǫlįį ts'ą̀' t'ee reh.

Aii łąįį tik tł'yah diinlii ts'ą̀' t'ee zhyą̀ą yeedeedàk àntł'it hàazhii, jyàanch'yaa ts'ą̀' *Gwazhał* taa inzhìi.

Ch'iitthàn łąįį tik hàa àhàa, łąįį ts'įį reh.

9.15 Gàa reh it'ee han shriit'agwą̀htsii.

Gwiizhìk reh yeedįį tankat reh, dinjii łyâa nitsìi vits'èe kwaa reh.

6.58 He got pretty smart on his own
and he thought about it for a very long time while he was there.
He got to be an elder, and he thought about it when he suspected that his parents must have come from some people somewhere.
They never told him.
7.13 They never did tell him anyway, because they only liked the place where they were living, you see?
They knew that he would want to go to where there were people, right?
7.29 And so he kept thinking for a long time.
He hunted for food all summer.
Every day he brought home food and dried it and made grease.
7.50 He brought back all kinds of game animals — sheep, caribou, grizzly bear.
He also built a dwelling for his parents.
It was just a hut covered with moss, banked with a gravel foundation.
8.07 He made a hut frame with willows and covered it with moss, and he made one big room.
It was a big round hut.
8.21 He gathered a lot of wood from far away with the three dogs.
He also made a big pile of dried willow.
He also did the same with the food.
8.48 It was many years later.
Whatever they needed, he prepared it for them.
So it was during the fall time.
So he hitched up his three dogs and started up the valley and crossed over the *Brooks Range*.
He was walking ahead of his three dogs.
9.15 So it was a huge river.
Meanwhile, down below on the ice, there was a very big man with no hat on.
So it was a big spear.

Gwiizhìk jidìi chiidzèe choo, aii zhrih ichyaa, aii zhrįh vikheeghàn.
Dinjik, shih, anything ch'ihlòk ahdzèe, ts'ą̀' gwizhrįh reh.
Chan, łyâa nint'aii.

9.36 Aii yeedįį reh ahaa ts'ą̀' t'ee reh, oonjit davàl kat dik'i' dàadlii.
Aiits'ą̀' gwiyeedak dazhoo ik nihdàk naatsùu ch'ìhłak chan niltsùu.
Yeendii zhyąą̀ k'igwâa'ee gwits'įį àhàa.
It'ee łyâa ninzhìt kwaa ahaa.
Aii gwiizhìk nihdìneetįį, gwiizhìk chiidzèe'ądak vàràhnyàa.

10.03 Aiits'ą̀' reh, gwinzįį, "Jùk łyâa gwinzįį ch'ihih'àa.
Łyâa gwintł'oo ch'ihih'àa," nyaa ts'ą̀' t'ee reh.[6]
Gwiizhìk yaaghà' ch'iinaa reh łąįį tł'yah dàadlii aii tł'i' tsįį reh doodii.
Àkwàt ch'a'àa agàa aii jidii in'àl, googàa yàandaii kwàa.
Oo'òk hee oohìlzhin į'.

10.23 Tr'ikhit nitsii kwàt nint'aii k'ìt vìyìih'ya'.
Kwàt yehkįį dàkhįį di'ik niltsùu.
Yits'ì' k'aatłak.
Aii dinjii yik'ìt t'ii'in gǫ̀ǫlįį kwàa.

10.40 Aiits'ą̀' reh it'ee łyâa nahgǫ̀ǫ yeeninzhii,
"Gwinzįį ch'ihih'àa," nyaa gwiizhìk chiidzèechoo ahaa, dzaa ch'ii'àn dhidii gwiizhìk hee yąhtsit, akhài' reh yideek'ìt reh gwìłdzàk.
Ch'adan hee nàatłèe.
It'ee aii chiidzah hàa yuhdzìi, googàa yahdzak kwaa yàakogwìł'ąįį.

11.12 Gohch'it t'ee łyâa nìndhaa dhidlit, yàandàii, *Ch'iteehàakwąįį* aii.
Aiits'ą̀' yaaghà' dik'i' gwiteet'ịh gwik'ìinlii.

6. It seems it is the other man, not Ch'iteehàakwąįį, who was thinking this. —AR
This reading is correct. —JE

He only carried that.

That’s his only weapon.

Moose, grizzly bear, or anything, he only spears it once, and that’s it.

Also, he was very strong.

9.36 As the big man was coming from down below, *Ch’iteehàakwąįį* put his arrows on his toboggan.

And he took off one layer of a double-layered caribou skin overcoat.

The big man was coming straight ahead from down below.

He wasn’t very far away.

While he made a move, he threw his atlatl-like weapon, they say.

10.03 He was talking to himself, “I’m going to eat really good.

I’m going to eat a whole lot,” that big man said.

Meanwhile *Ch’iteehàakwąįį* was sitting on his toboggan with his dogs in harness.

The big guy was eating something, but *Ch’iteehàakwąįį* didn’t know what it was.

He was alert and ready for him.

10.23 The big guy looked very huge and strong.

Ch’iteehàakwąįį took off his outer layer of his coat.

Ch’iteehàakwąįį was there ahead of him.

There was nobody equal to *Ch’iteehàakwąįį*.

10.40 When the man was almost near him,

“I’ll eat good,” the big man said to himself and threw his weapon at *Ch’iteehàakwąįį*.

The big man tried to hook him as he got near, but he missed him.

Ch’iteehàakwąįį moved fast.

The man kept on throwing his weapon.

11.12 *Ch’iteehàakwąįį* knew the big guy finally got really hot and sweaty.

So *Ch’iteehàakwąįį* had hidden his bow and arrows ahead of time.

Aii gohch'it ndàa ts'ą̀' gwintsàl cheendak, ts'ą̀' khan t'ii'in kwaa dhidlìt.

Ts'ą̀' it'ee dik'ì' nôonjìk.

11.27 Ndàa nìhłik neeyàhdàk, yigèe reh.

Aii googàa yaaghà' t'asharah'in nindhan kwàa.

Dinjii ajyàa t'inch'yaa kwàt iłts'ik kwaa reh.

11.29 Aiits'ą̀' t'ee gohch'it dèe it'ee łyâa veenjit gwìizųų gwich'in.

Ts'ą̀' yeendee njuu tee gwats'ą̀' ch'iindàk tr'ìinzhii.

11.54 Aii gwiizhìk t'ee ndàa nìhłik hee łyâa gwinzįį yigèe neeyàhdak.

Gwiizhìk k'i' tł'an gwats'ą̀' tthak vanàndhi'ee, gàa reh yaaghà' t'ihch'yaa nindhan kwàa.

Gohch'it oondee reh nàadii.

12.12 "Chan zhyą̀ą sheenjit gwiizųų," nyaa.

Gwiizhìk t'ee reh neeyuuhìidik reh.

Gohch'it yàa neech'itsyàhthat, gàa reh ts'iivii it'ee nàachįį.

Jyàa dĭizhìk.

"Chan zhyą̀ą vahshihîilgik," jyàa chan nyąą vàràhnyàa.

Jyàa nyaa gwiizhìk, it'ee vàa chats'ă khàgwighit t'agwàhnyaa łii vàràhnyàa.

12.33 Aii gwiizhìk it'ee łyâa gwinzįį gàa iihindii kwaa, gwiizhìk t'ee shrii choo di'įį vàràhnyàa.

Aii hàa jyàiinch'yaa ts'ą̀' hee (yaa'in) .

Jyàa vichi' dìnch'yaa gwiizhìk dzaa yeenìch'inddhaa, nàhąą?

12.48 Yachàa k'at ch'inddhaa.

It'ee reh.

So finally the big guy ended up a little tired and slowed down.

And just then *Ch’iteehàakwąįį* grabbed his bow and arrows.

11.27 He repeatedly shot arrows into his heart area.

Even then, he acted like he didn’t care.

He was a cannibal anyway, so he didn’t feel anything.

11.29 I guess the big man finally didn’t feel very good.

He started walking toward a big patch of spruce trees.

11.54 Meanwhile, *Ch’iteehàakwąįį* kept shooting arrows into his heart.

Although the arrows were all halfway into the big man, he acted like he didn’t feel anything.

He finally sat down nearby.

12.12 “I don’t feel so good, he said.

Meanwhile he was slowing down.

The big man was fighting him, but he was leaning against a spruce tree.

That’s what he did.

They say that he said to himself, “I’m very sleepy too.”

They say that’s what he said.

While he was saying that, what he really meant was he was going in and out of consciousness, they say.

12.33 While that was happening, he was hardly moving,

Meanwhile *Ch’iteehàakwąįį* got a big knife, they say.

With that, that big guy was like this (gesturing).

While his head was like this, *Ch’iteehàakwąįį* hacked him here with a big knife.

12.48 He slashed his throat.

That’s it.

Ch'iteehàakwąįį Nàhtryàa Hàa

13.15 Ts'ą̀' t'ee reh jyàanch'yaa ts'ą̀' dilik eenìneezhii ts'ą̀' reh di'ìk nanaatsùu ts'ą̀' it'ee chan hee neehòozhìi.

Aiits'ą̀' t'ee ahàa.

Ahaa, ahaa.

Akhài' reh, chan reh nàhtryàa drinhdeehàajàk gwak'at deedhizhii vàràhnyàa.

13.37 Aii chan oochii chyąą sheetryahtǫǫ reh, zhik drinhdeehaajak aii eenjit giitł'ì' deek'it.

Gwatsàl ch'iizhąą vitrìn gwèech'in, zhah yitsįį dił'ąįį vàràhnyaa.

Ts'ą̀' vàagwiindàii kwaa, nàhaa?

Aii jùu zhat gwak'at dahak it'ee drinhdàhaajak reh.

13.48 Toh zhrįh vizhìįkak reh.

Jyahts'ą̀' t'ee shih dhahkhwąįį deek'ìt gwąą'įį reh.

Aiits'ą̀' t'ee yeechiitthàn gwęętr'àa, nàhaa?

14.06 Akhài' reh ch'iichyaa toh jyàanch'yaa łee ts'ą̀' zhat naatth'ak, gwiizhìk hee yàhtsit jyàa diyinlik (yaa'in) ts'ą̀' reh aii nàhtryàa t'inch'yaa vàagwiindàii kwàa.

Aiits'ą̀' reh, aii gwichįh dą̀į' lęįį yitsìį ąątth'ak łee vàràhnyàa.

Vitsįį dah reh.

14.36 Zhyàa reh diinjik dah tr'iłtàa,[7] dzaa ch'iidàk khàriintthaii.

Ts'ą̀' reh vitsìį diinjik hàa ts'ą̀' kwat zhyàa tr'ìiheendii kwaa gwinyàa.

Vành dą̀į' hee dzaa ch'ii'ęę nàhtryàa.

"Hoii'! Gòhju' k'iteet'ineihłik łee shrǫ'," nyaa vàràhnyàa.

14.54 Nàhtryàa aii jyàa nyaa ts'ą̀' t'ee reh.

Diits'èehaa ts'ą̀' reh gwats'an tr'idiidiit'ee danàąhnaii akhài' reh, yaaghà' reh nìndhaa roh.

---

7. Johnny Frank uses the first person plural *diinjik* "our nose" instead of *viinjik* "his nose" when it is clearly Ch'iteehàakwąįį who purposely makes his nose bleed. This is a rhetorical and literary way of making the listeners feel they are part of the story. These pronouns shifts recur throughout the story. —KF and CM

Ch'iteehàakwąįį and the Wolverine

13.15 So he went back to his dogs, put his jacket back on,
and traveled on.
And so he's walking.
Walking, walking.
And then he also came to a place where *Wolverine* had a
place for sliding down, they say.
13.37 At the end of the sliding place was a sharp-pointed spear,
the place where he had worn a groove for sliding down.
And where he slid down he marked that sharp hook with
his poop, with snow on the tip of the hook, they say.
And we don't know about it, you see?
So whoever comes to that slide has to slide down.
13.48 Only the tip of the spear pierces [whoever slides down].
This is a place where *Wolverine* killed for food.
So *Ch'iteehàakwąįį* is braking as he's sliding down, you
see?
14.06 Then when *Ch'iteehàakwąįį* slid down to where the spear
was, he did like this while he caught it (gestures).
We didn't know it was *Wolverine*'s doing.
Before that, many of them fell into it, they say.
There was blood there on the tip of it.
14.36 So we just purposely made our nose bleed,
and pretended to be hooked up this way [through the
testicles].
So there's some nose blood on the tip of the hook,
and we just pretend we're limp and motionless, they say.
Early in the morning here's *Wolverine*.
"Aho, I did it again, as usual," he said to himself, they say.
14.54 So *Wolverine* said that.
Then he yanked the hook off of *Ch'iteehàakwąįį*,
who was still warm.

15.10 Aiits'ą̀' łyâa zhyàa tthak jyàa diyah'in googàa khiriltin gwinyaa.
Łyâa *some way* ts'ą̀' tr'iizhàk gwinyaa.
Aii gwiizhìk ch'aghwarh thah t'àa'ą̀įį, nàhtryàa aii.
"Ah! Nadhalzhòo," nyaa.
Ts'ą̀' t'ee reh diinanh gwahjòk tthak chan gwahjòk vàràhnyàa.

15.22 Datthak neediihaahtłòo gwiizhìk dinjii nìndhaa reh (adlaa).
Aiits'ą̀' zhik diindèe agàa goo'yaa vàràhnyàa.
"Nijìn nik'èe gwiljòk?" nyaa ts'ą̀' jyàa dii'in (yaa'in) vàràhnyàa.

15.44 Aii googàa zhyą̀ą jyàanch'yàa.
Aiits'ą̀' chan jidii tł'il ǫhtsùu choo reh chihvyaa k'it t'iinch'yaa, aii reh dinjii eenjit di'įį lee aii zhìt t'eedaną̀ąhnąįį vàràhnyàa.
Zhik gwîiłtin gwideetàa hee vandaa t'arąhndìi, aii chan oonin neehaatàl tthak tł'ìt vaadhàk vàràhnyàa.

16.13 Izhìk vijìi khàriindlòk gwinyàa.
Izhìk gwintsàl neeshrakràatł'ak, googàa,
"Hah! Nadhalzhòo,"
nyaa ts'ą̀' neekhwahdanaadhak.
It'ee chan diindih goohee'yąą reh (adlaa).

16.21 Gwiizhìk t'ee nàhtryàa *family* gwich'įį łee vigii nąįį agàa gǫ̀ǫlįį.
Aii t'ee zheekhwahdanàatsit vàràhnyàa.
Aiits'ą̀' oondee nijin jii khwah gwats'ą̀' hàatthat, izhìk zhat tth'an ch'ok khàłeedîįł'ee vàràhnyàa.

16.59 Aii tsįį neeyeeghwaa gwiizhìk gâahthak aii vinìch'iikak aii eenjit reh.

15.10 Then *Wolverine* really checked him all over his body,
but they say *Ch’iteehàakwąįį* held his breath
and pretended to be dead.
Some way they say he was still breathing.
On his waist band *Wolverine* had a stone axe.
“Ah! Nadhalzhòo,” he said.
So he’s tickling us all over, tickling us again and again,
they say.

15.22 *Ch’iteehàakwąįį’s* body was all limp and floppy and still
warm (laughs).
So *Wolverine* was even in heat with *Ch’iteehàakwąįį’s* eye,
they say.
“Where are you ticklish?” he said, and he was doing this
(gesturing) they say.

15.44 Even though he’s still like that [limp and pretending to be
dead].
And then too this big babiche bag that looked like a fish net.
Wolverine got that bag for humans so he threw us in it, they
say.
Whenever *Wolverine* hopped a little over a depression in
the ground,
Ch’iteehàakwąįį was too heavy for him,
and *Wolverine* also farted each time, they say.

16.13 We almost burst out laughing, they say.
Right there we made a little giggling sound, but then,
“Hah! Nadhalzhòo,”
Wolverine said, and he threw him down.
Now again he was in heat with him (laughs).

16.21 Meanwhile *Wolverine*’s family was living there with his
kids too.
He packed *Ch’iteehàakwąįį* back to his skin hut.
They had a place where they usually put their catch,
over there they say two sharp bones were sticking out.

16.59 *Wolverine* threw his pack sack at the sharp bones,
so that they poked into it.

Aii chan reh googàa tr'aatth'aa gwiizhìk shrak rihìlghaa, ts'ą̀' reh gweedak zhyą̀ą teet'ìh t'iizhìk (yaa'in) vàràhnyàa.

Aiits'ą̀' t'ee reh, aii oo'ęę neech'inghwaii gwiizhìk vigii nąįį reh,

"Nakhwatì' needineeghwaa,"[8] jyàa ginyàa.

"Âa, shįį ch'aghòo' hih'àa," jyàa ginyàa.

17.32 Aii gwiizhìk reh.

"Âa, dadhohnyàa! Nakhwan aii k'ihdąį' gwanaa ch'aghòo oojil, nakhwahan aii ch'aghòo' haadàa," nyaa.

Jyàa nyaa ts'ą̀' reh.

"Aiits'ą̀' reh yee'àn vazàrvii ijìi?"

Jyàa reh yàhnyàa.

18.00 Diighòo, diitsòk hàa khaht'aa aii łyâa *fresh meal* giyahtsii reh.

"Aii t'ôoju' nakhwahan aii ch'aghoo haadàa," jyàa nyàa.

Aii gwiizhìk reh shigii nąįį yee'òk dileedrìh[9] ginyaa reh dehtsii reh traa gaa'įį gavàhnyàa.

18.18 Yee'àt reh deedàk ts'iivii nìn'ee kat reh deekheegìilnàii.

Oodee shyah zhìt gwats'an gwèech'in ts'ą̀' oozhee ìitł'it reh dinjii ohtsùu zhìt dhidìi.

18.25 Aiits'ą̀' reh ohtsùu zhìt khàt'eeyą̀ąhnąįį, ts'ą̀' t'ee reh, "Vàa ch'aghòo khàraht'ii shrii oodì' da'at," àhnyàa.

Akhài' shų' yunkàntii.

Shų'yunkàntii ts'ą̀' reh ch'izhii shrii yats'ą̀' hîiłnąįį akhài' reh, aii hàa oozhee diik'àii gwahàat'uu akhài' zhyą̀ą reh daats'àk vàràhnyàa.

18.54 Aiits'ą̀' *Ch'iteehàakwąįį* dèenindhan gwik'ìt gǫ̀ǫlįį.

8. Literally, *Nakhwati' needineeghwaa* means "Your father is packing us," but actually it means "Our father is packing us." Here the pronoun shift is from second person to first person. But there is also a double shift at work in that the objective "us" also replaces "him." —KF and CM

9. *Dileedrìh* are half-dead clusters of reddish-brown branches, a.k.a. "witches' brooms," that grow in the top or on the sides of black and white spruce trees. They are the result of something biologists call spruce broom rust, a fungus. When chopped off, the branches are very good for building fires. —KF and CM

Ch'iteehàakwąįį was thrown but he ducked down.
So they say it happened that the sharp points went into the pack sack (gestures).
And so then, when he packed *Ch'iteehàakwąįį* home, meanwhile *Wolverine*'s kids said this:
"Your father is packing us," they say.
"Aa, I'll eat the testicles," they all said.

17.32 In the meantime,
"Ahh, be quiet! Yesterday you all ate some testicles, and now it's your mother's turn," he said.
So that's what he said.
"Where's that testicle knife?"
That's what he said.

18.00 They cut off our testicles and our penis and made that a really fresh meal.
"This time your mother will get the testicles," he said.
So he had his children go up in the trees nearby to gather half-dead reddish-brown spruce branches which they used for firewood.

18.18 They all climbed the nearest spruce tree and from up in the branches they looked down inside the packsack from up there and saw a man inside.

18.25 So they flipped him over out of the bag, and *Wolverine* asked his wife, "Give me the knife for cutting off testicles with."
But then she couldn't find it.
She couldn't find it so she threw him another knife.
Wolverine tried cutting the testicles off, but the dull knife just made a squeaking sound and wouldn't cut.

18.54 With that, he tried cutting out the crotch and noticed it was moving.

Gwiniheet'àl kwaa nìndhan gwik'ìt t'iinch'yaa ts'ą̀' shų' t'iyah'ìn.
Aiits'ą̀' yeediidì' hee yihîilnąįį ts'ą̀',
"Dak'àii gwatthoo yàh goot'aa reh t'oh'yà'."
Jyàa da'at àhnyaa vàràhnyàa.
19.15 Aiits'ą̀' da'at k'ii t'inyaa ts'ą̀' chan "Ch'izhuu gwą̂ąhchuu," nyaa ts'ą̀' tree ts'ą̀' di'nil'èe vàràhnyàa.
19.34 Aiits'ą̀' t'ee ch'izhii shrii yeenjit kàhą̀ąhtì'.
Aii gwiizhìk ch'aghwarh agàa giighàih tr'iilęę ił'ąįį, tsin ts'ą̀' neerihèonii jì' danàa yahaahthàl eenjit reh.
19.42 T'ôohju' yeenjì' jyàa dàhàazhìk.
Gwiizhìk hee yeedee tr'iinin nąįį reh,
19.56 "Oozhee nakhwatì' vęhndee needoo chan ch'ihîilya'," jyàa ginyaa gooràhnyàa.
19.59 "Needoo chan ch'ihîil'ya' jì' oodee vitsii inhaii,"[10] jyàa nyaa vàràhnyàa.
"Nijìn ch'idrii ts'an nehtthaa khaniiintin eenjit dèe?"[11] t'inyàa.
Nahdhak aii yeenjit nàhą̀ahti' gwiizhìk ch'aghwarh ił'ąįį tr'ą̀htsit vihiitsii tr'ąąhnąįį.
20.20 Zhyą̀ą reh gideech'ôolk'įį gwiizhìk yeedeedì',
"Ch'izhuu gwą̂ahchuu," nyaa.
Tree hàa oodì' jyàanch'yaa.
Oodì' khàiinghaa gwiizhìk aii t'ooghit khyą̀hnyaa t'ee.
Łì'hàa dinjii lęįį dhahkhwąįį zhat kagwìł'aįį reh.
20.33 It'ee reh łyâa khàiint'uu t'ahòo'yà' reh.[12]
Jidii iizuu nankat tthak jyàa dàh'in.
Aiits'ą̀' t'ee reh yaaghà' t'ee łyâa reh shreetryahtal zhrįh k'i' ch'ok di'ii kwaa vàràhnyàa.
Shreetryahtal ehjyàa dhidlii reh.

10. This may be an idiom or proverb of some kind. —KF and CM

11. Another possible idiom. —KF

12. The meaning of this sentence is obscure and very difficult to translate. —KF and CM

And that was the just the way *Ch'iteehàakwąįį* planned it and controlled it.

Wolverine was still trying to cut him, but his knife was no good.

So he threw it off into the corner and got mad at his wife.

"You should have cut both of the brown testicles with it."

That's what he told her, they said.

19.15 He made his wife mad and she said,"Ch'izhuu gwâ̜ąhchuu," and they say she started to cry and turned around.

19.34 So she went to find another knife for him.

Meanwhile *Wolverine* had a stone hammer ready next to him, so just in case *Ch'iteehàakwąįį* moved he could club us with it.

19.42 He was just about to turn around away from *Ch'iteehàakwąįį*.

Meanwhile, those *Wolverine* kids up there [in the spruce tree],

19.56 "Behind you, Father, down below, his eye is blinking again," they said, they say.

19.59 "If he blinks again, come to the point," he said, they say.

"Where did you get the hide-scraping tool from the heart?" he said.

Wolverine started to look around as *Ch'iteehàakwąįį* grabbed that stone axe over there and clubbed him with it.

20.20 It made a thumping sound while his wife was still crying,

"Ch'izhuu gwâ̜ahchuu," she said.

She was still crying over there.

She turned around to see him fall dead to the floor.

Wolverine had resided there, killing huge numbers of people.

20.33 That would really be his last killing.

He did that to all the bad [animals] all over the land.

And so only that shreetryahtal, he really doesn't have sharp-pointed arrows, they say.

That shreetryahtal weapon was left outside.

21.12 Vigii nąįį yi'èedee dîilk'įį t'ee reh vik'ì' aii
giveeteegwirìltrat ts'ą̀' reh gootaa'adàk akhài' zhik
nèekwąįį nąįį eegwîilnąą̀įį,
"Łee jì' nan aii ch'atrał shizhin naantłit," jyàa nyaa
vàràhnyàa.

21.22 Jyàa nyaa gwiizhìk aii tsyaa aii tr'iłdàii ts'ą̀' veejii aii reh
t'ee ch'atrał shizhin nàahaii roh.
Ch'atrał ginyaa ch'iitsii dzirh reh.[13]

21.36 Łì'hàa khe' ts'ą̀' neerahaatłak.
Neeràhdak googàa k'i' tsįį neekàk,
k'i' tsįį neekàk.

21.45 Gwiizhìk vachaa nąįį tthak neerąhdàk.
Yeezhee gwà'àn dhidlìi.
Viyihghan nąįį tr'inghan, eedąhzhrii vèegoodhàt.
Aiits'ą̀' vachan dachan khyąh tr'êetin vàràhnyàa.

21.56 Aii ch'itłèe tsal tseet'iriltsit aii reh vikhyąą tsan tr'iłtsąįį.
Łyâa ooch'ii'àn tr'eerii'oo gwiizhìk reh deezhàk
k'eegwaadhàk.
"Ch'iteehàakhwąįį, yaaghà' aldroo," nyaa vàràhnyàa.

22.08 Vats'ą̀' ihłok naraa'oo gwiizhìk dakwaiits'àt ìhłak k'at
ch'aachak łee vàràhnyàa.
Aii geh'àn t'ee vakwài' ch'iigwàt į'.
Aiits'ą̀' t'ee jyàa dìnch'yaa akhàyùunyàa.

22.28 Aiits'ą̀' oodàk t'iyàhnyàa,
"Dink'yùnzhit shrǫ', jyàa dàhąhtsii yùu," yàhnyàa.
Gwik'ìt t'ąhtsii vàràhnyàa.[14]

---

13. *Ch'iitsii dzirh* — how could they say "iron mitts"? —KP
Ch'iitsii dzirh is an object made out of stone for handling hot coals. I don't know why it's called gloves or mitts. —JE

14. The ending of this story is missing from the tape. —JE

21.12 *Ch’iteehàakwąįį* grabbed his arrows for the ones up in the tree, so he was going to shoot all but two of them.
“I’ll hit you with the copper gloves later,” he said, they say.
21.22 While he was talking, he shot the boy wolverine with an arrow and his older sister had what they call ch’atrał.
Ch’atrał means ‘metal gloves.’
21.36 Very slowly and jumping across.
Over and over he was shooting her with arrows even though she was blocking them, deflecting the arrowheads.
21.45 While this was going on, the boy wolverine’s brothers were all dead on the ground below.
His parents were dead too.
He was the only one still alive up there.
They say *Ch’iteehàakwąįį* put a wooden trap beneath the tree he was on.
21.56 In his pocket he had a little piece of knee fat which he used for bait on the wooden trap.
Each time *Ch’iteehàakwąįį* went away, they say the young boy wolverine climbed down and hollered to him,
“Look *Ch’iteehàakwąįį*, I’m trapped!”
22.08 When *Ch’iteehàakwąįį* came running back to his trap, they say the young boy wolverine chewed off one of his own toes.
So that’s why he’s got such stubby toenails.
22.28 Then *Ch’iteehàakwąįį* looked up to him and said,
“You will never grow up in your entire life.”
They say that’s why he’s still the same size today.

Johnny Frank

Vasaagìhdzak Dats'an Nąįį Hàa

<jfka401>

JF28.37 *Vasaagìhdzak* zhyàa vizheh chan gokwàa, va'at chan kwàa.

28.50 Zhyą̀ą nankak ch'ii'àn zhyą̀ą ahaa ts'ą̀' jidii k'adahak aii tthak hàa nìgwìi'ą̀įį.

Aiits'ą̀' reh ahaa, akhài' zhyàa reh.

Yeendaa zhat van dha'ą̀įį.

29.05 Van dha'ąįį yee'an tr'iinzhii gwiizhìk vakat dats'an daazhyaa tthak gǫ̀ǫlį̀į.

Yee'an[1] tr'iinzhii ts'ą̀' ànts'ą̀' gwitineezhìi.

29.20 Gwiizhìk ditr'uu ts'àt dats'ąą vàràhnyàa.

Aiits'ą̀' oo'àt gwà'àn nyą'shril lęįį yizhǐinlìi, ts'ą̀' khwàh yìlchaa, ts'ą̀' khwàh ghoo choo hee reh zhik van teeghàih teedik àn yiyàa'in tr'iinghwą̀įį kwàt jidìi gwandàii tthak neeyąą'ìk, googàa chan *Vasaagìhdzak* t'ii'in ts'ą̀' yàandaii vàràhnyàa.

29.40 Nyą' shril ghoo choo aghwaa ts'ą̀' gwintł'oo ch'eeghwàa.

"*Vasaagìhdzak*, aii jidii inghwàa?" jyàa reh giyàhnyàa.

Jyàa vàràhaanjyàa gwahtsii reh t'ii'in.

29.53 "Ch'ilik ihkhwaa reh t'ishi'ìn."

Jyàa dats'an àhnyàa.

Kwàt ts'ą̀' reh, "Nats'ą̀' teeriheedàa dineenjit ch'iinlìi."

Jyàa giyàhnyàa.

30.15 "Ą̀ąhą'," nyaa ts'ą̀' łyâa zhyą̀ą nan nizįį izhìk nǐinzhii ts'ą̀' t'ee reh khwàh yaaghà' reh nìin'ą̀įį.

Gwiizhìk dats'an tthak ch'iindàk yats'ą̀' jyàa dii'ìn.

Vindih tthak kwàt reh jyàa dìnch'yàa.

"Akwàt ch'oodzàa," nyàa.

Gwiizhìk ch'arahaadzaa dą̀į' dachan jyàa dìgilìk į'.

Kǫ̀ǫtèe tr'agwahtsìk, nan nihzhyąąhànaa'ee ts'ą̀' reh.

30.52 Kòǫtèe tr'agwahtsìk izhìk reh nìinzhìi, *Vasaagìhdzak* aii.

Gwizhìt gwachoo tthak dèeràdą̀ą'ą̀į'.

---

1. This should be *Yiyee'an*. —KP
It's a dialect difference. —JE

Johnny Frank

Vasaagìhdzak and the Dancing Ducks

<jfka401>

JF28.37 *Vasaagìhdzak* had no house of his own, and he had no wife.
28.50 He fooled around with anything he met in his path.
He was out walking one day.
And he came upon a lake out there.
29.05 He walked up to it when he saw all kinds of ducks on it.
He went back into the brush.
29.20 While he was approaching the ducks, they say he had a raggedy old caribou skin wrapped around him.
He put lots of moss into his pack, and he was walking alongside the lake where all the animals could see him, but any animal that saw him knew it was *Vasaagìhdzak,* they say.
29.40 He was packing lots of moss, so his pack was big and round.
And the ducks asked him, "*Vasaagìhdzak,* what are you packing?"
That's exactly what he wanted them to ask him.
29.53 I'm packing songs in my pack," he said to the ducks.
"We'll come to shore to you if you sing for us," the ducks said.
30.15 And *Vasaagìhdzak* said "Yes."
So he went to good dry ground and took off his pack.
Meanwhile, the ducks were coming in close to the shore.
After there was a crowd of ducks around him, he told them,
"Now dance!" he said.
Using sticks, he made a place for dancing.
And he made a teepee-like house with an opening for the doorway.
30.52 He put himself right by the doorway while all the ducks were inside.

31.03 "Akò' nakhweech'ihiihłyàa, akò' ch'oodzàa," jyàa nyàa.
"Nats'àhts'ą' vàa ch'araadzàa dęę?" jyàa giyàhnyàa.
31.19 "Gwintł'oo tr'įįltr'al ts'ą' vaa ch'araadzaa reh, ch'ilik łąą idèegwaahnyaa kwaa ts'ą' ch'araadzaa," jyàa dats'an àhnyàa.
Khàch'iin'ąįį gwiizhìk t'ee dats'an t'âanch'yaa tthak ch'ilik hàa shraagaahnyaa ts'ą' ch'agaadzàa.
Aii gwiizhìk kwàntee idîildii gwiizhìk gook'oh hantàa.
Gook'oh hantàa łee gwiizhìk deech'yàh aii khaiitsąį' nàhąą?
Aiits'ą' ilyąą dǫhlįį.
Akhài' zhyąą reh.
Yaaghà' dats'an k'ǫh hantàa.

<jfka403>[2]

0.47 Aiits'ą' gook'oh hantàa aii kwàt zhyąą yaaghà' ch'ii'àn hahjyàa.
Gook'oh tr'âą'al nats'àa gahahchyàa gǫ̀'?
Aii gwiizhìk ch'ilik hàa nagwankàk.
1.12 Gwiizhìk deech'yah ilyąą ts'à yąąh'in akhài' dats'an k'oh hantàa łee nìylii'in.
"Yaaghà' nakhwaghan t'inyaa łee!" jyàa ginyàa.
1.20 Ts'ą' hee kwat treecheegwihidiitìi.
Jyàhts'ą' googàa dats'an lęįį dìłkhwąįį vàràhnyàa.
Treecheegwidiitìi gwiizhìk kweetee nadhat ǫ'.
1.34 Dzaa gwee'àn zhyąą. . .teekat k'oohił'ee ts'ą' zhyąą jyàiinch'yaa ts'ą' reh, cheegalhaajyàa roh.
Aii gwiizhìk dats'an k'oh àhchàk, aii hantàa gwiizhìk reh.
Aii gwiizhìk gootł'èetah vilì'kaii natàl aii geh'àn nootsik, tèekwài' tsàlvìt, daadząįį nąįį hàa.
Aii geh'àn t'ee gootł'ì' ts'ìt'ya' gǫ̀ǫlįį (adlaa).
2.12 Jyàa kwàt reh yeendaa teeneegoodâąnàįį.
Yaaghà' dats'an iinghan zhrįh reh.

2. The story is continued onto a second tape. —CM

31.03 Then he said, "Now I'll sing, and you'll dance."
And the ducks wanted to know what kind of a dance he wanted them to dance.
"How do you want us to dance?" the ducks asked.
31.19 And he said, "It's a close-your-eyes-and-make-all-kinds-of-noise dance."
He started singing and the ducks were making all kinds of noise while they were dancing away.
Meanwhile he was sitting by the doorway wringing their necks whenever he got the chance, you see?
Among them was a white-fronted honker goose who always thought about his life.
So he got curious and opened his eyes a little and saw him over there wringing their necks.

<jfka403>
0.47 He was wringing their necks and piling them up to one side while they were dancing.
How could they make noise while he was breaking their necks?
Meanwhile, the dance was still going on.
1.12 The white-fronted honker goose opened his eyes a little when he saw *Vasaagìhdzak* doing that.
He hollered out, "This man is killing us!"
1.20 So they all ran for their lives.
Even so, they say he killed lots of ducks.
He was sitting at the doorway grabbing them by the neck.
1.34 They all ran out near him. That's when he grabbed them and wrung their necks. He kicked them hard on their butts.
And that's why the Arctic loon, the common loon, horned grebe, and red-necked grebe all have flat butts (laughs).
2.12 All the other ducks that were still alive flew back out on the lake.
He had lots of dead ducks by him.

2.21 "Âa. . . gwinzįį, dats'an gwintł'oo hih'àa," nyàa (adlaa).
"Dats'an gwintł'oo hih'àa," nyaa shòo dhidlit.
T'ee dats'an neeniin'àk, dats'an łęę reh.
2.26 Aiits'ą' reh, tthak khàyìinjoo kwaa ts'ą' yitsin tr'ànch'aadlii ts'ą' oozhee.
2.41 Oondaa gwîiłk'in lùh zhit ch'iizhàk hee łùht'ee nànyilii ts'ą' yak'àa gwîiłk'in.
Vakwài' zhrįh khàndhi'ee ts'ą' reh.
Gwintł'òo gwîiłk'in aii kǫ' geelèehàadlii ts'ą' gwineedhaa[3] izhìk łùh zhit yitsùu hàa jyâiinch'yaa ts'ą' łùht'ee yiinlìi.
3.00 Aiits'ą' t'ee łùh dhah yak'àa needhadhàt ts'ą' vakwài' zhrįh khàndhi'èe.
Aii gwiizhìk teevęę gwà'àn neehidìk.
Aii gwiizhìk dats'an aii łùht'ee ich'yàa, teetłòk nizįį ilìi niindhan eenjit reh.

Vasaagìhdzak Neegǫǫ Tsoo Hàa

3.10 Akhài' reh neegǫǫ tsoo reh yats'ą' tr'ìinzhii.
Yats'ą' tr'ìinzhii ts'ą' reh.
"Neegǫǫ, łyâa dats'an lęįį dhàałkhwaii t'ôonch'yàa.
Oonjìt łùh t'eiilii, vakaich'yaa," jyàa nyàa.
3.30 "Van dų̀hts'ąįį reh.
Nihchįį[4] oonjìt vits'eehòogìi, shehchįį t'inizhìk jì' nan aii gwintł'òo dats'an hiin'àa," jyàa nyàa.
Neegǫǫ àhnyàa.
3.42 Aiits'ą' reh, neegǫǫ aii aatłaa hee neekhwaaha'ak k'ìt t'ii'in roh.
Aiits'ą' reh, neegǫǫ chan nìinjigwaazhii aii eenjit nizįh kwaa vàràhnyaa į'.
4.00 Nèekwat reh *Vasaagìhdzak* neiin'àk į'.
"Ą̀ąhą'," yàhnyaa.

3. *Gwineedhaa* should be *gwinindhaa.* —KP

4. This should be *niłehchįį.* —KP

2.21 And he said to himself, "Ah, good! I'll have lots of ducks to eat" (laughs).
I'll eat lots of ducks," he said, feeling very happy.
That's how he fooled lots of ducks, lots of ducks.
2.26 He didn't pluck the ducks; he only gutted them.
2.41 He made a big fire and moved the hot ashes aside.
Then he put the ducks underneath.
3.00 He spread the hot ashes on top of them with only their feet sticking out.
He was walking along the shore while the ducks were cooking under the hot ashes, thinking that they were getting tender.

Vasaagìhdzak and Red Fox

3.10 A red fox met him on the shore.
And he told the fox,
"*Fox*, I've killed lots of ducks,
3.30 And I'm cooking them on the other side of this lake.
Why don't you and I race over to my cooking, and if you win, I'll give you lots of ducks to eat."
That's what he said to the fox.
3.42 So *Fox* was limping.
They say *Fox* is also very good at fooling people.
4.00 He fooled *Vasaagìhdzak* twice in his life.
Fox agreed to the race.
"Yes," he said.

"Kwàt shįį aii łyâa shakwài' iłts'ik ts'ą' shehkįį t'ihiinjyàa t'ôonch'yaa gwiizhìk shįį aii shakwài' iłts'ik duuyeh khant'ihnjii," yàhnyàa.

4.22 Aii jì' teevęę gwiingǫǫ ts'ąįį nìgwiin'ąįį, vàràhnyàa.

It'ee, neegǫǫ reh neech'iin'àk.

Vakwài' iłts'ik kwaa gàa reh t'inyàa (adlaa).

Gwiizhìk teevęę ninzhit ts'ąįį nigwee'ąįį.

"Ako'," nyaa ts'ą' hee neegǫǫ yee'an hee tr'akhwaaniin'ąįį vàràhnyàa.

Akhài' jyàa dii'in ts'ą' gwiteiinzhii ts'ą' neegǫǫ tsoo zhyąą dâanaii k'ìt t'iizhìk vàràhnyàa.

4.54 Oonjìt dats'an iłch'yaa aii datthak zhyąą tr'àl ąhjil ts'ą' yakwài' zhrįh gadąątsìt aii łùh zhìt needhazhàa.

Aii yakwài' łùht'ee needhazhaa.

5.16 Aiits'ą' ch'iinii nahgǫǫ vintł'èegwirin'ąįį ts'ąįį neehòozhii.

Aii gwiizhìk t'ee *Vasaagìhdzak* dat'àii hàa teevęę naagàl.

K'inidàk dòonch'yàa, yeendaa dats'an kwài' tth'aii khàndhi'ee roh.

5.32 Aiitł'ęę reh, zhat jyàiinch'yaa gwiizhìk reh, zhik ch'iinii t'oohjù' hee neegǫǫ tsoo khài' tr'àkhwaanǐin'ąįį ts'ą' yaaghà' ch'ii'ee nàadii ts'ą' neets'ąądâąjìl.

5.46 "Neegǫǫ vehchįį t'ishizhìk," nyaa ts'ą' yee'òk gwà'àn gadlòkyahchįį vàràhnyàa.

5.50 K'eejìt ninzhit dąį' hee neegǫǫ dats'an tthak tr'àl ìnlii, dats'an kwài' zhrįh oondaa t'inch'yaa gàa gàandaii kwàa (adlaa).

Aiits'ą' t'ee reh, łyâa needlòk yahahchìk.

6.19 Aiits'ą' reh, neegǫǫ, "Zhyąą neh'àn zhyąą cheedaaldak," yàhnyaa ts'ą' oondiindaa tł'oo hįįł'ee tsįį izhìk hee nàch'àghooniin'ąįį, "Dats'an nèehałchaa kwàa," yàhnyàa.

6.26 Izhìk nàch'àghòo'in'ąįį ts'ą' it'ee reh, ndàa nǐindlòk tł'ęę yeendaa dats'an ch'ìhłak kwài' òonjik, khàyìhìłchįį akhài' reh dats'an kwài' zhrįh.

Dats'an kwài' hàa gwiich'ok datthak reh.

6.32 *Nothing!* (adlaa).

"My feet are hurting and you will beat me in the race anyway," he told him.

4.22 So *Vasaagìhdzak* gave *Fox* the shortcut and he took the long way, they say.

Now, the fox fooled him.

He didn't know it yet, but *Fox*'s feet didn't hurt at all (laughs).

"Now!" he said, and they both started to race and the fox limped away.

But when the fox got behind the brush, they say he took off almost flying.

4.54 He got to the campfire in no time, bit off the ducks' legs, hid the cooked ducks, and put the legs back in the dirt to where they were before.

5.16 And then *Fox* went back to the path where he was racing.

Meanwhile, *Vasaagìhdzak* was racing for his life along the shore.

When he got to his campfire, he noticed the ducks were still there.

5.32 He was there when finally *Fox* came up limping and out of breath.

5.46 "I beat the fox," *Vasaagìhdzak* said and just rolled around laughing, they say.

5.50 *Vasaagìhdzak* didn't know that *Fox* was there way before he was (laughs).

Vasaagìhdzak just laughed and laughed.

6.19 And *Fox* told him, "I'm tired from the race because of you."

So he went to a grassy place at the point of a lake and went to sleep.

Vasaagìhdzak told *Fox*, "I'm not giving you any ducks anyway."

6.26 When *Vasaagìhdzak* finally finished laughing, he pulled out one of the ducks but pulled out only the feet.

All the rest were only duck feet also.

6.32 Nothing! (laughs).

Neegǫǫ tthak tr'àl yìnlii reh.

Tł'ęę t'oohjù' hee neegǫǫ ts'ą̀' shòo dhidlìt kwàa.

6.47 Aiits'ą̀' t'ee reh tł'oo khanjuu ts'ą̀' yeendaa tł'oo hį̂įlch'ok oondaa tsį̀į reh neegǫǫ tsoo ch'aghoo'ił'ą̀įį.

Gitr'igwîi'ee hàa oonjhjyàa neegwąą'ik ts'ą̀' gwik'eechii'àk.

"Neh'àn zhyą̀ą cheedaaldak," yàhnyàa (adlaa).

6.59 Aiits'ą̀' t'ee aii tł'oo zhit ch'iinaa yàanjoo ts'ą̀' jyàiinch'yaa aii, dàats'ą̀' chan tr'oonilì'.

Aiits'ą̀' t'ee kǫ' děinzhàa.

Tł'oo dàatłee.

7.13 Łat choo nàadoo gwiizhìk łat zhit ch'iindàa hee neegǫǫ tsoo yaaghà' ch'adą̀į' gwiteeneekaii gàa gàandaii kwàa.

7.27 Gohch'it yeendeedàa tthak neegǫǫ dhichįį ch'iindàa tthak geegook'in zhyą̀ą reh gwihiljii.

Âa, chan veetsingwaazhìk,

7.42 "Neegǫǫ shadats'àn sheenàa'įį tł'ęę neegǫǫ tsoo vàa gwàdhalk'in ts'ą̀' dhik'in," nyaa.

Ts'ą̀' chan nijìn yatth'an li' nyaa ts'ą̀' zhik gwà'àn gał òonjik ts'ą̀' yeezhee tł'oo tsal dhik'in tee chan yatth'an kàch'àdhàt, chan vatth'àn nąh'yà' kwàa (adlaa).

7.54 Zhyą̀ą geenjit kwaa dats'an łęę neegǫǫ ts'an heelyàa gwìłtsąįį.

Yats'an ch'in'àl kwaa reh.

8.03 "Shizhìt gwìłts'ik, gwintł'oo ch'ihih'àa," nyaa.

Ch'yaa vizhìk k'eegwiich'yaa ch'agwąąh'yà' kwàa (adlaa).

Now he found out what that fox did to him.
He was really mad at *Fox*.
6.47 So he started gathering grass while *Fox* was still sleeping out there, and once in a while *Fox* looked over his way and went back to sleep.
Vasaagìhdzak was now after him for what he did.
"I'm tired for nothing because of you!" he said (laughs).
6.59 He was sitting in the grass watching him while he was trying to get even with him.
Then he set fire to the grass.
The grass started burning.
7.13 The grass caught on fire and started burning full blast.
Vasaagìhdzak didn't know that *Fox* ran away when the fire first started.
7.27 The grass burned and *Fox* was gone.
And *Vasaagìhdzak* thought it was funny.
7.42 "*Fox* stole my ducks, so I burned him," he said.
He took a little stick and was feeling around in the burned part to see if he could find *Fox's* bones, but he didn't find any bones (laughs).
7.54 And so that's how *Vasaagìhdzak* gave *Fox* some cooked ducks.
He ended up getting nothing.
8.03 "I'm hungry. I'm going to eat lots," he said.
But he didn't even get a taste of them (laughs).

Vasaagìhdzak Dinjik Hàa

8.13 Gwiizhìk ch'ìhłan chan reh, dinjik iłdàii, dinjik iłdàii aii chan teevęę nah'aa vàràhnyàa.

Teevęę nah'aa ts'ą' khàyàdant'ii ts'ą' yeehagwaht'àa ts'à,'

"Jii chan aii hal'yàa," nyaa ts'ą' jyàa dìi'in vàràhnyàa.

8.36 Aii gwiizhìk zhik gwà'àn deetryà', dziitsal, dziigwat'an agàa, jidii shih a'àa datthak,

"Shitsii aii shats'an ąhtsìi," jyàa giyàhnyàa.

8.48 "Duuyee gwik'ìt t'ishi'in," nyàa.

Gwiizhìk t'ee ch'itseezhù' k'òont'aii naatsik ts'ą' dak'oh needhikhyùu.

8.59 Ch'ihdheeghwàt[5] chan nizįį iłtsąįį chan needee'ąįį.

Gohch'it ch'idzìt chan yik'it t'inch'yaa thaht'ìyee'ąįį,

"Jii shitł'èhthaa[6] heelyàa," nyaa ts'ą'.

9.10 Jyàa nyaa ts'ą' reh, dinjik ak'ìi t'inch'yaa gwiizhìk.

Aii gwiizhìk shìh kwaii agàa tthak, zhoh tthak, aii kwaii oozhrìk ts'ą' ch'ii'ęę tr'akhak roh.

9.20 "Jii hin'àa lèe tał'in?" nyaa ts'ą' gwiizhìk ch'ik'eh zhyąą gigeiit'ìi, nilįį hàa.

9.34 Gwiizhìk chan yeendaa gwà'àn teevęę gwà'àn dzan agàa reh neehaa'òl.

9.40 Izhìk hee jidìi tthak łyâa zhyąą yeet'iindhan yuudhàłchįį chan yik'èe gwahthat reh.

Gwiizhìk yee'àt reh ts'iivii.

"Jii hoh'àa lèe t'ał'in?" nyaa ts'ą' t'ee zhik tthak dinjyahkhit roh.

Kwàt zhik duuyeh tthak giits'ą' giindàh giyuunjìi.

9.55 Aiits'ą' yaaghà' ts'iivii choh nèekwąįį nihghàih nǐn'ee aiits'ą' tr'iinzhìi.

---

5. The *ch'ihdheghwat* or reticulum stomach of a large animal is used to store and carry other internal organs as well as blood during butchering. It's distinguished by its honeycomb-like texture. See Mishler and Frank, 2020:419.

6. *Shitł'èhthaa*, made from the *ch'idzit* or *omasum* stomach, is sometimes translated as a 'my skirt' instead of 'my baggy pants'.

Vasaagìhdzak and Moose

8.13 One time too, they say *Vasaagìhdzak* killed a moose with his arrow.
He was cutting it up, and each time he cut a piece, he said to himself, "I'll keep this part for this."
8.36 All the animals were wishing for moose.
The crow, camp robber, and other birds begged him for meat.
"Grandpa, give me that!" they said to him.
8.48 "No! I won't give you any," he said.
While saying that, he used the moose's caul fat
for a scarf over his head and around his neck.
8.59 And he used the reticulum stomach for his hat and put the omasum stomach on for a belt around his waist.
"This will be my baggy pants," he said.
9.10 He said this so he could make all the other animals hungry for it.
Once in a while he called the bear or the wolf over and said to them,
9.20 "Is this what you wish to eat?"
9.34 While doing that, he spread out the meat and fat all around him.
9.40 There was a muskrat out on the lake at the same time.
Everything obeyed him in those days.
There were spruce trees nearby.
"Is this what you wanted to eat?"
He made all the animals envious while he was saying this.
He knew they wouldn't come and get it.
9.55 So he walked over to two big spruce trees.

10.08 "Òi'hàa nats'àa dèegwąh tł'oo ch'ihih'àa jidìi shizhit aii datthak ahaltryąi'," nyaa.

Ts'ą' reh aiits'ą' reh dachan deetak ree neetł'intthaii vàràhnyàa.

Neetł'intthaii gwiizhìk, aii chan yideetak jyăiinch'yaa ts'ą' gwiizhìk, "Dachan nihts'ą', dachan nihts'ą'," nyaa vàràhnyàa.

Akhài' reh dachan nihts'ahts'ą' jyàa dĭizhìk.

Dachan deetak gwik'yăatł'at nàanąįį.

10.45 Aii "Dachan nihts'ą'," nyaa chan zhik gwandaii t'ȃąnch'yąą datthak chan yàa t'inyàa (adlaa).

Aii datthak yàa t'inyaa ts'ą' dachan vàa łineeghaa ts'ą' zhyąą tł'aachik k'ìt t'ii'in gwiizhìk hee yaaghà' jidìi t'aihnyaa datthak zhik dinjik igìinghàa.

11.02 Tthak zhyąą gwàhaljii[7] gwilìi, aii gwiizhìk yee'àt âa, zhyăąts'ii ts'ą' zhyąą dikì' zhrįh ha'ak ts'ą' dideeghàn zhrįh jyàa dăh'in vàràhnyàa.

11.11 Dachan deetak gwik'yâa tł'at nats'àhts'ą' gwats'an tr'iheehàa gǫ̀'?

Kwàt shih nąįį agàa tthak nilįį tthak ginàl zhyąą tth'an dagȃįį zhrįh yee'àt dhidlìi.

Aii gwiizhìk dachan nihk'yąą jyàa dineezhik.

Ts'iivii ąhtsit ts'ą' hȃątuu geh'an dachan dagǫ̀ǫ vàràhnyaa i'.[8]

11.33 Gohch'it reh vitsin jidii gîilii a'àa, vitsin aii tthak an heelyàa ti'ęę gwintł'òo ch'ihih'àa nyaa ch'yąą reh.

11.42 Gwandaa vitsin gwihiljii goodlit roh (adlaa).

Aiits'ą' t'ee yeezhee tth'an khàihłan nìnlii gwiizhìk hee zhik t'ah'in[9] datthak shòo hàa nihk'yąą.

11.55 Jyàa dèegwiizhìk.

---

7. I pronounce this *gwihiljii*. —KP

8. Twisted trees are common in the boreal spruce forest around *Venetie* and *Arctic Village*. They are not intertwined, but are twisted like corkscrews along their grain due to the extreme cold and dry climate and slow growth cycle. —CM

9. Today this would be pronounced as *zhik t'ii'in naii*. —KP

10.08 And then he said, "I will shit and clean out my stomach so I can eat lots."
He squatted down between two trees and told the trees,
"Trees, squeeze me. Trees, squeeze me," he said, they say.
And the trees squeezed him, and he was stuck there.
10.45 Every time he said, "Trees, squeeze me," the animals said the same thing too (laughs).
When the trees came together he was just stuck fast between them, and all the animals went for his moose meat.
11.02 All the meat was disappearing.
He was really angry.
He was only moving his head and body.
They say he was stuck.
11.11 How was he going to free himself?
Even the brown bear was there.
Everything was eaten up and just the white bones were left when the trees finally came apart and let him go.
He was so mad he grabbed the tree and twisted it.
They say that's why there are still twisted spruce trees.
11.33 According to his plan, *Vasaagìhdzak* was going to let out everything in his stomach so he could eat lots.
11.42 He ended up with nothing in his stomach (laughs).
So he gathered up all the bones while all the animals ran off.
That's what happened.
11.55 That's why the bears, wolves, and others eat moose today.

Aii reh jùk drin yaaghà' jidii zhoh, shih, jidìi shìh a'àa datthak aii shìh hee'àa eenjit t'iizhìk reh vàràhnyàa.
Aiitł'ęę yatth'àn khàihtan it'ee chan hàakit.
Yatthat, yatthàt, jyàiinch'yaa ts'ą' reh.
12.23 Yaghwài' ahtsìi.
Aii gwiizhìk tth'aii hee ch'a'aa kwaa.
Aiits'ą' t'ee, "Khwaii gwintł'òo hih'àa," chan nyàa.
"Ch'ihdheeghwàt shits'èe," nyąą.
Aii zhìt t'ee khwaii iłtsąįį.
12.58 Jidìi zhìt khwaii hahtsyàa gǫ'?
Zhik tthak gwihiljii.
Aii khwaii chan gwinzįį dak'àiitł'yaa reh deediyuâatł'įį vàràhnyàa.

Vasaagìhdzak Dzan Hàa

13.13 Khwaii tanh hih'àa niindhan geh'àn yeechìt chųų ts'ą' yàatr'iinzhii akhài' gwiizhìk dzan yeendòk ivyàa.
"*Vasaagìhdzak*, jidìi t'ah'ìn?" yàhnyàa.
"Khwaii t'ałin," yàhnyàa.
Aiits'ą' reh dzan t'àhnyàa,
13.41 "Shuu, jii sheenjit ąhtàn, hąhtan hęę?" yàhnyaa vàràhnyàa.
"Ą̀ąhą', kwàt nats'àhts'ą' reh hałtàn?" nyaa.
"Kwaa ji' shitsì' ąhchàa," yàhnyàa (adlaa).
13.49 "Ǫ̀hch'al shrǫh," nyaa vàràhnyàa.
Dzan jyàa nyàa, "Shitsii, shiyàa'an ch'azhrąįį hòohkhìi shrǫh aii jì' t'ee chyàhalghàa t'ôonch'yàa," jyàa yàhnyaa vàràhnyàa.
Jyàa yahnyaa,
"Aii ji' t'ee chyàhalghàa iihèech'al t'inch'yaa," yàhnyaa.
14.07 Aii googàa hee, tł'oovęę khai' dhidii gwiizhìk t'ee yeezhee nanzhrąįh khàhch'aa vàràhnyàa.
14.10 Aii zhik dèehee'yàa t'inyaa lì' yùunyàa.
Aii yiyeedak iintrat akhài' reh dzan chìlghàa

He pounded up the bones and boiled them and took the grease off the top.
He pounded and pounded the bones.
12.23 He still hadn't eaten but planned to eat lots of the grease he was making.
He made grease inside the thing he was wearing on his head.
"I have the fattest gut hat, and I will eat lots of grease," he said again.
12.58 What else could he use?
There was nothing else.
They say he tied up the bag with grease in it and walked down to the lake to freeze it.

Vasaagìhdzak and Muskrat

13.13 He thought he wanted to eat frozen grease.
As he walked toward it, *Muskrat* swam by and asked him,
"*Vasaagìhdzak,* what do you have there?"
That's grease," he told him.
Then he said to *Muskrat*,
13.41 "Nephew, can you freeze this grease bag for me?" They say that's what he told him.
Muskrat said, "Yes. How will I freeze it?
Just tie it on my tail," he told him (laughs).
13.49 *Vasaagìhdzak* told *Muskrat*, "Don't tear it."
Muskrat answered, "Grandpa, don't make any sudden moves because I might get scared and dive.
I might dive and your grease bag will tear open." They say that's what he told him.
14.07 *Vasaagìhdzak* was sitting on the shore and tore out a piece of sod, they say.
14.10 *Vasaagìhdzak* was curious to know what *Muskrat* would do if he did what *Muskrat* told him not to do.
So then *Muskrat* dove into the water and the grease bag tore open and went all over the water.

14.18 Khwaii dhach'aa ts'ą' hee teekat tthak reh gohch'it khwaii chan in'àl kwàa (adlaa).

Łì'hàa dzan ts'ą' shòo dhidlìt kwàa.

Gohch'it zhyąą vitsin gwìhiljii jyăiinch'yaa chan geełeehòozhìi.

14.32 Dinjik dìłtsii khàdiint'uu ch'yaa *one bite* gàa nąh'yà' kwàa.

Jyàa reh tèedhadhat į'.

Vasaagìhdzak Dzìitsal Nąįį Hàa

14.48 Kwàt chan, łyâa dziitsal gǫǫlįį chan gwak'at deedhizhii vàràhnyàa.

14.58 Aiits'ą' chan dziitsal giindih[10] kwàt zhyąą tthak jyàa dĭizhìk.

Giindih jyàa dĭizhìk ts'ą'reh, aii gwiizhìk reh tr'iits'ąhts'ą' dziitsal neeni'ee roh.

Aiits'ą' reh dzaa nihts'įį dindèe reh khąhjìl aii nahkàk vàràhnyàa (adlaa).

Aii nahkàk gwiizhìk dziitsal nąįį reh.

"Aii jidìi t'ąh'in dinintł'ìnlii, ghoo[11] tr'ahaa'yàa," giyahnyàa.

15.33 "Âa, duuyeh gwik'it t'ishi'ìn," nyàa.

Aii gwiizhìk jyàa diyah'in gwiizhìk ch'ii'ęę,

"Âa, shitsii, ęę," vàràhnyaa googàa duuyeh gwik'it t'ii'in.

15.45 Aii gwiizhìk jidii dzii, ree oozhrii ch'yąą aii reh yinjideegwîilzhìi.

"Shuu, dàkdhat hee gàa t'ąh'ìn," yàhnyàa.

16.02 Akhài' dàkdhat izhìk t'iyah'in gwiizhìk dziitsal yąhtsìt, gwiizhìk ch'ìhłak chan dziitsal yąhtsit ts'ą' vindèe kwàa.

16.06 Vindèe khăiinjil ts'ą' zhik gwà'àn chan zhyąą neetak ts'ą' jyàa dii'in vàràhnyàa (adlaa).

Jyàa dìi'in ts'ą', neeshrâahch'yaa adaatsii gwiizhìk chan neegǫǫ yats'ą' tr'ìinzhii.

Yats'ą' tr'ìinzhii ts'ą' reh yeedlàa.

10. In our modern dialect *giindih* is pronounced *giyindii*. —KP

11. *Ghoo* 'eggs' might also be written as *ch'aghòo*. —KP

14.18 *Vasaagìhdzak* also ended up not eating his grease (laughs).
He got real mad at *Muskrat*.
He walked away with nothing in his stomach.
14.32 He didn't get even *one bite* out of that big moose.
That's really what happened.

Vasaagìhdzak and the Birds

14.48 They say *Vasaagìhdzak* came to a place where there were lots of birds.
14.58 The birds all surrounded him.
They all surrounded him, and he didn't know how to fool them, so he took out both of his eyeballs and was juggling them, they say (laughs).
He was juggling them and the birds asked him, "What you have there, can you give them to us so we can keep them for our eggs?"
15.33 And he said, "Aa, no way! I won't do it."
The birds begged him, calling him "Grandpa," but they say he wouldn't do it.
15.45 While this was going on, some kind of a little mountain bird called *"dzii"* fooled him.
"Nephew, throw them up higher," it told him.
So he threw them higher and then a bird flew by and caught one.
16.02 Meanwhile, another bird caught the other eye.
His mind was still on the eye that was caught when the other one was caught too.
16.06 Now, he had no eyes at all and was walking around blind, they say (laughs).
He was doing that and was suffering when *Fox* came by.
He came by and was laughing at him.

16.34 Tł'ookàh zhrįh vindèe khăiin'ąįį ch'ii'àn tł'ookàh yindèezhal eenjit haahchik, "Hmm," nyaa.

Gwiizhìk yeedlàa eenjit jyàa dìyah'ìn.

Yąąh'in kwaa ts'ą̀' reh yich'eedaachii reh.

Aii googàa reh.

16.46 Gohch'it ndàa ts'ą̀' zhik chi'ii'an hatrak akhài' neegǫǫ tsoo ąhtsit vàràhnyàa.

16.56 Âa, ts'ą̀' t'ee reh, shineenjii yàhnyaa gàa "Nàkwaa," nyaa.

Aiits'ą̀', "Shitsii, yee'òk neenahǫįįh'ee, shitsì' oiintà' ts'ą̀' neenahǫįįh'ee," yàhnyàa.[12]

17.28 "Lyâa nineehįhdal kwàa," jyàa nyàa.

Akhài' reh, "Oo'òk k'eenihįįh'ee, shǫǫhkhwaa shrǫ̀'," yàhnyàa.

Aiits'ą̀' t'ee gwik'ìt t'iyah'in.

Yitsi' oontà' ts'ą̀' oo'òk khai' yàa neehidìk.

17.35 Neegǫǫ tsoo aii.

"Tr'ikhit gwintł'òo shitsì' oiintà', shitsì' ts'ąąhdàii," yàhnyàa.

17.44 Gwintsàl nehk'at nileezhyaa naanąįį gwiizhìk hee neegǫǫ tsoo yats'an tr'ineekàii (adlaa).

It'ee neegǫǫ tsoo khanâaghyų̀' gàa duuyeh jyàiinch'yaa ts'a' zhyąą zhik gwà'àn neehaandak ts'ą̀' vindèe kwàa, kwàt dèehee'yàa gǫ̀'?

Aiits'ą̀' gohch'it reh ts'iivii reh k'adêeljik vàràhnyàa.

18.10 "Nananh nik'ee gwit'èehaałch'yàa gòo'ąįį?" jyàa ts'iivii àhnyàa.

"Àąhà'," yàhnyàa, "jidìi dèe?" nyaa.

Akhài' "Dzìh," nyàa.

"Shananh dzìh' lèe?"

18.23 Ts'iivii yàhnyaa ts'ą̀' t'ee reh yakat neehaandak akhài' dzìh k'at daandak[13] aii chan dilìi.

---

12. Sarah says something softly in the background. —CM

13. Today we would say *daanjik* instead of *daandak.* —KP

16.34 He was poking him in the eye sockets and making fun of him.
Each time *Fox* poked him, he said, "Hmm."
Meanwhile he was laughing at him for that.
Fox was even rubbing up against him.
He couldn't see anything anyway.
16.46 He kept grabbing for him when, they say, he finally grabbed him.
16.56 And *Fox* begged him to let him go, but he said, "No way."
And *Fox* said, "Grandpa, I'll be your guide, just hold on to my tail."
17.28 And *Vasaagìhdzak* said, "I won't let go of you now."
But *Fox* said, "Don't kill me. I'll be your guide anywhere."
He held on to his tail and *Fox* slowly guided him around.
17.35 And *Fox* said to him, "You're holding on to my tail too hard; you're hurting it."
17.44 Just when his fingers loosened a little, *Fox* ran away (laughs).
Now he begged *Fox*, but *Fox* wouldn't come to him.
He walked around blind and was feeling around with his hands.
What can he do without any eyes?
They say he felt a spruce tree and asked the tree,
18.10 "Is there anything I can use on you?"
And the tree said, "Yes, what do you want?"
Vasaagìhdzak said, "Pitch."
And the tree said, "You mean the pitch on me?"
18.23 And so he felt around on the spruce tree and gathered pitch from here and there.

Aii natr'aa ts'ą̨' reh dindèe ginyąadri'[14] ts'ą̨' gohch'it vindèe nèekwąįį nihts'įį gąhtsii aiitł'ęę t'ee dindèe nìyinlii ts'ą̨' t'ee reh gwąąh'in (adlaa).

18.43 Gwiizhìk vindèe łyâa chidiinlee hàa dziitsal ghòo' yaa'įį roh.

Tthak reh vaghòo yinlįį (adlaa).

Vasaagìhdzak Tthaalit Hàa

19.00 Ch'ihłan chan shoh oohą̆ą'łi' vàràhnyàa.

Shoh oohą̆ą'łi', yats'ą̨' nakhâiichii gwiizhìk hee tł'it choo vâa naii vàrahnyàa.

Kheech'eechyaa akhài' shrak iltł'àt dǫhłįį.

19.13 Akhài' gwiizhìk tł'it choo vâa nàii.

Shoh yâa k'ii ts'ą̨' chan shoh gwiteetseendak.

19.21 Łi'hàa ditł'it ts'ą̨' shòo dhidlìt kwàa, ts'ą̨' yaaghà' gwîiłk'ìn ts'ą̨' chii dril oozhee chĭin'aii vàràhnyàa.

Chĭin'aii ts'ą̨' dâąhdrya' kat hee reh diti'èe'ìk zhak ąhtsit ts'ą̨' reh gatthahgwazhàa.

19.31 Vatthal gich'aazhik, ts'ą̨' "Khwinjihǫǫzii," nyàa.

"Jaghaii sheech'ahshii gò'?" nyaa ts'ą̨' reh dehłì' dak nôonjik ts'ą̨' t'ee reh gwats'an vatthal chan łìt choh dha'ąįį vàràhnyàa (adlaa).

Łit choh dha'ąįį ts'ą̨' reh (adlaa).

19.56 Aii gwiizhìk khaiinjii gwandàii datthak ch'a'àa kwaa reh, googàa gwandàii, nàhąą?

Gohch'it reh vatthal łìt choh gwats'an tr'âanąįį, zhik ahaa roh, aii vitłèe'ik zhyàanàįį ts'ą̨' aii oozhak k'êeljìk.

20.05 T'ee reh łìt choh reh dehłì' zhìt khăiin'ąįį roh (adlaa).

Aii khăiin'ąįį ts'ą̨' reh, "Shitsųų," zhyàą ch'ii'an nyaa vàràhnyàa.

20.32 "Yaaghà' nilįį gaih iinzhii łii agwàłąįį," nyaa vàràhnyàa.

14. Perhaps this is equivalent to *dindèe giyuuhàadri'*, meaning 'He measured it to see if it fit his eye socket.' —KP

He chewed it and gathered up enough to fit into his eye sockets.
He finally made them fit and put them in and now he could see (laughs).
18.43 While this was happening, the birds kept his eyeballs for eggs (laughs).

Vasaagìhdzak and His Scab

19.00 Once, they say, *Vasaagìhdzak* tried to kill a black bear too.
They say he was sneaking up on a black bear when he farted loud.
I guess he felt his fart coming while he was sneaking up.
19.13 Then he let it go.
The bear heard him and ran off into the brush.
19.21 He got so mad at his fart that he built a fire right there and put a flat rock into it, they say.
He put in a flat rock and waited until it got red hot.
Then he pulled down his pants and burned himself repeatedly.
19.31 His anus burned.
And then "I hope that will teach you a lesson," he said.
"Why did you let the bear get away?" he said.
And then he pulled up his pants.
Then after that they say he developed a big scab on his anus (laughs).
There was a big scab there (laughs).
19.56 He never ate anything in his life,
but he still lives, you see?
The big scab finally came off his anus while he was walking.
It fell into his pants, and he reached into his pants and took it out.
20.05 He took out a big scab (laughs).
And they said he was hollering, "Grandma!" out to nowhere.
20.32 He was saying "I found the dry meat you dropped!"
they say.

Gwiizhìk, "Shitsų̨ų̨," nyaa ts'ą̨' kheeshraadiitrak gàa reh vitsų̨h kwàa ch'ii'àn t'agwàhnyaa gwiizhìk lee vitsų̨h.[15]

20.48 Âa, yahaanjyàa gǫ̀'.

Aiits'ą̨' reh, "Yaaghà' nilį̨į̨ gaih ìinzhii agwàł'ą̨į̨," nyaa ts'ą̨' datthal łìt oontà' t'inyaa vàrànyàa.

Gwiizhìk ditsų̨ų̨ noozhrìk gàa reh, âa, yàhnyaa kwàa (adlaa).

21.09 "Shitsų̨ų̨ shizhìt gwìłts'ik googàa reh shį̨į̨ neehih'àa," nyaa ts'ą̨' datthal łìt neiin'àl aii zhrį̨h neiin'àl į̨' (adlaa).[16]

21.45 Dats'an łę̨ę̨ chan neeniin'àk dhiłkhwaii googàa ch'in'àl kwàa.

Kwàt dinjik chan dhìł khwą̨į̨ tthak khàdiint'uu googàa chan ch'in'àl kwàa.

Datthal łìt zhrį̨h neiin'al łyâa ninzhùk gweedhaa gwideezhak (adlaa).

Vasaagìhdzak King Hàa [17]

22.19 Aii it'ee vagwandàk hâą̨'aa gwats'ą̨' reh,
aii kwaiik'ìt gwachoo gwak'at deedhizhii.

King zhat dhidii.

Âa, *King* ts'ą̨' nizį̨į̨ shą̨ą̨'ee.

22.30 It'ee łyâa nankat tthak k'eedhiizhii tł'ee reh.

Ts'ą̨' reh it'ee tthak gaayii yahtsii aiits'ą̨' reh aii *King* chan reh va'at chan reh nih'àn *room* gwigwìi'į̨į̨ nàhą̨ą̨?

22.48 Gwiizhìk reh zhik gwà'àn, oo'àt ch'ii'ę̨ę̨ nihdèegwiidį̨į̨ izhìk reh k'àiich'ii dinjii k'ìt teedhitł'į̨į̨ reh.

---

15. This famous line from the story about Grandma leaving her dry meat reappears in Sarah's tale below. See note 19 below.

16. Kathy says something that makes Johnny laugh some more. —CM

17. This final episode in the Vasaagìhdzak cycle is an unusual and unique one which may have been influenced by European folklore. When I played the tape for the four surviving children in the Frank family in 1989, none of them had ever heard it, even though they all knew all the rest of the stories in the cycle. One member of the family thought the King was really a Chief. Of all the Johnny Frank stories then, this one seems closest to his own creative invention, an invention within the tradition. —CM

Meanwhile, he said "Grandma!" repeatedly, but he had no grandmother, so there was actually no grandmother to answer his call.

20.48 Nobody would answer his call.

And then, "I found the dry meat you dropped," he said, holding the big scab and calling his grandmother.

But they say she didn't answer (laughs).

21.09 He was saying "Grandma, I'm hungry so I will eat it."

So he ate his scab and that was all he ever ate in his life (laughs).

21.45 He fooled lots of ducks by killing them and ended up not eating any.

He also killed a moose and cut it up but didn't get to eat that either.

The only thing he really ate during his entire life was this scab (laughs).

Vasaagìhdzak and the King

22.19 Just before his stories ended, *Vasaagìhdzak* came to a big village.

There was a King there.

Ahh, he was being nice to the King.

22.30 This was after he traveled all over the place.

This King and his wife had two separate rooms, you see?

22.48 There was a dummy dressed up as a man at the doorway to the King's house.

Izhìk ch'ii'ęę aii *King* dhichįį gwiizhìk khai' gi'diintin ts'ą' reh ch'ii'ee jyàa dìnch'yàa.

23.04 Aii gwiizhìk reh, zhik gwà'àn jidii łyâa zhyąą nizįį oonyaa tthak *King* vizheh zhyąą *save* nilįį reh aii tthak teegwąhjii chĭinlii.

23.21 Chĭinlii ts'ą' reh aii gwiizhìk aiitł'ęę nijin zhat yàa dąį' gał hàa oozhok gineedîichik tł'ęę aii *King* aii yahaahkhwàa jì' eenjit reh.

23.38 Yiyèe'an tr'eech'ahchak dinjii k'ìt t'inch'yaa nąą'įį k'it t'ii'in yahtsìi.

Aiits'ą' reh, kwàt aii tł'ęę nihkąą t'ee reh vats'an zhrįh hiljìi.

Gwats'ą' khàa chan yeenjit gwak'ą'ąhtii, akhài' chan hee ch'ii'ęę nìneezhìi.

23.53 Toh hàa yàagwàt.

Aii yàagwat ts'ą' t'ee dhaałkhwąįį yuunyaa zhyąą dinjii k'ìt tèeyàatł'įį reh.

24.18 Aiits'ą' reh, aiitł'ęę reh t'inyàa, *King* aii.

Dèeheenjyàa łi' yùunyaa hàa reh.

Ya'at idîiltsąįį.

Zhik gwà'àn va'at ch'ah khąįįnlii aii ch'ìhłak nàazhii ts'ą' reh, "Aii dinjii neeshrâahch'yaa dhąąhkhwąįį dèeheech'yàa eenjit jyàa dąhthàn?" jyàa reh dakąį àhnyàa.

24.45 Ch'a'at idîiltsąįį ts'ą'.

Nih'àn *room* gwigwii'įį nàhąą?

24.55 Aiits'ą' reh, aii łyâa gwintł'òo ch'ąą'įį àkwàt jyàa dìnch'yaa ts'ą' akharòoheenjyàa jyàa reh yàhnyàa.

Vasaagìhdzak aii t'inyàa, googàa *Vasaagìhdzak* t'inyaa gàandaii kwàa.

"Yaaghà' gwà'àn *King* ts'àt ch'ìhłak aii vanôonjik ts'ą' t'ǫǫhłįį nàrąąhchįį," jyàa nyàa.

25.23 T'ee reh *Vasaagìhdzak* shòo dhidlit.

King ts'at vintł'èehàachal gwìltsąįį reh.

Aii nànaatsùu ts'ą' t'ee reh gwach'àa tthak neiin'at ts'ą' shrahtèeyìłjil.

While the King was sleeping, *Vasaagìhdzak* sneaked in quietly through the doorway.

23.04 Meanwhile he took everything that looked good to him, everything that the King had saved.

23.21 Each time he came after that, he felt around the doorway with a stick just in case the King tried to catch him and kill him.

23.38 The next day the King found out his things were gone.

So the King waited for him that night.

And when he came again, the King hit him with a cane.

23.53 He hit him with a short spear.

And he thought he killed him, but he actually hit the dummy instead.

24.18 *Vasaagìhdzak* then got the King's wife's clothes and dressed up like her and said to him,

"You killed the poor man. How come you just left him?"

24.45 He pretended to be the King's wife, you see?

They had two separate rooms.

24.55 And the King thought he would just leave him there since he already stole lots from him anyway.

That's what the King said.

But the King didn't know it was actually *Vasaagìhdzak* who had dressed up as his wife.

And she said, "We should put him in the King's blanket and put him somewhere."

25.23 Now *Vasaagìhdzak* made it so he could have the King's blanket too.

He was happy.

He took the blanket, went out, and took off the King's wife's clothes and went to a nearby village with the blanket.

Aiits'ą̀' geh'at kwaiik'ìt hee gwats'ą̀' hàazhii reh.
Izhìk gwats'an t'ee neerahąą'yàa kwàa.
25.35 Izhìk gwats'ą̀' hàazhii ts'ą̀' k'idik ts'ą̀' reh.
Aiits'ą̀' zhyą̀ą reh *King* reh yee'ęę tr'iinzhii reh.
Yee'àt khan datthak gwats'ą̀' hohjyàa, *King* akǫ̀ǫ danakhwahnyaa nyàa.
Aiits'ą̀' łyâa zhyàa ch'ìhłęę dzaa heedyàa kwàa, ts'ą̀' datthak khan sheenohjyàa jyàa nyàa.
26.22 Nyaa ts'ą̀' t'ee reh aii *King* vałąįįchòo chan aii kat chan dòodii ts'ą̀' reh *King* gwich'in, ts'ą̀' łąįį choh k'eeyahchik reh t'inyàa.
It'ee *King* t'inyaa gwinyaa ts'ą̀' khan oo'àn naroojyàa gwinyàa.
Tr'iinin nąįį hàa tthak t'igwìizhìk gwinyàa.
26.34 Aiitł'ęę zhyą̀ą oo'àt *King* t'avaràhnyaa reh akoo diinyą̀' kwaa reh.
Zhyą̀ą t'igwinyaa ts'ą̀' t'ee tthak nihkhaneegaajìl.
26.47 Łąįį choo hàa t'igiizhìk googàa k'eegwiich'yaa gwatsal gwakwaa zhee gwalaii.
Zhik gwà'àn shìh, gwach'àa, jidii tthak gwìhìljìi.
Izhìk gwats'an t'ee vakwaa vàràhnyàa.
27.02 Chan nankat neehidik kwàa.
It'ee.

Nobody would see him again from there anyway.
25.35 He arrived there as the King.
And he told everyone to come to the King.
He told them not one of them should be left behind and all should come to him.
26.22 At the same time, he looked like the King because he was sitting on one of the King's horses.
They say they all decided to leave right away since it was the King who gave the order.
All the children went too, they say.
26.34 Then the people found out that it was not true that the King wanted them there.
26.47 When they got there with horses, there were nothing but empty houses.
There was no food or clothing.
They say *Vasaagìhdzak* was never heard of after that.
27.02 And then he also died.
That's all.

Sarah Frank

Vasaagìhdzak Vagwandak

<sfkf2a>

SF0.09 Aiits'ą' *Vasaagìhdzak* aii ree vagwandàk ndàa nàa'àį'.
Izhìk łyâa tsingwąhch'yaa t'igiyàhnyaa į'.
Nankat neehidik ts'ą' ree jyàa dii'in nijin kwaiik'ìt gòo'ąįį ginyàa.
Izhìk it'ee *last* vagwandak ndàa nàa'ąį'.
Izhìk it'ee kwaiik'ìt gòo'ąįį łee k'idik.
K'idik ts'ą' it'ee dinjii naįį něiin'ak giyàhnyàa.
"Nakhwareheeghàa gwinyaa t'ǫǫhłįį gwà'àn ch'ijìnǫǫhjyàa," jyàa nyaa aiits'ą' it'ee gwik'ìt dinjii neiin'àk giyàhnyaa į'.
1.20 Ts'ą' it'ee gwik'it t'igiizhìk izhìk gwigwich'įį gwits'į' zhyąą geh'àt nigiinjil izhìk gwats'an gwik'èegąąhtìi.
Gwik'èegąąhtii gàa k'eegwiich'yaa gokwàa.
Aiits'ą' it'ee gwiizhìk adan aii zhat kwaiik'ìt nàhąą, gwats'ą' hiljìi.
Aiits'ą' gwik'èegąąhtìi gàa k'èegwiich'yaa gwik'ìgwaanjii kwaa ts'ą' it'ee datthak digizheh zhat gwits'eegohòojìl.
Akhài' ree zhik dinjii gwat'ąąhch'yaa aii datthak zhyąą gàh adan kwaii hàa tthak zhyąą tr'agwahąhdè' k'ìt t'igwiizhìk łii.[18]
Izhìk it'ee vagwandàk ndàa nàa'ąį'.
CF2.29 Gwit'eh gwilii dǫhłìi?
SF2.34 Hahde' k'ìt t'iizhìk ree giyàhnyàa.
CF2.38 Hậą'!
SF2.40 Izhìk gwats'an vagwandàk kwàa.
Datthal lìt neiin'àl giyàhnyàa (adlaa).
CF2.51 Aii łyâa zhyąą shįį jì' gàa veegwahaldak? (Adlaa)
SF2.54 Hậą'?
CF2.55 (Adlaa) Aii gwandak t'aihnyaa shįį jì' gàa veegwahaldàk.

18. The implication is that they mysteriously disappeared as a result of magic. —JE

Sarah Frank

The Story of Vasaagìhdzak

<sfkf2a>

SF0.09 Now this is the very end of *Vasaagìhdzak's* story.
They say it really happened in a funny way.
For whatever he was doing during his journey, they say there was a village.
This is the last story told about him.
So he came to this village.
They say after he got there he fooled the people by saying, "I heard that all of you are going to be killed.
Move to another place."

1.20 So they did exactly what he told them to do, and they were just living there.
They didn't move very far from there so they could still watch the place.
And they watched the place but nothing happened.
But in the meantime *Vasaagìhdzak* went to their old village.
After they watched the place and saw that nothing happened, they all returned to their houses back in the old village.
But when they got there, *Vasaagìhdzak* and the whole place had all disappeared.
That was the end of his story.

CF2.29 He must have hid everything?

SF2.34 They say it's like everything simply disappeared.

CF2.38 Yes.

SF2.40 That was the end of his story.
They say that *Vasaagìhdzak* even ate the very dried up scab on his butt (laughs).

CF2.51 I myself could even tell that story (laughs).

SF2.54 What?

CF2.55 (Laughing away) I meant that story. I said even I could tell that story.

Shitsųh łyâa zhyąą veetsinyăąhch'yaa.
Khik yeeshàaneegwaandak.

SF3.05 Jùu dèe?

CF3.06 Shitsųų t'aihnyàa.

SF3.07 Ôǫ.

CF3.08 Izhìk gwintł'oo yeeshàagwaandak, shįį jì' gàa veegwahaldak t'inch'yàa văihnyàa.

Nilįį gąįh t'inch'yaa yuunyàa ts'ą' neeyin'àl yàhnyaa hęę? (Adlaa)

KF3.17 "Shitsųų sheenjit nilįį gąįh nąąhtsit łee," nyaa vàràhnyàa.[19]

SF3.24 Oonjìt gwànaa ree, izhìk ree dinjik, dinjik łèe li'.

Aii oohâąhłi', akhài' gwiizhìk vilì' kaii hee dhitł'it giyàhnyàa.

Dhitł'ìt ts'ą' reh dinjik yits'ì' hìlghaa, nàhąą.

Ts'ą' it'ee yaaghà' zhat chìhkat gwîiłk'in izhìk gwakat gitł'eetthaii giyàhnyàa (adlaa).

Aiitł'ęę ree vatthal łit iłtsąįį aii it'ee vats'an tr'âanaii łee, aii it'ee zhik gwà'àn chan neehidik akhài' ree aii datthal lìt ineegwąh'ąįį łee (adlaa).

4.07 Yee'òk dziitsal kwaii, "Yaaghà' nakhwatsųh nilįį gąįh idiinzhii łee, oh'àa," nyàa.

Jyàa nyaa gàa vàh gwik'ìt t'igwii'in kwàa.

Aiits'ą' gohch'it ree, shų' nilii gąįh oh'àa jìhnyàa.

"Nakhwatsųh nilįį gąįh idiinzhii łee aii shų' oh'àa jìhnyaa àkwàt shįį hih'aa," nyaa ts'ą' datthal lìt na'àa ree giyàhnyàa.[20]

Aii jùu ndàh t'ii'in t'aràhnyaa lì' (adlaa).

KF5.00 Dziitsal nąįį reh.

SF5.01 Hâą?

KF5.03 Dziitsal nąįį andàh t'ii'in vàràhnyàa.

SF5.05 Ąąhą', aii dziitsal nąįį andàh t'ii'in reh.

---

19. Framed by "*nyaa varahnyaa*", this humorous folk adage is also used by Johnny in his episode of *Vasaagihdzak and His Scab* above. Kenneth uses it again in his 2014 video showing how to make and eat caribou dry meat. See Frank, 2014. Allusions like this out of context help other speakers recall the old stories. —CM

20. They're all laughing here. —LG

My grandmother really thought that was a funny story.
She told it to me many times.
SF3.05 Who's that?
CF3.06 I said my grandmother.
SF3.07 Oh.
CF3.08 Like I said, she told me about it so many times that even I could tell that story.
She said he thought it was dry meat so he ate it, huh? (Laughing all the time)
KF3.17 They say that he said, "My grandmother must have put that dry meat there for me."
SF3.24 Once long ago, I guess there were moose there, which he was trying to kill when he farted, they said.
He farted and frightened the moose away, you see.
Then he made a fire right there on the sand bar on which he sat down, they said (laughs).
A scab developed on his anus and then later fell off.
Later on he was in the same area and found it (laughs).
4.07 He told the birds, "Your grandmother left dry meat. Eat it."
But none of them ate it, and finally nobody was eating the dry meat, so he said,
"I'll just eat it myself because our grandmother left her dry meat for us, but nobody's eating it," so he said, and they say he ate his own dried up scab.
I wonder who saw him do that (laughing).
KF5.00 It was the birds.
SF5.01 What?
KF5.03 They say he did this in front of those birds.
SF5.05 Yes, the birds saw him.

CF5.09 Aiitł'ęę chan, "Yaaghà' *Vasaagìhdzak* datthal lìt na'àa," giyàhnyaa ts'ą̀' chan giyeedlàa gwich'in ǫ'.
"Hèę?"

SF5.15 Ą̀ąhą', jyàa giyàhnyàa.

CF5.09 They say that the birds were laughing at him and said,
"Hey, *Vasaagìhdzak* is eating the dried up scab from his own butt!"
"Right?"

SF5.15 Yes, that's what they said.

Johnny Frank

Dak Neehaa

<jfcmla>

JF27.27 Aii gwànaa nįįzhùk kwaa gwànaa reh, dinjii ch'ìhłak łyâa dazhan vàràhnyàa, aii shan reh gàagwiindaii kwàa.

Aii googàa dinjii dazhan vàràhnyaa reh, niheedhaa łii.

Izhìk jì', "Nìhihthaa," nyaa vàràhnyàa.

Aii Dak Neehaa òozhìi.

27.58 Aiits'ą', "Izhìk jì' nìhihthaa," nyaa ts'ą' t'ee reh.

"Aii jì' shak'ąą t'ahohch'yàa, geełèehohjyàa shrǫ̀'.

Nįįzhùk gweedhaa jì' gwànaa dak heechìisha'aa[1] t'ôonch'yaa, neegwihîishandaii t'ôonch'yàa."

Nyaa ts'ą' reh dinjii datthak yak'àa gwich'įį vàràhnyàa.

March nanh hee nìindhat.

<jfcm1b>

JF0.13 "Neehihdyaa t'ôonch'yaa," nyaa ts'ą' tthak nìgìyùl'in ts'ą' gohch'it khaii tthak giik'àa gwìch'ìį, *March* gwats'an dagogwaagǫ', gohch'it *June* nanh gwats'ą' datthak *July* zhìt gòhju' it'ee dakhaiichit dha'ąįį vàràhnyàa.

0.36 Aiits'ą' oondaa han tankak iłchįį gwiizhìk hee jyàanch'yaa gwìlgǫ̀', ts'ą' chan trìndąįį vàh gǫǫlįį vàràhnyàa.

Vakat hee ch'iits'ąą ts'ą' łuu làii kak hee zhyąą dhichįį ts'ą' vàh łuu hàajik.

1.01 Vàh łuu hàajik kwat ijìi lì' zhrįh, vàhgwiindàii kwaa jyàanch'yaa ts'ą' zhyąą jyàa dìgìnch'yàa.

1.14 Aiits'ą' gohch'it reh, "Drǫh shoonkeedzìi khadhoh'èe, k'èegwiich'yaa gôohtth'ak jì' shįį t'ihįįhjyàa," nyaa ts'ą' it'ee reh.

Oondaa nijìn tankak nàrąąhchįį izhìk łyâa gwik'èehǫǫhtyàa nyaa vàràhnyàa.

1. *Heechìisha'aa* is pronounced today as *heekìihisha'aa.* —KP

Johnny Frank

Dak Neehaa

<jfcmla>

JF27.27 Not too long ago, nobody ever heard of medicine, but there was this one man who was really a medicine man, they say.

Then he said, "I'm going to die," they say, and then he predicted the day he would die.

His name was *Dak Neehaa.*

27.58 And so he said, "I'm going to die" and predicted the day he would die,

And when he died, he told the people, "Don't leave but keep on living here because one day I will wake up again."

They say all the people kept on living there by him.

He died in the month of March.

<jfcmlb>

JF0.13 "I will come back again," he said.

So they lived by his body all winter and all spring from March until June.

They say he finally came back to life in July.

0.36 And spring came while his body was still lying on the ice.

They say the flies were bothering him, and he even had maggots on his body when finally the ice went out with him.

1.01 The ice went out with him, and he was nowhere to be found, but the people kept on staying there.

1.14 So he told them, "Listen for me and if you hear anything, it will be me."

They say he told them to watch for him out there on the ice where his body was laid.

1.37 Kwàt łuu hàajik gwats'an chųų lęįį gwįįlì' *flood* gwįįlì' tł'ee ndàa ts'ą' reh gweedhaa gwiizhìk khan hee reh zhik gwats'ą' chirîitth'ak.

Izhìk gwats'à' khàraajil akhài' yeendee nijìn narąąhchii.

Izhìk łuu hàajik ch'yąą izhìk hee reh ch'ilik hàa ch'aadzaa vàràhnyàa.

1.56 Chųų kak hee zhyąą *glass* kak ch'araadzaa k'ìt t'ii'in vàrahnyàa.

Aiits'ą' oondee nankak gwats'ą' oondòk ch'ahaadzàl.

2.13 Oondaa zhat gwats'ą' neech'aadzàl jyàa dǐi'ìn ts'ą' ndàk łeehaa, gòhch'it oondee nankak jyàa dǐi'in gwiizhìk dinjii lęįį zhyąą ch'its'êelzhii ts'ą' oondee ch'iindàk digizhit gwìłtsąįį izhìk ch'iindàk jyàa dǐi'in.

Gohch'it łąą oondee nankak deedhizhii gwiizhìk vikììtł'it tr'ąhtsit vàràhnyàa.

2.30 Tr'ąhtsit ts'ą' reh, shìh kwaa ts'ą' reh, dąįį ts'it tthaatłòk aii reh khèedii yaaghà' gwà'àn dha'ąįį łii.

Aii reh hìltłee ts'ą' t'ee reh dinjii nànâanąįį vàràhnyàa.

2.49 It'ee reh, va'at yach'àa yintł'ìneiinlįį ts'ą' dach'àa nànaazhii ts'ą' reh.

Jii vichìighai' aii reh jidìi łuh, teedlit hàa zhyąą tthak jyàa dìnch'yaa vàràhnyàa.

Aii eenjit va'at shreeyìnlìk.

It'ee reh, gwichįh dąį' gwinzįį gwandàii ch'yąą gwik'ìt t'inch'yàa.

3.18 Neegwadadhat shriit'ąąch'yąą vàa neegwâadhat gwiizhìk, "Chan hee nìhihthaa," nyaa vàràhnyàa.

3.33 Izhìk reh va'at vitì' hàa nąįį yuaahkat vàràhnyàa.

"Natsąhts'ą' gwich'ìighai' oo'ęę neiindik t'ini'ìn?

Zhyąą izhìk shràgǫǫlii jàghàii," vàràhnyàa akhài'.

"Yeedak diitì' gǫǫlii łee," jyàa nyaa vàràhnyàa.

4.12 Kwàt ts'ą' googàa vigii naii gàa yideent'aii geh'àn, googàa chan hee ch'adąį' deezhik gwik'ìt t'ineezhìk.

Chan hee nįįdhat ts'ą' chan hee dinjii neelįį vàràhnyàa.

T'ee nèekwat neezhii łyâa geetee nįįzhùk gwahadhak ts'ą' nìnèedhàk (adlaa).

1.37 Then the ice went out and there was lots of water and there was a flood.
Time went by and finally they heard something.
They all went to where his body was.
There where the ice went out he was singing and dancing, they say.
1.56 They say he was dancing on the water just like there was glass under his feet.
And then he danced back and forth toward the shore.
2.13 He danced back and forth until he was coming closer and closer, and when he finally reached the shore, there were lots of people standing there.
Then they say they just reached out and grabbed him by the back.
2.30 They grabbed him, but there was no food, except for a boiled porcupine that had been around since the previous spring.
He ate that and became a man again right there, they say.
2.49 Now his wife gave him back his clothes, and he wore them.
They say his hair was muddy and just had a lot of weeds in it.
His wife cleaned him up so he was the same as he was before he died.
3.18 They say a few years had gone by when he said,
"I will die again."
3.33 They say when he said that, his wife and his father asked him,
"How can you come back again each time after you die?
How do you solve that problem?"
"We have our father up in heaven," he said, they say.
4.12 And so he died once more even though his children tried to prevent it, yet it happened again.
He died twice more, they say, and sometimes it took a long time before he died again (laughs).

4.35 Aiits'ą', "Chan oondaa vankak nashohohchyaa yùu," nyaa ts'ą' t'ee reh gwik'ìt t'igiiyinlìk.

Izhìk chan hee vak'ąą tr'igwich'įį.

Gwiizhìk oondaa tankak gwazhrąįį ił'ąįį gwiizhìk tan vàa łihk'ìt teeya'àk, aii gohch'it chan tan chųų ąhkhan ts'ą' chan reh gwats'ą' hìljìi.

5.05 Tthak veech'iits'ąą, trìndąįį veech'iits'ąą tł'ee reh.

Aiitł'ęę chan hee reh yeendaa chųų kak ch'aadzaa łii.

5.26 "Chan hee dinjii lęįį naii yinêelzhìi, jyaanch'yaa nankak deedhizhii gwiizhìk chan giyąhtsit, izhìk chan giitthaatłok aii zhrìh shìh vizhìt.

5.51 Aii chan łì'hàa giik'èegwandaii ts'ą' gwandàii tthak giiyaahłii gooràhnyaa gwik'ìt t'iizhìk.

Kwàt aiits'ą' izhìk tł'ęę dach'àa nànaazhii ts'ą' gwinzįį gwandàii.

Vatthąį' tthak chan nizįį.

Aiitł'ęę t'ee gwaandak yeedàk hee diitì' gǫǫlįį łii, łyâa shrôonch'yaa łii.

"Chan neehihdyaa t'ôonch'yaa gaa oo'ęę neehihdyaa kwaa."

Digii dalàk naii, àhnyaa vàràhnyàa.

6.14 Aii reh khee gwànaa yeendaa niizhìt kwaa gwànaa jyàa dǐizhìk aii t'ee oondee *Vashrąįį K'ǫǫ* gęhdee vatth'ank'ìt gòo'ąįį.

Shant'ee googàa gwąął'in t'inch'yàa.

SF6.27 Yeendaa lidįį goovee'ałtsii gaa shi'in, yee'at nilįį oo'at drah kat doodlii ch'yaa łaii tsal chan ya'aa łee.[2]

JF6.38 *Aah shit!*

AW6.49 Oo'at zhat deehihłyaa.

JF6.59 Izhìk gwànaa, gehnaa nįįzhìt chan akòo dìgwii'in kwaa.

Gàa jii t'agwaihnyaa gwànaa łyâa shriit'ąhshyùk neegwihiidhak.

Dinjii nàdhak tł'ęę googàa oo'ęę nidìk.

Vatthąį' tthak anlìk.

Vatth'àn zhrįh, aii googàa reh oo'ęę nidìk.

2. Sarah interrupts the story here by coming to the door and announcing a small crisis with the puppies.

4.35 Each time he died, he told the people, "Put my body out on the ice again."
And they did that.
They always stayed close by his body each time.
His body was in sight out on the lake at all times until finally spring came, and the ice moved back and forth until he disappeared.
5.05 The flies bothered his body, and there were maggots all over him.
Then they noticed him dancing again out there on the water.
5.26 Lots of people surrounded him once again while he danced.
They grabbed him and fed him just as they did before.
5.51 He put on his clothes and became himself again.
His flesh also became good.
After that he told stories saying there was a father in heaven and that it was really fun there.
"I will die again, but this time, I will not come back."
He said that to his children and to his relatives, they say.
6.14 This happened years and years ago, and his grave is up above *Arctic Village*.
I've even seen it myself.
SF6.27 [Interrupting] I'm making tea for everybody, but the meat we have up on the cache is being eaten by the puppies again.
JF6.38 Aah, shit!
AW6.49 I'll go out there and put it further up.
JF6.59 At the time this man died but kept coming back to life.
What I'm saying is there was a long interval that followed.
Yet afterwards what happened to him happened to other people too.
People would die but they came back alive.
Their bodies decomposed.
There were just bones left, but even so they still came back to life.

Gwichįh dąį' gwandàii gwik'ìt t'inch'yaa ts'ą' izhìk gwànaa gwįįlì'.
7.28 Aii shitsųh *Ndìk* khaiinjii yanah'yą'.
Aii dinjii nèekwat neezhii reh *Dàk Neehaa* òozhìi.
Łyâa dinjii nizįį inlì' vàràhnyàa.
7.57 Aii t'ee Neets'uuch'in.[3]

3. *Neets'uuch'in* is a Gwich'in contraction for *Neets'ee Gwich'in.* —AR
Johnny uses it again at the beginning of the second version of the *Tł'èevì Tì'* story, but not in the first version which follows. There is a break in the tape here before the *Tł'èevì Tì'* story begins. —CM

Before that time, it kept on happening, but they still came back to the way they were when they were alive.

7.28 My grandmother *Ndik* almost saw this man.

This man that died twice was named *Dak Neehaa.*

He was really a good man, they say.

7.57 He was from *Arctic Village*.

Sarah Frank

Kǫ̀'ehdan
Ch'eechyah Ch'ìhłak

<sfkf2a>

SF7.55 Aii *Kǫ̀'ehdan*[1] aii veegwarahaandak?

KF7.58 Ą̀ąhą̀'.

SF8.07 Aii it'ee ch'adą̀i' gwànaa ree jyàa dìgii'in ts'ą' shìh gaahkhòk.

Shìh gaahkhok ts'ą' it'ee jùu datthak ch'ihee'àa geegwitr'it t'agogwah'in t'agooràhnyàa.

Shih tsal ginghan ts'ą' it'ee ree vikeegahch'yàa.

8.44 Aii *Kǫ̀'ehdan* aii it'ee. . .oondaa shìh gahvir, nàhąą.

Shìh gahvir gwiizhìk it'ee di'ìk dazhoo ik zhrįh nàgaazhii t'agoogàhnyàa.

Gwiìndhaa ts'ą' ree di'ìk niltsùu ts'ą' ts'ee ehdan oondaa shìh gahvir jyàa digii'in.[2]

9.11 Aii gwiizhìk it'ee Ch'eekwaii it'ee goo'àt nǐinjil łee gooràhnyàa.

Izhìk gàhgiindàii kwàa.

Oozhee vikeegahch'yàa gwizhrįh.

Aii gwiizhìk it'ee zhyą̀ą khan hee ree gook'ą̀ągahàajil, nàhąą?

9.36 Aiits'ą' ts'eehdan di'ìk gàa nìneehaachal gàa gògòontrìi.

Aiits'ą' it'ee ts'eehdan ree jyàa dìgii'in.

Ts'eehdan jyàa dìgii'in ts'ą' ree, vachaa chan.

Dagachaa hàa łi'hàa nihk'ìt t'igii'in googàhnyaa į'.

Łyâa zhyą̀ą duulèe ginlįį.

10.14 Aiits'ą' it'ee gook'ą̀ąrahàajil ts'ą' it'ee ree.

It'ee ree k'ageheenjyàa gwizhrįh.

Aiits'ą' it'ee dagachaa hàa t'ee łyâa diits'an tr'igiiin'oo googàhnyàa.

Aii gwiizhìk it'ee gwats'an tr'igiin'oo ts'ą', geedąhzhrįį reh, datthak gooringhàn.

---

1. *Kò'ehdan* means 'Without Matches' or literally 'No Fire.' —CM

2. I don't know if Sarah means that he just removed his top clothing or stripped down to nothing at all. —LG

Sarah Frank

Kǫ̀'ehdan
First Version

<sfkf2a>

SF7.55 Are we going to tell about *Kò 'ehdan*?

KF7.58 Yes.

SF8.07 A long time ago this is what they did when they killed lots of game.

What we say about them is that everybody worked together after they killed game so that they could have a big feast.

They were all cooking food.

8.44 *Kò 'ehdan* was busy boiling meat, you see.

What they were saying is that his coat was made of fur.

Fur was the only clothing they had.

It was too hot so he took off his fur clothes.

And he was busy cooking without his fur clothes.

9.11 Meanwhile they didn't know they were being ambushed by the Inuit.

That's what they say about them.

They were too busy cooking when they were attacked.

9.36 He didn't even have a chance to put on his coat.

So he left without his coat.

That's what happened and his younger brother was also with him.

They say he and his younger brother were the same — both were very fast.

They were hard to compete with.

10.14 When they were attacked they had to fight.

Now they would have to defend themselves.

So they say that somehow he and his younger brother got away.

The Inuit killed everybody except those two.

10.44 Aiits'ą' gehdąhzhrįh gwats'an tr'igiin'oo ts'ą' it'ee gehdee ddhah, ddhah kat chii dhidlii, nàhąą?

Jyàa dinch'yaa izhìk k'iidàk googàa khàgaa'oo ts'ą', oodee chiikat dagòo'ąįį izhìk hee deegaa'òo.

Aiits'à izhìk gwats'an it'ee oodàk jidii shrąh gał aii k'ìt t'inch'yaa oodàk it'ee googohshrąą.

Gàa vachaa aii it'ee dzaa gii'àii kat gwiłshrąą ts'ą' it'ee nineegiival aatsìt aii it'ee yeezhee gaahkhwąįį.

Aii gwiizhìk aii dinjii oodee zhat nàdhàt.

Aiits'ą' it'ee łyâa duuyeh k'èegwiich'yaa t'igiyilii gàhgiindaii ts'ą' ree datthak gwigwinghan o'.

Aiits'ą' it'ee adan jyàa dĭizhìk ts'ą' àkwàt it'ee ree giidrąįį neehàanjik kwàa.

11.57 Aiits'ą' it'ee ree neegihiijyàa, nàhąą.

Neegihiijyaa izhìk chan jii datthak ts'ee'hdan ree.

Aiits'ą' it'ee Ch'eekwaii ch'ìhłak aii it'ee jidìi tsee dzirh gwich'in dazhoo jyàa dąhjyaa aii it'ee oozhee yeenjìt nĭinlii giyàhnyàa.

12.24 Aii it'ee t'èelnaii, aiits'ą' it'ee reh oo'at kwank'ìt neegwąą'yà'.

Zhik tr'igwaghan izhìk neegwąą'yà' izhìk chan vaghwaii giyàhnyaa aii it'ee zhik gwà'àn zhah t'eh gwizhĭinzhii łee, aii chan.

Izhìk dąį' jyàa dìgii'in ts'ą' aih kat jidìi vihtr'ih[3] giyàhnyaa aii it'ee gwanàngahchìt googàhnyaa į'.

Aii gwik'ìt t'inch'yaa zhangaa'yùu ts'ą' zhat neegihiidàl.

Akhài' it'ee jii giikwaì' aii kat neegihiidàl.

Nats'ąhts'ą' googàa iiheendyàa gǫ̀'.

Aiits'ą' it'ee googàa jèiinch'yaa gèhch'it it'ee geelèegohòojìl.

Aiitł'ee it'ee khàneezhii gàa jii datthak ch'iitsii ch'ok hàa giikwaiichan khàndiin'yùu rǫh.

13.52 Aiits'ą' ninijii kwàa.

Kǫ' tsal chan adàh gwizhyăanąįį gwìch'in, akwaa gwìch'in.

3. *Vihtr'ih* is our word for obsidian, traditionally used for making projectile points. —KF

10.44 So as they were going along, both of them climbed to the top of this rocky mountain just the way they were, you see?
So finally they got to top of that really rocky area.
While they were up on top, the Inuit were trying to hook onto their snowshoes from down below them.
They had a long stick with a hook on the end of it.
Finally, they did hook his younger brother's snowshoes, so they dragged him below.
Kò'ehdan stood up there while they were killing his brother.
They knew they couldn't get to him, and since they killed everybody else, they left him alone.
11.57 They were all leaving, you see.
Meanwhile he didn't have anything on from the waist up.
But they say that one Inuit left him a long pair of beaver fur mittens.
12.24 The mittens really came in handy for him.
So he went to check out the camp.
Back where they say everybody was killed, they say his sister-in-law was still there.
She had crawled underneath the snow during the attack.
In those days when they went to war they got some real sharp-pointed pieces of obsidian and fixed them to the bottom of their snowshoes.
That's what they say about them.
So that's what they all had on,
and they walked over the snow with them.
Then they walked over her foot.
Even so, she didn't move.
She stayed that way until they all left.
Finally she crawled out, but her whole foot had been stabbed with those sharp obsidian points.
13.52 She couldn't stand up.
But maybe she had saved a small ember from the fire.

Zhik kǫ' chan zhahgaatik izhìk gwà'àn it'ee kǫ' tsal ineegwàh'ąįį.

Aii hàa it'ee zhat it'ee khàneegwîilk'ii dǫ̀hłįį.

Łyâa veenjit gwìizųų.

Aii hàa khèegwîilk'in ts'ą̀' jèiinch'yaa gwiizhìk.

Izhìk it'ee łat khaneejuu ts'ą̀' it'ee izhìk gwits'eehòozhìi.

14.35 Aiits'ą̀' yąąh'yą̀' akhài' ree łyâa ninijii gàa veegògwàntrìi.

Aiits'ą̀' it'ee gwintł'oo nihts'ą̀' gintrìi tł'ǫǫ it'ee zhik tr'ìnjàa aii t'iyàhnyaa,

"Nahzhrįį zhik tsin ts'ą̀' gwihindàii jì' izhìk gwankeehinhàii, shįį aii it'ee łyâa sheegògwàntrii," yàhnyàa.

15.10 Jyàa yàhnyaa ts'ą̀' it'ee ree jyàa dìnch'yaa tł'ǫǫ it'ee ree yeelèehàazhii.

Khaii dąį' hee zhik shrahtèegadal, nàhąą.

KF15.22 Ą̀ąhą'.

SF15.23 Izhìk ch'ìhłak it'ee gwankeehàazhii.

Izhìk gwà'àn ahaa gwiizhìk it'ee geh ts'ą̀' tr'ahak giyàhnyàa.

Aii yeedàk gał jyàa dilik ts'ą̀' geh aii zhah t'eh k'igwaadhàk nàhąą?

Izhìk it'ee jyàa dinjik dąį' vak'ąą nitsigwaraatàl į', aih hàa.

Aiitł'ęę it'ee oozhee tr'oondak į'.

16.04 Jyàa dïi'in aii geh dhàh tsal aii hàa it'ee jii videeghàn kat jyàa dìiyah'in aii jyàa dìi'in ts'ą̀' it'ee aii hàa gwintsàl nindhaa dhidlìt.

Aii geh dahkhòk hàa.

16.32 Aiits'ą̀' gwiizhìk khaii dąį' tr'ahàandii ch'yąą gwinjik ahàa.

Akhài' ree dèiinch'yaa, jùk vanh chan tr'ahàandii łee izhìk kwank'ìt k'idik.

K'idik ts'ą̀' it'ee yeendaa izhìk dąį' oondèk tth'an kwat jèiinch'yaa į'.

Aiits'ą̀' oondee shìh deek'it gogwàh'įį izhìk gwà'àn tth'an dhidlii łee, aii zhik tr'ahàandii izhìk chan tthai' oozhee kwànchit tsal dhidlii ginyàa.

Aii hàa it'ee khàneegwîiłk'in łee.

Or maybe she found a small coal from the fire they put out.
But I guess she started a fire for herself.
She felt very bad.
After she started a fire for herself she stayed there.
Kò'ehdan now saw smoke rising so he went over there.
14.35 After he saw her he knew it was hard for her to get up at all.
They both just wept together, and then the woman said to him,
"Go and try to survive and just leave me.
I can't do anything."
15.10 After she told him that, he stayed for a while and then finally left her there.
You see this was way back in the winter when everybody traveled far apart from one another.
KF15.22 Yes.
SF15.23 He started his journey towards that one area.
They say that while he was on his way he came across some snowshoe hares.
He held the stick up and the hares dove down under the snow, you see?
When they do that we stomp on them with our snowshoes.
After that we just pick them up.
16.04 That's how he collected fur to cover himself.
He stayed warm that way, by killing snowshoe hares.
16.32 While doing that he followed the old trail from way back in the early part of the winter.
Suddenly he came across a camp site that had been used that same morning.
They had just left that very day.
In those days they always left bones around the fireplace.
So he found the food area and found some bones there, and there they say he also found some embers that were still hot.
So he started a fire with them.

Aiits'ą̀' it'ee oondèk tth'an dhidlii kat hee gwatsal gwaajyàa.

17.33 Jèiinch'yaa tł'ęę t'ee zhyą̀ą kǫ' hàa chan vich'iinjii nàhąą, ts'ą̀' zhyą̀ą oo'àn hìltth'àt.

Aiits'ą̀' niizhyùk hee vàa'atgwee'è' tł'ęę it'ee tr'ineedhàt.

Tr'ineedhat ts'ą̀' it'ee chan hee zhik van tsal kat gwà'àn gwidį̀į tsal chan in'àl dǫ̀hłįį.

Aiitł'ęę it'ee ree tąįį hàazhii.

Jùk vành tr'ahàandii gwinjik.

18.12 It'ee hàazhii ts'ą̀' reh izhìk dą̀į' gògwàntrii ts'ą̀' chan niizhùk gahadàl kwaa t'agooràhnyàa.

18.33 Aiits'ą̀' reh it'ee yeendaa nàngaandii łee, zhik oonjìt tąįį hee njì' gwàa'ą̀į' hee shyąąghan adant'ee jidii tsal hàa adant'ee gwich'įį.

Nìnjik dahtłii t'ee aii nįhjyàa ghat k'idik izhìk hee it'ee yats'ą̀' nihděiinzhii gàa,

"Łyâa sheerigooghan t'ishe'ìn," jyaa yàhnyàa.

It'ee yee'àn it'ee khàginjihheetraa eenjit chyahahaii akhài' zhak neeyą̀htsìt.

SF19.13 "Oondaa jidìi tsal shantł'ăhtsìt tł'ęę t'inih'in," yàhnyàa.

Aiits'ą̀' it'ee gwik'it t'iyinlìk.

Aiitł'ęę it'ee ree chĭinzhii ts'ą̀' it'ee ree zheh gwitee khàginjii intrat ǫ'.

"Yee'àt sheegwarooghan t'ôonch'yaa *Kǫ̀'ehdan* shoozhrį̀' heelyàa, aii yaaghà' *Kǫ̀'ehdan* k'idik," jyàa hiinjyàa yùu yàhnyaa, giyàhnyàa.

19.57 Aiits'ą̀' it'ee akǫ̀ǫ dinyaa ts'ą̀' zheh gwitee khàginjii' intrat.

Âa, zhik datthak tr'âak'įį ts'ą̀' àkwàt zhyą̀ą ch'iinjì' vats'à' jyàa dìgwìizhìk.

Aii shyąąghan vizheh gwach'àa gwatsal aii googàa gàh nichigogwâątil gooràhnyàa.

20.27 Izhìk it'ee aii gwitee ch'ii'àn hee googàa it'ee chèhìltłèe.

Aiits'ą̀', "Jùu shik'it t'iizhìk jì' aii shijyàa heelyaa," nyąą dǫ̀hłįį.

Aii chèhìltłee akhài' dinjii ch'ihłęę lą̀ą yik'ìt t'iizhìk vàràhnyàa.

After that he started to chew on some bones.

17.33 He stayed that way and he felt the heat from the fires, you see, and he just fainted.

He was unconscious for a long time and finally woke up.

After he woke up I guess he found some more food around that small lake, and he ate that too.

So then he followed the trail.

It was a fresh trail from that same morning.

18.12 So he left.

In those days it was hard going, so they didn't travel too far.

This is what they say about them.

18.33 So everybody stopped to make camp, and this one old woman who was always the very last one, made camp with what little she had.

Kò'ehdan sneaked into her house without anyone noticing.

"I'm the only survivor from the ambush," he said to her.

She started to run outside to announce this, but he stopped her.

SF19.13 "Let me have something to eat first," he said.

So that's what she did.

After that she went outside and spoke up real loud.

Before that, he already told her to say,

"I was the only survivor from the ambush and everybody was killed and my name will be *Kò'ehdan*,
so just say, '*Kò'ehdan* is here.'"

So that's what she announced real loud.

19.57 And so she announced it by saying it loudly.

Aa, when they all heard her, they rushed over to her.

And they say that everybody rushed over so fast that the poor old woman's house was nearly torn apart.

20.27 Although it happened so fast, he still got away from them.

He must have said, "If any one of you move as fast as me, you will be my friend."

And they said one of the men did move as fast as he did.

It'ee ree shreenyàa gwahahgǫ̀' gwats'ą' datthak shìh keegii'in gooràhnyàa.

21.04 Shìh keegii'in ts'ą' shìh lęįį giłtsąįį.

Aii jyàa digiizhìk ts'ą' gwiizhìk it'ee gwiłgǫ̀' nàhąą?

Aii *Kǫ̀'ehdan* aii va'at chat[4] goonjik gooràhnyaa į'.

Aii adàh neegihilchįį izhìk hee t'iyàhnyàa.

Itree gwiizhìk ch'ii'àn gavahneeyèedyaa, aiits'ą' it'ee t'iyàhnyàa,

"It'ee nijìn k'įh neehaa'ee gàa t'ôonch'yaa," jyaa yàhnyàa.

Da'at t'ahnyàa.

21.54 It'ee ree oo'àn neegohòojil nàhąą.

Aiits'ą' it'ee shìh shreenyàa gwahahgǫ̀' gwats'ą' shìh lęįį giłtsąįį.

Aiitł'ęę it'ee dinjii lęįį gwinyąą t'ôonch'yaa zhat gwànaa.

Aiits'ą' it'ee ree shìh lęįį giłtsąįį ts'ą' it'ee ree yee'àn gahàajil.

22.26 Tr'injàa nąįį zhrįh zhat.

Aiits'ą' it'ee oo'àn gahàajil.

Oo'àt nijìn *Chųų Choh Vęę* kwaiik'ìt gogwàa'įį.

Izhìk, izhìk gwats'ą' ch'ii'àn chan *Van Choh* dha'ąįį ginyàa.

Aii ęhdàa hee datthak gwigwich'įį.

22.55 Aii gwiizhìk it'ee aii van ch'iidąą ts'ąįį ìgiinjil ts'ą' it'ee nihk'yąą veelin niinzhit, nàhąą?

Aiits'ą' zhik ts'ąįį, ts'ąįį gwintsàl nahgwàn.

Aii tr'ìnjàa t'aihnyàa?

Aii t'ee jyàa digweheenjyàa eenjit gwak'ąąhtii reh.

Aii Ch'eekwaii adàh neeyihìlchįį.

Aii, aiits'ą' oo'àn drin hee shik oo'àn ninidik, ninidìk jyàa dii'in akhài' it'ee gook'yàanjik.

It'ee gook'yàanjik ts'ą' it'ee ree gaveenìiyinzhii ts'ą' t'igiyàhnyàa,

"Oo'àt Ch'eekwaii nąįį zhik gwà'àn łyâa gwintł'òo goohàa tsèehinih'yàa.

24.00 Nèhkak giveenjit hąhtsyàa ts'ą', aii hàa gwintł'oo tsèegehee'yàa.

4. *Chat* is the same as *chan*. —LG

It was springtime before the snow melted, and it's said that they all were busy hunting for game.

21.04 They hunted and saved lots of food.

While they were busy doing that, the snow all melted, you see?

They say the Inuit took *Kò'ehdan's* wife with them too.

While they were taking her away, he said something to her.

She was crying and followed them.

That's when he said to her, "Be sure and mark your trail and you will be back."

He told his wife this.

21.54 Now they all went back, you see.

So they saved lots of food before the snow melted.

There were lots of people in those days.

After they saved enough food, they started to travel toward the place where they were supposed to be.

22.26 There were only those women there.

So they all left.

They say there was a village by the *Arctic Ocean.*

Near that place they say there was a big lake.

That's where they were all living.

22.55 So they went to the far end of that lake because it was long on both sides, you see?

But on one side it was a little shorter distance.

Remember that woman I was talking about?

She kept a sharp lookout.

The Inuit captured her.

But then she took a walk each day until she realized that they were nearby.

She knew about them so she came up to them, and they told her this,

"Keep the Inuit busy by playing games.

24.00 Make a ball for them and really play a long time with them.

Dàhthee oo'àn vàh gooheelyaa gwats'ą' jyàa dagavąh'in," yàhnyàa.

Izhìk oo'àn jyàa dìi'in izhìk it'ee chat shìh tsal goovantł'àhchàk.

Aiits'ą' łì'hàa, łì'hàa gook'ìt gwahaandal gwits'ì', dik'èegąąhtii reh.

24.34 Aiits'ą' it'ee jyàa dìi'ìn oo'àn ninidìk gòhch'it ree it'ee oo'àn neezhii ts'ą' it'ee ree dèeyàhnyaa gwik'it t'iizhìk

Nèhkak iłtsaii ts'ą', it'ee nèhkak goots'ą' chǐin'ąįį ts'ą' it'ee aii hàa tsèegii'in, tsèegii'in gwiizhìk gook'èegąąhtii reh.

Gòhch'it dinjii goolàt nąįį it'ee geheechyàa gwats'ą' jyàa dìgii'in ts'ą' gòhch'it ree datthak t'igiizhìk gàvàhnyàa.

Datthak it'ee gîiłchųų aii gwiizhìk it'ee ree aii *Kǫ̀'ehdan* vǎihnyaa aii vijyaa goodlit vǎihnyaa aii hàa ch'ii'àn gwats'ą' geedaa,

25.33 "Yit! Łąą zheh tik zhak needhiizhii gwiizhìk it'ee at'ôohju' hee k'eeriidàl," nyaa giyàhnyàa.

Zheh tik goochįh googàa tthak gwiinghan reh.

Aiits'ą' it'ee datthak jyàa dìgiizhìk ts'ą' it'ee łyâa zhyąą datthak giviinghàn.

26.03 Googiinghàn.

Aiits'ą' aii dinjii dzirh yeenìinlii vǎihnyaa, aii it'ee yeenìde'dìin'ąįį giyàhnyàa.

Jyàa dòonch'yaa gweedhaa gwiizhìk zhat,

"Khehłan ondì' shrǫ'," yàhnyàa.

26.23 Gwik'ìt t'ii'ìn.

Aiits'ą' drin hee neehidik jyàa dìi'ìn.

It'ee ree datthak gwigwiinghan nàhąą.

Aiits'ą' aii dinjii t'aihnyaa ree yeedąą hee needyàa.

It'ee ree zhat k'èegwiich'yaa t'ôonch'yaa gik'yàanjik ts'ą' oodee zhat kagwìł'ąįį giyàhnyàa.

26.50 Aii zhrįh gîiłkhwąįį kwàa.

Łyâa zhyąą datthak googiinghan reh.

Jyàa teedhadhat vàràhnyaa į'.

KF27.07 Shitsųų aii *Kǫ̀'ehdan* tr'ohkit kǫ̀'neeha'ak hęę?

Do that with them until they all get tired and fall asleep,"
they told her.
She also gave them a little food to eat.
And so they were very, very cautious not to get caught.
24.34 So she went back and forth,
and finally she did what she was told to do.
She took the ball out to them, and they played and played.
Meanwhile they watched them.
She kept it up until one by one they were falling asleep.
Finally they all were sound asleep.
Meanwhile *Kò'ehdan* and that one man he had chosen for
his friend and everybody were charging toward them,
and this is what he said before anyone got there,
25.33 "Yit! I already killed everybody in three different houses,"
that's what they said about him.
He meant he killed people in three houses before anyone
else got there.
26.03 So they killed everybody.
I said before that one Inuit had given him some mittens.
They said *Kò'ehdan* also warned him.
He told him, "When this time of year comes around,
don't stay around the village too much."
26.23 His friend did what *Kò'ehdan* told him to do.
He moved around a lot during the day.
Everyone else was killed, you see.
Then that man came back down later on.
He knew something was wrong, so they say he stayed
away.
26.50 He was the only one who survived.
Everyone else was just killed.
They say this is what happened to *Kò'ehdan.*
KF27.07 Grandma, that *Kò'ehdan* was carrying a hot ember
at first, huh?

SF27.14 Ąąhą̀’.

KF27.15 Aii geh teegwąhjii izhìk dąį’ it’ee vakǫ̀’ nàanaii gwìch’in hę̀ę?

SF27.26 “Vakǫ̀’ nàanaii izhìk gwizhrįh gwintsàl iitrìi,” nyąą vàràhnyàa.

KF27.35 Aii vakǫ̀’ nàatthaa ts’ą̀’ lèe?

SF27.37 Ąąhą̀’.

SF27.41 Izhìk gwats’an it’ee gwâahk’ii kwaa zhyą̀ą neehidik t’aràhnyàa.

Aiits’ą̀’ yaaghà’ vichįh tr’ahàandii k’idik văihnyaa izhìk t’ôohju’ hèe gwìilk’in, izhìk it’ee kǫ’ ts’ą̀’ gàa oo’àn hìltth’at giyàhnyaa reh.

Jyàa teedhadhat vàràhnyàa.

KF28.06 Aii va’at vàiinyaa aii lèe *Nihtineeraach’yaa* òozhii?

SF28.18 *Łihteerąhdyàa*.

KF28.20 *Łihteerąhdyàa*. Jyàhts’ą̀’ it’ee voozhrį̀’ aii shaaghan reh hę̀ę?

SF28.25 Ąąhą̀’.

KF28.33 It’ee łyâa viginjik ndàa nàa’ąį’ gwich’in izhìk gwats’à’ hę̀ę?

SF28.37 Ąąhą̀’, izhìk it’ee vagwandàk ndàa nàa’ąį’ į’.

SF28.50 Nah aii jùu dinjii nąįį t’agàhnyąą lì’.

Neegąįį Tsal[5] reh googàhnyàa.

Aii agàa jyàa dìgii’in googàhnyaa į’.

Izhìk it’ee ch’ijù’ zhat ch’iinii gahàajil ts’ą̀’ it’ee yaaghà’ dinjii gwich’įį it’ee gwà’àt nìgiinjil łee gooràhnyàa.

Izhìk it’ee Neegąįį Tsal dyąhch’į̀’ aii łąįį di’įį giyàhnyàa.

Łąįį neeyahahchik giyàhnyàa.

29.31 Aii it’ee, “Tr’igwinghan jì’ tr’injàa sheenjit tr’ooheendal,” nyaa eenjit it’ee tąįį hee łąįį yehiłchii giyàhnyąą aii łąįį t’aihnyaa aii łat giłtsin ts’ą̀’, zhit gwà’àn traa goonjii izhìk hee.

Łat giłtsin ts’ą̀’ zhyą̀ą łat tsii zhyą̀ą łąįį tr’iyàatsit giyàhnyàa.

KF30.06 Aii lee aii dyąhch’į̀’ vilìk kwaii lèe?

SF30.09 Ąąhą̀’. Łąįį tr’iyàahtsit gwiizhìk chąąvał zhìt dhidii dǫ̀hłį̀į.

5. According to Alexander and Alexander (2005:178), the Neegąįį Tsal were from upriver and came over to fight the last war at *Shoo*. —CM

SF27.14 Yes.

KF27.15 While he was getting snowshoe hares, that's when he dropped his hot ember, right?

SF27.26 They say that he said, "When I dropped my only hot ember, that's the one time I cried a little bit."

KF27.35 Because his hot ember went out, right?

SF27.37 Yes.

SF27.41 So it's said that after that he went without a fire until he came across the old camping place.

That's when he finally built a fire, but he fainted.

So that's what happened to him, they say.

KF28.06 His wife's name is *Nihtineeraach'yaa?*

SF28.18 *Łihteerąhdyąą.*

KF28.20 *Łihteerąhdyąą.* Was that the old woman's name?

SF28.25 Yes.

KF28.33 So that's how his story really ends, huh?

SF28.37 Yes. That's the end of his story.

SF28.50 I don't know which tribe they meant before that.

They were called the Neegąįį Tsal people.

They did the same thing too.

They say as usual they came over until they reached close enough to where people were at.

They say that one little old Neegąįį Tsal man had dogs.

His dogs pulled him around, they say.

29.31 They say he told them, "When you kill everybody, be sure and give me one of their women."

So he followed behind them with his dogs.

So you see they got near to the place where some people were living.

Suddenly his dogs sniffed the smoke from the camp and just took off, they say.

KF30.06 You mean that old man and his dogs?

SF30.09 Yes. When the dogs took off he was sitting inside the toboggan.

Jèiinch'yaa ts'ą' oo'àt tr'igwich'įį zhat kwàntee zhyąą łąįį yàatsit giyàhnyàa.
Aiits'ą' it'ee zhyąą it'ee goo'àt niriinjil gik'ìganjik ǫ'.
Datthak zhyàa kheeghan agàa tineegwigwìłtrat ts'ą' gwiizhìk yaaghà' dyąhch'į' aii chąąvał zhŭudii gwiizhìk ree t'igii'in ǫ'.
Aiits'ą' it'ee zhyąą aii dyahch'į' giyąhtsit gooràhnyàa.
"Dzanah," dzaa dee'àn jii datthak nihts'įį kat gwigwìłtràt.
Aiits'ą' dzaa vineedohdhàa jyàa diizhìk nàhąą aii yeedàk gwąąh'in aii gwiizhìk dzaa gweedaa googàa dah gǫǫlįį.
31.04 Jèiinch'yaa ts'ą' it'ee łąįį giyàa nihkhan nąąhjil ts'ą' ch'ii'àn giyàh gwik'eeniinzhit gooràhnyàa.
Oo'àt hee valàk naii jèiinch'yaa tee neełąįįyàatsìt.
Nik'èe iłts'ik lèe t'aràhnyaa lì'?
31.32 Gwitineełąįį yàatsìt.
Izhìk hee jii datthak dah jyàa dìi'in googàa,
"Łąą gwinzįį shik'ìt gwaanjik kwàa," nyaa giyàhnyàa.[6]
Izhìk hee zhak hee veedlòk diinyaa tth'ak giyàhnyàa.
KF31.44 Giyeedlàa?
SF31.45 Ąąhą'.
Aiits'ą' it'ee gook'ìgwanjik ǫ, jyàa dìgwiizhìk ts'ą' it'ee zhat gàa gogwąąh'yą' kwaa ts'ą' it'ee ch'iinjik jyàa dìneegiizhìk gooràhnyàa.
Aii chat gwandak tsyąąhch'yaa.
KF32.03 Aii veegwahandak shrǫǫ, aii?
SF32.05 Aii gwinzįį vanaldàii kwaa t'inch'yàa.
Jyàa dìgiyinlik gwinyaa, gwinyaa gàa.
Aii gwinzįį vagwandak analdàii kwaa į'.
Deenyaa geh'àn t'igiyìnlik gooràhnyaa į'.
Tr'ìnjàa ǫǫheendal eenjit jyàa nyaa izhìk geh'àn.
It'ee łat khàa giyîiłkhwąįį gooràhnyaa į'.

6. They're all laughing here. —LG

They say his dogs pulled him into camp like that.
That's how they found out they were going to be attacked, so they all grabbed their weapons.
As all this was happening, the old man was just sitting there in his toboggan.
So they grabbed him, they say.
And "Look here."
From here and all the way around they cut him (gesturing).
His eyebrow was like this.
And he looked like he was looking up and blood was running down this way.

31.04 They say that's how they turned his dogs around and chased his dogs back with him.
That's how he looked when his dogs returned to his people.
I wonder if they meant he was hurting?

31.32 So his dogs pulled him back, and he was just covered with blood.
They say even after what happened to him he said,
"It's good. They didn't even know I was there." (laughs)
When they heard that they were all really laughing at him.

KF31.44 They laughed at him?

SF31.45 Yes.
So they say once they were found out, they just turned around and went back.
They didn't even get to see the place.
It was a funny story too.

KF32.03 Can you tell that story?

SF32.05 I don't remember all of that story.
They say that's what happened to him.
But I don't remember all of it.
They say there was a reason why they did that to him too.
It's because he was saying that he was going to get a woman, I guess.
They also say they killed him with smoke too.

Kǫ̀'ehdan
Ch'eechyah Nèekwąįį

<sfrflb>

SF23.58 *Kǫ̀'ehdan* aii gàa łyâa dinjii gwandàii needhidlìt.

24.26 Aii *Kǫ̀'ehdan* nąįį gooringhan gwinyàa, izhìk dąį' vachaa aii hàa nihk'it t'igii'ìn.

Łyâa duulèe ginlįį.

Aiits'ą' zhik gwigwich'įį.

Izhìk it'ee ch'atthąįį gaghan dąį' t'ee aii shìh vikeegahch'yàa hàa gwinzįį nihłineech'agaa'àl į'.

Aii gwik'it t'igii'ìn.

Dagachaa hàa nihts'įį gwigwich'įį ts'ą' vikeech'agahch'yàa.

Aiits'ą' gwinìndhaa nàhąą.

Aiits'ą' it'ee dazhoo ik nàgàazhii aii neegiltsùu, thał zhrįh nàgàazhìi.

Aii jyàa dìgii'in yeendaa vikeech'agahch'yàa.

Gwiizhìk it'ee gook'àa rahàajìl.

25.36 Aiits'ą' it'ee gooringhan gooràhnyaa į'.

Aiits'ą' vachaa chan yàh.

Aii jyàa dìinch'yaa ts'ą' it'ee geedązhrįį gwats'at tr'igiin'oo nàhąą.

Zhat t'ee datthak gooringhan.

Gwats'an tr'igiin'oo ts'ą' jùunch'yaa ddhah nǎazhii.

Chiikak trijit deegaa'oo googàhnyàa.

Vachaa chat tr'ahaahkhwàa kwaa akhài' aih zhùu'yùu nàhąą, aih zhùu'yùu aii hàa chiikak deegaa'oo gwiizhìk oodàk jyàa dìgiyah'in gii'àii kat gwìłshràa.

Aiits'ą' neevalgiyaatsìt.

Giichaa giyehzhee giichan dìłkhwąįį.

Aiits'ą' dąhzhrįh.

26.38 Aiits'ą' it'ee adan chan t'igiyah'in gàa àkwàa.

Aiits'ą' akhagiyùunyaa nàhąą.

Kǫ̀’ehdan
Second Version

<sfrflb>

SF23.58 *Kò’ehdan* had really come back and survived.

24.26 At the time when they had war with *Kò’ehdan* and his people, his younger brother was very fast like him.

They were the bravest ones.

And so they were living there.

They killed many big game animals, and whenever this happened, they put on a big feast for everybody.

That’s what they were doing.

Both *Kò’ehdan* and his younger brother were staying across from each other.

And they were busy cooking and it was just hot, you see.

They were wearing fur clothing, so they took off their tops.

And as they were busy cooking and doing this and that, they were attacked.

25.36 They say they were all killed.

His younger brother was with him.

The two of them escaped just the way they were, you see.

But the rest of them were all killed.

After they escaped there was a mountain.

They say they climbed up on top where it was really rocky.

They probably wouldn’t have killed his younger brother, but when they got on top of the mountain they were shooting at them with hooks attached to the end of ropes.

And here they hooked one of his younger brother’s snowshoes, you see, and pulled him back down.

Kò’ehdan watched them kill his brother right below him.

So then he was all alone.

26.38 And then they tried to do the same thing with him, but they couldn’t do it.

So they just left him there, you see.

Aiits'ą̀' t'ee neegihiijyàa izhìk t'ee Ch'eekwaii ch'ìhłak it'ee jidii tsee dzirh yeenìinlìi.[7]

27.17 Gii'at chan òonjik ts'ą̀' adahàa neegahaachìi.

Aiits'ą̀' aii itrèe.

Itree ts'ą̀' gavàa neeyèedyàa.

Aii zhrįh akhagôonyaa reh.

Aiits'ą̀' itree gwiizhìk gavàa neeyèedyaa ts'ą̀' da'at t'ahnyaa dohłii,

"It'ee nijìn k'įh neehąą'ee gàa t'ôonch'yaa," jyàa da'at àhnyàa.[8]

Izhìk geedant'ee chan akǫ̀ǫdiginyàa.

Aiits'ą̀' it'ee łyâa neegohòojìl.

28.08 Aiitł'ęę gwàndàa hee neeneezhìi.

Neeneezhii gàa kwànk'ìt hee łat tsal khăiint'aii łee gwits'eehòozhii.

28.28 Akhài' aii vachaa va'at, aii it'ee zhah t'ee inzhii łee.

Aih kat jidìi ch'ok aii aih kat gaadlii.

Jyàa dàgah'in googàhnyaa į'.

28.52 Aii hàa it'ee jii yiikwaiichan kan'yùu łèe.

Ts'ą̀' jii vakwaiichan datthak ìizųų.

Ts'ą̀' t'ee yeendaa, yeendaa kǫ̀' tsal hàa neegwîiłk'in aii it'ee ts'ą̀' tr'ineezhìi.

Âa, gwintł'òo gintrìi, aiitł'ęę it'ee zhik tr'injàa t'iyàhnyàa,

"Shaghwaii it'ee łi'hàa gwihįhdàii kwaa, nan aii zhik nijìn nitsaii agookwee'àii ts'ąįį zhyąą teiinhàii," yàhnyàa.

29.55 Gwik'ìt t'igiizhìk, aiits'ą̀' aii vaghwaii jii vakwaiichan datthak ìizųų ǫ'.

Aiits'ą̀' it'ee zheedąį' hee dee'àn gahàandii ch'yąh izhìk dee'àn tąįį hàazhìi.

Izhìk hee t'ee ddhahkat dąhshyaa nilįį aii it'ee kǫ̀' zhìt dìłk'in ts'ą̀' aii it'ee neeha'àk.

Jyàa dĭi'in gwiizhìk it'ee nijìn geh nah'in dąį' t'ee yeedak toh jyàa dilìk.

---

7. I just couldn't hear what she said about the mittens that one Inuit left behind for him. —LG

8. I don't know the meaning of this. —JE

As they were leaving, that's when one of the Inuit left him a pair of beaver fur mittens.

27.17 They kidnapped his wife, and she left with them.

So then she was crying.

She was crying and following them.

He was the only one left.

As she was crying and following them, he told his wife, "You will return."

They were saying the same thing too.

So finally they left.

28.08 He finally came back down.

He saw a little smoke rising from the old camp, and he went there.

28.28 It was his younger brother's wife who had crawled under the snow.

They wore something pointed and sharp on their snowshoes.

And they say they stomped on the snow with it.

28.52 With that they cut through her foot.

And her entire foot was no good.

But she went ahead and built herself a little fire and that's how he found her.

After they both cried a lot together, the woman said to him,

"My brother-in-law, I know I will not live, but you should go in the direction where other people could be."

SF29.55 His sister-in-law's foot was in bad shape.

And *Kò'ehdan* couldn't do anything to help.

So he followed the old trail people had left back in the winter.

He lit a hollow piece of wood and carried it with him.

Aiits'ą' zhah zhìt k'igwaadhàk.

Aii it'ee yakat nichigwiilyuu ts'ą' t'ee aii geh dahkhwat aii k'ìighai' ch'a'àa.[9]

Yadhàh chan jii dideeghàn kak jyàa dàh'in ts'ą' it'ee yaaghà' khaii dąį' hee tr'ahàandii ch'yaa izhìk chan hee gwankeehàazhìi.

31.20 Vànhdąį' tr'ahàandii łee izhìk kwànk'ìt k'idìk.

Izhìk it'ee oondàk shìh deek'ìt gwà'àn gîilii dàl tth'an eiinch'it[10] łee, ts'an jidìi gîilii tsal kwat t'ee in'àl łee giyàhnyàa.

Aiits'ą' it'ee yeendaa gwîiłk'in ch'yąą vàa àn nàgwàatth'àt.

Vàa ànàgwaatth'at ts'ą' van hee t'ee tr'ineedhat gàaneeneenjìk ts'ą' it'ee ree vànhdài' tr'ahàandii t'ôonch'yaa ree tąįį hàazhìi.

Ninzhùk gwahàadhat kwaa gwìch'in roh.

Aiits'ą' it'ee shyaaghan aii oonii taįį hee zhah kwan ahtsik zhìt hee dhidii łèe.

Aii it'ee nihjyàa ts'ą' tr'ìinzhii łee giyàhnyàa.

Shyaaghan it'ee ree gwandak hàa kwàntee khàginjiheetraa ts'ą' yeegwahaandàk.

Aiits'ą' chyàhahaii akhài',

"Gîilii tsal shizhyą̌htsìt, aiitł'ęę t'inih'ìn," nyàa.

SF33.04 Gwik'ìt t'iyìnlìk.

Jidìi tsal yintł'ą̌htsit aii in'àl tł'ęę t'ee shyaaghan chàhàzhii ts'ą' reh,

"Yaaghà' *Kǫ̀'ehdan* shahaiinjyàa yùu," yàhnyàa.

Aiits'ą' it'ee kwaiitee khàgiinjih'iintrat.

33.23 "Yaaghà' *Kǫ̀'ehdan* veeragooghan łee k'idik," jyàa nyàa.

Yit! Dinjii naii datthak łąą giits'ą' chyàhkhâanaii ts'ą' t'ee aii zhah kwan t'ǎihnyaa aii googàa datthak khàdagaanaii googàhnyàa.

33.51 Aiits'ą' it'ee ree ch'ii'àn vats'ą' jyàa dìgwiizhìk.

9. He was smashing down on the snow wearing snowshoes to kill a hare which ran underneath the snow. —JE

10. *Eiinch'it* is 'that very moment.' —JE

While he was doing that he came across some snowshoe hares.
He held his short spear over them and then they disappeared under the snow.
So all he did was stomp all over and kill them.
That's how he ate.
He wrapped the snowshoe hare fur around himself for a coat and kept following the old winter trail.
31.20 Finally he reached the place where people had just left that very morning.
So they say he looked around and found a place where they had food.
And he found some crumbs and bones,
and he ate a little bit from that.
After that he built a fire and fell over unconscious.
After he came to and was well aware of everything,
he followed the trail of the people who had left earlier.
He didn't know how long he was there.
He met an old woman who was too slow to keep up with her people who had moved earlier.
She was staying in a snow igloo.
That's whom he met up with, they say.
The old woman was going outdoors to holler out and announce him.
But he told her,
"First give me something to eat and then go ahead."
SF33.04 That's what she did.
After she give him a little to eat and he ate it,
the old woman went outside and he already told her to say, "*Kò'ehdan* is here."
So she hollered out and said,
33.23 "That *Kò'ehdan* is here, the only one who survived from the war."
Yit! Then everybody charged over to him.
They say even her snow igloo was stomped all over.
33.51 Everybody just went to him.

Ch'ii'àn it'ee ree chìhìltłèe.
Izhìk hee t'inyaa vàràhnyàa,
"Dzaa jùu chyàhadhaltłee jùu shik'ìt tàltłee jì' aii shijyàa heelyàa," nyaa ts'ą̀' gwik'ìt t'iizhìk.
Akhài' dinjii ch'ìhłak yik'it t'iizhìk.
It'ee ree shreenyą̀ą gwats'ą̀' gweedhaa datthak shìh keegii'ìn.
Shìh keegii'in ts'ą̀' it'ee shìh nitsii gòonjik.
Aiitł'ęę it'ee chųų vęę gwats'ą̀' gahàajìl.
Gahàajil gwiizhìk it'ee gwìłgǫ̀' gwinyą̀ą.
Aiits'ą̀' it'ee zhik van łyâa ninjyàa jèiinch'yaa aii oondaa vatł'an gwà'àn hee gwigwich'įį googàhnyàa.
Ch'eekwaii nąįį.
SF35.23 Aiits'ą̀' it'ee zhik tr'ìnjàa aii[11] jyàhts'ą̀' geegoolii geh'àn geenjit datthak gwak'ą̌ąhtii dǫ̀hłį̀į.
Akhài' van vęę chųų hìltł'it izhìk ts'ąįį nahgǫǫ gwiinzii nyąą t'ii'in.
"Zhik ch'ìh neeshahooghwąįį aii chųų keehàdhaltł'it t'ishi'in," gavàhnyàa.
36.13 Aiits'ą̀' it'ee chan shih tsal oo'ęę nini'įį zhyą̀ą giveeninidik.
Aii tr'injàa jyàa àgàhnyaa jèiinch'yaa ts'ą̀' goohaa tsèeni'in.
Ts'ą̀' nehkaii gooveenjit aii hàa goovaa tsee'ne'in jyàa dagoovąh'in àgàhnyąą ts'ą̀' t'ee gwik'ìt t'iizhìk.
Âa! Ninzhùk tsèegii'in gòhch'it dinjii ch'ìhłęę k'ìgwaadhàk.
It'ee nichik t'ii'ìn.
37.07 Gòhch'it it'ee łyâa zhyą̀ą datthak dinjii neegwąą'in kwàa.
Aiits'ą̀' it'ee *Kǫ̀'ehdan* it'ee aii naii gwats'ą̀' gahàajil nàhąą.
"Giłchųų gwiizhìk zheh tik zhak needhiizhii gwiizhìk t'ôohju' hee shijyàa naii shatąįį k'eedàl," nyàa.
Datthak zhyą̀ą gooringhan googàhnyaa t'agavaihnyàa.

11. This woman was Kǫ̀'ehdan's wife. —CM

So he jumped out of there.
That's when he said,
"Whoever can make the same moves as I do will be my friend."
And there was one man who did it.
They were getting lots of food in before spring came.
After they got enough food, they left for the ocean.
After they left, the snow all melted.
They say those Inuit were living by this long lake.
SF35.23 That woman must have known this was going to happen, so she watched everything.
When she was packing water she dumped water in the direction which was shortest distance towards them.
She kept taking hikes, sometimes to get wood and other times just to urinate.
That's when she dumped water in the shortest direction.
Even when they asked her why she did that, she told them,
"The mosquitos were bothering me."
36.13 She even sneaked a little food to them.
That's when they told that woman to play games with them.
So she made a ball for them and she played with them.
She did what they told her.
Oh, they played for a long time.
Pretty soon one man after another would disappear after having fallen asleep.
37.07 Finally all of them just went to sleep,
and they didn't see even one man left.
So *Kò'ehdan* and them went there, you see.
They attacked them while they were sleeping and *Kò'ehdan* said, "I already killed everybody in three houses before the rest of my friends even got here."
They say they killed everybody.

SF37.46 Datthak googinghàn, aiits'ą'aii dinjii tsèe dzirh intł'èiinlii aii, aii jyàa dòonch'yaa gwiizhìk khehłan oindì' shrǫ̀' àhnyàa giyàhnyą̀ą.

Aiits'ą̀' nihk'yàa gwizhrįh neehidìk.

It'ee ree datthak googinghàn, nàhąą, aii dinjii t'ee k'ii'ęę needyàa.

Izhìk dą̀į' lèe gwaatr'àl t'ôonch'yaa gǫ̀'.

Gwaatr'àl gàa kwaa ginyaa į'.

38.30 Aiits'ą̀' it'ee ęęneedyaa gàa łyâa tr'agòhch'it ts'ą̀' it'ee zhyą̀ą gwi'ęę nàazhìi.

Oodaa "Aanàii" yàhnyàa, googàa gwik'ìt t'ii'in kwàa.

Aiits'ą̀' t'ee zhik gwà'àn jyàa dìgiyahnyaa łee nalàk naii t'inch'yaa gaanandàii gwats'ą̀' jì' izhìk gwats'ą̀' hinhhaii giyàhnyàa.

Gwik'it t'iizhìk giyàhnyàa į'.

Aii zhrįh chan gwandàii.

Datthak googinghàn.

Jyàa *Kǫ̀'ehdan* khadeh'an nineedhivįį gwinyaa t'agwaihnyàa.

Jyàa digiizhìk į'.

SF37.46 After they killed everybody,
Kò'ehdan had already warned that guy that left him the beaver fur mittens not to stick around this time of the year.
So he was always out somewhere.
After the ambush, you see, that man was coming back.
It wasn't brushy back then.
At the time they say there was hardly any brush around.
38.30 He was coming back, but he knew something was wrong, so he stopped.
Kò'ehdan told him, "Come here!" but he wouldn't do it.
So they told him to go where his other relatives were living.
They say that's what he did.
He was the only survivor.
Everybody else was killed.
What I'm saying is they say that's how *Kò'ehdan* had his revenge in war.
That's what happened.

Johnny Frank

Òol Tì' Goghwaii Haa

<jfka405>

6.51 Zhat gwanaa łyâa dinjii gǫǫzhįį ǫ'.

Zhat dąį' *Gwichyaa Zheh. . .Òol Tì'* chan yeejìt *Old Crow* chan *President* nilįį.

7.05 Aiits'ą' aii jidìi ch'adhàh, tsèe dhàh, aadzii, tł'il jidìi tthak zhat dąį' dinjii yat'ąąhch'yaa datthak vitsyàa naii lęįį roh.

Zhat dąį' *Old Crow* dinjii *10,000* hanjii àanch'yąą gwinyàa.

Aii datthak t'ee vitsyàa naii lęįį khwąh choo tr'ih t'agah'in kwàa.

7.31 Khwąh choo kat tąįh gwich'in k'iinii teekat nihts'ìneegah'òl.

Aii gwiizhìk yeezhee *Tsìik'ì' Tì'* chan, dinjii lęįį roh.

Aii k'ii tr'ihchoo zhìt, tr'ihtsal hàa, k'àiich'i' tthak hàa k'iinjì' teendì' geehihiidàl, dąhthee *Òol Tì'* goodihêehaa gwats'ą' reh.

Aiits'ą' oonjì' *Ch'iteenjii' Ddhak* goodigiidàl.

Aiits'ą' zhik khwąh choo jyàa dinch'yaa aii kat deegadàl.

7.57 Vakat jidìi shìh nizįį tthak, tsèedhàh datthak, aadzii, tł'il, ch'adhàh inzhii tthak.

Aii gwiizhìk zhik tr'ih zhit k'iinjì' lęįį geelyaa.

Aii jyàa dinch'yaa tr'ih zhìt tr'agadàl ts'ą' aii zhit gadàl ts'ą' tr'ih hàa gwìinjì' geegihiidàl.

Yaaghà' khwąh adàa kwaii chan yeedì' Gwichyaa Gwich'in yeedì' khwąh hàa zhrįh idzii nilįį gąįh, khwaii hàa jyàa dìgìi'in.

Aiits'ą' t'ee oonjit k'àiich'ii gǫǫlįį.

8.31 Aiits'ą' tr'ikhit gwintsìi veegòo'ąįį.

Aii voondee chan *Dik'ehzhazhal* òozhìi, *Òol Tì'* reh.

Aii chan dinjii gwintsìi veegòo'ąįį nilįį.

Chan łyâa nàgogwaahnàii.

Łyâa zhyąą *champion.*

Johnny Frank

Òol Tì' and Goghwaii

<jfka405>

6.51 At that time people were really smart.
At *Fort Yukon. . . Òol Tì'* was chief, and he was also like the President at *Old Crow*.
7.05 And so they had animal skins, beaver pelts, sun-bleached caribou hides, and babiche, all those things.
Òol Tì' also had a large band of people at that time.
Old Crow had a population of around 10,000, they say.
Òol Tì's band had a big raft, and on top of it was a big pile of things.
7.31 They came down with a big raft, and on it was a big pile of things.
At the same time *Ts'iik'i' Tì'* was on his way upriver with a birchbark boat and canoe full of things.
They met *Òol Tì'* on the way up to *Old Crow* at a place called *Ch'iteenjii' Ddhak.*
And when they met, they stopped next to their big raft and got on.
7.57 The big raft was full of good food, all kinds of fur, caribou hide, babiche, and smoked tanned skin.
The people that were on the raft just got on their boat.
And they got on their raft and were on their way to see the people at *Fort Yukon*.
The raft was full of dry meat and grease on top of it.
That way *Old Crow* people got lots of things.
8.31 *Òol Tì'* was a rich and powerful man that way.
His oldest brother was named *Dik'ehzhazhal.*
He was rich and powerful too.
They were both fast and strong as well.
They really were the champions.

8.47 Aii gwiizhìk *Goghwaii* reh tsyaa tsal shrìit'ąhtsii nilįį vàràhnyàa.

Aii tsyaa tsal shrìit'ąhtsii nilįį ts'ą' t'ee reh izhìk zhat dhidii.

It'ee k'ì' agàa di'įį dhidlìt.

Aii nąhjyàa tr'iinin nilįį dąį' chan ditii dhìłkhwàii.

9.04 K'ì' tsal vitì' yee'agwàh'ąįį hàa vitii yìnlįį yeedlàa, aii k'aii shryah tsal, tth'an k'ì' ch'ok tsal lęįį dizhyǎadlii, yeetak hee yanant'įį hee yiłdàii.

Dihch'į' neech'ahaaghaa gwiizhìk kwàt zhyąą k'ì' dach'ok eentrat.

Ditii dhìłkhwąįį (adlaa).

9.22 Łyâa dinjii ada'âiilii *Goghwaii* gwinyąą ginjih ìizųų.

Aii zhìt oozhrii geh'àn reh t'ii'ìn.

Aiits'ą' reh zhat dinjii gǫ̀ǫlįį.

Kwàt tr'ikhit gwintsii veegòo'ąįį.

Ts'ą' zhyąą oo'òk tr'injàa veeraadii googàa veenjit nizįį dąį' gàa òondàk.

9.50 Zhyąą gwich'in tthak tr'ìnjàa hàa nìgwìi'àii googàa reh.

Zhik veeraadii dąį' yàa nìgwii'àii gwinzįį.

Kwàt jàghaii vigii tsal gǫ̀ǫlįį gàa chan aii chan òonjik kwaa ts'ą' aii ya'at zhrįh òonjik?

10.06 Aii vakąį' chan reh nats'àa reh òozhii chan.

Aii chan łyâa duulèe nilįį reh.

10.29 Voondee yee'àt gwich'įį ts'ą' *Goghwaii* gwiizhìk tsyaa shrìit'ahtsii nilįį.

Ch'aghwarh ginyąą dąį' dàa'ąįį tsal jyàa dinch'yaa reh, aii di'įį.

Łyâa vagwàntrii reh.

Aii gwiizhìk reh aii khàgwǎachįį.

10.47 Aii khàgwǎachįį ts'ą' yeedì' hee, vàa nihts'eeriin'òo.

Ts'ą' tr'iinin tsal zhyąą dhidii gwizhrįh t'inch'yàa.

10.54 Aii chan shin k'ąąhtii, aii *Òol Tì'* voondee chan yeh'àt gwich'įį.

Tr'iinin gweedhaa tthak vàa itrèe.

Aii shų̀' nahshų' geetèe hee gàa itrèe.

8.47 At that time, they say *Goghwaii* was just a young man.
He was there at *Old Crow* during that time.
He had his very first bow and arrow.
When *Goghwaii* was younger, they say he killed his uncle also.
9.04 I guess his father found a little bow and arrow for him.
I guess he must have found a bone arrowhead.
He sneaked up behind him and shot him.
The old man was running around with pain while he shot him repeatedly.
He killed his uncle that way (laughs).
9.22 *Goghwaii* was a really mean man, they say.
And that's what his name meant too.
There were lots of people at *Old Crow*.
Òol Tì' was rich and powerful.
And if he saw a married woman he liked, he would take her just like that.
9.50 He bothered all the women.
Isn't it bad enough that he bothered those married women, yet he would not take their children?
He took a man's wife once and left her child behind.
10.06 I also forgot that woman's husband's name.
He was a very good hunter too.
10.29 *Goghwaii's* older brother lived next to him when
Goghwaii was still just a young man.
He had a little stone axe on him.
It was the kind that was really hard to get.
10.47 *Òol Tì'* took a woman away once.
Then he went downriver with her without her little baby.
10.54 *Òol Tì's* older brother (*Tsiidàadlii*) also took care of the baby one whole summer.
Sometimes he had such a hard time trying to stop the baby from crying that he cried with the baby.

11.08 Aii gwiizhìk t'ee reh vachaa[1] tr'ikhit tr'ìnjàa lęįį oonjìi.

Nihts'įį reh zheh gwachoo kwàt zhyąą va'at naii dèedąą'ąį' vàràhnyàa.

11.19 Nich'it naii reh.

Aiits'ą̀' gohch'it reh t'iyàhnyąą vàràhnyàa:

"Zhik tree gwiizhìk shin t'ąhthee jyàa jìinyaa gàa t'ee dinjii neenaa'in jì' t'ee dinjii zhyąą neehaan'yàa dąhłįį," jyàa yàhnyaa vàràhnyàa.

It'ee reh vachaa tr'ahaahkhwàa gwats'ą̀' ch'ah'ee reh t'inyaa.

11.54 Aiits'ą̀' t'ee reh *Tsiidàadlii* reh, *Tsiidàadlii* tree kwaa ts'ą̀' t'ee reh k'ideegwaanaii.

Gwiizhìk t'ee reh dagwadàl hàa, gwitr'it t'agwaa'in gàa t'ôonch'yàa.

Gohch'it t'ee ch'anchàl vàrahnyaa oonjik ts'ą̀' ddhah dha'aįį.

Jèiinch'yaa aii taa gweedįį k'iidąą t'ee drindìi kǫ' hàazhàa.

Zhik Vantee Gwich'in[2] tthak yahąąh'yàa eenjit reh.

12.10 Aiits'ą̀' t'ee reh, yeedì' *Natâadlii* vàrahnyaa, łyâa van nitsìi giyàhnyàa.

Ye'eedìt hee dì' nàa'ąį' ginyàa.

Aii chan izhìk vakwaiik'ìt gòo'ąįį reh.

Neetąįį gàgàhnyàa.

K'ǫǫ gwintsìi gwinyaa aii t'ee vak'ǫǫ reh, *Òol Tì' Vak'ǫǫ*.

Ch'ihłòk gàa dachan gąąh'in kwàa reh.

T'ee lèe łuk gǫ̀ǫlįį ts'ą̀'.

Aiits'ą̀' reh, oodì' shraahîiłkhwàt.

Tsiidàadlii reh.

Aii chan łyâa dinjii valàràa gǫ̀ǫlįį nilįį k'it t'inch'yaa reh.

1. Apparently this younger brother to Òol Tì' is Goghwaii, but the text is confusing about just how all three men are related to one another in the struggle which follows. It would seem that Tsiidàadlii was the oldest, followed by Òol Tì', and then by Goghwaii. This relation is thrown into disarray, however, when Goghwaii later addresses Òol Tì' as *shitii* 'my uncle' instead of *shoondee* 'my older brother,' but he may be using this term sarcastically. —CM

As I remember it, my grandfather called the oldest one K'i'dàadlii rather than Tsiidàadlii. —KF

2. Vantee Gwich'in are the *Old Crow* area residents on the Canadian side. —JE

11.08 *Òol Tì's* younger brother bothered lots of women.
He had two houses full of wives, they say.
11.19 They were all young women.
They say he finally told him while he was crying:
"You do this all summer long, and I suppose you won't do anything about it when you see them again."
He said this because he wanted his younger brother killed.
11.54 Then *Tsiidàadlii* stopped crying.
He started to prepare his things.
He finally grabbed some kind of weapon.
Then they say he came down this one side of the mountain like lightning.
So all the *Old Crow* people would see him.
12.10 They say that *Natâadlii* is a large lake, and they say his village was at the very end of this lake.
It's a long lake, and it ends way down that way.
They called it *Neetą̨įį*.
They say there was this big creek which belonged to *Òol Tì'* so they called it *Òol Tì's Creek.*
There's no timber there.
Tsiidàadlii walked down there because there were lots of fish.
Tsiidàadlii was a rich man.

Chan łyâa zhyąą *champion.*

12.56 Aiits'ą' reh oodit k'idik akhài' reh zhik gwà'àn dihch'ì' ch'ihłęę reh, *Dyąąhch'ì' Ch'itsyàh* òaazhii.

Aii reh yandaktł'iłgǫǫ nihk'yąą veek'ì' gǫ̀ǫlįį.

Aii reh nèekwąįį reh gee'iltìn.

Aii ch'ìhłak reh *Dyąąch'ì' Ch'itsyàh* antł'aanaii.

13.09 "Aii shats'ą' tr'àł neegwąh'èe," àhnyąą.

Va'at hàa k'eeriinjik roh.

Aii yaaghà' *Dyąąch'ì' Ch'itsyàh* aii chan hàa gwaandak ts'ą' yats'at nôonjik van jì' nàa'ąį'.

Yats'ą' tr'àł neeheedyaa eenjit reh.

It'ee reh *Òol Tì'* nèheedhaa, aiits'ą' t'ee reh.

13.35 Łyâa shriit'tąhshyùk gwahàadhat.

Gwiizhìk hee reh yeechìt ch'iidįį hee reh.

Van kat hee dzan dhàh ik aii hàa vakak shree ha'ak ts'ą' ch'iidįį hee tr'iinkwąįį vàràhnyàa.

13.49 Aii gwiizhìk yaaghà' *Tsiidàadlii* yaaghà' gwich'įį.

Kwàntee hee vadzaih dhàa gihdǎątsùu, gihdêiinvyaa, nàhąą?

Izhìk ch'ii'àn chiiyèech'yà' gwatsal jyàanch'yaa googàn chîitsįį ts'ą' chìnàatłàk.

14.02 Gwe'ęhjyàa chan it'ee dinjii haahkhwàa geenjit *trainìng* nilįį t'ii'ìn.

Aiits'ą' t'ee yeechìt tèedhàkwąįį.

"It'ee reh tr'ìnjàa vits'ì' tr'àl neezhii łee ts'ą' reh, yaaghà' tr'ìnjàa k'ineh shooiindii,"[3] jyàa reh nyaa vàràhnyàa.

Aii tr'ìnjàa kaiihàh'yà' akhài' reh haljii.

Aiits'ą' oo'òk yìłdii t'inch'yaa yuunyaa ts'ą' reh, tr'ìnjàa k'ineh shooiindii nyaa ts'ą' reh.

14.40 Ts'ą' t'ee reh yee'àn yeevan neehòozhìi.

Ahkài' yaaghà' gwe'ęę reh jyàhts'aii tr'àłtee dhidii łee reh gwiizhìk yeechùk van vee gòo'ąįį.

Vahk'ah gòolįį.

Izhìk hee reh aii tr'ìnjàa yee'òk hee than nìindhat yàhnyaa ts'ą' yehzhee nàadìi.

3. The meaning of this is 'Came to take back the woman.' —JE

He was also a champion.

12.56 So he arrived there and there was this one old medicine man named *Dyąąch'i' Ch'itsyah.*

Tsiidàadlii had some kind of a two-bladed axe under his arm.

And he had two of them.

He gave one of them to *Dyąąch'i' Ch'itsyah.*

13.09 "Make some fog for me," he told the old man.

He did this because someone took his wife away.

He told *Dyąąch'i' Ch'itsyah* what happened before.

He planned to go to her through the brush at the end of the lake.

Now this was before *Òol Tì's* death.

13.35 Just then, someone [*Òol Tì'*] started coming across the lake.

The sun was sparkling on his muskrat skin jacket, and they say he had paddled up from down below.

13.49 Meanwhile, *Tsiidàadlii* was living on this side of the lake.

The front of his house was covered with caribou skins so that the doorway was very small, you see?

But he got in and out of the doorway backwards.

14.02 He was training and getting ready for combat.

Then the man paddled to shore not far from him.

"I'm looking for that woman, but she's gone missing," he said, they say.

14.40 So he walked along the shore.

That woman was somewhere in the brush up along the bank.

There was a bank there.

Tsiidàadlii already told the woman earlier to hide at a certain place, so he sat on the shore below where she was hiding.

Aiits'ą' yahaahkhwàa yàandaii eenjit shrôondaii t'iyàhnyąą.

15.18 Aii *Òol Tì'* chan łyâa nàgwaah'naii reh.

Duuyeh zhyąą ch'ahahdàk vàràhnyàa.

Aiits'ą' reh yitł'èets'àl kak dêel'yuu ts'ą' nàdhat gwiizhìk t'ee k'iłtąį' dzaa ts'ąį reh.

K'iłtąį' dzaa gwąąh'ee ts'ą' yeendàk hee jyàanch'yaa vàràhnyàa.

15.45 Aii gwiizhìk t'iyàhnyaa, "Shitii, yaaghà' shakwài' ch'àa hàa łyâa shitèedhaangìt.

Gwach'àa tłìk vizhyaa tr'iinhaa, aii shats'ą' hoiinlyaa jyàa reh noihnyàa," jyàa reh yàhnyàa.

Jyàa nyaa ts'ą' t'ôohju' t'ee łyâa yee'àn neenìi'ąįį ts'ą' zhik ts'ąįį reh *Tsiidàadlii* nàdhat roh.

Yeechùk teevęę gwìin'èe.

Vahk'ah dìh dzahts'ąįį digèe yats'ąįį gwił'ąįį ts'ą' reh.

Aii gwizhìk aii *Goghwaii* văihnyàa reh ditr'uu ts'at dats'ąą.

Aii reh gwideetak nĭinzhìi.

Gwiizhìk ch'aghwarh chan thah t'àa'ąįį reh, adan t'ee ch'ijyàa heelyàa, dinjii tr'ahaahkhwàa ch'ijyàa heelyàa t'ii'ìn.

16.26 Gwiizhìk jyàa yàhnyąą,

Dak neenee'ąįį gwiizhìk t'ee k'ì' khai' hąąkhyuu ts'ą',

"Aii veenoh'ìt hee khàch'iriintthàii," jyàanch'yâa.

Gwiizhìk hee aii voondee chan t'iyàhnyaa,

"Vik'eeshraiidraa nichyàa t'iinch'yaa vàhanandàii yùu," yàhnyaa vàràhnyàa.

K'i' dhàh vizhìt rihdlii, aiits'ą' deenjì' vitły'àa hàa dachan veedhitin t'inch'yàa.

16.59 Aii dik'ìt shraiidraa[4] òozhii, aii łyâa nichyàa t'inch'yàa.

"Aii ǫhdak shrò'," yàhnyaa vàràhnyàa.

Izhìk yàandaii ts'ą' veechìi t'ìgwìnyąą.

Yee'àt dak nìl'ąįį ch'yąą gwintł'òo khan ch'ihìlghàa vàràhnyàa t'aihnyàa.

4. I think *dik'it shraiidraa* may be a reference to *k'i' dhàh* 'quiver.' —KP KP is correct. —JE *K'i'dhàh* glosses as 'arrow skin' —CM

He did that on purpose so she would get killed instead of him.
15.18 That *Òol Tì'* was very quick and agile.
They say he never missed with his arrows.
So he stepped on *Tsiidàadlii's* pointed tunic to pin him down and then aimed his bow.
He was standing there, facing upstream, stepping on one side of his bow while he had a bunch of arrows hanging from him, they say.
15.45 While doing that, he said to him, "Uncle, give me your used clothing because I'm all raggedy."
He turned away and *Tsiidàadlii* was standing on this side and the lake shore on the other side had a bank along it.
Òol Tì' had his armpit exposed on the side where he was standing.
He had a hammer-like weapon on his belt.
Goghwaii came in between to be on *Tsiidàadlii's* side to kill *Òol Tì'*.
16.26 While talking with him,
he was standing there selfishly looking up as
Goghwaii quietly took out his bow and said,
"He sure doesn't know what I have in mind for him."
His older brother said to him,
"Remember how wide the quiver is," they say.
Arrows were kept inside of it and a rope was attached to a piece of wood on it.
16.59 It was called a quiver, and it was really wide.
"Don't hit that quiver," he said, they say.
He knew about it and was glad for that, they say.
I'm saying he was standing there selfishly looking up when *Goghwaii* startled him, they say.

Yegèe hee reh yìłdàii.

17.20 Danzhit łùh vee hee zhyąą drindhìhìłdòo!

Hàa k'i' khàanąįį hàa yidik tr'ălgìk googàa ch'adąį' hee khąh'ee łee vàràhnyàa.

17.29 Izhìk chan łyâa yeenjit oohìlzhįį.

Yidik tr'ĭltłee hàa googàa chalghàa.

Googàa jii yatthài ch'iinjì' tr'ach'ąhdàk vàràhnyàa.

Aii gwiizhìk zhyąą yuhjìi kwàa.

It'ee yigèe yìłdàii yàandaii roh.

Aii gwiizhìk zhyąą deedàk k'ì' zhìt ch'ahahdàk gohch'it dąąts'ą' zhyąą ch'ats'ą' vàa gwihizhit zhyąą yeech'iidàk googàa zheedà'ahdàk vàràhnyàa.

18.09 Aii gwiizhìk *Goghwaii* yats'ą' drindàatłee, ch'aghwarh yichlitsįį ahnàii.

"Jùk shitii virinjik gwìch'in?" yàhnyaa, ts'ą' yichìitsįį dàa'ąįį ahnàii.

Aiits'ą' vichìit'ik vichiighài' chan łineerìłchàa.

Gweenjì' dàa'ąįį deek'ìt.

Aii googàa *Goghwaii* zhrįh zhat ch'aghwarh di'įį gàagwiindàii nàhąą?

Izhìk geh'àn nankat gwiindàii tthak shizhi' *Goghwaii* vàa *trouble* gwiinlì' t'inch'yàa.

Òol Tì' tr'ôołkhwąįį gwinyąą.

It'ee dinjii yeedì' tsyaa hìlgìk.

Zhyąą kwàt yeedìt vanlaii kwàt zhyąą va'at naii tthak oondàa vankat gwàndàa khaihîilnąįį gwinyąą.

Tthak tèeneegoogaadàl googàa reh.

Kwàt ts'ą' reh, daga'at hàa yeendàk tr'àl giin'òo.

19.12 Aiits'ą' oonjìt *Teedląįį Zheh*[5] gwà'àn hee tr'àl zhìt tr'igiin'òo.

Izhìk gwich'in gahàhłì' agàa *Òol Tì'* dhìłkhwąįį t'ii'in giyàandàii.

Ts'ą' neegiiniin'àk ts'ą' giyèełkhwąįį roh.

Aii ch'ùn t'ee *Vantee*[6] gwìnjì' datthak nihłigeeghan.

5. *Teedląįį Zheh* was an old village near *Old Crow*. —JE

6. *Vantee* refers to the entire area around *Old Crow*. —JE

He hit *Òol Tì'* with an arrow right in the armpit.

17.20 All that was seen was a cloud of dust when *Òol Tì'* jumped over the cliff!

They say he ran to the edge of the cliff, but *Òol Tì'* already had his bow and arrow out.

17.29 But *Tsiidàadlii* was really watching out for him.

Even so, he got hit too, but he barely missed him.

They say he just stopped shooting because he knew *Òol Tì'* got hit already anyway.

Meanwhile, *Òol Tì'* continued shooting back while he was wounded.

They say he was shooting arrows up into the sky because he was dying and didn't know it.

18.09 Then *Goghwaii* jumped off the cliff and hit *Òol Tì'* in the head with his stone axe weapon, shaped like a tomahawk.

He said, "I wonder if we hurt my uncle?"

And then he split his head open with an axe.

He tied his hair over his split-open head to close it.

Everybody knew that *Goghwaii* was the only man to own an axe, you see?

That is why *Goghwaii* had trouble all his life.

They killed *Òol Tì'* they say.

A young man ran down alongside the lake and through that area to spread the news.

They say all of *Òol Tì's* wives tried to commit suicide by running out into the lake, but they kept pulling them back to shore.

19.12 And then *Tsiidàadlii* and his wife took off to nowhere from there and somehow came to *Teedląįį Zheh.*

They tried living there but everyone knew *Tsiidàadlii* helped kill *Òol Tì'*.

And somehow they fooled him and killed him there too.

Nàantsąįį, Ch'itsyaa[7] naii hàa.
Republìcan, Demòcrat naii hàa.
Izhìk gwanaa reh *Demòcrat* naii datthak chit nilįį t'ôonch'yàa, *whole Alaska.*
19.52 It'ee nihłagahaaghan t'ee.
It'ee reh veh'àn dinjii tthak nihłeeghàn.
Izhìk gwàts'an t'ee *Goghwaii*, aiitł'ęę khaii aii vitì' *K'azheezhal* vàràhnyàa.
Dinjii gwintsìi veegoo'ąįį t'inch'yàa.
Kwàt eedan veh'àn vachaa tr'ôołkhwàįį vàagwiindàii.
Ts'ą̀' t'ee *Republìcan* naii tthak giyeenjit khàihłak nahtsìk.
Giits'eehiidàl gàa giyą̀ąnjat.
Niveh gàa yąąjat, dįhchi'ì' nilįį gàa.
20.43 Ch'ihłan tr'igiinìinjil googàa zhyą̀ą niveh iłèehòozhii vàràhnyàa.
Izhìk gwàts'an it'ee *Òol Tì'* ndàa nàa'ąį.
Òol Tì' dinjii gwintsìi veegòo'ąįį t'aràhnyàa.
21.20 Dinjii tthak nihłigeeghan tł'ęę kwaiik'ìt gwintsìi tik tthak nihłigeeghan t'inch'yàa, *Old Crow* reh.
Łì'hàa yeenaadą̀į' dinjii gǫ̀ǫlįį gwinyàa.
Aiits'à' reh, aii *Goghwaii* chan viti' tr'ôołkhwàįį.
Yaaghà' *Òol Tì'* vigii naii reh, aii naii giyiiłkhwaii.
Aii gwats'ą' khaiits'ą' oodee hee tthał ghàih gwich'įį.
K'azheezhal, *Goghwaii* vitì' it'ee łyâa *Goghwaii* nitsìi reh, vachaa chan, vijùu chan.
22.25 Aiits'ą' reh, aii gwiizhìk yèe'ęę *Ch'atthą̀įį Keehaa* vàràhnyàa.
Òol Tì' vichiikàį' aii chan łyâa zhyąą *President* nilįį reh,
Aii tthai ghàii gwich'įį, izhìk gwats'an nihkheeneegiidàl.
Akhài' yaaghà' *Òol Tì'* vigii naii digitii goonilì' łee ts'ą' yaaghà' nìneegiijyàa.

7. *Nàantsąįį* is a Gwich'in kinship unit or sib which Johnny associates with the American Republican party. *Ch'itsyaa* is a Gwich'in sib which Johnny associates with the Democratic party. For more on Gwich'in sibs see McKennan, 1965:60-65. —CM

That was one reason a war broke out around *Old Crow* between the Nàantsąįį and the Ch'itsyaa — between the Republicans and Democrats.

The Democrats were in the lead that time in Alaska.

19.52 They had a war.

Because of *Goghwaii* there was war everywhere.

They say his father's name was *K'azheezhal,* and he was a rich and powerful man also.

Everyone knew it was because of *Goghwaii* that his younger brother died.

The Republicans (*Nàantsąįį*) were against him.

They went after him.

But they were afraid of him, even though he was an old man.

20.43 They say a whole army came after him once, but he got away from them on foot.

Now that was the end of the story about *Òol Tì'.*

As they say, *Òol Tì'* was a rich and powerful man.

21.20 Three different villages made war against each other around *Old Crow.*

They say there were lots of people living there a long time ago.

And then even *Goghwaii's* father was killed.

Òol Tì's children killed him.

At that time *Goghwaii* got bigger and stronger.

His father *K'eezheezhal* was living by the border of the *Brooks Range.*

Goghwaii was growing up, along with his younger brother and younger sister.

22.25 *Òol Tì's* son-in-law, named *Ch'atthąįį Keehaa* was the chief, they say.

He lived by the border, and sometimes they exchanged visits with each other.

It was there that *Òol Tì's* children were trying to kill their own uncle, *K'eezheezhal.*

Aii googàa reh *Goghwaii* dagachaa hàa, łyâa zhyąą nakhwareheeghàa t'igwii'in jì' gwizhrįh nich'itsùhthat gavàhnyàa.

Duuyeh *Goghwaii* vik'ìt t'igwii'in gwiizhìk t'igwinyàa.

Aiits'ą' reh, niveh naii ch'iinįį tthak kwàt zhyąą azhrąįį chyah niin'ęę gwinyąą reh.

Datthak zhyąą googhoo t'eegàaghaa, k'ì' tri'iilęę, toh, shrii hàa reh.

Gàh giginkhii kwaa ts'ą' reh.

23.25 Gwiizhìk dyąąhch'ì' aii gahaahkhwàa eenjit t'igii'in gàa giinaajat roh.

Aiits'ą' reh, *Goghwaii* chan łyâa ìizųų gàagiindàii.

Ts'ą' aii chan tr'iihàhdak giindhàn.

Aii jidìi geelyaa aii noh'ìt it'ee reh khach'iriinthaii gwiizhìk

Goghwaii zhyąą reh lafoo nilįį k'ìt t'ii'in.

Zhyąą gwak'ǎahtii reh t'ii'ìn.

23.56 Tr'ǫąąhdàk akhài' googàa chalghàa ts'ą' vanànghoo tsal tł'an łàa nàch'arąhdàk vàràhnyàa.

Khàdhazhral gwiizhìk vijùu chan geeghaii neehidìk.

Aii k'i' gwats'an tr'iniingyųų, aii oozhee gwit'ěiinzhàa,

"Tì'yaa, yaaghà' nakhoondee tr'iłdàii, diitsįn gwats'ą' k'i' hiljì'i," jyàa ginyaa ts'ą' khàgiinzhràa.

24.24 Dyąąhch'ì' vagwaanjat ch'yąą chyàantłee ginyàa.

Niveh t'âanch'yąą tthak kwàt zhyąą shrahtèeshrìłjil.

Zhik ch'ìhłęę zhyąą łyâa tr'iniinzhii akhài', aii vizhį' reh.

Vachaagii yìnlįį.

24.57 Aii łyâa vàa gwiindàii aii reh tr'inìinzhìi.

Tr'inìinzhii ts'ą', oo'àt dee'àn tthał nìin'ee ts'ą' dįhch'ì' ahàa.

Tsyaa deegwììt'aii ahaa googàa ahaa kwaa eenìriin'oo k'ìt t'iyìnlik, vàràhnyàa.

25.12 "Shitii, khai' hishidluu," akhàshoiinyąą yàhnyàa.

Gwiizhìk hee yichiitth'àn gidiinjir vàràhnyàa, k'i' hàa.

Aii gwiizhìk zhik dinjii hanjii *one hundred* ch'iinaa tthak dįhch'ì' k'àn ch'itsèhìłthat dąį' neekhigehìljil rǫh.

Goghwaii and his younger brother were warned by their father that they should not fight unless they had to.
Nobody fought like *Goghwaii* anyway.
They said there was an army there.
They all had bows and arrows and spears and knives ready.
But nobody said a word.
23.25 They came to kill the old man, but they also knew *Goghwaii* was really a bad one too.
So they planned to put an arrow into him.
They all had their bows and arrows ready.
Goghwaii was acting foolish while he was watching out.
Someone shot him.
23.56 He ducked down fast, but he got shot right in the back, they say.
He screamed and his younger sister yanked out the arrow and put it into the ground and said,
"Father, my older brother is shot and the arrow has gone into his intestine."
24.24 They say an old man whom everyone was afraid of ran out.
The army just ran in all directions because they were afraid of him.
He ran after one of them.
It was one of his own younger brother's children.
24.57 The young man was running fast.
But they say the old man made him look like he was not moving at all and caught up to him in nothing fiat.
25.12 He was begging for mercy, saying, "Uncle, please let me die on my own; leave me alone."
The old man shot him in the head, they say.
About one hundred men were scared off when this old man started fighting.

Kwàt aii ch'a'àn ahaa zhrįh dhìłkhwaii reh zhat gwats'ą' hiljìi.
Aii *Goghwaii* reh, aii gootì' Nàantsąįį t'aràhnyàa.
Aii gwiizhìk vanàn zhit khah naatsìk ręh.
Aii gwizhìk vitì' oondìt ditłįh eenìnidìk.
Izhìk vitłįh tr'oochìt akòodiyàhnyąą,
25.59 "Shitłįh, chan oonii nanoonizhį' shrǫ'.
Yaaghà' tr'iinin naii t'ee łyâa chideeshąąhjii t'ôonch'yàa.
Zhyąą oondùk zhyąą jyǎanch'yà," yàhnyaa googàa chan oonìn neehòozhii dǫhłįį.
It'ee reh tr'ahaahkhwàa.
Aii chan shan ts'an t'iizhìk vàràhnyàa.
Ditłįh kweetee gwats'an oozhàk jyàa diizhìk gwiizhìk yee'àt njyaa[8] gwinyąą shryah[9] yeendak niveh zheh jyàa dòonchyaa reh.
Oonèedee chan jyàa dòonch'yaa gòo'ąįį rǫh.
Izhìk gwizhìt dinjii lęįį nihděiinjìl, łyâa zhyàa *champion* naii.
26.36 Chan zhat nìnidii jì' gwinyaa.
Gwiizhìk yeenii needyaa dàį' tthak k'i' hàa nihdèegiinjìl.
Yee'òk tr'ineezhii gwiizhìk t'ireheelyàa gìnyàa.
"Tr'iinin naii chidęęshąąhdak nyaa ch'yąą akǫǫ'įįnch'it," ts'ą' jyàa yàhnyàa.
Ts'ą' zhik gwà'àn tr'eeshrąądąąkhwat, gwiizhìk oo'àt aii shryah kwaii kwaiitee ch'ii'àn khàgwèedįį.
Izhìk k'i' tsįį hàa jyàa dòonch'yaa gwinyàa.
K'i' hàa chyǎant'òo nàgwàanąįį gwiizhìk yizhìt tr'antłee vàràhnyàa.
27.11 Oonjit zhyàą dinjii, aii k'i' t'âanch'yąą vik'iitł'ųų hee t'iizhìk nàhąą?
Gwiizhìk oonjì' jyàa dǐizhìk akhài' jii vanchòh reh tr'iłdàii vàràhnyàa.
Tr'igiinìinjil, zhah tsal kat łyâa tr'aagal gwinzįį rǫh.
Tr'igiinìinjil googàa ndàa jyàa dìi'in.

8. *Njyaa* is a hut used by the army. —JE

9. I thought this word was *shrah* instead of *shryah*. —KP

But he only killed one man who was on the side.
Meanwhile, *Goghwaii* had a hard time with his back.
It kept getting full of pus inside.
Goghwaii's father went over and visited his relatives once in a while.
His relatives first told him,
25.59 "My friend, don't come back over again.
These children are really getting on my nerves.
Just stay over there," he said to him.
I guess he must have gone over again later.
Because he would soon die.
They also say that he got hit by witchcraft.
He went over to his relative's house which was a skin hut.
He had one like that too.
Lots of men were already there.
They were all champions hoping that he would come over again.
26.36 They saw him coming over, they say.
So everybody went inside to wait for him with their weapons.
They planned to get him when he got close to the house.
He came over and spoke to his relative,
"I thought you said these children get on your nerves?"
He started to walk away very fast.
They say lots of arrows were sticking out of the opening to the skin house.
The arrows started flying but somehow he got ahead of them, they say.
27.11 The arrows missed him, you see?
They say he happened to look over like this very quickly and that was when he got hit in the thumb.
They all started chasing him on the snow, but he got ahead.

Oonjùk vanank'ah k'ąhnjik gwinìgwiin'ee.
Jyàa dòonch'yaa.
Izhìk hee *Vizhuu K'i'*, *Goghwaii* vachaa reh.
Gwiizhìk *Goghwaii* aii oodee, oozhee ch'iinii viti' neerineedàa gwiizhìk k'iłtąį' kat tree hàa hatrak gàa oozhee vanank'įį khah khatł'àk vàràhnyàa (adlaa).
27.55 Gwiizhìk *Goghwaii* gwinzįį gwandàii t'iin'in jì', ch'ìhłęę gàa oonìn neeheedyaa kwàa.
Aiits'ą' reh, izhìk ch'iinii t'ee vitì' neerahkhàa, aii chan shan hàa tr'ǫąąhdàk geh'àn tr'iłdàii reh.
Yit! Gwidįį jyàa dǐizhìk, vidik niłilzhrùu, vigii chyaa aii, "Shii nak'àa neech'ołchyaa," yàhnyaa.
"Nakwaa, shįį gàa neech'ahalchyaa nan neehindii," yàhnyàa.
Aii k'i' k'eeshraavii gik'èechì'[10] ontà' reh, aii dah tan choo dhidlìt łee aii khǎiinzhaa łee vàràhnyàa.
28.32 Dazhoo ik naatsąu vidrihtsįį tr'igwìłdàii gàa reh giidąądak[11] kwàa.
Yeezhee ch'iinìn tr'ineezhii gwiizhìk aii dąhthee ch'iidàk kì' vàroonjyaa k'it t'ii'in googàa reh k'ì' iłèehàazhii.
Aii gwiizhìk ch'ii'àn tr'ineezhii gwiizhìk k'ì' hàa vik'ìh'àn aant'òo[12] jyàa dàrah'in googàa ęhdaa dąhthee hee needyaa vàràhnyàa.
Aii dįhchì' aii gwiizhìk dinjii ìhłęę dazhan zhik gwà'àn neehidik,
"Ijìi deeyąhthàn?" jyàa vàràhnyàa ts'ą' t'ee zhyąą zhik ch'iinìin hee gwits'ěehaa ch'iinìn k'i' ìintrat vàràhnyàa.
Łàa zhik khan hee neetł'eedeedìi.
Yakwài' teetł'an nach'ąhdàk reh.
Jyàanch'yaa gwiizhìk giits'ą' hàajìl.
29.27 Zhik tsyaa aii gwiizhìk łyâa zhyąą tsyaa naii tthak yahâąjil googàa oodee gwìizųų gòo'ąįį gwats'ą' t'ii'ìn.

10. *Gik'èechì'* is a certain part of the arrow that he is holding. —JE

11. He did not feel the arrow forced into him because of his coat. —JE

12. *Vik'ìh'àn aant'oo* means they were shooting arrows in front of him because he was running too fast. —JE

Over there, on the side of the hill, there's a creek flowing down that way.

It looks like this.

Vizhuu K'i' ('His Son's Arrow') [was] *Goghwaii*'s younger brother.

They said that when *Goghwaii* saw his father being chased down there he cried and tried helping him by trying to shoot arrows, but pus would burst out of his back each time (laughs).

27.55 If only *Goghwaii* had been in good health at that particular time, the ones who were chasing his father would not have made it back over.

If not for witchcraft, his father would not have been hit at all either.

Yit! Now he was at the foot of the hill and his son was up on top.

"Let me do it," he said.

"No. Let me give it [the weapon] to you," he said.

Part of an arrow had pierced his hand, and they say his hand was all bloody and frozen.

28.32 He was wearing a caribou skin parka so when they hit him in the chest, he didn't feel it.

They said that all the men were shooting a hail of arrows at him, but he stayed way ahead of them all the way over.

There was a medicine man among them too and they say he said to himself, "What's wrong with him?"

And they aimed at him and shot him right in the spot and through his foot.

They went to him while he was wounded there.

29.27 There was a young man (*K'azheezhal's* son) who was also being chased there.

But he was fast and got away.

Aii gwitee neezhii ts'ą̀' t'ee k'eegaajìl.
Gwiizhìk yeezhee dhidii ts'ą̀' reh łyâa giyintsą̀į'.
29.59 Aii googàa veh'àn vachaa tr'ôołkhwąįį kwàt khai' dizhi' chan dhìłkhwą̀įį.
Aiits'ą̀' reh geenjit k'eegwaadhat aii gòhch'it aii ookyąą nee'oo zhyą̀ą tree hàa giinêelzhii oochit vik'į̀' vakwą̀į' ìin'ee reh.
30.07 "Yehdàk nitsųų nìhee aii dèeyahaanjyàa gwik'ìt akhàrooheenjyàa," jyàa ginyàa.
"Akwaa jì' tr'ahaahkhwàa," jyàa ginyàa.
Aii ch'ii'ęę needyaa gwiizhìk reh.
"Shachaa, gwichit ał'ii, neetł'eehałchal, kheeshidluu, akhàshoiinyàa," jyàa yàhnyąą vàràhnyàa.
Akòodinyąą kwaa jì' gweheezyàa.
30.44 Vachaa, "Dzaa nahaa," jyaa yàhnyaa.
Googaa giitsin ch'ijiinjir ik'ee ganaandaii go'.
K'i' hiłtraa ts'ą̀' yitsii nich'iinjir varahnyaa.
Yidrihtsii nach'ahdah vàràhnyàa.
Yehzhee zhat tree gahnyaa tł'ęę nìneegaajìl.
It'ee dinjii neeshąhąą'yàa kwàa.
Tł'ęę khaii tthak chan nihkhaiinjit niveh gaatsii ts'ą̀' reh nihłanjih geenihłagoolìi, niłèh'an dinjii lęįį.
31.05 Dinjii gǫ̀ǫlįį t'igwinyàa, yeenaa dą̀į'.
Kwàt yaaghà' ts'ąįį *Goghwaii champion* nilį̀į.
Jùhts'aįį chan *Dachan Naatąįį* vàràhnyàa chan *champion* nilį̀į.
Aii t'ee *Genèràl.*
Niveh chìt aiits'ą̀' zhik *Goghwaii* hàandii ts'ąįį datthak gok'ąąhtìi.
Oondaa nìrinjik ts'ą̀' shryah choh tr'ahtsìk rǫh.
Aiits'ą̀' tr'injàa naii, dinjii chan hàa tthak tǫǫ tthak gàgąąndàii.
31.38 Niveh gèeroolii khaii tthak tthąįį gwadąįį tr'iłchųų gwinyaa t'iihnyàa.

K'azheezhal was wounded and was still sitting down there.

They didn't want him to die.

29.59 It was because of him that his younger brother was killed.

He killed his own relative too.

They just stood around him crying while he had an arrow stuck through his foot.

30.07 "Your grandmother went up for a while and we'll see what she wants us to do with him," they were saying.

"Otherwise, we'll have to get rid of him," they were saying.

"My younger brother, this thing I use for a blanket. I'll give it to you. I'm going to get very cold," he told him, they say.

It would be better if he didn't say that.

30.44 His younger brother [said], "Look here," he told him.

But even so, *Goghwaii* stabbed him in the stomach.

They say he drew out his arrow [from the quiver] and stabbed him in the stomach with it.

Everyone who was standing near him cried and then slowly walked away.

They fought against each other all that winter.

They were always on the lookout for each other.

31.05 It's been said that long ago there were lots of people.

Goghwaii was the champion on one side.

And *Dachan Naatąįį* was also the champion on the other side, they say.

Dachan Naatąįį was a general, the head of the army.

They were all watching out for *Goghwaii.*

Wherever they settled down, they put up a big *shryah* (skin hut).

The women and their children kept watch at night.

31.38 What I'm saying is they say they all had a hard time getting enough sleep for fear that they would be attacked.

Akhài' reh yaaghàt *Goghwaii* vats'an tr'ìnjàa reh vành dąį' t'ôohju' oonjìt gwintsàl khaiyahkąįį gwiizhìk hee khàshraa'intrat vàràhnyàa, "Gòhch'it dee *Dachan Naatąįį* naii geedaa," nyaa ts'ą'.[13]

<jfka402>

0.11 "Gòhch'it dèe zhyąą *Dachan Naatąįį* naii geedàa," gwinyąą ts'ą' àkwàt shryah choo dha'ąįį.

0.17 Aii ch'iizhàk kwàt zhyąą k'ì' zhrįh teegwagwąhtà'.

Ts'ą' t'ee aih hàa ch'iizhàk nihdèetsiląątłit k'it t'igwii'ìn.

0.39 Gwiizhìk dinjii ch'atąįį zhyąą nihts'ahts'ą' geedàa reh.

Goonkàt gokwàa reh.

It'ee łyâa nįįzhùk kwaa tr'iinjil gwiizhìk *Goghwaii* ǫǫkeegàaya' gàa *Goghwaii* hiljìi.

0.47 Aii vàgwąąjat reh.

Hiljii, it'ee łyâa nahgwàn tr'iinjil gwiizhìk it'ee *Goghwaii* zhik chǐinzhii ts'ą'.

Njyaa òozhii,[14] aii tsyaa vaihnyąą.

Njyaa ts'ą' tr'iinzhii gwiizhìk nihk'yàa dèe'in vàràhnyàa.

Gwiizhìk k'i' tthak *ready'* nilįį reh t'ii'ìn.

Goghwaii nah'gǫǫ ahaa gwiizhìk yihtrăngìk.

Ts'ą' zhyąą k'i' hàa jyàa dìi'in googàa atrak k'ìt t'ii'in.

1.35 Gwalàii oozhee vakwaiitł'ęę gwizhrįh gohòotraa vàràhnyàa.

K'i' khài' t'iinjìk gwakwaa googàa t'ee vakak k'ì' gwąąh'yà' kwaa ts'ą' nihděenzhii reh.

Ìinch'it oochyąą neezhìi, zhat dąį' jyàanch'ii reh dzaa gweedąą chan ninjyàa nàngìłt'àii.

Tik dìlįį, aii chan vantł'eeghwàa vàràhnyàa.

1.41 Łyâa zhyąą k'igwaanaii ìinch'it oozhaa neeshiizhàa.

Dèiinch'yaa jii googàa veetł'at dànch'iriłchaa łee ts'ą' vivìt chan dzaa vik'èech'araagyųų łee vàràhnyàa.

13. This story continues over onto another tape: <jfka402>. —CM

14. Njyaa was a member of the army led by Dachan Naatąįį. He may have been a mercenary. —JE

There was this one woman on *Goghwaii's* side who was up at dawn one morning and hollered out, "*Dachan Naatąįį* and his army are coming!"

<jfka402>

0.11 "*Dachan Naatąįį* and his army are coming!"

0.17 After that warning, they say, everyone got excited and ran inside their skin houses with bows and arrows.

So many people were running here and there that it looked as though there was a snowstorm.

0.39 *Dachan Naatąįį* and his army were near now, looking for *Goghwaii.*

There was no space between the army that was coming.

Meanwhile, *Goghwaii* was nowhere to be seen.

0.47 They were scared of him anyway.

They were very close when *Goghwaii* walked out.

He started walking toward a man I'm calling *Njyaa,* watching out all the while.

Meanwhile, they were all ready with their weapons.

The fighting started and *Goghwaii* got away like a flash.

He didn't even get hit at all.

1.35 They say he came back out again.

The arrows weren't slow, but none of them hit him, so he went back inside.

At that time, men used to wear this clothing which hangs down on the front.

There were three strips of cloth, and they say it was called *vantł'eeghwaa*, a kind of codpiece covering his crotch.

1.41 He disappeared into the skin house but came right back out with torn clothing hanging on him.

Even his sleeves were torn off, they say.

Aiits'ą' nihk'yàa k'i' ontà' ts'ą' nihk'yàa khiizhaa
vàràhnyàa.
It'ee reh oo'àt nijìn k'ii'àn tr'eedàa gwiizhìk t'iizhìk it'ee
zhat *stop*.
Jyàanch'yaa dąhzhrii chinidik jì' gwahaljii gwahahtsyàa
t'ii'in reh.
2.20 Aiits'ą' reh (adlaa),
"Oo'àt zhat gwitee chit aii reh t'inyąą.
Shin dąį' nihłigeeghan?"
Aii Ch'itsyaa naii hàa dàanch'yąą niłeeghan, nàhąą?
Aii tthak neegihiichìi.
Akhài' reh *Goghwaii* vitsyàa aii naii reh dinjii ìhłak
gwàndaa t'âanch'yąą gôołkhwąįį łèe.
2.27 Aii gwideek'ìt dinjii neerahohchyaa ts'ą' gwinzįį neegòolì'
jyàa ginyàa.
Aiits'ą' naagąįį ik vàràhnyàa, jyàa dąhchyaa t'igiyàhnyàa.
Aii chan łyâa ninjyàa reh.
Aii t'ee k'oh nàrahchaa, aii t'ee niveh naii tthak gìiyeelyàa.
Kwàt yaaghà' geedant'eh shryah zhìt gwizhit zhyaa.
3.11 Naagąįį ik zhyąą tąih gwìch'in dha'aii t'igwinyàa.
Aii jyàanch'yaa ts'ą' niht'įį gihilìi.
Izhìk googàa chan *Goghwaii* naagąįį ik zhyąą khaanzhii
vàràhnyàa.
3.23 It'ee shrôondaii (adlaa), yee'àt t'ii'in gwanaagąįį ninjyàa
dąį' jii k'iłtài' aii chan vits'į chan shrii gwìch'in, nàhąą?
Niveh eenjit t'inch'yaa kwàt aii hàa oozhee yìigòk.
Aii gwiizhìk dìlch'yąą naii tthak yee'òk jyàanch'yaa
datthak k'ì' hàa tr'ǫąąhdàl jì' googàa datthak ch'ìhłęę
zhrįh nah'in kìt t'inch'yaa vàràhnyàa.
3.35 Aii gwiizhìk yeezhee yee'àn neehahchaa gwiizhìk yits'ìį
teech'ant'ìi yatl'an yee'àn hee zhee t'àdhak yeezhee
adan aii yich'ìitthak jyàa dàh'in vàràhnyàa.
Aiitł'ęę oozhee gwideek'ìt kwàt zhyąą chihkat
k'itôonch'yaa gwinyàa, naagąįį.

He ran out and looked around once in a while, shooting at people, they say.
At last, everything stopped.
If he continued doing what he was doing, he would have killed almost everyone anyway.
2.20 The chief on the enemy side said (laughs),
"Remember I said they fought last summer?"
Between the Ch'itsyaa clan, anyway, they went and counted the people that were killed, you see?
And they found out that *Goghwaii's* side killed one more than than the other side so they said they wanted to settle their differences so they could stop being enemies.
2.27 They say they wanted to give up one more man to make up for that one extra man they killed.
At that time, they say the army used to carry around with them a beaded tunic.
It was really long too.
They wore this around their necks in case they decided to become friends again.
3.11 So they could trade beads.
But *Goghwaii* cheated and kept all the beaded clothing just to make them mad.
3.23 The tips of their arrows were for their enemies so they were as sharp as a knife, you see?
With that, he poked at the beaded tunic.
In the meantime, they say he kept watching for enemies.
3.35 He walked around undoing all the beads and dropped them into one big pile and then they say he sifted them up and down off the ground in his hands.
After that the beads looked like rocks on the ground.

4.00 Aiits'ą' dinjii łyâa vit'èegwahaahch'yàa kwaa zhik gwitee gwandàii, jidìi *hobò* reh, aii t'ee reh, gootsa' chìnąąhchįį.

Aii chìnąąhchii akhài' yee'at łagwadąąnaii reh yee'àt jidìi ch'àa reh ch'ilt'aii gwinyàa, t'ee niveh vàa *fine* tr'ookwàt reh t'arah'ì n.

It'ee reh gwinzįį neegweedhàt.

Googàa gweedhaa datthak giyuunilì', aii geh'àn t'ee chan tr'àl inzhìi.

4.49 Tr'àl inzhii ts'ą' oonjìt *Tł'oo K'at*[15] gàgàhnyąą oonjìt *Old Crow* njì' khįį.

Old Crow vijųų *Tł'oo K'at* gàgàhnyąą izhìk hee t'ee *Ch'ôonjik* ch'iidì' zhyąą ddhah jyàanch'yaa nàhąą?

4.56 Izhìk neech'ąątąįį izhìk it'ee dagachaa hàa gwigwich'įį.

Aii gwiizhìk t'ee niveh giyeenjit niveh ahtsìi.

Gwiizhìk khaihłan nìinjyaa.[16]

Goghwaii eenjit iłts'ik naii.

5.08 Kwàt ch'adhàh zheh gwach'ok gwagwąh'įį ts'ą' reh tthak gwineeyàh tr'aantłoo.[17]

Jàghaii t'inch'yaa kwàt gwiizhìk gavàh chan shìh gǫǫlįį.

5.23 Aii gohch'it t'ee reh, aii digik'į aii t'ôohłįį nìginlii jì' gweheezyàa.

Aii ch'adhàh zheh, ch'adhàh teet'įh izhìk digik'ì' nìgiinlii łee.

Aii gwiizhìk yeedįį t'ee reh njuu tr'iinlìt k'ìt t'igwìizhìk gwinyąą.

Zhik chįį ahaa aii t'ee zhyąą nakhwàa tr'ahâak'yaa t'igwii'in nyąą vàràhnyàa.

Neegiyan'ee reh t'igiyàhnyàa.

5.44 Aii ch'adhàh zhee gwizhit reh oonjìt reh gaadìi.

15. *Tł'oo K'at* is on the north side of the *Porcupine River* just above *Old Crow*, the site of a historic Gwich'in settlement which has been the subject of archaeological investigations. See Morlan 1973. —JE and CM

16. This word *nìinjyaa* should be *niginjyaa.* —KP
It means 'gathering.' —JE

17. *Gwineeyàh tr'aantłoo* refers to enemies — people standing everywhere around the huts, surrounding the camp. —JE

4.00 Sometimes there is a worthless man around, a hobo.

Goghwaii took one of those men out to them.

They paid their obligation that way by giving them a chance to make up for the one extra man they killed during the fighting.

Now, both sides were even, but they still tried to kill *Goghwaii,* so he took off somewhere.

4.49 They were walking to this brushy place they call *Tł'oo K'at* near *Old Crow.*

It's on the *Porcupine River* where the caribou usually cross, you see?

4.56 Anyway *Goghwaii* and his younger brother went there to stay where the animals crossed.

They were gathering an army together while he stayed there.

They were *Goghwaii's* enemies.

5.08 *Goghwaii* and his younger brother had a big skin house, but they were surrounded.

In the meantime, they had lots of food too.

5.23 Finally, if only they could have put their bow and arrows away.

Instead, they put them against the side of the skin house.

Meanwhile they say there was a whole army coming toward them.

There were so many, they say they looked like a moving island.

The head of the army came and said they only came to visit them, they say.

They were trying to trick them, they said.

5.44 They were both sitting inside the skin house.

Ch'adhàh zhee gwintsìi ts'ą' oojìt reh gaadìi, shrii zhrįh.
Gook'ì' aii ch'adhàh teet'įh dhidlìi.
Aii gwiizhìk kwàt zhik ch'adhàh zheh gwindìh dinjii kat dąhthee gwinyàa.
Tthak tòh, k'ì' hàa *ready* nilįį reh.

6.13 Łyâa jùk tr'ahaahkhwàa jyàa giyûuhaanjik googàa giveeyèezhii.
Aii gwiizhìk *Ch'ôonjik*, *Porcùpìne* reh, yaaghà' deetthàn gwindìh jyàa dòonch'yaa gwinyàa.
Gwiizhìk t'ee łuu hàajìk, ch'iinįį łuu nihdìijii reh, dąįį, kweetee chan nèekwąįį yihdĕiindìi.
Aii gwiizhìk vachaa veeghaii dhidìi.

6.46 "Nats'ąą dèeshe'in shik'ìt t'i'hini'yàa yùu," dachaa àhnyaa.
Aiits'ą' reh, jyàanch'yaa gwiizhìk oondìt nèekwąįį naii, gwiizhìk gwatsal gwizhrįh chiyèech'yą.
Àntsʼą' tthak ch'ii'àn dinjii gǫǫlįį reh.
Dàhthee gwà'àn tthak dinjii.

7.16 T'ôoju' jyàa dĭizhìk gwiizhìk dzaa dachaa keets'ahhìłkaii.
Ts'ą' oondaa teetł'an nàatil.
Gwats'an oo'àt ch'ii'àn vakwaiitł'ęę gwizhrįh goohòotraa vàràhnyàa.
Vachaa chan vik'ìt t'iizhìk.
Zheedòhònyàa, jyàa dìgwiizhìk googàa reh ch'ihłęę gàa ch'ihìłdak kwaa gwinyàa.
Yeech'iitthàn han gwats'ą' dih reh jyàa dìgiizhìk.

7.36 Hàa ch'iitthàn tr'iłuu'àldzìk.
Hàa ch'adài' hee yeech'iiniiłuu adàa kat ch'iinjì' hee reh.
Tryah zhuu chųų kat aagal k'it t'igii'in gooràhnyąą.
Yeedì' geendih hee k'ìgògwanaii gooràhnyàa.

7.49 It'ee reh dinjii eegeezhìi.
Aiits'ą' t'ee, chan łyâa Ch'eekwaii dìitth'ak vàràhnyàa.
Ts'ą' yee'àn *Chųų Choh Vęę* zhyąą gwik'èegwigweheendàii gwats'ą' gahàa'oo.
Gook'į' chan kwàa.
Gwiizhìk hee Ch'eekwaii lęįį giłdràt.

The skin house was big, and they were sitting there with just their knives.
Their bows were left outside and their arrows were still stored inside their quivers.
They say at that moment people were standing everywhere surrounding the tent for as far as the eye could see.
Each one was ready with a short spear and a bow and arrow.
6.13 This time they really came to kill *Goghwaii* for sure, but he got away again.
The *Porcupine River* was right there, and the ice was just about to go out.
Two men were blocking the doorway while the two brothers were inside.
6.46 *Goghwaii* told his younger brother, "Just do what I do," he said.
Just a small opening was allowed through the doorway.
The outside of the tent was crowded with men everywhere.
7.16 He made a signal to his brother with his elbow and before anyone noticed, they were out the door in a flash, they say.
His younger brother did what he did too.
There was a roar from the crowd, but they say not even one of them had a chance to shoot.
They were gone in a moment over the cliff toward the river.
7.36 Everybody ran to the cliff.
But they were away on the moving ice like young land otters, they say.
They say they disappeared around the bend of the river after that.
7.49 They both escaped.
And they say *Goghwaii* really spoke Iñupiaq too.
So they decided to try to make it over to the *Arctic Ocean.*
Again, they had no bows or arrows.
Meanwhile there were lots of Inuit.

8.17 Izhìk dąį' Ch'eekwaii, *Dinjii Zhuh* hàa duuyeh zhyąą nihłaa'in roh.

Aii googàa s*ometime* nihtee jyàa dìgìich'yaa gàa, aiitł'ęę gwàndàa nihłigiighàk.

Zhyąą jyàa dìgìnch'yaa ts'ą' oo'àt k'eegii'òo.

8.27 Łyâa Ch'eekwaii dìitth'ak reh.

Shrii hàa giits'ą' chĭinjil, akhài' reh goots'ą' ginkhii.

"Yaaghà' shalàk naii shahaahkhwàa geegwitr'it t'agogwah'in ts'ą' *some way* ts'ą' goots'į' tr'àl'iida'oo[18] t'igwii'ìn.

Nakhwak'ìighai' tr'igweheendàii ghat t'igwii'ìn.

Nakhwàa tr'igweheech'yàa," jyàa gavàhnyàa.

8.57 Ts'ą' ąąhą' ginyąą ts'ą' t'ee reh nih'àn Ch'eekwaii zheh nihdèegiin'òo.

Zhyąą tth'an zhrih ginlii łee gavàhnyàa.

Aiits'ą' reh, aii Ch'eekwaii vigii gǫǫlįį hàa gwigwich'įį, aii t'ee gootłįh reh.

Aiits'ą' reh, it'ee łyâa zhyąą goothąį' neegòhòlìt, *Goghwaii* it'ee łyâa neehooshizhì' nindhan roh.

9.28 Gwinzįį gooch'agah'aa tthak gwinzįį gook'èegąąhtìi.

Googàa *Goghwaii* it'ee łyâa neehooshizhì' nindhan roh.

Aiits'ą' t'ee reh, dachaa t'àhnyàa.

"Juk tǫǫ neehihdyaa t'ôonch'yàa.

Gehdee gwàdàk gàagiindàii izhìk shoonkat neehindyàa," yàhnyaa.

"Oozhee nitłįh gavàa gwich'įį jèiinch'yaa tthak giłchųų gwiizhìk goochàa k'eech'ąhtrìt," jyàa yàhnyaa.

9.53 Jyàa dìgòovìnlìk.

Adan t'eh ditłįh, goo'at naii hàa tthak reh jyàa dìnlìk.

Aiits'ą' reh, gook'ì' chan gòonjik nàhąą?

T'ee neegahòo'òo, vành khachyaazhii akhai yee'àt zhat zhyąą dinjii kwaa gwąąh'in.

Akhài' *Goghwaii* neegahòo'oo łee, zhik vàa gwich'įį tthak zhat dhidlii.

18. *Tr'àl'iida'oo* is an old-fashioned word. —KP

8.17 The Indians and Inuit were always enemies toward each other.
Sometimes they lived among each other, but they always ended up fighting.
The two brothers finally arrived over there the way they were.
8.27 But *Goghwaii* spoke Iñupiaq anyway.
The Inuit came out to them with knives, but he spoke really well to them.
"Our own relatives tried to kill us, but somehow we got away.
We came for your help so we can survive.
We'll stay with you," he said to them.
8.57 The Inuit agreed and each of them stayed with a different family.
They say they were very skinny.
And so they stayed and even gained their weight back.
At last *Goghwaii* wanted to leave.
9.28 The Inuit fed them well and took good care of them.
But *Goghwaii* still wanted to leave, so he told his younger brother that he would sneak away that night and wait for him.
Somewhere on the way over he told his brother,
"Cut the Inuits' throats while they're sleeping before you come after me."
9.53 So his brother did what he was told to do.
He killed the whole household.
Then they even took their bows and arrows and left, you see?
The other Inuit woke up and found out what happened.
They were very mad at them.

Gwintł'òo Ch'eekwaii naii iłts'ik giłtsąįį gavàhnyaa t'agavaihnyaa, agàa neegoogąhk'ii reh.

10.29 Aiits'ą' t'ee neegahòo'oo ts'ą' yaaghòk hee k'ineegii'òo.

Dinjii tee neegii'oo ts'ą' t'ee reh jyàa dòonch'yàa.

Aiits'ą' reh, googàa chan hee googàa neegiyuunilì' nàhąą?

Aiits'ą' chan hee goots'ì' tr'àl neegii'òo.

Aiits'ą' yee'àt *Bartèr Islànd*, izhìk gwats'ą' *Łeeridiidàl* gwinyaa gòozhii gehnaa dąį'.[19]

11.01 Łi'hàa Ch'eekwaii gǫǫlįį.

Yeenjìt *Hudson Islànd*[20] gàràhnyąą chan.

Ch'iinjì' Ch'eekwaii gǫǫlįį gwinyąą.

Aiits'ą' t'ee reh, oonjìt dinjii gôołkhwąįį[21] nàhąą?

11.36 Kwàt ts'ą' zhik Ch'eekwaii tthak nihłàa gogwaandak t'inch'yàa.

Aiits'ą' izhìk hee dagachaa hàa k'eegii'òo.

Ch'eekwaii naii tthak chan yàandàii.

Chan łyâa nint'aii vàràhnyaa ts'ą' giyàandàii.

Aiits'ą' akwàt zhik gwich'in tthak dłòk hàa zhyąą giinòoghaa.

Dinjii chyah tł'an hee dagachaa hàa nih'àn nàgàdhàt.

Gooroohkhwaa googàhnyaa łee ts'ą' reh.

11.54 Izhìk t'ee gwiizhìk shrii di'įį, *Goghwaii.*

Izhìk chan hee t'ee k'ì' nôonjik kwàa.

12.12 Chan hee k'ì' ehdan nàanàii.

Aiits'ą' Ch'eekwaii nint'aii nèekwąįį naii nihts'įį yigìn ooheendal.

Oo'ęę ahaa dąį' hee giyàhnyàa.

12.33 Aii gwik'ìt łyâa dinjii nitsii nèekwaii aii naii tr'ahaahkhwàa, vachaa chan gwik'ìt t'ireheelyàa, jyàa ginyaa.

Giinòoghaa gàa nihts'įį nint'aii naii yeenĩin'òo.

---

19. *Barter Island* in the *Beaufort Sea* was formerly called *Łeeridiidàl.* The Inuit village of *Kaktovik* is found on this island today. —JE and CM

20. *Hudson Island* is probably a mispronunciation of *Herschel Island*, another historic Inuit village east of *Barter Islànd* and near the mouth of the *Firth River* on the *Beaufort Sea*. —CM

21. This word *gôołkhwąįį* means 'they killed a man.' —JE

After all, they even fattened them up.

10.29 Then the two brothers made it back to their own people somehow, but their own people still tried to kill them, you see?

So they went away again.

Over by *Barter Island* is a place called "Where we gather."

11.01 There were lots of Inuit there.

There was another place called *Hudson Island* [*Herschel Island*].

There were lots of Inuit there too, they say.

Remember the Inuit they killed?

11.36 Anyway all the Inuit around there already knew about them.

And so *Goghwaii* and his brother arrived there.

They arrived and of course all the Inuit knew him too.

They all knew that he was strong, they say.

Then they were surrounded and met by the Inuit.

They were in the middle of the crowd.

I guess the Inuit had a plan to kill them.

11.54 Meanwhile, all *Goghwaii* had was a knife.

He didn't have his arrows.

12.12 So, once again he was without them.

Two strong Inuit planned to grab him by the arms on each side.

I guess they must have planned it long before they arrived.

When *Goghwaii* was coming, they told those two strong Inuit to grab him.

12.33 What they say is two of the biggest Inuit had planned to kill him, and they also planned to do the same to his younger brother.

They surrounded him with their two strongest men on both sides.

"Shitłįh" giyàhnyaa ts'ą' giyàashragwąąhch'yàa.

Gwiizhìk hee giyeenjit oohìlzhin reh.

Dinjii dachan k'ìt t'inch'yaa tł'an reh.

Łąą gwats'an dinjii tr'oohaa gokwaa googàa gwats'an tr'iinzhii vàràhnyàa.

Izhìk it'ee goorahaahkhwàa ginyaa łee.

13.30 Dinjii deetik gokwàa, oozhee diitth'àn deetak gwatsal gwizhrįh aii googàa yeezhàk diitth'àn deetak jyàa dii'ìn.

Vinkeekwaii rahaadhàk googàa diikwài' yakak gwąąh'yà' kwaa vàràhnyàa.

It'ee reh *Goghwaii* yee'àt ch'ii'àn tr'ineezhii.

Izhìk t'ee vachaa gwats'ą' hìljìi.

Vachaa aii tr'ôołkwąįį łee.

13.53 Aiits'ą' yaaghà' k'inidik gàa łyâa shoo nilįį kwàa.

Vachaa hiljii izhìk geet'iindhan kwàa.

Ts'ą' t'ee reh yaaghòk gwats'an gwich'in naii hàa tthak.

Oonjìt Ch'ôonjik Gwich'in naii hàa tthak kwàt zhik gooyèhghan naii goolàràa gǫǫlįį.

Naagąįį ik ch'iinjì' tthak gwitèegaadlìi.

Tthak gwitèedhidlii ts'ą' t'ee niveh onkwàt ts'ą' yee'àt ch'ii'an ddhah tah gahàajìl.

Adan chan niveh chìt nilįį.

14.24 Aiits'ą' yaaghà' jùhts'ąįį chan *Dachan Naatąįį* vàràhnyàa.

Aii chan gwik'ìt t'ii'in gàa reh aii gwik'ee'ìt ąhch'yaa łee vàràhnyàa.

14.33 Oo'àt ch'ii'àn oodee ddhah kat nihtak geeneeriidàl, aii gwik'ìt t'igii'in kwàa.

Inidzii Ch'eekwaii gwinyàa.

Maybe three to four thousand.

Oodìt gehdìt *Bartèr Islànd* chan.

Izhìk gwats'ą' niveh ahtsii t'ii'ìn.

Oodee geek'įį ch'ii'àn gwintł'eek'ah reh khàgaajìl.

14.53 Akhaì' zhyąą yeendaa chųų choh vęę deedì' zhyąą tsił ddhah khàradąą nąįį.

They called him "Shitłįh," their so-called Indian "friend," teasing him.
But they were closely watching out for them.
They were in the middle of the crowd.
At the same time, they say they were ready for him.
There was no way he could get away, but they say he got away again that time.
13.30 There was no way out through the crowd for *Goghwaii* to escape, but somehow he got out by crawling.
People tried kicking him but not one foot touched him, they say.
He escaped after all and walked away.
But that's when his younger brother got killed.
13.53 And so he got away, but he was very mad.
His brother was dead and he didn't like it.
Still, his parents were rich.
They gave out beaded clothes to all the people there and to all the *Porcupine River* people.
He bought an army like that.
And they went over the mountains.
He was the head of the army.
14.24 On the other side was a man named *Dachan Naatąįį,* who did the same, they say.
14.33 This time they didn't go through the valley, though.
They say there were lots of Inuit.
Maybe there were three or four thousand of them.
Near there also is *Barter Island*, which also had that many Inuit.
That's where he planned to start a war.
14.53 They got up to the top of the ridge on the side and there was the ocean in the distance.

K'iidì' tthak kwàt zhyąą t'agwąhtsii tthak hàa ch'agwąhdok tthak Ch'eekwaii naii reh.

Ch'eekwaii lęįį gwizhìt gwich'įį reh.

Gwiizhìk yeezhee ch'iitthàn gwinìidlan oozhee ch'iidįį hee zhyąą khàgaajìl.

Łyâa gwiizhìk gwi'it deehiindak reh.

Ch'iidįį Ch'eekwaii tr'ìk khał tr'avał' aatsit akhài' reh zhyąą dinjii khăa'in k'ìt t'inch'yàa.

Aiits'ą' reh, jyàa dìnch'yaa gwiizhìk, "It'ee reh vadzaih adôo'įį," nyàa.

Ts'ą' t'ee reh gwikhyųų gwa'an hee zhyąą vadzaih nàgwahjìi k'ìt t'igii'in.

15.35 Yaaghà' ts'ąįį ch'ii'àn geegǫh'ìt ch'ii'àn nàràdąągwat reh!

Aiits'ą' reh, di' ts'ą' geendii k'eegwaadhàk googàa reh zhit ch'iidii geendih khè ts'ą' tr'eekìitthak vàràhnyàa.

Łyâa dinjii t'ii'in niindhàn, gwiizhìk chan vadzaih k'ìt t'igwii'in roh.

Jyàanch'yaa ts'ą' t'ee reh, tseenjyàa vak'ǫ̂ǫtì'i.

Gwiizhìk oodìt gehdìt reh.

Ch'eekwaii naii shriit'ąąch'yąą gwich'įį gwinyàa, k'aii tee.

Oozhee yeendàa chan łyâa zhyąą dàanch'yąą *thousand* naii gwich'įį reh.

Oodįį jyàa dìi'in gohch'it reh oodįį neegwąą'in kwaa.

Gwiizhìk hee zhyąą deetthàn hee geendih tr'ach'ąąn dii.

Oochìt k'aii tee gwiizhìk łat gwinyàa.

Aii eenjit k'il kàheet'ii'in łee vàràhnyàa.

16.29 Zhik t'agwąhtsii, jyàa dìgwìizhìk.

Aii Ch'eekwaii naii lęįį gwich'ii łee.

Zhyąą reh nìtrèegwirigwìiltik gwizhrįh gwinyàa.

16.43 Aiits'ą' oondaa *Hudson Island* kat Ch'eekwaii nąhkat, zhyąą tsił làii kat ch'iidì' kwanh choh reh t'inch'yàa.

Dinjii lęįį vizhìt gwizhrįh t'inch'yàa.

16.55 Aiits'ą' t'ee reh dêetthàn gahàajìl.

Aiits'ą' gwintsàl tł'oo gwazhàł dąąk'at gwinyàa.

Aiitł'ee t'ee dzaa zhat gwats'ą' gahàajìl.

All they saw were snowdrifts all along it.
It looked like shining armor all along the coast.
There were a lot of Inuit living there.
Goghwaii and his men continued moving until they got to a steep valley.
Then all of sudden an Inuit woman came around the bend pushing a sled.
She stopped and kind of suspected she had seen them.
But *Goghwaii* told his people, "Pretend to be caribou."
So they say they pretended to be digging lichens out of the snow.
15.35 Over the hill beyond those pretending to dig like caribou, lots of people were hiding.
That woman pretended to leave but came around the bend again and again, watching just to make sure, they say, but they continued to act like caribou anyway.
From where the woman was, lots of Inuit lived not far down from her.
There were thousands of them up ahead.
When the woman stopped coming around the bend, *Goghwaii* and his men started going again toward that bend.
And they say they noticed a little smoke coming out of the willows.
The woman must have been gathering wood for that fire, they say.
16.29 The army moved up closer and spread out and found out there were lots of Inuit living there too.
They killed them all in a moment, they say.
16.43 In the distance was the main village on *Hudson* [*Herschel*] *Island* where there were only snowdrifts, and on top of those drifts were big igloos.
There there must have been lots of Inuit inside each igloo.
16.55 So they continued coming down.
They say there were small hills on the way down.
So they stopped on the way down.

Akhài' łyâa zhyąą tr'ikhit ginlęįį, kwàt reh gwintł'òo googweheech'yàa nàhąą?

17.04 Aiits'ą' reh, eedan aii niveh chìt nilįį ts'ą' t'inyaa vàràhnyàa,

"Dzaa juuhch'yàa, gwiizhìk shįį zhrįh oodąą giveenìhihshyàa," nyaa vàràhnyàa.

Zhyąą tsił làii, aih t'èegwąąhch'yaa kwaa reh.

Yaaghà' gwà'àn tsiłchoo aii khànoht'ìi ts'ą' aii dagadǫǫhłyaa ts'ą' vit'įh gwintsìi gohtsii.

Tthak gwik'ùhjyàa.

Ootthàn nìhihshyàa ts'ą' gwikyąą gavàa neehihdyàa.

"Goots'įį neehihdyaa," nyaa vàràhnyàa.

Dinjii ehdàk nàa'ąį' ts'ą' zhik t'àhtsii tthak zhyąą k'ì' hìltłoo gwinyàa.

I don't know how many hundred.

Aii gwiizhìk oodiindàa hee gwazhrąįį a'aa vàràhnyàa.

17.56 Oondaa łąą t'ee gwats'ą' nahgǫǫ ahàa.

Gwiizhìk hee zhyąą ehjyàa gwà'àn tthak hee zhyąą reh zhah.

Kat gwaghootìlzhrąįį nàgwàanaii gwinyàa.

It'ee *Goghwaii* khèeraa'in reh.

Izhìk khaihłan nàdhàt.

Nàdhat ts'ą' ootthàn goots'ą' ginkhìi.

18.18 "Kwàt yaaghà' shìh ehdan goodhaii nàdaalnaii, nakhwats'ą' nalghal t'ishe'in."

Jyàa nyaa ts'ą', neegoovan'ee t'agavàhnyàa.

"Łąą k'ooshinyą' k'ìt tihch'yaa kwaa," nyaa gwiizhìk k'iłtąį' toh aiits'ą' ch'iidąą ahaa t'inyàa.

18.29 Dinjii t'ą̌ąhch'yaa naii tthak ch'iikyąą kwàt zhyąą vats'ą' tthak zhyąą geeraanjìk k'ìt t'ôonch'yaa.

Njuu zhyąą vik'įh alaa k'ìt t'igwii'in.

Gwiizhìk ch'iidàk khanàandaii ts'ą' neetoh'ahkhàa.

18.50 Aii gwiizhìk vik'įh chan dinjii khałeenàhoch'ok k'ìt t'inch'yàa.

It'ee łàa tsił jyàa dìrînlìk ohts'ąįį łihts'èeriltłòo.

Since there were so many, they were afraid they would be seen, you see?

17.04 Since he was the leader of his army, they say he said to them, "Stay here, I'll go down to them myself."

The area was just tundra, and snowshoes were not needed.

He told them to cut up snowdrifts and pile them high so they could hide behind them.

He said to stay behind them.

He said he would go down and lead the Inuit back up.

"I'll lead them back up here," he said, they say.

The whole place was swarming with people, each one holding bows and arrows.

I don't know how many hundred.

Then they say they saw a dark spot moving off in the distance.

17.56 Meanwhile, he was just walking right close to the village when all the Inuit came out.

From a distance, they say he looked like a black streak.

That meant they saw *Goghwaii* coming.

Goghwaii stopped right where he was and started talking to them from a short distance.

18.18 "I have no food.

I need your help, and I was forced to come here," he said.

He was fooling them.

"I'm in no shape to fight for myself," he said.

He was using his bow as a walking cane, pretending to limp and walking toward them while he was talking.

18.29 All the Inuit started moving after him.

It looked like a big island moving behind him.

He was trying his best by walking fast ahead of them.

He was using his bow for a cane.

18.50 In the meantime, lots of Inuit were also right behind him.

He was trying to get them to come near his army, they say.

Izhìk gwiizhìk ch'iidàk needyaa gwiizhìk it'ee łyâa zhyąą veenirinjyàa gwahtsii vàràhnyàa.

Łyâa deedàk gwikiilee dhizhii, gwiizhìk hee k'inilghàa ts'ą' k'i' khąąhnaii vàràhnyàa.

Gwiizhìk zhik t'agwąhtsii tthak k'ì' hàa jyàa dìgwìizhìk.

Vashraih dąątth'at k'ìt aii njuu dha'aii k'ìt t'ôonch'yaa gwinyąą.

19.27 K'i' hàa khàtreedha'ąįį gwiizhìk gwìhìljii nàgwàanaii gwinyàa.

Zhat zhyąą nan kak ch'iitthàn gòo'ąįį k'ìt t'ôonch'yaa tthak Ch'eekwaii iłchįį t'ôonch'yaa.

Aiits'ą' ye'èendàa chųų choh vęę izhìk ch'iindàa ts'ąįį hàazhii vàràhnyàa.

19.36 Yaaghà' ch'ìhłęę ye'èendàa.

Ch'iindàa dinjii tthak zhyąą *line up.*

Fence ginlįį ts'ą' reh.

Oondaa ch'iindàa jyàa dìgiizhìk ts'ą' nihts'aii gahàajìl.

Jidìi gąąh'in datthak gaghan.

Gwiizhìk yeeneenjì' rch Ch'eekwaii tr'ìk nèekwąįį naii googàa ch'iinjì' hìlgik gwinyàa.

Aii tr'agwaghan gwiizhìk jyàa gwinyàa.

Izhìk chan gwâahch'įį ts'ą' yeenjì', k'eejìt dąį' t'igwìizhìk reh.

20.01 Yeenjì' k'igwaanąįį tł'ęę oonii neeshraadąąhkhwàt.

Ch'adąį' hee t'ee oonjì' dąhthee gaagal gwiizhìk goot'èe dhìzhìi.

Khaihłęę gavàa gwihîiłnaii tł'ee oo'ęę neezhii t'ii'in vàràhnyàa.

20.23 Yaaghà' deedì' chan Ch'eekwaii tr'ìk tik, aii chan ìhłęę oodì' gook'įh nànàhòzhìi

Aii chan vàa gwaraandak, oodì' hee k'ìgwaanaii vàràhnyàa.

Shriit'agwąhshyuk gwihìłthat ts'ą' yeedįį tr'eeshraadąąhkhwat vàràhnyàa.

Chan hee givinghan reh.

Yaaghà' *Bartèr Islànd* gwats'ą' reh t'igii'ìn.

Aiits'ą' t'ee datthak łąą gwigwinghàn.

Just when he was near his army, he turned around fast and suddenly took out his arrows, they say.
And then his whole army came out of its hiding place.
They say the whole place was like a moving island.
19.27 With the arrows flying, all that could be heard were cries and people dying everywhere, they say.
It looked like a big piece of land there because there were so many Inuit lying around dead.
And then they say he went a ways off to the ocean shore.
19.36 His army lined up all the way to the shore.
They were like a fence.
They all went to the shore and spread out on both sides.
They killed everyone in sight.
They say that while this was going on, two Inuit women ran away.
While the fighting was going on, *Goghwaii* overheard someone telling about the two women.
20.01 He went after them and was back in no time.
They say this meant he had already killed both of them, no matter how far away they were.
20.23 He also heard about three more women who escaped the other way.
And he went after them too, they say.
He was gone for a while and came back, they say.
He killed them also.
The women were trying to go to *Barter Island.*
And so he killed everybody.

20.40 Aiitł'ee t'ee *Barter Islànd* nìneegiidàl t'iginch'yaa reh.
Tǫǫ dąį' hee jyàa dìgiizhìk.
Gwintsàl gwîindhaa gwigwìłtsąįį goorahnyaa t'agwaihnyàa.
20.52 Zhyą̀ą chųų vęę tsił kat t'ôonch'yaa kwàt zhik vanh yahahkàa.
Duuyeh tǫǫ nìch'itsirahthat t'ôonch'yaa.
Vành yahkàa gwiizhìk gwizhrįh nìch'itsigahthàt.
Nijìn tsił kat ts'ooghaih izhìk hee tthak gîilk'įį.
Ts'ą̀' jyàanch'yaa gwiizhìk khàyahahkàa reh.
21.13 Tseerii'in k'ìt t'igwii'in gwinyàa.
Łyâa lęįį *thousand* diłkhwąįį vàràhnyàa.
Ch'iidì' kwaiik'ìt gwintsìi tthak, *not one live.*
21.36 Gwiizhìk t'ee dàa nàgwąąhjìk tł'ee t'ee, "Tthak gwit'eh agàa tthak nǫ̌ǫhtii," nyaa vàràhnyàa, aii *Goghwaii.*
"Gwit'aanghaa gǫ̀ǫlįį jì' eenjit."
"Àąhą'," vàràhnyàa.
21.48 "Jyàa dàgwą̀htsii shachaa deek'ìt jyàa dìneegweheenjyàa googàa it'ee sheenjit gwinzįį. Akò' neerohoojyàa," nyaa vàràhnyàa.
Kwàt ch'izhii naii ts'ą̀' geheedàa ts'ą̀' jyàa dìgeheelyàa t'iginch'yaa gàa yaa'àt t'iizhìk aii naii zhrįh nyaa giyàhnyaa.[22]
Khaiinjii chųų vęę tthak neegaajil googàhnyàa.
It'ee reh.

22. The meaning of this is: "They would do the same to whomever was coming down – another tribe or group." —JE

20.40 They also went to *Barter Island.*
They went at night.
I'm saying they really put up a hot little war.
That's what they say about them.
20.52 Along the ocean it is all tundra.
They never fought during the night.
They started fighting at dawn.
They all hid behind the snowdrifts.
Then they would wait for daylight.
21.13 When there was fighting going on, it looked like they were playing, they say.
They say he killed about a thousand people.
Not one person was left alive in the big village.
21.36 After the fight was over, "Look underneath everything," *Goghwaii* said, they say.
"In case there's any place where they could hide."
They said, "Yes."
21.48 And then he told his army, "I feel better now that I got revenge over my younger brother's death. Let's go!" he said, they say.
They could have killed anyone they met on their way home, but they say he said he wanted to kill only the ones who killed his brother.
They say he went all along the *Arctic Coast* and came back.
That's all.

Johnny Frank

Goghwaii

<jfcm2b>

JF0.15 *Òol Tì'* tr'ôołkhwąįį, ąįįts'ą' gwanaa gweedhàa ts'ą' Vantee Gwich'in nąįį datthak gehnjìt Dagǫǫ hàa datthak zhik zhyąą niłigiighan ts'ą' gwizhrįh t'igii'ìn.[1]

0.47 Aii chan Ch'itsyàa, Nàantsąįį nąįį hàa gǫǫlįį ts'ą' nihtee t'igiich'yaa ts'ą' gohch'it ndàa niłagahòoghan ts'ą' gwinzįį googàa neegwadadhat gwinlęįį łyâa gwinzįį gąhchųų kwaa gooràhnyàa.

1.05 Tthak tr'àhahchųų dąį' tthah diichì' yeezhak tr'oontà' ts'ą' tsįį chìraadhàk ts'ą' dàk kheechìraadhàk.

Jyàhts'ą' t'ee shin, khaii hàa gweedhàa gwinyàa.

1.20 Aii gwik'ìighai' gwats'an gwinzįį neegahòlit łyâa dinjii lęįį àn dhidlìt.

Geedan niłigeeghàn.

1.36 Izhìk dąį' *Goghwaii*, dagachàa hàa łi'hàa dinjii vik'ìt t'ii'in kwaa ginlįį ts'ą' reh.

Gweedhàa tthak goorahàahkhwàa giveegǫǫkàt rantii googàa łyâa gògwàntrìi.

1.52 Aiitł'ęę gòhch'it t'ee łyâa zhyąą chìgeendak k'ìt t'inch'yaa ts'ą' chan yee'àt chųų vęę chan Ch'eekwaii ts'ą' gahàa'òo.

2.07 Zhik niveh iłtsąįį, giveenjit iłtsąįį izhìk goorîiłkhwąįį kwàa.

Gwidigiin'oo ts'ą' daganlì' zhrįh hàa reh gogwandàii.

Ts'ą' reh gooshìi kwaa ts'ą' neeshreegâahch'yàa.

Oo'àt k'eegii'òo hee Ch'eekwaii, dinjii Ch'eekwaii nàatł'įį zhyąą chųų vęę di'oo'ee reh.

Aiits'ą' ch'iitthàn gwazhrąįį gee'aa, toh gii'įį ts'ą'.

2.31 Izhìk hee reh, łyâa reh Ch'eekwaii gîitth'àk.

Shrii zhrįh hàa goots'ą' galgihìłjìl, akhài' reh aii *Goghwaii* ootthàn chìilnąįį ts'ą' goots'ą' ginkhìi.

---

1. The Vantee Gwich'in are the people from around the *Old Crow* area of the northern *Yukon Territory*. The Dagǫǫ or Takudh are an extinct band of Canadian Gwich'in who inhabited the upper *Porcupine River* in the mid-19th century.
—CM

Johnny Frank

Goghwaii

<jfcm2b>

JF0.15 After *Òol Tì'* was killed, the Vantee and Dagǫǫ Gwich'in fought one another for a long time.

0.47 Some of them were Ch'itsyaa and some were Nàantsaii, and they lived in the same place, and they fought for many years during this time, but they didn't even get a good night's sleep, they say.

1.05 When everyone slept at one time, they put awls beneath their heads to keep themselves awake.

They did this all summer and all winter, they say.

1.20 Things became better between them after that, but lots of people were killed.

They fought one another.

1.36 At that time, there was nobody like *Goghwaii* and his younger brother.

People were always trying to kill them, but it was really hard to do it.

1.52 *Goghwaii* and his brother got very tired of it so they went over to the Inuit living on the coast.

2.07 Neither one of them got killed even though the Inuit formed an army to get them.

The brothers got away with just their bare hands and survived.

They had no food and were in poor health when they arrived.

There were lots of Inuit all along the *Arctic Coast*.

So they were walking toward them using short spears.

2.31 They both spoke the Iñupiaq language too.

The Inuit ran up to them with knives, but *Goghwaii* talked to them.

2.50 "Akhài' łyâa khai' shalàk nąįį googàa diihàahkhwàa gwankàgantii aii gwits'ì' zhyąą gwee'àn neerihii'òo ts'ą' diishìi kwaa dineegògwàntrii t'igwii'in.

Nakhwats'ą' gwiizųų t'igwihee'yàa kwaa t'ôonch'yàa.

3.05 Zhyąą gwintsàl nakhwàa t'igwihèech'yaa tł'ęę dineenjit gwinzįį ts'ą' nakhweełèerihee'àl," jyàa gavàhnyaa ts'ą'.

"Ą̀ąhą'," giyàhnyaa akhàgiyuunyàa.

3.15 Aiits'ą' gavàh yìgwìich'įį, vachàa chan vàh ts'ą'.

Aiits'ą' nih'àn reh Ch'eekwaii tłįh gaa'įį.

3.26 Gwinzįį gook'aandak, gòhch'it t'ee łyâa zhyąą neegaak'ìi gaadlìt.

Goghwaii heezyaa (adlaa).

Łyâa gwinzįį neegaak'ìi ts'ą' t'ee giveenjit gwinzįį ts'ą' t'ee reh dachàa hàh gwaandàk.

3.46 "Nìhkàa vành łì'hàa vành dą' hee nèehìidà'àl t'ôonch'yaa, zhik vàh gwinch'įį aii geegwahandak kwàa.

Jyàanch'yaa giłchųų gwiizhìk goochàa k'eech'ąąhtrit jì' gahàahchyaa kwaa t'inch'yàa," dachàa ahnyaa vàràhnyàa.

4.10 "Kwàt shant'ee yaaghà' vàa gwihch'įį nąįį tthak jyàa dìhihłyàa," ts'ą' jyàa dachàa àhnyaa ts'ą' t'ee reh khàa ts'ą' reh gwinzįį gaachįį kwàa.

Nìhkèe vành gwìizųų t'igihee'yàa gwats'ą' t'iginch'yaa akwàt.

4.18 Aiits'ą' t'ee reh vành dąį' hee reh vachàa Yahdii nah'in k'iighai' vành dąį' hee khai' khàchèe'ąįį ts'ą' yaaghà' iłchųų nąįį zhyąą chàa k'èech'iłtrit ts'ą' gwizhrįh reh.

4.46 Jyàanch'yaa ts'ą' neehotł'įį ts'ą' t'ee reh yik'ì' chan òonjìk.

Adan t'eh oo'àt ditłįh hàa gwich'įį aii adant'eh jyàa dìnlìk ts'ą' zhyąą tsił làii kat reh zhyąą neegohòo'oo ts'ą' ijii lì' reh gaadlìt.

5.10 Àkwàt aiitł'ęę, neegwadadhat ch'ìhłak reh oo'àt gwigwinch'ì' gooràhnyàa.

Kwàt łyâa zhyąą Ch'eekwaii àgwąhtsii Ch'eekwaii dìitth'ak vàràhnyàa.

2.50 "Our own relatives tried to kill us, and that's the reason why we're here.
We won't do anything bad to you because we're in such poor health and have no food.
3.05 We want to live here for a little while until we regain our good health," he told them.
So they say the Inuit said "Yes" and decided not to kill them.
3.15 And so *Goghwaii* and his younger brother stayed there.
And then they became close to the people they stayed with.
3.26 The Inuit took good care of them, and they even gained weight.
They didn't know what *Goghwaii* had in mind for them, though (laughs).
Finally they were back in good health, so he told his brother this:
3.46 "You and I are leaving early tomorrow morning.
Cut their throats while they are sleeping so they won't say anything."
That's what he told his younger brother, they say.
4.10 "I'll do the same to the people I'm staying with," he told his brother.
They didn't sleep very well that night because they would do something bad the next morning.
4.18 So *Goghwaii's* brother woke up quietly early the next morning by looking up at the Big Dipper in the sky and cut the people's throats like there was nothing to it.
4.46 *Goghwaii* got up and got dressed and did the same.
He took their bows and arrows and walked away on the snowdrifts, and nobody knew what happened to them.
5.10 They stayed with the Inuit there for a year, they say.
They say *Goghwaii* spoke their language very well too.

5.23 Aiits'ą' yaaghà' hee k'ineegii'oo, ts'ą' t'ee k'ì' agàa Ch'eekwaii gîiłkhwąįį k'ì' ts'an gaa'įį roh.

5.34 Chan hee ninzhuk gwahàadhak, chan hee valàk nąįį giyàa teeneegwiin'ąįį.

Chan hee tr'àl neegii'òo.

Aiits'ą' yee'àt *Barter Island*[2] ch'ii'àn hee gahàa'òo.

5.56 Ch'eekwaii zhyąą dachan k'ìt t'inch'yaa, ch'adąį' hee googwandàk zhat k'aadhàk gwik'iitł'ųų reh t'igii'ìn.

6.06 Ch'eekwaii hàa gwinch'ì' aii inghan tł'ęę reh łyâa nint'aii giyàandàii.

Ch'eekwaii zhyąą dachan k'ìt t'inch'yaa tthak zhyąą goonôoghaa zhyąą łanagoodii'ee ts'ą' reh.

6.25 Ch'eekwaii nèekwąįį gôołkhwąįį ts'ą' gooriheeghàa googàhnyaa ts'ą' reh.

Aii Ch'eekwaii k'yąą gavàh ginkhii gwiizhìk t'ee oohìlzhìn.

Nint'aii giyàandaii ts'ą' łi'hàa Ch'eekwaii nitsii nèekwąįį nint'aii giits'ąįį na'ahchįį.

6.41 Dzaa gweedàk giigìn eeghaii nàdhàt.

It'ee giyuunyaa ts'ą' Ch'eekwaii nint'aii gàa yigìn ch'ìhłak iihàhchàa eenjit reh.

6.51 Aii zhik t'ee gwak'ąhtii zhyąą diideetak gwìltł'àt.

Zhyąą nàdhat googàa dèehee'yàa *figùre* gwìłtsąįį reh t'inch'yàa.

7.04 Ch'eekwaii khàshràantrat gwiizhìk Ch'eekwaii nint'aii ch'angwàhts'ąįį yigìn ąhtsìt.

Ch'angwąhts'ąįį chan aii jyàanch'yaa googàa aiitł'ęę danlì' tr'inliijii vich'yàa nànthâal nąįį vàràhnyàa.

7.24 Kwàt zhyąa ch'iidàk nìrìilzhii gwizhrįh googàa yeezhòk diitth'àn tee hee k'ìgwaanąįį ts'ą' k'ąh iłchįį ts'ą' diikwaiichàn tee, diitsèhtak gàa ch'ii'àn.

Oo'àt dinjii àn nàa'ąį' gwats'ą' tthak googàa dinjii eh'àn tr'ìneezhii vàràhnyàa.

2. *Barter Island* is located in the *Beaufort Sea* off the northern coast of *Alaska*. The modem Inuit village of *Kaktovik* is located there, and its residents are probably the direct descendants of those whom the Gwich'in fought in the protohistoric period. —CM

5.23 And so they got back, and they even took the Inuit's bows and arrows for their own.

5.34 A long period of time went by when his own relatives didn't get along with him again.

So *Goghwaii* and his brother took off somewhere.

They went over to *Barter Island*.

5.56 There were lots of Inuit there, and they already heard about their coming, but *Goghwaii* didn't know about this.

6.06 This happened after they killed the other Inuit they stayed with, and these Inuit knew he was very strong too.

This time the Inuit rushed up to them and surrounded them so that there was no way out.

6.25 They say they planned to kill both of them because of what they did before.

Goghwaii was alert and was speaking to them in their language.

The Inuit knew he was very strong, so they chose two strong Inuit men for him.

6.41 The two strong Inuit men stood right here on each side of him.

Now they thought they could grab his arms on either side.

6.51 But *Goghwaii* was watching out for them.

He was standing in the middle of the crowd and figuring out what he would do.

7.04 One Inuit gave a warning by letting out a loud cry, and the two Inuits grabbed both of his arms.

He somehow freed his hands, and they say he even skinned his arms doing that.

7.24 He made it out of the huge crowd by crawling through their legs, sometimes crawling sideways.

Somehow he got away from the crowd, they say.

7.41 Aii gwiizhìk vachàa aii reh, oochìt dinjii nint'aii neekwąįį yąhtsit aii reh zhat gwats'ą' hiljii vàràhnyàa.

7.52 Aiits'ą' t'ee zhik dineh'àn tr'ìneezhii, tr'agwazhrąįį k'i', k'i' hàa ch'ii'àn hìłshùu k'ìt t'ii'in[3] googàa ch'ii'àn k'i' hàa ant'òo.

Aii zhrįh drinjir dhidlii t'eh ànts'ą' ch'ii'àn tr'ìneezhii k'ìt t'iizhìk vàràhnyàa.

K'i' hadàl googàa gwandaa t'agwąhkhan neehidik reh.

8.12 Aiitł'ęę oo'ęę neezhii ts'ą' t'ee reh ch'ihłęę gwatsal valàk nąįį giik'àa t'inyaa geh'àn gwinzįį idìk tł'ęę t'ee giihàa tineegwa'àk.

8.32 Oo'ęę neezhii ts'ą' t'ee reh vachàa oo'àt gwats'ą' hiljii ts'ą' t'ee zhik vitì', vitłįh hàa tr'ôolkhwąįį.

Aii goolàràa gǫǫlii, naagąįį gii'įį, aii ik tr'inghan tł'ęę aii ts'an tr'àl inlii aii hàa t'ee niveh oiinkwàt.

8.47 Neets'uuch'in nąįį gàa.

Aiits'ą' t'ee yee'àt ch'ii'àn tr'ahàajil gwinyàa oo'àt *Ch'ųhnjik* garàhnyaa reh, yaaghat *Nizhihgijii Vatthàl* gwinyàa aii *Shrii Tł'it* t'agwaràhnyàa.

Shrii Tł'it, Dizhèe Tł'it, Dizheenjik gwitł'it.

9.12 Aii ch'ii'an gahàajil ts'ą' reh, oo'àt chan łyâa zhyąą, izhìk gwats'an dinjii t'ee Ch'eekwaii, Dinjii Zhuh hàa gwinzįį nihłaa'in kwaa gwinlęįį neegwadadhat gwin'è' gwinyàa.

9.30 Aiits'ą' oondàk ddhah tee Ch'eekwaii nąįį gwich'įį łi'hàa dik'èegąątìi.

Izhìk chan gàandaii ts'ą' yaaghà' gwà'àn ànts'ą' gwinlęįį yeedak ddhah kat ts'ąįį gwinìginjil gooràhnyàa.

9.45 Aiits'ą' zhik ch'ii'àn antł'it gwitł'it hee zhyąą ch'atthąįį adagâa'įį.

Ts'ą' ch'ii'àn ànłigeedàa ts'ą' gohch'it ch'iindàa *Chųų Vęę* gwats'ą' yìich'ya' izhìk ch'iitthàn k'àii chyah nąht'aii gwinyaa han gwintsìi.

10.01 Aii gwiyeedak ch'ii'ęę geeghanh k'įį reh khàgaajìl akhài' yeezhee k'àii chyah kat Ch'eekwaii hanłiłt'aii gwinyàa.

3. Today the word *t'ii'in* would be pronounced *t'igwii'in.* —KP

7.41 Two other strong men grabbed his brother at the very same time, and they say that's when he got killed.

7.52 And so *Goghwaii* got away from the crowd of Inuit, although they all tried their best to hit him with arrows.

Somehow he got away under the flying arrows, they say.

8.12 Then he came back by himself.

But his younger brother was killed.

8.32 His relatives and his father who were killed before were rich and had beads.

Beaded tunics and outfits were made for him which he hid somewhere.

He bought an army with these beaded tunics and outfits.

8.47 Even the Neetsuu'chin people from this area were part of it.

So they say the whole army went over to *Nizhihgijii's Caribou Fence*, at the place called *Ch'ųhnjik* (*'Charred Wood Creek'*).

And the *Shrii Tł'it* river.

The *Shrii Tł'it,* the *Dizhèe Tł'it,* the *Coleen River* valley.

9.12 They went over that way.

It was in this area that the Inuit and Indians didn't get along for many years, they say.

9.30 Then there were other Inuit living in the mountains who were alert all the time.

He also was aware of them so they went over another mountain through deep snow, they say.

9.45 So they traveled along a steep mountain pretending to be caribou.

Then they finally came into view of the *Arctic Ocean.*

They came near a big river where they say there were willows along the banks.

10.01 When they arrived at the end of that steep mountain, below them in the brush was an Inuit village, they say.

Gwiizhìk yeendaa *Chųų Choh Vęę* deedì' zhyąą tsił dagàįį kat gwahàa'ee t'ee zheh gwaghoo reh t'ôonch'yaa gwinyàa.

10.19 Łì'hàa Ch'eekwaii lęįį.

Aiits'ą' reh yeezhee k'àii khyųų gwats'an Ch'eekwaii tr'ìk ch'iidįį k'il kàhèe.

Ch'iidąą zhyąą reh vadzaih gwits'èech'in kwaa gwiizhìk oodeedąą zhyąą reh dinjii gwìch'in niił'in vàràhnyàa.

10.45 Aiits'ą' kwàt zhyąą geenoh'ìt k'eegwaanąįį ts'ą' geendih tr'eechìitthak vàràhnyàa.

"Aii gwiizhìk zhyąą vadzaih adôo'įį ts'ą' zhik gwà'àn zhyąą khàntł'eedhoh'ee," jyàa nyaa vàràhnyàa.

10.57 "Nijìn gwìdi' tr'ineezhii jì', gwiizhìk hee ch'iitthàn nakhwat'àii hàa drindàhohdàa ts'ą' zhik han nihts'įį teet'įh jyàa dàhǫhjyàa," nyaa vàràhnyàa.

11.08 "*Line up* hohłyàa," ts'ą'.

Jyàa dìi'in gohch'it t'ee reh gwintsàl gatr'agwąąhłįį k'ìt t'ii'in ts'ą' reh nèenjik reh neehidiindìk t'ee reh k'il tsal dąąch'yaa reh khał kat deedhilii.

Ts'ą' t'ee reh ch'iidì' gèendih gwik'ee ch'eeluu gwiizhìk hee ch'iitthàn ddhah ndįh reh gwindìłuu'iinjìk k'ìt t'igwiizhìk gwinyàa.

11.33 Aiits'ą' zhik han nihts'įį teedik dì'aii gwiizhìk yi'eedìt hee łinèegàatsìt.

Aiitł'ęę reh khai' zhyàa jyàa dìgwiizhìk zhyąą Ch'eekwaii nąįį lęįį zhat gwigwich'įį łee aii tthak ginghàn.

11.46 Ooch'iindàa tł'oo gwazhàl khànkìgatthaii gwiizhìk t'ee ch'iidì' gwintsìi ts'ą' reh łuu ddhàk gwakat dàraanjaa k'ìt t'ôonch'yaa gwinyàa.

Aii ghootìlzhrąįį gwinyàa.

They saw smoke coming out of their houses.

They say that at the same time, they could also see round igloos along the Arctic coastline from where they were.

10.19 There were really lots of Inuit living there.

Then they spotted an Inuit woman coming alongside the brush gathering wood.

She acted like she saw humans up on the ridge, but she wasn't sure because she didn't expect to see caribou there, they say.

10.45 So the woman walked away, they say.

But she kept coming back to make sure of what she saw, so *Goghwaii* told them, "pretend to be grazing caribou," they say.

10.57 *Goghwaii* told his people, "Run down the ridge once the woman disappears.

Then spread out along the river and make sure nobody sees you," he said, they say.

11.08 So, "Line up that way."

That Inuit woman moved about acting like she was suspicious, but finally she put a few dry willows on her sled and left.

And that was when *Goghwaii's* people came down the mountain ridge like an avalanche, they say.

11.33 So everybody lined up alongside the river.

And then they just killed all the Inuit in the village.

They say those Inuit were good hunters too.

They knew there was another big village not far from there.

They had already seen it from the ridge, and that was where *Goghwaii* and his brother had killed Inuit before.

11.46 They came near the village crawling in the high grass, and when they peeked out from the grass, they say the village of igloos looked like mountains of broken pack ice piled along the shore.

They say the Inuit were like a dark mass, standing there among their igloos.

12.12 Aiits'ą' izhìk zhat jyàa dòonch'yaa gwiizhìk it'ee reh *Goghwaii figure* gwìłtsąįį.

"Dzaa gwats'an nihk'yąą tsił khàndanoht'ii aii nihkat dòhłii ts'ą' ch'iikyąą vìgwèech'in kwaa ohtsìi.

Ts'ą' veegoh'ìt nihts'įį ch'ii'àn tthak gwik'yùhjyàa," nyàa vàràhnyàa.

12.46 Oondàa gwiizhìk giveenìhihshyàa nyaa vàràhnyàa.

Aiits'ą' t'ee deetthàn hàazhìi.

Oochìt Ch'eekwaii ch'iindàa gwazhrąįį a'aa giyąąh'in ts'ą' łąą it'ee reh narahąąh'yàa gąhthee inzhii gwiizhìk hee zhik zhah daagąįį datthak tanzhrąįį nàgwaanaii gwinyàa.

Nàgwaanaii ts'ą' ch'iichyąą kwàt zhyąą njuu gwìch'in gaa'ee nàgwaanàii.

Aii gwiizhìk reh oochìt zhat nagwazhrąįį' ąh'ee vàràhnyàa.

13.20 Tòh di'įį ts'ą' ahàa, it'ee neech'an'ee reh t'ii'ìn.

13.29 "Shishìi kwàa, it'ee łyâa sheegògwàntrìi chan nakhwats'ą' nalghal t'ishi'ìn," jyàa nyàa.

K'ahooshinjii t'ihch'yaa kwàa, Ch'eekwaii nąįį shrii zhrįh hàa tr'ahaahkhwàa ginyaa ts'ą' ch'iindàk kwàt zhyąą njuu tr'iinlìt k'ìt t'igwiizhìk.

13.52 Gwiizhìk oochìt nagwazhrąįį'ąh'ee vàràhnyàa.

Ts'ą' t'ee vats'ą' nahgwàn tr'eedàa gwiizhìk it'ee k'adeedii'in gàa reh dinjii vah gwiindàii reh tłįh a'įį dhìłkhwàįį.

14.04 It'ee gwàdak tr'eetǒąąhkhàa.

Łì'hàa zhyąą vijìh veenìriinjil ts'ą' goots'įį neetoaahkhàa oodeedąą tsił nihk'ìt taradąąt'uu jyàa dòonch'yaa izhìk dzaa gwats'ą' reh t'ii'ìn.

14.21 Jii kwat zhyąą gwit'įh ch'ii'àn zhyąą reh vashrąįh dąątth'ak k'ìt t'ôonch'yaa gwit'įh zhyąą tseenaazhii reh.

14.30 Aii zhìt ch'iichyąą it'ee łąą veenìrinjyàa gwiizhìk gwik'ìitł'it k'inidik vàràhnyàa.

14.39 K'inilghàa shrii khàahnaii vàràhnyàa.

Gwiizhìk kwat zhik tthak nàràajìl.

12.12 *Goghwaii's* army was waiting while he was figuring out what to do next.
"Cut up the snowdrifts here and pile them up on both sides.
I'll be coming from down there, and it will be hard for them to see you.
So hide down behind them," he said, they say.

12.46 While they were doing that, they say, *Goghwaii* went out there to meet the Inuit.
He started walking down to them.
And just when he came into view, they say all the Inuit spotted him.

13.20 He was using his cane as he was walking toward them, trying to fool them.

13.29 "I have no food and I'm in poor health," he told them.
He had no choice but had to go there, he told them.
He said he was in no shape to defend himself or fight.
The Inuit planned to kill him with their knives, and everybody surged toward him like a moving island.

13.52 While he was standing out there, they say, people recognized who he was.

14.04 But just when they got near he turned around and started to walk fast back up toward his army still using his cane.
His army was hiding there behind the snowdrifts.

14.21 Behind the snowdrifts were so many people that they looked like a moving mountain.
They say they were all hiding.

14.30 Just when the Inuit caught up and were closing in on him, he got back to where his warriors were hiding, they say.

14.39 He turned around quickly and grabbed his knife, they say.

Zhyą̀ą vahk'ah ch'iitthàn nìn'ee k'ìt t'inch'yaa aii zhìt ch'iichyąą zhyą̀ą njuu k'ìt t'igwiizhìk vàràhnyàa.

14.55 Nahts'ą̀hts'ą̀' k'i' hàa ahshìi k'ìt t'igwii'in, zhyą̀ą gwihiljii nàgwaanaii ts'ą̀' t'ee reh.

Yeendaa kwaiik'ìt gòo'ąįį gwats'à' ch'iindaa tr'inzhii łyâa zhyàa teetł'an tr'iinjil gwiizhìk it'ee oondaa k'idik vàràhnyàa.

15.12 Yaaghà' ch'angwą̀hts'ąįį chan *Dachan Naatąįį*.

Aii chan niveh chìt, *Général,* aii chan vik'ìt t'igwii'in kwaa reh.

Aii t'ee jyàa dìgiizhìk gwiizhìk kwàt t'ee *line up* ginlii t'igii'ìn.

15.27 Oondaa łineegàatsit reh, aii googàa yeenjì' Ch'eekwaii tr'ìk tik nąįį reh yeenjì' googàa galhìłjil gwinyàa.

15.38 Oondaa tsił ch'akwanh dha'ąįį aii chan łuu hàa giyahtsii t'inch'yàa.

Aii gogwaghan gwiizhìk reh t'igiizhìk googàa t'ee gavàa gwiindàii.

Aii t'ee oonjit *Neegwachoonjik* gàràhnyaa,

Ch'eekwaii tr'ikhit gǫ̀ǫlįį dą̀į' reh.

15.52 Aiits'ą̀' reh t'igii'ìn.

Gwiizhìk yee'àt *Bartèr Islànd* gwinyaa chan *town* jyàa dàgwą̀htsii gòo'ą̀įį, izhìk gwats'ą̀' chan Ch'eekwaii tr'ik nèekwąįį nąįį yeediidì' hìlgìk.

16.03 Oondaa gohch'it tr'igwinghan gwiizhìk vàa gwaraandak, Ch'eekwaii tr'ìk tik nąįį yeenjì' galhìłjil gwinyàa.

Yeenji' tr'iinzhii zhyą̀ą tan kat zhyą̀ą k'eehehndik k'ìt t'inch'yaa ôoltł'ee k'it t'iizhìk vàràhnyàa (adlaa).

16.19 K'eejit dą̀į' hee Ch'eekwaii tr'ìk gwik'ìt gal'ą̀hjil reh.

Gwahàadhat kwaa yeenii tr'ee shraadą̀ąhkhwat, it'ee givinghan reh.

Aiitł'ęę chan yeedì' chan, dinjii nèekwąįį nąįį gook'ìh nànàhò'òo.

There was a bluff and down below it looked like a big island covered with spruce trees moving towards him, they say.

14.55 The arrows fell down together like snowflakes until there was nobody left alive.

Then he started walking down towards the village, and his warriors were only halfway down by the time he was already there, they say.

15.12 On the other end was a general named *Dachan Naataii.*

He was another general on *Goghwaii's* side.

Everybody was lined up going down.

15.27 When they arrived down there, they found out that somehow three Inuit women had escaped, they say.

15.38 Also all the igloos out there were made of ice.

While they were killing everybody, these women escaped.

This was when there were lots of Inuit living in the village called *Neegwachoonjik.*

15.52 And then there was another place called *Barter Island.*

It was a big town, they say, and two more Inuit women escaped to there too.

16.03 When everybody was killed, his people told him about those three Inuit women, they say.

He went after them in a flash, they say (laughs).

16.19 The women had left long ago, but he came back in no time, meaning he had already killed them.

When he came back, he went after the other women too, even though two men had already started to follow them.

16.33 Izhìk chan vàaragwaandak[4] chan yeedi' k'igwaanaii vàràhnyàa.

Gwintsàl gwihìlthat ts'ą̀' yeedįį tr'eeshraadą̀ąhkhwat vàràhnyàa.

16.40 Tthak givinghan reh.

Aiitł'ęę t'ee *Bartèr Islànd* deedì' tthak gahàajil chan gwintsii gwigwinghàn.

Izhìk t'ee vachaa gwats'ą̀' hiljii reh.

16.56 Izhìk k'inidik vàràhnyàa.

17.09 Zhat chan hee tǫǫ nàgwaatth'at gwiizhìk hee t'ee jyàa dìgiizhìk.

Gwindii tsił eenoh'ìt gîilch'įį nats'àa goorahąą'yàa gò?

It'ee łąą gwiihàanii gwintsàl Ch'eekwaii lęįį tr'ôołkhwąįį gwinyaa t'iihnyàa.

17.29 Aii ndàa gwàa'ąį' t'ee łyâa zhyąą yeenjìt dąą ch'yaa *hundred* tr'ôolkhwąįį kwàt yaaghà' chan roh.

17.38 Izhìk t'inyaa, "It'ee shachaa deek'ìt neegàhòlìt akò' neerahoojyàa," nyaa vàràhnyàa.

17.51 Dachàa deek'ìt łyâa dinjii lęįį dhiłkhwąįį vàràhnyàa.

Izhìk gwats'an giyàa nineegwìn'ąįį kwaa.

Aiits'ą̀' gohch'it zhyąą ch'oonjih hàa neeshrâahch'yaa dhidlìt, gwandaii chan dhahkhwąįį kwàa.

18.07 Gwiizhìk t'ee shìh kwaa, ts'ą̀' gwiizhìk shik zhyąą giihaahkhwàa giyeegǫǫkàntii.

Gwiizhìk it'ee yaaghà' *Tr'igoozhrìk Tì'* aii t'ee vigii aii òonjìk.

Tr'igoozhrìk Vinh reh, aii vigii.

18.25 *Tr'igoozhrìk* oozhii aii t'ee khèedąį' gwànaa reh, ninzhùk kwaa gwanaa t'agogwàhnyàa.

Aii t'ee oonjùk tth'aih gwandàii łee.

18.36 Shįį tr'iinin ihłįį gwànaa.

18.44 Neehidik veegògǫ̀ǫtrii[5] neech'idzah'ak gwiizhìk, aii geh'àn t'ee giyûułkhwąįį łąą giihàahkhwàa kwaa akhài' reh.

---

4. I think today *vàaragwaandak* would be *vàa gwaraandak* —KP
The tape shows a contrast between this line and the pronunciation in 16.03. —CM

5. The word *veegògǫ̀ǫtrii* is usually pronounced today as *veegògwàntrii.* —KP

16.33 They told him about those other two women also, they say.

They say he went after them and it took only a little while before he got back too.

16.40 That meant he killed both of them as well.

Then they went down further, killing all the way to *Barter Island.*

That's where his brother got killed.

16.56 They say he arrived at *Barter Island* during the night.

17.09 They were hiding behind snowdrifts around the village.

How could anybody see them?

When they started killing, they say, lots and lots of Inuit were killed.

17.29 Hundreds of Inuit were killed there, and the same number were killed at the other village.

17.38 "All right. Now that I've had my revenge over my younger brother, let's go home," he said, they say.

17.51 They say *Goghwaii* killed lots of people over the death of his younger brother.

They never bothered him again after that.

He suffered so much from after effects from all the killing he did that he couldn't even kill animals after that.

18.07 There was no food, and everybody tried to kill him all the time.

Meanwhile, he married *Tr'igoozhrik Vinh,* who was the daughter of *Tr'igoozhrik Tì'.*

18.25 Many years later, I discovered that they were still alive over there.

18.36 That's when I myself was a child.

18.44 Finally, they were killed because they got so old they couldn't walk anymore.

Johnny Frank

Tł'èevì' Tì'
Ch'eechyah Ch'ìhłak [1]

<jfcmlb>

JF8.15 Aii *Tł'èevì' Tì'* dinjii nèekwąįį vigii gǫ̀ǫlįį yàh gwich'įį.
Ch'ìhłęę chan łyâa dinjii nint'aii nilįį vàràhnyàa. Nitsìi.
Aiits'ą' oondàk *Gwazhał* ghài' hee shin gwigwich'įį.
Akhài' Ch'eekwaii ęęgoonah'yà' łii ts'ą' reh.

8.42 Aiitł'ęę Ch'eekwaii oo'àn neegiijil Ch'eekwaii niveh hàa goots'ą' gahàajìl.
Two hundred àgąąch'yąą gooràhnyąą.

9.07 Gwats'ą' gahâajil ts'ą' giveek'eegiidàl *Tł'èevì' Tì'* aii reh, nąhjyàa Ch'eekwaii, Dinjii Zhuh hàa nihłiighan tthak gineegaandàii.
Aiits'ą' reh, zhyąą "Shijyàa," googàhnyaa ts'ą' zhyąą.

9.26 Ch'eekwaii naii neegavan'ee ts'ą' reh gavàa shragwagwąhch'yàa, aagaa zhyąą Ch'eekwaii k'yąą chigidlii hee gaa t'iginyąą ts'ą' reh.
Zhyąą govaashragwąąhch'yaa googàa *Tł'èevì' Tì'* aii gàadandàii.

9.37 Aiits'ą' dijyàa naii reh t'àhnyaa,
"Naaghat deegii'in tsinteediigan'ee k'ìt t'igii'in zhyąą oodhǒozhin.
Zhyąą googohshįį k'ìt t'ohch'yàa."

10.00 Jyàa nyaa googàa aii nèekwąįį naii giveechìi t'igwinyaa kwàa.
Gwiizhìk eedan aii reh shrii shriit'ąhtsii di'įį.
Aii dzaa divìt zhyah'ee ts'ą' reh ootthan chųų, chųų giheenjyàa dąį' googàa aatłaa tthak jyàa dìgii'in.

10.16 Ts'ą' aii *Tł'èevì' Tì'* łyâa tthak gavàandàii.

1. A full English version of the way Johnny told the story of Tł'èevì' Tì' in 1933 was published by Robert McKennan (1965:67-68). It's surprising how many details of the 1972 and 1973 versions which follow here coincide with that telling forty years earlier. This is testimony to the excellent translating skills of McKennan's interpreter, John Fredson, and the remarkable stability of the narrative itself. The two variants recorded here by myself and Kathy Alexander less than six months apart illustrate some subtle differences in style and performance. —CM

Johnny Frank

Tł'èevì' Tì'
First Version

<jfcm1b>

JF8.15 There were two men living with *Tł'èevì' Tì'* who both had lots of children.

They say one man was also very strong. And tall.

They all lived close to the *Brooks Range* in the summertime.

After that the Inuit came sneaking up on them.

8.42 They went back over and returned with a whole army.

There were two hundred of them, they say.

9.07 And they all came over to them.

But *Tł'èevì' Tì'* remembered all the wars between the Inuit and Indians from before.

And then they pretended to call them "my friend" when they came.

9.26 They even taught them Inuit songs and were being friendly.

But *Tł'èevì' Tì'* knew what was going on.

9.37 And so he told his two friends,

"These Inuit are here to fool you.

Watch out for them and stay alert."

10.00 But they say the other two were not listening and were not interested.

Tł'èevì' Tì' had a big knife up his sleeve.

They watched them each time they left to get a drink of water.

10.16 And *Tł'èevì' Tì'* knew all about that.

Adan t'eh gavàh t'ii'ìn.
Aii gwiizhìk vigii nèekwąįį naii zhrįh gǫǫlįį,
Tł'èevì' aii vachaa, vàh chan.
Aiits'ą' va'at chan łyâa zhyąą *champion* nilįį.
Googàa nihłiriheeghàa.
Izhìk gwik'it t'igwihee'yàa kwaa, gwik'ìt t'igwiheèyàa nijìn shrit jyàa nìindhan ts'ą' gwizhrįh eedan aii reh t'ee łyâa nihłiriheeghàa gooriheeghàa eenjit t'igwii'in k'ìt gàandàii ts'ą' reh zheh gwizhìt googàa nihdìnidii kwàa.

10.55 Ts'ą' ehjyàa kwàt zhik ch'adhàh zheh gwach'ok gwii'ąįį.
Aii ch'adhàh teet'įh hee dik'į' nĕinlįį.
Oonaa dinjii lęįį niveh adàa dąį' hee.

11.13 Aiits'ą' t'ee reh, Ch'eekwaii naii giyuuheendal googàa gwits'ì' gwak'ą̆ąhtii ts'ą' gòhch'it hee t'ee reh dinjii nint'aii gavàh gwich'įį văihnyaa.
Aii reh Ch'eekwaii gàa nint'aii giyàandaii ts'ą' reh dinjii tik reh yąhtsit gwinyaa vàràhnyàa.

11.42 Kwàt ch'ìhłęę chan nèekwąįį naii yąhtsìt, *Tł'èevì' Tì'* aii reh.
Aii googàa reh vizheh dinjii lęįį googàa gwideetak ch'ii'àn gwatsal dinjii ghwahk'at ch'ii'àn, googàa reh chìhìltłee vàràhnyàa.

12.00 Aiits'ą' t'ee yee'àt nanchyàh kak izhìk hee nĭinzhii jèiinch'yaa gwiizhìk it'ee k'ì' hàa tthak giyuhjii.
Łyâa zhyąą *four yard,* jyàa dąhthee gwà'àn gookhyųų neeyihìidik gwiizhìk giits'ą' k'ì' hàa vàa ahtsin k'ìt t'ii'ìn googàa giyàhdak kwaa.
Ts'ą' nįįzhùk gweedhaa gwiizhìk aii dinjii nitsìi aii chan zhyąą googàa nehkaii giyìłtsąįį.

12.40 Aiits'ą' reh ch'ìhłęę aii khan tr'ookhwąįį.
Gwiizhìk va'at aii chan aii dinjii nitsìi tr'oontà'.

He had only two children, *Tł'eevì'* and her younger brother.
His wife was also really a champion.
But there was going to be a war.
He didn't know if there was going to be war or not, but *Tł'èevì' Tì'* knew that the Inuit were there to kill them, so he didn't go inside the house, not trusting them.
10.55 So he put his bows and arrows in between layers of skin on the side of the skin house.
He put them in there before many Inuit arrived.
11.13 And so he was really watching out for the Inuit.
Finally the Inuit knew that one man was very strong.
They say that three Inuit grabbed him because they knew he was strong.
11.42 Two other Inuit grabbed the other man, who was *Tl'èevì' Tì'*.
There were still lots of people inside his little house, but he went out like a flash among the crowd, they say.
12.00 So he got out to a wide open place while everyone was shooting at him with their arrows.
He was only about four yards away, and the arrows came to him like rain while he paced back and forth.
But they didn't hit him.
But meanwhile during that moment they wounded that big man.
12.40 So that other guy was killed quickly.
Meanwhile *Tł'èevì' Tì's* wife killed another big man outside.

Gwiizhìk aii tòh[2] hàa tr’iigok gwiizhìk ęhjyàa chan, aii chan dinjii dhagwat vàràhnyàa.

12.55 Aii gwak’ą̀ą tr’oonąhdak akhài’ vamà’ aii tr’iłdàii vàràhnyàa.

Aiits’ą̀’ oochìt chųų ts’ą̀’ ch’ehìlghaa ts’ą̀’ chųų zhìt tĕiinzhii.

Izhìk jèiinch’yaa ts’ą̀’ vakak tąąnaii ts’ą̀’ veenjit gwinzįį.

13.13 Gwiizhìk aii vigii tsyaa tsal, veejii chan vàa ts’ą̀’, zhyą̀ą łì’hàa zhyą̀ą nànch’àa’ee ts’ą̀’ reh gwit’eh chan gokwàa.

Geenoh’ìt chan gokwàa.

Izhìk jyaànch’yaa oochìt han teeghàih sheih tsal dą̂ąk’at aii eenoh’ìt tseeginiichįį gooràhnyàa.

Aii tr’iinin nèekwaįį naii.

13.34 Aii gwiizhìk gootì’ tr’ohjìi ts’ą̀’ dinjii t’ą̂ąch’yaa datthak k’ì’ lęįį di’įį datthak gòhch’it giyeeną̀ąhnii ts’ą̀’ k’ì’ nèekwąįį, ch’ìhłak hàa zhrįh tr’agoonąhthak ts’ą̀’ t’ee zhik jùu vikì’ kwaa naii ch’iindàk nanchyàh kat neehiijyàa.

Ch’iindàk tł’yaach’aną̀ąht’aii łyâa reh giinjyàa reh gwinyàa.

14.02 Aiits’ą̀’ it’ee tthak ch’iindàk tr’ineegiijil, gwiizhìk hee ch’adhàh teet’įh dik’ì’ ną̂ąhtsit ts’ą̀’ t’ee, aii shrii t’ăihnyaa zhrįh chan.

Akwàt aii k’ì’ aii reh dinjii nèekwąįį gòodhąįį niyahaathal jì’ àkwàt tik naii hàa.

14.28 Aii zhrįh teehahdàk eenjit t’ii’in vàràhnyàa.

Aiits’ą̀’ shrii hàa tthak gooheeghàa eenjit tr’ał tee chan gokwaa ch’iindàk zhyą̀ą geegǫh’it gokwaa ch’iindàk.

Kwàt aii tr’iinin nèekwąįį t’ee gavąąh’in, aiitl’ęę zhik geegwaandak aii gogwandàk aii nizįį aii t’ee zhik eeragwaandàk.[3]

2. The Gwich’in *tòh* was a short spear with a point made from sharpened caribou horn hafted to a wooden shaft. It is often translated as ‘cane’ even though it bore only a slight resemblance to a walking cane. To my knowledge, no examples of this important weapon and hunting tool have ever been collected and preserved in a museum setting. —CM

3. This sentence doesn’t make much sense. —JE

At the same time, the big man was being tortured with a short spear, they say.

12.55 They say *Tł'èevì' Tì's* wife was shot in her breast with an arrow.

So she ran for the water down at the river and went into it.

And she felt better with the water on it.

13.13 Meanwhile, the young boy and his older sister were there.

There was no place to hide.

They say they were hiding behind a small hump of ground down by the river.

Those two children.

13.34 Their father was being shot at until they only had one or two arrows left.

Whoever had one or two arrows left started to leave.

All the Inuit left in single file.

They say there was a really long line.

14.02 Then when they had all left, I'm saying *Tł'èevì' Tì'* ran back to his skin house and grabbed his bow and arrows, and his knife as well.

The arrows were saved in case two or three people cornered him.

14.28 They say he planned to shoot them in case they cornered him.

So he could kill them all with his knife, but there was no brush around and no place to hide up there.

The two children saw them and their story is good and that's what I'm telling about.

14.53 Aiits'ą' oozhee tr'iinin han nèegweedįį neekhangiijyàa izhìk reh dzaa gǫh'ìt gwatsal izhìk it'ee Ch'eekwaii ch'ìhłak k'ì' hàa t'ee yeenjit nĭinzhii łee googàa gàandaii kwàa.

15.07 K'iitthàn ahaa gwiizhìk hee yųąąhdàk googàa hilghaa vàràhnyàa.

Ch'ii'àn tr'anaantłee gwiizhìk yats'ą' k'ì' ìintrat, akhài' oondìt tł'eedik gwatsal khèhshii gwiizhìk ch'iindàa yazhràk aii yizhìt ch'ąhdàk.

15.30 Aiits'ą' yats'ą' nĕiinzhii.

Aiits'ą' tòh, tòh łyaa nizįį di'įį, aii hàa nahgǫǫ yeenìnidìk aii yits'inaatłak gwiizhìk zhàk ts'ą' shriiyuudąąhshyà' googàa yiigok kwàa gwalàįį hee yitrìl tł'ęę nìłtrit vàràhnyàa.

15.50 Aiits'ą' vitsin veekhagwaanaii ts'ą'.

Aiits'ą' ganaaandak gwiizhìk t'ee yeendee ndak dinjii tthał niin'ęę aii ch'iindak haazhii vàràhnyàa.

16.00 Ch'iindàk zhyąą vashraihdąątth'ak k'ìt t'inch'yaa ineegwazhraih ee'aa ts'ą' ch'iindàk gwahaljii gweetthal ch'iindàk.

Gòhch'it łyâa oondee łyâa nįįzhìt hee ch'iidàk teetsik gwatsal k'àii dòk trał tsal ghoo dha'ąįį, izhìk tik naii t'ee vàh tr'ałtĕiinjil vàràhnyàa.

16.27 Àkwàt t'ee gooch'įh neehidik gaa reh zhik gwà'àn nahgwàn tǫǫ gǫǫlįį ts'ą' reh ch'atr'àł chan gǫǫlįį.

Ts'ą' yee'àt nihłàa gaadzit tth'ak givîitth'ak ts'ą' t'ee giveełeehòzhìi.

16.43 Aii dinjii *two hundred* ndàa t'ąąch'yaa datthak dinjii ìhłęę zhrįh givinghàn.

Gookhàihkwài' agàa reh.

Tł'ęę oonaa neezhii ts'ą' oodee nijìn tr'ohjìi ch'yąą nìneezhii ch'iidàk kwàzhyąą[4] k'ì' kat nan gàa gwinzįį ìch'in kwàa, aii khaihłan nĭinlii dìłk'in.

Aii nyàa, tǫǫ hee dhidii vàràhnyàa.

4. *Kwàzhyąą* is short for *àkwàt zhyąą.* —KP

14.53 The children saw two Inuit hiding in ambush for *Tł'èevì' Tì'* when they crossed the river near them, but *Tł'èevì' Tì'* didn't know about it.

15.07 While walking down, they say, they aimed at him but missed him because he moved so fast.

He ran and shot at one of them while he was climbing over a little bank and shot him in the stomach.

15.30 Then *Tł'èevì' Tì'* came close to him.

He had a good short spear, which he used to jab him with, and they say he finally slashed him open around his stomach.

15.50 Then his whole intestine came out.

Then *Tł'èevì' Tì'* went after the people who were still walking in a single file a long distance away, they say.

16.00 The hills all looked like they were moving.

Tł'èevì' Tì' could be seen on the side of them until he got rid of most of the Inuit.

Finally, when he reached the little creek where there was lots of brush, three Inuit escaped into the brush, they say.

16.27 He followed their tracks but it got too dark and foggy.

He heard them whispering, but he walked away.

16.43 Just this one man killed almost two hundred people, even their main chief.

Tł'èevì' Tì' came back to where they were shooting at him earlier.

The ground was covered with arrows, which he picked up and used to build a fire.

He sat by his fire all night, they say.

17.18 Aiitł'ęę vành t'ee oochìt tr'iinin naii nôonjik ts'ą' da'at, t'ee gwinzįį neegwâanaii ts'ą' da'at chan mà' kat k'ì' khàneiintin ts'ą' aii chan chųų hàa yakat gwik'ee'ąhtryàa ts'ą' t'ee veenjit gwinzįį.

17.45 Łyâa dinjii lęįį dhìłkhwaįį vàràhnyàa, *Tł'èevì' Tì'*.

Aiitł'ęę khaii chan Ch'eekwaii lęįį gwi'ęę gwich'įh hàajil gwinyàa.

Aii t'ee *Gwazhał* ǫhts'aii łyâa git nitsìi dha'aįį izhìk eegaih gwigwich'įį.

Shrôondaii aii git nitsìi vęę ootthàn *Chųų Choh Vęę* gwats'ą' gwèech'in tthak.

18.11 Izhìk khaii divii eech'idiintł'įį ts'ą' reh khaii gwich'įį.

Voondee chan vàa ts'ą' *Tł'èevì' Tì'* voondee *Khàiidhiiluu* oozhii aii reh.

18.24 Aii chan Ch'eekwaii naii łyâa giihił'èe, nàhtryàa gi'gwàdhan lęįį aghan ts'ą' khàihkwaii giyàa'įį.

18.36 Izhìk chan Ch'eekwaii niveh lęįį k'eedàl.

Oodìt reh giyuundee, khàihkwaii ąįį, aii reh oaahkàt.

"Nachaa łyâa dinjii lęįį dhiłkhwaįį, khàihkwaii gwintsìi veegòo'aii chan dhìłkhwàįį.

Neerookhwaa jàghàii?" giyàhnyàa.

Akhài' aii *Khàiidhiiluu* łyâa geet'indhan kwàa.

"Shachaa dhŏohkhwąįį jì' yeenjit nanjuughat ch'ii'àn tr'iheedàa ts'ą', nankat tthak nikhweenjit niveh oohihkwàt ts'ą', yaaghà' *Chųų Choh Vęę* deedì' tthak tr'iheedàa ts'ą' tthak gwahaljii tr'agwahahtsyàa.[5]

19.14 Shachaa dhohkhwaa shrǫ'," gavàhnyaa ts'ą' it'ee nats'ąątèe ginyąą naii ts'ą' goolat naii gàa tree gooràhnyàa, ts'ą' akhàgògònyàa.

Aiitł'ęę googàa zhat gwigwich'įį *two hundred* andaa t'agâąch'yaa ts'ą' drin hee giyàhtsèe'in ts'ą' oodòk git kak gòodhaii nìgiihaahthal jì' eenjit jyàa digiyah'in googàa gòodhaii nìgiyaahshìi kwàa.

19.42 Neekaii agàa tthak t'igiyah'in googàa tthak geiigavahtsìi.

19.48 Aiits'ą' reh gòhch'it zhyąą akhàgiyuunyàa.

5. There are obvious parallels here with the story of Gogwhaii. —CM

17.18 After that, in the morning, he got his children back, washed his wife's wound, and took the arrow out of her breast.

She felt much better after that.

17.45 They say *Tł'èevì' Tì'* killed many people.

And they say more Inuit came over again after that, in the winter.

They lived on the other side of the *Brooks Range* beside a really big glacier.

Tł'èevì' Tì' stayed in a place overlooking the *Arctic Ocean* on purpose.

18.11 He stayed there and lived by snaring Dall sheep that winter.

His older brother, whose name was *Khàiidhiiluu,* was with him too.

18.24 The Inuit had respect for him because he killed lots of wolverine, and they thought of him as their chief.

18.36 An army of Inuit arrived there too.

They asked his brother,

"Your younger brother really killed lots of people.

He also killed a big chief.

May we kill him?" they said.

But *Khàiidhiiluu* really didn't like that and refused.

He told them, "If you kill my younger brother, I will go all over the country and buy myself a big army and come back along the whole *Arctic Coast* and kill everybody.

19.14 Don't kill my younger brother," he told them, and they just had no choice.

Some even cried and decided not to do it.

They still stayed there, and all two hundred of them played with him out on the glacier every day trying to corner him, but they just couldn't do it.

19.42 They even played ball with him, but he beat them all.

19.48 So they finally just quit.

Aiits'ą' *Khàiidhiiluu* aii chan gookhàihkwài' t'inch'yaa aii akǫǫ dàgàvàhnyąą ts'ą' t'ee łyâa zhyąą akhàgògoonyàa.

Tł'èevì' Tì'
Ch'eechyah Nèekwąįį

<jfka401>

JF0.34 Neets'uuch'in[6] oondòk hee ddhah tee neegihiidàl ts'ą' nàgaazhrìi shin, goo'at gavàa ts'ą'.

Dinjii nitsìi łyâa niint'aii chan kwàt ch'izhii dinjii chan.

Aii dinjii nitsìi aii reh vik'ii gǫǫlįį ts'ą' gàa gàandaii kwaa vàràhnyàa.

0.57 Shragwąąhch'yaa gwizhrįh.

Kwàt *Tł'èevì' Tì'* vàràhnyaa łyâa dinjii nitsìi kwaa reh.

Shin googàa reh ch'igii dhàh ik vits'èe gǫǫlįį di'įį vàràhnyàa.

1.09 Aiits'ą' ch'atah t'agwah'in dàį' łyâa ninzhìt googàa ch'atah nidìk.

Run and jump, pole a long way.

Akwàt chan łyâa natsàl, googàa chan łyâa khan neehidìk.

Aii hàa oondòk ddhah tee gwigwich'įį gwiizhìk ts'iivii kwaa, *Gwazhał* gwinyàa.

Rocky Mountàin gwats'ą' nahgwàn reh.

K'àii chan kwàa.

Ts'iivii chan kwàa.

Zhyąą nan chyàh laii kat.

1.50 Aii gwiizhìk reh, gwigwich'įį gwiizhìk reh, yeenaa Ch'eekwaii *two hundrèd* ąąch'yaa ch'iinaa tr'ìinjìl.

2.00 Gohch'it reh *Tł'èevì' Tì'* aii t'agavàhnyàa.

"Zhik łyâa niveh nilįį tthak zhyąą oohàdhoozhìn, nakhwak'ì, nakhwazhrii hàa tthak oohàdhoozhìn, zhyąą nakhwàa shragogwàąhch'yaa gwiizhìk nakhwagiheeghàa gàa t'igii'ìn," jyàa nyaa vàràhnyàa.

2.18 Jyàa gavàhnyaa gàa zhik nèekwąįį nąįį gaveechìi t'igwinyaa kwàa.

6. Neets'uuch'in is Johnny Frank's way of saying Neets'ee Gwich'in, 'the people living around *Arctic Village*.' —AR

Since *Khàiidhiiluu* was their chief, he told them to quit trying to kill *Tł'èevì' Tì'*.

Tł'èevì' Tì'
Second Version

<jfka401>

JF0.34 During the summer time the Neets'ee Gwich'in traveled around in the mountains.

And they took their wives along with them.

There were two men.

One was tall and very strong, and the other one was strong too.

The tall strong man did not know how to get mad, they say.

0.57 He was always kind.

They say the man named *Tł'èevì' Tì'* was a small guy.

He wore a young caribou skin coat with a hat attached to it even in the summertime, they say.

1.09 And he was really good at running.

He could run and jump a long way over rough terrain, even though he was a small man.

They were living on the tundra near the *Brooks Range*, they say.

There were no willows.

There were no spruce trees.

It was close to the *Rocky Mountains*.

1.50 They were living on the wide open tundra when about two hundred Inuit came to them.

2.00 Finally *Tł'èevì' Tì'* said this to them.

"Be aware of the warriors. Have your bows and arrows ready.

They will pretend to be nice, but they will kill you all," *Tł'èevì' Tì'* said, they say.

2.18 He kept warning his people, but those two men didn't listen.

Shòh hàa ch'iidàk kwàzhyą̀ą jyàa dìgii'in googàa *Tł'èevì' Tì'* zhat dhidii kwàa.
Gwiizhìk shrii jyàa dą̀htsii di'į̨ vàràhnyàa.
Aii dzaa ch'iinjì' gwik'yą̀h'èe.
2.38 Gohch'it dik'ì' chan łyâa nagwąą'į̨ izhìk hee dik'ì' gwit'eenlìi, aii gwiizhìk reh geedan aii k'ì' datthak chan neegahaazhik t'igii'ìn shrii hàa.
2.53 Aiits'ą̀' t'ee reh, yee'àt chan dee'àn dinjii choh nàdhàt.
Ch'eekwaii nąįį łyâa shrǫąąhch'yaa vàràhnyàa.
Gwitł'ee jì' gwîindhaa gwahą̀ąh'yàa gwiizhìk, ts'ą̀' reh.
Ch'eekwaii agàa ch'ilik eegiyųąąhtan ts'ą̀' giyàa dìlk'į̨.
Aii gwiizhìk łyâa *ready* gilìi.
3.11 Vitì' aii gwehkį̨ dą̀į' giyàandaii łèe.
Aiits'ą̀' aii eenjit ch'andą̀į' gį̨lį̨ ts'ą̀' aii chan goodhaii nàgahaadhàl gwankàntii googàa łąą goodraii neehidik kwàa.
3.23 Zhat vigii nèekwaįį naįį chan gǫ̀ǫlį̨.
Tł'èevì' aii chan vitì' tsyaa tsal, vachaa chan vàa, ts'ą̀' va'at chan.
3.36 Kwàt ts'ą̀' aii va'at chan łyâa duulèe nilį̨.
Gàa aii tsyaa tsal nèekwąįį zhyą̀ą goohìlzhìn.
Aiits'ą̀' da'at oonii geedàa dą̀į' hee, "K'eegwiich'yaa gǫ̀ǫlį̨ jì', zhik gwà'àn àndhat gwà'àn khài' gavàa neehiindìk," yàhnyàa.
3.53 Gohch'it t'ee treegwigwihîiłtìk.
Gwiizhìk dinjii ch'ilik oonjii dàk a'èe, ch'yąą nihts'į̨ vigin tr'oontà' gwiizhìk ch'iindàa toh vizhìt nizhriitthàii.
Nihts'į̨ dinjii ineetàl gàa ch'adàį' hee reh vizhit ch'iriitthaįį t'ii'ìn.
4.15 Ch'į̀hlę̨ chan reh, aii chan nihts'į̨ vigìn tr'ąhtsit ch'yą̀ą akòodiriinlìk łee ts'ą̀' gwiizhìk eedan aii reh zhik gwà'àn zhyą̀ą neehidìk.
4.30 Jyàiinch'ii shrii zhrį̀h oohìlzhin ts'ą̀' zhik jyàiinch'yaa ts'ą̀' k'ì' tr'oohahdàa jì' tthak chan gwak'ą̌ąhtìi.
Aii googàa gootee gook'èevę̨ gwà'àn neehidìk.

They were greeting the Inuit happily, but *Tł'èevì' Tì'* stayed back.

They say he had a big knife.

He had it on him.

2.38 He hid his bows and arrows, while the others carried their knives.

2.53 And so the tall man was there.

They say he was having a good time with the Inuits.

He didn't know what he was getting himself into later.

The Inuit sat with him and taught him Inuit songs.

3.11 They were getting ready to fight while doing so.

They knew his father from before.

So they were scared of him, and they tried to get him to go along, but he kept away.

3.23 *Tł'èevì' Tì'* had two of his children there.

He had a daughter named *Tł'èevì'* and a son who also had a younger brother and that younger brother had a wife.

3.36 His wife was a hard-working woman.

The two young boys were aware of the Inuit too.

He told his wife, "If you see something happening, stay away over on the side."

3.53 Finally the fighting started.

And the tall man who was learning Inuit songs was held by his two arms and his body was slashed with a short spear.

He tried getting away by kicking with his feet, but it was too late.

4.15 They did the same with the other man.

They grabbed both of his arms while he was walking around.

Tł'èevì' Tì' had nothing but his knife on him.

4.30 He was on the side watching the fighting and watched out for arrows in case someone tried shooting him.

His two young sons were hiding down by the river.

Aii gwiizhìk vigii tsal nèekwaįį nąįį oochìt vahk'ah chan kwaa reh.

Oochìt han gwintsàl jyàa dàgwąhtsii, dana'aagyùk reh.

Little bank, it's a gravel.

Izhìk tsèeniidichįį nyàa.

5.12 Aii *Tł'èevì'* reh, aii ch'idrèe kwaiitryah tsal zhùu'yùu.

"Ch'iitthàn, kwaiitryah tsal shigii ch'iitthàn dìłnyàa izhìk t'ee łyâa nint'aii shiłtsąįį," nyaa vàràhnyàa.

Gwiheendàii gwinkeehàazhìi.

Yats'ą' àkwàt zhyąą gavàa chǐinzhii, zhyąą yee'òk zhyąą jyàa dìi'ìn.

5.35 Aii gwiizhìk reh va'at, aii reh zhik dinjii ch'ìhłèe tr'ôołkhwaįį gwinyàa, aii k'àa reh dinjii dhagwàt.

5.43 Aii gwiizhìk t'ee k'ì' hàa gwak'ǎąhtii googàa ch'adan gwats'an tr'ǫąąhdàk aii tr'injàa.

Aii geełeehòolchįį hàa t'įį ts'ą' jyàa dǐizhìk, akhài' jii vamà' aii oo'òk hàats'àk aii tr'iłdàii vàràhnyàa.

5.56 Aiits'ą' yeezhòk chihkat nǐinlaii izhìk hee chit ch'yǎaghàa, vach'oo k'ì' een'ee ts'ą' reh.

Zhat jyǎiinch'yaa gwiizhìk ch'iidàk hee zhyąą nihłant'įį tthak jyàa dinch'yaa, gookhyųų ndàk neehidìk.

6.13 Oodàk gookhyųų nidhiizhii dąį' gook'ì' nąhjii t'agavah'ìn.

Aiitł'ęę gwadąą neihdyaa łąą k'il kat neehihdik k'ìt łąą k'ì' t'inch'yaa, nyąą vàràhnyàa.

Nahdak tthak, k'ì' trąįį hàa neehidik reh.

6.34 Gohch'it zhik t'agwahtsii tthak kwàt zhyąą nankat ts'it ch'òo hàa gwiich'ok k'it t'ôonch'yaa, nyąą vàràhnyàa.

Googàa tr'ahdak kwàa.

Dzaa ch'iizhaa t'iinch'yaa googàa duuyee giyàhdak reh.

6.47 Jyàa dìi'in ts'ą' aii jùu vik'ì' kwaa it'ee reh ch'ii'àn tr'inidìk, k'ì' ch'ìhłak zhrįh akhǒonjik ts'ą' oo'àt chųų vęę hee k'ì' ch'ìhłak gwats'ą' t'eehaahch'yàa reh t'ii'ìn.

7.05 Ch'iindàk jyàa dìgii'in ts'ą' oondàa nihłagwąì'in ts'ą' aii jùu vik'ì' kwaa zhat digizhaa zhìt k'ì' kwaa, aii zheedàhtràk.

Jyàa dìgii'in gooràhnyaa į'.

There was a little bank there, made of gravel.
That's where he said he was hiding.
5.12 *Tł'èevì'* had a small pair of caribou leg skin boots on.
"When I heard my kids crying out desperately down there, I really got stronger," he said, they say.
He went among them while they were fighting.
5.35 Meanwhile, they say, his wife stabbed a man over a man who was already dead.
5.43 *Tł'èevì' Tì'* was standing around watching for arrows.
Even so, they say, his wife got hit in the breast with an arrow.
5.56 She ran to the little creek and dove into the water with the arrow still in her breast.
While that was going on, *Tł'èevì'* Tì' was over on the side watching out.
6.13 They say he was walking back and forth on the side while he was being shot at.
He did that so they would run out of arrows.
6.34 When he came back down, they say, he said the arrows on the ground were like a mattress, there were so many of them.
It looked almost like porcupine quills lying on the ground.
They shot at him many times, but he didn't get hit, even though sometimes he was near to where the arrows landed.
6.47 Whoever ran out of arrows just walked away to go back to the ocean.
They usually just saved one arrow to go back to the ocean with.
7.05 From a distance someone would wave their arms, which meant they were out of arrows.
That's what they did, they say.

"It'ee shik'ì' kwaa," nyaa reh t'ii'ìn.

7.12 It'ee neeheedyaa gwizhrįh.

Jyàa dìgii'in ch'iindàk.

7.19 Gohch'it dàa ts'ą' ch'iindàk nanchyàh kat łyâa ninzhùk ch'iindàk tthak tł'yaa chaganą̌ąht'aii ts'ą' aii gwiizhìk yeezhee han ch'iindàk chan chųų diigwàtk'ìt nàa'ąį' gwinyàa.

Oonjìt chan shih gwintsàl dadlàn.

Little bank.

Izhìk chan needyaa akhài' Ch'eekwaii khęhkwaii reh.

Zhyąą naagaįį zhrįh niliį reh.

7.55 Aii zhrįį yats'ą' nihkheiidiintin łèe roh.

Yeedąą dinjii zhyąą tòh hàa zhrįh yeedaa dinjii aghàn.

8.09 Aiits'ą' yaaghà' gwà'àn dik'ì' dhidlii ch'yąą kwàt reh, han geeghaih gwit'eh.

Gwiizhìk hee, needyaa gwiizhìk oozhee nan jyàa shizhìk shataa hee naadàk yàhnyaa vàràhnyàa.

8.17 *Tł'èevì' Tì'* t'inlìk.

Ch'ii'àn tr'anaatłee łąą yeendìt vahk'ah tsal dį' hee oodàk jyàa dïizhìk gwiizhìk hee ch'iindàa hee yizhìt ch'ąhtłee.

Aii shan hàa chan k'ì' oonii jyàa dïinlìk,

8.34 "Zhyąą nats'an ałtsii t'ał'in," jyàa yàhnyaa ts'ą' yàa khanànaatrak vàràhnyàa.

Akwàt dìyàhnyaa kwaa jì' reh tr'ahaahkhwàa roh.

8.43 Aiits'ą' t'ee ch'iindàk, aii *Tł'èevì'* goohan[7] chan chųų zhìt nehkaii niliį ts'ą' chųų zhìt k'ïlt'àii.

9.00 Aii gwiizhìk chan tsyaa tsal yaaghà' zhat.

It'ee . . .[8]

Gwiizhìk ch'iindàk goohàaghàn ts'ą' zhyąą k'ì', shrii hàa zhrįh.

9.05 Izhìk hee ch'iindàk hee vazhraįį daatth'ak ginch'yaa gwiizhìk azhrąįį tsal goots'an anaadhàl.

Ch'iindak zhyąą gwihiljii gweetthal ts'ą' ch'iindàk.

7. Johnny identifies the woman above as Tł'èevi' Tì's wife but Tł'èevì's mother is clearly one and the same person. —CM

8. This is an aside which breaks the frame. Johnny is responding to something Sarah says or does. —CM

Every once in a while someone waved his arms and said, "I have no more of my arrows."

7.12 That meant he had to leave.

Finally there was long line of Inuit going away across the tundra.

7.19 They say the creek below was about as deep as our knees, and the little bank on the other side was a little bit steep.

Tł'èevì' Tì' was walking around there when the leader of the Inuit crept up to him.

That Inuit had on a beaded outfit.

7.55 *Tł'èevì' Tì'* still had his bows and arrows hidden away by the river.

The Inuit was creeping up on him while *Tł'èevì' Tì's* only weapon was his short spear.

8.09 The Inuit shot at *Tł'èevì' Tì'* with his arrows.

Tł'èevì' Tì' bent down real fast, and the arrows missed him.

8.17 He did that to *Tł'èevì' Tì'*.

Then the Inuit ran and was trying to run over a little bank when *Tł'èevì' Tì'* caught up to him and slashed his short spear into his body.

Using his medicine powers, he even got his bow and arrows back.

8.34 "This is just to give you a lesson," he told him, as he was killing him repeatedly, they say.

Even if he didn't say that to him, the Inuit would have been killed anyway.

8.43 *Tł'èevì's* mother was still lying in the water wounded.

9.00 The young boy was still there, also.

That's it. . .

Meanwhile, *Tł'èevì' Tì'* was killing all the Inuit one by one using just his arrows and knife.

9.05 You could see them from a long ways off, and once in a while, you could see them falling one by one until there were none left.

9.17 "Yeendee deetthan k'ąhnjik tr'igwìin'ee izhìk k'àii tr'àl ghoo tsal dha'ąįį," nyàa.

9.26 Izhìk t'ee tik nąįį zhrįh t'ee vàh gwiteiinjìl.

Aii zhrįh akhŏonyàa.

9.34 Łyâa dinjii lęįį dìłkhwąįį vàràhnyaa į'.

Aiits'ą' t'ee reh yeendòk zhat ddhah kat Dinjii Zhuh tthak giheeghàa ghat t'igii'ìn.

Dèegwildàii dèegwiheezyàa geenjit dinjii vęhdàa kwaa k'at deegaajìl.

9.44 Aiits'ą' t'ee van ts'ą̀' hàazhii gwiizhìk t'ee tǫǫ nàgwàanąįį.

Tǫǫ nàgwàanąįį ts'ą' reh yeekyùk da'at, vanchil dazhoo hàa chųų dhah iłtsąįį ts'ą' k'ì' khăiintin ch'ii'àn gwideek'ìt gwak'ą'ąhtryaa.

Ts'ą' t'ee reh veenjit gwinzįį.

10.15 Aiits'ą' yeedeedàk kwàt zhyąą ch'oo hàa nankat gwiizhoo k'ìt t'ôonch'yàa. K'ì' reh.

Traa kwàa.

Aii yeendaa kìnàazhik tǫǫ hee.

"Aiinyàa dhiidìi," nyaa vàràhnyàa.

10.24 Zhik tr'iinìn nąįį kwàntee nìgiyinlii ts'ą' jùu oondee tik akhŏonyaa aii jùu oonaa tǫǫ yeeneeheedyàa jì' eenjit zhrįh.

Tǫǫ datthak needįįhshyaa ts'ą' dhiidii ts'ą' gavaał'yà' kwaa nyąą vàràhnyàa.

10.41 Aiitł'ęę oo'àt k'eegiidàl izhìk hee reh chan hee Ch'eekwaii lęįį.

Aii ch'adan Ch'eekwaii lęįį t'inch'yaa łii gogwaandak[9] ts'ą' t'ee reh.

Dinjii tthak diiriighan.[10]

"Diikhwan zhrįh tr'agwandàii," àgàhnyàa.

11.11 Aiits'ą' t'ee reh, "Gwitł'ee khaii jì' goots'ą' riheedàa ts'ą' neegoorihęę'ee ts'ą' gooriheeghàa," jyàa ginyaa gooràhnyàa.

---

9. The word *gogwaandak* should be *geegogwaandak*. —KP
This is a dialect difference. —JE

10. Today we say *tr'inghan* instead of *diiriighan*. —KP

9.17 "There's a little creek with thick round brush back that way," he said.

9.26 Three Inuit got away into that brush.

They say he killed many of them.

9.34 There were really lots of people killed, they say.

The Inuit had planned to kill all the Indians who lived in the mountains in the first place.

It's a good thing *Tł'èevì' Tì'* was there because nobody could beat him.

9.44 So by the time he went over to the lake, it was dark.

When it got dark his wife was over there with a piece of animal skin with the hair on.

She made some hot water and took out the arrow and washed her wound with that skin.

After that, she felt better.

10.15 Near there up on a hill, the arrows were stacked up like piles of porcupine quills.

There was no wood around there.

He made a fire out there in the dark.

"I'm sitting around the camp fire," he said, they say.

10.24 The children piled the arrows up near the fire.

They say he waited up all night for the three Inuit he left behind just in case they came back, but they didn't.

10.41 When the three Inuit got back to their people, there were still many of them left.

Everyone else was killed.

"We're the only ones left alive," they told their leader.

11.11 And they what they said was, "Next winter, we're going there again to fool them, and then we'll kill all of them."

Ts'ą' t'ee reh eedan zhrįh zhuundàk zhat khaii voondee chan *Khàiidhiiluu* òaazhii vàràhnyaa *Tł'èevì' Tì'*.

11.23 Aii chan Ch'eekwaii nąįį tthak yeet'iindhàn.

Nàhtryàh lęįį dhahkhwaii ts'ą'.

Khèhkwàii giyàa'ìi.

11.40 Aii oo'ęę eenineegiidàl, izhìk geenjit doondee ts'ą' hàazhii ts'ą' reh zhat gwich'įį.

Zhat git choo dha'ąįį ginyàa, izhìk hee t'ee. . .

Yit!

11.47 Ch'eekwaii nąįį git kat nehkaii hàa giyàa tsèe'in.

Nijìn goodhaii nìgiyaahnaii jì' giihaahkhwàa reh.

Drin hee giyàa neetsèe'ingwaazhik googàa tthak goondaa t'iiyinch'yaa.

12.00 Geetèe hee giinoodąąndàl googàa reh zhyąą gootah reh tr'iyahàatłak roh.

Goochi' ehdòk hee gwiizhìk hee zheehaatłak gwiizhìk giyùhdak googàa k'ì' aghàa gwiizhìk ahchak giyàhnyàa.

12.19 Łyâa dinjii *champion world* nankat indì' reh.[11]

Aiitł'ęę aii voondee reh, "Nachaa dinjii lęįį dhiłkhwąįį ts'ą' neeroohkhwàa, dèenindhàn?" jyàa giyàhnyàa.

12.30 Akhài' reh, "Nakwaa," nyàa.

"Shachaa dhoohkhwąįį jì', zhik Dinjii Zhuh datthak teech'ihihłyàa ts'ą' yee'àt chųų vęę niriheedàa ts'ą' jii nanvęę tthak nakhweenjit nihts'eeriheedàa ts'ą' ch'ìhłęę gàa gwiheendàii kwaa t'ôonch'yàa," jyàa gavàhnyaa gooràhnyàa.

12.55 Goolàt nąįį gàa tree gooràhnyàa.

"It'ee nats'àatee, *Khàiidhiiluu*?" gògwàntrii t'iinyàa.

"Akwàt nachaa tr'ahaahkhwàa kwaa," zhyąą shàgàhnyàa.

It'ee khaiinkǫǫ.

It'ee *Tł'èevì' Tì'* vagwandàk.

11. This should be "world *kat*" or "*nankat,*" not "world *nankat*." It's redundant the way it stands. —KP

They say *Tł'èevì' Tì'* went up to his older brother *Khàiidhiiluu.*

11.23 All those Inuit liked *Khàiidhiiluu too.*

This was because he killed lots of wolverine.

They thought of him as their chief when they came over to him.

11.40 *Tł'èevì' Tì'* went to live with his brother because of that.

He was living on a big glacier, where he . . .

Yit!

11.47 The Inuit played ball with him on the glacier.

They were trying to corner him so they could kill him.

They played with him every day, but he was still stronger than everyone.

12.00 Sometimes they surrounded him, but he got out by jumping over their heads.

They say he jumped up and grabbed the flying arrows.

12.19 He was the world champion during his lifetime.

Khàiidhiiluu was the older brother of *Tł'èevì Tì'.*

The Inuit told him, "Your younger brother killed lots of our people.

Do you want him killed for it?"

12.30 *Khàiidhiiluu* said, "No."

"If you kill my younger brother, I'm going to use my medicine and get all the Indians to come over to the ocean to kill you all!"

They say that's what he told them.

12.55 Some of them even cried, they say.

The Inuits said, "Now what, *Khàiidhiiluu?*

We can't kill your younger brother *Tł'èevì' Tì',* so we'll just have to leave him alone."

This is what I heard.

Now that's the end.

That's *Tł'èevì' Tì's* story.

Sarah Frank

Shyaaghan Shìh Hàa Ch'eechyah Ch'ìhłak

<sfcm>

SF0.30 Nizhìk dąį' hee, shyaaghan than adahzhrįį gwich'įį.
Aiits'ą' zhik gwà'an tthaa eenjit gyah diintł'ii ts'ą' tthaa khat gwich'įį.

0.59 Aiits'ą' jyàa dii'in gwiizhìk zhik dinjii gǫǫlįį gaa aii zhik gwà'an tthak neegihiidal gwizhrįh.
Aii tthak neegihiidal gwizhrįh.
Aii tthak ch'igehee'àa gǫǫkatneegihiidal.
Aiits'ą' aii shyaaghan t'aihnyąą, et'ee neehidik veegogǫǫtrii ts'ą' zhyàa dhidii.

1.23 Aiits'ą' zhik gwà'an tthaa tsal khat dich'iintł'ii ts'ą' tthaa tsal iilòk aii kwaii ahgąįį.

1.34 Akhài' jidii khwanh zhìt nyą' shril hàa khwanh kwat di'ii aii zhìt dhidii ts'ą' oondaa chan zhyàa gwiiłk'à'.
Aii dhidii jyàa diinch'yaa gwiizhìk vindįį chan dinjii kwàa.
Aiits'ą' zheh gwizhìk khaa nihdineezhii ts'ą' tł'ee cheendak ts'ą' gichinąą'aii.

2.08 Aii gwiizhìk reh ehjyàa gwà'an reh gwandaii neehidik k'it t'igwinyąą gwiitth'ak.
Aiits'ą' t'ee jyàanch'yaa khai' tr'iinzhii ts'ą' t'ee oo'àn zhik ch'adhah gihdeenvyaa aii jyàa diinlik ts'ą' oo'àn gwaa'in akhai' yee'at gwà'an shìh neehidik t'inyąą łee.

2.38 Shìh neehidik t'inyąą łee ts'ą' t'ee jidii zhik gwà'an aat'oo.
Aat'òo vakat va'aatr'ii aii jyàa dąhjyàa ts'ą' aii gǫǫdak aii *roll* gahtsik giiyaiidoo ts'ą' jyàa digiiyah'in aii neegahaazhik.

3.03 Aiits'ą' t'ee shìh ęhjyàa neehidik t'inyąą łee ts'ą' t'ee tł'yah zhat dąį' tł'yah ch'adhah chat tł'yah gahtsii, giiyąą tł'yah ts'ą'.

SF3.15 Aii tł'yah gahtsii ts'ą' aii jyàanch'yaa tł'yah njyah di'ii.
Aii hàa t'ee zhik kwantee deehin dachan kat jyàa diiyah'in ts'ą' tthak tł'yah hàa nigwidįįłchaa.

Sarah Frank

The Old Woman and the Grizzly Bear
First Version

<sfcm>

SF0.30 A long time ago, an old woman was living alone in the woods. She set snares for ground squirrels and was living on them.

0.59 While she was doing that, the rest of the people traveled around looking for food to eat.

The old woman had a problem walking.

So I'm saying all she did was live in one place.

1.23 She snared ground squirrels and dried the meat.

1.34 She had a hut insulated with moss and had a fire in the middle of it.

She lived in the hut, and no one else was living near her.

Then one night she came home tired and lay down to sleep.

2.08 She heard some kind of animal moving outside.

She got up slowly and lifted up her doorway flap, which was made out of skin, looked outside, and saw that it was a grizzly bear.

2.38 She saw it was a grizzly bear.

At that time, they usually had a piece of birch bark this long (gesturing) which was twisted and rolled up.

3.03 And so it was a grizzly bear that was outside her house, and at that time, they usually had a skin rope which was braided.

SF3.15 She had that kind of rope, so she tied the long rope onto a piece of wood in her doorway, wrapping it every which way all over her doorway.

3.31 Aiitł'ee jyàa diizhìk gwiizhìk t'ee aii aat'oo aatr'ii t'aihnyąą oondaa kǫ' zhìt ch'iindaa jyàa diinlik ts'ą' vitsįį daak'in ts'ą' vitsįį jii gwintł'oo jyàa diizhìk.

Nihk'yaa jyàa dii'in gwiizhìk et'ee yee'at shìh zhik geh ch'adhah gihdeenvyaa yaa'ìi aii jyàa diinlik, gidįįgyųų.

4.02 Ch'ii'ee shìh t'ii'in łee, aiits'ą' ch'ii'ee nihdeehahaii ahkai' jii vichi' zhrįh gǫǫkak gĕiin'ee.

Aiits'ą' gwiizhìk t'ee yeendàa jidii aat'oo aatr'ii aii oonjik ts'ą' t'ee jii vantsįh ch'iinji' hee jyàa diiyiinlik ts'ą' jii tthak viniiyuuanjik k'it'iinch'yaa naanaii.

4.31 Jyàa diizhìk ts'ą' t'ee, jii aat'oo chan gwintł'oo daak'in ts'ą' t'ee yee'àn tr'iinzhii gwiizhìk gwiintsàl tǫǫ gǫ̀ǫlįį.

4.43 Gwiintsàl tǫǫ gǫ̀ǫlįį ts'ą' t'ee ch'ii'àn kǫ' hàa ahtsii tthak ak'an ts'ą' jii tthak ak'an ts'ą' t'ee ch'ii'àn ahaa gwiintsàl tǫǫ gǫ̀ǫlįį ch'ii'àn ahaa kǫ' hàa k'iighai' yik'ą̆ątii ts'ą' ch'ii'àn neehidik.

5.04 Jyàa dii'in akhai' oo'àt ch'ihłan gwizhrįh dhidii aii gwiizhìk jii kǫ' tthak vah daa'àii roh.

Aiits'ą' t'ee jii datthak vah kǫ' t'iizhìk ts'ą' vaghai' agaa tthak dhik'in.

5.23 Aiits'ą' t'ee iłchįį.

Aiitł'ee tǫǫ gwiintsàl įįnchi' tł'ee vanh drin gǫ̀ǫlįį gwiizhìk et'ee nijin t'iinch'yaa izhìk yahgwats'ą' haazhii akhai' shìh, jii datthak vaghai' tthak kwàa dhidlit łee, dhik'in ts'ą'.

5.47 Aiits'ą' aii shìh chan gwandaii kwàa, iłchįį.

Aii shyaaghan shoh dhidlit vàràhnyąą.

SF5.55 Shyaaghan shoh dhidlit, aiits'ą' et'ee shoh nilii ts'ą' t'ee aii shìh et'ee jyàanch'yaa shìh ak'ii t'inch'yaa ts'ą' jyàanch'yaa khaiiyidiint'uu ts'ą' t'ee gwįįzii, khaii gwiink'oo geenjit gwįįzii jyah diltsaii vàràhnyàa.

Aii vagwandàk lyâa nizįį.

3.31 After doing that, she lit up one end of her rolled up birch bark, and it started to burn on one end.

3.47 She was swinging her torch back and forth sideways while the grizzly tore off her skin doorway.

4.02 The bear was trying to come in, but only its head was actually inside.

Meanwhile, the old woman took her torch and pushed it up one of the bear's nostrils, and then the rest of its body lit up.

4.31 The birch bark lit up brighter.

It was getting dark outside.

4.43 The bear was burning up while it was walking about, and the old woman could tell where it was walking because of the light moving around in the dark.

5.04 While it was doing that, the bear went to one place and sat down.

Its whole body caught on fire, and the fire burned off all of its hair.

5.23 And then it died.

She slept for a while that night, and the next morning, she went back to where the grizzly bear was and found its hair had all burned.

5.47 The bear was not alive.

The old woman was happy, they say.

SF5.55 She was pretty happy because the grizzly bear was fat, so she butchered it and saved it for the winter, they say.

Now that's really a good story.

Shyaaghan Shìh Hàa Ch'eechyah Nèekwąįį

<sflgla>

SF20.39 Shyaaghan naii zhik neerihinjìk izhìk goot'àii gwi'it'aahgwan.
Ąįį geh'àn t'ee nijìn gwà'an tthaa gǫǫlįį nàgoogahchik.
Izhìk hee tthaa eenjit khyą̀h gaalii.
Aii tthaa gǫǫlįį gįį eenjit googàa dinjii goot'ǎadhàk gooràhnyaa t'iginch'yàa (adlaa).

21.12 Aiits'ą̀' t'ee jii shyaaghan khaiits'ą̀' gwiizhìk adahzhrįh kwan zhìt gwich'įį ts'à tthaa kee'ìn.
Akhài' shìh yeek'idik łee giiyàhnyaa adahzhrįh dhidii gwiizhìk chan chiitąįį gwintsàl too gòo'ąįį.
Kwan zhìt nihdèegweedii chan vadzaih dhàh neegąąhvyàa, ąįį t'ee ginděiivyàa gaa'įį.
Łąįį gàa khaldii kwàa.
Khàa gǫǫlįį ts'ą̀' t'ee zhee gwizhìt dhidii.
Akhài' yee'àt zheh gwindii k'èegwiich'yaa t'igwinyaa gwiith'ak.

24.00 Jyàa doonch'yaa łyâa geenjit gwik'èegąąhtii.
Ts'ą̀' t'ee dèegwinyaa niindhan ts'ą̀' oo'àn khài' chìkîintthaii ts'ą̀' gwąąh'ìn.
Akhài' zhyą̀ą ya'ghà' gwà'an shìh neehidik łee.

24.15 Nihdìneezhii ts'ą̀' tł'yah nìltł'yaa òonjit.
Zhat dą̀į' tł'yah niltł'yaa zhrįh tł'yah gàa'įį.

24.40 Ąįį tł'yah niltł'yaa hàa kwàntee nihk'yąą nànyaazhùu.
Aįįtł'ee jidìi aat'oo aatr'ii gahgąįį ąįį chan khìk neegahaazhik.
Giyàa gwaahk'ik dą̀į' han dàatłak geh'àn ts'ą̀' łyâa giik'ąąhtii.

The Old Woman and the Grizzly Bear Second Version

<sflgla>

SF20.39 Sometimes they say old women would lose their strength as they traveled.

Because of that the people would leave them behind where ground squirrels were plentiful.

There the old women would trap for ground squirrels.

Because of the ground squirrels they caught, people were able to benefit from their efforts, they say.

21.12 So once in the fall, this old woman was living by herself in a sod hut and trapping for ground squirrels.

And so they said say a grizzly bear came to her as it was getting to be a little bit dark outside, and she was there alone.

Right inside that sod house, by the entrance, there was a caribou skin hanging.

That's what they had for a door.

She didn't even have a dog with her.

It was night time and she was back inside the house.

And then they say she heard something right outside, around the house.

24.00 At a time like this they would watch closely for things like that.

So, wondering what was making the noise, what they say is she got up and cautiously poked her head out to look.

And right out there was a grizzly bear prowling around.

24.15 She went back in and got a braided skin rope.

At that time that was the only kind of rope they had.

24.40 And she tied that braided rope back and forth across the entrance.

Then she got a roll of birch bark, the kind they dry and always keep with them.

They really took good care of that because it ignited quickly when they wanted to build fires.

Ąįį aat'oo aatr'ìi dàhk'ii gwiizhìt t'ee shìh kwàntee ch'adhàh neiivyaa hàa nilee hêelnaii.

Ts'ą̀' tł'yah nànoozhùu teetak k'ii'ęę tr'ikìinzhaa.

25.32 Gwiizhìk ąįį aatr'ii kǫ̀' zhik kìyiintthaii ts'ą̀' dàak'in.

Daak'ik dą̀į' nihk'yą̀ą t'injìk.

25.55 Jyàa dǐizhìk gwiizhìt ąįį zhìt dizhìt kìyąhshaa.

Gwint'aii t'iyìnlik ts'ą' zhyą̀ą ànts'ą̀' cheevaghwàhêelnaii.

Ąįįtł'ee t'ee shyaaghan chìinzhii ts'ą̀' aakin yàa'įį

Gwiizhìk gwints'al tǫǫ gǫ̀ǫlįį ts'ą̀' zhik gwà'an gwizhrįh hee kǫ̀' neeha'ak yą̀ą'in.

Ąįį datthak yak'ąąhtii.

Gohch'it t'ee kǫ̀' hehłan dha'ąįį naanaii ts'ą̀' nàatthaa'.

Aiitł'ee nihdìneezhii ts'ą̀' nàachįį.

Vàndą̀į' hee heekìlnaii ts'ą̀' chìinzhii.

27.53 Nijìn kǫ̀' nàatthaa gwąąh'yą̀' izhìk gwats'ą̀' hàazhii akhài' yaghà' k'ii'àn nankat shìh vantsįh vinìn kwaii hàa iłdų̀ų zhyą̀ą k'ii'àn k'ilt'àii.

Lyâa shìh nitsìi dìlkhwąįį vàràhnyàa.

Ąįįtł'ee t'ee nìyił'aa ts'ą̀' oo'àn neeyinlii.

Yinìlįį datthak iłgąįį ts'ą̀' chan tthaa kee'in kwaii hàa łyâa dinjii yit'eelnaii vàràhnyàa (adlaa).

So while she was lighting the birch bark, the bear struck the skin hanging over the doorway with its paw.
It stuck its head into the rope mesh across the entrance.
25.32 Just then she stuck the birch bark into the fire, and it burst into flame.
When it caught on fire, you know, it rolled open.
25.55 When it rolled open, she shoved it right into its face.
She did it with such force that the bear just rolled out of the way.
Then the old woman went outside and watched.
It was rather dark, and all she could see was the light from the sparks on the bear moving around.
She kept an eye on it the whole time.
Finally, the sparks stopped moving around and went out.
Then she went back inside and fell asleep.
Early the next morning she got up and hurried outside.
27.53 She went to the spot where she had seen the sparks go out, and right there on the ground was a bear, lying down, with its face completely scorched, snout and all.
It was really a good edible big bear she had killed, they say.
After that she butchered it and took the meat home.
She dried all the meat.
With that and the ground squirrels she caught, the people really benefited from her efforts, they say (laughs).

Sarah Frank

Shyaaghan Nàa'in Hàa Ch'eechyah Ch'ìhłak

<sfcm>

SF6.36 Chan shyaaghan ch'ìhłak aii chan gwik'ìt t'inch'yàa.
Adąhzhrįh gwich'įį' ts'ą' tthaa oonilį'.
Oo'òk tthaa tsal teech'aląį' aii oondaa ikhyąą.
Gwiizhìk it'ee k'il ninjyàa, aii oondaa yitsįį gwizhrįh jyàa dìyah'in ts'ą' yîiłk'à'.

7.02 Aįį gwiizhìk gwintsàl tǫǫ gǫǫlįį ts'ą' t'ee.
Han gwinjik vàh tąįh jèiinch'yaa, gweedì' nǐnląįį.

7.20 Aiits'ą' jyàa[1]... dĭi'in ts'ą' yeendàa gwîiłk'ą' ts'ą' tthaa ikyąą.
Gwiizhìk it'ee ooch'iitthàn[2] k'il jèiinch'yaa daatin ąįį noondàk, ąįį jyàa dăh'in vàràhnyàa.
Ąįį t'ee naa'in t'ii'ìn.

7.56 Ąįį shyaaghan hàanìgwii'aii t'ii'ìn.
Aii gwiizhìk tthaa ikhyàa.
Jii tthaa vàt ąįį t'ee oondaa kǫ' kat gwintł'oo yąhkhyàa.

8.15 Gwintł'òo nindhaa yìltsąįį tł'ęę t'ee zhik traa noondak izhìk ch'iitthàn gwik'yăanaii akhài' chan yeechìt gwà'àn chan neetrèegwahaathàk vàràhnyàa.
Akhài' aii naa'ìn t'ii'in łee vàràhnyàa.
Naa'in.

8.47 Tthaa trìk nindhaa dzat vindèe hee naanąįį t'ii'in łèe.
Aiits'ą' jèiinch'yaa zhyąą yeechìt khàtł'yăh'ee ts'ą' jèiinch'yaa vàràhnyàa.
Jèiinch'yaa gwiizhìk jidìi t'ii'in yuunyąą eenjit yuukeehàh'yą' akhài' naa'in.

9.08 Dazhoo ik naatsùu ts'ą' yeechìt dee'àn khàtł'yąh'ee vàràhnyàa.

1. Sarah interrupts the story here to ask a question of someone across the room.

2. *Ooch'iitthàn* is a contracted word meaning *oo'àt ch'iitthàn.* —AR. This is one word. —KP

Sarah Frank

The Old Woman and the Brushman
First Version

<sfcm>

SF6.36 This one old woman was in the same situation as the other one.
She was living alone and snaring ground squirrels.
The few ground squirrels she caught in snares, she was singeing.
She was using a long dry willow stick to poke the willows.
7.02 It was beginning to get dark.
She was up on top of the river bank.
7.20 Below her the current was running strong.
Meanwhile she was busy singeing a ground squirrel in the fire.
She had some dry willows piled by her, and a brushman was bothering them, they say.
The brushman was doing that.
7.56 He kept annoying the old woman.
Meanwhile, she kept singeing the ground squirrel.
She put the ground squirrel's guts on the fire to make them hot.
8.15 She really made them hot and then she took a long willow and threw them down below where the firewood was piled up, they say.
They say he was moving around very noisily.
That brushman.
8.47 The insides of the guts she threw down there splashed right in his eyes.
They say he was kneeled down there.
While he was like that the old woman was curious to know what it was, so she went to see.
She knew it was a brushman.
9.08 They say he was wearing a caribou fur coat and was kneeled down.

9.20 Gwiizhìk t'ee zhik gwà'àn gał òonjìk.
Aii dząą hee yichì'itsįį ch'ąhkhaa vàràhnyàa.
Yîiłkhwąįį (adlaa).

Fig. 12. Johnny Frank in Venetie, circa 1960. Photo courtesy of Richard Birchell.

9.20 So in the meantime, she grabbed a stick.
Then she hit him over the head, they say.
And killed him (laughs).

Fig. 13. Sarah Frank in Venetie, circa 1980. Photo courtesy of Lawrence Roberts.

Shyaaghan Nàa'in Hàa Ch'eechyah Nèekwąįį

<sflgla>

SF28.50 Shyaaghan ch'ìhłak chan naa'in diłghwąįį giiyàhnyàa.

Aii chan reh tł'eedik gwîiłk'ą' ts'ą' it'ee izhìk chat tthaa ikhyąą.

Izhìk chat it'ee gwintsàl tǫǫ neegwiilik ginyàa.

29.14 Ąįįts'ą' it'ee oondaa tthaa ikhyąą ąįį shrilii.

Izhìk dąį' daa'ąįį chan gǫǫlįį kwaa, nàhąą.

Zhik gwà'àn k'il njyah ąįį oondàa giitsįį ts'aii chigiiyiitthak ts'ą' nihts'ą' ts'ą' giiyeelee.

29.34 Ąįįts'ą' it'ee vitł'eech'iik'ik aii gwik'it t'iinch'yaa chiinlii ąįį yakha' vashrąį' t'eh gwats'an k'iizhąą ąįį k'il daak'ą' ąįį jyàa da'in giiyàhnyàa, naa'ìn.

29.52 Ąįįts'ą' gwiintsàl tǫǫ gǫǫlįį ts'ą' yidik tr'ahshii kwaa, nàhąą.

Ąįįts'ą' zhyąą yeenjit gok'aantii.

Ąįįts'ą' it'ee ąįį tthaa ts'ik hałii giiyàhnyàa akhài' vitrik ąįį kwat yeendaa kǫ' kat vee niinlii ts'ą' reh datthak yąh khyąą.

30.19 Datthak nindhaa dhidlìt.

Ąįįtł'ee it'ee ąįį tthaa trik t'aihnyaa it'ee zhìk t'ii'in izhìk k'iizhak yinaahtii dahlįį k'iizhak hee jyàa diyiinlìk.

Tthaa trik dhah vindee nandhitł'ik rǫh.

30.41 Ąįįts'ą' it'ee yeekit zhak gwà'àn hee neetreegwahaatak yàhnyàa giiyàhnyàa.

Gwiintsàl vanh gweech'in reh ootthan t'ohjuh hee gwaa'ìn dohłįį akhài' reh yeekit zhìk dee'àn reh nàa'in.

Dazhoo ik k'ùu tsal naatsùu ts'ą' dee'àn khàtł'yąh'ee ginyàa.

31.10 Chan yîiłghwąįį giiyàhnyàa t'aihnyàa (adlaa).

The Old Woman and the Brushman
Second Version

<sflgla>

SF28.50 This one old woman I heard about once killed a brushman.

She had a campfire on the edge of a steep river bank and was singeing ground squirrels.

They say it was just before dark.

29.14 And she was singeing ground squirrels.

There were no axes at that time, you see?

They only used long dry willow sticks to burn.

29.34 As the long willows burned up, she kept putting more of them into the fire, but they say a brushman was pulling on them.

29.52 It was beginning to get dark, so she didn't try to look for him, you see.

She was watching out for him.

So they say she put the ground squirrel guts on the fire to make them hot.

30.19 She made them really hot.

Then she threw them in the direction where he was pulling on her wood.

The hot guts splashed right into his eyes.

30.41 They say he was moving about very noisily.

The light was dim so she went to look over the river bank and saw the brushman.

They say he was wearing a worn out fur coat and kneeling down rubbing his eyes.

31.10 Again what I'm talking about is that they say she killed him (laughs).

Johnny Frank

Shyaaghan Tsal Łuk Choh Hàa

<jfmhla >

JF6.57 Shyaaghan tsal łyâa dazhan vàràhnyàa.
Aii than hee vigii nąįį tthak, vakàį' hàa datthak àn dhidlìt, googàa lyâa nįįzhùk nankak gwandàii vàràhnyàa.

7.13 Dazhan ts'ą' jyàa dìnch'yaa than t'inch'yaa.
Googàa chan jidìi ch'atth'anh gǫǫlįį gwinyaa.
Dinjii tr'àł zhît gǫǫlįį gwinyąą googàa aii chan nah'in kwaa ts'ą' reh.

7.29 Aii dazhan k'iighai' reh k'èegwiich'yaa gwąąh'in kwaa ts'ą' dąhzhrii than gwandàii.

7.36 Łyâa nihts'įį tòh di'įį, googàa *fifty yard* gwizhrįh ahaa ts'ą' *she knock him down.*

8.09 Izhìk chan oo'àn t'eehaadhàk, jyàa dii'in ts'ą'.
Googàa khaii hee tr'eenjyaa hee oonii tąįį hee łì'hàa gwîink'oo googàa idluu kwaa ts'ą'.

8.21 Googàa nihk'it gwinzįį gwandaii.
Łyâa dinjii lęįį vàh gwandàii datthak shin yaghan, googàa chan shin yaahkhwąįį kwaa ts'ą' shyaaghan natsal chan nilįį vàràhnyàa.

8.38 Aiits'ą' aii *Chihtł'ee Vàn* vàràhnyàa aii ts'an hàhdląįį deedì' van, han gwinjik van tik dhidlìi, van nitsìi kwaa, aii veegòodląįį.

8.52 Izhìk reh shin tthak teeghaii hee tth'an jàł hàa chihjàl ił'ąįį vàràhnyàa.

8.59 Łuk ch'ìhłak khàhchik aii łąhch'yaa nįįzhùk t'ąąhch'yaa.
Akhài' aii van shrìit'ąhtsii reh vizhìt łì'hàa ts'iivii nitsìi ndaa t'ąhtsii neerąhnjik choo vizhìt iltin łèe.

9.15 Aii iłdràt vàràhnyàa.
Aii teeghaii neehidik oondaa ch'iinaa yats'ą' neehîil'ee yidiindak[3] tr'inidìk.
Ts'ą' t'ee reh tth'an tòh di'įį aii łąh yeenjit iłtsąįį vàràhnyàa.

3. The word *yidiindak* should be *yandak* —KP

Johnny Frank

The Little Old Woman and the Big Fish

<jfmhla >

JF6.57 This little old woman had really magic power, they say.
Her husband and all of her children died, but she lived on alone for a long time, they say.

7.13 Because she had magic power, she was like that.
But she didn't even see any ice bears around, they say.
And she didn't see any brushmen or Naa'in, they say.

7.29 It was because of her magic powers that she didn't see any of these, and she lived alone.

7.36 She used canes on both sides of her, but she still could walk only fifty yards before she fell down.

8.09 She would fall down, and when they traveled during the winter, she stayed way in the back.
Even when it was cold, she didn't get cold.

8.21 Anyway, she was still in good health.
The people who lived with her all died from old age, but she didn't get old, and she kept on being a little old woman, they say.

8.38 They say there's this lake called *Chihtł'ee Van (Chandalar Lake),* and from this lake is a creek which flows through three little lakes into the river nearby.

8.52 They say she spent all of her summer fishing there on the shoreline using bone hooks.

8.59 She caught one fish now and then and lived on it.
The biggest lake had a lake trout bigger than a tall spruce tree in it, with a northern pike inside of it.

9.15 They say she spotted it.
She hooked the fish and then held on to the line while walking along the shore.
And she had a bone spear which she made a big hook out of, they say.

9.33 Aiits'ą' vyah di'įį aii chan yitł'yàa iłtsąįį ts'ą' kwàt aii tth'an tòh aii gał tr'oohòotak łiyìłtł'įį ts'ą' łąh yìłtsąįį, (yitł'yaatr'aałchaa) ts'ą'.

9.47 Aiits'ą' neerąhnjik zhuu dhìłkhwąįį aii ghàn yeek'it ch'iint'ìi[4] yakak gìitł'įį, ts'ą' reh oondàa yihîiłnaii.

Akhài' aii łuk nitsii niyiił'in ts'ą' t'ee reh yuunjik.

10.05 Yùunjik ts'ą' t'ee reh yik'yąąnjìk.

Ts'ą' reh, "Ch'iinaa gwats'an tr'anoozhì' shrǫ̀' zhyąą oo'àn ginkhii hàa yeendaa łuk shatth'anłąh ts'an tr'anoozhì' shrǫ̀'," nyaa ooch'ii'àn zhyąą zhral vàràhnyàa.

10.27 Àkwàt zhik łąh tł'yàa aii chan,

"Łuk yûųhtal shrǫ̀'," chan nyaa ts'ą'.

"Łuk nôǫhtal shrǫ̀'," aii chan tł'yàh agàa àhnyąą vàràhnyàa.

10.37 Aiits'ą' gwiizhìk ch'iinaa yàh t'àii t'àh'ìn, gwiizhìk łuk aii ch'iinaa khài' oo'àn neegijìk ts'ą' łideeyahłàk.

Gohch'it łyâa zhyąą teeghaii ch'iinaa chìl'ąįį yìłtsąįį.

10.57 Aii gwiizhìk oo'àn neegijìk ts'ą' ch'iindàk łiyahchyaa gohch'it aii łąh tł'yàa nìndąįį ts'ą' gineeyahchàa.[5]

11.07 Aiitł'ęę t'ee reh, "Yaaghà' łuk haałkhwàa veenjit shits'ïinyaa," nyaa ts'ą' ch'ii'àn zhyąą zhral vàràhnyàa.

11.15 Aiits'ą' t'ee reh dzaa nijìn łuk vidrìi dha'ąįį gàandaii izhìk hee ts'ee vàa tr'oogit tth'an zhųh tsal.

Aii hàa dzaa khàyadangìt gwiizhìk, "K'èegwiich'yaa t'oona'yà' shrǫ̀'!" łuk àhnyàa.

11.34 Ts'ą' gwiizhìk łyâa dzaa yidrìi keehaagòk ts'ą' reh.

Akhài' gohch'it reh yidrìi dhagwàt łee ts'ą' t'ee reh łuk choo gòhch'it t'ee reh hahchyàa, ts'ą' ditł'ì' hàa jyàa dïizhìk.

Akhài' oondàa nankak ch'iindàk zhyąą tèedaghàii dhatthaii gwiizhìk iłchįį vàràhnyàa.

12.01 Aiits'ą' t'ee reh łàh tł'yàa gìłchaa ts'ą' t'ee reh yidrìi dha'ąįį izhìk ch'iizhàk t'ee łì'hàa shrii neeshrâahch'yaa di'įį vàràhnyàa.

---

4. Today *yeek'it ch'iint'ìi* would probably be written as *yik'ich'iint'ùu* —KP

5. A grandfather clock chimes in the background. —JE

9.33 So she had a skin rope that she tied to her short spear and tied whatever sticks she could find to the bone spear to use as a hook.

9.47 So she had a small lake trout which she cut in half and tied to the hook side of the bone spear and threw it out into the lake.

That big fish saw it and grabbed it.

10.05 She felt the fish grabbing her hook.

She talked to the fish saying, "Don't let go of my bone hook!"

They say she was talking and hollering.

10.27 She talked to her fishing line, too, saying

"Don't let that fish break you," and she kept right on talking.

"Don't let that fish break you," she said, they say.

10.37 She kept tugging on the line with the fish, slowly taking it to shore.

Finally she got its head on the shore.

10.57 She kept talking to it while slowly guiding it to shore, and tying it after each pull.

11.07 After that she hollered and spoke out loudly to nowhere, saying, "Help me kill that fish!" they say.

11.15 Then she repeatedly jabbed the fish where she knew its heart was, using a little bone hook that she used for killing marmots.

While doing that, she talked to the fish. "Don't you do anything!" she said.

11.34 Meanwhile, she repeatedly jabbed for its heart.

When she finally struck its heart, the big fish swung its tail back and forth and forced itself up onto the shore.

That's where it died, they say.

12.01 She tied the rope nearby and they say she had with her a little poor-looking dull knife.

12.13 Googàa reh yitsin tr'ìch'iint'uu izhìk gwats'an t'ee ch'a'àa.
Aii gwiizhìk reh oodòk ddhah nitsìi ǫhts'ąįį łyâa ts'ee gǫ̀ǫlįį.
Dinjii gǫ̀ǫlįį izhìk oodąą neerąą'ìk vàràhnyàa.

12.32 Oodaa neerąą'in akhài' łuk choo iłàa łee reh.
Aii tthak àn ts'ą̀' chan dinjii hàa giindàii, nihłaa giindàii roh.

12.45 Aii tthak goolàt nąįį ch'andàii' aanąįį ts'ą̀' àkwàt zhyą̀ą shyaaghan tsal vats'ą̀' t'igwìizhìk.
Ts'ą̀' aii łuk choo zhyą̀ą vik'eech'arąąhtrit ts'ą̀' zhyą̀ą gohch'it tthak khàridìint'ùu.

12.55 Âa! Dinjii lęįį googàa giithą̀į' łuk ts'ik dril ahtsii aii hàa googàa ch'agąįhk'ìt gwachoh gwagòo'ee gwigwìłtsą̀įį.

13.10 Gwats'an łyâa zhyą̀ą khaii tthak łyâa zhyą̀ą dinjii nàatł'įį googàa khaii tthak yakwàn gwiindàii vàràhnyàa.

13.15 Aii shyaaghan tsal gwandàii tthak chan vik'ii gǫ̀ǫlįį kwaa.
Ts'ą̀' "Shats'àroonyà'," chan nyaa kwaa.
Ts'ą̀' zhyą̀ą gwinzįį gwandàii, ts'ą̀' jyàanch'yaa.
Ts'ą̀' nįįzhùk gwiindàii vàràhnyàa.

12.13 Still, she used that to cut its stomach open and then she ate off of it.

Meanwhile, there were a lot of people living nearby on a big mountain hunting for marmots.

They all watched her from up there, they say.

12.32 They looked again and were surprised to see her big dead fish.

They all told each other since they already knew each other, and some of them got scared.

12.45 All of her relatives came down to the little old woman as the big fish was being cut.

They finally finished cutting it up.

12.55 Aa! There were lots of people there cutting it up into strips and hanging it, and the whole place was covered with smoke drying caches.

13.10 Everybody really ate from it all winter long, and yet they were living all winter at her house, they say.

13.15 That little old woman never got mad in her entire life.

And she never said "Help me," either.

And she was always in good health.

And they say she lived for a very long time.

Sarah Frank

Ch'atth'anh [1]

<sflglb>

SF0.09 Aii ch'atth'anh it'ee zhat gwanaa dąį' shìh kwaa dinjii anlìi nàhąą.

Aiits'ą' dinjii kwaii a'àa.

Aii geh'àn iìzųų ilìk t'agàhnyàa.

LG Ą̀ąhą'.

SF0.30 Izhìk dąį' it'ee łyâa vagǫ̀ǫlįį giyàhnyaa t'inch'yaa, nàhąą.

Izhìk it'ee dinjii, dinjii ch'ìhłak it'ee vigii tsyaa ch'ìhłak chat vàagwandàii giyàhnyàa.

Aii t'ee oo'òk neehidik akhài' it'ee aii shìh t'aihnyaa aii t'ee k'adeedhizhii łee giyàhnyaa.

Aiits'ą' it'ee aii dinjii dìłkhwąįį, nàhąą.

Aiits'ą' t'ee vik'ìgwàanjìk, ts'ą' it'ee giyeenjit khaihłak iłtsąįį.

Vitì' aii it'ee oo'àn yats'ą' hàazhìi.

Yats'ą' hàazhii ts'ą' gwiizhìk łyâa dinjii gǫ̀ǫlįį gwinyàa.

SF1.41 Yats'ą' hàazhii ts'ą' it'ee oo'àt yigii a'àa, nàhąą.

Aii gwiizhìk it'ee oo'àn yats'ą' tr'iinzhii łee.

Aiits'ą' yaaghà' chan aii chan haałkhwàa niindhan eenjit it'ee aii chat t'ee ts'ą' tr'iinzhii dǫhłįį.

Aii gwiizhìk oo'àt dinjii lęįį gwich'įį aii gwats'an t'ii'ìn.

Aiits'ą' it'ee zhik k'ii'àn shìh aii yats'ą' hàazhii.

SF2.21 Aii ts'įį tr'ineezhii ts'ą' t'ee gwinzįį yeenìnhàii kwàa.

Aii ts'įį needyaa ts'ą' t'ee oo'àt nihts'įį zhyąą dinjii jyàa diizhìk gwinyaa.

---

1. *Ch'atth'anh* is the name given to a grizzly bear that refuses to den up in the fall. It is a fearsome animal because whenever it enters a lake or river, the water freezes on its coat and provides it with a protective shield of ice. This shield makes it nearly impossible to kill with a spear or bow and arrow, and Sarah explains all this on <sflg2b>: 12.16-14.02. Robert McKennan (1965:152-153) published two Ice Bear stories in English which were told to him by Henry John, and I collected one from the late storyteller, Moses Peter, on October 8, 1972, which was recorded in Gwich'in but published only in English translation (see Mishler 1973). Sarah's story here is rather different from all of these, but similar to one told

Sarah Frank

The Ice Bear

<sflglb>

SF0.09 It was a long time ago when people were dying from starvation, you see.
And so that was when the ice bear ate people.
So they're talking about how it became very mean.
LG Yes.
SF0.30 They say there were really lots of them around then, you see.
So at the time, they say this man had one son living with him.
They say that while his son was out hunting or just walking, he met up with a grizzly bear.
And so the bear killed the young man, you see.
Then when the people found out about it, they all got together and went after the bear.
But the young man's father went after him first.
So he went to him, but they say there were lots of people there.
SF1.41 You see he went to him while that bear was still eating his son's flesh.
The bear thought he was going to kill this man too, so the bear went after him.
But they say he came from a place where lots people were living.
So the bear came toward him.
SF2.21 But then he turned around and led the bear toward the place where all the people were.

1. (cont.) by Laura Pascal of *Fort McPherson, N.W.T.* and read on CHON-FM in *Whitehorse* by Ruth Carroll in November, 1992. Ice bears have terrorized villagers even in modern times. Moses Peter, a resident of *Chalkyitsik*, killed one of them in December, 1963 (E.M. Peter, *Tundra Times,* March 23, 1964), and the fresh tracks of another one were seen around *Arctic Village* during the winter of 1969-1970 (Josephine Peter, *Tundra Times,* April 1, 1970). See the recent photo (Fig. 14) of one taken by Yukon wildlife photographer Peter Mather. —CM

Nihts'įį gihîilzhii nàgàanąįį.

Aiits'ą' aii gwideetak k'ii'àn hee t'ee yits'įį needyaa giyàhnyàa.

It'ee łàa dinjii tł'an k'ii'àn neezhii gwiizhìk it'ee zhik dinjii nąįį zhyąą datthak giits'ą' tr'agal'ąhjil łee ts'ą' giinan datthak gwiteegwìłtrat, nàhąą.

LG Ą̀ąhą'.

SF3.06 Izhìk it'ee daganlį' hàa shìh gîiłkhwąįį googàhnyàa.

Jyàa dìgiizhìk googàhnyàa.

Izhìk it'ee gwizhrįh vagwandak ndàa nàa'ąį' (adlaa).

SF3.26 Dihch'į' gwilęįį vits'į'į needyaa aii chat haałkhwàa niindhan akhài' łyâa gwìizųų gwąąh'yà' vàràhnyaa t'aihnyàa (adlaa).

Jèiinch'yaa daganlì' hàa reh giyùunjik ts'ą' ree giyîiłkhwàįį.

LG3.45 Khandigiyâągyųų dohłii.

SF3.47 Ą̀ąhą', jyàa dìgiyinlìk googàhnyaa į'.

SF3.54 Àkwàt chat ch'adan chan.

Aii chat yaaghà' *Shyaaghan Ndìk*[2] aii chan ch'izhii shyaaghan chan vàa.

Aiits'ą' it'ee aii khaiits'ą' kwan ginghàn.

Aii zhìt gwigwich'įį ts'ą' it'ee geh'àn gahàandii.

Gwitł'ęę aii shyaaghan nąįį neegooheendal gwats'ą'.

Gahàandii ts'ą' izhìk nìgiindii gwats'an it'ee jyàa dìginch'yaa nàhąą.

SF4.38 Aii gwats'an it'ee oo'àt kwan dhidlii aii geeghaih chan tthał zhyą̌h'oo ts'ą' vadzaih ginghàn.

Aii it'ee jidìi dachan hàa jyàa dìginlìk gwiizhìk shìh nìgiinlii nàhąą.

Aii jèiinch'yaa eełèegahàandii t'igii'ìn.

Aiits'ą' izhìk gwats'an it'ee goo'at nìgiindii gwats'an t'ee aii shyaaghan nąįį ts'igòolįį ts'ą' ree khan ree shyaaghan nąįį ineegiijyàa.

2. Shyaaghan Ndik was a Dì'hąąį Gwich'in woman, one of the wives of Diitsii Giitł'uu. See Appendix A below. —CM

Meanwhile, they say the people just suddenly lined up on two sides.
So he led the bear right in between them.
They waited until he led the bear into the middle of them.
Then they all ran and grabbed hold of him.

LG Yes.

SF3.06 They say they grabbed every part of his body and killed the bear with their bare hands.
That's what they did, they say.
That is the end of this story (laughs).

SF3.26 That bear really thought he was going to kill the poor old man too, but they sure tricked him good.
That's what they say about him (laughs).
They just grabbed him by their bare hands and killed him.

LG3.45 They must have torn him apart.

SF3.47 Yes, that's what they did to him, they say.

SF3.54 Another time too.
Old Woman Ndik had another old woman staying with her.
It was late in the fall time.
Everybody had built a sod hut and was living in it.
After that they all went somewhere.
Meanwhile they left those two old women behind until they could return to get them.
After they left and went so far, they all made camps and stayed there, you see.

SF4.38 They say there was also a caribou corral right near to where they built their sod huts.
Before this happened, they killed lots of caribou in the corral and just stored all the meat right there by the corral, you see.
After they made camp, they were afraid something might happen to the two old ladies, so they went back in a hurry, and on the way back they came across a bear track.

SF5.19 Shyaaghan ineegiijyàa akhài' it'ee dòonch'yaa dzaa tąįį gwinjik ch'ii'àn ree shìh gwik'ìinzhii łee ts'ą̀' oo'àt kwan dhidlii ch'ii'àn gwik'ìinzhii ginyàa.

Zhat ch'ii'àn neereedàa ts'ą̀' ree łyâa veenjit gwak'aantii giyàhnyàa.

Aii googàa ree tr'aah'in kwàa.

SF5.45 Aiits'ą̀' it'ee yeezhee shyaaghan nèekwąįį nąįį zheh gwizhìt dhidii ch'yąą aii nąįį khan neegaa'in, akhài' aii shyaaghan nąįį gogwandàii.

Gogwandàii ts'ą̀' it'ee chineegeejìl ts'ą̀' t'ee yeedee shìh dhidlii ch'ii'dàk gwats'ą̀' gwik'ìinzhii łee ts'ą̀' aii shìh kwat ajyàa aii ghài' dhidii łee giyàhnyàa.

Izhìk dhidii ts'ą̀' it'ee dinjii shòo ahtsii kwaa t'ii'in ts'ą̀' gwik'ìt giits'an gwìłtsąįį gooràhnyaa į'.

LG Ą̀ąhą'.

SF6.27 Aii ch'iidàk nijìn gwąąh'in ch'iidąą ch'ooghwan hàa diits'ą̀' tr'iinzhii giyàhnyàa.

LG Mmm hmm.

SF6.38 Aii gwiizhìk it'ee zhyą̀ą ginlęįį t'igii'in ǫ'.

Gwiizhìk it'ee zhyą̀ą giinoodį̀įljil łee ts'ą̀' it'ee tthak giinan datthak gwitee gwìłtràt.

Jii giidzèe agàa, datthak giinan gwitee gwìłtrat ts'ą̀' jii giidzèe oonjit nàhąą?

Aii teegogwąhtą' nats'ą̀ą hee'àl gò'?

Aii jyàa dìgiyinlìk ts'ą̀' t'ee zhik giitth'àn kwaii hàa datthak teegwìłtrat ts'ą̀' jèiinch'yaa dak neegiyìłkhaa ts'ą̀' it'ee giihàagwihiiłnąįį.

Daganlì' zhrįh hàa. (Lillian adlaa)

SF7.18 Izhìk chat shìh jyàa dìriinlìk gwinyaa ǫ'.

<sflg2b>

SF12.43 Ąįį jyàa dìgii'in geh'àn t'ee zhat gwànaa dą̀į' shìh, shìh it'ee dinjii a'àa ts'ą̀' it'ee, it'ee ch'atth'anh gwįįlì' ginyàa.

Aii dinjii a'àa ts'ą̀' vatthą̀į' ch'atth'anh ilìk.

Aiits'ą̀' it'ee ìizųų ilìk ǫ'.

Ts'ą̀' jii vaghài' kat tthak jii zhyą̀ą łuu zhrįh adaatsìk.

SF5.19 They say the track was heading right in the direction where all the sod huts were.

They say they were very alert for that bear as they were walking.

But they still didn't see him.

SF5.45 They hurried up and checked on those two old ladies that were staying in one of the sod huts, but they were still alive and so they went out.

They say the bear went up to where the meat was and that it just stayed there by the meat, eating it.

LG Yes.

SF6.27 They say it really made the people angry when he did that to them.

LG Mmm hmm.

SF6.38 But they sure got back at him over it.

When he saw them, he growled and charged toward them.

But there were so many of them, they surrounded him and they grabbed onto every part of his body, even his ears, you see?

How could he bite them if they held on to his ears?

Then they grabbed his arms and legs.

And then they flipped him over on his back and killed him.

With their bare hands. (Lillian laughs)

SF7.18 That's what happened to this bear, they say.

<sflg2b>

SF12.43 They say when a bear eats people it turns into an ice bear.

In those days there were lots of ice bears.

A bear's fur turns to ice because it eats human flesh.

Then it turns bad.

So what it does is go in and out of open water until its fur is all covered with ice.

13.42 Aiitł'ęę it'ee iłts'ik kwaa ts'ą̀' t'ee dinjii aghan t'aràhnyàa.

LG13.51 He', ąįį gàa vàashandàii kwaa łii reh.
Jyàhts'ą̀' eh'àn.
Jàghaii ch'atth'anh ginyaa t'iginyaa nihthan łee.

SF14.02 Izhìk gwànaa dąį̀' łyâa vigwįįlį̀' giyàhnyaa į'.
Izhìk gwànaa dąį̀' chat dinjii gitsii kwaa, nàhąą.
Dinjii nàdhak dąį̀' chat gitsii kwàa.[3]
Aiits'ą̀' kwat a'àa ts'ą̀' ìizųų ilìk t'agàhnyaa.
Aii t'ee ch'atth'anh agàhnyaa t'iginyàa.

3. McKennan says that Gwich'in burials on an elevated cache inside a split hollowed-out log occurred only after the introduction of the steel axe, but since large trees were scarce in the *Chandalar* country "this method of interment could not have been used very often" (1965:60). Osgood says that "The *Peel River* Kutchin consider interment on an elevated cache or stage as the normal method of disposing of the dead" (1936:145). Sarah's remarks indicate that perhaps the platform cache method was once widely practiced and customary among the Neets'it Gwich'in also, even without the log coffin. —CM

13.42 After that it never gets sick, and then it just preys on humans.

LG13.51 Huh, I didn't even know that. So that's why. I often wanted to know why they called them *ch'atth'anh*.

SF14.02 They say there were lots of them around in those days.
You see in those days they never buried people.
When people died they didn't bury them.
Then these bears ate the dead bodies, and they're talking about that's why they turned so vicious.
So they say that's why they're called *ch'atth'anh* or "ice bears."

Fig. 14. Ch'atthanh (Ice Bear), Klukshu River, Yukon, 2020. Photo by Peter Mather.

<sfrf1a>

SF36.29 Ch'adąį' shitsii oondàk dinjii lęįį nąįį niinjìk dąį'.
Dinjii lęįį nąįį gaatsii t'ôonch'yàa?

SF36.48 Nijìn dąį'?

RF Łyâa ninzhìt dąį' hee dǫhlįį?

SF36.52 Aii dinjii ehłik gwinyaa dąį' lèe?

RF Ą̀ąhą'.

SF36.58 Izhìk dąį' dinjii tr'ohchìt ts'ik hàagiindàii kwaa dąį'.
Dinjii lęįį èhłik ginyàa.

RF37.08 Aii shitsii gàa gwitee t'ii'in?

SF *No.*

SF37.13 Aii ti'yąą zhrįh.
Ti'yąą chan ts'ą' yaaghà' *Paul Solòmòn vitì',* aii nąįį hàa tsyaa ginlii gwànaa t'ee dinjii ehłik ginyàa.
Ch'iindàk tthał ghàih tr'igwich'įį.

RF37.30 Aii nijìn gwà'àn hęę?

SF37.32 Nijìn yeendee oondee *Arctìc Villàge* yeendòk ch'iinaa datthak dinjii gwandàii.

37.43 Izhìk gwàndàk datthak hee tr'igwich'įį nyàa.
Izhìk hee âa, khaiits'ą' dinjii heełee łii gwintl'ôo ch'atthąįį lęįį tr'îiłkhwąįį nyàa, ti'yąą geeneegwaandàk.
Izhìk it'ee drah choh kwat chiitąįį doodlii nyàa.
Gwiizhìk it'ee *Gwichyaa* Gwich'in, ootthàn gogwąąh'yą' ts'ą' k'ineegiidàl akhài' ts'ik hàa k'ineegiidal gavàhnyàa.

38.29 Aiits'ą' it'ee zhyąą dinjii ałts'ik nàgwaadhàk nyàa.
Dinjii ałts'ik gwichįh hàagiindàii kwàa. Aiits'ą' zhyąą giveenjit gwìizuu ts'ą' yaaghà' ch'ak'ǫh ts'ą' zhyąą cheegiidàl aii hàa noonlyàa gwìizųų dinjii dats'an gwìltsąįį nyaa t'aihnyàa.

38.52 Aiits'ą' łyâa zhik tthał ghàih dinjii gwich'įį.
Aii zhik tthał ghàih dinjii datthak èhłik nyàa.

39.06 Aii ti'yąą geeneegwaandàk.
Dinjii zhyąą ree hàa chį' haadhàk nyàa.
Aiits'ą' dèegwihee'yàa gàhgwiindàii kwaa ts'ą' it'ee zhyąą dachan tsiik'ìt tr'agwahtsii nyàa.

<sfrf1a>

RF36.29 My grandfather once talked about people dying off.
Did they bury all of them?

SF36.48 When was that?

RF It must have been a long time ago.

SF36.52 Was that when they say people died from an epidemic?

RF Yes.

SF36.58 That was the first time people didn't know anything about sickness. And they say lots of them died from that.

RF37.08 Was my grandfather there?

SF No.

SF37.13 Only my father. My father and *Paul Solomon*'s father were young men then. They say lots of them died.
They were living by a caribou fence.

RF37.30 Where was that?

SF37.32 All the way up toward *Arctic Village*.
People were living all over that area.

37.43 He said we were all living around there.
My father said that before the people died, we killed lots of caribou. He told us about it.
He said there were lots of meat caches all over.
That was when they took a trip to visit the *Yukon Flats* people.
But when they returned he said they came back with that sickness.

38.29 He said people got sick.
We never heard of anyone getting sick before.
He said that they went out in the cold and got worse.

38.52 All those people living by the caribou fence died.
That's what my father told us.

39.06 Father said people just died off instantly.
We didn't know what to do so we built a cellar, he said.
That's where we piled them.

Izhìk gwizhìt zhyàą dinjii nihkak deerahłii nyàa.

Aii it'ee jidìi shìh, shìh aii dinjii a'àa, aii it'ee ch'atth'anh ilìk ginyaa t'iginyàa, zhat gwànaa.

39.44 Ch'atth'anh ilìk ts'ą̀' aii chan it'ee veenjit gwìizųų ts'ą̀' zhyàą dinjii a'àa roh.

Aiits'ą̀' veenjit gwìizųų ts'ą̀' it'ee zhyàą teeddhaa hee teenaa'òo. Aii it'ee ch'atth'anh ilìk ginyàa.

40.09 Gwintł'òo dinjii lęįį ehłik nyaa geegwaandàk.

Gwintł'òo gwìizųų nyaa t'aihnyàa.

Dinjii tr'itsii kwaa nyàa.

Zhyàą dachan tsiik'it gwachoh tr'agwahtsìk zhyàą nihkat deegoorahłii gooràhnyàa. Jyàhts'ą̀' gwizhrįh.

40.42 Ts'ik hàagiindàii kwaa ts'ą̀' ree t'igii'ìn.

Gwintsàl dinjii lęįį ehłik ginyàa.

Aii tthał ghàih gwich'įį nąįį datthak.[4]

4. This commentary marks a transition into the *Famine in the Early Days* story, first version, which Sarah tells without interruption. —CM

That's what the bear ate, and it turned into an ice bear.
That's what they said about it in those days.

39.44 After the bear turns into an ice bear it doesn't feel good, so it eats human flesh. And then too it doesn't feel so good.
It goes in the open water until it becomes an ice bear, they say.

40.09 He told us how so many people had died from that sickness.
He said it was so bad that they didn't even bury them.
They built a large log storage cellar and just piled them up in there. That's all they did.

40.42 They did this because they didn't know anything about sickness.
They say that lots of people died off.
All the people along the caribou fence died off.

Sarah Frank

Deenaa Dąįį' Shìh Kwaa[1]
Ch'eechyah Ch'ìhłak

<sfrfla>

SF41.11 Nąhjyàa it'ee chan yaaghà' shitsųų *Mil Vahan* giyàhnyàa.
Aii it'ee ti'yąą chįh dąį' hee gwats'an gwandàii t'aihnyàa.
Aii chat shàhgwaandak hee t'inyàa.
Êe' gwintł'òo shìh ehdan dinjii lęįį àn dhidlit nyàa.
Ch'aga'àa kwaa ts'ą'.
Googàa neegihiinjik gàa reh gògǫǫtrìi.
41.51 Aiits'ą' zhyąą nijìn nirinjik zhyąą dinjii làt nąįį tthak it'ee ahchìk.
Deegooreheelyàa zhyąą jèiinch'yaa geełèerahadàl nyàa.
Dinjii *lęįį* ehłik nyaa, aii shitsųų chan shàhgwaandak t'aihnyàa.
42.18 Izhìk it'ee jyàa diginch'yaa shrahtèegadàl, nàhąą.
Shrahtèegadàl nijìn giveenjit gwiheezyàa jì' gwats'ą' shrahtèegadàl gavàhnyàa.
Googàa aii goolàt nąįį neeraa'in kwaa gavàhnyàa.
42.37 It'ee shìh kwaa dąį' givehdànagąįį.
Izhìk it'ee zhik chan, thok adan chan dinjii hàajil aii nąįį chat, goolàt nąįį zhyąą diiłèerahadàl ginyàa.
Shitsųų shàagwaandak t'aihnyàa.
Jyàa digwii'in nyaa, aiits'ą' it'ee dinjii ch'ìhłęę reh it'ee geedant'ee geheedluu gwats'ą' reh.
Va'at vigii ch'ìhłak gǫǫlįį yàhnyàa.
43.29 Vigii ch'ìhłak gǫǫlįį ts'ą' it'ee zhyąą it'ee ch'ii'àn hàazhii.
Ninzhyùk hàazhii kwaa ts'ą' it'ee giveegògwàntrii ts'ą' t'ee izhìk it'ee nìgiindii łii gavàhnyàa.
Dzaa chan zhyąą tąįh tsal dha'ąįį k'ìt t'ôonch'yaa gwats'ą' ch'ii'àn it'ee nįįvyah zheh gwigwìltsąįį dǫhłįį.
44.02 Aiits'ą' it'ee oondaa tr'ijit, traa tsal khèedìlk'ìn.
Googàa jidii gihèe'aa gǫ'.

1. Johnny Frank also knew this story and told a brief English version of it to Mike Holloway. See <jfmhlb>. —CM

Sarah Frank

Famine in the Early Days
First Version

<sfrfla>

SF41.11 Long before that, my great-grandmother, whom they called *Mil's Mother*, was living way back before my father's time.
And she told me this.
She told me how so many people had died from starvation because of nothing to eat.
But still they kept on traveling with what little strength they had.
41.51 So whenever they camped overnight, the next day they had to leave behind the ones who had died.
She said that they just left them there.
They just left them like that.
I'm saying many people died there.
42.18 When this happened, she said they all went their separate ways to where they might have a better chance to survive, you see.
Yet she said many of them never returned at all.
42.37 If there was no food, they starved.
So they just went in different directions, but they still kept dying.
That's what my great-grandmother told me.
So she said that's what was happening with this one man and his wife and their one child.
43.29 So they just went in different directions from each other.
They didn't go very far until it was too hard for them to go any farther, and she said that they made their camp there.
It looked like there was a little hill there and so they pitched their skin tent toward it.
44.02 Somehow this man built a little fire.
But there was nothing to eat.

Traa tsal khèegìilk'in ts'ą̀' it'ee zhyą̀ą gavàa oo'àn nàgwaatth'at łii gavàhnyàa.
Aiits'ą̀' aii tr'iinin ch'ìhłak gii'įį aii goodeetak dhidii ts'ą̀' it'ee gwiizhìk gavàa àn gwahàadhat.
Aiits'ą̀' aii it'ee t'inyaa dǫ̀hłįį.
Itree ts'ą̀' it'ee, "Ne'ęę, jidìi ch'akwaiigǫhtsan[2] gwaatsan," nyaa.
Ts'ą̀' it'ee itree ts'ą̀' gooteetak dhidìi.
Aiits'ą̀' it'ee gàh neeniinjìk dǫ̀hłįį, zhik tr'ìnjyàa aii.
Gàh neeniinjik łii ts'ą̀' it'ee yeendaa gwigwîiłk'in ch'yąh, aii traa tsal nihk'àa neehiilìi, akhài' ree zhyą̀ą dzat ch'iinii zhyą̀ą dinjik nagwàl aii tr'iin'ee łii, aii kat it'ee gwigwîiłk'in łii gavàhnyàa.
45.27 Gwigwîiłk'in łii, aii it'ee ahtsan t'inyaa łii yàhnyàa.
Âa!
Aiits'ą̀' it'ee łyâa gwinzįį tthak yik'yǎandàii ts'ą̀' ree dèiinch'yaa dinjik nagwàl kat gwigwîiłk'in łii aii ahtsan t'inyaa łii.
Aiits'ą̀' gwinzįį k'ìjìljik tł'ęę t'ee yeendee vakąį' vàa àn nàgwaatth'at gàhneeniinjii kwaa, nàhąą.
Aii it'ee zhyą̀ą k'àahàazhii dǫ̀hłįį.
Akhài' aii dinjii chan . . .[3]

<sfrflb>

SF0.06 Shìhîiłkhwąį' t'ii'in yuunyàa.
"Ijìi dèeni'in t'ine'ìn?
Zhyą̀ą khai' ts'ą̀' hee tr'eheedluu nihthan dèene'ìn," nyàa.
Akhài' it'ee zhyą̀ą.
"Dòonch'in ts'ą̀' dèe?" t'inyàa.

2. The *ch'akwaiigǫhtsan* is an olfactory gland in the hoof of a moose that helps it communicate with other moose, especially during the rut. Caribou also have these interdigital glands. —KF and CM

3. Story continues onto the B side of the same tape. —CM

So he built a little fire and suddenly they all fell asleep unconscious, she said.
While they were sound asleep that one child was sitting in the middle of them and this is what she was saying.
She was crying and saying, "Mama, I smell a singed hoof."
And she kept on crying right there in between them.
So the woman finally became conscious.
And after she came to, she was fixing the fire that she built before when she came across a moose leg that was sticking out, and discovered that's what she had built the fire on.
45.27 She said that's what they built fire on and that's what she smelled.
Ah!
So she really checked it out well and then she realized they built their fire on top of some moose legs.
So after she checked it out, she just fell over on her husband who still hadn't awakened, you see.
She must have thrown herself on her husband.
And he thought. . .

<sfrflb>

SF0.06 He thought she was trying to kill him.
Then he said, "Gee, I thought we were going to die slowly.
What are you trying to do?"
Then she told him.
She said, "What are you saying?"

"Yeendaa ch'angwàl[4] chi'in'ee kat tr'igwîiłk'in łee, aii eenjit t'ishi'ìn," jyàa yàhnyàa.

0.41 Ts'ą̀' it'ee yats'ą̀' dak khàkěe'ą̀įį.

Datthak gwinzįį gwąąh'in akhài' zhyą̀ą ree dinjik nagwàl ch'iindàa jèiinch'yaa kat gwigwîiłk'in łèe.

Aii khaiits'ą̀' dinjik nihłoankee haa'oo, nàhąą.

Dinjik nihłaaghwąįį, akhài' jii vijì' aii nihłą̀ą jyàa dǐizhik ts'ą̀' nihts'at tr'inidii kwàa, zhyą̀ą dinjik nèekwąįį zhat iłchįį łee.

Aii it'ee ts'ą̀' nìgiindii t'igii'in łee gavàhnyàa.

1.32 Âa, gwintł'òo shòh gaadlìt gavàhnyàa.

Aiits'ą̀' it'ee aii chat vak'àa gwâak'ą' ts'ą̀' dhich'yaa, nàhąą?

Aiits'ą̀' it'ee jidìi tsal khèegaatsìt ts'ą̀' aiitł'ęę aii dinjik t'aihnyaa nèekwąįį reh.

2.09 Aii t'ee giitthąį' tsal khą̀htr'it aii hàa t'ee yaaghà' dinjii it'ee nìneegijii kwaa nąįį, oo'àn shìh tsal hàa oo'àn goots'eehòozhìi.

Aiits'ą̀' it'ee jidìi tsal goots'ą' hiłchit zhik gwandàii nąįį.

Goolàt naii ch'adą̀į' hee kwaa gavàhnyàa.

2.45 Aiits'ą̀' aii naii t'ee jùu gwandàii tsal nilįį naii datthak zhat gwats'ą̀' gahàajìl.

Jyàa dǐizhik ch'iighai' gogwandàii goovàhnyąą t'aihnyàa.

Izhìk t'ee *Mil Vahan* shàagwaandak t'agwaihnyàa.

3.10 Dinjii lęįį anlìi nyą̀ą, gàa gogwandàii gavàhnyàa.

Gwintł'òo gògǫ̀ǫntrii ch'iinaa gwinìindhàt gwinyąą t'ôonch'yàa.

3.44 Aiits'ą̀' it'ee giighàih, izhìk dą̀į' gwintł'òo ch'aga'àa kwaa t'agooràhnyàa.

Giighàih nǐinjil ts'ą̀' digwigwìl'gǫ̀'.

Gwich'ìighai' dinjii làt naii gwandàii nyąą t'aihnyàa.[5]

4. The *ch'angwàl* refers to both the metacarpal and metatarsal, a.k.a. the cannon bones. The meat and tendons of these bones are a Gwich'in delicacy. See Mishler and Frank (2020: 424).

5. This marks the end of the story. —LG

She told him, "We built the fire right out there where a moose's cannon bones are sticking out."

0.41 So then he woke up to her.

After he checked out everything, he found that he did build the fire on top of a moose's legs.

There were two moose that got in a fight during the rutting season in the fall, and somehow both of their antlers got stuck together.

So there were two dead moose that they camped on top of.

That's what she said about them, you see.

1.32 Ah, she said they were so happy.

Since the fire was right on top of it, some of tendons were cooked, you see?

2.09 They cut some meat off and ate a little bit of it.

After that they cut off some more parts and took some back to the people that couldn't go any farther.

He fed a little bit to those people that were still alive.

He told them some of the others had already died though.

2.45 What few survivors were left all went back with him.

She said that's what they did and that's how they survived.

This is what *Mil Vahan* told me about.

3.10 She said lots of people died, but she said some survived.

They say people really had hard times in those days.

3.44 At that time we say that people didn't eat much.

So that's how they survived through the cold winter until spring break-up.

That's how many of those people survived.

I mean that's what she said.

SF4.06 Âa, gwinlin gwìizuu gwinyaa gwagwandàk gǫ̀ǫlįį t'ôonch'yàa.
Dòoghai' tr'iinin chiitee ilìk.
Viyèhghan kwaa, aii naii googàa geetàk akharoonjìk ginyaa t'ôonch'yaa, nàhąą.
Izhìk it'ee geetàk geeneegogwaandak dąįį' gitree ts'ą̀' geegogwaandak t'agavaihnyàa.

5.09 Shitsųų jyàa nyàa ch'ìhłan shìh ehdan tr'eedàa nyàa.
Izhìk chan tr'injàa nìindhat nyàa.
Aii chan deereheelyàa vàh gwiindàii kwaa ts'ą̀' drah veeriłtsąįį kat dèeriłchįį yàhnyàa.
Aiits'ą̀' vigii tsal chan gǫ̀ǫlįį yàhnyàa.
Aii chan gwandàii ts'ą̀' vitsùu rąhchįį ts'ą̀' veełèerahàandii t'ee nyàa.
Gogǫ̀ǫntrii gwinlęįį t'igwee'yą̀' gwinyąą t'ôonch'yàa.

6.03 It'ee jùk zhyą̀ą łyâa shrôonch'yaa tr'agwandàii gàa chan dęhtł'yaa kat t'igwinyaa, shìh ehdan tr'agwahąąh'yàa gwits'ireedaa[6] gwìch'in t'ôonch'yaa shìh kwaa.

RF6.28 Datthak ts'ą̀' gwak'oorehèedàa.

SF Ą̀ąhą'. Aii jùk gwits'ireedaa t'ôonch'yàa.

RF6.39 Aii jùu zhrįh K'eegwaadhat k'injikhit naii zhrįh ch'idiheedàa.

SF6.56 Ą̀ąhą'. Jùk shrôonch'yaa tr'agwandàii gàa gògǫ̀ǫntrii diidivee gòodlii, googàa K'eegwaadhat oodiitą̀' k'ìt t'inch'yaa naii zhrįh.
Aii chan ts'ą̀' shìh kwaa chan jii nèekwąįį łyâa tr'agwahąąh'yàa gwizhrįh, hee?

RF Ą̀ąhą'.

6. *Gwits'ireedaa* is how Sarah says it, but it's now been changed to *gwats'à'reeda* by the younger people. — JE

SF4.06 They say there were many terrible stories like that.
Even the kids became orphans.
They even said that when the kids' parents died they just left the children behind to die, you see.
When they recalled these incidents they just wept as they told each other about it.
That's what my grandma said.

5.09 My grandma said that one time they were traveling with no food.
That time, she said, one woman died.
They didn't know what to do with her so they built a raised, open cache.
That's what they laid her on.
She had a little baby too, she said.
He was still alive but they put him inside her clothing with her and left her there, she said.
They went through many heartaches.

6.03 Today everything seems to be fun in our lives, but in the Bible it says we will see famine again.

RF6.28 We all will go through it.

SF Yes. It's in the future for us.

RF6.39 Only people that believe in God will survive.

SF6.56 Yes. Right now we have a happy life, but we never know what's in the future for us, except for the ones who hang on to God.
This one and famine, these are two things we will really face someday, right?

RF Yes.

Deenaa Dą̀į' Shìh Kwaa
Ch'eechyah Nèekwąįį

<sflg2b>

SF0.18 Ąįį shitsųų *Mil Vahan* t'ee ąįį yagahà' ti'yąą ąįį chįh dą̀į' gwats'an gwandàii t'aihnyàa.

Ąįį it'ee shah gwaandàk.

1.00 Deenaa dą̀į' shìh kwaa dą̀į' dinjii hàa neeshreegwâahch'yaa t'igwinyàa.

Ch'ìhłan khaii shìh kwaa gwiizhìk tr'eenjyaa gwinyàa.

Shìh kwaa ts'ą̀' geetàk dinjii zhehk'ąą ch'ìhłak datthak gàa gookwàa gwilìk.

1.30 Jyàa dìgii'in gwiizhìk geenjyàa.

Aiits'ą̀' oondaa nìriinjik chan jidìi gihee'àa gàagiindàii kwàa.

Ts'ą̀' zhyą̀ą oondaa nìriinjik ts'ą̀' gwagwâahk'ìk.

Gàa łyâa kǫ̀' k'èegąąhtìi.

Jyàa dìgii'in hàa tr'eedàa ts'ą̀' geedàa.

Gòhch'it t'ee łyâa gògǫǫtrii ts'ą̀' dinjii làt tth'aii gwintsàl eenjit gwinzįį izhìk dą̀į' t'ee ch'aga'àa kwaa ts'ą̀' łyâa zhyą̀ą goozhràk gàa kwaa googàhnyàa.

2.01 Aiits'ą̀' vadzaih dhàa dazhoo aii làt khàraht'àa aii t'ee dagazhràk kat deenìn nìgiyahchaa ts'ą̀' vak'àa tł'yah dàrahchàa.

Aii k'iighai' googàa gwintsàl diineenjit gwinzįį ts'ą̀' shragwarâadhan ginyàa.

Aiits'ą̀' jyàa dìgwii'in ts'ą̀' googàa dinjii làt tèech'ìdlì' gwiizhìk zhyą̀ą gwats'an tr'aradàl ginyaa.

2.35 Łyâa zhyą̀ą nehshrit t'igii'in reh.

Aiits'ą̀' chan hee nìrįįdii ginyàa, łyâa t'ee gwats'an tr'eegiheedàa gògǫǫtrii.

Akhài' dinjii ch'ìhłęę. . .

LG2.58 Ą̀ąhą'.

Famine in the Early Days
Second Version

<sflg2b>

SF0.18 I'm saying my great-grandmother, *Mil's Mother*, was from farther back than my own father.

That's who told me this story.

1.00 This story is about famine that took place a long time ago when it's said that a band of Gwich'in was undergoing great hardship.

They say that one winter they were traveling along, moving from one place to another with no food whatsoever.

Sometimes during this famine an entire family would perish.

1.30 Yet they kept on moving while this was happening to them.

They would reach a place to spend the night, still not knowing what they would eat.

All they could do was stop and build a fire.

They really took good care of the flint they had for starting fires.

While this was happening to them, they kept on moving.

Finally times got really bad.

Some people still had a little strength, but not having eaten yet, their stomachs got really flat, they say.

2.01 Then they would cut a piece of caribou fur off and, laying it across their bellies, they would tie a rope around it to keep it in place.

They say just that would make them feel a little better and more comfortable.

And in the meantime, they say, while some of the people were dying off, others would continue to survive.

2.35 It got to the point where they were just barely making it.

Again they stopped to rest, and this time it was really difficult for them to start off again.

But there was this one important man. . .

LG2.58 Yes.

SF2.59 Dinjii ch'ìhłęę, vigii ch'ìhłak ts'ą' va'at aii hàa t'ee zhyąą dagats'àt, aii t'ee dazhoo ts'àt, ts'ą' nįįvyaa kwaii hàa zhrįh geelìl.

Zhyąą zhik dinjii kwaii iiheendii kwaa ts'ą' adan ąįį dàa tr'ineezhìi.

Dàhthee giveegwìgwiheetrii gwats'ą' t'igii'ìn.

3.43 Aiits'ą' t'ee geedàa akhài' giveegògǫǫtrii ts'ą' ninzhùk gahàajil kwàa.

Aiitł'ęę zhyąą yaaghà' ch'ii'àn tąįh tsal dìlk'at k'ìt t'įįchyaa.

Aiits'ą' ch'ii'àn zhah tsal khàgiindhàt, ts'ą' t'ee nįįvyaa gwanàgôołjìk.

Aiits'ą' it'ee ree yeendaa chan traa tsal heegîilk'in.

Ts'ą' zhyąą jyàa dìgįįch'yaa gwiizhìk ch'aga'àa kwàa.

Gwiizhìk gwâak'ą' gwinyàa khehłee oo'àn gihìltth'at łii.

4.45 Jyàa dìgiinch'yaa ts'ą' gavàa àn gòo'ąįį, ąįį gwiizhìk googii zhrįh gootsįį gaandàii łii.

Aii tr'iinin zhyąą itree, itree ts'ą' t'ee t'inyaa giyàhnyàa.

"Ni'ęę, yeendaa ch'akwai' gwaatsan!" nyaa ts'ą' itree.

5.45 Jyàa dìnyaa ts'ą' gòhch'it t'ee vahan yats'ą' gàa neeneenjìk.

Chan hee tr'iinin itree ts'ą' jyàa nyàa,

"Ni'ęę, yeendaa ch'akwài' gwaatsan gwaatsa!"

6.23 Aiits'ą' khàkee'ąįį ts'ą' yeendaa gwâak'ą' kǫ' aii nihk'yàa hàak'in ąįį nihkat deenahłii akhài' ree dzaa ch'iinii zhyąą dinjik kwài' kha'iin'ee kat gwâak'ą' łii.

Ąįį ch'akwài' dhàh ndùh ahtsan t'inyaa łii.

6.52 Aiits'ą' gwindii datthak neehaandak akhài' zhyąą dinjik nagwàl kat gwigwîiłk'in łii.

Ąįį dìlk'at t'ee dinjik t'įįch'yaa łii.

7.24 Aiits'ą' t'ee yeendee vakài' gàa neeneenjii kwaa ąįį zhyąą shòh hàa yak'àahàazhìi.

SF2.59 There was this one important man who, with his wife and only child, just packed up their blankets, their skin blankets, and their skin tent on their sled, and they kept pulling that, kept on going.

Because no one else in the band was moving, he went on himself.

They kept on going, not knowing how far they would get.

3.43 So they were going along; it was really hard for them, and they didn't get very far.

After a while they noticed an area that had a little hump-shaped hill.

And so they dug a little snow out on the side of that hump.

And they pitched their skin tent there up against that hump.

Next they built a small fire.

And they stayed that way, still without eating.

As they sat in front of the fire, both parents passed out.

4.45 And while they were in that condition, their little child was still awake.

The child was just crying and crying.

"Mom, I smell some kind of fur burning!" the child said, crying.

5.45 He kept repeating this over and over again until finally his mother came to in response to his crying.

Again the child cried to her, "Mom, I smell some kind of fur burning."

6.23 So when his mother got up and went to pile up the embers from the fire, which had become scattered, she noticed that the fire was burning on top of a moose hoof sticking out from below.

And the fur on the moose hoof was burning; that's what the child was saying he smelled.

6.52 The mother felt all around the moose hoof and discovered they had built the fire on top of a lower moose leg there.

And she realized that hump was an entire moose.

7.24 Very excited, she went over and threw herself down on her husband, who was still passed out, to wake him up.

Akhài' yats'ą' gàh neeneenjìk, aiits'ą' t'iyàhnyàa, "Ijìi khài' ts'ą' tr'iheedluu nihthan nats'àa dèeni'in t'ini'ìn," nyàa.

Shìhîiłkhwąį' yuunyàa.

8.09 Dòonch'in ts'ą' t'agwàhnyàa, "Yeendaa dinjik nagwàl kat tr'igwîilk'in łii eenjit t'ishi'ìn," va'at yàhnyàa.

8.31 Aiits'ą' t'ee vakąį' yats'ą' dàk kheekèe'ąįį.

Ąįį ch'angwàl kat ch'àt dhich'yaa khàgąht'uu tsal neegįį'àl hàa gàa neeginįįjìk k'ìt t'igiizhìk.

Aiitł'ęę nèhkàa vàn dąį' neeyaakàa gwiizhìk khàkìgaazhii.

Ąįį vakąį' gwįįzii datthak gwąąh'in ahkài' dinjik nèekwąįį t'inch'yaa łii.

10.01 Zhik vikhyųų gwâak'à' ts'ą' vakat neegwaaghwan gwà'àn t'ee nilįį khànìłt'ùu.

Aiits'ą' t'ee oo'àt dinjii làt eełèegahàajil gwits'eeyihiłtsìt.

Oo'àt k'inidik gàa ch'adąį' hee goolàt nąįį kwàa.

Goolàt nąįį nèhshrit gwandàii ąįį nąįį t'ee shìh tsal hàa t'ee eek'inidìk.

Shìh tsal gavàntł'ahtsìt.

10.52 Ąįį gįį'àl ts'ą' gàa neegineenjìk k'ìt t'igwiizhìk ts'ą' oo'àn giyàa neehòojìl.

Ąįį vik'iighai' dinjii làt neegwiindàii vàràhnyàa.

11.08 Ąįį dinjik khaiits'ą' hee nihłankeehaa'òo, dąį' nihłaaghwąįį, aii vijì' nihłìlzhrak ts'ą' oo'àn gahàajil ąįį agogwąh'ąįį t'igwinyàa.[7]

SF14.27 Aiits'ą' jyàa dìgwii'in ts'ą' it'ee aii k'ìighai' ąįį dinjii tsal naii gwandàii nyàa.

Ąįt'ee łyâa diikhwan dinehnaa ti'yąą ąįį chįh dąį' gwats'an gwandàii t'inyaa ąįį *Mil Vahan*.

7. Becausc of a lengthy three-minute digression in the conversation that follows this sentence, part of the text has been cut and placed into Sarah's *Ch'atth'anh lce Bear* story.

And finally, when he became conscious, he said to her, "I thought we were just going to die slowly! Why are you doing this?"

He thought she was trying to do him in.

8.09 And his wife said, "How can you say that?

What's happened is that we built our fire on top of a moose leg.

That's what I'm trying to tell you."

8.31 So she got her husband up.

They cut out little pieces of cooked tendon from the moose leg cannon bone and ate them.

With that, they felt a little of their strength returning.

The next morning they got up at dawn.

Her husband carefully checked all around, and that's when he discovered there were actually two moose there.

10.01 So on the side of the hump where the fire was, in the area which had thawed, that's where they cut some meat.

Then he took some back to where they had left the others.

When he arrived, already more people had died off.

To the few who were still barely alive, he came back with a little food.

He gave the little food that he had to them.

10.52 After they ate it and felt they were regaining some strength, they went back over with him to where the two moose were.

So in this way he helped some of the people survive, they say.

11.08 They say the two bull moose had been fighting in the fall during the mating season, had apparently locked antlers, fallen and died, and that's how they were found.

SF14.27 So this is what happened, and very few people survived even after they found the two moose under the snow.

All this happened even before my time or my father's time.

So *Mil's Mother* is from way back before my father.

Ąįįt'ee it'ee łyâa neeshrâahch'yaa izhìk dąį' it'ee diikhwan t'ee chan diinee gògǫǫntrii gàa ree vik'èerąąhtii t'aihnyàa.

LG15.14 Izhìk hee gwaandak?

SF15.15 Ą̀ąhą', izhìk hee diihàagwaandak t'aihnyàa. It'ee łyâa dinjii lęįį ch'a'àa kwaa gwilìk ąįį it'ee chan jidii zhik gwà'àn vadzaih, ch'atthąįį k'eh?

LG15.29 Ą̀ąhą'.

SF15.30 Jidìi tsal jyàa dąhtsìi googàa k'èegąąhtii, nyaa.

Aii it'ee ch'ara'àa kwaa gàa diizhìk vàh jyàa dàrah'in yàhnyàa.

Łyâa gwįįtsàl *hard time* zhik gògǫǫtrii gwinyaa ǫ'.

15.51 Aiits'ą̀' it'ee jyàa dìgwii'in nyàa.

SF16.00 Izhìk shin hee zhyąą neegihiidàl gwizhrįh t'igii'ìn, ch'ihłok ch'iizhàk gwigwich'įį kwàa.

Zhik k'ǫǫ gòodlii izhìk it'ee dąįį gwahgǫ̀' gwiizhìk it'ee chųų gwilìk, nàhąą.

Zhik it'ee zhik k'ǫǫ hee łuk tsal ąįį chan gaahkhwąįį k'ìighai' gwizhrįh ch'aga'àa.

Àkwàt tthaa khàh'oo dąį' chan ąįį k'ìighai' gwizhrįh chan jidìi tsal tr'a'àa nyàa.

16.39 Łyâa gògǫǫtrii geegwaandak t'aihnyàa.

Aiits'ą̀', "Diivàt zhìt gwihiljįį dąį' dazhoo tsal it'ee dzaa tr'iłtsùu," nyaa t'aihnyàa.

17.04 Âa dinjii lęįį ch'a'àa kwaa ts'ą̀' dinjii lęįį anlìk k'ìt t'inyaa t'aihnyàa.

Gògǫǫtrii ąįį diilàk nyaa diyèhghan naii gògǫǫtrii gwachoh gwats'an tr'idiigìinlii t'įįch'yàa.

She was the one who told us about it.
She was very old and not well.
Although we were poor, we still took care of her.

LG15.14 Was that when she told stories?

SF15.15 Yes, I'm saying that's when she told us stories.
They say that when the time comes when many people are really starving for so long, they used some little piece of fat which they saved from a caribou or any large game animal.

LG15.29 Yes.

SF15.30 They say that although they didn't eat, they licked on this piece of fat.
They say this was the hardest time of all for them.

15.51 She said this is what they did.

SF16.00 During the summertime they never stayed in one place but were always on the move.
When the water raised from melting snow, they usually stayed near some slough, you see.
They ate the little fish they caught from the slough.
And she said if the ground squirrels were out, then they ate them too.

16.39 As I said, she talked about the most difficult times they had.
As I said, what she said was, "When our stomachs were so empty, we wore a little piece of fur on our chests."

17.04 Like I said, she was saying that they lost many people from starvation.
It was the hardest time, she said, but our parents survived through that hardship.

Johnny Frank

Taa'ii Tì'[1]
Ch'eechyah Ch'ìhłak

<jfka405>

JF0.37 *Òol Tì'* oonjìt *Old Crow* hee, aii gwanaa łyâa nankat gògwàntrìi, aiits'ą̀' *same time,* yaaghà' *Valdez* reh.[2]

Russian aii tr'oochìt izhìk zhat dąį' teetr'ihchoo iłìt.

1.00 Gwats'an k'àiich'i' łyâa ninzhyùk gwiinli' ǫ'.

Tr'oochìt tr'ihchoo teedhidlìt aii k'ìinjik neehòolìt kwàa.

Aii vananh ch'iitsii aii jii *Alaska* kat gwich'in datthak yit'ą̌ąhch'yà' reh (adlaa).

1.26 Shrii, tthoodzyah, tòh, k'i' tsį̀į dha'ąįį, jidìi tsal ginch'ii tthak, dachan èet'ìi gii'įį, aii googàa tthak khàgidiint'uu ts'ą̀' reh.

Aiits'ą̀' k'àiich'ii oonìn ch'izhii chan neegòonjìk.

Izhìk gwats'an t'ee k'àiich'ii naagąįį kwaii tthak gǫ̀ǫlįį.

1.36 Làraa gǫ̀ǫlįį gàagwiindàii kwàa.

Naagąįį nihłehts'ì' *colòr* nilii ts'ą̀' aii zhrįh Dinjii Zhuh tthak yuukwàt.

Tseedhah dàanch'yąą gahtsii tthak naagąįį ch'iitsii hàa zhrįh.

Zhat dąį' oo'àt zhat gwakhàihkwài' t'ee *Taa'ii Tì'* òozhìi.

Łyâa dinjii gǫǫzhįį reh.

2.15 Aii t'ee tr'ihchoo zhìt yuuheendal kwaa gàa (akoo), aii *Taa'ii Tì'* zhat *Russiàn* nąįį teedhijil oo'òk tr'injàa veerîilk'įį nąįį googàa tǫǫ hàa nìgwìgwìilìi.

Tr'ihchoo zhit dinjii lęįį, *ship* choo zhìt.

1. This version of the *Taa'ii Tì* story is actually a preface to the longer story of *Òol Tì' and Goghwaii*, which appears earlier in this volume. It was performed and recorded at the same time on the same tape.

2. *Valdez* is the modern city located on one arm of *Prince William Sound* and founded during the Gold Rush era. It's unlikely that the Russians established a presence there, although they did build trading posts in the Alutiiq villages of *Chenega* and *Nuchek*, also located in *Prince William Sound.* —CM

Johnny Frank

Taa'ii' Tì'
First Version

<jfka405>

JF0.37 There were some hard times at *Old Crow* during the time *Òol Tì'* was living there.

The Russians came to Valdez about that same time.

They landed their ship for the first time.

1.00 Lots of things were available from them for a long time after that.

The first boat did not go back, and the Alaska Natives used up all the steel on it (laughs).

1.26 They brought knives, ice chisels, canes, spear heads, axes, and lots of useful little stuff, saws, and milled lumber.

Then they went over again to pick up more things.

And this time they brought back lots of beads.

1.36 We didn't know anything about money.

The only thing the Indians bought were different kinds of colored beads.

They traded many furs for beads and stoves.

The chief there was a man named *Taa'ii' Tì'*.

He was really wise.

2.15 When the Russians landed there, they fooled around with Indian women during the night.

There were lots of men in the big ship.

2.26 Aii khaihkwaii nilįį, *Taa'ii Tì'* aii inee gavahnyaa googàa nihk'ìt t'igii'ìn.
"Aiits'ą' chan jùk gwats'an chan akòodeekhwa'yàa kwàa," jyàa gavàhnyąą.

2.39 Gwint'aii ginkhii ts'ą' reh.
Aii gwiizhìk reh jùu gǫǫzhii nilįį tthak yatthài' jyàa dàh'ìn:
"Natthài' datłok jàghaii gwiint'aii ginįįkhìi?" yàhnyàa.
President k'ìt t'inch'yaa, t'inch'yaa kwàt vik'ii t'igwinyàa, hôołtin kwaa ts'ą' ch'iindàa gîiłchųų.

3.04 Aiitł'ee, nihkèe vành, "Łyâa chan gwik'ìt t'akhwa'yàa kwaa," gavàhnyaa, googàa chan oo'òk tr'iinjàa tthak veerîilk'įį googàa hàa nìgwìgwìilii reh.
Aiits'ą' oo'òk gwich'in nąįį giyàh gwaandak.

3.15 Gwiizhìk oozhee giłchųų roh.
Yaaghà' gwà'àn zheh gwadhàa zhìt giłchųų jèiinch'yaa ts'ą' datòo òonjik ts'ą' gootąagìt.
Gwiizhìk khàgiizhràl.

3.25 Vatthąį' datłòk gàa àndhat shuuch'îił'ąįį kwaa t'inch'yaa kwàa, t'inch'yaa[3] zhrįh gavàhnyąą ts'ą' gootăagìt.
Aiits'ą' reh dǫǫ nąįį oonìn tr'ihchoo neehahłaa zhrįh akhŏonyàa.

3.34 Giveenjit gwìizųų kwàt dèegeheenjyàa gǫ̀'?
"Aiits'ą' nijin gwats'an t'akhwa'in gwits'ee khwajyaa," goovahnyaa.

3.50 "Izhit dąį', danàa neehindii," giyàhnyàa.
Aii *boss* aii hàandàii.
Zhik tr'ihchoo k'ahndak, t'inch'yaa dǫǫ zhrįh, nàhąą?

4.02 Aiits'ą' aii *boss* reh, oonìn danàa neehindii yàhnyąą.
"Ą̀ąhą'," nyàa.
Aiits'ą' oonìn gavàa hàazhìi (adlaa).

4.27 Aiitł'ee oonjìt reh *President* dhidii eenihdèe giyąąhchįį.
Tr'ihchoo oondìt *Alaskà* neiinlìt dinjii dàanch'yąą dizhìilk'įį datthak vành ch'ihłòk tthak giviighan t'inch'yaa.

---

3. This *t'inch'yaa* is superfluous. —KP
But it's needed because it's told from the storyteller's point of view. —JE

2.26 The chief named *Taa'ii'Tì'* told them not to bother the women, but they still did it, so he told them,
"Don't ever do that again!"
2.39 He spoke very loudly.
The Russian men he was talking to at that time were feeling his body muscles like this (gesturing) and said to him:
"You have weak body, why are you talking?"
He was like a President himself so he was really mad when they told him that.
He didn't say another word until everyone went to bed.
3.04 The next morning, he reminded them, "Don't do it again," but they still fooled around with the women, even the married women.
The people in the village told him about it.
3.15 The Russian men were sleeping at that time.
They were all sleeping in tents, and *Taa'ii'Tì'* got his short spear and stabbed all of them.
They all cried out in pain.
3.25 While doing that, he reminded them that they underestimated him and that his body was not weak.
He only spared four men who would take the ship back over (to *Russia*).
3.34 They didn't like it, but what would they do about it?
"So since you kept on doing it, go on back to where you came from," that's what he said to them.
3.50 So the four men said to him, "Leave with us."
They knew their own captain.
Only those four men were sailing the ship, you see?
4.02 The captain of that ship asked him to return with them.
"Okay, yes," he said.
So he went back over with them (laughs).
4.27 When they arrived (in Russia) they took him to the President there.
Taa'ii'Tì' told him about the shipload of men that went over in Alaska and how he killed them all that one morning.

4.32 Jàghaii t'ii'ìn ginyaa akhài' gahaahchìi kwaa nàhąą?
Geedan googwitr'it geh'an t'agoorah'in ts'ą' reh.
Aiits'ą' aanàii yàhnyaa ts'ą' adan chan yuaahkat akhài' gwinzįį yàagwaandàk.
"Àkwàt dzaa jùk k'eegwaadhat inlįį gwik'ìt shant'ee oonjìt zhat k'eegwaldhat t'ôonch'yaa," yàhnyąą.
5.02 Aiits'ą' reh tr'injàa veerîilch'įį googàa tǫǫ gwitee gwąąch'yaa hàa nìgwìilii, zhat vakąį' dhichįį googàa.
Aiits'ą' shàa gogwaandak ts'ą' reh akòodakhwa'in kwaa jyàa gavaihnyàa.
Gàa aii googàa nihk'ìt t'igii'ìn.
Nèekwat akoodagavaihnyàa googàa.
5.19 Jii natthài' datłòk jàghaii zhyąą gwint'aii ginkhìi, jyàa shàgàhnyaa ts'ą' dłòk hàa sheegeedlàa, aiitł'ęę datthak giviighan.
5.25 Dzaa k'ineedàl nąįį nàh gogwahaandak.
Aii geenjit akhàgavoiihnyaa t'inch'yàa, jyàa yàhnyaa.
Łì'hàa shoo dhidlìt, aii *President* reh.
Aiits'ą', "Jùk gwats'an chan, chan akôodigehee'yàa jì', zhyàa łyâa datthak givinghan," jyàa yàhnyaa łee (adlaa).
5.51 "Łì'hàa dinjii nizįį inlįį.
Aii geh'an dzaa dinjii shàa gwahaandak googàa gwadhąhtsąįį," yàhnyàa.
Aiits'ą' *ship* choo zhìt teetł'an k'àiich'ii nàa'ai', aii tthak yats'an iłtsąįį.
"Jidii vit'èegwąąhch'yaa, *every year* datthak jyàa danahał'yàa," yàhnyàa.
6.13 Aii hàa oo'àt *Tanàna* izhìk chan *Tsìik'ì' Tì'* vàràhnyàa.[4]
Chan zhat dąį' dinjii kwaiik'ìt ch'ìhłak gàa *2 to 3000* dilįį ǫ'.
Dinjii ahchìi kwàa.

4. Tsìik'ì Tì' was an Indian fur trader and middleman from the *Fairbanks* area, apparently not Gwich'in. —JE and CM

4.32 The President asked the four men why *Taa'ii' Tì'* did what he did, but they kept quiet, for it was their fault after what they did over here.

Then the President told *Taa'ii' Tì'* to come to him, and right there *Taa'ii' Tì'* told him what the men did over in Alaska.

"I'm chief over in Alaska just like you're the leader here."

5.02 *Taa'ii' Tì'* told the Russian President that his men sexually molested the married women every night while their husbands slept.

"Someone told me about them so I warned them not to do it again.

But they still did it.

I warned them twice about it.

5.19 They made fun of me, saying how weak I was, and it was no use speaking loudly to them, and that's why I killed them.

5.25 Those four who came back with me can now tell the story.

And that's the reason why I spared them."

That's what he told him.

That President was glad to hear about it.

"If that ever happens again, you have my permission to kill them all," he said (laughs).

5.51 "You're a good man.

That's why you even had these men tell me about it," he told him.

Then he even gave *Taa'ii' Tì'* half a shipload of things.

He told him, "I'll give you everything every year from now on."

6.13 There was a man named *Tsìik'ì' Tî'* living on the *Tanana River*, they say.

At that time, there were two to three thousand people in each village.

Nobody died.

6.25 Aii *President*[5] nilįį chan *Tsììk'ì' Tì'* oozhii.
Aii chan *Taa'ii Tì'* eenìnidìk.
Aii k'àiich'ì' tthak yats'an nahtsìk.
Aiits'ą' aii tsèedhàh giyahtsii tthak gwinjihkhee jyàa dìgiya'ìn.
6.35 Aiits'ą' aii *Tsììk'ì Tì'* chan yaaghà' *Gwichyaa*[6] oo'ęę nìnidìk, yaaghà' chan *President* nilįį chan *Drihtsììn Tì'*.[7]
Aii chan tsèedhàh vitsyàa nąįį yahtsii tthak chan *Tsììk'ì' Tì'* vintł'èeyaraazhik, jyàa dìgii'in k'àiich'i' àn łireelyaa gwiizhìk vit'įį yinlįį gwinjihkhee àn łeedàa (adlaa).

Taa'ii Tì'
Ch'eechyah Nèekwąįį

<jfka402>

JF10.30 Łyâa nįįzhit dąį' hee, *long time Taa'ii Tì' Valdez* ghàih *ship* choo ch'iinįį teegił łìt.
Aiits'ą' oonìn chųų choh kat k'ìinjik tr'ihchoo neegahahłaa googàa goveegogwàntrii.
10.43 Gooveegogwàntrii ts'ąįį zhyąą jyàa dìginch'yaa ts'ą' Dinjii Zhuh aii k'ìighai' gògwandàii.
Aii *Taa'ii' Tì'* łyâa dinjii gwintsìi veegòo'ąįį nilįį.
Vitsyàa naii lęįį.
Aii reh *ship* kak, jidìi ch'iitsii, gwatsàk, dachan vàa'iit'ii, *anything* aii datthak.
Dinjii Zhuh tthak łâa ch'iitsii shrii, tòh, k'èechì' daa'ąįį, *handmade axe too.*
11.30 Vitł'ìhtsii nêelghwat aii chan *steel* nilįį kwaa ts'ą' *sulfûr, iron* nilįį, aii googàa tr'ikhit daatł'òo.
Duuyeh tr'ookwàt.

---

5. Johnny Frank uses the English word President as a synonym for a powerlul chief, which in Gwich'in is *khàihkwaii.* —CM

6. *Gwichyaa* and *Gwichyaa Zheh* 'Flatlands' or 'Flatlands House' both refer to *Fort Yukon.* —CM

7. Drihtsììn Tì' was a fur trader at *Fort Yukon.* –JE

6.25 The chief's name there was *Tsìik'ì' Tî'*.
He went over to *Taa'ii' Tì'* all the time to pick up things.
Ts'ìik'ì' Tì' traded fur with them.
6.35 *Ts'ìik'ì' Tì'* came to *Fort Yukon* where another chief by the name of *Drihtsìin Tì'* was living.
His men gave all their furs to *Tsìik'ì' Tì'*.
So they got lots of fur and they traded lots of things for it (laughs).

Taa'ii Tì'
Second Version

<jfka402>

JF10.30 It was a very long time ago when *Taa'ii Tì'* and his men landed a big ship near Valdez.
It was hard for the Russians to take their ship back across the ocean.
10.43 They were having such a hard time that they stayed and lived off the Indians.
Taa'ii' Tì' was a rich and powerful man.
He had a big following.
And on his ship, he had lots of things like stoves, nails, saws, knives, canes, and axes.
11.30 The hand-made axes were not made of steel but of iron and sulfur.
They were really expensive.

Aiits'ą̀' nindhàh dą̀ąch'yąą zhat dą̀į' tr'ookwàt, aii lęįį gwats'an tr'ahtsìi.

Aii gok'aa chan naagąįį agàa gwats'an trahtsìi.

Tł'ee t'ôohju' diits'an rahtsìk.

Aiits'ą̀' łyâa Dinjii Zhuh datthak yit'ą̌ąhch'yàa.

12.05 Tyąh choh chan.

Tyąh choh vizhit diishryaa'àii chan gǫ̀ǫlı̨̀į.

Aii chan Dinjii Zhuh datthak yii'ı̨̀į.

Kwàt chan tthoodzyah agàa, *ice chìsèl.*

Aii chan jyàa dąhjyaa ts'ą̀' gwats'an gahtsìi, *Russiàn* nąįį.

Aii chan zhik gwà'àn dinjii gwintsii veegòo'ąįį naii zhrįh ts'an nilı̨̀į.

12.26 Dinjii neeshrâahch'yaa duuyeh yuukwàt.

Aiitł'ee t'ee reh, *Russìan* naii lęįį *ship* zhǐilk'ı̨̀į.

Datthak, zhik gwà'àn Dinjii Zhuh gǫ̀ǫlı̨̀į.

Kwàt aii googii chan gǫ̀ǫlı̨̀į.

Aii nich'it veerîilch'ii, aii googàa tthak hàa nìgwìgwìilii.

13.02 Aii dinjii łąįį k'ìt t'agoonyą̀ą.

Ts'ą̀' reh àgąąnjat kwaa ts'ą̀' *troublè* gǫ̀ǫlı̨̀į ts'ą̀' chan Dinjii Zhuh gàandaii kwàa.

Gwiizhìk geedan aii nakhweh'àn gwehèelyaa jyàa giindhan aii geh'àn gąąjat kwaa t'igii'in.

Akhài' aii *Taa'ii'Tì'* khàihkwaii nitsìi nilı̨̀į.

"Akǫ̀' tr'ìnjàa hàa nàgooh'àii kwàa," goovàhnyàa.

13.23 Googàa chan nihk'ìt t'igii'in gęhdaa chan akòo dàgòovàhnyàa.

Akòodàgàvàhnyàa tł'ee zhik gwà'àn juu va'at t'arah'in datthak aii akòodàhnyàa.

"Chan nakhwàa nineegwigwii'aii jì', shah goondàk," jyàa gavàhnyàa, goondàh reh.

Gwint'aii ginkhii ts'ą̀' ginjih hatrak ts'ą̀' reh.

Akhài' tth'aii googàa chan nihk'ìt t'igii'ìn.

Aiits'ą̀' *Taa'ii'Tì'* vàaragwaandàk.

It'ee *ready* dhidlìt, gwak'ąąhtìi.

We couldn't afford to buy them.
They bought lots of fur.
We gave them lots of fur.
We traded our fur for beads.
The Indians really used them.
12.05 Big pots too.
Big pots which were shiny on the inside.
All the Indians owned one.
There was also a spear which was used as an ice chisel.
It was this long (gesturing).
I'm talking about the Russians who gave these things out.
Rich people were the only ones who had these things.
12.26 Poor people couldn't buy them.
After that, there were lots of Russians who were from the ship.
There were also lots of Indians.
The Russians fooled around with the Indian married women.
13.02 They thought of the Indians as dogs and were not afraid of anyone.
The Indians didn't know anything about trouble.
The Russians were not afraid because they thought the Indians would get the blame instead of them.
Taa'ii' Tì' was the boss.
So he told them, "Now, stop bothering the women."
13.23 But they still did it anyway.
So then he told them again the next day.
"If they bother you again, let me know," he told the husbands.
He said that in front of the men, using a loud voice.
But the Russians still did it anyway.
So the husbands told *Taa'ii' Tì'* about it, and he got ready and watched them.

13.59 Khàa heechyàa gwats'ą̀' gwak'ąąhtii gàa oo'òk yaa'an zheh tr'injàa datthak jyàa dìgii'in goonah'yà' ts'ą̀' t'ee nàachį̀į.

Tǫǫ gwiinzįį inchį̀' kwaa ts'ą̀' vành it'ee reh toh, niveh eenjit reh.

Aii òonjik ts'ą̀' zhik gwa'an giłchųų gwiizhìk datthak gavaghàn.

Aiits'ą̀' dinjii dǫǫ zhrįh reh akhoonyàa.

"Łyâa gwìizųų t'inizhìk," giyàhnyàa.

14.46 "Inee," nakhwaihnyaa kwàt googàa t'akhwa'in.

"Nakhwan aii gwìizųų t'akhwa'in t'ôonch'yaa," gavàhnyaa.

Nijìn gwats'an t'akhwa'in gwits'eekhwajyàa gavàhnynaa.

Ts'ą̀' t'ee reh *sail bàat* ch'iinjik neegiłtsą̀įį.

Ship choh zhyą̀ą reh, tr'ihchoo nìivyaa zhrįh neehiilak aii t'agah'in gàa nizįį neegiyìłts'ąįį ts'ą̀' t'ee tr'ihchoo gehìłìt.

"Nik'èe diinàa neehindyàa?" giyàhnyàa.

"Ą̀ąhą'," nyaa ts'ą̀' reh gavàa neehòozhìi.

"Oondìt k'eegwaadhat choh nilįį hąąh'yàa," jyàa giyàhnyaa.

15.17 Aiits'ą̀' t'ee oonìn neegiyą̀hchįį ts'ą̀' t'ee reh, *President* zheh nihdèegiyąąhchįį.

"Jii dinjii tr'ihchoo oonìn neiinłìt aii gwidinjii tthak inghan t'inch'yaa,

Nan dèevahaiinjyàa geenjìt nats'ą̀' tr'ehìłch'įį t'arah'ìn," jyàa ginyàa.

15.52 Nats'àhts'ą̀' geh'àn t'anakhwah'ìn ginyaa akhaì'reh gahaahchìi kwàa.

Aiits'ą̀' reh, "Aanàįį," yàhnyaa, ts'ą̀' yats'ą̀' nĭinzhii ts'ą̀' gwinzįį yuaahkàt akhài' gwinzįį yàagwàandak, *Taa'ii' Tì'*.

Nijìn zhat nìgiinjil dą̀į' gwats'an oo'òk tr'ìnjàa tthak veerîilk'įį googàa khik drin, tǫǫ hàa nìgwìgwìi'àii.

"Àkwàt shįį zhrįh geenjit k'eegwaadhat ihłįį."

13.59 He watched them before he went to bed and saw them doing it.
Then he went to bed.
He didn't sleep too well.
He got up in the morning and took a short spear like they usually use in war and walked among the Russians while they were sleeping and killed them.
He only let four men go.
They told him, "What you did was really wrong."
14.46 Then he told them, "I said 'No' to you but you kept right on doing it.
Go back to where you came from," he told them.
And so they returned with their sailing ship.
They had a big ship, which they fixed, and they left.
But before they left, they asked *Taa'ii' Tì',*
"Could you come with us?"
And he said "Yes."
"You will see the big boss over there," they said to him.
15.17 And so they took him in the ship to see the President at his house.
"This man killed all the men on the ship that went over, and it's up to you to do whatever you want with him," they said.
15.52 The President asked the men why this man killed so many of them, but they were quiet.
So he ordered *Taa'ii' Tì'*, "Come here."
And that's when *Taa'ii' Tì'* told him why he did it.
He told him how the Russian men fooled around with married Indian women day and night.
"I'm the only one in charge here."

Kwàt reh shitsyàa naii "At t'ah'in ts'ą' reh akò' akòodakhwa'in kwaa," jyàa gavaihnyàa.

16.11 Aiits'ą' ch'ìhłęę reh *boss* aii shanlì'òonjik ts'ą',

"Natthąį' datłòk, jàghaii gwint'aii gininkhii?" jyàa shàhnyàa.

"It'ee geet'iihthan kwaa," nyàa.

16.32 "Shant'ee reh k'eegwaadhat choo t'ihch'yàa.

Kwàt geet'iihthan kwaa t'inyaa ts'ą' reh gwinzįį dhiichįį kwàa.

Jyàanch'yaa ts'ą' vành gwats'ą' giveenjit khàdhalchį'.

16.46 Vành yahkàa gwiizhìk toh noodhiijìk.

Goots'ą' hìdhiizhii ts'ą' giłchųų gwiizhìk tthak givihghàn ts'ą' dǫǫ naii zhrįh akhǒiihnyàa, geeneegogwahaandak ts'ą' nihts'èegeheedàa geenjit akhàgavoiihnyaa t'inch'yàa."

Jyàa nyaa yàhnyàa.

17.00 Àah, łyâa shoo dhidlìt.

It'ee łyâa zhyąą giveenideech'îin'ąįį.

Aiits'ą' *ship* choh zhit k'àiich'ì' shats'an hąhtsyàa jì' shitsyàaa naii łyâa lęįį t'ôonch'yàa.

Jii *ship* teetł'an jùk shats'an dhąhtsąįį *every year* jyàa dàshahah'yàa.

17.36 "Shits'ìhinjyàa, shan t'ee shitsyàa naii datthak vàh ts'ìhihjyàa.

Aii chan ànts'ą' chan geh'òk ch'adan gwich'in naii chan *friend* nihłaraa'įį datthak vàa nihts'ìreheenjyàa," yàhnyaa.

Łyâa zhyąą gwinzįį ginhè' ts'ą' kwàt zhyąą ch'iinii zhyąą veeneegwirǐnlìi.

Aii gwiizhìk nan kat ch'ii'àn *ocean* gwadàl àn łich'eetthal reh.

Łyâa vagǫ̀ǫlįį.

Aii tyąh choo gàa shant'ee nał'ya'.

18.02 Zhyąą tyąh choo hee zhyąą, *rivèt* tik ts'ą' hàa nihtr'aatsàk, diitįį t'aihnyàa.

Jyàa dąhtsii reh, nał'in googàa nehshrit neehih'ak t'aihnyàa.

So I told my friends, "Don't do what you're doing to them any more. [Stop the killing.]"

16.11 He told him about himself being the boss over there and what they were doing to his men's wives.

Then he told him about the time one of their bosses came up to him and took his hands, saying, "You have a weak body, so why are you speaking so loudly?" he said to me.

"And I didn't like it," he said.

He said, "I'm one of the big chiefs over there, and I didn't like the way they were talking to me.

So I couldn't even sleep that night.

16.46 I got up at dawn and grabbed my short spear.

I went to them and killed them while they were sleeping, and I spared only four men so they could tell you about it themselves."

That's what he said to him.

17.00 The President was really satisfied with what *Taa'ii' Tì'* did.

Taa'ii' Tì' then suggested that the President send over a big ship every year so he could help out his own people back home.

17.36 *Taa'ii' Tì'* told him, "You'll help me with things, and then I'll help my people.

We'll all be friends and help each other," he said to him.

The President agreed and *Taa'ii' Tì'* started to get things from him across the ocean by ship.

Lots of things became available.

I even saw the big steel pots myself.

18.02 I'm talking about a big pot that had three rivets on it.

It was a very thick pot, this big (gesturing), and I'm saying I could hardly carry it by myself.

Diitįį ts'ą' aii googàa Dinjii Zhuh yuukwàt yaa'įį t'aihnyàa.
Shin, khaii hàa tr'eeghwàa (adlaa).

18.24 Videetł'yàa chan łyâa nitsìi.
Ch'iitsii tłìk shrii choh jyàa dąhtsii chan reh.
Aii t'ee łùh shrii giyàhnyaa reh.
Aii chan łyâa zhyąą shįį shik'ìt t'inch'ii naii yuuheekwàt t'aihnyaa kwàa (adlaa).

19.00 Aii gwik'ìighai' t'ee *Alaskà* kat łyâa niizhùk ch'iitsii t'eegwąąhch'yaa gwinlì' aiitł'ęę *Amerìcàn* naii k'eedàl ts'ą' *Alaskà sell* iłtsàįį.
It'ee reh.

It was very thick, and the Indians made a habit of buying it.
We carried it on our backs both summer and winter (laughs).
18.24 Its handle was very big too.
There was a big steel knife also.
They called it a flour knife.
People like me couldn't afford to buy it (laughs).
19.00 For that reason, Alaska has used steel for a long time.
The Americans came later on, after the Russians sold Alaska.
That's all.

Johnny Frank

Johnny Vich’ilik

<jfcm2b>

JF19.03 [Ch’idlii Ch’ilik No. 1 (Page 260)]

<jfka401>

JF13.41 *Khàgohòonjik Tì’.*
That guy’s name is Khàgohòonjik Tì’[1]
All winter, no animal, see?
Well one man pay something.
“You make medicine for caribou.”
“Well,” he said, “all right.
Tomorrow go up and make second camp, see?”

14.16 “Oondaa nìreheenjyaa jì’ izhìk gwats’ą’ datthak shàa hohjyàa,” nyàa.
Aiits’ą’ t’ee vàarahàajìl.
Aii tr’ìnjàa nąįį gwitł’ęę jì’ oonii heedàa reh.
Shih kwaa kwàt reh, vadzaih k’įh chan gokwàa.

14.29 Aiits’ą’ reh, “Akò’ oondaa gwiintł’òo gôohk’ii,” nyàa.
Aiits’ą’ yee’òk traa hàa gahandak kwànchyàa choo giłtsąįį.
Òihàa dinjii lęįį reh.

14.46 Kwànchyàa choo gwinjyaa gwigwìłtsąįį ts’ą’ izhìk *one side* reh zhah khàgidiindhàt, *pile* giłtsąįį jyàa dąhtsii reh.
Aiits’ą’ t’ee reh, “Nakhwant’ee gàa shàa chŏohłii,” nyàa.

15.09 [Ch’idlii Ch’ilik Nos. 2A and 2B (Pages 260-261)]

15.32 Nyaa ts’ą’ zhìt shree nee’aa ts’ąįį zhyąą gooneedęędhàa.
Gwiizhìk tthak łangoodii’ee gwiizhìk reh.
Aiits’ą’ diideetak gěiinzhii ts’ą’ chan shree k’ihkheii gwikhyuu neehaa ts’ą’ nèekwat needąązhii tł’ęę yeezhee ch’iizhàk hee jyàa dĭizhìk.

15.55 Vadzaih *cow* nilįį reh.
Aii reh yijì’ oontà’ reh.
Jyăiinch’yaa reh.
Vadzaih reh, ghàt.
“Datthak gwinzįį noh’ìn,” jyàa nyaa ts’ą’ reh.

1. Khàgohòonjik Tì’ was a famous Gwich’in medicine man. —JE

Johnny Frank

Johnny's Songs

<jfcm2b>
JF19.03 [Sings Song No. 1 (Page 260)]
<jfka401>
JF13.41 *Khàgohòonjik Tì'.*
There was this guy called *Khàgohòonjik Tì'.*
All winter long there was no food.
So one man paid a medicine man for caribou.
The medicine man said, "Well, all right.
14.16 Tomorrow go up and make a second camp, see?"
"All of you follow me over there," he said.
So they went with him.
The women walked far behind.
There was no food and no caribou tracks anywhere.
14.29 And then, "Build a big fire," he said.
There were lots of people.
14.46 So they quickly gathered and piled up a lot of wood in no time.
They made a big pile of snow on one side of the fire.
And then he said, "You all sing along with me."
15.09 [Sings Songs No. 2A and 2B (Pages 260-261)]
15.32 They sang while he walked outside of the people in a clockwise direction.
The people were in a *Circle*, all of them touching each other.
Next he went inside the *Circle*, walked around twice inside the *Circle*, and bent down.
15.55 He held up a cow caribou's antlers.
He was shaking them.
"Look at them good," he said to them.

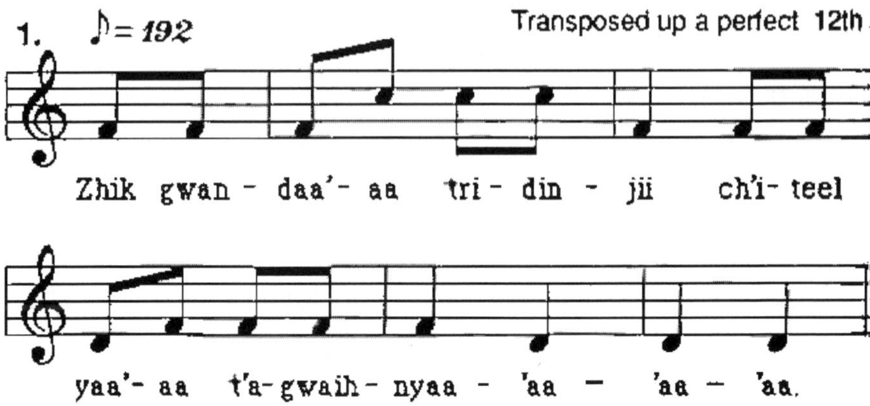

(Note: This is a dream song made by a man named Viłeenjik to predict the coming of the white man. —CM

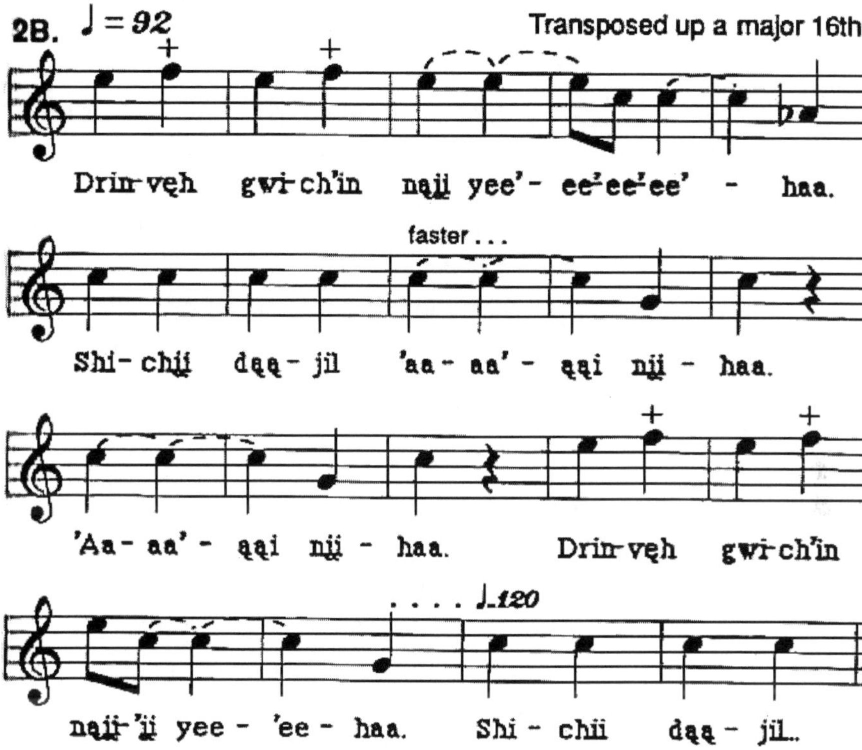
2B. ♩= 92
Transposed up a major 16th
Drin-vęh gwi-ch'in nąįį yee'- ee'ee'ee' - haa.
faster . . .
Shi- chįį dąą - jil 'aa - aa' - ąąi nįį - haa.
'Aa- aa' - ąąi nįį - haa. Drin-vęh gwi-ch'in
. . . . ♩. 120
nąįį-'įį yee - 'ee - haa. Shi - chii dąą - jil..

Yijì' oontà' dzaa ęęgwâą'ąį' vadzaih zhyąą reh khadąą'ai'.

16.13 Zhyąą dinjii yats'ą' hakhak gàa nah'in ts'ą' reh, it'ee reh, "Gwinzįį noh'yà'?" jyàa gavàhnyàa.

16.23 "Datthak ts'ą' gwinzįį hǫǫh'yàa jidìi vadzaih t'inch'yaa tthak vàahakhwandàii," agàa gavàhnyàa.

16.25 Aiits'ą' "Ą̀ąhą̀'," giyàhnyàa, "It'ee tthak tr'ąąh'yà'," giyàhnyaa ts'ą' yijì' oontà', zhat yitsįį ąhtrat ts'ą' zhat zhyąą gwihiljii ginyàa.

16.35 Gwiizhìk zhik gwà'àn tr'oochìt yak'ohchan goonjik yuu yaghài' tr'inlii yeezhee zhat gwà'àn vadzaih ghài' ginyàa.

Gwiizhìk zhat gwihiljii.

16.45 Aiitl'ęę t'ee t'agavàhnyaa, "Nijin ts'ąįį vidrihtsįį gòo'aįį ts'ąįį shàa goondàk," nyaa vàràhnyàa.

Aiits'ą' "Izhìk ts'ąįį," vàràhnyàa.

Akhài' "Akwaa jì' zhik ts'ąįį jùk it'ee yihilkąįį.

17.18 Zhik nành jyàa dąhthee nihk'yąą ts'ąįį jyàa dǫ̀hłìi, *line up* ohłįį ts'ą' gàa nihzhit dǫǫjyàa," nyaa vàràhnyàa.

Vadzaih k'įh gwarąąh'in kwaa reh.

Akhài' vadzaih k'įh zhat gǫ̀ǫlįį gwalą̀įį riinjìl.

17.26 Aiits'ą' oondaa jyàa dìgwiizhìk ts'ą' nihts'ąįį gahàajìl.

Yit![2]

Gwintł'òo vadzaih lęįį.

Jidìi zhoh, neegǫǫ, aii gàa tthak.

Jidìi viyee'an jyàa dìgwiizhìk roh.

17.39 Aii tthak nihts'an deedaa diideetak kwàa.

Nijìn ch'ii'àn geeheehàa gǫ̀'?

Zhoh googàa reh, neegǫǫ agàa.

Vadzaih dìlch'yąą dazhoo chyàa k'it t'inch'yaa.

Tthak ch'ìhłak gàa gwandàii kwàa.

17.57 "Drinvęę Gwich'in," nyàa.[3]

Zhat vadzaih aii reh.

Dinjii reh t'àhnyàa.

---

2. *Yit!* is a word expressing surprise. —CM

3. Johnny is anthropomorphising the caribou here, comparing them to another tribe of Indians. Drinvęę Gwich'in would be the "Sunrise People." —CM

He was holding the antlers, and he held them this way (geturing).
16.13 People came to him to look at them.
"Did you look at them good?" he asked them.
16.23 And he told them, "Now that you've seen it, you should know what kind of a caribou it is," he told them.
16.25 And they all said "Yes" and "We saw it all," while he was still holding the antlers, they say.
16.35 Then he pushed them away and they say the caribou that had been there just disappeared.
There was nothing left there but the caribou hair which he pulled off before.
16.45 Then he said, "Tell me which direction the tip of its chest is pointing towards?"
And they said, "In that direction."
"But if not, it's going to be dawn in that direction."
17.18 And they say he said, "Go spread out and line up facing the dawn."
They couldn't figure out why they would do that since they couldn't see any caribou tracks.
But they went out and came to a lot of caribou tracks.
17.26 They did what he told them to do and came to lots of caribou.
Yit!
Lots of caribou came.
Even the wolves, foxes, and all the others.
The animals were trapped in the middle of the people.
17.39 They had no way of getting away.
How would they get away?
Even the wolves and foxes.
The caribou were everywhere that you could see.
There was nothing but fur all over the place.
Not a single one of them was alive.
17.57 In his song saying, "*Drinvęę Gwich'in*,"
he meant the caribou.

18.12 "Diikhwan tǫǫ gwats'an tr'inlįį kwaa t'ôonch'yaa, eedan tǫǫ gwats'an nilįį.
Drin gweech'in gwich'in nąįį," nyàa.
"Yeendaa kǫ̀' tr'izhyąąhjil," jyàa nyaa ts'ą' ch'idlìi.
It'ee nizįį.
18.23 [Ch'idlii Ch'ilik No. 3 (Page 266)]
18.45 Jyàa nyaa gwiizhìk ch'izhìn t'èe oontà' jyàa dàh'in.
Gwiizhìk yuundaa gwâak'a' reh, nìivyaa zheh.
Aii kǫ̀' ts'ìį a'ee vit'įį ts'ąįį kǫ̀' dąį' gwizhrįh jyàa dìnyàa.
Gwiizhìk *Gwichyaa* Gwich'in nąįį tthak shan hàa giihaahkhwàa gwankàgantii gàa shų̀' t'igiyàh'ìn.
Gweedhaa tthak.
19.06 Aii eenjit lęįį nąįį t'iyah'in gik'yàanjik t'inyaa łèe.
Aiits'ą' reh, jyàiinch'yaa t'ee tr'ahahchųų nìgwiindhàt.
Ch'ijì' aii t'eh chan vakat tsuh tsal, *feather* aii tsal tł'yah tsal vàrahchàa.
19.23 Zheh gwiteegwąąch'yaa ts'ą' nihkheekhwadii[4] nąįį reh.
Aii di'il jyàa dàh'in gwiizhìk, aiitł'ęę reh,
"It'ee tr'ahahchųų," nyaa ts'ą' t'ee reh.
"Gwinzįį oo'àt ęhjyàa k'eiich'ì' shrohłii," nyàa.
Łąą jyàa dìgwiheenjyàa gàashandàii kwaa reh.
Kwàt jùk gweendàa dazhan gwinyaa. . .
Nothing!
Shįį gàa shagadhan kwaa nąįį dazhan àgàhnyaa t'iginyaa roh.
Izhìk gwanaa lyâa gìnt'àii.
19.55 Ditseet'ìt chan ch'izhii khàneen'ąįį.
19.56 [Ch'idlii Ch'ilik No. 4 (Page 267)]
Nyaa ts'ą' jyàa dii'ìn.
20.09 [Ch'idlii Ch'ilik No. 5 (Page 267)]
20.19 Jii *Alaska* kak nihts'įį dì' vats'àn jyàa dìi'in reh t'agwàhnyàa.
Łyâa vik'ìinjiidhat t'aihnyàa.

4. This should be *niłeehoodii*. —KP
Another dialect difference. —JE

18.12 "We are not the night people.
They are the night people.
We are the day people," he said, "who came out of the fire."
That's how he sang it.
Now, that's it.
It's good.
18.23 [Sings Song No. 3 (Page 266)]
18.45 He sang this song while he was holding an eagle feather and shaking it.
He was sitting inside a skin hut with his back toward the fire.
The *Fort Yukon* people tried to kill him by using witchcraft, but they couldn't do it.
All of the time.
19.06 He found out about that.
And so when it was time to sleep, he had a set of caribou antlers with a little feather attached to them by a little string.
19.23 This was given out to all the married couples.
He was holding the string of feathers in his hand and said,
"We will sleep now," he said.
"Fix all the things outside," he said.
I didn't know this was going to happen.
They say medicine power today is nothing compared to those days.
Even I have less power.
They were really powerful back then.
19.55 Again he took something out of his pocket.
19.56 [Sings Song No. 4 (Page 267)]
He was singing like that.
20.09 [Sings Song No. 5 (Page 267)]
20.19 What he meant in this song was that his two legs were dangling on either side of Alaska.
I really believed him.

3.
♪ = 184
Transposed up a perfect 11th
Daii' yee - yaa', daii' yee - yaa', daii yee yaa' oo -
zhrii, oo-zhrii, gǫǫ-łįį-įį-įį-įį Daii' yee- yaa', daii'
yee - yaa' daii' yee- yaa' oo - zhrii, gǫǫ-łįį Gǫǫ -
laii- aii- aii- aii - aii- aii Daii' yee - yaa' daii
yee- yaa', daii yee- yaa' oo - zhrii, gǫǫ- łįį Gǫǫ...

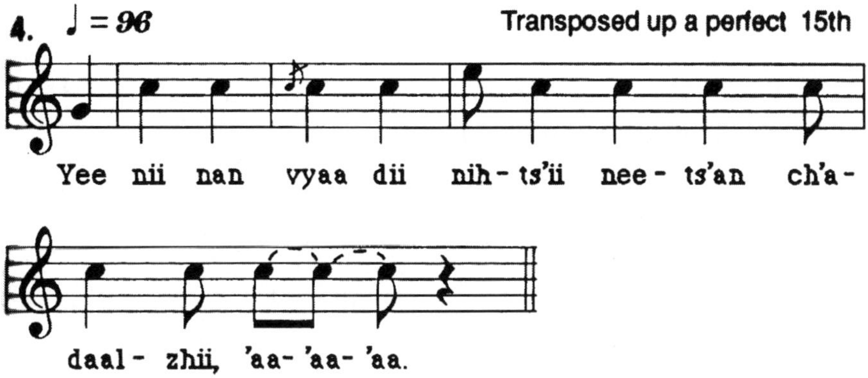
4.
♩ = 96
Transposed up a perfect 15th
Yee nii nan vyaa dii nih - ts'ii nee - ts'an ch'a-
daal - zhii, 'aa- 'aa- 'aa.

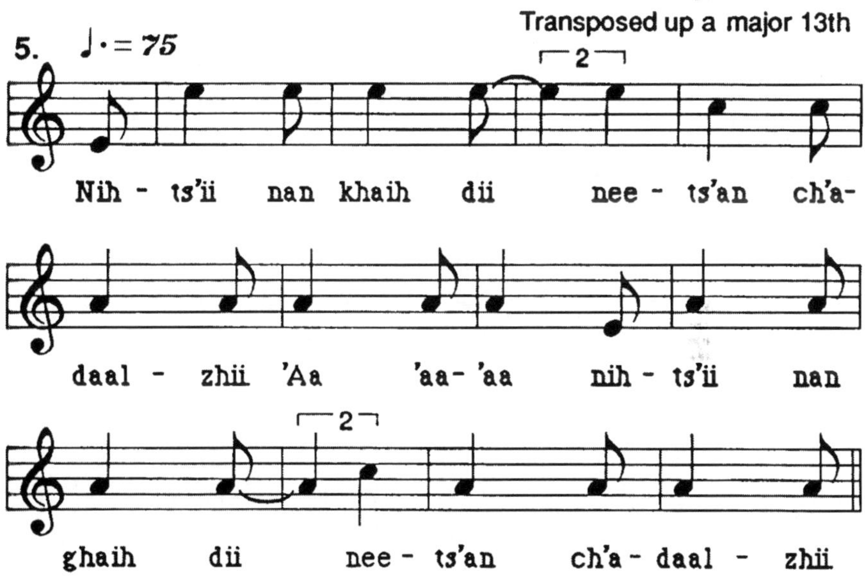
5.
♩. = 75
Transposed up a major 13th
2
Nih - ts'ii nan khaih dii nee - ts'an ch'a-
daal - zhii 'Aa 'aa- 'aa nih - ts'ii nan
2
ghaih dii nee - ts'an ch'a - daal - zhii

Nats'àa khaii datàn zhit gǫ̀ǫlįį kwàt zhyą̀ą ch'ak'òh t'it tr'igwich'ìį.

Kwàt lą̀ą jyàa dàgwą̀htł'oo ahtr'aii nizįh kwaa tr'ahąąh'yàa drąįį ninjich'ihthat kwàa.

20.40 Yeenjit diits'įį chan gwich'ìį.

Tr'îiłchųų gwiizhìk hee ahtr'aiivii choh gǐinzhii k'it t'igwinyàa.

Zhyą̀ą *flat* gǫǫlįį, zhyą̀ą ts'iivii choh tee tr'igwich'įį ch'yąą zhyą̀ą lyâa zhyą̀ą tł'oo làii kat tr'igwich'įį k'ìt t'ônch'yàa.

21.00 Gwiizhìk yeendìt dee'àn ddhah vijuu deedì' chan han shriit'agwą̀htsii aii k'àii choh tr'àl ch'iidì' zhyą̀ą gwit'iłtaii.

21.07 Gwintł'òo tr'agwaanduu tagwanaii t'iihnyàa.

Vanh khàchyàraazhii ts'ą̀' *nothìng.*

Aii gwiizhìk yeendit dakhachee'aii.

Aii *Chief Jonàs* vitsii vitì' reh.[5]

Aii t'ee lyâa yeenjit ch'ichìt nilįį.

21.37 Aii reh "Shitii," ą̀hnyàa.

Vitii neeshrâahch'yaa yuunyaa k'ìt.

21.55 "Shitii gwilęįį t'ee lèe oochìt t'ee lèe gwinzįį neegwąą'yą̀' lì', yaaghà' ch'izhìn choh nankat ch'iidì' noodîilnaii, łyâa zhyą̀ą shalàk vàa tr'agweendaii gwìch'in," jyàa reh nyàa.

Ch'izhìn ts'an vyàa hàa reh.

21.59 Ts'iivii tsal tee tr'igwich'įį zhyą̀ą reh, tsił kat reh gòo'ą̀įį.

Kwàt yaaghà' gwà'àn dinjik dhàh gąįh ęhjyàa dhidlii tthak chan hiljìi.

22.15 Kwàt yi'eendìt dì' han gwìin'èe.

Aiits'ą̀' reh yaaghà' ch'adhàh tthak ahtr'aii yahàadlii łee jyàa reh gwinyàa.

22.32 Oondìt ch'iinaa zhat k'ą̀hnjik gwatsal.

"Oonjit veenǒhjyàa," jyàa reh nyàa.

---

5. Chief Jonas, also known as Ch'akal, lived at *Fort Yukon* and was the father of Mary Thompson. —JE.
John Fredson recited Chief Jonas's *Second Address on the Death of Hudson Stuck* for Edward Sapir. See McGary 1982:62-63. —CM

We were living there because of the cold winter.
I never thought a big hurricane-like wind was coming up.
20.40 *Khàgohòonjik Tì'* was living across the river from us.
And during the night we heard a big wind come up.
The place where we were living was flat, but there was big spruce timber.
21.00 When the big wind came, it was like living on a flat grassy place.
On the other side of us was a big mountain, with a wide river near it and brush alongside it.
21.07 I'm saying it was a really bad wind.
When we woke up in the morning, it was calm outside.
Khàgohòonjik Tì' woke up across the river too.
He was the father of *Chief Jonas's* grandfather.
He was bossy to him.
21.37 He called him "My father's brother," as though he was being nice to him or had no pity for him.
21.55 He said, "I wonder if my poor uncle got home safely, because the big eagle came by headed down river, which might mean my uncle got lost somewhere."
He used the eagle's power to know that.
21.59 There were snowdrifts in the small stand of spruce timber where we were.
All the dried moose hide outside our house was gone too.
22.15 The river across from us was kind of far away, and they say all the moose hides were blown over there.
22.32 There was a little creek near that river.
"Go over and pick them up," he said.

Veechìi t'igwinyaa kwaa ts'ą' reh.

22.50 Aiits'ą' reh, jùu vach'adhah haljii nąįį datthak, yeenin reh k'ìgwaajil ts'ą' yeenii reh tthak reh neegiyeelyàa.

Aii eedan viinyą'[6] ts'an, gàa zhik ahtr'aii yùunjik kwàa.

Oonjit k'ąhnjik gwatsal tthak zhyąą gwik'ìinjil łee reh.

Aih kwaih googàa yi'ee'àt gwà'àn dhidlii.

23.21 [Ch'idlii Ch'ilik No. 6 (Page 272)]

Jyàa chan reh.

24.13 Aii Han Gwich'in nąįį, vitì' niindhat ts'ą' ch'izhii dinjii yahkhan nôonjìk, aii reh vitsųų aii nìindhat.

Aiits'ą' aii vitsųų yìinlii niindhat, aii k'at tr'igwidìi ts'ą', ch'ilik iłtsąįį.

Ts'ą' zhik viti' neeyiilįį, aii chan niindhàt.

24.46 Shitsųų aii daghwaii *Tr'iheetìl* vàràhnyaa aii gwinzįį yidehk'ìt gwiłtsąįį, gwinzii videhk'ìt gokwàa, akhài' reh.

Aii shyaaghan chan nindhat ts'ą' reh vaghwaii *Tr'iheetìl* aii eedan aii gwinzįį tthak gwank'yąą niłtsąįį k'ìt t'inch'yàa.

24.58 Aiits'ą' łyâa ch'ilik nizįį iłtsąįį vàràhnyaa.

Nankat vagwandàk gǫǫlįį t'aihnyàa.

Daghwaii gwadàl, nyàa.

"Gwinzįį nǐinzhii," giyàhnyàa.

"It'ee nàts'àa tee, shitsųų?" nyaa.

Ts'ą' ch'idlii t'inyàa.

25.23 Vitì' niiindhat.

Ch'izhii Han Gwich'in chan yahan nôonjìk, aii chan ti'yąą àhnyàa.

25.44 Akhài' gwahàadhat kwaa ts'ą' nìvichį' àanąįį.

Aii chan k'at deech'įįłtsąįį gàa jùk akòodinyaa kwàa, nan geh'àn zhrįį t'inyàa.[7]

25.56 [Ch'idlii Ch'ilik No. 7 (Page 273)]

Jyàa nyàa.

KA26.29 Aii jùu?

---

6. He's mad about something and uses *shan,* a shaman's song, to do it. —KP

7. This should be *gwizhrįį tiinyàa*. —KP

They say he didn't look too happy.

22.50 Whoever lost their moose hides went over there and brought them back.

Khàgohòonjik Tì' wasn't taken away by the wind because it was his own doing.

All the moose hides were lying along the creek.

Even all the snowshoes were blown away.

23.21 [Sings Song No. 6 (Page 272)]

That man sang this song.

24.13 The song meant a Han Gwich'in man's father died and another man married his mother.

And then his grandmother died, and so he was mourning her when he made this song.

His stepfather also died.

24.46 My grandmother had a brother-in-law named *Tr'iiheetil* who made a good place for her because she didn't have a good place of her own.

That old lady also died, and her brother-in-law *Tr'iiheetil* felt like he did good by what he had done for her.

24.58 They say there was news all over the country about the good song he made.

I'm saying he sang about his sister-in-law's belongings,

"You are in a good place," as they say.

"What now, Grandma?" he said.

This is what he meant in his song.

25.23 His father died.

Another Han Gwich'in whom he called his father remarried his mother.

25.44 He also died soon after that.

I wouldn't tell anyone about this song, but I'm doing it for you.

25.56 [Sings Song No. 7 (Page 273)]

That's what he said.

KA26.29 Who sang that?

6.
♩. = 54
Transposed up a major 14th
Ee - ee- ee 'aa- tsųų shii- tsųų - ųų - ųų
Ch'oo- ts'oo daa-ghwaii hoo - til shoo- t'oo nii-
tł'oo dee- niin - lii Hee- ee- ee- ee-
ee - ee - ee- ee aa' - aa - tsųų shii - tsųų
Hee - ee aa' aa - tsųų shii- tsųų - ųų - ųų Shoo-
ts'oo daa- ghwaii hoo - til shoo- t'oo - nii - tł'oo dee-
niin - lii Hee - dee - gii yah-
nuu' - uu' - uu' - uu' aa - tsųų shii - tsųų
Hee' - ee' aa' - aa tsųų shii - tsųų

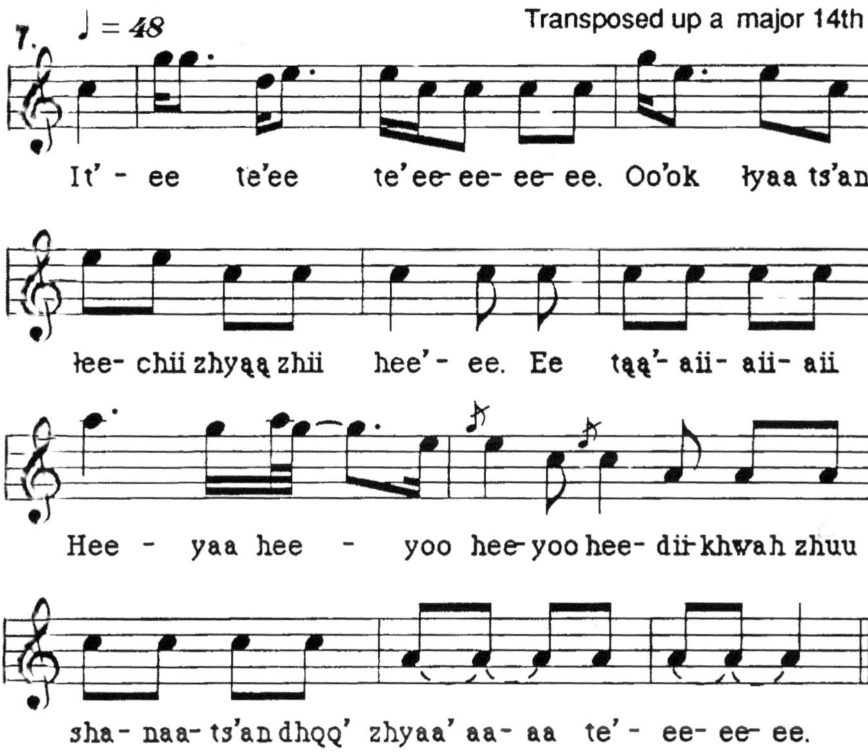
7.
♩ = 48
Transposed up a major 14th
It' - ee te'ee te'ee- ee- ee- ee. Oo'ok łyaa ts'an
łee- chii zhyąą zhii hee' - ee. Ee tąą'- aii- aii- aii
Hee - yaa hee - yoo hee- yoo hee- dii- khwah zhuu
sha- naa- ts'an dhǫǫ' zhyaa' aa- aa te' - ee- ee- ee.

JF26.30 "Ch'ahaalzhyąą sheenats'an dhàanzhii t'inizhìk,"[8] ditsii àhnyàa.

27.00 [Ch'idlii Ch'ilik No. 8 (Page 276)]
Jyàa nyaa ts'ą̀' khik dazhàn.

27.29 Aiitł'ęę chan hee.
Aii "Shįį t'ihch'yaa," nyàa.
Gwiizhìk deedàk gwik'ìneech'ii'ą̀įį.
Aii "Shįį t'ishi'in," nyaa reh.
Aiitł'ęę chan:

27.51 [Ch'idlii Ch'ilik No. 9 (Page 277)]

28.14 Jyàa nyaa ts'ą̀' drin ch'ìhłak zhit ch'ilik nèekwąįį zhrįh idlii tł'ęę łì'hàa ahtr'aii nint'aii yeedì' gòiihak, giyàhnyàa.

28.19 Nàrahaazhrii geenjit ch'ilik yąhįį reh.

<jfkalb>

24.21 [Ch'idlii Ch'ilik No. 10 (Page 278)]

<sfcmlb>

29.46 [Ch'idlii Ch'ilik No. 11 (Page 278)]

8. This song line means something like "Ducks gather around me with your wings." —KF

JF26.30 "*Ch'ahaalzhyąą sheenats'an dhàanzhii t'inizhìk.*" He sang that to his grandfather.

27.00 [Sings Song No. 8 (Page 276)]

That's what he said, and he was a medicine man.

27.29 And after that again.

"It's me when the sun rises and sets."

That's what he's saying in his song when he works his medicine.

"It's me who's doing this," he said.

Then he sang another song like this:

27.51 [Sings Song No. 9 (Page 277)]

28.14 He sang two songs in one day.

Then a big wind would come up, they said.

28.19 He uses it for a hunting song too.

<jfkalb>

24.21 Sings Song No. 10 (Page 278)]

<sfcmlb>

29.46 Sings Song No. 11 (Page 278)]

8.
♩· = 60
Transposed up a major 14th
Ee - ee, yeenjit doo - daii- aii- aii - aii
shii'- ii yaa'- va - ga- noo - chih- dii - yii - yee.
Gwii-yee-haa hii- yee haa, hii- yee haa hii- yee.
Gwii-yee- haa hii- yee. Gwii-yee- haa hii- yee haa
hii-yee. Yeen- jit doo - daii- ii yoo - shii yee yaa'
va - ga- noo - chih dii- yii - yee. Hii- yee- ho'
hii - yee- haa hii - yaa- haa hii - yee.

9.

♪ = 184
Transposed up a major 10th
Doo nih- łii ee- eh - nan ni- zhee- ee kha- naih - dii
aii- yaa- yaa. Daa- nih- łik aii- yaa nan- zhit hee
kha- naih - dik aii- yaa- yaa. Aii- yee- yee- yee
it'- ee yaa shii ee- eh - nan .daa- nih- łik aii- yee
nan- zhit - aii kha - naih - dik aii - yee - yee.

(Note: This song was apparently composed by Ch'akwaii Kat to break the magic spell of a bad medicine man named Tsyaa Ch'aa. Ch'akwaii Kat sang the song while hiding under a blanket. Johnny tells a story that goes with this song, but the story was recorded only in fragments. —CM)

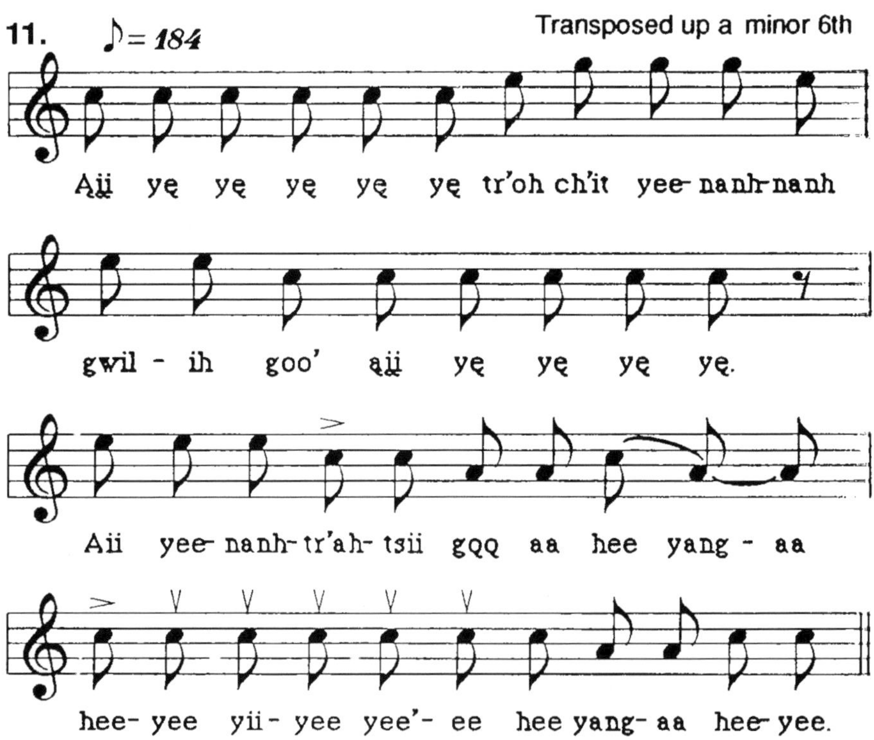

(Note: This song was made by the medicine man Gahałik to heal a bullet wound he inflicted on a friend with a muzzle loader. Johnny tells the story that goes with this song in English only. —CM)

<jfcm22a>

27.00 [Shigwii Shyaavin's War Song]

(Note: This song was made by an old woman named Shigwii Shyaavin who used her medicine to start a war of revenge against the Inuit. —CM)

<jfcm2a>
20.25

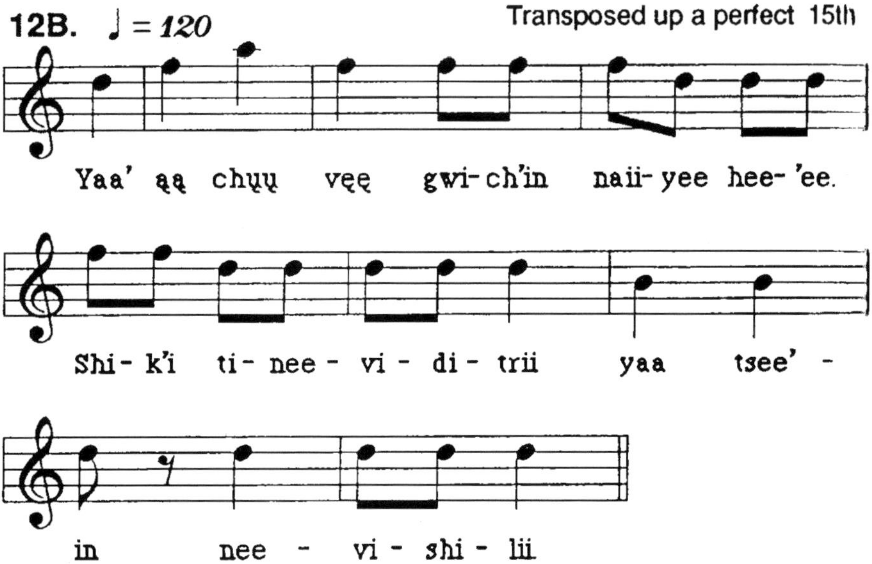
12B. ♩ = 120
Transposed up a perfect 15th
Yaa' ąą chųų vęę gwi- ch'in naii- yee hee- 'ee.
Shi- k'i ti- nee - vi - di - trii yaa tsee' -
in nee - vi - shi - lii

<jfcm2a>
28.59 [Medicine Song for War]

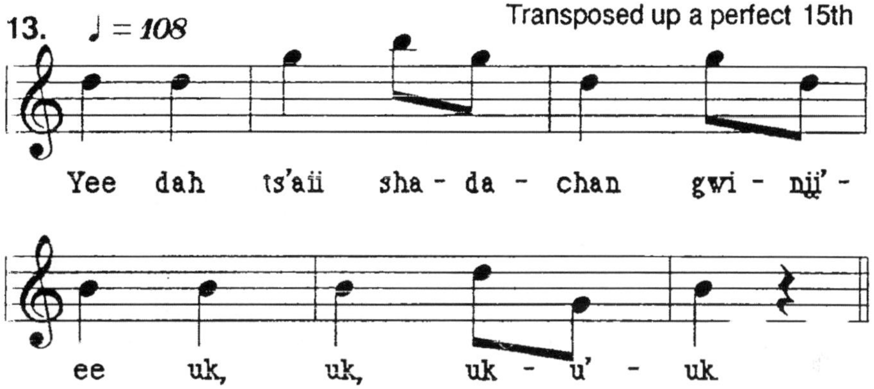

<jfcm2a>
21.18 [Medicine Song Calling for Caribou]

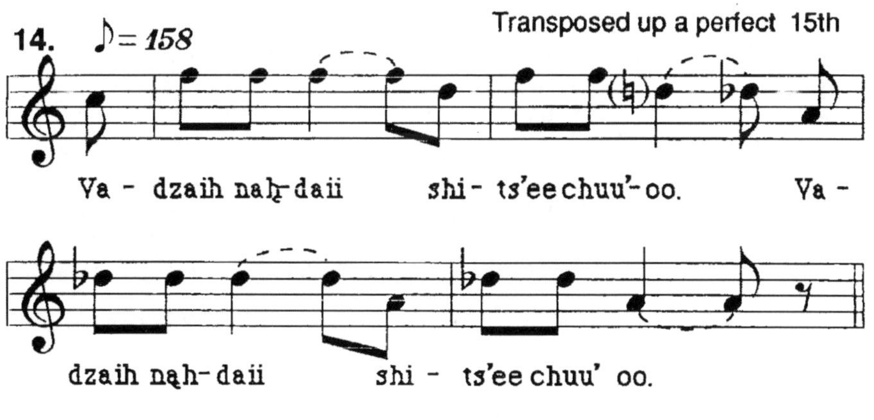

Fig. 15. The Frank family in Arctic Village, July 19, 1927. Left to right are Johnny, Dina, Sarah, Dan, Nathaniel, Joseph, Allah, Hamel, Lucy Ch'igwich'in (Johnny Frank's mother), and Jessie Natthąįį. Photo by J.B. Mertie, Jr., courtesy of U.S. Geological Survey Photographic Archives, Denver.

Part II
Life Histories

Our work with the taped recordings of Johnny and Sarah joins and perpetuates a recent trend in producing Gwich'in Athabaskan biographies and autobiographies. We hope it will encourage other elders to record and share their life stories. Katherine Peter, the senior Gwich'in member of our project team, was among the first Alaska Natives to write and publish an autobiography, *Neetsąįį Gwindaii* (1992), in her own Native language. The efforts of Bill Pfisterer (1982) to record the life of the late Belle Herbert of Chalkyitsik (also a Gwich'in speaker) over a period of just a few weeks resulted in a mosaic of people, places, and events going back more than one hundred years. More recently, Pfisterer also published a splendid panoply of Porcupine River stories told in English by the late Richard Martin (1993). Martin was a compelling and genuinely comical Gwich'in storyteller whom I also had the good fortune to record in Chalkyitsik during the early 1970s.

The following notes about the lives of Johnny and Sarah are not intended to replace or summarize their own life histories, which are skillfully portrayed in their own words. Rather, they provide a rough chronological sketch of their family's movements within the Gwich'in tribal homeland where they raised their family and made their living. Archival research and lengthy interviews I had with the four surviving Frank children — Nathaniel, Hamel, Dan, and Maggie — and with grandson Lawrence Roberts led to additional life history material and photographs that augment Johnny and Sarah's own personal accounts.

Sarah's mother was named Mary Ch'idįį; her father, John Vandeegwizhįį, was an Episcopal church lay reader. Although some family members insist that Sarah (who was basically monolingual) lived to be 105, the Thirteenth U.S. Census (Bureau of the Census 1910) indicates that she was born in October, 1892. If accurate, this early census would have made her ninety-six at the time of her death on June 15, 1988. If Sarah was actually 105 at her death, she would have been born in 1883. As Sarah herself said, however, during those days none of the Indians in that area had calendars or kept track of the years, much less the days and months, so there is no way any of these dates can be precise. In later years Sarah celebrated her birthday on September 28.

The Twelfth U.S. Census (Bureau of the Census 1900) gives Johnny's birthdate as August, 1880, making him ninety-seven at his death on December 27, 1977. But the Thirteenth U.S. Census (Bureau of the Census 1910) says he was born in November, 1884, four years later. The Parish Register at St. Stephen's Episcopal Church in Fort Yukon shows he was nineteen years old in 1905, which would move his birth year up to 1886. By his own reckoning, Johnny believed he was born in 1880, and he celebrated his birthday on October 18.

Johnny was the son of Frank or "From," whose Indian name was Dritzhuu, and Lucy Ch'igwihch'in. On his father's side, Johnny descended from the Di'hąįį Gwich'in, a tribal group that historically occupied the central Brooks Range west of Gold Camp, particularly the upper Middle Fork and upper North Forks of the Chandalar River, and parts of the Middle and South Forks of the Koyukuk River. This legendary group was almost wiped out by warfare with the Koyukon Athabaskans living on the Koyukuk and the Iñupiat, an Inuit group on the North Slope. The few remaining survivors intermarried with the Neets'it Gwich'in living in the area around present day Arctic Village near the headwaters of the East Fork. (See McKennan 1933, 1935, 1965: West 1959; Hall 1969, 1975; and especially Burch and Mishler 1995). The Franks, Tritts, and Roberts families, as well as some of the Johns and Peters, had a common Di'hąįį ancestor named Diitsii Giitł'uu who had six different wives. (See the Frank family genealogy in Appendix A to this volume.)

During the Alaskan gold rush, the geologist Frank Schrader (1899) found a band of seven Gwich'in hunting Dall sheep and drying meat on Robert Creek, at the portage between the headwaters of the North Fork of the Chandalar and the Middle Fork of the Koyukuk. While Schrader gave the names of several of these people (Robert, Horace, and Phoebe and two girls named Emma and Mary), not enough is known yet about their family history to determine whether they were Di'hą̨į̨ or Neets'it Gwich'in or a mixture of both. This same Robert and his family shows up in the Twelfth U.S. Census (Bureau of the Census 1900) along with Johnny Frank's family and several others at a location described only as "Gens du Large (Chandalar) River."

Schrader was one of the few white men who ever met the Gwich'in living in the area that many of McKennan's sources (McKennan 1933;1965:23-24) described as the former Di'hą̨į̨ homeland, far west of their current territory. Although Schrader photographed these people, his published report never mentions meeting them. I finally discovered his original field notes ninety-four years after they were written. Schrader learned from a group of prospectors staying at Chandalar Lake that the tribe's first chief was named Peter and the second chief was Frank. This must have been Johnny Frank's father, Frank Dritzhuu. The Twelfth U.S. Census (Bureau of the Census 1900) lists Frank's birthdate as April, 1851. Like Sarah's father, Old John, Frank Dritzhuu was recognized as a church lay reader in the Arctic Village area (Tritt n.d.).

Details of Johnny and Sarah's life before their marriage are almost completely lost, although Sarah, who was Neets'it Gwich'in, recalled being raised at her father's cabin on Old John Lake and rather vividly described a long trip with Old John to Fort Yukon during the height of the gold rush around the year 1900. She also recalled being married to Johnny at St. Stephen's Episcopal Church in Fort Yukon by the Reverend William Loola, the first ordained Gwich'in deacon in Alaska. If the official census records are correct, Sarah was eighteen years old at the time of her marriage, and Johnny was about twenty-five. The Thirteenth U.S. Census (Bureau of the Census 1910) indicates that the couple had already been married for three years, which would suggest a marriage date of 1907. Their first-born child, Lucy, however, was not included until the Fourteenth U.S. Census (Bureau of the Census 1920), where her age is shown as eleven years.

Sarah says that after the wedding they returned to her father's cabin at Old John Lake for a short while before moving to Tryahtł'it (on Otter Creek north of Christian Village), where they set up a residence for two or three years before moving to the Ch'at'oonjik (the Koness River) and to Gwak'an Zheh on the Sheenjik. The house Johnny built at Tryahtł'it was dug into the side of a hill and was remembered as being very warm. Elijah Henry also had a cabin there. Albert Tritt built a store at Gwak'an Zheh in 1907, and the Franks lived there for a while also. Sometimes ammunition was so scarce during these years that bullets had to be recycled. Johnny,

Fig. 16. Sarah Frank's father, Old John (Vandeegwiizhįį) in Fort Yukon, 1925. Frederick B. Drane Collection in the Archives, Alaska and Polar Regions Department, University of Alaska Fairbanks.

who had a reputation as a sharpshooter, claimed that he once shot two dozen hares using the same slug.

The Koness River, also locally known as the Nest River, attracted the Gwich'in for its abundance of game animals. This supply must have been very reliable because Johnny and Sarah raised their family there, at least seasonally, for about twenty-two years — from about 1909 until 1930 or 1931. Details of their house on the Koness are sketchy at best, but it still appears on an early U.S. Geological Survey map (see Mertie. J.B. 1927a: Plate 1). It was located directly east of Old John Lake at a caribou crossing and just north of Tth'ah Neekaii, a big pointed rock outcropping.

There were several Indian log houses on the Koness, and the Franks were neighbors at various times to Albert Tritt, Gilbert Joseph and Maggie Divi' (Johnny's older sister), and Dihch'i' David. Johnny's mother, Lucy Ch'igwihch'in, lived next door to Johnny and Sarah. Apparently Johnny's father, Frank Dritzhuu, had also lived in the Koness River valley near Ddhah Dzak mountain, and this may have been where Johnny Frank was raised. Still, the men had to look for game every day, no matter how cold the weather, and sometimes the whole family traveled together to find animals.

Also on the Koness is a site called Johnny Frank's Stone-lined Meat Caches, documented by the Cooperative Park Studies Unit in 1979 and listed on the National Register of Historic Places. This site is just east of the East Fork of the Koness River on a hillside in the western foothills of Index Mountain. These meat caches and an associated butchering site were apparently in use during the 1840s and were rediscovered by Johnny and used by him for storing caribou meat during the early 20th century.

It was while the Franks were living on the Koness River, but during a summer visit to Arctic Village in 1927, that they met a team of geologists from the U.S. Geological Survey, led by John Mertie and Gerald Fitzgerald, who were surveying the area around Arctic Village. Mertie's photographs and Fitzgerald's field diary represent the first systematic efforts to document the lives and culture of the Neets'it Gwich'in band (see Mishler 2018). Twelve Indian families were gathered in Arctic Village that spring. The families took turns giving potlatches to the rest of the village and then everybody danced all night to the fiddle playing of Albert Tritt and Jim Christian.

In his diary, Fitzgerald (1927) says he first met Johnny Frank while mushing dogs on the trail between Fort Yukon and Christian Village on March 31, 1927, and that Johnny talked about the trail between his house on the Koness River and Caribou House, also known as Last Timber. With temperatures on this trip ranging from -20 to -50 degrees Fahrenheit, Fitzgerald finally arrived in Arctic Village on April 19. He did not see Johnny again, however, until May 14, when the Franks all arrived in Arctic Village with five dog teams. They had just come in from the Koness River and had a hard time traveling. On May 18 Fitzgerald wrote, "Johnny Frank comes over and tells us stories of Indian war time, strong men, brush men, etc.—Raven and the light." And on June 26 he wrote, "Rain all night and almost all day — cloudy — Johnny Frank tells Indian stories."

There were a lot of caribou in the area at the time, and most of the Arctic Village men were either hunting or packing meat back to the village with dog packs. On June 3, Fitzgerald observed that Johnny and his family left to dry meat. Apparently they liked to go above the timberline where they found more wind to dry the meat and fewer insects. Sarah stayed behind in the village, and on June 9, Fitzgerald says he pulled one of her teeth. On the 14th Johnny Frank returned to Arctic Village, apparently with his dry meat in hand.

On June 29, 1927, a meeting was held at Esaias Simon's place to make plans for the Fourth of July. Johnny and Fitzgerald were put in charge of the games. Starting at noon they had jump races, sack races, three-legged races, a greased pole climbing, and a pillow fight on a swing bar pole. At 4:30 p.m. there was a big potlatch dinner followed by a dance at Esaias's house. On the 5th there was another potlatch followed by another dance lasting until midnight. On July 14 Fitzgerald and Johnny floated down the East Fork in a canoe to meet John Mertie, Fred Clark, and Mike Wheeler, three more geologists who were on their way to Arctic Village to work with Fitzgerald. On July 19, Mertie took twenty-two pictures of all the Indian families residing in Arctic Village, including the Franks (see Mertie, J.B. 1927b and Mertie, Evelyn 1982. See also Mishler and Frank, 2023, Chapter 2). Included in the Frank family photograph are two old women whom the Franks cared for — Lucy Ch'igwihch'in (Johnny Frank's mother) and Eleanor Treenaats'yaa (Chief Christian's mother).

As it turned out, both of these old women met tragic deaths. Eleanor Treenaats'yaa died in a fire at Arctic Village one night while the wind was blowing. She was alone at the time, and no one knew there was a fire until they awoke the next morning and found her cabin reduced to ashes. There was nothing left to do but gather her charred bones into a coffin and bury her.

Many years later, during the 1940s, Lucy Ch'igwihch'in also died from a fire. She was standing next to a hot stove inside a canvas tent when her dress caught fire. Everyone else in camp had gone down to the river to greet an airplane and couldn't get back to help until after she was very badly burned. They sent her to Fairbanks on the plane, and she died at the hospital there.

On July 20, 1927, the Franks headed back home toward the Koness River, and the team of geologists followed with six pack dogs. After making an exploratory loop through the Brooks Range east and north of Arctic Village, Fitzgerald and Mertie and their men arrived in the village again on August 15. In his diary entry for August 17, Fitzgerald wrote that Sarah's father, Old John Vandeegwiizhįį, walked all the way in from Old John Lake to Arctic Village, a distance of fifteen miles, just to bid farewell to them. What made this walk noteworthy was Fitzgerald's observation that Old John was ninety-five years old at the time. On August 19 the geologists said goodbye and pushed off down the East Fork of the Chandalar in two moose skin boats.

According to Sarah, it was during the 1920s that the Neets'it Gwich'in were visited a number of times during the Christmas and New Year holidays by Iñupiat from the Arctic North Slope. Although the Iñupiat had been enemies of the Gwich'in in the past, those whom the Franks met played many games and traded the Western-made goods they had obtained from trading with whaling ships. Johnny Frank learned to sing several Iñupiat songs, and Nathaniel, Johnny and Sarah's oldest son, almost married one of the Iñupiat women who fell in love with him. Hadleigh West (1963:259) says that every August until 1928 the Gwich'in around Arctic Village made an annual trip north to trade with the North Slope Iñupiat. The Gwich'in traded wolf, wolverine, and caribou skins for ivory fish hooks, beads, tobacco, tea, and manufactured goods such as guns, ammunition, stoves, knives, and pots and pans.

Sometime around 1930 or 1931 the caribou didn't migrate through on schedule, and the Franks were starved out of their long-time home on the Koness River. All of their dogs there died except for one puppy named Tłak Trik. For a while they moved back to their old place at the mouth of Otter Creek, then spent some time on the Sheenjik River, and also lived for a couple of years in and around Arctic Village. One summer the weather was so cold that hundreds of baby caribou died, truly a bad omen for people who depend on caribou meat for much of their food.

In 1933, the anthropologist Robert McKennan, who was familiar with the work of the Mertie-Fitzgerald survey party six years earlier, flew to Arctic Village and floated down the East Fork to Chandalar, the original English name for Venetie, where he arrived on July 27. While there, McKennan interviewed Johnny Frank, Old Robert, and several others. McKennan was so impressed with Johnny's traditional knowledge that he recorded many of his stories and gathered a wealth of ethnographic information for his classic study *The Chandalar Gwich'in*. Accompanying McKennan on this trip was the bright young scholar, John Fredson, who served as his translator. Fredson later became the first certified school teacher in Venetie and worked with the Franks and others to secure the Venetie Indian Reservation. (See Mackenzie 1986 and Mishler 1982.)

Then in the spring of 1934, after a falling-out with some other families, the Franks left the Arctic Village area and headed south until they came to Gold Camp (Ddhah Ohts'aii) on the East Fork of the Chandalar River, about thirty-eight miles north of Venetie. Sarah remembers that Johnny was led to this place by a vision, but Nathaniel recalls that Johnny's father, Frank Dritzhuu, was already living there alone when they arrived and kept going back and forth between Gold Camp and Ackerman Lake. Shortly after they arrived in Gold Camp, however, Johnny and Nathaniel went across the river and killed five moose. With this kind of good luck, the Franks never went back to the Koness River except once to reclaim the floor boards of their old cabin for making a coffin.

Gold Camp was so named in the late 1930s after Moses Cruikshank, Johnny Frank, and some of their friends sank two or three holes in the creek with a steam boiler (Cruikshank 1986:71-

72). The results were disappointing. Johnny told me that he dug such a deep shaft that he needed a ladder to descend into it. One day he climbed out to take a lunch break and when he returned he found the walls of the shaft had caved in. He was cured of gold fever when he realized that he would have been killed if he had been inside the shaft when it collapsed.

Through their stories of the first school in Venetie in 1937 and 1938, we can grasp something of what it was like for Johnny and Sarah to give up a centuries-old seasonal round of foraging in exchange for life in a village. As we listen to and read their stories, we sense their dilemma of wanting their children to attend school to learn about the larger western world and at the same time trying to stay focused on the land and harvest the healthy wild food it provided. Sarah vividly recalls the time when they brought their large family to Venetie for the winter just so the enrollment there could be boosted enough to keep the school open and keep John Fredson employed as the teacher.

After other Gwich'in families settled there and the school could stand on its own, the Franks returned to Gold Camp and traveled to Venetie only occasionally to visit family and friends. They remained at Gold Camp for the next forty winters, not leaving their home there for good until Johnny's health began to fail in the mid-1970s.

From Sarah's narrative and Bureau of Indian Affairs (1980; 1983) field site records, it's clear that the Franks underwent hardship wherever they lived, even at Gold Camp, where they eventually built four cabins. The first of these, now in ruins, was constructed on the west bank in 1935. The next year they built another one on the east bank on what later became part of the Venetie Reservation, but it proved to be too low and close to the river. This one is also gone now. Finally, in 1942 they built two more cabins on the west bank. Nathaniel, the oldest of the Frank children, recalls the family arriving in Gold Camp in the spring of 1934, but judging from McKennan's account the Franks were already in the Venetie area the previous summer. During the Gold Camp years, after most of their birth children were grown and married, Johnny and Sarah adopted and raised Sarah John and raised two of their own grandsons, Stanley Frank and Lawrence Roberts.

Dan Frank said that in 1937 or 1938, when he was about thirteen years old, he developed a boil on his side so big that he couldn't buckle his belt. He didn't go to Fort Yukon to see a doctor because his parents were afraid they wouldn't be able to pay the doctor and the hospital costs. There was also some concern that good medicines were not being prescribed. Finally, Sarah covered the boil with an ice pack, filed down a small knife, and lanced it. The pus that drained out filled a one-pound coffee can. Dan cried, but the wound healed.

Hamel remembered that Johnny also built log cabins at several other locations near Gold Camp. One of these was about thirty miles to the west on the eastern end of Ackerman Lake (Neetęędrat Van), where the family often lived in the summer. Others were located at Ch'idrii (Heart Mountain), where Your Creek joins the Middle Fork of the Chandalar; at Kiidrii Choh (Big Rock Mountain) north of Gold Camp on the East Fork of the Chandalar; at Łinitsigwaa'ee (a tributary of the Ch'aghaihchanjik); and at Neech'aa T'oo Git, on a glacial creek called Łuut'eechanjik (another western tributary of the Ch'aghaihchanjik). Still another cabin was started on the Ch'aghaihchanjik itself but was never finished.

Fig. 17. The Frank family in Venetie, October, 1989. Left to right are Dan Frank, Maggie Roberts, Hamel Frank, and Nathaniel Frank. Photo by Craig Mishler.

The Ch'aghaihchanjik, shown on most maps as the North Fork of the East Fork, empties into the East Fork just below Gold Camp. Although Gold Camp was generally an excellent place for hunting big and small game and setting traps during the winter, occasionally the family faced hardship and had to look elsewhere for food. Some of these hard times came because the Franks shared their reserves with others who were less fortunate and sometimes because game animals were scarce. One of the family's favorite retreats in times of hardship was at Łinitsigwaa'ee.

During the spring, right after break-up, many Gwich'in families around Arctic Village, Venetie, Fort Yukon, Chalkyitsik, and Old Crow went to the lakes to hunt muskrat and ducks. Around Gold Camp, however, there are not many lakes for muskrat, so the Franks would leave their cabin and move to places like Van Choh to take advantage of these resources. Each spring they would also go up the East Fork of the Chandalar into the mountains to hunt moose and northward-migrating caribou and make dry meat. They spent a lot of time traveling around Neetr'ee Ddhaa and Yeechyah Tł'ee Ki', accompanied by a few dogs carrying dog packs. The packs were made out of tanned caribou leg skins, and each dog was able to pack thirty to forty pounds of meat. However, during the month of June most

Fig. 18. Nathaniel Frank packing moss for chinking the logs of the first school in Venetie, c. 1937. Photo courtesy of Dan Frank.

subsistence activities, except for drying caribou meat, came to a halt. The Franks and most other Gwich'in families were forced to remain in one place because melting snow made the ground too soft and wet for travel.

In July and August they began moving through the mountains again, looking for Dall sheep and southward-migrating caribou, which still usually show up in early August. For the Franks, sheep meat was the greatest delicacy and was highly sought after. One of Johnny's favorite sheep hunting areas was around Ch'idrii (Heart Mountain), just north of Ackerman Lake on the Middle Fork of the Chandalar River. After hunting sheep and southward-migrating caribou, the Franks would float back down to Gold Camp in a couple of skin boats full of dry meat for the winter. In the fall Johnny would take his furs to Fort Yukon to trade for Gold Shield brand tea and coffee, Eagle brand canned milk, sugar, tobacco, and gun shells.

Fall was also a favorite time of the year to hunt moose, and Johnny was famous for catching big bulls in his rawhide snares. Joe Wagner, an Episcopal Church lay worker who stayed at Gold Camp several times for a month or more in the early 1970s, remembers Johnny sitting on the roof of the cabin in the evenings, calling moose with his voice and scraping moose antlers together. The homestead at Gold Camp, like the one on the Koness River, was primarily a wintering place. When moose and caribou weren't around, the Franks lived off birds and small game, snaring or shooting ptarmigan, hares, lynx, porcupine, and, in the summer, ground squirrels. Grayling and northern pike (jackfish) were also available in the East Fork, where Johnny built a fish trap.

Johnny and Sarah were devout Christians, and Sarah talks a great deal about the early missionaries and the prophesies of the Bible. Their grandson. Lawrence Roberts, whom they raised at Gold Camp until he was seven years old, likes to tell the story of how his grandfather's faith in God once got them a moose. Lawrence said he was hunting with his grandfather one time in June, 1962, when they were almost completely out of food. Johnny was still grieving over the accidental drowning of his grandson Buddy Frank in Chalkyitsik the month before. The East Fork of the Chandalar was very high and muddy, making it impossible to catch grayling. They decided to walk down the East Fork about twelve miles from Gold Camp to a place where moose were known to cross the river. When they got there, they spied a big bull moose standing on the opposite bank.

However, they were frustrated because the current was too swift and the water too deep to chance a crossing on foot, and they had no canoe. The moose just stood there and seemed to stare at them for a long time. Then it started walking downriver, and they couldn't follow it because there was a creek coming into the river below them on their side, and the water in this creek was very high also. As Lawrence tells it, Johnny dropped down on his knees to pray, and Lawrence did so also. Johnny said (in Gwich'in), "Dear God, you've got to give me this moose. You took ten of my fourteen children, and my grandchild, and right now I've got to have this moose in order to survive. Don't take this away from me."

When they stood up, Lawrence saw that the big bull was continuing to move downriver and away from them, and that's when he thought to himself, "What's the use?" The next moose crossing was another ten miles downriver. But just when it seemed totally hopeless, the moose suddenly turned around and came back upriver, never stopping until it reached a place just opposite to where they were standing on the bank. Then it started crossing the river. It swam part way across and started drifting down, but then it came to a sand bar, regained its footing, and eventually came right up to them. The bull wasn't frightened even though it could see them very clearly, and it just stood there while Johnny shot it at close range, toppling it with a single shot. Then Johnny fell down on his knees and prayed again to thank God.

Lawrence went back up to Gold Camp to get their dogs, and by the time he got back, his grandfather had the moose meat all cut up into small chunks and ready to put inside the dog packs. "Those dogs were a part of us," Lawrence says, "and I remember every one of them. Shinlįį was the mother, and the other six were all her pups. They were named Leader, Granger, Vat'aii, Blackie, Gray, and Diamond. And those dogs were so big and so strong that between them they packed out that whole bull moose."

Another story illustrates the way Johnny Frank and other Gwich'in respect animals. Lawrence remembers that one spring at

Gold Camp they had no meat, just a little flour and rice, and he would go out every day to fish for grayling and to check his rabbit snares. One day he found a rabbit still alive in one of his snares. He let it go and chased it just to see if he was fast enough to catch it. Soon he did catch it, and then he let it go and chased it again. This time when he caught it, he killed it, but for a long time after that he couldn't catch anything at all.

He was sleeping in a tent outside his grandparents' cabin one day when Johnny woke him up. Johnny asked him, "Did you catch a rabbit and let it go again?" Lawrence was surprised and scared and answered, "No." A little while later, while they were eating at the table, Johnny told Sarah that he had a dream, and in his dream he saw Lawrence catch a rabbit and let it go and chase it again. When Lawrence overheard this he confessed. Johnny said, "Don't you ever abuse animals again. And don't ever waste meat." After Lawrence told the truth to his grandfather, his luck came back to him, and he was able to get fish and game again.

A few years later, in September, 1964, Johnny and Sarah and Lawrence were hunting moose on the Middle Fork of the Chandalar when they found themselves in trouble. They went up about fifteen miles in a boat with their son Hamel and their grandson Kenneth, and Hamel shot a moose. They packed the meat down to the boat, and Hamel and Kenneth took the boat and the meat back to Venetie. They left a little bit of the meat with Johnny, Sarah, and Lawrence, thinking they would eventually walk back to the village on their own.

But several weeks passed. Johnny, Sarah, and Lawrence were way overdue, and Hamel couldn't go back to look for them because ice started running in the river, making the water mushy, a condition called *neezhri'*. Then, to make matters worse, it started snowing. Lawrence killed a porcupine right next to their tent and that was all they had to eat for the next week. The ice got worse, so they started walking down along the river and decided to go overland across some hills to shorten the distance. They had three dogs with them but nothing to feed them except the porcupine bones. The snow soon came up to Johnny and Sarah's knees and up to Lawrence's waist, and they had no snowshoes with them. They walked about fifteen miles overland, and shot only one tree squirrel and one grouse. They camped on the hilltops but couldn't see anything because of the blizzard and thick overcast.

The weather also made it hard for those who were searching for them. Hamel had alerted the State Troopers, and one of the troopers flew out from Fort Yukon with pilot Cliff Fairchild. Johnny and Sarah and Lawrence heard the plane passing overhead but couldn't see it. Johnny finally told Lawrence to build a big fire, and that's when they were finally spotted. Fairchild and the trooper made a food drop, and they fed themselves and the dogs with canned food.

Although they were never lost, they had a hard time getting back to the river, and when they did, they camped next to the river in the area of Taih Troo'ee. Lawrence walked up and down the river looking for spawned-out salmon to feed the dogs. In the meantime, the trooper notified the Venetie National Guard, which sent out three or four dog teams to rescue them. The dog teams followed a trail up the other side of the West Fork until they got close to where the Franks were camped, and they exchanged gunshots to signal their arrival and location.

But the only place the soldiers could find to cross the river was about a half mile above where the Franks were camped. They had to grab each other's hands and wade across the ice-choked river to reach the far side. One man slipped and almost drowned, but six made it across. They spent all day building a wooden frame for a boat and covering it with the waterproof canvas wall tent that Johnny and Sarah and Lawrence were staying in. At last they succeeded in getting everyone safely across to where the dog teams were, and they returned to Venetie the next day.

In the summer of 1976 Johnny and Sarah were flooded out of their cabins at Gold Camp when the East Fork water rose high above its banks. The old village of Venetie was also flooded at this time, prompting many people to start building new cabins on higher ground. Johnny and Sarah were dramatically rescued by helicopter, and Judy Erick remembered that when Johnny got off the helicopter in Venetie, he started passing out candy to all the children. Nevertheless, after the flood subsided, Johnny and Sarah returned to Gold Camp.

These close calls, just three of dozens faced by the Franks over their long lives, suggest how thin the margin of safety is in the Alaskan wilderness, even for people who know the land intimately and take every skilled precaution to insure their own survival. Johnny and Sarah's ability to beat the odds and live to a ripe old age is a testament to their resourcefulness, ingenuity, physical toughness, and emotional inner strength in times of danger and starvation. Gwich'in elders are so highly respected by succeeding generations in part because they have repeatedly met this challenge.

Sarah Frank

Old John Vizheh[1]

<sfdlBIA338a>

CF1.03 Jii zheh nijìn dą̀į’ gwìltsąįį gàagǫǫdàii gįįdhan į’.
What year reh?

SF1.14 Izhìk łyâa gògǫ̀ǫtrii t’inyàa. Ę̀ę, nijìn dą̀į’.
Zhat gwànaa dą̀į’ łyâa zhyą̀ą *year* gwinyaa, shreedrìn gaa hàagwiindàii kwaa gwànaa t’igwirı̀įlìk.

CF1.45 Dzaa gwiłtsąįį dą̀į’ nagwànlįį?

SF1.50 Izhìk dą̀į’ zhat gwìłtsąįį dą̀į’ shigii ch’ìhlak gǫ̀ǫlįį ǫ’.

CF2.23 “Jàghaii nitì’ dzaa geet’įįdhan t’įįch’yàa?” yàhnyaa.

SF2.31 Yeendaa *Van Choo*, aii vę̨ę łuk gǫ̀ǫlįį nàhąą izhìk gwat’ą̌ąhch’yaa eenjit geet’įįdhan į’. Aii gwik’ìighai’ gwizhrįh gwįįzįį ch’aga’àa. Àkwàt yaaghòk gwà’àn, yeedòk chan, tthaa chan, aii chan gǫ̀ǫlı̀į.
Aii kwat hàa ga’àa aii zhrįh, gàhànts’ą̀’ giihee’àa kwàa.
Aii zhrįh ga’àa dzaa gwįįzįį googwìłnjik eenjit dzaa zheh gwìłtsą̀įį. Aii gwichįh dą̀į’ it’ee dinjii gǫ̀ǫlįį.
Ch’ijùk hee gwaldàk. Gwįįzįį gwandak ałtsii kwàa.
Gàa yaaghà’ jii ti’yąą dzaa zheh gwahahtsyàa gwats’ą̀’ tr’ohchìt jii vitsii?
Tr’ootsyaa aii t’ee tr’ohchìt dzaa zheh gwìłtsąįį ǫ’.

CF3.44 Dzaa lee?

SF3.45 Ą̀ąhą’, aiitł’ee dzaa neegwąą’in kwàa. Aiits’ą̀’ t’ee ti’yąą zheh gwìłtsą̀įį. Aii *last.*

CF3.59 Yaaghà’ vitì’ tr’ohkìt dzaa zheh gwìłtsąįį?

SF4.05 Ą̀ąhą’, aii tr’ohchìt zheh gwiłtsą̀įį. Izhìk it’ee aii jyàa diizhìk, nàhąą?

CF Ą̀ąhą’.

1. This conversation took place on July 17, 1979, at the site of Old John’s cabin on *Old John Lake*, where Sarah and several other *Arctic Village* elders were flown to by a Bureau of Indian Affairs helicopter. They gathered in front of the ruins of the cabin for an afternoon of reminiscing. There were many people involved in the conversation, but our interest here is primarily in the memory and knowledge of Sarah Frank. Therefore, only Sarah’s words and those of Caroline Tritt-Frank, her interpreter, have been transcribed. Others present included David Libbey, Abraham John, Moses Sam, Martha James, James Gilbert, and Myra Kay (see Fig. 27). —CM

Sarah Frank

Old John's Cabin

<sfdlBIA338a>

CF1.03 They (the BIA) want to know when they built this house. What year?

SF1.14 It's really hard to say when it was. They did it during the time when they say we didn't know anything about years or calendars.

CF1.45 Were you born when *Old John* built this place?

SF1.50 Yes. I already had one child at the time he built it.

CF2.23 He (*David Libbey*) asked, "Why did your father like it here?"

SF2.31 You see that *Van Choo* [*Old John Lake*] over there.
There are lots of fish in it and he liked to depend on it.
That's how he ate so well. Also there are lots of ground squirrels around here and up above the area.
That was all they ate. Other than that they didn't have anything to eat. They lived well just by eating that.
That's why he built his house here.
There were lots of people here when they lived here.
I'm telling this wrong. I am not telling the story right.
Before my father built this house, his grandfather *Tr'ootsyaa* built here first.

CF3.44 Right here?

SF3.45 Yes, but afterwards he just left the place.
So my father the last one who built the house.

CF3.59 Was his father the first one to build this house?

SF4.05 Yes, he was the one who built it. Did you ask, when did he build this house?

CF Yes.

SF4.27 Jii vitsii tr'ohchìt zheh gwìłtsąįį dąį' it'ee vizhìt khàłêiijii iłtsąįį. Jidìi zhik gwà'àn tł'oo.

CF Ąąhą'.

SF4.34 Jèiinch'ii ts'ą' łuh, oozhòk nankat łùh.

CF Ąąhą'.

SF4.39 Aii hàa nihtee tthak nąhtraa ts'ą' it'ee hiidàr gwìch'ìn.

Jyàa dàhtsii roh. Aiits'ą' dzaa vigihdêiinvyàa gǫǫlįį gàa zhyąą gihdêiinvyàa kwàa.

Aii gwizhìt iłtsàįį. Aii zheh gwìłtsąįį gwizhìt ił'ąįį.

CF4.59 Aii lèe ch'iitsii eenjit t'ą̆ąhch'yaa?

SF Hąą?

CF5.02 Jidìi eenjit yat'ąąch'yàa? Aii jidìi iłtsàįį.

SF5.04 Ch'iitsii gwìch'in giizhìt gwîiłk'ą'.

CF5.05 Ch'iitsii. Aii chan juu t'iizhìk t'iinyàa?

SF5.11 *Tr'ootsyaa*. Jèiinch'ii tł'oo. Tł'oo hàa chan aii łùh hàa t'iyįįlìk, aii hàa yizhìk[2] iłtsąįį nał'yą' į'.

CF6.02 Nijìn gòo'ąįį? Aii zheh t'agwąįįnyàa?

SF6.03 Aii nijìn gòo'ąįį yeedòk gwà'àn nijin gòo'ąįį lì'.

Giyàhnyàa.[3]

CF6.13 Ǫ̂ǫ, aii gwadachàn làt hęę?

SF6.18 Jyàa dĭizhìk łee roh.

6.59-17.40[4]

CF17.47 "Jii zheh nijìn dąį' *Old John* gwat'ą̆ąhch'yaa akhàgoonyàa?" yàhnyàa.

SF17.53 Izhìk gwat'ą̆ąhch'yaa akhàgoonyaa aii t'ee zhat dąį' dinjii dzaa gwee'àn dinjii lęįį nąįį gwandàii.

Akhài' t'ee datthak shìh kwaa gòodlit. Ch'atthąįį gaah'in wàa. Aiits'ą' t'ee jii vitsii nąįį, *Paul Solomon* gootì', dinjii lęįį nąįį yeenjì' *Old Crow, Circle* datthak gwats'ą' gahàajìl, tr'ohchìt *Gwichyaa* shigąhjil, shìh kwaa ts'ą'.

---

2. *Yizhìk* is the same as *yiyìk,* meaning 'stove pipe.' —JE
It's translated here as 'chimney.' —CM

3. At this point Alice Peter reminds Sarah about how Old John took the logs from his father's old house. And that's what he built the house with. —LG

4. A section on visiting the Inuit is included below in Part III.

SF4.27 When his grandfather built this house, that's when he built the fireplace, using some grass.

CF Yes.

SF4.34 With this kind (she points to something) and dirt, dirt from the ground.

CF Yes.

SF4.39 So he mixed it together and wetted it down.

The stove looked like a heater. It was this big (gesturing).

There was a door on it, but it was not a door, just an opening.

When he built the house, this is what he had inside.

CF4.59 Is that what he used for a stove?

SF What?

CF5.02 What he built, what did he use it for?

SF5.04 It looks like a stove and they built a fire inside.

CF5.05 This stove. Who did this?

SF5.11 *Tr'ootsyaa*. With this kind of grass.

He did it with grass and mud.

With that mixture I saw him build a chimney.

CF6.02 Where was this located? I mean that house.

SF6.03 Where was it at? Up above from this area.

That's what they said.

CF6.13 Ooh, so some of these logs were from there?

SF6.18 So that's what he did.

6.59-17.40

CF17.47 "When did *Old John* stop using this house?" he (David Libbey) asked her.

SF17.53 Food became scarce while there were still lots of people living here.

That's why he stopped using this place. There were no big game animals. So his grandfather, who is *Paul Solomon Sr.'s* father, and many others went to *Old Crow* and *Circle*. Many of them left for the flatland areas because food was scarce.

CF19.07 Łyâa, izhìk gwànaa dąį' âa, *what year* t'ôonch'yaa nik'èe gàanandàii? nàhnyàa.

SF19.13 Łąhch'yaa gàhgwiindàii kwaa t'iihnyàa.

It'ee łyâa t'iihnyàa.

Jii nah, jùk geełeehìdhiizhii izhìk gwats'ą' geegwahaldak ǫ'.

Aiitł'ęę nakhwan chan nijìn gàakhwandàii geegoondàk.

Aii jì' gwinzįį dęhtł'yaa gahahtsyàa.

CF20.27 It'ee tseenjyàà gwandàk.

SF20.28 Aiits'ą' t'ee nijìn dąį' geełeehìdhiizhii izhìk gwats'ą' gwaldak t'iihnyàa.

Aiits'ą' aii dinjii gǫ̀ǫlįį, aiits'ą' dzat gwee'àn oochìt *Arctic Village* gwà'àn datthak łuk ghat dinjii gwat'ą̌ąhch'yaa googàa khaii gwį̂įk'oo ts'ą' shìh kwàa.

Shìh kwaa diinyaa?

CF Ą̀ąhą'. Aii geegwandak hęè. . .?

SF21.26 Ą̀ąhą'. Aiits'ą' t'ee dzaa izhìk dąį' dzaa gwee'àn ti'yąą vitsii aii ti'yąą aiits'ą' chan aii nąįį hàa t'ee dzaa zhat dinjii tthak geełèehàajil ts'ą' dzaa gwik'ìitł'ųų tr'agwandąįį.

Akhài' diikhwan chan diihàa gògǫǫtrii.

Ch'atthąįį tr'ąąh'in kwàa.

CF21.51 Hmm.

SF22.26 Aiits'ą' jyàa dòonch'yaa ts'ą' diikhwąhzhrįh tr'îilch'ii.

Akhài' diikhwant'ee diishìi kwàa. Aiits'ą' t'ee yaaghà' *Van Choh* ooch'iitthàn t'ee tr'ahàandii, ti'yąą nąįį.

Oochìt *T'aa Dha'ąįį* gwatthan tr'ą̂ąhaa aii gwats'an chan *Zheh Gwatsal* ch'iitthàn tr'ahàajil ǫ'.

CF23.00 Tr'ohkìt nijìn noohàa diinyàa?

SF23.04 Dzaa.

CF *No,* dzaa hadhòojil tł'ęę reh?

SF23.06 *T'aa Dha'ąįį.*

Izhìk dąį' t'ee sheejii *Rachel, Christian Choh* nąįį *Zheh Gwatsal* gwigwich'įį łii. Aii giveek'eeriidàl.

24.15 Izhìk gwats'an t'ee chan, aii chan vishìi gǫ̀ǫlįį kwàa.

CF19.07 Do you know when that was? Did he say what year?

SF19.13 I'm saying I really don't know.

Listen, I will talk about what happened before I left this place.

Then you tell about what you remember.

That way everything will be written down in order.

CF20.27 Okay, you can talk some more.

SF20.28 As I said, I will talk about what happened before I left this place.

There were lots of people using the fish from around here and *Arctic Village*, but it was too cold that winter, so food was scarce.

CF Yes. Could you tell about. . . ?

SF21.26 Yes. At the time my father's father and his grandfather and a lot of other people were living here, but they all left this place.

And we stayed behind, but we also had a very hard time getting food.

There were no large game animals around.

CF21.51 Hmm.

SF22.26 As we stayed there, it got worse, so my father and his family started traveling down toward that way.

From here at *Van Choh* ['*Old John Lake*'] we stopped at this place called *T'aa Dha'ąįį* ['Cottonwood Placed on the End'] and made camp. From there we traveled down toward *Zheh Gwatsal* ['*Christian Village*'].

CF23.00 Where did you say you made your first camp?

SF23.04 Here.

CF No, after you left this place.

SF23.06 *T'aa Dha'ąįį.* When we arrived at *Christian Village*, my older sister *Rachel* and *Chief Christian* were living there.

24.15 They hardly had any food either.

Aiits'ą' *three times* vàh tr'ąąhaa tł'ęę ts'ą' t'ee tthàn ts'ą' *Gwichyaa* gwats'ą' rahàajil ǫ'. Izhìk dąį' gwats'an dzaa neegwąąl'in kwaa ǫ'.

CF Hęę.

SF24.36 Duulèe jyàh dàłtsii dǫhłįį, aii gwànaa t'agwaihnyàa.

<sfdlBIA338b>[5]

CF41.10 Hey shitsųų, nahan nijìn dąį' nįįdhat t'inch'yàa?

SF41.18 Łąhch'yaa nįįdhat ts'ą' vanaldàii kwàa.

Shigii ch'ìhłak gòodlit jìhnyaa?

CF Ąąhą'.

SF41.27 Aii nitsìi kwaa, natsàl gwiizhìk ch'adąį' nįįdhat į'.

Izhìk gwizhrįh ganaldàii.

Àkwàt łyâa shreedrìn haashandàii kwaa t'ôonch'yàa.

CF41.42 Jidìi chyaa tsal *or* nich'it tsal?

SF41.44 Nich'it tsal aii t'ee *Lucy*[6] t'aihnyàa. *Ambrose* va'at t'aihnyàa.

CF42.11 Dąhtsii?

SF42.12 Êe, jyàa dąhtsii.[7]

CF42.16 Dàk dhidii? Neehidik?

SF42.18 Neehidik, vagwantii t'aihnyàa. Aii ni'ęę niheedhaa, aii gwats'ą' gwànaa dąį' t'ee t'iizhìk. Aii gehjųų gwànaa nįįdhat į'. Aii ni'ęę chan oodee gwizhìt gwįįch'į'.[8]

CF43.06 Oodee gwich'įį gwiizhìk nįįdhat hęę?

SF43.14 Oodee gwich'įį gwiizhìk veenjit gwìizùų.

Aiitł'ęę vijuu gwànaa hee, zhik gwà'àn neerihiinjìk izhìk it'ee dzaa nirįįdii izhìk t'ee nįįdhat į'.

CF43.38 Khaii *or* shin?

SF43.44 Shin, khaiits'ą' duulèe, *Septembèr or Octobèr* hàa ch'ìhłak nanh t'iizhìk į'. Khąįįts'ą' gwats'ą' gweedhaa.

---

5. At this time Sarah was visiting her mother's grave with the same group of people listed above. —CM

6. They actually say Luhsii instead of Lucy. —KP

7. She makes some kind of hand gesture. —LG

8. *Aii oodee gwizhìt gwiich'į' nyaa t'ee oodee* Old John *vizheh t'agwàhnyàa.* —LG

So we only stayed there three days and then we traveled down to the *Yukon Flats*.

That was the last time I was at this place.

CF Huh.

SF24.36 What I'm saying is that maybe I was this big at that time (using hand gestures).

<sfdlBIA338b>

CF41.10 Hey Grandma, when did your mother pass away?

SF41.18 I really don't remember when she died.

The time when I said I only had one child?

CF Yes.

SF41.27 She was just a child when my mother died; that's how I remember.

I didn't know anything about calendars back then.

CF41.42 Was it a boy or a girl?

SF41.44 I'm saying she was a girl; her name was Lucy.

I'm saying she became Ambrose William's wife.

CF42.11 How big was she?

SF42.12 Oh, she was this big (gesturing),

CF42.16 Was she sitting or walking?

SF42.18 I'm saying she walked and was very active. It was before my mother died when it happened. She died after that. My mother also lived in that house up there [referring to *Old John's* house].

CF43.06 Did she die while she was living in that house up there?

SF43.14 She was living up there when she started to feel bad.

But we still traveled around here until she died.

CF43.38 Winter or summer?

SF43.44 Summer, maybe fall, in September or October, one of those months.

Gwiizhìk t'iizhìk. *July* ndàa nàa'ąį'.

CF44.18 Iłts'ik ts'ą̀' nįįdhat?

SF44.20 Ą̀ąhą', vizhìt shìh gwitr'it t'agwa'ìn kwaa ts'ą̀' nįįdhat.[9]

<sfdlBIA337a>

SF0.36 Izhìk dą̀į' hęę dząą vanàrąąhjìk gwats'an dzat gwee'àn neegwaal'in kwaa ǫ'.

CF0.54 Jìi t'ee tr'ookìt naan' in?

SF0.56 Ą̀ąhą'. Juk tr'ohchìt naal'in t'ishi'ìn. Izhìk dą̀į' chan ti'yąą nàhąą. Ti'yąą chan dinjii zhik gwà'àn nìrihiidàl hee, geetàk Drinzhìt dą̀į' dinjii eenjit khàgiinjìi. Aii hàa dinjii tee chan neehidik nàhąą? Ch'eekwaii tee agàa tthak neehidik į'. Aiits ą̀' khèhłan t'ôonch'yaa kwàa. Aiits'ą̀' gòhch'it zhyą̀ą vakat khan neegwąąl'in kwàa. Ts'ą̀' jùk gwizhrįh vakat neegwąąl'in t'ishi'ìn.

CF1.58 Yaaghà' jidìi t'inch'yaa? Dachan vakat?

SF2.00 Zhyą̀ą vakat gwinìn'ee į'.

Jyàhts'ą̀' tth'ank'ìt gwakak shrigwigwilìk į'.

CF Hą̀ą.

SF2.23 Jèiinch'ii dachan chan gwanàgatthak valàt kwat chat dats'an agàa giikat aghan į'. Łuk agàa.[10]

CF2.35 Ą̀ąhą', nał'in ijìi.

SF2.37 Jyàa digìyàh'in į', gwik'ìighai' vigwiheech'yàa eenjit t'igiyah'in dǫ̀hłįį. Ch'izhii tr'ahahtsyàa vakat nìneerįį'ąįį jì' văihnyaa t'aihnyàa. *Cross* vakat nìneerįį'ąįį jì' łyâa heezyàa. Geenjit *try* gwahałtsyàa lèe.

CF4.17 *Hey,* jùk khàa oonjìt kwànk'ìt gwits'eegohòojil jì' jèiinch'įį veenjit tr'ohtsyaa oiinyàa, nàhnyàa.

Aii jì' oonaa neegiiheechyaa, dząą gwinìgiiheetthal eenjit.

SF4.28 Ą̀ąhą', aii jì' heezyàa shitseii, łyâa gwįįzįį t'igwinyàa.

CF4.38 "Ą̀ąhą'," nàgàhnyàa.

9. If Sarah's mother died while Lucy was still a toddler, this would probably have been about 1909 or 1910, a couple of years after Johnny and Sarah's marriage in 1907. —CM

10. For photos of similar grave pole carvings see McKennan, 1965: Plates 25 and 26.

It was just before fall. Maybe late in July.

CF44.18 Did she die from sickness?

SF44.20 Yes, the food wasn't digesting in her stomach and she died from that.

<sfdlBIA337a>

SF0.36 After she was buried here, I never saw this place again.

CF0.54 Is this the first time you came here after that?

SF0.56 Yes, this is the first time I ever returned to see it. You see at that time my father was always on the go, and when Sunday came he did church services for people. He did the same for the Inuit when he traveled among them. So we never stayed in one place. That's why we never returned here. So this is the first time I have returned.

CF1.58 What are these things here? On the wooden pole?

SF2.00 They just stick them on the pole.
This is how they fixed the graveyard.

CF Yes.

SF2.23 They used this kind of pole.
They put different kinds of carved wood on the tip of it.
Sometimes they used ducks or even fish.

CF2.35 Yes, I've seen it.

SF2.37 They do this so the grave will be marked. I'm saying I'm asking him if we could mark it with a cross. It will be good if we put a cross on it. I will try for it.

CF4.17 Hey, (translating) they said they wanted to make a cross for you when we return to the camp tonight.
Then they will bring it back and put it on the grave.

SF4.28 Yes, that will be good, my grandchild.
It really sounds good. I will appreciate it.

CF4.38 "Yes," they said.

SF4.40 Aii jì' łì'hàa gwįįtł'oo shòo hihłyàa, gwįįzįį.[11]
Aiits'ą̀' oonjìt shigii tsal chan vineegwaràh'ąįį jì' aii chan gwik'ìt t'iriheelyàa hą̀ą?

CF5.01 Ą̀ąhą'.

SF5.31 Oonjìt *Ch'at'oonjik* ginyaa izhìk gehdìt chan izhìk t'ee shigii tsal dhichįį. Aii t'aihnyàa. *Joseph* òozhìi.

CF5.39 Ą̀ąhą'.

SF5.40 *Nahnaa* chan òozhii.

CF Ą̀ąhą'.

SF6.10 Dzą̀ą gwee'àn neegwahą̀ąl'yàa kwaa aii dzą̀ą gwee'àn neeshagahahchik łì'hàa, *Thank you.*
K'èegwaadhat ' t'igwii'in jì' łyâa giveenjit tsèe'in ihłįį į'.

CF6.48 Âa, geedan chan ideechìi t'igii'in gwìch'in roh.

SF6.56 Ą̀ąhą', łì'hàa geenjit shòh ihłįį.

CF7.01 Geedan chan "Mą̀hsi'," nagàhnyàa.

SF7.02 Ą̀ąhą', gwįįtł'òo geenjit shòh ihłįį.
Aii geh'àn tr'igwihdìi kwaa k'it t'ihch'yàa, ts'ą̀' dzą̀ą gwee'àn neehihdik t'ishi'ìn.

CF7.13 Hą̀ą.

11. Today we say *gwįntł'oo* and *gwinzįį.* —KP

SF4.40 Then I will be very happy, good.
Up that way, for my other little one, will they do the same thing for him?

CF5.01 Yes.

SF5.31 Over at *Ch'at'oonjik,* south of this place, my child is sleeping. That's who I mean. His name is Joseph.

CF5.39 Yes.

SF5.40 *Nahnaa* is his other name.

CF Yes.

SF6.10 I didn't think I would ever see this place again but they brought me here. Thank you. By the grace of God they are doing this, and I'm very happy about it.

CF6.48 Ah, they are happy to do that for you.

SF6.56 Yes, I'm very happy about it.

CF7.01 They said, "Thank you" to you too.

SF7.02 Yes, I'm very thankful and happy. That's why I don't look sad seeing this place again.

CF7.13 Yes.

Fig. 19. Stanley Frank (seated in doorway), Maggie Frank Roberts, Sarah Frank, and Johnny Frank, circa 1950. Photo courtesy of Paul Williams Sr.

Fig. 20. Left to right are John Christian, Johnny Frank, Neil Sam, and Christopher Johnson with a trapped wolf at Gold Camp, late 1960s. Photo from Kenneth Frank collection.

Sarah Frank

Shalàk Naii

<sfkfla>

CF21.37 Shitsųų, nitì' doozhii t'inch'yàa?

SF21.42 Ti'yąą lèe?

CF Ą̀ąhą'.

SF *Old John.*

CF21.47 Vanaljìk gwiizhìk łąą.

SF21.49 *John* oozhii. *Vindehgwìizhìi* chan òozhii.

KF21.59 Nahan aii yù'?

SF22.00 Ni'ęę chan *Màry* òozhii į'. *Mary Ch'idįį* adąhzhrįį tsyaa nąįį tee vagòodlit. Nich'it nilįį ts'ą̀'. Aii geh'àn jyàhts'ą̀'giyuuzhrii t'igiyàhnyąą.

CF22.26 Aii ànts'ą̀' *Lena Vahan* nąįį hàa shàa khik nihtineegiidàl. *Lena Vahan* aii doozhii łèe? *Mary Dzan*?

SF Ą̀ąhą'.

SF22.42 Aii chan *Màry Dzan* oozhii į'.

KF22.50 Shitsųų, nahan vahan aii nats'àhts'ą̀' gavoozhrì' t'inch'yàa? Gooyèhghan?

SF22.56 Aii gavoozhrì' it'ee gwinzįį hàashandàii kwaa t'inch'yaa nàhąą.

CF23.03 Nitsųų nąįį lèe? Tr'iinin inlįį dąį' hee gookwàa?

SF23.09 Ą̀ąhą'. Tth'aii hee shakwàa gwiizhìk gwànaa gookwàa gwìch'in roh.

KF23.16 Nitì' ts'ąįį aii yù'?

SF23.21 Aii ti'yąą vitsii ginyaa. Vitsii giyàhnyàa. Aii t'ee voozhrì' *Kǫ̀'dah Ty'aa* chat ginyaa ts'ą̀' *Kǫ̀'nii'àk* chan. Ąįį hàa t'ee nihkheegaadii googàhnyàa.[1]

KF23.47 *Kǫ̀'dah Ty'aa* ts'ą̀' *Kǫ̀i'nii'àk* hàa lèe?

SF Ą̀ąhą'.

KF23.55 Aii it'ee nitì' vitsųų nąįį ree?

1. Other sources indicate that Sarah's father's father was Kǫ̀'nii'àk, but that her mother's mother was Kǫ̀'dah Ty'aa. See Sarah's side of the genealogy in Appendix A. —CM

Sarah Frank

My Relatives

<sfkfla>

CF21.37 Grandma, what was your father's name?

SF21.42 My father?

CF Yes.

SF *Old John.*

CF21.47 I just remembered it too.

SF21.49 His name is *John Vindęhgwìizhii* too.

KF21.59 What about your mother?

SF22.00 Also my mother's name was *Mary*. She was the only girl that was born among a family of boys. That's why they named her *Ch'idii.*

CF22.26 That one and Lena's mother. I always get mixed up with them. What is Lena's mother's name? *Mary Dzan?*

SF Yes.

SF22.42 Her name is *Mary Muskrat.*

KF22.50 Grandma, what are your mother's parents' names?

SF22.56 I really don't know their names, you see.

CF23.03 Your grandmothers? Did they die when you were a child?

SF23.09 Yes. Maybe they died before I was born.

KF23.16 What about on your father's side?

SF23.21 They say my father's grandfathers are named *Kǫ̀'dah Ty'aa* and *Kǫ̀'nii'ak.* They were both married.

KF23.47 You mean both *Kǫ̀'dah Ty'aa* and *Kǫ̀'nii'ak?*

SF Yes.

KF23.55 That's your father's grandmothers?

SF24.04 Ti'yąą vitsii nąįį ree. Aii t'ee yaaghà' shitsųų *Mil Vahan* aii shàh gwaandàk. Aii it'ee zhat gwànaa ti'yąą chįh dąį' gwats'an gwandàii t'arahnyą̀ą.

KF Ą̀ąhą'.

SF24.21 Aii *Mil Vahan.* Aii it'ee shàagwaandak dąį' jyàa nyàa. Âa, gwintł'òo dinjii gǫ̀ǫlįį nyaa t'inch'yàa. Khaii neerihiinjìk ch'iindàa gàa chuuluh tik łąą nǐin'ee t'ee nyaa. Aii njik datthak tr'eedàa. Oondaa gwitsįį nìriindii jì' nikheetee ts'ą̀' ch'irihee'àa t'igwinyaa kwaa nyàa. Nehshrit jidìi tsal zhrįh ga'àa nąįį reh. Aii shitsųh shàagwaandak t'agwaihnyàa.

KF25.01 Aii nijìn ts'ąįį nitsųų nilįį?

SF25.06 *Mil Vahan* lèe?

KF Ą̀ąhą'.

SF25.08 Aii t'ee yaaghà' ti'yąą sheek'aii yàhnyàa.

KF Ôǫ.

KF25.17 Nitì' vitì' vahan aii goovoozhrì' anandàii?

SF Goohàashandàii kwaa nǎihnyàa.

KF25.33 Nitì' vitsųh aii anandàii gàa vahan aii anandàii shrǫ̀ǫ noiihnyaa t'iihnyàa.

SF Akwàa.

CF25.42 Aii *Mil Vahan* vǎiinyaa jùu t'aiinyàa?

SF25.45 Ôǫ, *Mil Vahan* vǎihnyàa, aii ti'yąą t'ee sheek'aii zhrįh yàhnyàa. Zhat gwànaa dąį' ch'oozhii èediigwąąhtan kwaa roh.

Aii ti'yąą vitsii aii t'ee vicheii nąįį gwilìk dąį' òozhri'aghan giyàhnyàa. Gàa aii chan gwinzįį gavàhshandàii kwaa į'.

Yaaghà' *Albert Ginkhii* goohan aii chan oozhrii giyàhnyàa į'. Aiits'ą̀' yaaghà' *Màry Dzan* gootì', aii gootì' goohan *Mary Dzan* goohan, goohan taihnyàa.

Aii chan Dinjii Zhuh k'yą̀ą gootòo'ahzhrì' googàhnyàa. Googàa gwinzįį ganaldàii kwàa.

CF27.22 lt'ee zhrį' ginlęįį ts'ą̀' shàanihtineegiidàl t'agavaihnyàa, geetàk hee. Gavoozhrì' hàashandàii gàa reh.

SF Ą̀ąhą'.

SF24.04 That's my father's grandfathers. And my grandmother *Mil Vahan* told me that. She was living way back before my father's time, as they would say.

KF Yes.

SF24.21 When *Mil Vahan* told me about this, she said there were many people then. When they traveled in the winter they had three trails. Everybody followed those trails. If we made a big camp overnight, there was hardly ever any food.

We just barely got by with what little we had. What I'm saying is this is what my grandmother told me.

KF25.01 Which side is she, your grandmother, from?

SF25.06 You mean *Mil Vahan?*

KF Yes.

SF25.08 My father called her "my aunt."

KF Ooh.

KF25.17 Do you remember the name of your father's father's mother?

SF I said I don't know.

KF25.33 You remembered your father's grandmother, but I thought maybe you might remember his mother. That's why I asked.

SF No.

CF25.42 Who did you say *Mil Vahan* was?

SF25.45 Oh, my father only called her "my aunt." During that time they hardly taught us our relations.

At that time they say my father's grandfather named his grandchildren as they were born. I didn't know them either. But they say he named *Albert Tritt's* mother.

And also *Mary Dzan's* father, and her father's mother too.

And *Mary Dzan's* mother too. That's who I mean. They say he called them all with Indian names. But I still don't remember them.

CF27.22 I know most of their names but there's too many. So I get all mixed up.

SF Yes.

CF27.35 Aii *John Fred* giyàhnyàa vitì' vahan hàa tth'aii haashandaii kwaa.

SF27.46 *John Fred* viti' aii t'ee *Fred.*[2]

CF Ąąhą'.

SF28.01 Aii t'ee *Fred* òozhii į'. Aii va'at chan, *John Fred* vahan aii chan *Louisà* òozhii į'. Aii t'ee gavàashandàii.

CF28.17 Aii jùu vigii nąįį t'iginch'yàa?

SF28.23 Aii t'ee gooyèhghan nąįį hàashandàii kwaa năihnyaa t'iihnyàa.

CF28.27 Ǫ̂ǫ, hah.

SF28.32 Aii *John Fredsòn vitì'* aii t'ee *Fred* oozhii į'. Aii ni'ęę zhrįh gootee goojùu nilįį. Aiits'ą̀' oondee dèegą̀ąch'yaa gavàashandàii kwàa. Ch'ìhłak chan oonjìt.[3]

CF29.07 Aii jì' it'ee łyâa nalàk giinlii łee hęę̀?

SF29.09 Ąąhą'. Łyâa shalàk nąįį į'. Shee'ii nąįį t'aihnyàa. Àii *Fred.*

KF29.18 *Fred* aii lèe nahan vijùu nilįį lèe văiinyàa?

SF Ąąhą'.

KF29.27 Aii *Louisà* văihnyaa aii ts'aįį nàkwàa?

SF Ąąhą'.

KF29.31 Aii *Fred* aii ree hęę?

SF29.33 Ąąhą'. Aii *Fred* aii t'ee ni'ęę voondee į'.

KF Ąąhą'.

SF29.48 Ginlęįį t'iginch'yaa gàa gwinzįį datthak gavàashandàii kwaa į'. Aii ti'yąą goohan, gooyèhghan nąįį googàa chan hàashandàii kwaa t'ôonch'yaa, nàhąą.

CF30.23 Shitsųų, shitsii *Johnny* gwandàii jì' dèegwìłkhan nàa *argue* heelyàa lì' hęę̀?

SF Ą̂ą.

CF30.31 Ą̂ą, gavàanandàii gàa oiints'ìt t'iinyaa nàhaanjyàa t'inch'yaa hęę̀?

SF (Adlaa, gwintł'oo geedlàa.)

KF30.37 Nijin gihįįkhìk hee datthak vàa ch'ats'ą̀' t'iinyaa ǫ', hèe?

SF Ąąhą'.

KF30.42 "Chan hee lèe ch'ats'ą̀' t'inyàa," nàhnyaa ǫ'.

---

2. *Anàrak òozhii.* —KP

3. The last part of this statement is inaudible. —LG

CF27.35 I still don't know *John Fred's* father and mother yet.

SF27.46 *John Fred's* father was named *Fred*...

CF Yes.

SF28.01 His name was *Fred*. His wife, *John Fred's* mother, was also named *Louisa*. I knew her.

CF28.17 Whose children were these?

SF28.23 I told you I didn't know their parents.

CF28.27 Oh yeah.

SF28.32 *John Fredson's* father's name was *Fred*. My mother was the only sister they had. I don't know how many of them there are. One of them is still alive somewhere.

CP29.07 They're your relatives then?

SF29.09 Yes. They're really my relatives. I'm saying that *Fred* is my mother's brother.

KF29.18 You're asking if your mother is *Fred's* younger sister?

SF Yes.

KF29.27 He's not on *Louisa's* side?

SF Yes.

KF29.31 But on *Fred's* side, huh?

SF29.33 Yes. That *Fred* is my mother's older brother.

KF Yes.

SF29.48 There's lots of them but I don't hardly know all of them. I don't even know my father's parents, you see.

CF30.23 Grandma, if my grandpa *Johnny Frank* was living now, he would probably argue with you, huh?

SF Yes.

CF30.31 He would say that you remember, but that you just lie about it, huh?

SF (*Sarah* laughs. They all laugh.)

KF30.37 He always disagreed with you when you told stories, huh?

SF Yes.

KF30.42 He'll also say, "You don't say it right."

Łyâa dzaa dhidii jì' łyâa zhyą̀ą duuyeh gàa ginkhii t'ôonch'yaa hę̀ę?

SF Ą̀ąhą'.

KF30.51 Jaghaii jyàanch'yaa t'inch'yaa?

SF30.53 Jèiinch'yaa t'inch'yàa, chan veechìi gįįkhii kwàa.

<sfdlBIA338a>

SF26.44 Ginjik ninjyàa neenjit ałtsįį?

CF Jidìi eegwaldak nįįdhan datthak eegwandàk. Nizįį.

SF27.00 It'ee jii t'agwàihnyaa, it'ee dą̀hthee dą̀į' gèełeehìdhiizhii aii ree it'ee geegwahaldak t'iihnyàa.

CF Ą̀ąhą'.

SF27.09 Aiits'ą̀' jii nàhąą? Jii ti'yąą t'iyàhnyaa. Ti'yąą chan dzat gwee'àn gwiindàii, nijìn dą̀į' lì'? *English* gįįkhii tr'ohchìt tr'ąąh'yą̀' ǫ'. Izhìk dą̀į' gwats'an jii dęhtł'yaa kat. Dzaa gwee'àn vidęhtł'yàa neehih'ak į'. Dęhtł'yaa. Jìi t'ee tr'ohchìt t'ee. Mmm. Nijìn nìi'ąįį?[4] Jìi t'ee tr'ohchìt t'ee eech'agwęęhtan ts'ą̀' jii t'ee tr'ohchìt *English* gįįkhii nąįį dzat tr'ohchìt gwąą'in giyèech'ǫąątan į'.

29.46 *Bible* gwandàk tthak vitee dhidlii dzaa vitsįį. Shàh ìch'in kwàa. *Sunday* vakat keegwąąh'in. Łyâa zhyą̀ą jii googàa gwįįzįį gwąął'in kwaa t'ôonch'yaa, nàhąą.

CF Hę̀ę.

SF31.05 *Sunday* gwats'an *one week* vizhìt khàgiriinjii. Gwintsàl ginjih hàandàii dhidlìt, nàhąą?[5]

Aiits'ą̀' gitree hàa googàa datthak khàgigiinjii t'agooràhnyàa, izhìk gwànaa.

Jùk diikhwan tr'agwandàii diihàn nąįį, aii nahnjyàa gooyèhghan nąįį gwandàii izhìk gwànaa t'agwaihnyàa.

4. There's a crackling sound and then a zipper sound in the background. —LG

5. *Ginjih nyaa dą̀į' t'ee* Biblè *ginjik t'àhnyàa.* —LG

If he was here he wouldn't give you a chance to talk, huh?

SF Yes.

KF30.51 How come he's that way?

SF30.53 I don't know why he's like that.

<sfdlBIA338a>

SF26.44 Am I making the story too long?

CF You tell about everything that you want to tell about. It's good.

SF27.00 As I said, I will tell about what happened before I left this place (*Old John Lake*). I was just telling about how long ago it was that I left this place.

CF Yes.

SF27.09 So you see? I was talking about my father. My father lived here, but I don't remember the exact year Maybe when they first saw the English. That was the first time they got a prayer book. I've got his prayer book with me somewhere here. Mmm. Where did I put it? This was the first prayer book that the English preachers taught to people around here.

29.46 There's a short Bible story in it. I can't see well. Look for Sunday on it for me. I can't see well even with glasses, you know.

CF Right.

SF31.05 Starting Sunday, we prayed every day for one week. He was just beginning to learn about the Bible, you see?

They say they even cried when they prayed in those days.

I'm talking about the time our grandparents were living.

35.09 Izhìk gwànaa geegwaldak t'iihnyàa. Aiits'ą' izhìk nàhąą? Izhìk dęhtłyąą eedoodîiltin gwats'anh it'ee chan gįįkhii, chan dinjii eenjit khàgiinjìi. Aiits'ą' gįįkhii chan, jyàa dinyaa ts'ą' gwizhìt łyâa gwįįtł'òo gwitr'it t'agwąh'yà' į'. Dzaa gwee'àn dinjii tee neehidik ts'ą' yee'àn Ch'eekwaii tee googàa datthak neehidik ts'ą' Ch'eekwaii nąįį eenjit googàa eenjit tr'igįįkhii gwahtsii ts'ą' khàgiinjìi. Aii gwalàįį it'ee neeshrâahch'yaa dhidlìt ts'ą' ree it'ee vakwàa į'.

CF38.38 *Old John* nik'èe *vipicture* ni'įį nàhnyàa?

SF38.42 *Vipictùre*[6] shi'įį kwaa į'. T'ǫǫhłįį *vipicture* dhitin dǫhłįį. Aii *Old John* ti'yąą. Aiits'ą' vijùu nèekwąįį nąįį gǫǫlįį, aii nąįį zhrįh gavàashandàii. Aiits'ą' jii ti'yąą vijùu aii gii t'ee *Albert Tritt* tįįch'yàa. Aii gwats'an chan yaaghan nąįį chàn.

CF39.38 *Wait, wait,* chan t'iinyàa lèe. Nitì', *right?*

SF39.42 Ą̀ąhą'. Ti'yąą aii vijùu *Josèph*[7] *Vahan* òozhìi, aii vigii t'ee *Albèrt.*

CF *Wait,* nitì' aii vijùu?

SF Ą̀ąhą'.

CF Aii vijùu jàghaii?

SF39.58 Vigii nąįį t'įįch'yaa naihnyàa. *Albert Tritt.*

CF Ôǫ.

SF40.30 Aii vijùu nèekwąįį gwą̀ąlįį, aii ch'ìhłak. . .

CF Aii jùu vijùu nèekwaii gwàlįį?

SF40.36 Ti'yąą.

CF *Okay,* ą̀ąhą'.

SF40.40 Aiits'ą' jii ch'ìhłęę *Josèph* vahan văihnyàa.

CF Ą̀ąhą'.

SF40.44 Ch'ìhłak chan *Louisà* oozhìi, aii vigii chan it'ee *John Fred* ijìi. Aii t'ee *Louisà* vigii į'. Aii t'ee ti'yąą vijùu nąįį ts'anh gwandàii nąįį.

6. *Vipicture* is an interesting example of a Gwich'in pronominal prefix attached to an English noun. —CM

7. They actually say Joses instead of Josèph. —KP

35.09 I'm talking about those days. So right there, you see? My father taught himself about the Bible. After that he started to preach. He prayed for people. He really worked hard on it. He traveled among the people around here, and even went among the Inuit. He went and traveled among the Inuit and prayed for them. He kept this up until he got old, and then later on he died.

CF38.38 Have you got any photographs of *Old John*?

SF38.42 I don't have his picture. Maybe somewhere there is one.

My father, *Old John*, had two younger sisters. One of my father's younger sisters is the mother of *Albert Tritt*.

And there are others too.

CF39.38 Wait, wait, say it again. Your father, right?

SF39.42 Yes. My father's younger sister's name was *Joseph Vahan,* and her child's name was *Albert*.

CF Wait, did you say she was your father's younger sister?

SF Yes.

CF What about it?

SF39.58 I'm telling you that's whose children they are. One of them is *Albert Tritt*.

CF Oooh.

SF40.30 He had two younger sisters and one of them is . . .

CF Who has two younger sisters?

SF40.36 My father.

CF Okay, yes.

SF40.40 I said that one of them was named *Joseph Vahan.*

CF Yes.

SF40.44 The other sister's name was *Louisa*. Her child's name was *John Fred*. He was the son of *Louisa*. So he was from my father's younger sister.

SF42.43 Aii *Louisà* vigii *Mary* Dzan òozhii aii ts'an t'ee vagòodlìt, aii t'ee *Lenà Albèrt* t'inch'yàa.

CF43.07 Aii *Louisà* vigii aii dòozhìi?

SF43.12 *Meezhrii.*[8]

CF *Mary?*

SF *Meezhrii Dzan.*

CF43.20 *Mary Dzan. Mary Johnsòn, okay.*

SF Aii t'ee *Louisà* vigii į'.

SF43.49 Aii t'ee *John Fred* t'ee ch'ìhłak aii t'ee *Mary Dzan* vachaa.

SF44.11 Akǫ' it'ee jyàa dàgwąhtsii gwizhrįh.

<sfkf2b>

CF5.03 Nigii nąįį t'agavăihnyaa, it'ee shri' ginlęįį ts'ą̀' goolàt nąįį gàa anandàii kwaa? năihnyàa.

SF Ą̀ąhą'.

CF Hęh.

SF5.47 Shigii *Lucy* aii it'ee chit. Gwats'ąįį chat tr'iinin gàa aii it'ee gwandàii gàa nehshrit shats'an tr'irąąhchįį. Aii gwats'an it'ee *Nathaniel.* Gwats'ąįį it'ee *Frank,* gwats'ąįį *Joseph* gwats'ąįį tł'ee t'ee *Allah.* Gwats'ąįį *Agnès.*

KF6.06 Aiitł'ęę chan *Dorothy?*

SF Jùu văihnyàa?

KF *Dorothy.*

SF6.16 Akwàa, *Dorothy* shigii òozhįį kwaa ǫ'.

KF Ą̀ąhą'.

SF6.22 Shigii *Allah* vigii aii *Dorothy* oaazhii ǫ'.

KF Ą̀ąhą'.

CF6.38 Shitsųų nigii ìhłak *Nishuk* òozhii lèe t'inch'yàa?

SF *Nishuk*? Nàkwàa.

CF6.45 Ôǫ, aii chan ch'oozhrį' dìhtth'ak t'aihnyàa.

SF6.47 Aii *Nishuk* aii t'ee yaaghà' nakhwatsii *Johnny* vachaa aii it'ee *Nishuk* òozhìi.

CF6.58 Aii dinjii dèiinch'yaa t'agàhnyàa?

8. Meezhrii was the old Gwich'in way of pronouncing Mary. —CM

SF42.43 *Louisa* had a daughter named *Mary Dzan.* And her child is *Lena Albert.*

CF43.07 What was *Louisa's* daughter's name?

SF43.12 *Meezrii.*

CF *Mary?*

SF *Meezrii Dzan.*

CF43.20 Ooh, *Mary Dzan, Mary Johnson*, okay.

SF She's *Louisa's* daughter.

SF43.49 *John Fredson* was one of them, and he was *Mary's* younger brother.

SF44.11 That's all for now.

<sfkf2b>

CF5.03 I said you had so many children that you can't remember all of them.

SF Yes.

CF Oh.

SF5.47 My daughter *Lucy* is the oldest one. There was another after her but it didn't live. After that there is *Nathaniel*, next is *Frank*, then *Joseph*, and then *Allah*. After that is *Agnes.*

KF6.06 After that too is *Dorothy*?

SF Who did you say?

KF *Dorothy.*

SF6.16 No. I didn't have a child named *Dorothy.*

KF Yes, okay.

SF6.22 My son *Allah's* daughter's name is *Dorothy.*

KF Yes.

CF6.38 Grandma, was one of your children named *Nishuk?*

SF *Nishuk?* No.

CF6.45 Oooh, I heard of that name.

SF6.47 That *Nishuk* was the younger brother of your grandfather *Johnny.*

CF6.58 What was the man like?

SF7.06 Dinjii tłìk choh zhyą̀ą niłįį dǫ̀hlį̀į (adlaa).

CF7.14 Shoondee *Willìam* aii *Lincòln*[9] natsàl dą̀į' *Nishuk* zhrįh àhnyaa geh'àn t'aihnyàa (adlaa).

SF Ôǫ.

CF7.25 Jùu t'agahnyaa lì' nihthan t'iihnyàa.

SF7.32 Ch'adą̀į' gwats'an jyàa dìgwii'in jì' aii jì' *family* nąįį lęįį gihidęętł'oo t'ôonch'yaa, nàhąą. Googàa gwik'ìtnt'igwii'in kwàa.

CF Ą̀ąhą'.

<sfkf2b>

KF22.06 Shitsųų, aii jaghaii shaghwaii vǎiinyaa t'iinyàa?

SF *Albèrt* lèe?

KF Ą̀ąhą'.

SF22.14 *First time* sheejii òonjik į'. Aii eenjit shaghwaii vǎihnyaa t'aihnyàa.

KF22.25 Neejii nats'àa voozhrį̀'?

SF *Leerà.*[10]

KF22.34 Aii ts'an googii gǫ̀ǫlįį lèe t'inch'yàa?

SF22.38 Aii ts'an vigii nèekwąįį zhrįh gòodlit akhài' aii khaihłęę gookwàa.

KF22.31 Gavoozhrį̀' gǫ̀ǫlįį aii nąįį?

SF22.54 Ch'ìhłak zhrįh *Abràhàm* òozhii. Tsyaa tsal aiits'ą̀' ch'ìhłak aii vàashandàii kwàa. Aii yeenjì' hee gwà'àn hee neegihiidàl izhìk hee vagòodlit ts'ą̀' khan vakwàa.

Aiits'ą̀' aii voozhrį' hàashandàii kwàa.

CF23.27 Tr'oochit neejii eiindì'?

SF Ą̀ąhą'.

CF23.30 Aiitł'ęę t'ôohju' hee shitsųų *Saràh Ghoo* òonjìk?

SF Ą̀ąhą'.

CF Ôǫ.

SF23.34 Aii sheejii vakwàa tł'ęę t'ee aii *Saràh* chan nôonjik į'.

CF23.41 Dą̀ąch'yaa *time* geiindì'? Dǫǫ?

SF Hąą?

9. Caroline is talking about her brother, Lincoln Tritt. —CM

10. Leerà is another pronunciation for Laura. —AR

SF7.06 He was big and sort of sloppy-looking (laughs).

CF7.14 When *Lincoln* was little, my older brother *William* always called him *Nishuk* (laughs).

SF Oooh.

CF7.25 I always wondered who he was.

SF7.32 If only we kept a family tree on every family from long ago, all our relatives' names would be written down, you see. But we never did.

CF Yes.

<sfkf2b>

KF22.06 Grandma, how is he your brother-in-law?

SF You mean *Albert* (*Tritt*)?

KF Yes.

SF22.14 He was married to my older sister first. That's why I called him my brother-in-law. This is why I say it.

KF22.25 What is your older sister's name?

SF *Leera.*

KF22.34 Did they have any children?

SF22.38 They had two children, but they both died.

KF22.31 Did they have names?

SF22.54 One of them was named *Abraham*. He was a boy, but the other one I didn't know. They were traveling far away when he was born, but he died right away.

I don't know his name.

CF23.27 He was married to your sister first?

SF Yes.

CF23.30 After that he married my grandmother, *Sarah Ghoo?*

SF Yes.

CF Oooh.

SF23.34 After my older sister died, then later on he married *Sarah*.

CF23.41 How many times was he married? Four?

SF What?

CF23.45 Dąąch'yaa *time* geiindì' t'inch'yàa.

SF23.47 *Two times* geiindì' t'inch'yaa ǫ'. Hęę?

CF23.55 Dęę (adlaa).

SF23.56 Àkwàt it'ee *two time* geiindì' į'.

CF Chan shoaakat? (Adlaa)

SF24.01 Aii sheejii tr'ohchìt òonjìk. Aii vits'ì' kwaa tł'ęę it'ee yaaghà' sheejii *Saràh* chan nôonjik t'inch'yàa.

CF24.14 Ąąhą'. Lyâa zhyąą shàa nihtineegiidàl t'ee.

KF24.22 Łyâa zhyąą neejii nilįį lèe t'aiinyàa? Aii *Saràh*?

SF24.28 Sheejii deek'ìt needhidii ts'ą' sheejii vàihnyaa į'.[11]

KF Ôǫ.

SF24.38 Aii sheejii *Leerà*. Aii t'ee chan ni'ęę aii tr'ohchit dinjii yuunjik. Aii *Nidik* òozhii. Aii *Dįhch'į' Davìd* gwinyaa aii vigii. Aii t'ee tr'ohchìt ni'ęę òonjìk.

Aii gwats'an it'ee aii vigii nąįį t'aihnyaa *Leerà*, *Mary, Albert.*

Aiitł'ęę yaaghà' ti'yąą neeyùunjik izhìk gwats'an aii t'ee shoondee *James (Jimmy John)* ts'ą' *Jyaalii*, shįį, ts'ą' *Petèr, Christian.*[12] Jyàa dàrąąch'yaa ts'ą' it'ee yaaghà' *Old John* vigii nąįį tr'aadlìt ǫ'.[13]

25.51 Gwichįh dąį' chan vigii gwinlì'. Aii it'ee *Mary, Leerà, and Albert.* Gwichįh dąį' chan vigii dǫǫ nąįį gòodlit į'. Aii dinjii *Dįhch'į' David* gwinyaa aii vigii reh.

KF26.51 Jyàhts'ą' t'ee voozhrį' hęę? *Dįhch'į' David* vigii hęę?

SF Ąąhą'.

KF26.58 *Nidik* lèe vǎihnyàa?

SF27.00 Ąąhą', *Nidik*. Aii *Nidik* vachaa chan *Josèph* òozhìi.

11. This sentence illustrates how classificatory kinship works for the Gwich'in. Kinship ties are not determined as much by blood lines as by generational and situational relationships. —CM

12. James John, Charlie John, Peter John, and Christian John. These were Frank's brothers. —JE

13. Sarah's mother was first married to Nidik, the son of Dihch'ì' David. Their children were Laura, Mary and Albert. Sarah's mother was then remarried to Old John. Their children were James, Charlie, Sarah, Peter, and Christian. —JE

CF23.45 How many times was he married?

SF23.47 He was married twice. Is that right?

CF23.55 I don't know (laughs).

SF23.56 Yes, he was married twice. Right?

CF You're asking me? (Laughs)

SF24.01 He married my older sister *Leera* first. After she died, then later on he married my older sister *Sarah*.

CF24.14 Yes. I really get all confused with them.

SF24.28 That *Sarah*, was she really your older sister?

SF24.28 She replaced my real older sister so I called her my older sister.

KF Oooh.

SF24.38 My older sister *Leera* is from my mother's first marriage to this man named *Nidik,* whom they say was the son of *Old Man David*. He was married to my mother first.

I said these are her children from that marriage: *Leera*, *Mary*, and *Albert*.

Later on my father married her and that's when my older brother *James* (*Jimmy John*), *Charlie*, myself, *Peter*, and *Christian* were born. That many of us came from *Old John*.

25.51 So she had children from before. They are: *Mary*, *Leera*, and *Albert*. They say she had four children before from that *Old Man David's* son.

KF26.51 What was his name? The son of *Old Man David*?

SF Yes.

KF26.58 Did you say, *Nidik?*

SF27.00 Yes, *Nidik.* That *Nidik* had a younger brother named *Joseph*.

Aii t'ee chan yaaghà' *Myrà Ch'atąįį Gwatrat*[14] gwinyaa ijìi?

KF Ą̀ąhą'.

SF27.20 Aii t'ee vigii į'. Vahan chan *Suuzan* òozhìi. Aii chat *Tr'ootsyaa* vigii.

CF27.41 Shitsųų *Myrà Ch'atąįį Gwatràt* gǫ̀ǫ neeshrą̂ąhch'yaa gwich'in.

SF27.44 Ąą, giyàhnyaa į'. Oonjit *Old Crow* gwà'àn hee nìneezhii k'ìt t'igiyàhnyàa.

Khaii dąį' yaaghà' vàanòodlit diiginjìk k'ìt ginkhii?[15]

CF Ą̀ąhą'.

SF28.04 Aii yeegwaandak t'aihnyàa.

CF28.06 Aii chan lèe nalàk oonjìt gwà'àn dìlk'įį lee nàagwaldak t'ôohju' hee gwik'yǎanjìk nàhnyàa?

SF Ą̀ąhą'.

CF (Adlaa)

SF28.19 Aii shii oaałkàt. Ti'yąą voondee ąįį *Vitì'ìsharąąhthan* giyàhnyàa. Aii t'ee òonjit hee vanàgwąąhthat aii oaałkàt. Akhài' izhìk gwats'an t'ôohju' hee gwinzįį gàandaii kwaa. Gàa shàhgwaandàk. Oonii gwandak yììtsąįį łii shats'ą' nǐin'ąįį łii. Aii tr'oodąį' gwànaa oodhǎałch'ìį. Aii nįįzhit kwaa gwànaa dąį' vakwaa k'ìt t'iyàhnyàa. Vigii nąįį gǫ̀ǫlįį dǫ̀hłįį.

CF Ą̀ąhą'.

SF29.21 Yeendaa gòhch'it zhyąą vizhìt kǫ̀' kwaa?[16]

KF29.49 Łyâa t'ee duulèe nanzhrįh łyâa zhyąą gineehaandàii goo'àii.

Nan jì' gwizhrįį gwik'ìteech'idireheetł'òo t'agwaihnyaa, jùk reh.

SF30.17 Gavoozhrì' łyâa zhyąą gwinzįį hàashandaii kwàa. Shàh gogwaandak kwaa roh. Dèegiinch'yaa t'iginch'yaa lì'.

14. The late Myrà Ch'atąįį Gwatrat was also known as Myra Kay, who resided in *Old Crow*. —CM

15. Sarah is probably referring here to John Ritter, former Director of the Yukon Native Language Centre. —CM

16. It's fall time and Sarah talks as if she's getting chilly, hinting that she would like someone to build a fire. —CM
There are loud ambient noises from Kenneth putting wood in the stove. —LG

Have you heard of *Myra Ch'atąįį Gwatr'at?*

KF Yes.

SF27.20 She was his daughter. And her mother's name was *Susan.* And she too was the daughter of *Tr'ootsyaa.*

CF27.41 My grandmother *Myra Ch'atąįį Gwatr'at* must be doing poorly now.

SF27.44 Yes, that's what I heard. They said she's back in *Old Crow.* That's what this white man that speaks our language told me.

CF Yes.

SF28.04 That's who told me about her.

CF28.06 He's the one who told you that you have relatives over there and that's how you found out you have relatives there?

SF Yes.

CF (Laughs)

SF28.19 I asked him. My father's older brother *Viti'isharąąhthan* moved over there. That's who I asked him about. He didn't quite understand, but he told me some. Later on he sent back a cassette tape to me. I listened to it recently. It sounded like he died not too long ago. He probably had lots of children.

CF Yes.

SF29.21 There must be no fire in the stove?

KF29.49 I really think you're the only one who can remember things.

I'm saying you're the only one we can write down information from.

SF30.17 But I don't know everybody's names. They never told me. I wondered what was wrong with them.

Aiits'ą' jùk nàhąą? Dzaa jùk tr'agwandàii. Ch'adąį' *Shyaaghan Dìk* gwinyaa ǫ', gwîintth'ak roh?

KF Ąąhą'.

SF30.46 Aii vigii nąįį *Drit* ginyàa. *Ch'aadzaa Vahan* chan goojùu.

Aiits'ą' *Drit Zhuu* chan aii it'ee łyâa zhyąą nakhwatsii. Aii *Drit* văihnyaa chan oondee vats'an yaaghà' *Ninà Robert* nąįį, *Abraham* nąįį, tthak giits'an gwandaii į'. *Shyaaghan Dìk* ts'anh gogwandàii nąįį.

Aii nąįį jùk lęįį tthak, lęįį t'iginch'yaa, nàhąą.

CF31.32 Aii *Drit* văihnyaa it'ee shitsii *Albèrt* vitì' t'inch'yaa oiihnyàa?

SF31.37 Vitì' aii eenjit t'aihnyaa gò'. *Drit* reh.

CF Ąąhą'.

SF31.43 Àkwàt *Drit Zhuu* aii chan yaaghà' nakhwatsii *Johnny* aii chat *Drit* ts'an gogwandàii į'. Aiits'ą' yaaghà' shigii nąįį chan, nàhąą.

CF Ąąhą'.

SF31.58 Aii nąįį *Drit Zhuu* àkwàt *Drit* hàa ts'an lęįį nąįį gwandàii ǫ'.

Goojùu *Ch'aadzaa Vahan* văihnyaa aii t'ee chat yeechìt *Jessie*[17] nąįį giits'an gwandaii į'. Aii *goofamìly*[18] nąįį lęįį nąįį gogwandàii t'inch'yàa.

CF32.29 Oodìt *Ninà Robèrt* jùu ts'an tr'igiinjil gavaiinyàa?

SF *Ninà?*

CF32.35 Ąąhą'. *Ninà Robèrt* lèe?

SF32.41 *Nina* aii it'ee yaaghà' *Albèrt* aii nąįį hàa tthak khehłak nąįį, k'ìt t'igiinch'yaa į'.

CF32.53 Izhìk gàa gàashandàii kwaa t'iihnyaa ǫ'. Nats'ąhts'ą'?

SF32.57 *Famìly* ginlįį ts'ą' goots'an nihzhyąą neech'idiijìi, nàhąą?

Aii goots'an tth'ai' dinjii lęįį gwandàii jìhnyaa t'iihnyàa.

CF33.10 Hę'.

17. Probably a reference to Jessie Williams of *Venetie*. —CM

18. The word *goofamily* represents the convergence of an English noun with a Gwich'in prefix. *Goo-* is the plural third person possessive. —CM

But right now, you see? Those who are living here. Have you heard of *Shyaaghan Ndik* from a long time ago?

KF Yes.

SF30.46 They say her children are the *Tritts*. *Ch'adzaa Vahan* was their younger sister. *Drit Zhuu* is your real grandfather. But *Drit, Nina Robert*, and *Abraham* are all his relatives. They're all descended from *Shyaaghan Ndik.*

There are so many of them and more, you see.

CF31.32 I thought *Drit* was my grandfather *Albert's* father?

SF31.37 That's his father, and that's what I said. Yes, *Drit.*

CF Yes.

SF31.43 *Drit Zhuu* is your grandfather Johnny's father. So all my children are from there, you see.

CF Yes.

SF31.58 Many of them descended from *Drit* and *Drit Zhuu.* Their younger sister *Ch'aadzaa Vahan* I named is related to *Jessie Williams* and them. Many of their relatives and their families were living then too.

CF32.29 That *Nina Robert*. Where did you say she came from?

SF *Nina*?

CF32.35 Yes, *Nina Robert*?

SF32.41 *Nina's* mother and *Albert Tritt* were all in the same family.

CF32.53 I didn't know about that. How?

SF32.57 They're family, and from there we had many generations, you see? And many living people descended from them.

That's what I was saying.

CF33.10 Huh.

SF33.14 Aii *Albèrt* goohan aii it'ee *Josèph Vahan* òozhii į'. Aii it'ee ti'yąą vijùu. Jyàa dìginch'yaa į'. Sheejii *Rachèl* nąįį ti'yąą t'ee shee'ii àgàhnyàa gǫ̀'. *Shyaaghan Ndìk* ts'an gwandàii nąįį, aii nąįį nihzhyąą neegidiijii ts'ą̀' jùk goots'an dinjii gǫ̀ǫlįį jìhnyaa t'iihnyàa.

CF Ą̀ąhą'.

KF34.28 *Elijàh* vitì' *Henry* oozhii hę̀ę?

SF Ą̀ąhą'.

KF34.34 Aii *Henry* aii jùu vahan t'inch'yaa lì'?

SF34.42 Łąhch'ii duuyeh vàashandàii. Diinehkįį dą̀į' gwats'an gogwandàii t'iginch'yàa.

KF34.53 Aii *Shyaaghan Ndìk* ts'an t'iginch'yaa kwaa aii jì' hę̀ę?

SF34.59 Ą̀ąhą', *Shyaaghan Ndìk* ts'an tr'igiinjil kwàa.

Fig. 21. Johnny Frank in Venetie, old village, with potato garden, circa 1958. Photo from Kenneth Frank Collection.

SF33.14 *Albert's* mother's name was *Joseph Vahan*. And she was my father's younger sister. That's how it is. My older sister *Rachel* and them called my father uncle. So as I was saying, that many people today come from *Shyaaghan Ndik's* generation.

CF Yes.

KF34.28 Was *Elijah's* father named *Henry*?

SF Yes.

KF34.34 Who was *Henry's* mother then?

SF34.42 I don't think I know. They were from long before us.

KF34.53 They're not from *Old Woman Ndik* then, right?

SF34.59 Right, they were not from *Old Woman Ndik*.

Fig. 22. Sarah and Johnny Frank harvesting potatoes in Venetie, with BIA school in background, circa 1960. Photo courtesy of Richard Birchell.

Johnny Frank

Johnny Frank Vagwandak

<jfka406>

JF0.31 *Old John Lake* [1] gwinii njùhts'aii *five mile* t'ee shagòodlit ǫ'.
Nìivyaa aii gwik'ìt *Van Choh* ts'ą̀' *two mile* chan *Old Jimmy,*[2] shiiyàhghan reh.

SF0.55 *Old John,* aii ti'yąą t'aràhnyąą.

JF1.00 Aii chan vagòodliti'.
1880 gwiizhìk shagoodlit.
October 18 chan shibirthdày.[3]
Izhìk gwats'an dàhthee goohihshryàa gwats'ą̀' gaashandaii kwàa.

1.31 Aiitł'ee dzaa gweedì neerihiinjìk t'ee shats'aii shachaa vagòodlit.
Gweeddhaa tthak zhyąą̀ tr'eedàa gwizhrįh t'igwii'ìn. Shin, khaii hàa nihk'ìt.

1.50 It'ee łyâa ihtsàl, shachaa vagǫ̀ǫlįį ts'ą̀' chan Gwichyaa Gwich'in lęįį łąįį hàa k'eedàl.
Izhìk khik ganaldàii, it'ee łyâa ihtsìi kwàa.
Łąįį gàa łyâa sheenjit nitsìi.

2.10 *Ddhah Dzak* aii t'įh oondee *Ch'idrii* [4] izhìk hee ti'yąą dink'ìshahthàt.
Gweedhaa shin hàa ch'iindàk jyaa digwii'in.
Khaiits'ą̀' dinjik gǫ̀ǫlįį oonąą neeriidàl ts'ą̀' shin chan oondàk ddhah tee.
Vachooshii'ee gwàandak.

2.45 Khaii hee tr'eenjyaa hee dazhootthał tsal, tr'iinin datthak reh, shįį zhrįh kwàa.

---

1. *Old John Lake: Arctic Village geeghaih Van Choh.* —JE

2. Old Jimmy, also known as Jimmy John, was Sarah Frank's brother and Johnny Frank's brother-in-law. Johnny makes a rare mistake here by calling Old Jimmy his father-in-law, and Sarah gently corrects him. Even Homer nods. —CM and KF

3. *Shibirthdày* is an unusual convergence of forms in that it has a Gwich'in prefix attached to an English noun. —CM

4. *Ch'idrii* is a mountain located on the *T'eedriinjik* (the Middle Fork of the *Chandalar River*). It was Johnny's favorite place for hunting Dall sheep.

Johnny Frank

Johnny Frank's Life Story

<jfka406>

JF0.31 I was born not far from *Old John Lake*, about five miles on this side.

My father-in-law, *Old Jimmy*, was born two miles toward the big lake.

SF0.55 *Old John* is my father.

JF1.00 He was born there too.

I was born in 1880.

October 18 is my birthday.

I don't know how long I will live from here on.

1.31 We traveled down this way (toward *Gold Camp*) after my younger brother was born next to me.

We were constantly moving, summer and winter alike.

1.50 I was still small when my younger brother was born.

That's when lots of *Fort Yukon* people arrived with dogs.

I always remember that particular time.

I was still small because the dogs really seemed big to me.

2.10 I was raised by my father up at *Ch'idrii* mountain which is behind *Ddhah Dzak* mountain.

We were always moving back and forth during the summer.

We came back in the fall for moose and went up into the mountains during the summer.

Vachooshii'ee told the story.

2.45 Children used to wear skin clothing.

Jyàanch'ii gwach'àa tr'ąąh'in kwàa.
Dazhoo tthał, dazhoo ik hàa, dazhoo dzirh chan.
Oozhee tah tr'aa'į googàa dazhoo nilįį reh.
3.09 Łąhch'yâa diit'ìgwįn'ee kwàa.
K'ìt diinàa t'ôonch'yàa, zhat gwanąą reh.
Aii gwànąą *muzzlè loader* gǫǫlįį gwànaa.
3.24 Aii chan vikì' gǫǫlįį kwàa łì'hàa gwinzįį kwàa.
Aii deechì' kwaa dąį' t'ee chan reh dinjii zhìgwìłts'ik.
Googàa *some way* ts'ą' tr'agwandàii tr'agwahtsìi.
3.45 Tr'iinin ihłįį gwànaa gwats'an dąį' yeendak *Arctic Village* vijuu ch'iindàk *Dachan Lee*[5] ch'iindàk łyâa tthał gǫǫlįį, *fence.*
3.58 Dinjii tthak tthał ghàii gwichįį k'ìighai' łyâa shìh gǫǫlįį kwat aii ch'atthàįį tthak yee'àn *Gwazhał*[6] taa naa'òo dąį' t'ee łyâa khaii dinjii gwinzįį gwandàii kwàa.
Łąįį lęįį gàa ihdàndhagąįį reh.
4.27 Googàa dinjii tthak gwinzįį gwandàii.
Aiits'ą' gohch'it reh it'ee ch'ahałk'ee eenjit nìgwiindhat ts'ą' *muzzlè loadèr* hàa chiitsal kwaii oaałk'èe.
Chiitsal ta'àałk'ee, łì'hàa gwintsìi sheegòo'ąįį k'ìt t'įįhthan.
4.45 K'ì' chan shi'įį kwàt chiitsal chan ta'ałdàk.
It'ee gwiizhìk ihtsìi gwilìi.
Aii gwiizhìk it'ee *Gwichyaa Zheh* łyâa *steamboat* gǫǫlįį gwinyàa.
5.12 Dinjii chan gǫǫlįį gwinyàa.
Fourteen year old ihłii gwiizhìk dinjii *Yukon* dì' zhyąą dinjii dachan gwich'in zhyąą nin'ee t'igwinyaa łèe.
Tr'oochìt *Gwichyaa* gwąął'yà' 1897.
5.40 Izhìk gwats'an t'ee ch'athąįį ta'àałk'ee ts'ą' jùk drin tth'aii nihk'ìt.
Izhìk dąį' chan dhałts'ik kwàa.

5. *Dachan Lee: Arctic Village gęhjuu ddhah.* —JE
Dachan Lee means *Tree Line.* —CM

6. *Gwazhał: ddhah naaht'aii t'arahnyąą.* —JE

We didn't see this kind of white man's clothing.
When we traveled during the winter, I wore fur pants, a fur jacket, fur mittens, and even fur insoles.
3.09 We were never sick in those days.
That's how we felt at that time.
In those days, there were lots of muzzle loaders.
3.24 It was no good when there were no shells for them.
People went hungry when there were no shells.
But somehow we still survived.
3.45 When I was a child, there were lots of caribou fences up on *Dachan Lee* mountain near *Arctic Village*.
3.58 All the people lived along the fence.
That was the only way there was meat.
When animals went back over the *Brooks Range*, people had a hard winter.
Even lots of dogs starved to death.
But people still survived somehow.
4.27 And then finally, I grew up and got old enough to have my own muzzle loader.
I shot birds and was proud of myself.
4.45 I also had a bow and arrows, and I shot birds with those too.
Meanwhile, I was getting bigger.
And then they say there were lots of steamboats at *Fort Yukon*.
5.12 They say there were lots of people there.
When I was fourteen years old, it's said there just were so many people that they stood like timber all the way down the Yukon.
I saw *Fort Yukon* for the first time in 1897.
5.40 I've been shooting big animals from that time to this day.
I was never sick during that time.

5.55 *Captain Ray*[7] vàràhnyąą zhat iindì', vagwandàk gǫ̀ǫlįį.

Aii *Canadian general* choo t'agàhnyaa.

Dinjii, *Gwichyaa* tąįį kat *Old Crow* Gwich'in nąįį tthak gooshìi kwàa.

Zhyąą oochìt indì' ts'ą' *ordèr* ahtsii zhyąą dinjii antł'àhchaa ts'ą' vałchii oondàa ch'iinaa jyàa darah'in.

Zhyąą *free, only man, Captain Ray.*

6.35 Łì'hàa dinjii gwinzįį k'eełtįį.

Aii ch'âałk'ee gwats'an chan yeendee neereejil ts'ą' t'ee łąą diigwahąhjii kwaa ts'ą' reh, lęįį chan diinàa gwich'įį gòodlìt.

6.55 *Peter Vitsiich'ìi'ee*, *John Neeshòoch'it*, *Jilzhìt*, shąą *Łikyaadòk*, *Petèr Ts'ik*[8], ti'yąą voondee chan, aii vigii nąįį hàa datthak t'ee yee'àt zhat gwizhrįh tr'agwandàii.

7.21 Łyâa gwinzįį ndàa tr'eedàa.

Aii t'agwaihnyàa, *twelve year old* ihłįį gwànaa reh.

Shitsụh, ti'yąą vahan, aii t'ee gwandàii.[9]

Aii t'ee ti'yąą khaii hee reh ts'at ch'adhàh zhìt yeelil, tr'eenjyaa hee.

7.53 Łąįį yatth'àn deetak ee'tthaii ts'ą' yatth'àn khąhkàt rọh.

Aiits'ą' shin hee googàa tr'eenjyaa dihnyaa dąį' chan yeeghwàa.

Jyàa dagwąhtł'oo gògwantrii ch'iinaa tr'injìl.

8.13 Aii łyâa gehnaadài' gwats'an gwandak datthak hàandàii.

Nankat gwich'in tthak yàandàii.

Nèekwat Ch'eekwaii, Dinjii Zhuh aghan dąį' nèekwat vàa gwiriinghan, googàa khaihłee chan gwidiinzhii reh.

Lyâa *smart.*

---

7. Captain Patrick Henry Ray of the U.S. Eighth Infantry wrote from *Fort Yukon* on January 5,1898, that he had delivered flour, meat, and rice to thirty-two destitute families of the *Chandalar* and *Porcupine River* bands, whom he felt were "victims of the gold craze." Apparently big game was extremely scarce due to the large number of animals killed by white prospectors. See Ray 1898. —CM

8. John Neeshòoch'it was Mary Joseph's father. —JE
Photos of Peter Ts'ik a.k.a. Peter John taken in *Arctic Village* in 1927 are displayed in Mishler (2018, 2023). —CM

9. According to the Frank family tree, this was Shyaaghan Ndik, whose English name was Sarah. —CM

5.55 They say there was lots of news about *Captain Ray.*
They talked about him as a big Canadian general.
The *Fort Yukon* and *Old Crow* people had no food at that time.
All he did was make out an order and give it to people, and they got a toboggan load of food.
For free. He was the only man who did that.
6.35 He took good care of the people.
We moved back up (to the *Arctic Village* area) about the time I started shooting big animals, and I was doing good when lots of people came to live with us.
6.55 *Peter Vitsiich'ii'ee (Chief Peter), John Neeshooch'ii, Jilzhit,* my brother-in-law *Łikyaadok, Peter Ts'ik (Peter John),* my father's oldest brother, and his children, and ourselves were all living there.
7.21 We were doing fine.
I was twelve years old then.
I'm saying that my grandmother, my father's mother, was still living then.
During the winter when we traveled, my father used to haul her around in an animal hide blanket.
7.53 A dog tripped her once and sprained her leg.
So they say he packed her around on his back when we were traveling in the summer.
That's the kind of hard life we've been through in the past.
8.13 My grandmother knew all the old stories from a long time ago.
Everyone knew her.
She had been through two wars when the Inuit killed all the Indians, but she lived through two wars and survived.
She was very smart.

8.37 Aii yaaghà' *Dihch'ì' Naavee*[10] vàràhnyaa, *Oolam Ginchii* gootì'.

Aii łyâa deendaadąį' gwats'an vàràhnyaa googàa sheejii yàhnyaa reh.

One hundred twenty year gąhkhyuk gwiindàii t'aràhnyàa.

9.02 Googàa viginjìk t'igwin'ee kwàa.

Tth'ai hee gàa neehidik akhài' łąįį yatth'àn khąhkàt rǫh.

Gweedhaa tthak, vành khachii'ak, kǫ̀' ts'ą̀' nidik, jyàanch'yaa ts'ą̀' drin tąhthee gwaandak, gwaandak.

9.25 Deenaadài' nehłiriighan hagàa tthak geegwaanda.

Nìhkèe vành chan jyàa diheenjyàa reh.

Vindii dinjii kwaa googàa reh.

Tr'iinin tsal nèekwąįį geetee dhidii googàa jyàhts'ą̀' ch'anjàa hàa tr'agwaandak k'ìt t'inyaa reh t'inyàa.

9.53 Aiits'ą̀' oondòk gwizhrįh t'ôonch'yaa ts'ą̀' reh.

Ch'atthą̀įį datthak yee'àn *Gwazhał* taa naa'oo ts'ą̀' Neetsųųch'in[11] nąįį tthak nihk'yą̀ą shrahtèe dhijil t'ôonch'yàa.

10.05 *Paul Solomon* nąįį gàa yeenjì' *Circlè* gwà'àn agàa, Tanana agàa goolàt nąįį, *Old Crow* k'iinjì' agàa.[12]

10.31 Aiits'ą̀' it'ee łyâa tthak geenjit ihsįį dhiidlìt.

Dzaa *Vįįhtąįį 1900* gwiizhìk t'ee dzaa k'eeriidal.

Aiits'ą̀' łyâa reh, sheegwâa'aii kwaa ts'ą̀' geenjit ihsįį ihłįį.

11.06 Aiits'ą̀' t'ee reh, goodhiinjìk ts'ą̀' reh, *1907* reh goodhiinjìk.

Aiits'ą̀' *Vashrą̀įį K'ǫǫ* oondàk neeshizhii ts'ą̀' aiitł'ee t'ee shigii ch'ìhłak gòodlit ts'ą̀' *Ch'at'oonjik* hee zheh gwàdhaltsąįį, izhìk *twenty nine year* zhat gwiich'ì'.

11.38 Tr'iinin *eleven* shi'įį gòodlit, izhìk zhat giwiich'ì'.

Gòhch'it łyâa gwandaa nizįį dhiidlit.

11.55 Chishinjii chan kwàa.

---

10. *Dihch'į' Naavee, ginkkii William viti' t'arahnyąą. Oolam Ginchii* Priest William *ginkhii t'arahnyąą.* —JE

11. Neetsųųch'in is Johnny's way of saying Neets'ee Gwich'in. —AR
Or perhaps it's his way of saying Neets'it Gwich'in. See Part II Introduction above. —CM

12. He mentions Paul Solomon here because that's the interviewer's (Kathy Alexander's) great-grandfather. —KP

8.37 They say there was also this old man *Dihch’ì’Naavee,* who was the father of *Priest William* (*Loola*).

He was known to be very old, but he called my grandmother “my older sister.”

It’s said she lived to be around 120 years old.

9.02 There was nothing wrong with her speech either.

She was up and around on her own before a dog tripped her.

From the time she got up, she sat by the fire and told story after story all day long.

9.25 She told stories of all the old-time wars.

She did this day after day.

Even when there was no one sitting by her.

She even told stories to two little kids as though they were grown-ups.

9.53 We lived there for a long time without going anywhere.

When all the animals went over the *Brooks Range*, that’s when the *Arctic Village* people left and went their separate ways.

10.05 Even *Paul Solomon* left.

Some moved to *Circle*, some to *Tanana*, and some to *Old Crow.*

10.31 I was now pretty good at everything.

We arrived here in *Venetie* in 1900.

And now I was really good at anything, and there was nothing wrong with me.

11.06 Then I got married in 1907 and moved back up to *Arctic Village.*

I had one child when we went back to the *Koness River* and built a house where I stayed for twenty-nine years.

11.38 I had eleven children that time.

I was now good at everything.

11.55 I never got tired.

Kwàt tsyaa shą̌ąht'aii chan gǫ̀ǫlį̀į kwàa.
Aii googàa than gwizhrįh ndàa àdàalchyaa ts'ą̀' aii gwiizhìk dęhtł'yaa chan eedoodadhàaltin tł'ęę aii shik nał'ìn.
Forty-two year datthak *Bible* nał'yà'.
12.20 Aiitł'ee reh, dinjii tee neihdik gàa dinjii łyâa gwinzįį gwandàii kwàa.
Aii tee t'ihch'yaa geet'iihthan kwaa ts'ą̀' reh than gwizhrįh shik gwihch'įį.
12.33 Than gwizhrįh chan shit'ìgwiin'ee kwaa.
Ts'ą̀' reh, oodee shigii nąįį tthak dink'ǐinjìk ts'ą̀' tr'ìnjàa gootee gîįlch'ìt.
Aii googii nąįį ànts'ą̀' chan gii neegwiilìi.
Łyâa niizhùk gwihdàii roh, *ninety-three year.*
One hundred gęhdàa hihshyaa, gàashandàii.
13.07 Aii *Ch'at'oonjik* gwiich'į̀' jìhnyą̀ą.
Khyą̀h t'ał'in, łyâa niizhìt khyą̀h t'ał'in.
Łyâa zhyą̀ą shilìk chan nizįį ts'ą̀' vał nidii oondàk nihchik, *seven hundred fifty pound.* Geetèe *eight hundred pound* ch'ihłòk neeshilil.
13.28 Shàh chan dinjii kwaa ts'ą̀', *Nathaniel* aii reh tr'oochìt, shichį' vagòodlìt, t'ee *Ambrose* yeiindì'.
Aii gwats'aįį vineegòhodlit aii niindhat.
Aii gwats'ąįį nilįį t'ee *Nathaniel.*
14.03 Aiits'ą̀' oondee gwich'in nąįį łyâa gìizųų.
Aii gwits'į̀' gweenaa neehòoshizhįį izhìk it'ee dzaa ni'izhii, 1936.

14.34-34.18[13]

34.35 Aii tr'iinin ihłįį gwanaa k'eedài' geenàagwaldak łì'hàa gògwantrii t'igwinyàa.
Tr'ìnjàa, tr'iinin choo aghwaa gwiizhìk nįįvyaa chaavał chiindàa oąąhjik shrììts'ą̀' ch'iindàa t'ee tr'eenjyaa.
34.58 Łì'hàa gwinzįį kwaa tr'iniinjìl.

13. There is a long digression in the story when Johnny talks about how they worked to get a school established in *Venetie*. This segment has been included in a separate section below. We rejoin this story when Johnny returns to memories of his childhood. —CM

There was no one else as strong as me.
I made my own living alone out there in the brush.
I taught myself how to read and study all the time.
I've read the whole Bible for forty-two years.
12.20 After that, I tried living with other people, but they seemed to be in poor health.
So I went back to living alone in the brush.
12.33 I never got sick when I lived alone out there.
All my children grew up, and each one of them got married.
Now their children have their own children, so I've been living for a long time.
I'm ninety-three years old now.
And I know I'll pass one hundred.
13.07 I trapped when I was living on the *Koness River*.
I went trapping a long ways off.
I had good dogs, and I took along a very heavy toboggan, sometimes seven hundred fifty pounds at a time, sometimes eight hundred pounds.
13.28 Nobody went trapping with me.
Ambrose (*William*) was married to my daughter.
The next child died.
And then *Nathaniel* came along.
14.03 The people back there (in *Arctic Village)* were hard to get along with.
Because of that I moved away in 1936.

14.34-34.18

34.35 Like I mentioned a little while ago, when I was a child, it's been said that life was very hard.
A woman even packed her big child on her back while pushing a heavy toboggan.
We've traveled so many times in the past.
34.58 And I've had one of the hardest lives.

Googàa reh jùk shit'ìgwin'ee kwaa dzaa gweendàa dhiidìi (adlaa).

Łyâa zhyąą *high word* eenaagwaldak gàa gwik'ìt geegòo'ąįį kwàa.

Vàanoodlit nąįį gàa yàandàii kwaa àkwàt nats'ą' jùk *United States, Russiàn* zhrįh *Bible* hàa giindàii.

35.59 Aii gwiizhìk nąhjyàa jìhnyaa oonjit ch'àa chan kwàa.

Dinjii geetèe nihts'įį gwiich'įį googàa chuutyah nèekwąįį zhrįh gwats'an nilįį, nàhąą?[14]

Jyàa dòonch'yaa ts'ą' k'èiich'ii kwàa.

Yaaghà' ch'iitsii k'ìk daatin aii k'ìt'inch'ii, aii zhrįh reh dii*Zheh* k'aa ch'ìhłak t'eegwąąhch'yaa.

Friiban trąįį ch'ìhłak chan.

Jyàa dàgwàhtł'oo gògwàntrii yeenaa gwiin'è'.

Kwàt jùk laraa tr'ahahtsyàa zhyąą dèegwąhtsii gwiindhan gògwgąhtsii tr'ooheendal googàa dinjii yàandàii kwàa.

36.39 Shįį reh *old pensiòn* gàa łąhch'yaa nitsìi kwaa t'aałch'yaa gàa tr'iitsaii hįhjii kwàa.

14. Two skin tents that faced each other sharing the same fireplace is what they called *nihts'įį gwigwiich'įį.* —KP
See an early description of this by Frederick Whymper 1868:222. —CM

But there's nothing wrong with me, and I'm still sitting here (laughs).

There's absolutely nothing wrong with me.

I would tell you more using harder words that even the white man cannot understand.

Only the people of the United States and the Russian people know about the Bible.

35.59 As I said, during the hardest times we were having, we had no white man's clothes.

Two households together owned only two cups, you see?

We had nothing in our houses.

We only had one tin plate in our house.

And also one banged-up old frying pan.

That's how hard it was.

People nowadays can get as much money as they want, but they still don't know how to go about it.

36.39 I don't get very much of an old age pension, but I still have everything.

Fig. 23. Johnny Frank in Venetie, circa 1962. Child unidentified. Photo from Kenneth Frank collection.

Fig. 24. Johnny Frank with a trapped wolf at Gold Camp, late 1960s. Photo from Kenneth Frank collection.

Sarah Frank

Sarah K'èejit Nilįį Dąį'

<sfrf2b>

RF0.44 Gàa chan *start* neeroolį' gwintsàl hęę? Nijìn nagòodiit izhìk tr'ohkìt.

SF0.58 Tr'ohch'it aii oonjìt *Shiinjik* dee'àn gwįį'ee gęhjìt tr'ał choh dha'ąįį' ǫ', ddhah. Aii gęhjìt dee'àn han gwìin'ee.

Aii *Dizhèenjik*[1] gàgàhnyaa į'. Dinjii Zhuh k'yaa goozhrįį.

Izhìk gwà'àn it'ee shagòodlit ǫ'.

RF1.34 Nitì', nahan nats'àhts'ą' gavoozhrį'?

SF1.38 Ti'yąą it'ee *John* òozhii į', *Old John.* Aiits'ą' ni'ęę chan *Mary.* Adanzhrįh tr'ìnjàa nilįį, nàhąą. Aiits'ą' tsyaa nąįį tee vagòodlit aii geh'àn it'ee *Mary Ch'idįį* giyàhnyaa į'.

Zhik tsyaa nąįį ch'aga'àa dąį' giirahtee t'igii'in nàhąą, izhìk gwaazhrii t'inch'yàa.

RF2.31 Aii nitì', nahan nąįį hàa gootì' aii nik'ee gavàanandàii?

Nats'ąą gavoozhrį'?

SF2.44 Gootì' aii t'ee gwįįzįį gavàashandàii kwaa t'inch'yaa, nàhąą.

Shàh gogwaandak kwàa.

RF3.05 Aii izhìk nagòodlit diinyaa izhìk dąį' dèegii'ìn?

SF3.25 Aii shagòodlit jìhnyaa izhìk it'ee oonjìt *Dizhèenjik* izhìk gwà'àn tr'igwich'įį nyàa. Shoondee *Paul Solomòn*[2] aii shàh gwaandak t'agwaihnyàa. Aii *Paul Solomòn* vitì' aii ti'yąą hàa łì'hàa nakheet'igiindhan. Aiits'ą' gweedhaa nihłàa gwigwich'įį į'.

Izhìk it'ee oonjìt khaiits'ą' tr'igwich'įį izhìk it'ee nagòodlìt shàhnyaa į'. Izhìk gwànaa dąį' tr'iinin gwilìk, nàhąą, garagwaahkìi kwàa ǫ'.

Nijìn tr'iinin gwilìk gàh gwiindàii kwaa ts'ą' gweedhaa t'ôonch'yàa.

1. The *Dizhèenjik* is the *Coleen River.* See Caulfield (1981b). —CM

2. *Shoondee* means 'my older brother,' but here it is a classificatory kin term designating someone older than Sarah in her own generation but not a blood sibling. —CM

Sarah Frank

Sarah's Childhood

<sfrf2b>

RF0.44 Let's start over again. Where were you born?

SF0.58 The *Sheenjik River* runs this way and there is this big brushy mountain. Right above there is a river called the *Coleen*. I was born in that area.

RF1.34 What were your father's and mother's names?

SF1.38 My father's name was *John*, *Old John*. And my mother's name was *Mary*. She was the only girl that was born in a family of boys, you see. That's why they named her *Mary Ch'idįį*. You see, when the boys ate, they grabbed everything before her, leaving her just the crumbs.

That's what she was named after.

RF2.31 Do you know both of your parents' fathers' names?

SF2.44 I really don't know, you see. They never told me.

RF3.05 When you were born what were they doing?

SF3.25 When I was born they said we were living on the *Coleen River*. That's what my older brother *Paul Solomon* told me. *Paul Solomon*'s father and my father really liked each other. That's why they always went places together. So they were living there the fall when I was born, he said.

In those days when a child was born, you see, they never recorded the birth date. So we never knew when children were born as time passed.

RF4.38 Nats'àhts'ą̨' ch'oozhrį̀' gahtsìi? Dinjii Zhuh k'yàa ch'oozhrį' gahtsii? Nan nik'èe noozhrį' gǫ̀ǫlįį?

SF4.45 Shįį shoozhrį' kwaa ǫ'.

RF Qǫ.

SF4.50 Aii shagòodlit tł'ęę gwànaa it'ee Indlis[3] ginkhii nąįį yeendòk zhik neegihiidàl ǫ'. Gàa gwinzįį goonaldàii kwàa. Aii gwik'iighai' it'ee tr'ohchìt gwàndak hàagiindàii gaadlìt į'.

Aiits'ą̨' izhìk it'ee jyàa dìginch'yaa, ts'ą̨' dinjii tee neegihiidàl.

5.35 Aii ginkhii nąįį *Mr. Moodỳ* chan ginyàa. *Mr. Gaamii* aii it'ee Indlis ginkhii nąįį. Aii nąįį it'ee oondòk tr'ohchìt dinjii hàh gogwaandak. Aii K'eegwaadhat gǫ̀ǫlįį ginyàa. Aii nąįį tr'ohchìt gwandak giłtsą̀įį.

6.15 Izhìk gwats'an dinjii tee jyàa t'iginch'yaa ts'ą̨' giihee'àa tsal googàa kwaa ts'ą̨' Dinjii Zhuh tee gwigwich'įį t'agooràhnyàa. Izhìk dą̀į' diiginjìk googàa zhìt giginkhii t'agooràhnyàa. Aii Indlis ginkhii nąįį.

6.42 Jyàa digee'yà' googàhnyaa į'. Aiits'ą̨' izhìk it'ee jyàa digii'in ts'ą̨' ti'yąą gàa *three times* gogwaanch'yaa giinkhii ǫǫ'ęę nǎąhchįį t'inch'yàa. Aiits'ą̨' khàa hee gogwaandak, dinjii eenjit chan khàgigiinjii. Jyaa dìginyaa izhìk gwànaa. Izhìk hee ch'ilik tsal kwaii datthak ìgìdlìi.

RF9.04 Aii nagòodlit dą̀į' oondee izhìk khaii gwiizhìk nagòodlit *or* shin?

SF9.13 Khaiits'ą̨'. *September* nanh. *September 28,* ginyàa. Izhìk gwizhrįh gwinyąą gòo'ą̨įį.

<sfcm>

CM9.40 Nitì *Old John?*

SF9.42 Ą̀ąhą'.

CM *You tell me about him?*

SF Hąą?

CM9.45 Gwandàk, *you tell me? Old John* vagwandàk?

3. *Indlis* is the old Gwich'in way of pronouncing *English*. —CM

RF4.38 How were they given a name? An Indian name? Do you have an Indian name?

SF4.45 No, I don't have an Indian name.

RF Oh.

SF4.50 After I was born some English preachers traveled around here.

I don't remember them well. That's how they first got the Word of God. So that's what they did, and they traveled lots.

5.35 That preacher's name was *Mr. Moody* they said, and also *Mr. Canham*. They were both English preachers. They said there was a God. They were the first ones who told us about it.

6.15 Although they had very little to eat, they still lived among Indian people after that, they said. These English preachers even learned to speak our language. That's what we say about them.

6.42 So that's what they say they did. At that time my father brought a preacher around three times. They spoke to people and they prayed for people. That's what they did in those days. They even learned to sing some short songs from the songbooks.

RF9.04 When you were born, were you born in the winter or summer?

SF9.13 It was in the fall, September. They say September 28. That's what they say about it.

<sfcm>

CM9.40 Was *Old John* your father?

SF9.42 Yes.

CM Can you tell me about him?

SF What?

CM9.45 Can you tell me a story? *Old John*'s story?

SF9.50 Ti'yąą lèe? Ǫ̂ǫ, vagwandàk[4] (adlaa).

10.00 Łyaa gwįįzįį gwąąndak kwàa. Gwįįzįį diihàa gwaandàk.

Aii, *Old John, long time he say*, shitsii nyaa, aii vagwandàk nyaa khìk eengwaandàk. Aii zhyąą zhik gwà'àn nankak neegiheedàl hee jidìi gwandàii gaahkhwąįį. Aii eenjit gwizhrįh giyeegwaandàk. Jii ti'yąą chan ts'ą' shitsųų *Mil Vahan* aii hàa nihłàa gogwaandàk. Izhìk hee (adlaa) nakhwatsii *Toł*[5] ginyàa.

10.52 Nakhwatsii *Toł* jyàa dii'in ginyaa eegogwaandàk. Izhìk tr'iinin ihłįį gwiizhìk t'iginyàa. Izhìk hee ąįį eenihłàa gogwaandak hee oozhee ch'iinaa nĭnląįį, nàhąą? Dząą chųų jyàa dĭi'in. Chųų lęįį izhìk chii choh oondàa rahahjyàa k'ìt t'iginyàa (adlaa).

Toł ginyaa nakhwatsii *Toł* ginyaa ree t'iginyàa (adlaa).

Tr'iinin ihłįį gwiizhìk t'iginyaa ts'ą' sheetsin deegidlii izhìk gwizhrįh gǫǫaldàii.

Aii nankak neegihiidàl izhìk hee, k'ì' zhrįh hàa t'igii'in, nàhąą. Aii zhrįh ch'atthąįį gohjìi. Izhìk geenjit duulèe nilįį dòhłįį. Aii eenjit giyeegwaandàk t'inyàa.

12.16 Chihłan chan nįįvyaa zheh tr'igwich'įį ganaldàii ǫ'. *No tent, caribou skin they make a tent, that's all. I remember. Gee, hard time. Nothing, no blanket too. Caribou skin they made blanket, that's all, and parkii.*

13.07 Aii chan dząą chįį gilzhìi. Vadzaih dhàh chan chyăh gaa'įį.

Sometime dinjii lęįį khehłòk neegihiidàl. Khehłòk neegihiidàl izhìk hee, nijìn shìh gwintł'oo gaahkhwąįį.

Aii dąį' chan izhìk ninghyùk gwigwich'įį. Ninghyùk gwigwich'įį ts'ą' ąįį shìh gà'àa.

Aii gwiizhìk chan, âa tsee'in, tr'ìnjàa, dinjii, tsyaa, nich'it jii tthak tseegii'ìn. Âaa, *fun* gogwahtsìi. Tseegii'in hàa jyàa dìgii'ìn. *Sometime, sometime* chan tł'eevalk'ìt reh gogwahtsii izhìk chat dinjii tr'ìnjàa kwat hàa datthak chat avàl. Hàa łyâa *fun* gogwahtsii t'ee.

4. *Łyâa veetsingwąąhch'yaa ts'ą' adlàa.* —LG

5. *Toł* is just the splashing sound of the water. —LG

SF9.50 Oh, my father's story (really laughing).

10.00 He hardly every told stories to us. He always told this story about his grandfather. It was mostly about how they used to move around to hunt for animals. But my father and my great-grandmother, *Mil's* mother, used tell stories to each other. That's what our grandfather *Toł* said.

10.52 They talked about what our grandfather did. When they said this I was only a child. As they were talking about him, below them was a creek going down, but the water was like this. Into the deep part of water they threw a big rock.

And they said, *"Toł."* They were just saying our grandfather *Toł's* name by doing that (laughs). I was only a child at the time, but I remember saying that sounded very funny to me.

They were still using bows and arrows when they moved around a lot. They shot game with that. Maybe he was good at that. That's why they told a story about him.

12.16 I remembered once we lived in a skin hut. There was no tent. Skin huts are made out of caribou skin. I remembered that. Gee, we had a hard time. We didn't have much. There were no blankets. They made blankets out of caribou skins. And parkas.

13.07 They also used them for their pillows. They used caribou skins for their mattresses. Sometimes lots of people traveled together. When they came to lots of food as they all traveled together, they stayed in together one place for a long time. They lived there until they had eaten all the food.

During this time the women, men, and young men and young women all played games. Oh, they all had fun.

They all played games. Sometimes they built swings. And everybody would swing. They sure had fun.

14.30 Aiits'ą̀' it'ee izhìk gwats'an k'iinaa gweedhàa. Aii shitsųų *Mil Vahan* văihnyaa. Aii ti'yąą tth'aii vakwàa gwiizhìk vagòodlit łii. Aiitl'ęę it'ee gwintsàl ihtsìi nyàa. Jyàa dăłtsii gwiizhìk it'ee ti'yąą chan vagòodlit nyàa. Izhìk it'ee vitsii aii, ti'yąą vitsii.

Ąįį vindehgwahalzhyaa oo'ę̀ę sheenohchìi yàhnyàa.

15.41 Izhìk gwats'an k'iinaa gweedhaa ts'ą̀' it'ee shįį aii *maybe I was that big that time.* Yeendòk dinjii lęįį neegihiidàl.

Zheh chan gokwàa. Shin, khaii hàa nihk'ìt datthak.

Nijùk datthak neegihiidàl. Izhìk datthak ch'igihee'àa eenjit gwizhrįh.

Daagǫǫ, geh, vadzaih, divii, aii zhrįh gàh gwihiljìi. Łuk chan. Ąįį chan ch'eedąįh hàa zhrįh giyuugit.

Ąįį jyàa digii'in ts'ą̀' k'iinaa gweedhàa. Dinjii tsyaa nitsìi naii googàa zhyąą nilįį gahch'yàa.

16.55 Aii jyàa dąhtsii zhrįh datthak gootèegahchàk.[6] Nilįįchų̀' *that's all.* Ts'ik gàa kwàa. *There's no tea, nothing.* Łyâa *hard time.*

CM17.34 Gògòntrii.

SF Mmm hmm. Gògòntrii. Izhìk gwats'an it'ee shįį, nàhąą?

Shįį chan it'ee diik'iidhàt, googàa k'èiich'ii datthak kwàa.

Lìdii googàa kwàa, *no sugar, no tea, nothing. That time* jidìi nankak, nan ts'anh jidìi jak deenich'ùh, natł'àt, nakàł, nitsįh jii kwat tthak dinjii ya'àa.

18.46 Gwintł'òo *hard time.* Aiits'ą̀' izhìk gwanaa t'ee ihtsìi gòodlit tł'ęę.

Duulèe *1907* dąį' dinjii shòonjìk ǫ'. *That time* shigii naii *fourteen* gwįįlį' ǫ'.

Jii *ten* datthak gookwàa. Jùk dǫǫ naii zhrįh. *Nathaniel, Hamel, Dan, Maggie—that's all. Four* naii zhrįh jùk gwandàii. *Gee!*

6. *Gootèegahchàk* means 'they were served individually.' —JE

14.30 So as time passed, as I said before, my great grandmother, *Mil's Mother*, was born. My father wasn't born yet. *Mil's Mother* said she was not very big. I was this big, she said, when *Old John* was born. That's when my father's grandfather told someone to bring him to me so I could stay busy keeping an eye on him.

And so the time passed.

15.41 After that I came along. Maybe I was this big (gesturing) at that time. Lots of people traveled up that way.

There were no houses. They did the same whether it was winter or summer. They traveled for a long time. They only did it for food.

It was only for ptarmigan, hare, caribou, and sheep. And fish too. They could only catch fish with spears.

They did all this as the years went by. Young men cooked meat and drank the broth with it.

16.55 They were served individually and could eat only so much meat and drink the broth with it. That's all. There was no sickness. They really had a hard time making a living. There was no tea, so it was a pretty hard time.

CM17.34 A hard time.

SF Yes, a hard time. After that, I was growing up, but still there were lots of things we didn't have, you see? There was no sugar and no tea, nothing. At that time everything we had was from on the land. Berries from the land, blueberries, blackberries, cranberries, salmonberries, and rosehips. They ate all of these.

18.46 We faced some very hard times. So it was during these times when I grew up.

Maybe in 1907 I was married. I had fourteen children altogether.

I lost ten of them. Today I have only four children left: Nathaniel, Hamel, Dan, and Maggie—that's all. Just those four are still living. Gee!

<sflg2a>

SF7.09 Àkwàt jidìi eegwarahaandàk?

LG7.15 Nakhwan aii nats'àhts'ą' tr'oochìt vàanòodlit nakhwatee gwąąh'in ree? Aiięęgàa *Tł'oothał* [7] ginyaa, nàhąą.

Gàa nan chan reh nan chan nats'ąhts'ą' tr'oochìt vàanòodlit nah'in dąį' nats'ąhts'ą' dèegavoiinyaa ts'ą' nats'ąhts'ą' ninjich'iindhat izhìk geegwandak jì' gàa gwįįzįį.

SF7.45 Aii *Tł'oothał* vàràhnyaa ree dinehnaa hee tee'yą' t'aràhnyàa. Ąįįts'ą' tr'ohchìt yeendòk yeendee *Old John Lake* gwà'àn gwizhrįh tr'agwandàii ǫ'. Ąįįts'ą' izhìk gwats'an it'ee gwiizhìk *nineteen* dąąch'yaa t'igwii'in izhìk tthak geeragwaandak jì' łyâa gwiheezyàa izhìk gàhshaandàii kwaa ǫ'.

8.28 Shreedrìn gàa reh. Zhat gwànaa dąį' shreedrìn tr'eechyaa kwàa.

Ąįįts'ą' izhìk it'ee yeendòk gwizhrįh tr'agwandàii. Ąįįts'ą' it'ee vàanòodlit gǫǫlįį ts'ą' chat gàagwiindàii kwaa ǫ'.

Izhìk dąį' it'ee vàanòodlit, vàanòodlit t'ee tr'îitth'ak googàa *Gwichyaa* chan ts'ą' oonjìt *Zheh Gwatsal* [8] ginyaa gwìnji' izhìk gwìnji' it'ee vàanòodlit gilęįį kwàa.

9.16 Aii naii it'ee zhik gwigwich'įį, nàhąą, izhìk dąį' k'eiich'ii tsal jidìi dink'ee chì' chan. Ąįįts'ą' kǫ'. Ąįįts'ą' lìdii, *rice* , songąįį, łùh, jii zhrįh gǫǫlįį ǫ'. Ąįį chat duuyeh dinjii datthak yii'įį t'aihnyàa.

9.51 Aii tsal zhrįh goots'an tèegwąąch'yaa vàanòodlit naii.

Ąįįts'ą' ęę *Gwichyaa* it'ee yaagha'ęę ch'ìhłan khaii dząą yeedee *Van Choo* vęę gwà'àn dinjii gwich'įį izhìk dąį' it'ee łyâa shìh kwaa dinjii lęįį t'aihnyàa.

10.30 Gavoozhrì' łyâa tsyàąhch'yaa. Dinjii lęįį aii naii gogwandàii.

---

7. *Tł'oothał* is the central figure in a traditional Gwich'in folk narrative about the coming of the first white man. I recorded a version of this story from Ambrose William, Johnny and Sarah's son-in-law, when I visited them in *Gold Camp* in 1972. However, this text has not been transcribed for inclusion here. A short English-only variant appears in Charles Keim's collection from *Old Crow*. (1964:99) —CM

8. *Zheh Gwatsal* is *Christian Village*. —LG

<sflg2a>

SF7.09 What should we talk about?

LG7.15 How did the white men come among your people? They talk about that man *Tł'oothał* too, you see.

Tell me about the time you first saw a white man, what you thought to yourself about him. It's good if you can talk about that.

SF7.45 About that *Tł'oothał,* they say that happened before our time. From the beginning we all lived up that way or around the *Old John Lake* area. It would really be good if I could remember the years, but I don't know the years.

8.28 There are calendars. At that time we didn't know how to use a calendar.

So back then we only lived around this area. So we didn't know much about white men.

We did hear about some white men living around *Christian Village* and around the *Fort Yukon* area.

9.16 At the time they lived there, you see, we needed things like shells, matches, tea, rice, sugar, and flour. That's all they had. I'm saying very few people had any of these things.

9.51 That's all we used from the white men.

So one winter people were living here by the shore of *Old John Lake*. I mean lots of people. There really was no food.

10.30 Some of them really had funny names. There were many people living back then.

Ąįįts'ą' it'ee khaii ch'ìhłan khaii łyâa gògǫ̀ǫtrii khaii gwĭindhàt. Shìh kwaa ts'ą̀' khaii gwìizhit.

Ts'ą̀' it'ee gohch'it, t'ee yaaghà' ąįį dinjii t'aihnyaa naii chįhdą̀į' gwànaa ti'yąą naii gogwandàii ąįį ehnaa gwandàii naii t'aihnyàa.

11.03 Ąįįts'ą̀' izhìk it'ee shìh kwaa. Ts'ą̀' t'ee yeenjì' van tee ginyaa izhìk van tee ts'ąįį nin tsal eenjit gwįįzįį goo'ąįį izhìk ts'ąįį datthak zhyą̀ą gahàajil į'. Izhìk it'ee gwįįzįį ganaldàii. Yeenjì gahàajil ts'ą̀' aii gwats'an oonjìt *Eaglè* ginyaa aii gwà'àn. Ąįįts'ą̀' yeenjì', yeenjìt *Old Crow* ginyaa ąįį chan tth'aih gokwàa.

11.46 Ąįįts'ą̀' *Circlè* gwizhrih izhìk chat dinjii t'įįch'yaa. Izhìk gwizhrįh gàashandàii. Ąįįts'ą̀' yeenjì' it'ee shìh kwaa, nin tsal kwàa. Nin tsal googàa gąąh'in kwàa. Ąįįts'ą̀' it'ee yeenjì' gahàajil. Aiits'ą̀' ti'yąą zhrįh ąįį t'ee yeedee *Van Choo*[9] vęę tr'igwich'įį izhìk dą̀į' it'ee shrìit'ałtsii t'agwaihnyàa. Izhìk tr'igwich'įį izhìk tth'aii hee vàanòodlit tr'ąąh'in kwaa ǫ'.

12.25 Ąįįts'ą̀' izhìk hee tr'igwich'įį ts'ą̀' reh. Ti'yąą aii zhik nihk'yą̀ą datthak neehidik gàa gwandaii nah'in kwàa.

Ąįįts'ą̀' it'ee *Gwichyaa* tthàn t'ee izhìk oochìt t'ee *Captain* zheh gwinyaa ąįį t'ee *Gwichyaa* dhidìi. Aii izhìk ts'ąįį it'ee gahàajìl.

LG12.57 Aii jùu văiinyaa *Captàin* aa?

---

9. *Van Choo,* literally 'Big Lake,' is the popular local name for *Old John Lake*, but it's generic and could refer to any lake. There's another *Van Choo* close to *Venetie*. The unique formal name for *Old John Lake* is *Van K'eh Dee*. —CM

That one winter we had the hardest time. We had no food as winter went by.

The people I mentioned earlier were the people alive during my father's early days.

11.03 So now there was no food. So they all decided to go to where there were lots of lakes. They say it was a good place for small game animals. So everybody left for those areas. I remember it then. At that time there were people only around *Eagle* and *Old Crow*, but *Old Crow* had not been established yet.

11.46 *Circle* was where they had some people too. That's all I know. So when they went down there, there was no small game. They didn't even see any small game.

So they all left to go there and just my father's family stayed behind along the shore of *Old John Lake*. I was getting pretty big by then. While we lived there we hadn't seen any white men.

12.25 So we stayed on. My father went all over the area, but he saw no game. They say this guy named *Captain* was at *Fort Yukon*. So they traveled down that way.

LG12.57 I'm asking who was this *Captain*?

SF12.59 *Captàin Ray* aii *nineteen. . .* dąąch'yaa t'ii'in dąį' googàa vàashandàii kwaa t'aihnyàa.[10] Izhìk chat dinjii gwats'ą' hàajìl, yeenjì' van tee chan izhìk gwats'an t'ee dząą gwee'àn dinjii kwàa.

13.18 Akhài' it'ee tsin ts'ą' yaaghà' *Drit* naii aii naii gogwandàii shitsii *Dihch'ì' Davìd* yaaghà' izhìk dąį' zhat gwanaa gwich'in naii gàa chat gwįįzįį hàashandàii kwàa.

K'eedąį' jùu dinjii dèe vats'an dohthaa lèe t'inch'yaa văiinyaa łèe?

LG13.45 Ôo, *Tr'ìnjàa Vi'* năihnyaa ijìi.

SF13.48 Ôo, *Tr'ìnjàa Vi'*?

LG Ąąhą'.

SF13.64 Aii naii aii naii t'ee gogwandàii gwànaa izhìk it'ee t'igwii'in t'iihnyàa. Ąįį *Shyaaghan Ndìk* vàràhnyaa ch'yąą chan ąįį naii gogwandàii gwànaa t'igwii'in t'iihnyàa. Ąįįts'ą' izhìk it'ee ti'yąą aii gòhch'it ǫǫ'ęę neezhii nin tsal kwàa. "Ąįįts'ą' it'ee yeetthàn *Gwichyaa* ts'ąįį tr'ahoojyàa," nyàa.

14.33 Izhìk ts'ąįį tr'ahàajìl. Ąįįts'ą' łąįį chan ch'a'àa kwaa gwįįzįį ch'a'àa kwàa. Diikhwant'ee chan googàa ch'iitthàn tr'eedàa. Gwiizhìk it'ee *Zheh Gwatsal* ginyaa izhìk t'ee *Christian Choh* ąįį t'ee *Zheh Gwatsal* gwigwich'ìį. Sheejii *Rachèl* naii.

15.01 Ąįįts'ą' izhìk ch'iitthàn tr'eedàa, oo'àt ddhah kat ch'ii'àn tr'eedàa izhìk *T'aa Dha'ąįį* ginyaa izhìk tr'ąąhaa gwats'an ànts'ą' chat ddhah taa riinjìl. Ąįįts'ą' gehchìt gwàtthàn it'ee tr'ihęęhaa gwiizhìk ti'yąą ąįį diits'ìį hàhàk. Ąįįts'ą' *Zheh Gwatsal* k'idik łèe.

LG15.29 Khaii t'akhwa'in?

10. Captain Patrick Henry Ray of the U.S. Army 8th Infantry arrived in *Fort Yukon* on September 12, 1897. Less than a month later he and Lt. Wilds took charge of the supply warehouses of the Alaska Commercial Company and the North American Transportation and Trading Company and defended them against a mob of destitute gold miners. See Ray's Account in Ray and Richardson, 1900:519-560. Ray left *Fort Yukon* by dog team on February 22, 1898. These dates help pinpoint the year when Sarah and her father Old John went to *Fort Yukon* for the first time. Sarah was probably about six years old. —CM

SF12.59 Captain Ray. It was 19. . . something. I don't even know. There were some people who went there too. There were hardly any people around here after they left for the *Old Crow* area.

13.18 But somehow the *Drit [Tritt]* family stayed on, and also *Old Man David*, but I can't remember some of those people's names from that time.

Not too long ago — who did you say we came from?

LG13.45 Oh, I told you *Tr'injaa Vi'*.

SF13.48 Ooh. *Tr'injaa Vi'?*

LG Yes.

SF13.64 This happened when they were all still living. They say all this happened while *Old Woman Ndik* and them were still alive. So one day my father returned home. There was no small game, so he said, "Let's go down toward the *Yukon Flats* area."

14.33 So we left in that direction. Our dogs were not well fed. We all walked down. *Chief Christian* was living at the place called *Christian Village*. That was my older sister *Rachel* and them.

15.01 We went down that way, over the mountains. On the way we stayed overnight at the place called *Cottonwood Grove*. From there we went over the mountains again and made camp. But my father continued on down alone until he reached *Christian Village*.

LG15.29 Was this during the winter?

SF15.30 Ą̀ąhą' shreenyàa, shreenyàa t'igwii'in drin diinzhìt. Ąįįts'ą̀' it'ee *Zheh Gwatsal* hee ti'yąą k'idik łèe. It'ee tr'ohchìt vàanòodlit nał'yà' gwats'ą̀' gwaldak t'iihnyàa. Aiits'ą̀' it'ee ree khàa ts'ą̀' it'ee tr'ihę̀ęhaa shrigwilii ni'ę̀ę.

Ąįįts'ą̀' nihdèerįįjil tr'igwîiłk'in nihdèeriinjil gwiizhìk, yee'àt łąįį ch'ik'yàanjik tth'ak roh. Akhài' sheejii *Rachèl* t'ii'in łèe.

16.23 Diits'ą̀' łąįį yihìltsit łèe. Ąįįts'ą̀' zhat danàh naahaa aiitł'ęę nìhkàa it'ee tthàn vachąąvàl kat agàadîiriik'įį. Ts'ą̀' ree oochìt *Zheh Gwatsal* ree k'eeriidàl. Izhìk chan *four days* gavàa tr'ą̂ąhaa gwìch'in. Ąįį gwats'an it'ee tthàn ts'ą̀' chan *Gwichyaa* chat gwats'ą̀' rahàajìl.

17.02 *Gwichyaa* gwats'ą̀' rahàajìl. Ąįįts'ą̀' it'ee izhìk chat ookyùk gwàtthàn tr'âahàa, izhìk chan ti'yąą *Gwichyaa* gwats'ą̀' hàazhii diits'ìį. Izhìk gwats'an chan dachąąvał nèekwaįį diidirîiljìl. Izhìk it'ee tr'ohchìt t'ee łùhgąįį, łùh, sungàįį, lìdii, ąįį zhrįh it'ee tr'aa'in ǫ'. Ąįį thał k'eegilik hee shee tsin gwąąhch'yaa ch'yàą'. Ąįįts'ą̀' ree.

LG17.50 Neetsingwąąhch'yaa nats'àhts'ą̀' łùhgąįį nintł'èegahtsìt?

SF17.55 Ą̀ąhą', łùhgaįį diitèegiłtsìt. Aii tr'a'àa ree diishìi kwaa t'iihnyàa. Ąįįts'ą̀' it'ee tr'ą̂ąhaa aiitł'ęę nìhkàa it'ee ree, drin diinzhìt aiitł'ęę nìhkàą it'ee *Gwichyaa* k'ineediigaadàl.

Izhìk it'ee tr'ohchìt vàanòodlit tr'ąąh'in ǫ'.

18.14 *Gwichyaa* k'eeriidàl ree vàanòodlit gǫ̀ǫlįį kwàa. Vàanòodlit ànihłik gilęįį kwaa zhrįh *Gwichyaa* gwigwich'ìį.

Izhìk jyàa dìgįįch'yaa, izhìk it'ee tr'ohchit vàanòodlit tr'ąąh'in ǫ'.

19.13 Aiitł'ęę zhat khaii *one year Gwichyaa* tr'igwįįch'į̀'.

Tr'igwįįch'į̀' izhìk it'ee vàanòodlit arąąjat ch'yàą. Oo'òk neerihiidàl hee goorąąjat roh. Goorąąjat ts'ą̀' gooragwąhshįį. Ąįįts'ą̀' izhìk it'ee jyàa dìgwii'in ts'ą̀' *one year* zhat tr'igwįįch'į' ǫ'.

SF15.30 Yes. It was springtime when the daylight was getting long.
So my father got to *Christian Village*. I'm talking about everything else before I tell you about seeing white men for the first time. So late in the evening we finally finished making camp. Then we went inside and built a fire. Then suddenly the dogs noticed something. Here it was my older sister *Rachel*.

16.23 She came up with a dog team. After she stayed overnight with us, the next day we traveled back with her. We even rode on her toboggan on the way back until we got to *Christian Village*. We stayed four nights with them.
From there we went all the way down to *Fort Yukon*.

17.02 So we left to go to *Fort Yukon*. On the way down we made camp, and again my father continued on to *Fort Yukon* ahead of us. Then they came back and got us with two dog teams. That was the first time I had ever seen crackers, flour, sugar, and tea. That was the first time I had ever seen cloth pants. They sure looked funny to me.

LG17.50 So it was funny, but how did they give you crackers?

SF17.55 Yes, they passed the crackers to us. What I'm saying is we ate them because we didn't have any food. So after we stayed overnight, the next day the daylight lasted so long we got to *Fort Yukon* that very day.
That's when we saw our first white men.

18.14 When we got to *Fort Yukon* there were hardly any white men. There were just a few still living around there.
That was how we first saw white men.

19.13 We lived there in *Fort Yukon* for one year. We were really scared of white men while we were living there. When we walked around we were afraid of them. Since we were so afraid of them we stayed out of their sight. We stayed there for one year and did what had to be done.

19.54 Aiitł'ęę it'ee khaii gwìindhat tł'ęę shreenyàa izhìk dąį' it'ee *Captain Ray* įįdi' jìhnyaa t'iihnyàa. Ąįįts'ą' ąįį chan yaaghà' *Captàin Ray* ts'ą' *American* gįlįį łee roh.

Ąįįts'ą' *English* naii chan.

20.25 Aii naii hàa it'ee *Gwichyaa* nihk'èhnjì' it'ee gwigwich'įį łee. Izhìk ąįį naii khaiinjii niłigeeghan į'. Aii chan nan eh'àn.

Khaiinjii niłigeeghàn. Ąįįts'ą' zhik gwatah gavàa gwahàadhat ts'ą' it'ee tł'ęę t'ee yeedì' nijìn *Nome* gàgahnyaa gwìdih gwìch'in izhìk gwìdì' it'ee ree làrąą agogwąh'ąįį łèe.

Aiits'ą' âa, *it's good* ts'ą' izhìk gwats'ą' vàanòodlit hijyàa. Gwįįtł'oo vàanòodlit gǫǫlįį.

21.11 Ch'igeeghwaa, khał geelil geetàk chat łąįį nèekwąįį.

LG21.18 Łąįį choh hàa?

SF21.19 Łąįį choh kwàa, zhyąą łąįį. Ąįįts'ą' ąįįtł'ęę ch'igeelil jyàa dìgii'in ts'ą' it'ee gihijyàa. Vàanòodlit lęįį naii gàa àn dhidlìt t'agwaihnyàa. Goodhąįį nàgaadhàk.

21.48 Ąįįts'ą' jyàa dìgwii'in ts'ą' it'ee ch'iinjì' *Circlè* gwats'ą' rahàajìl. *Circlè* gàa chan zhat dąį' vàanòodlit zhat kwàa.

Vàanòodlit gǫǫlįį kwàa, łyâa lęįį kwaa naii zhrįh. Aįįts'ą' izhìk it'ee tr'igwich'įį. Ąįįts'ą' vàanòodlit naii googàa geedant'ee łyâa neeshreegâahch'yaa į'. Jyàa dìgįįch'yaa t'igich'yàa. Ąįįts'ą' nin gihijyàa, gihijyàa.

Izhìk dąį' t'ee oonjìt *Circlè* tr'ohchìt tr'agwąąh'yà' t'igwinyàa. Aiit'ee Dinjii Zhuh naii zhak kwaiik'ìt gwigwich'įį t'igįįch'yàa. Ąįįts'ą' izhìk gwats'an it'ee, it'ee vàanòodlit jyàa dìi'in, nàhąą. Ąįįts'ą' vàanòodlit gwilii. Izhìk googàa tth'aih vàanòodlit gwįįtł'òo gǫǫlįį kwaa ǫ'. Izhìk hee googhàii tr'ihee'àl googàa goorąąjat ch'yąą.

LG23.33 Giveh'òk hee noh'òo?

SF23.34 Ąąhą'. Ts'ą' izhìk hee it'ee tr'ohchìt t'ee vàanòodlit jyàa dlìi'ìn.

19.54 Then the winter passed. What I'm saying is that spring *Captain Ray* was there. This *Captain Ray* was an American. Then there were some English from *Canada* too.

20.25 They each had a place of their own. They almost fought each other over the land. They almost fought.

Somehow they stopped. At that time they discovered gold around the *Nome* area.

Oh, it sounded so good, so the white men were all leaving to go there. There were lots of white men.

21.11 Some were packing and pulling sleds and some had two dogs.

LG21.18 With horses too?

SF21.19 There were no horses, just dogs. They pulled their sleds and left. I'm saying lots of white men died that way because there was no way to survive. They became desperate.

21.48 There were no white men in *Circle* then. There were just hardly any white men around there, just very few of them.

So we stayed there. Even the white men were poor.

That's how they were. They kept leaving and leaving for the south.

It was the first time we ever saw *Circle*. There were Indians living in that village when white men started moving in, you see. Then more white men came. Even then there weren't that many white men around. That was when we were still afraid to pass them on the road.

LG23.33 You passed them at some distance?

SF23.34 Yes. So this is what white men did. And then the steamboats traveled along the *Yukon River*, you see.

Ąįįts'ą' *steamboat* neehiilak, nàhąą. *Steamboat* chat gǫ̀ǫlįį ts'ą' ąįį eenjit *Yukon* gwiinjik hee zheh gogòodlìi. Izhìk hee traa tsii gaghàn.[11] *Steamboat* talak izhìk gwats'an it'ee k'eiich'ii tsal gǫ̀ǫlįį ǫ'.

<sfws105Ab>

MR45.42 Aii jidii *store,* jidìi ch'ookwàt zheh gòo'ąįį?

SF45.53 *NAT. NAT store.*[12]

MR Izhìk tr'ookìt izhìk t'ee tr'ookìt ch'ookwàt zheh gwąąh'in hęę?

SF Ą̀ąhą'.

MR46.14 Izhìk dąį' aii ch'ookwàt zheh dòonch'yàa?

SF46.30 (Adlaa.) Ch'ookwàt zheh zhyąą jùunch'yaa dachan zheh gòo'ąįį gwizhìt reh, zhyąą dzaa gwik'ìt t'ôonch'yàa, aiits'ą' zhik vakat, jidìi *countèr* dachan tyąh ch'iidì' nįį'ee aii kat gwizhrįh izhìk reh ch'arookwàt.

MR Aiits'ą' izhìk aii ch'ookwàt zheh gwąąh'in dąį' jidii aii shrìt ch'andaa eet'indhàn nàhnyàa?

SF47.18 (Adlaa.) Jidii shìh, *anỳthing* kwàa, łuh, songąįį, *mush, rice*, aii songąįį, lìdii. Aii zhrìh gwìch'in ǫ'. Aiits'ą'... jidìi *bacon* chan. Aii zhat dąį' tsingwąąhch'yaa tsingwąąhch'yaa ch'aroonkwàt, jùk geevàagwahaldak t'inyàa. Izhìk dąį'.

MR47.53 Aii jùu hàa?

SF47.57 Shachaa nąįį hàa. Shachaa nèekwąįį nąįį. . .

MR Aii jùu nąįį?

SF48.03 *Petèr, Christian* hàa. Aii shįį nąįį hàa.

MR Ch'ìhłak aii nats'ąhts'ą' onzhrìi?

SF48.12 *Christian.*

MR48.17 Aii jidii ookwàt?

11. Many Indians earned money or received trading goods by cutting and selling cords of firewood to the steamboats. All of this wood was cut by hand. —CM

12. The North American Trading and Transportation Company store in *Fort Yukon* was nicknamed the NAT store. It was a major competitor of the Alaska Commercial Company and set up a post at *Circle City* about 1895. It sold its fleet of Yukon River steamboats at St. Michael's in 1906 and sold all of its stores along the river by 1912. See Kitchener (1954). —CM

There were lots of steamboats. That's why they had houses along the *Yukon*. They would cut cords of wood. After the steamboats started coming up, we started getting more things.

<sfwsl05Ab>

MR45.42 What was the name of the store there (in *Fort Yukon*)?

MR45.53 NAT. The NAT store.

MR Was that the first store you ever saw?

SF Yes.

MR46.14 What was the store like?

SF46.30 (Laughs.) The store was built with logs and had a counter, and we would buy over the counter.

MR What did you like most at the store?

SF47.18 (Laughs.) Just food that we needed, like flour, sugar, oatmeal, rice, especially tea and sugar. That's all I think.
Bacon too. I'll tell you about the funny way we would buy.
Back then.

MR47.53 You and who?

SF47.57 Me and my little brothers, my two little brothers.

MR Which ones?

SF48.03 *Peter*, *Christian*, and me.

MR What's the name of the other one?

SF48.12 *Christian*.

MR48.17 What did he buy?

SF Oo'àt gwà'àn łuk ghat tr'igwich'įį. Izhìk łuk gąįh, łuk gąįh *sell* tr'ahtsii ǫ'. Zhat *store.*

MR48.38 Aii, aii jùu vats'ą̀' *sell* yuhtsìi?

SF *Store* gwidinjii.

MR Dèegwą̀htsii yuukwàt?

SF48.57 T'agwą̀htsii yuukwàt lèe gàashandàii. Gàhgwiindàii kwàa. Gàhgwiindàii kwaa ts'ą̀', nàhąą.

MR49.08 Aii jidìi gwit'įį nakhwan tł'ěiinlìi?

SF Aii t'ee tik tr'įįlįį ts'ą̀', nàhąą. Tthak jidìi gweheenjyàa gàawiindàii kwaa ts'ą̀', datthak tik tr'iinlįį ts'ą̀' songą̀įį zhrįh tr'òonjìk.

<sfrfl a>

SF2.53 Akhài' izhìk ch'ìhłan khaii shìh kwaa gòodlit jìhnyàa. Izhìk dą̀į' it'ee yeenjì' Vantee ginyaa gwats'ą̀' datthak dinjii jyàa dǐizhìk. Aii gwats'an yeenjì' *Old Crow* gwìnji' *Circlè* kwaii nàgaajil, aii datthak k'ìh neegogwąą'yą̀' kwaa ts'ą̀' jùk datthak gookwàa.

3.29 Izhìk dą̀į' it'ee ti'yąą zhrįh. Aii *Van Choh* vęę gwà'àn tr'igwich'įį. Izhìk shoondee chan, aii chan. Izhìk it'ee diikhwan chan łyâa zhyą̀ą ti'yąą nihk'yą̀ą hee gwà'àn nintsal jì' eenjit neehidìk. Googàa nintsal kwàa.

4.07 Zhik gwà'àn daagǫǫ kwàii. Aiits'ą̀' it'ee łyâa gwìizuu danàh gweedhaa ts'ą̀' it'ee yeetthàn *Gwichyaa* ts'ąįį gahàajìl.

4.24 Ti'yąą nąįį. Aiits'ą̀' *Gwichyaa, Zheh Gwatsal*[13] chan *Christian Choo* gwich'įį. Aii nąįį ch'iitthàn tr'eedàa izhìk ìt'ee ti'yąą aii diits'įį hee hahàk. Aiits'ą̀' aii gwandak ahtsìi ts'ą̀' it'ee łąįį danankàrìlìk. Aii hàa it'ee *Gwichyaa* hee k'eeriidàl.

5.03 Aii *Christian Choo* googhàih chan *four days* tr'âak'ì'. Aii gwats'an it'ee tthàn ts'ą̀' *Gwichyaa* gwats'ą̀' chan tr'ahàajìl. Jyàa dòonch'yaa gwiizhìk łyâa khyu' năazhrìi. *Christian* chan. Aiits'ą̀' adan t'ee chat vishìi kwàa.

13. *Zheh Gwatsal* is *Christian Village.* —LG

SF We were fishing and living somewhere, and we were selling dry fish, dry fish to the store.

MR48.38 Who did you sell to?

SF To the store manager.

MR How much did he pay for it?

SF48.57 I don't know how much. We don't know, you see.

MR49.08 What did he trade you for?

SF The three of us didn't know what to buy, you see. So all three of us just got sugar.

<sfrf1a>

SF2.53 As I said before, that one winter we ran out of food. That's when they say many people left this place and went over there. Some ended up over in *Old Crow* or *Circle* and most of them never returned, and they died there later.

3.29 That was when my father was still alive. And we were living at *Old John Lake*. My older brother was there also. And we were too. My father kept hunting for small game. But there was no small game.

4.07 There weren't even any ptarmigan. After a while everything got worse, so we decided to go down toward the *Yukon Flats*.

4.24 My father and them went toward the *Flats*. And that *Chief Christian* was living at *Christian Village*. As we traveled down, my father went ahead of us, and he broke the news about us. And then a dog team came to take us to *Fort Yukon*.

5.03 We stayed by *Chief Christian* for four days. From there we went down to the *Yukon Flats*. We went there just the way we were. We hunted but had no luck. *Christian* was in the same situation. He didn't have any food either.

5.31 Aiits'ą' t'ee tthàn ts'ą' tr'ahàajìl. Ts'ą' oochùk *Shiht'èendik* ginyaa gwatthan nìriinjìl.

Izhìk gwatthan drin hee ch'ara'àa kwaa tr'eedàa t'iihnyàa.

Łąįį gwilęįį nąįį tr'ijit nehshrit gah'àl.

6.04 Âa, aii it'ee ne'ęę aii jidìi ch'ich'iighąįį vàh ch'arahkhii gii'įį. Aii jèiinch'ii tsal aii yichų' tsal ahtsìk. Aiits'ą' dazhoo t'ùu tsal chat yizhìlìi. Aii it'ee łąįį taahthàk. Aii zhrįh.

6.30 Aii ch'iighai' it'ee tr'ijit gah'àl. Âaa, zhik *Gwichyaa*, zhik *Shiht'èendik* ginyaa gwatthan nìriinjìl. Gwiizhìk it'ee ti'yąą aii diits'įį hee *Gwichyaa* gwats'ą' hàazhìi.

Aiits'ą' aii gwaandak, ts'ą' t'ee chąąval nèekwąįį it'ee ookyąą diineenàgaajìl. Jyàa dìgii'in ts'ą' *Gwichyaa* gwats'ą' hee datthak neediigiinlìi.

7.12 Aiits'ą' *Gwichyaa* chan khaii nèekwat *two years* it'ee tr'igwinch'ì'. Tł'ęę it'ee chan oonjìt *Circlè* gwats'ą' rahàajìl. Izhìk dąį' it'ee làrąą gǫǫlįį lèe t'igwii'ìn gǫ̀'.

Làrąą kwaa t'igwii'ìn. Làrąą gǫ̀ǫlįį ts'ą' gàagwiindàii kwaa reh.

7.47 Aiits'ą' it'ee izhìk dąį' ree yeedì' nijìn hee lì'. Nats'ąą hee gogoozhrįį lì', yeedì'. Izhìk gwà'àn hee làrąą aragwąh'ąįį, ginyąą. Dinjii Zhuh ch'ìhłak googàa iihàanii kwaa t'agwaihnyąą. Làrąą hàa giindàii kwàa. Aiits'ą' t'ee ch'iinjì' chuuluh chyah nĭin'èe. It'ee zhat gwidì' Vàanòodlit nąįį gwats'ą' hijyàa reh.

8.29 Izhìk it'ee *first time* làrąą agwarąh'įį gwinyàa. Izhìk gwits'eegehijyàa nąįį t'ii'ìn. Goolàt nąįį lęįį àn dhidlìt.

Geetàk hee Vàanòodlit ch'eeghwaa ts'ą'. Geetàk chan khał geelil ts'ą'. Geetàk chan łąįį nèekwąįį tł'yah dàgąąhdìi.

Âaa, gihijyàa.

9.01 Izhìk hee Vàanòodlit nąįį goorąąnjàt ch'yąą t'iihnyàa (adlaa).

Tr'ohchìt goorąąh'in roh. Ch'irîitth'ak draii googàa kwaa t'agwaihnyàa. Vàanòodlit nąįį tr'ąąh'in dąį' goorąąjat ch'yąą (adlaa). Zhat dąį' Vàanòodlit lęįį nąįį àn dhidlìt t'agwaihnyàa.

5.31 So, we went down farther. We went as far as to what you call *Shiht'èendik.*

As I said, we were traveling in the daytime without eating.

The poor dogs were just barely walking.

6.04 Oh my mother had this rotten animal brain that she used for tanning skins. She made a little juice out of it and then she put in an amount of cut up skins That's what she passed out to each of the dogs.

6.30 That's why they had very little strength to walk. So we reached the *Flats* around what you call *Shiht'èendik.*

My father went ahead to *Fort Yukon*. Then he spread the news, and two dog teams came and took us all up to *Fort Yukon*.

7.12 So we lived in *Fort Yukon* for two years. And after that we went to *Circle*. At the time there was no money. We didn't know anything about money in those days.

7.47 At that time we heard about this unknown distant area. I don't remember the name of the place. During that time somewhere in this unknown area they discovered gold.

Not even one Indian made a move to go there. They didn't know anything about money. And there was a wide trail toward there. Swarms of white people kept going there one after another.

8.29 That was the first time they discovered gold, they say. So that's where they all traveled to. Many of them died off.

Some white men traveled on foot with a pack. Some of them pulled a sled, and a few of them traveled with two dogs in harness. Oh they were just constantly going, one right after another.

9.01 I remembered we were just afraid of white men then (laughs).

You see that was first time we saw them. As I said, we didn't know a thing about English then, so when we saw white men we got scared of them (laughs). I'm saying that's when many white men died.

9.55 Goodhaii nàgaadhàk. *Circlè* chan ninzhyùk tr'igwinch'į'. Izhìk dąį' t'ee òonjit kwaiik'ìt gòo'ąįį.[14]

RF Ą̀ąhą'.

SF10.14 Aii ddhah ch'iinjì' nìin'ee vakat tr'ąį̀ł, tr'ąį̀ł tsal googàa kwàa. Ddhah làii zhrįh ch'iinjì' dhidlìi. Oondìt *Hot Spring* gàgàhnyaa,[15] izhìk it'ee gwà'àn agàa neegihiinjik t'agavaihnyàa, ti'yąą nąįį.

10.42 Izhìk gwà'àn chan oo'àn ddhah kat nàgàandìi. Gwiizhìk *Danzhìt Khǎįįląįį* gàgàhnyàa. Aii zhyąą ddhah deetak gwatł'at ch'iinii *Khǎįįląįį* t'agogwàhnyaa łii roh.

11.06 Jyàa dìgwii'in ts'ą' oonjìt zhat chan nèekwat khaii tr'igwinch'į' gwìch'ìn. Aiitł'ęę it'ee gwinii neerahòojìl. Izhìk dąį' shoondee *Philip* aii va'at gǫǫlįį. Aii nı̃indhàt. Aii eenjit oonjì' nàgaajil t'agavaihnyàa, ti'yąą nąįį.

11.42 Gwinii khan neereheedàa kwaa gwìch'in akhài' aii shoondee chan gàa khǎiinjii àn dhidlìt. Dąįį gwahgǫ̀', gwahgǫ̀' tł'ęę tr'ihtsal hàa nìhìlzhrìi akhài' nàaghàa. Aiits'ą' *islànd* tsal kat nehshrit tèedhizhii łii. Nats'ąhts'ą' gwats'at tr'eeheedyàa gǫ̀'. Aiits'ą' khǎiinjih vakwaa t'aihnyàa. Aiits'ą' it'ee zhazhat tr'ihchoo tsal gǫǫlįį aii hàa t'ee gwinii tr'ihchoo nihts'eegąąhłìt łii.

12.35 Akhài' aii hàa t'ee giigwąh'ąįį. Nehshrit gwandàii ts'ą' t'ee yaaghà' gwikyąą hee tèegiyiłchįį łii. Aii geh'àn it'ee gwinii khan neerohòojil t'agwaihnyàa.

12.56 Aiitł'ęę *Gwichyaa* izhìk gwà'àn hee chihvyàa chàgaadlii ts'ą' reh łuk tr'oonjii ts'ą' ree. Aiitł'ęę łyâa vijùu gwànaa hèe izhìk t'ôohju' hee gweechyąą tineeridhijìl.

13.19 Izhìk dąį' yeendee *Old John Lake* ginyaa *Vashrąįį K'ǫǫ* gwà'àn dinjii t'inch'yaa nąįį datthak kwàa. Datthak yeenjì' gahàajìl ree. Gwìizųų nàgwatth'at t'iihnyàa.

RF13.38 Chihvyàa chìgiłtsùu jiinyaa *Gwichyaa Zhee* gwà'àn?

SF13.42 Izhìk dąį' lèe?

RF Ą̀ąhą̀'.

---

14. I'm not sure what she says here. —LG

15. Sarah is apparently alluding to *Circle Hot Springs*, a popular resort located between *Fairbanks* and *Circle*. —CM

9.55 Most them were stranded or something. So we lived in *Circle* a long time. It was just a village then.

RF Yes.

SF10.14 There was no brush on that mountain there then. The mountain was all bare. What they called that *Hot Spring*, we even traveled around there with my father and them.

10.42 Around there too we traveled to a mountain called *Danzhit Khą̌įįlqįį*. It's a creek between two mountains.

11.06 We were doing this and that until we stayed two winters there. After that we started to travel back. That was when my older brother *Phillip* had a wife. She died.

That's the reason we went there in first place, my father and them.

11.42 We probably would not have returned that soon, but we almost lost my older brother. It was springtime and after break-up he went hunting with a canoe, and he tipped over. Then he just barely made it to a small island.

There was no way he could leave that island. He almost died there. There were lots of small boats around. So they went down with a boat.

12.35 That's how they found him. He was just barely alive when they brought him halfway up.

As I was saying, that's how we came back a lot sooner than we planned to.

12.56 After that we stayed around the *Flats* and put a fish net in to get many fish. And then years later we came back up here.

13.19 At that time all the people around *Old John Lake* and *Arctic Village* were gone. They all went to the east. I'm saying it became very difficult for them.

RF13.38 You said they set fish nets around *Fort Yukon*?

SF13.42 You mean at that time?

RF Yes.

SF13.44 Ą̀ą̀hą̀’, chihvyàa[16] zhrįh.

RF13.46 Jidii k’it t’inch’yaa chihvyàa?

SF13.50 Shii chihvyàa reh.

RF13.53 Vakwàa?[17]

SF13.58 Ą̀ą̀hą̀’. Khèedą̀į’ shii chihvyàa zhrįh hàa łuk keegii’ìn. Izhìk dą̀į’ it’ee gwats’ą̀’ gwànaa izhìk it’ee yaaghà’ shitsųų *Màry* aii t’ee shàhgwaandàk. Zhik *Yuukòn* nàhąą?

Chihvyàa chat kwaa ts’ą̀’ zhat gwànaa *Yuukòn* zhik nijìn *slough* k’ìt t’ôonch’yaa, izhìk it’ee neegogwahtsìk łii ts’ą̀’ ah, giyàhnyàa.[18] *Gwichyaa* k’àii łyâa ninjyàa. Dzaa gwats’an duulèe yeenjìt zheh ts’at gwats’ą̀’ jyàa dą̀htsìi.

14.50 Aii t’ee ch’iinìn neegogwatsìk ts’ą̀’ aii chigilik łii. Aii shitsųų *Màry* shàagwaandak reh. Aii nał’yą̀’ kwàa.

15.04 Aiits’ą̀’ t’ee łuk vizhìjyàa ts’ą̀’ t’ee kheegiyinlii ts’ą̀’ oonjìt vitł’į̀’ tł’at didhachaa izhìk gwizhrįh giitł’at deech’a’at ts’ą̀’ giizhìt łuk goondàk. Aii łuk tsal gwizhìt jyàa nihtèegaazhìk. Jyàa dìgwii’in nyàa.

Aii ch’iighai’ łuk keegii’in reh. Chihvyàa chan kwaa ts’ą̀’.

Aii vijuu gwànaa yaaghà’, oochìt zhat tr’igwinch’į̀’ jìhnyaa dą̀į’ t’ee chihvyàa gǫ̀ǫlįį.

15.47 Aiits’ą̀’ chihvyàa chàgaadlìi. Aii hàa t’ee łuk keegii’ìn. Aii dą̀į’ tr’il gahtsii chat gàagiindàii kwàa. Tł’ęę vijuu gwànaa t’ôohju’ hee tr’il gahtsìi.

16.31 Gògòontrìi ch’iinii gwinįįdhat t’ôonch’yàa.

RF16.36 Zhik gwà’àn łuk daagąįį eenjit tr’il tsal gahtsii, aii yų̀’?

SF Hąą?

RF16.42 Łuk daagąįį eenjit tr’il tsal gahtsii ijìi? K’ǫǫ gwà’àn.

SF16.49 Tr’il gahtsii kwaa. Da’anlee hee?

RF Da’anlee reh.

---

16. *Chihvyàa* is a gill net. —CM

17. I’m not sure what Sarah said here. —LG

18. This *ah* was something to catch fish with, either a trap or a dip net. —KP

SF13.44 Yes, only a fish net.

RF13.46 What kind of fish net?

SF13.50 It was a dog salmon fish net.

RF13.53 Nothing?

SF13.58 Yes. Years ago they only used dog salmon fish nets. Before that my grandmother *Mary* told me there were no fish nets on the Yukon River, you see? What they did in those sloughs along the Yukon was build a fish trap.

They said they used long willow branches. In the *Flats* they have long willows with thick brush that are as long as from where I'm sitting here to that corner of the house (gestures).

14.50 That's what they lay in the water across the slough, and somehow they catch fish with it. That's what my grandmother *Mary* told me. I've never seen it done.

15.04 So the fish got caught in it, and then they took the fish out and they tied string around the tail end of the trap that they made out of those willow branches. So the tail end, that's where they take the fish out.

They shared the fish with one another. She said that's what they did. That's how they caught fish. There were no fish nets then.

As I said before that, years later when we were living there, that's when they had lots of fish nets.

15.47 So they set fish nets in the river. That's how they fished then. At that time they didn't even know how to make fish wheels. Years later they started making fish wheels.

16.31 Everything happened the hard way at that time.

RF16.36 Around there they make a small fish wheel for whitefish. What about that?

SF What?

RF16.42 Did they make a small fish wheel for whitefish? In the sloughs?

SF16.49 Not a small fish wheel. Do you mean a fish trap?

RF Right. Fish trap.

SF16.53 Da'anlee gogwahtsìk aii t'ee dzat gweendàk *Vantee* łuk daagąįį eenjit. Da'anlee gogwahtsìk ts'ą' ah, chìga'ak.

Aii t'ee zhik łuk gwizhìjyàa.

17.21 K'ǫǫ gwintsìi kwaa dąį' chan ah gahtsik! Aii chìga'ak aii chat łuk vizhìjyàa ts'ą' reh. Aii kwat it'ee shriijaa kwat reh. Aii dąį' łi'hàa łuk kat gidhi'ee t'ôonch'yàa. Dzaa gàa ree yeedee *Van Choh* dha'ąįį gàa łuk daagąįį jyàa dąhtsii gǫǫlįį. Aii eenjit da'anlee neegogwahtsìk, yeedee. Ch'iinjì' tł'in jyàa dòonch'yaa ch'iinjì' datthak łuk gǫǫlįį t'iihnyàa.

RF18.25 Jùk aii łyâa ch'akwàa?

SF18.26 Jùk łyâa vakwàa. Tth'aii hee vigwehèelyaa gwìch'ìn.

Henry[19] aii teet'eegąąhnąįį ts'ą' aii gwits'ą' nĭinzhyaa[20] tthak ginyąą i'.

RF18.53 Jyàa ree dìgwiizhìk ginyàa?

SF18.56 Ąąhą'. Aii t'ee łyâa łi'hàa ganaldàii gwànaa reh.

RF19.03 Deegii'in chan teet'eegiyaanàii?

SF19.06 Da'anlee geh'àn reh. Da'anlee łuk dehjyàa aii eh'àn nihk'įį diginyaa dǫhłįį. Izhìk geh'àn teet'eerąąhnàii giyàhnyàa.

Izhìk gwats'an it'ee łuk kwaa gòodlit. Âaa, adzii łuk t'iihnyàa.

19.33 Łuk daagąįį tsal reh.[21]

<sflg2b>

SF17.36 Zhik ganaldàii tr'inin ihłįį ganaldàii googàa łyâa gògǫǫtrii ǫ'. Vàanòodlit ts'an jèiinch'ii tsal googàa tr'ąąh'in kwàa t'agwaihnyàa. Aiits'ą' dachan, dachan giyàa zheh gwahtsìk, ąįį jyaa ree dįįch'yàa, it'ee nìgiinjii t'igii'ìn.

Jyàa dìgiyilìk ts'ą' dzaa gwee'àn dachan nèekwąįį oodìt kwàntee chan.

19. Henry John was a famous medicine man who lived in *Venetie*. —CM

20. I don't know what this word *nĭinzhyaa* means. —LG
It means that Henry John put a curse on the creek that someone threw him in. —JE

21. Sarah stops the story to speak to someone who walks into the house. —LG

SF16.53 Up this way was where they built fish traps for whitefish.

They built the cone-shaped fish trap and also used the willow branches that they used to catch fish with. That's how they caught fish then.

17.21 If the slough was too small then they used the willow branches kind of trap. They set this in the slough and the fish ran into it. Usually they caught grayling in it. Sometimes there were just fish all over the place. Even up here at *Big Lake* there were lots of whitefish then. They used to build a fish trap for them there. I'm saying there were lots of fish all the way around that bend of the lake.

RF18.25 Are there fish in it now?

SF18.26 There are none now. It could still have fish in it, but *Henry John* fell in it and cursed it or something like that, I guess.

RF18.53 They say that's what happened, right?

SF18.56 Yes. I remember when it happened.

RF19.03 They pushed him unexpectedly and he fell in?

SF19.06 I told them it was because of the fish trap. They got in an argument over the fish that were in the trap. They said that's why they pushed him and he fell in. Ever since then there haven't been any more fish in that lake. But boy I tell you there used to be lots of fish then.

19.33 It had lots of small whitefish.

<sflg2b>

SF17.36 What I remember as a child is that even then we had a hard time. Like I said, we didn't see much of the white man's things. At that time they had caribou hide shelters. They called them skin huts, and that's all they lived in. The poles they put up the house with were about this long (gesturing). And then they set up camp.

They put two poles together here and then the front top.

18.28 Dachan nèekwąįį jyàa dìgilìk. Oondee chan. Aiits'ą' nihts'įį gwigiich'įį. Aiits'ą' jyàhts'ą' zheh gogwahtsìi. Ąįį gwadachàn tr'iilęę iltsąįį chan neegahaazhìk.

LG18.50 Ôo, ą̀ąhą̀'.

SF18.52 Ąįį hàa oodok hee dàngogwąąhtł'uu tł'ęę it'ee ąįį vadzaih dhàh nįįvyaa vaihnyàa, ąįį it'ee giiyeenihts'įį nyaa ts'ą' gwinìgiyąąhtthàk.

19.06 Ą̂ą tr'agwâahk'ik gòogǫǫtrii ginya t'agavaihnyàa. Ąįį jidìi chii tł'yaa[22] k'it ree giyàhnyaa.

LG Ą̀ąhą'.

SF19.18 Ąįį kat chii jyàa dìgii'in ąįį ts'an kǫ̀' tsal tr'ijyàa, nàhąą. Ąįį k'iighai' it'ee gogwâahk'ik.

LG19.30 Ąįį tł'yahk'it jùk nijìn gwà'àn vagǫ̀ǫlįį lì' hęę?

SF19.33 Oondòk *some plàce* gwà'àn vagǫ̀ǫlįį gwìch'in googàa jùu dèe yinkeehi'ìk gǫ̀'. Jidìi chii gwiyeendaa dilų̀' kwàa.

Gwįįtł'òo dilų̀' kwaa nilįį. Ąįį chan azhrąįį. Aiits'ą' zhyąą datłok k'ìt t'įįch'yaa nał'in į'.

20.09 Ąįį it'ee zhik gwà'àn, aat'oo aatr'ii ąįį chan łi'hàa k'èegąąhtii i'. Aiits'ą' zhik aat'oo kat jidìi ghoo zhrąįh[23] dhidlii ijìi?

LG Ą̀ąhą'.

SF20.26 Ąįį chan łyâa t'eegąąhch'yaa į'. Aiits'ą' dąį' dįį' jidìi aat'oo kat jidii ghoo zhrąįh dhidlii, ąįį it'ee chan giyųųndak.

Ts'ą' giyatthat, giyatthat jyàa dìgiyah'in ts'ą' datłòk giyahtsįį. Aiitł'ęę it'ee ąįį it'ee zhik giits'ą' jyàa dąhthan, nàhąą. Ąįį gwiizhìk it'ee jii jyàa dìgiyah'in ts'ą' ąįį kat kǫ̀' tsal dǎadhàk, nàhąą. Dihjyàa ąįį hàa it'ee gwîik'ik ginyàa. Ąįį hàa tr'agwâahk'ik ginyàa.

LG21.15 Àkwàt shii ąįį jidìi aat'oo kat jidìi daagąįį tsal dhidlii, daagąįį tsal nilįį ijìi.

SF Ą̀ąhą'.

LG21.22 Ąįį hàa t'igiyah'in oiihnyaa łii. Aii jidìi daagąįį dril ree.

22. This *chii tł'yah* is the name for flint. —LG

23. This *ghoo zhrąįh* is the hard, round fungus that grows on the trunks of birch trees. Northern Dene throughout Alaska's Interior use these fungi to start fires and then mix the ashes with their snuff. The result is a very powerful chew. —CM

18.28 So they put two poles together. And another one way in the back. So two families lived across from one another. So that's how they built their house. They carried ready-made poles for the house with them.

LG18.50 Oh, yes.

SF18.52 They all helped each other as they tied it together and put it up and covered the poles with caribou skins.

19.06 They said it was hard to build a fire in those days.
They called that flint *chii tł'yah.*

LG Yes.

SF19.18 Somehow they hit it or rubbed it against the rocks, and it made sparks, you see. And that's how they started fires.

LG19.30 Those flint rocks—where do you think they can find them now?

SF19.33 They must be around up that way today. It's not a very hard rock. It's not a hard rock. It's black. It looks like it's soft. I saw it.

20.09 And those birch trees. They sure took good care of that birch bark. And you know that black round stuff [fungi] on birch wood?

LG Yes.

SF20.26 That too they really needed. They took these black round things from birch trees, and they pounded them. They pounded them like this until they were soft. After that they held them like this toward the sparks. And that's how they started fires, they say. They say that's what we started fires with.

LG21.15 I thought they used that small white flaky stuff on birch wood.

SF Yes.

LG21.22 I really thought that what they used was that thin white flaky stuff.

SF21.25 Ą̀ąhą’, aii kwàa. Ąįį aat’oo aatr’ii ąįį chan giyahgąįį nàhąą. Aiits’ą̀’ *roll* giyahtsii ts’ą̀’, jyàa dąhjyaa chan neegahaazhik į’. Ąįį chan giik’iighai’ khan gwâahk’ik geenjit. Aii jyàa dìgìi’ìn.

LG21.49 Shii ąįį ch’ats’ą̀’ hee ninjich’ihthat, nats’ą̀ą k’ii’àn ninjich’ihthat t’ihch’yàa, shįį.

SF22.03 Ąįį it’ee shitsųų vagwandàk t’aihnyàa.

LG Ą̀ąhą’.

SF22.09 Aiits’ą̀’ izhìk ganaldaii ch’adhàh zheh tr’igwich’įį, izhìk it’ee ànihłik hee ganaldàii ǫ’. Chadhàh zheh, âa neerihiinjìk.

LG22.25 Nìivyaa zheh, reh?

SF22.26 Ą̀ąhą’, nìivyaa zheh. Aįįts’ą̀’ izhìk hee jyàa dìgwii’in êe’ gògǫǫtrii t’igwinyàa.

LG22.40 Gàa chan goolàt naii giveenjit dòhłįį t’ôonch’yaa kwaa dòhłįį hęę gogogwaa’èe, zhat gwànaa dą̀į’ gwalàt kwat.

SF22.47 Ą̀ąhą’, goolàt naii ąįį naii gook’iighai’ dinjii gwandàii.

LG Ą̀ąhą’.

SF22.53 Ąįį naii łyâa giveenjit gwįįzįį. Dinjii gook’iighai’ gogwandàii, nàhąą. Aįįts’ą̀’ jùk datthak jidìi tsal tr’a’àa tsal hàa jyàa dàgoogah’in, nàhąą. Gook’èegąąhtii ts’ą̀’ gwik’iighai’ it’ee gwįįzįį. Izhìk it’ee hèedą̀į’ nįįzhìt kwaa gwànaa it’ee yaaghàt ąįį t’ee yaaghàt nitsųh sheejii *Saràh* aii it’ee gavàh gwįįch’ì’ į’.

LG23.37 Shitsųų *Saràh Ghǫǫ* lèe?[24]

SF Ą̀ąhą’.

<sfkf2b>

CF8.21 Nįįvyaa giyàhnyaa zhit gohch’įį ch’adą̀į’ neekhwanjik dą̀į’

SF8.26 Tr’iinin ìhłįį dą̀į’ it’ee nìivyaa zheh tr’igwich’įį ǫ’. Izhìk dą̀į’ ch’iitsii chan kwaa zhyą̀ą oondaa gwâak’ą’ gwizhrįh. Nįįvyaa zhìt. Izhìk it’ee łyâa ganaldàii ǫ’.

KF8.42 Jidìi hàa gwiits’ąįį t’ôonch’yaa?

SF8.45 Dachan hàa. Dachan ts’ik.

24. Saràh Ghǫǫ was one of Albert Tritt’s wives. A photo of her appears in Mishler (2018) and in Mishler and Frank (2023); Fig. 2.11.—CM

SF21.25 Yes, but no. They also dried the birch bark, you see. And then they rolled it up this long and carried it with them. With this the fire started faster. That's why they did this.

LG21.49 Here I really thought different.

SF22.03 I'm saying this was my grandmother's story.

LG Yes.

SF22.09 I remember when we lived in a skin house. I remember about it here and there in places where we set up camp.

LG22.25 That's with a skin house, right?

SF22.26 Yes, a skin house. Oh, they said it was hard the way they did things.

LG22.40 But some of them were used to it, and it didn't bother them in those days.

SF22.47 Yes, other people survived because of them.

LG Yes.

SF22.53 Because they were well. You see, people survived because of them. They fed them a little food and they survived. It was years later. That's when I lived with your grandmother, my cousin *Sarah*.

LG23.37 You mean my grandmother, *Round Sarah*?

SF Yes.

<sfkf2b>

CF8.21 A long time ago when you traveled around, did you live in what's called a skin house?

SF8.26 I was just a child when we lived in a skin house. At that time we didn't have any stoves. There was only a campfire inside the skin house. I really remember that.

KF8.42 What was it made of?

SF8.45 Wood. Narrow poles.

KF8.50 Łaavii gwich'in ree hę̀ę ?

SF8.52 Ą̀ąhą'. Dachan ts'ik geenjit gahtsìk, ąįį khaii hee chan neegahaazhik ǫ'. Aii hàa it'ee nìginjìk.

CF9.03 Shitsųų, aii lèe jìints'ik lee giyàhnyàa?

SF9.06 Ą̀ąhą', jìints'ik giyàhnyàa.

KF9.09 Aii dachan reh hę̀ę ?

SF9.10 Ą̀ąhą', aii oodee dachan dzaa nihts'įį łagahtł'ùk ǫ'. Gwiditit deenìn dachan tak njaah aii chikhâa'ee giyàhnyàa. Aii kat k'iindàa dzaa dachan jyàa dìgilìk, jyàa dìgiyilìk. Aii t'ee nįįvyaa giinôaahdak ts'ą̀' reh.

KF9.41 Aii lee ch'adhàh reh hę̀ę?

SF Ą̀ąhą'.

CF9.45 Shitsųų, shàagwaandak, aii ch'adhàh t'eegaahch'yaa geetàk hee chan nidigiyaatsìi' yàhnyaa hę̀ę ? Giikat gwà'àn ch'it'èe k'ìt t'inch'yaa geedzâiilii.

SF9.55 Ą̀ąhą', aii it'ee giikat jidìi zhik gwà'àn nin tsùu. Aii giikat gànahtł'ùu.

CF Ą̀ąhą'.

SF10.11 Chat giyatsaii. Aaa, nìįvyaa gwinzįį vìyìich'yą' nilįį.

KF10.19 Jidii giikat ahtsìk dìinyàa? Tsaih hàa?

SF10.30 Giikat lèe gwahtsìk. Zhyą̀ą łangiidąąhkàį' izhìk gwizhrįh chan giyatsàii. Giyatsaii ts'ą̀' it'ee jii jidìi ch'itsùu aii dòk tsal chan giikat nilįį. Jyàa gwizhrįh dìgiyah'in vanaldàii.

CF10.57 Aii ch'adàį' gwànaa łąįį nagadąątsį' googàhnyaa hę̀ę?

SF Hąą?

CF11.04 Łąįį. Łąįį łyâa gęhdàa kwaa nagadąąhtsį' googàhnyaa ch'adàį' gwànaa hę̀ę ?

SF Ą̀ąhą'.

CF11.08 *Ribbon* k'ìt t'inch'yaa hàa gàa ree.

SF11.12 Ą̀ąhą'. Izhìk tr'ikhit chan nigiidąątsì' t'agoogàhnyaa dǫ̀hłįį hèe? Izhìk gwànaa jidìi łąįį yindha'ąįį chat gwànlįį. Goonàn tah chan. Ch'iitsii ghoo tsal daalàii k'it t'inyàa.

KF8.50 Was it *łaavii,* some kind of dry wood?

SF8.52 Yes. They made narrow poles for it. And even when they traveled in the winter they carried the poles with them. That's what they traveled with.

CF9.03 Grandma, what did they call those extra-narrow poles?

SF9.06 Yes, extra-narrow, that's what they say.

KF9.09 That was the wood, right?

SF9.10 Yes, they tied two poles together way up high. On those they laid another pole they called the main support pole. On that pole they put another pole like this (gesturing). That's what they wrapped their skins on.

KF9.41 That's the hide, right?

SF Yes.

CF9.45 My grandma says that sometimes they put decorations on those skins, right? They would hang feathers on them.

SF9.55 Yes, they sewed something like feathers on them.

CF Yes.

SF10.11 They painted them up. They made the skin house so pretty.

KF10.19 How did they say they make that paint? With ochre?

SF10.30 They made something. They lined paint only on the stitches holding the skins together. After they lined paint, they hung the bulk of the feathers on it. That's how I remember it.

CF10.57 A long time ago they say they decorated their dogs, right?

SF What?

CF11.04 The dogs. They say that a long time ago they really decorated their dogs, huh?

SF Yes.

CF11.08 They even used something like ribbon too.

SF11.12 Yes. They must have gotten carried away with their decorations, and maybe that's why they said that about them. At that time they used dog ring collars. They had wide straps over their backs. There was this round metal and it rang just like bells.

Aii ch'adąįį' ch'ihłòk jèiinch'yaa łąįį tł'yàa iighàn. Aii dzaa vigin chan chiits'ii làii ghoo daalàii. Nèekwąįį dòhòchàa. Gwiizhìk goonàn kat chan nèekwąįį. Ąįį kwat daalàii k'ìt t'inyàa. Ch'ihłòk gwizhrįh jèiinch'ii iighan.

Aii chan vàanòodlit chat giyùunjik ch'yąą. Ch'adhàh łąįį tł'yàa reh.

CF Hâą.

KF12.13 Aii lèe shitsii yit'èehaahch'yaa oiinyaa?

SF Ąąhą'.

KF12.20 (Adlaa.) Shòo nahtsii kwaa gwiizhìk gwilìi t'ah'ìn?

SF12.26 Geenjit vats'ą' khàgihkhìk dąįį' chan vik'ii t'iihnyaa ǫ'. Aii zhyąą ree zhyąą nał'in.

KF12.38 Shitsųų aii lèe oo'òk gwich'in ts'ą' k'ii'àn geedàa dąįį' izhìk gwats'ą' nagadàl aii łąįį kwaii ch'izhii łąįį tł'yàa nìdìiltsį' aii gwakat nàgàazhik. Aiitł'ęę hee kwaiik'ìt gwats'ą' gaha'oo lèe t'iinyàa?

SF13.05 Aii łąįį vijì' chat ohotł'įį zhòk ghoo hàa vijì' tr'ahtsìi. Aii vakat chan jidìi *ribbòn* gwìch'in aii chat vijì' jyàa dąchjyaa aii kat.

CF13.32 Aii kwaiik'ìt gwats'ą' geheedàa dąįį' aii jidìi łąįį tł'yàa t'èegąąhch'yaa aii giłèegehilik ts'ą' aii ch'izhii aii gwakat nìgilik hèę ?

SF Ąąhą'.

CF13.43 Kwaiik'ìt k'eegeheedàl gwats'ą' reh. It'ee łyâa gwigwehił'ee ts'ąįį reh.

SF13.49 Geetàk hee shik łąįį kat ch'iindàak'ii kak jèiinch'yaa į'. Aii Ch'eekwaii tee chan łąįį tł'yàa gwantł'èerinlii ǫ'.

Vàanòodlit tee chan.

14.19 Aii ree vanàn tah ch'adhàh t'ųų jyàa dąhts'ik nihk'ęhndaa vanàn tah deenìn jèiinch'yaa. Aii gwintł'òo tr'ahtsii vàgwàntrii į'.

KF14.47 Dèiinch'yaa chan vàgwàntrii t'inch'yàa?

SF14.49 K'eerâahkaii roh. Tł'il hàa k'eerâahkaii. Nihtr'eerąhkąį'.

Vanàn tah agàa.

At one time they made dog harnesses like that. Around their collars they had bells that jingled. Usually they put two bells on them.

And then there were another two bells on their back. It was so jingling-like. I made that kind only one time.

Some white men took them. That was a dog harness made of skin.

CF Oh.

KF12.13 Did you think my grandpa was going to use it?

SF Yes.

KF12.20 (Laughs.) He makes you angry, but still you do nice things for him, right?

SF12.26 If I said anything to him then he got mad. So I just let him be.

KF12.38 Grandma, before they reached the place where the people were, they switched to the fancy dog harnesses. You're saying after that they continued on to the village, right?

SF13.05 They made antlers out of ball yarn, then they strung ribbon from that.

CF13.32 So before they reached the village they switched to the fancy ones, right?

SF Yes.

CF13.43 This was before they reached the village. That's how much they respect it.

SF13.49 Sometimes it looked like it was set on top of the dogs.

They gave it to the Inuit, and white men too.

14.19 With this one they sewed two straps on the back of the dog.

This was the hardest one to make.

KF14.47 How come it was hard to make?

SF14.49 Because we sewed it. We sewed it with babiche, and we sewed it in so many places.

Sarah Frank

Sarah Tr'iinin Nąįį Di'įį Dąį'

<sfrf2b>

RF18.22 Aii k'eejìt ohłįį dąį shitsii hàa tr'ookìt nihłòodhoojìk nijìn hee nihlòodhoojìk?

SF18.24 *Vįįhtąįį* tąįį ree. Izhìk dąį' it'ee dzaa oondòk *Old John Lake* ghat gwà'àn gwizhrįh tr'agwandàii. Akhài' dzaa *Vįįhtąįį* izhìk k'eeriidàl ts'ą' dzaa tr'igwich'įį izhìk it'ee nihłaròonjik ǫ'.

RF19.07 Nihlàakhwandàii kwaa gwikįh?

SF19.13 (Adlaa.) Ą̀ąhą'. Izhìk dąį'gwilin hee tr'igwich'įį t'ôonch'yàa. Izhìk it'ee zhik neerihiidàl gwizhrįh t'igwii'in ǫ'.

RF19.36 Dzaa niłàdhoonjìk aiitł'ęę nats'àhts'ą' niłàdhoojìk? Geenakhwarąhchįį?

SF19.47 Nihłaròonjìk, aiitł'ęę aii khaiits'ą' gòodlìt.

RF19.50 Ginkhii hàa lèe?

SF19.52 Àkwàa. Nihłaròonjik ts'ą' it'ee khaiits'ą' gòodlìt. Aiitł'ęę it'ee *Gwichyaa* hee ootthàn nàraa'oo. Izhìk it'ee *Willìam* ginkhii *Loola* vàràhnyaa aii it'ee nihkhèe danahchįį į'.

RF20.25 *Gwichyaa Zheh* gwats'ą' hòojil?

SF20.29 *Gwichyaa* gwats'ą' rahàa'òo. Izhìk it'ee nihkhèe diirąhchįį ǫ'. Aiitł'ęę ookyąą neerii'òo.

20.47 Aiits'ą' it'ee dzaa *Vįįhtąįį* hee tr'igwich'įį. Akhài' aiitł'ęę it'ee chan yeendàk *Old John Lake* izhìk hee chan gwits'ee rohòo'òo. Izhìk gwà'àn it'ee hee gwizhrįh tr'igwichįį.

RF21.13 Shriit'agwąhkhyùk gooch'į'?

SF21.14 Ą̀ąhą'. Aiitł'ęę it'ee *Tryahtł'it* hee gwats'ą' rahàa'òo. Aiitł'ęę diigii tik nąįį gǫ̀ǫlįį gwiizhìk.

RF21.27 Izhìk it'ee lèe *twenty-two years* gooch'į'?

SF21.31 *Tryahtł'it* lèe?

RF21.32 Ą̀ąhą'.

Sarah Frank

When Sarah Had Her Children

<sfrf2b>

RF18.22 When you both were young where did you and Grandpa get married?

SF18.24 At *Venetie*. At that time we lived only around *Old John Lake*. Then one time we came to *Venetie* and were living here, and that's when we got married.

RF19.07 You didn't know each other before?

SF19.13 (Laughs.) Yes. At that time we lived in many places.
We were always on the move.

RF19.36 When you got married did you have a ceremony?

SF19.47 After we got married that fall.

RF19.50 A big preacher?

SF19.52 No, after we got married it was fall time already. After that we went to *Fort Yukon*. That's where the Indian preacher *William Loola* married us.

SF19.52 You went to *Fort Yukon*?

SF20.29 We went to *Fort Yukon*. That's where they married us.
After that we came back here.

20.47 We were living at *Venetie* until we went back up to *Old John Lake*. So that's where we stayed.

RF21.13 You lived there for a long time, huh?

SF21.14 Yes, until we went to *Otter Creek*.
We stayed there until we had three children.

RF21.27 Did you live there twenty-two years?

SF21.31 You mean at *Otter Creek*?

RF21.32 Yes.

SF21.33 Âa, ninghyùk tr'igwįįch'į'. Dąhkhyùk tr'igwįįch'į' gwaghàih tr'eechyaa kwaa ǫ'.

RF21.39 Ch'ìhłan shitsii shàa gwaandak it'ee *twentỳ-eight years* gwich'in roh.

SF21.45 Oonjìt *Ch'at'oonjik* t'agwaihnyàa.

RF21.46 Ǫǫ.

SF21.48 *Ch'at'oonjik* izhìk it'ee *twentỳ-eight years* tr'igwįįch'į'.

RF21.54 Zhik *Tryahtł'it* t'agwaihnyaa izhìk gwats'an izhìk gwats'ą' hòojil?

SF21.58 Ąąhą'. Aii *Tryahtł'it* gwats'an it'ee *Ch'at'oonjik* nìriindii Tr'igwich'įį łyâa kwaiik'ìt gwinzįį. Jidìi nin tsal kwaii gǫ̀ǫlįį. Aiits'ą' it'ee *twentỳ-eight years* oonjìt zhat tr'igwįįch'į'.

<sfwsl05B>

MR50.57 Aii naròonjik tł'ęę dèegwąhkhan tr'iinin ni'įį?

SF51.06 *Two year* ts'ą' reh.

MR52.38 Aii duulèe jyàhts'ą' ganandàii gwich'in nàhnyàa, duulèe *Gold Càmp* gwats'ą' *move* hohłyàa gwats'ą' dąhthee hee nihłòodhoojìk t'ôonch'yaa nyàa.

SF52.52 Diigii nąįį *five* goodlit gwiizhìk *Gold Càmp* nìriinjìl. Tr'ohchìt shòonjik tł'ęę, dzaa gwiizhìk shòonjik, aiitł'ęę gwats'an it'ee. . .

MR56.18 Nijìn nihkheenàkhwarąhchįį?

SF56.20 *Gwichyaa* hee, *William Ginkhii* nihkheedanąhchii.

<sfws105Bb>

MR5.29 Aii naròonjik dąį' tr'ookìt *Gwichyaa Zheh* gwąąh'yą' lèe t'ôonch'yàa, *or* gwikįh dąį' chan gwąąh'yą'?

SF5.36 Gwats'ą' dąį' gwąął'yą' t'ôonch'yàa. Tth'aih sharoonjii kwaa dąį' *Gwichyaa* gwąął'yą'. Izhìk t'ee ti'yąą gavàa dhiidìi, *Gwichyaa* tr'oochìt gwąął'yą' gwats'an chan *Circle* chan gwąął'ya'.

6.01 Izhìk gwats'an t'ee k'ìinjik neereejil ts'ą' t'ee dzaa gwee'àn chan tr'igwiinch'į' t'ôonch'yàa.

MR7.53 Aii *Circlè* oonjì' nàdhoojil dąį' *Circle* dèegii'ìn, gwitr'it gǫ̀ǫlįį?

SF21.33 We lived there a long time. I can't say how many years we lived there.

RF21.39 That one time my grandfather told me it was twenty-eight years.

SF21.45 I'm talking about the *Koness River* up there.

RF21.46 Oh.

SF21.48 The *Koness River* was where we lived for twenty-eight years.

RF21.54 Did you move there from the place called *Otter Creek*?

SF21.58 Yes. We moved from *Otter Creek* to the *Koness River*. It was a nice village then. There was lots of small game. So we lived there twenty-eight years.

<sfwsl05B>

MR50.57 How soon did you have your first child after marriage?

SF51.06 After two years.

MR52.38 He (*Mike Holloway*) is trying to figure out what year you got married by asking you how long it was after you got married before you moved to *Gold Camp*.

SF52.52 We moved to *Gold Camp* after having five children. After we got married, then. . .

MR56.18 Where did you get married?

SF56.20 *Preacher William* [*Loola*] married us at *Fort Yukon*.

<sfws105Bb>

MR5.29 Was that your first time at *Fort Yukon* when you went there to get married?

SF5.36 I had been there before. I went to *Fort Yukon* way before I got married. I was still living with my father and mother. We went to *Fort Yukon* and then to *Circle*.

6.01 We came back down and lived around here too.

MR7.53 When you went over to *Circle*, what did you all do over there? Were there any jobs?

SF8.01 Gwitr'it gokwaa zhyąą dinjii khaihłok gwich'įį. Jyàa dìginch'yaa ts'ą' *school* chan gokwàa, *school* chan gokwàa, ts'ą' zhyąą khaihłok dinjii t'inch'yàa.

Adagogwaandàii. Zhat gwinzįį ts'ą' aiits'ą' gilęįį ts'ą' zhat gwigwich'įį t'agavaihnyàa.

8.49 Łuk keegii'in ts'ą' dats'an goonilì', ch'atthąįį goonilì' kwaii hàa jyàa dìgii'in ts'ą' zhyąą *town* shriit'agwąhtsii gòo'ąįį. Izhìk dąį' lèe làraa geechyàa? Izhìk dąį' t'ee yeedì' làraa aragwąh'ąįį gwinyąą. Aii ch'iinii łąą chuuluh jyàa dąhchyaa ch'iinii nǐin'èe, googàa Dinjii Zhuh iihàanii kwàa.

MR9.27 Aii nijìn dèe *gold* gogwąh'ąįį łii?

SF9.29 Yeedì' *Wisemàn*[1] izhìk gwìdì', làraa aragwàh'ąįį gwinyàa. Vàanòodlit ch'iinii hijyàa.

MR10.39 Aii *gold* gogwąh'ąįį dąį' izhìk gwànaa dąį' naròonjik tł'ęę t'igiizhìk *or* narooheendal gwats'ą'?

SF10.52 Gwats'ą' hee.

10.53-14.46[2]

SF14.47 Izhìk jyàa digwiizhìk tł'ęę t'ee aii shoondee chan nǐindhat ts'ą' shaghwaii *Darlene* chan nǐindhàt. Aiitł'ęę t'ee ti'yąą nąįį jii han gwinjik ch'iindàk neegohòojil ts'ą' oondee *Arctic Villàge* k'eeriidàl nàhąą? Izhìk gwats'an t'ee zhat ch'iindàk gwizhrįh tr'igwich'įį.

MR15.16 Aii dzaa nǐindhat lèe t'inch'yaa? Noondee?

SF15.18 Ąąhą'. Aii chan nǐindhat ts'ą' *Darlene* chan nǐindhat aiitł'ęę t'ee yeendàk neerohòojìl.

MR15.48 Aii nihłoodhoojìk dąį' *Gwichyaa Zheh* ootthàn nàdhoo'oo hęę?

SF15.53 Ootthàn nàraa'oo ts'ą' khanh chan oochyąą neerii'òo.

MR16.07 Nahan chan izhìk dąį' gwandàii?

SF Ąąhą'.

MR16.12 Gàh aii yù'? Nahan, nitì', noondee nąįį gàa gogwandàii?

1. *Wiseman* is a small mining town settlement on the *Middle Fork* of the *Koyukuk River*, about one hundred miles northwest of *Venetie* in the central *Brooks Range*. A gold rush occurred there in 1907-1908. See Robert Marshall's classic, *Arctic Village* (1933).

2. Section not transcribed. —CM

SF8.01 There were no jobs. People just lived in one place and there was no school. People just lived in a group there, trying to make a living because it was good there for animals.

There were lots of people living there.

8.49 They fished and hunted ducks and moose. The town was big. Nobody cared about money. That was the time we heard of a gold rush somewhere downriver. A wide winter trail (stampede) came down from there. But none of the Indians went for it. At that time, people didn't think money was important.

MR9.27 Do you remember where they found gold?

SF9.29 There was talk about a gold rush somewhere around *Wiseman*. Lots of white people started coming this way.

MR10.39 When they found gold at that time, did it happen after or before you got married?

SF10.52 Before.

10.53-14.46

SF14.47 My older brother died shortly after that and also my sister-in-law *Darlene*. After this happened, my parents and I came back through this way along the river going back up to *Arctic Village*, you see? From then on, we only lived up that way.

MR15.16 Did your oldest brother die here [in *Venetie*]?

SF15.18 Yes. He died and so did *Darlene*, so after that, we went back up.

MR15.48 Did you go to *Fort Yukon* when you both got married?

SF15.53 We went down and came back up right away.

MR16.07 Was your mother living at that time?

SF Yes.

MR16.12 Who else was living? Were your parents and your older brother still alive?

SF16.19 Aii tthak gogwandàii gàa ni'ęę aii oondàk neeriijil izhìk it'ee oondee *Old John Lake* izhìk vęę tr'igwich'įį izhìk t'ee ni'ęę chan nĭindhàt. Aiits'ą' ti'yąą zhrįh.

17.20 Izhìk oondòk jyàa dìgwiizhìk gwats'an it'ee jii, izhìk gwats'an t'ee *Arctic Villàge* zhat dąį' dinjii kwàa. Zhyąą zhat tr'igwich'įį kwàa. Aiits'ą' t'ee ch'iinjì' tr'ahàajil izhìk it'ee oondee *Old John Lake,* izhìk t'ee tr'iinin tr'ohchìt shi'į'.

17.57 Aiitł'ęę t'ee chan hee deetthàn ts'ąįį tr'ahàajil ts'ą' oochìt *Tryahtł'it*, izhìk gwà'àn gwizhrįh chan niinzhùk tr'igwinch'į'.

18.18 Izhìk hee chan diizheh gòo'ąįį, aii t'ee zhat dąį' Vàanòodlit shìi kwaii gǫǫlįį kwàa. Aiits'ą' ch'atthąįį nin tsal zhrįh ch'andaa t'èegwąąhch'yàa aii eenjit t'ee zhik zheh ch'iinii. Vadzaih hah'òo eenjit it'ee gwinzįį ts'ą' izhìk t'ee tr'igwich'ii t'ihnyąą. Shaghwaii *Halvìr* nąįį hàa, *Dihch'į' Tsal* nąįį gàa tthak izhìk gwà'àn gwizhrįh tr'igwich'įį.

MR19.03 *Anàazhrii Tsal* reh hęę? Aii *Henrỳ* òozhii gàa *valast-nàme* aii yu'? *Albèrt Tritt* chan lèe vaiinyàa?

SF Izhìk dąį' oondàk kwaiik'it gokwàa.

MR22.07 Aii izhìk dąį' jùu *chief* nilįį? Aii oondìt *Tryahtł'it* gwinyaa?

SF22.16 *Chief* gǫǫlįį kwàa.

MR22.28 Nijin dąį' gwats'an t'ee *chief* gahtsìk t'iginch'yàa?

SF22.33 Aii t'ee izhìk gwats'ą' it'ee geegwaldak t'iihnyàa. Aiits'ą' izhìk gwats'an *Tryahtł'it* chan dąąch'yaa khaii lęįį tr'igwinch'į', izhìk chan *twenty five years* tr'igwiinch'į', *Ch'at'oonjik*. Izhìk gwats'an t'ee yaaghà' *Arctic Village* gwats'ą' rahàajil, izhìk yaaghà' nee'ii *Eziàs* vaihnyàa.

23.15 Aii niti' hàa jyàa diginyaa naihnyaa ìjìi? Aii hàa t'ee geegiginkhii akhài' dinjii łagwàłjik ts'ą' t'ee *Arctic Village* kwaiik'ìt gòodlìt, zheh chan gwigwinghàn.

MR24.32 Izhìk chan dąhyùk gooch'į' t'ôonch'yàa?

SF Nijìn?

MR *Ch'at'oonjik.*

SF16.19 All of them were living, but when we came back up and were living at *Old John Lake*, my mother also died there. So there was just my father.

17.20 After that happened there was nobody at *Arctic Village*; nobody was living there. We continued traveling, and it was at *Old John Lake* that I had my first child.

17.57 We continued traveling south of there to *Otter Creek*, and we stayed there for a long time.

18.18 We had our house there. There was no white man's food at that time. We only subsisted on moose, caribou, and small game. The caribou migrated through there. I'm saying that's why we had our house there and were living there. My brother-in-law *Halvir* (*Albert Tritt*), *Old Man Tsal,* and my family were living there.

MR19.03 Is that who they call *Anaazhrii Tsal?* I know his name is *Henry* but what is his last name? Did you also say *Albert Tritt* was living there?

SF Yes, there were no villages around there at that time.

MR22.07 Who was chief at that time? At that place they call *Otter Creek*?

SF22.16 There was no chief.

SF22.28 When did they start having chiefs?

SF22.33 I'm telling you stories before we started having chiefs. From then on, we stayed at *Otter Creek* for many winters. And then we moved north of there to the *Koness River*, where we lived for twenty-five years. From there, we moved to *Arctic Village*. Remember I mentioned your uncle *Ezias* (*Simon*) earlier.

23.15 Remember I mentioned him and your father always talking about it? They both gathered people together and started *Arctic Village*, and they also built houses.

MR24.32 How long did you stay there?

SF Where?

MR *Koness River*.

SF24.38 *Twenty-five years* zhat tr'igwiinch'į', tr'iinin lęįį tr'ii'ìi, nąhąą? Aiits'ą' dąįį chan lęįį tr'ii'ìi.

<sfws105Bb>

MR40.23 Tr'ookìt tr'iinin ni'įį dąį' neegògwàntrii? Tr'iinin ni'įį neegògwàntrii?

SF40.29 Ąąhą'. Khaiinjih *doctòr* nał'in kwaa ts'ą' tthak shigii gwilìk t'ôonch'yàa. Łyâa gwìizųų gwąął'in ch'yąą.

MR40.50 Aii jùu nits'ìnyàa?

SF40.51 Aii tr'ìnjàa nąįį reh.

MR40.54 Aii jùu nąįį?

SF40.55 Aii oondee sheejii *Saràh* chan.[3]

Aii tr'ìnjàa nąįį tthak zhat dąį' tr'iinin gwihilìk dąį' tthak nihts'ìgiinyaa t'inch'yàa. Nihk'èegąątìi. Izhìk gwik'it t'iginch'yaa tr'ìnjàa lęįį nąįį nihk'ąątii t'ôonch'yàa.

41.30 Gwats'an nijìn gògòontrii k'ìt t'ôonch'yaa dąį'? Aii dąį' chan oondee sheejii *Sarah* chan jyàa diì'ìn. Aii chan diizhìt tr'iinin goondak. Tr'iinin nįįzhùk hàa tr'iłts'ik dąį' *doctor* k'ìt t'igii'ìn.

MR42.30 Ch'adąį' gwànaa goolàt nąįį tr'iinin khyų' gii'įį hàa chan nàgadhak lèe t'inch'yàa?

SF42.39 Ąąhą', gàa lęįh kwaa nąįį jyàa diì'in gwìch'in. Tr'iinin shų' googwilìi dąį' aii geetèe tr'iinin hàa nàdhak gàa lęįį t'ii'in kwàa.

42.56 Geetàk hee gwizhrįh jyàa dìgwinjìk gwinyàa. Aii zhyąą gwîihtth'ak reh. Yaaghà' shitsųh, *John Fred* vahan, aii t'ee shandàh jyàa diizhìk. *John Fred* vahan.

43.21 Aii t'ee nitsìi kwaa nàhąą? Aiits'ą' vats'ąįį chan tr'iinin gwehèelyàa.

Aii t'ee, aii hàa t'ee jii zhyąą vizhìt k'àiich'ii andoo k'ìt t'igwinyaa giyàhnyàa. Ts'ą' aii hàa, aii tr'iinin vizhìt ts'ą', aii hàa t'ee vakwàa, izhìk t'ee shandàh t'iizhìk.

MK43.38 Aii lèe chąąvał zhìt văinyaa ch'yąą?

SF Ąąhą'.

MR44.05 Aii ijùk t'iizhìk, *Gold Camp* gehdìt?

3. This is Sarah Tritt, a.k.a. Sarah Ghoo, the wife of Reverend Albert Tritt. —JE

SF24.38 We lived there for twenty-five years. We had lots of children, you see? And lots of black flies too.

<sfws105Bb>

MR40.23 Did you have problems giving birth to your first child? Did you have a long and hard labor?

SF40.29 Yes. I didn't see a doctor during any of my pregnancies or childbirths. I remember having really bad times being sick.

MR40.50 Who helped you?

SF40.51 The women.

MR40.54 Who were they?

SF40.55 Like my older sister *Sarah* (*Tritt*).

Women always helped each other when someone was in labor. They helped one another.

41.30 Whenever someone went through long and hard labor? *Sarah* was the one that acted like a doctor. She even reached inside the woman and took out the baby.

MR42.30 Did anyone ever die from having hard times giving birth?

SF42.39 Yes, but not too many of them. Some died from complications but not that many.

42.56 Sometimes we only heard of someone doing that. My grandmother, the mother of *John Fredson*, did that right in front of me. *John Fredson's* mother.

43.21 *John Fredson* was small at that time, you see? It happened with the child that came right after him.

They say they even heard a sound inside her belly during her labor. She was pregnant and she died during childbirth right in front of me.

MK43.38 Was she the one you mentioned that died in a toboggan?

SF Yes.

MR44.05 Where did it happen? Was it below *Gold Camp*?

SF44.09 Ąąhą’. *Gold Càmp* gehdìt zhik *Gwat’òodląįh* ginyaa ijìi? Oodìt zheh gehdìt k’iidì’ ddhah tsal dhitìn. Aii gwats’ą’ k’iidì’ tan kak t’iizhìk.

44.46 Aii zhik jyàa dìheenjyàa kwaa gwìch’in gàa zhik dinjii lęįį zhat nǐinjìk nàhąą? Aii ch’ìhłak nàrah’an, kwàntee jyàa dǐi’in gàanìgwìi’aii giyàhnyàa. Aii łyâa t’iyinlìk giyàhnyaa t’aràhnyàa.

45.09 Aii t’ee yaaghà’ nitii *Henrỳ* vijùu *Annie Ch’its’ų’* giyàhnyaa aii reh.

Aii reh yùunjik giyàhnyaa t’igiyàhnyąą.[4]

53.56 Gwįhdàii datthak *hard time* zhìt gwizhrįh gwiindàii t’ôonch’yàa (adlaa).[5]

MR58.42 Aii tr’iinin gwandàii lèe t’inch’yàa?

SF58.44 Aii t’ee gwandàii kwaa ts’ą’ t’ee shats’an tr’iyǎąhchįį. Nâą, zhyąą diineełèegahàa’òo, aiits’ą’ t’ee t’ashàhnyàa, “Shijùu, yaaghà’ googà’ diiroonyaa kwàt yaaghà’ traa chan kwàa, tr’iinin nąįį chan traa oonjii gagąhtsii kwàa. Traa chan kwaa ts’ą’ t’ee yeedàk traa tsal khàhihtthàa gwiizhìk oodąą neiinchìk,” shàhnyàa. Aii gwik’ìt t’igwìizhìk ts’ą’ traa lęįį tr’òonjìk. Aii chan tthak dàa’ąįį hàa vik’èech’araachil ts’ą’ diikwàntee chan traa lęįį nìriinlìi. Datthak K’èegwaadhat gǫǫlįį gwinyaa, aii k’ìighai’ t’igwii’ìn.

60.24 Khaiinjih *two day, two night* hàa tthak àłts’ìk.

Gàhshandàii kwàa. Gàhshandàii kwaa gòodlìt. Aii jyàa gwizhrįh t’agwąhsų’ t’igwìizhìk googàa aii shįį tr’ohchìt dhałts’ik akhài’. . .

61.10 Aii k’ìighai’ datthak K’èegwaadhat gǫǫlįį gwinyaa łi’hàa t’igwinyaa gwìch’in jyàa nihthan. *Lucy* vats’ąįį yehèelyaa aii t’iizhìk.

4. Short sections not transcribed. —CM

5. Short sections not transcribed. —CM

SF44.09 Yes, you remember that place called *Gwat'oodląįįh* down below *Gold Camp*? That small mountain downriver from the cabin? It happened on the ice just in front of that mountain, so they say.

44.46 I don't think it would have happened, but lots of people died in that area, you see? One of their spirits was going around, and people even heard it outside of their houses, they say. The spirit took it, they say.

45.09 Your uncle *Henry's* sister, *Annie Ch'itsų's* spirit, took the baby, they say. She really did.

53.56 I had a hard life all my life (laughs).

MR58.42 Did the child live?

SF58.44 The baby was stillborn when she took it out from inside of me. Look, our husbands just left us alone there, and she said to me, "My younger sister, no one cares for us and there is no wood. The children are too small to help. There's no wood, so bring it into camp while I chop it." And I was doing that and had lots of wood. She and I split all the wood and piled it outside our house. They say we did it all because of God's help.

60.24 I was in labor for almost two days and two nights.

I don't remember. I don't remember how it turned out. I went into a coma. A miracle happened to us, and I went into labor first but. . .

61.10 That's why I think it's true that they say there really is a God. That was the child after *Lucy*.

61.56 Aii vats'ąįį t'iizhìk ts'ą̀', nah, gwintł'òo ihtree roh. Aii tr'iinin gwandàii kwaa ts'ą̀' vagòodlit, nàhąą? Aiits'ą̀' gwintł'òo ihtrèe.[6]

62.22 Ihtree ts'ą̀' jyàa diihnyaa akhài' t'ee aii tr'iinin dzaa ts'ąįį shigin kak deeneeriłchįį łii. Shintł'èerąhchįį. Aiits'ą̀' t'ee zhat gwats'an chan vits'eehòoshizhii ts'ą̀' t'ee. . .

Fig. 25. Johnny Frank unloading moose meat at Venetie, circa 1960. Photo courtesy of Richard Birchell.

6. This tragic event must have occurred around 1910, since daughter Lucy was born in 1909 and Nathaniel came into the world in 1911. Sarah was about eighteen at the time. See the Frank Family Tree in Appendix A. —CM

61.56 It happened with that child. Look, I cried and cried. That baby was a stillborn, you see? So I cried lots.

62.22 I cried and what I said was another baby was given back to me here. I dreamt about a baby being put back in my arms.

Then I became pregnant again soon after that. . .

Fig. 26. David Frank (Neerahadhak) with Johnny Frank dressed up as General MacArthur in Fort Yukon, circa 1951. Acc #95-030-149, Rebecca Drane Collection, Alaska and Polar Regions Archives, Rasmuson Library, University of Alaska Fairbanks.

Sarah Frank

Sarah Ts'ą̀' Shyaaghan Nąįį Hàa Mil Vahan

<sfws105Fa>

SF9.16 Aiits'ą̀' aii *Mil Vahan*, aii t'ee hèedài' gwànaa. Nitì' shòonjik tł'ęę, oondee *Vashrą̀įį K'ǫǫ* hee k'ineeriidàl.[1] Izhìk hee t'ee zhik gwà'àn t'ee neeshrâahch'yaa tsèeniichįį.

9.44 Aiits'ą̀' t'ee diits'ą̀' nihděiinzhii ts'ą̀' t'ee diihàa gwich'įį aii shitsųh.

DF Hmm.

SF9.53 Neehidik kwàa, aiits'ą̀' khaii neerihiinjìk chan chąąval zhìt tr'iłdii ts'ą̀' neerahahchik izhìk hee. Geetèe hee diihàa gwaandak t'agwaihnyą̀ą.

DF Hmm.

SF10.13 Khaii neerahahchik tł'ęę chan vijuu gwànaa it'ee łyâa veegògwantrii izhìk t'ee chan Ch'eekwaii naii oo'ęę nineedàl.

10.27 Nitsųh *Maggie* chan, aii chan hàa gwich'įį. Jyàa dàràh'in.

It'ee łyâa veegògwantrii, izhìk it'ee aii *Maggie* naii khagiyìldìi, izhìk it'ee, gwiizhìk *Chųųvęę* gwats'an Ch'eekwaii naii oo'ęę k'eedàl.

10.51 Aii t'ee oonjìt *Ch'idzèe*[2] ginyąą izhìk gwìnji' t'ee khaii gwigwich'įį. Izhìk hee chan gwats'ą̀' gahàajil roh.

Nitsųh *Maggie Gilvìt* hàa.

11.14 Izhìk gwìnji' it'ee nįįdhat į'.

DF11.16 Hmm.

SF11.17 Izhìk t'ee Ch'eekwaii naii yanǎąhjìk t'inch'yàa.

DF Hmm.

SF11.52 *Aii Shitsųų Mil Vahan* aii t'ee ti'yąą chih dąį' vagǫ̀ǫlįį.

---

1. *Vashrąįį K'ǫǫ: Arctic Village t'agwarahnyaa.* We call *Arctic Village* after this small creek which flows into the East Fork of the *Chandalar River*. —JE & CM

2. *Ch'idzee—Sheenjik gwa'an ddhah oozhri' t'arahnyąą.* 'Its Ear'. This is the name of a mountain toward the *Sheenjik River*. —JE

Sarah Frank

Sarah and the Old Women
Mil Vahan

<sfws105Fa>

SF9.16 And so back during the time of *Mil Vahan.* Not long after your father and I got married, that poor thing was old and frail, and we came back to *Arctic Village*.

9.44 My great-grandmother, *Mil's* mother, moved in with us.

DF Hmm.

SF9.53 She couldn't walk, so whenever we traveled, we hauled her around in a toboggan. I'm telling you the stories that she used to tell us.

DF Hmm.

SF10.13 We used to haul her around with a toboggan. Not long after that, she was too old to move around, and that's the time the Inuit used to come over.

10.27 She also was staying with your grandmother *Maggie*. Some Inuit came over from the *Arctic Coast* when she was about to die.

10.51 Your grandmother *Maggie Gilbert* and *Gilbert Joseph* were living at *Its Ear Mountain* during the winter, and that's where they took her. They were living with the Inuit there.

11.14 She died right around there.

DF11.16 Hmm.

SF11.17 The Inuit buried her there.

DF Hmm.

SF11.52 My great-grandmother *Mil* was born before my father.

Treenahtsyàh[3]

<sfkf2b>

SF36.13 Shyaaghan goonàandak nilįį, aii *Treenahtsyàh.* Ąįį nąįį k'iighai' gwinzįį gaandaii t'iginyąą.

CF36.24 Łyâa zhyąą shyaaghan dhidlìt giyàhnyaa, aii hee?

SF Jùudèe?

CF36.29 *Shitsųų Treenahtsyàh* t'aihnyàa.

SF36.35 Neeshrâahch'yaa ts'ą' shyaaghan dhidlìt. Aii it'ee diikhwan it'ee vik'èerąąhtii gwiizhìk yaaghà' vigii *Christian Choo* nąįį yaaghà' vitseii nąįį chat gǫǫlįį googàa giik'ęęłtįį kwaa t'inch'yàa.

CF Hęę.

SF37.07 Aii it'ee tr'ohchìt t'ee oondee *Vashrąįį K'ǫǫ*. Vitseii nąįį gǫǫlįį googàa giyiłèehiidàl. Izhìk hee t'ee oonjìt *Ch'at'oonjik* gwinyaa, izhìk it'ee diihàa gwits'eehòozhìi. *One year* datthak kharaadi' į'. Aiitł'ęę it'ee shreenyàa yaaghà' k'ìteeriłchįį. Aiits'ą' datthak zhik gwigwich'įį ǫ'. Aiitł'ęę gehjųų gwànaa chan hee t'ee izhìk it'ee łi'hàa neeshrâahch'yaa. It'ee łyâa vagwandàii gàa łyâa neeshrâahch'yaa aii googàa chan it'ee giyiłèehoojìl. Aiits'ą' it'ee chan hee it'ee *Ch'at'oonjik* gwits'eerihiijyaa. Ts'ą' aii shyaaghan zhrįh dzaa dhidii ǫ'.

38.27 Nats'àhts'ą' chan veełèereheedàa gǫ'? Chan hee adàh neerihiłchįį. Akhài' it'ee izhìk it'ee łyâa vàagwąą'ąį' łii dǫhłįį. Jidìi tthak danaa kwaa googàa ch'iinjì' neereedàa hee tąįį hee vàa ihshyaa t'agaihnyąą. Izhìk hee it'ee dòonch'in zhyąą. *Vashrąįį K'ǫǫ* ree gagàhnyàa. Izhìk, "*Jesus* k'ineeheedik jaghaii dèe zhyąą datthak giłeegehijyàa," nyąą.

39.19 It'ee vagwandàii làt kwaa t'inyàa.

CF Ąąhą'.

---

3. Treenahtsyàh, whose English name was Eleanor, was Chief Christian's mother, and appears in the Frank family photo taken in 1927. See Fig. 15. —CM

Treenahtsyàh

<sfkf2b>

SF16.13 *Treenahtsyàh* was an old woman that told many stories. I learned a lot from her.

CF36.24 They say she lived until she grew very old, right?

SF Who?

CF36.29 My grandmother *Treenahtsyàh.*

SF36.35 She really aged poorly. We were the ones who took care of her and her children. Like *Chief Christian* and them. She had many other grandchildren, but they never took care of her.

CF Huh.

SF37.07 From the very beginning in *Arctic Village* her grandchildren used to leave her alone by herself there. She went with us to what you call the *Koness River.* We kept her there for one year. It was springtime when we took her back over to *Arctic Village*. Everybody was living there then. Later on she really got worse. She began to lose her mind, but still they left her alone by herself. Again we were going back to the *Koness River*. But the old woman was still there. And we couldn't just leave her there.

38.27 How could we take off without her? So once again we took her with us. She must have been near death then. As she was traveling with us during that spring, she kept falling. I used to walk way behind the others with her as we traveled back. That's when she was saying about what they now call *Arctic Village*. "That's where *Jesus* is going to return. Why do they leave the place?" she said.

39.19 She was beginning to lose her mind then.

CF Yes.

SF39.25 Jyàa deheenjyàa łee reh. Aii gwiizhìk it'ee zhik *Vashràįį K'ǫǫ* gehdee *Van Choh* dha'ąįį jyàa nàa'ąį'. Izhìk gwà'àn it'ee nitsii vadzaih inghàn. Aii oonjì' neereheelyaa eenjit vak'at dànrahgàįį. Aii gwiizhìk it'ee łyâa *Vashrąįį K'ǫǫ* geełèehakhaii geet'iindhan kwàa. "Zhat *Jésus* k'ineeheedik t'ôonch'yaa. Jaghaii datthak geełèegehijyàa?" nyàą.

40.10 Aiits'ą' yeendaa aii gwà'àn tthak aii nilįį vakat dàdhagąįį, tthaa chan naak'ìi roh. Aii tthaa chat tr'ahgàįį. Aii njyąh tr'aatsìi. "Dòonch'in zhyàą shìh kwaa gwits'eegihiidàl?" nyàą. Aiits'ą' nilįį ałvir dàį' chan ch'ik'eh gwitee ahchàk. Tthaa tłat chan vee ałvìr.

40.48 Tthaa ch'ìhłak veedàłchik zhyàą datthak a'àl. Nilįį chan gwik'ìt t'ał'ìn. Googàa aii ch'ìk vehzhee geełèehalzhik aii gwiizhìk it'ee, "Dòonch'in zhyàą shìh kwaa gwits'eegihiidàl?" nyàą. Łyâa gwìizųų t'inyaa ts'ą' it'ee *Vashràįį K'ǫǫ* chan ootthàn vàhnìneerahojil į'. Izhìk gęhdìt it'ee *Albèrt* chan ts'ą' *Gilvit*, *Jimmy, Titùs* aii datthak gęhdìt shìh gahgąįį gwigwich'įį. Izhìk oonìn yeenjit nòozhìi, nitsii. Googàa chan oodąą han neegogwąą'in kwàa.

42.09 Ts'ą' chan hee oodàk giveeneedhizhìi. Izhìk at'ôohju' hee it'ee dinjii nąįį yàhneejìl. Gwiizhìk oodee tr igwich'įį. Izhìk chan yaaghà' shyaaghan dhidii diigìitł'ìt. Aiits'ą' it'ee t'ôohju' oodąą neegiijil dinjii nąįį. Izhìk tǫǫ it'ee t'ee vàa zheh gòok'in į'.

CF Hęę'.

SF42.49 Jyàa deheenjyàa eh'an t'inyaa łii. Diikhwan aii nihts'ą' deediinyaa ts'ą' geegwaraandak jì' łyâa shoo heelyaa t'inch'yaa, nàhąą.

CF Ąąhą'.

SF39.25 Something was going to happen to her. Meanwhile your grandfather killed some caribou near the very end of this big lake above *Arctic Village*. We wanted to take that caribou meat with us so we were half-drying it. Yet she really didn't want to leave *Arctic Village*. She said, "That's where *Jesus* is supposed to return. Why is everybody leaving?"

40.10 So all the meat was half-dried, and the ground squirrels were fat, so they dried ground squirrel meat. They were saving some for their travel ahead. She also said, "Why do they go where there's no food?" And when they boiled meat they put some fat in with it. They even boiled fat ground squirrel.

40.48 They dished her up a whole ground squirrel and she ate it all. She did the same with meat. As I put her dishes away she said, "Why do they want to go where there's no food?" She was just getting pretty bad so we all went back down to *Arctic Village* with her. Not too far down from there is where *Albert*, *Gilbert*, *Jimmy*, *Titus*, and all of them were drying meat and living. So your grandfather went over there for her. But they never checked on her.

42.09 So he went back over there again. This time some of them came back with him. But we stayed there. And meanwhile the old woman was all by herself. So the men returned from checking on her. That's when she burned to death after her house caught on fire.

CF Huh.

SF42.49 So that's what was going to happen to her. That's why she said that. If she and I tell about it, I'm sure she'll mention me, you see.

CF Yes.

Lucy Nahthąįį Hàa

<sfkfla>

SF0.09 Ninjiraanąįį chan łyâa gwit'èegwąąhch'yàa. Àkwàt chan shyaaghan *four* nąįį gook'èerąąthtìi. Ch'ìhłak ginlįį ts'ą. *One year* gook'èerąąhtìi. Izhìk chan nitsii vahan aii łyâa zhyąą shyaaghan ghoo zhyąą nilįį, ak'ìi.[4] Aiits'ą' chaavał zhìt dhidii ìizùų. Nijìn gwintsàl chuuluh jyàa dǐnch'yaa it'ee jyàa dǐnjik. Âa, shat'àii hàa oihtà' googàa shàh jyàa dǐnjik. Vàh dachąąvał taghàl.

1.02 Izhìk hee ch'ìhłan chaavał zhit tr'avaghòo àanàii. It'ee zhik tsił khyųų gwintsàl jyàa dòonch'yaa nàhąą. Izhìk chuuluh kat t'ee vàa chaavał taghàa. Łì'hàa shat'àii hàa goitą' googàa, gwiizhìk chan tr'iinin ihkhwaa ǫ'. Ąįįts'ą' it'ee gòhch'it geet'ihthan kwàa. Ddhah kat gwatah rijyàa roh, ts'ą' t'ee ląįį nąįį chan shik'èegogwahthat roh. Izhìk chan hee chaavał zhìt shàa tr'avaghòo aanàii. Aiitł'ęę łąįį nehshrit zhak oodhiijìk ts'ą' it'ee goots'ìgįįhkhìi. Gwiizhìk it'ee k'iinii chuuluh njik ch'idzee'aa aii shyaaghan.

2.27 Gwiizhìk oozhee chaavał zhìt, oozhee aat'oo k'iindàa jèiinch'yaa nàhąą. Dzaa viteetak gwatsal gwànlįį. Aiits'ą it'ee ch'ik, shrii kwaii hàa gwizhìt dhidlii tee gwaał'in akhài' shrii gwintsàl diitįį vachan ch'ìitsii reh, jyàa dąhtsii (yaa'in). Aii t'ee khałtin ts'ą' t'ee k'iizhàk chaavał deetak gwankeitthaii vatąį' łoonaii chan akwaa ǫ' diitįį roh. Aiits'ą' it'ee tł'yah hàa vatąį' kat gwinlęįį adhałtł'ìį. Shyaaghan vàa chaavał tineeghàl.

4.00 Khaii, shin hàa chan neerihiinjìk. Izhìk ch'ìhłan t'ee zhah kwaa gwiizhìk chan khał hàa tr'ahàandìi. Shin kat zhah kwaa gwiizhìk ląįį tł'yah dahk'ii ts'ą' ree chaavał hàa tr'ěenjyàa.

KF4.37 Nijìn gwà'àn hee t'akhwah'in?

SF4.40 Oondee *Vashrąįį K'ǫǫ* ddhah kat ree.

4. Sarah is referring here to Johnny Frank's mother, Lucy Ch'igwihch'in. —CM

Lucy and Nahthąąį

<sfkfla>

SF0.09 We had to think fast sometimes. We were taking care of four elderly women, one at a time. We took care of them for one year. Your grandfather's mother was a really small, round-like, and fat old woman. It was hard for her to get in the toboggan. Every time the trail tipped a little bit to the side she fell off. Oh, I hung on tight, but it still happened. The toboggan tipped over.

1.02 One time she rolled off the toboggan. All the toboggan did was hit the side of the snowdrift on the trail. I hung on tight with all my strength, but I was packing a baby on my back. Finally I didn't like it. We still had to go over the mountains, but my dogs minded me well. Again she rolled off the sled. After that I finally stopped the dogs by just talking to them. Meanwhile that old woman was crawling along the trail behind me.

2.27 The bottom of the toboggan was made of birch wood, and here there was a crack between the birch wood, you see. So I was searching in the toboggan where all the cookware was, and I found a knife with a thick blade and the metal handle was this big (gesturing). So I took it out and stuck it in the crack in the wood in the bottom of the toboggan. The handle of the knife is strong because it is so thick. Then I tightened the rope around her many times. After that the old woman never tipped the toboggan over again.

4.00 Both winter and summer we traveled. One time we started our journey with a sled when there was no snow. It was like summer while we were traveling with dogs harnessed to a sled.

KF4.37 Where was this?

SF4.40 It was back there in the mountains near *Arctic Village*.

<sfws105Ca>

MR2.33 Aii ijùk ts'ąįį shrìt dhoodìi?

SF2.36 *Tryahtł'it* izhìk tr'aadìi. Yaaghà' nahgwàn chan diighàih dinjii kwaa gwiizhìk yaaghà' nitì' vahanh, aii zhrįh danàa dhidìi. Akhài' aii chan t'ee diits'ą' shòo dhidlìt kwaa ts'ą' chan dineełeehòozhìi. Aiits'ą' łyâa sheejii *Saràh* hàa zhrįh zhat tr'aadii reh.

4.11 Łì'hàa khaiinjih gwihndàii datthak *hard times* gwąął'yà' t'ôonch'yàa.

MR6.36 Izhìk dąį' dąhkhyùk shìh khwa'į' kwaa shrǫǫ yindhàn? Dąąch'yaa *months?*

SF6.41 Khaiinjih *one month* tthak gwinzįį ch'irin'àl kwàa. Tr'iinin nitsìi nąįį googàa tthak zhyąą k'angilt'aii ts'ą' gwizhrįh t'iginch'yàa.

16.10 Zhat gwats'ą' geełèeriheedàa kwaa akhài' nitsųų *Nahthąįį* nàhąą? Neehidik kwaa aii neerahahchik, nàhąą? Aii vak'àa gòodhaii nàgwàanàii. Neehidik kwaa ts'ą' neerahahchik, nàhąą? Aii gwiizhìk łąįį tthak chan zhyąą àn dhidlìt, nàhąą?

17.14 Zhat dąį' tr'agwandàii shìh chan gǫǫlįį kwaa, nàhąą? Aiits'ą' shyaaghan nąįį vak'ąątii kwaa k'ìt t'inch'yaa nąįį, *four* nąįį. Jii chan tr'oochìt neerahahchik.

18.09 Izhìk zhat dąį' diikhwan aii? Oonjìt *Ch'at'oonjik* tr'igwich'įį, nàhąą? Aiits'ą' khaiits'ą' vadzaih gǫǫlįį ts'ą' shìh lęįį tr'iłtsąįį. Dachan tsiik'ìt jyàa dàgwąhtsii datthak shìh dèedàa'ąi' tr'iłtsąįį. Shìh lęįį tr'ii'įį akhài' yaaghà' *Vashràįį K'ǫǫ* gwich'in ch'atthąįį gąąh'yà' kwaa ts'ą' aiits'ą' gooshìi kwaa, nàhąą? Aiits'ą' oonjì' dineenìneegiidàl aii nąįį gòodhaii nidiigadąąhnąįį t'igwìizhìk.

MR18.49 Nakhwashìi kwaa nàgwaanaii gwiizhìk jàghaii V*ashràįį K'ǫǫ* gwits'eekhwajil kwàa?

SF19.01 Nitì' aii gitr'îi'ee roh. Tr'ihijyàa gitr'îi'ee aiits'ą' gwiizhìk diishìi kwaa gwilìi, nàhąą? Aiits'ą' googàa gehnjì' ts'ąįį tr'ahoondì' nyaa izhìk chan łyâa gwìizųų gineedhihłyàa. Ch'iinjì' tr'ahoojyàa kwaa văihnyàa. Googàa nihk'ìt

<sfws105Ca>

MR2.33 Where were you two living?

SF2.36 We were at *Otter Creek*. No one was nearby either. Just your father's mother (*Lucy*) was with us, but she got mad and took off. So there was just my older sister *Sarah* and me staying there.

4.11 It seems like I had hard times all my life.

MR6.36 How long do you think you all had no food? How many months?

SF6.41 We hardly ate for one month. Even the bigger children only lay in bed.

16.10 We could have kept staying there, but your grandmother *Nahtthaii* couldn't walk, you see? So we were stuck there with her. She couldn't walk so we carried her when we traveled, you see? All the dogs died off too, you see?

17.14 There was no food at that time, see? We took care of four old ladies. She was the first one we took care of and we had to carry her.

18.09 The reason we were living there? We were living on the east side of the *Koness River,* you see? Because the caribou were plentiful that fall, we saved lots of meat. The wooden storage we made in the ground was full of food. We had lots of food but the *Arctic Village* people didn't get any caribou, so they kept coming to us for food and that got us in trouble, you see? That's why it happened.

MR18.49 How come you didn't go to *Arctic Village* when you had no food?

SF19.01 Your father refused. He refused to leave even though we were running out of food, you see? He wanted to move north instead, and I had a dream that if we moved, something really bad would happen to us. I told him I didn't want to go that way, but we went anyway. That's ch'iinjì' tr'ahàajil izhìk t'igwìizhìk. Zhat chan naazhrìi gàa gwandàii nah'in kwàa.

MR20.37 Aii izhìk dą̀į' *Arctic Villàge* gwats'ą̀' ninghìt geh'àn *Arctic Village* aii gwats'ą̀' gahàa'oo kwaa hęę?

SF20.43 Ą̀ąhą', izhìk chan shìh kwàa. Gooshìi kwaa datthak ts'ą̀'. Datthak giłèegahàajìl.

28.15 Aii *Treenahtsyàh* chan ts'ą̀' shitsųh *Mil Vahan* chan, *Nahthą̀įį*, yaaghà' nitì' vahan, jii nąįį łyâa zhyą̀ą khaii googàa chąąvał zhìt goorìłdii, neegoorihilùu. Shįį sheh'òk hee tr'eelìl.

28.49 Dèegwą̀htsii *hard time* tr'agwąąh'in googàa aii shyaaghan neeshrâahch'yaa zhyą̀ą vak'ą̆ątii kwaa aii nąįį tr'oondak aii k'èerąąhtii t'agwaihnyàa.

MR30.19 Izhìk dą̀į' jùu nąįį *Arctic Villàge* gwich'įį łìi?

SF30.23 Nijin dàį' dèe?

MR30.27 Aii shyaaghan dhik'in dą̀į'. Jùu nąįį zhat gwich'įį?

SF30.32 Zhat gehndìt gwigwich'įį. *Halvàr* chan ts'ą̀' *Gilvìt*, *Gabriel, Jimmy, Titus* nąįį hàa gehnjit gwigwich'įį googàa oonìn giveenìdhizhii ts'ą̀' aii shyaaghan nǫhjii gavàhnyaa googàa gwik'it t'igwii'in kwàa.[5] *Two times* oonìn giveenìdhìzhìi.

32.29 Zhat dą̀į' yaaghà' *Christian Choh famìly* nąįį, *Elijàh* nąįį chan aiits'ą̀' yaaghà' *Halvàr* nąįį chan.[6] Aii yaaghà' t'agą̂ąch'yaa naa! *Titùs* nąįį chan. T'agą̂ąch'yaa? Łì'hàa zhyą̀ą aii shyaaghan nąįį eełèegahadàl. Tthak gootsųh yinlįį nąįį reh. Gwiizųų.

MR33.47 Aiitł'ee nakhwashìi kwaa gòodlit aiitł'ęę hee reh hę̀ę?

SF Ą̀ąhą'.

MR Aiitł'ęę t'iizhìk lèe t'inch'yàa?

SF Jùu?

MR33.55 Aii shyaaghan *or* gwats'ą̀' hee?

5. The people Sarah refers to are Halvar (the Rev. Albert Tritt), Gilvit (Joseph), Gabriel Peter, Jimmy John, and Titus Peter (Kias Peter's and Naomi Tritt's father). —JE

6. The people Sarah is talking about are Chief Christian's family, Elijah Henry, and Halvàr (Rev. Albert Tritt). —JE

where we ran out of food. He hunted there but didn't get anything.

MK20.37 They didn't go to *Arctic Village* because it was too far, right?

SF20.43 Yes, they moved away too because there was no food there.

28.15 We took care of *Treenahtsyàh*, also grandma *Mil Vahan*, *Nahthaii*, and your father's mother (*Lucy*). We even hauled them around in the winter time. It was always me who pulled her along.

28.49 No matter how hard a time we had, we always took care of those poor old women. I'm talking about the poor old ladies we took in.

MR30.19 Who all was living at *Arctic Village*?

SF30.23 When was that?

MR30.27 When the old woman *(Tr'eenahtsyàh)* burned to death, who all was living there?

SF30.32 They lived right across from her. There were *Albert*, *Gilbert*, *Gabriel*, *Jimmy*, and *Titus* living there across from her. *Johnny* went over to them two times and told them to pick up the old woman, but they didn't do it.

32.29 There was *Chief Christian* and his family. Also *Elijah's*, *Albert's*, and *Titus's* families. See how many people there were? They always left that old woman by herself. And she was grandmother to all of them too. It was bad.

MR33.47 Did that happen after you ran out of food?

SF Yes.

MR Did it happen to her after that time?

SF Who?

MR33.55 That old woman, was it before or after?

SF34.07 Aiitł'ęę t'iizhìk? Aiitł'ęę t'ee gehnjìt *Ch'at'oonjik* tr'igwich'įį, nàhąą?

MR Mmm hmm.

SF34.07 Izhìk gwats'ą' dąį' t'ee chan datthak giyeełèehàajìl, aiits'ą' jyàa dinch'ii zheh gwaddhàa ch'àa tsal, nąhvyàa zhìt tseeniichįį. Aiits'ą' t'ee oonjì' adàh neerihìlchįį ts'ą' *one year* kharaadì'.

MR34.36 Izhìk lèe *Arctic Villàge* t'igiyìnlik?

SF Àąhą'.

SF34.53 Aii *Christian Choh* vigii chan kwaa, nàhąą? Googàa aii dahan eełèegihiidàl.

MR35.06 Nats'àhts'ą' oonjì' nǫǫhchįį, chąąvał hàa?

SF35.08 Ch'iinjì' shin gwinìindhaa ts'ą' khai ts'ą' vàh neereedàa. Nahgwàn tr'ahadàl.

36.03 Izhìk it'ee ch'iinjì' vàh neereedàa, nàhąą? Izhìk t'ee jyàa dòonch'yaa ddhah kat t'ôonch'yaa ts'ą' ch'iitthàn chii nąht'aii łee. Aii deetàa tr'ihijyàa. Izhìk it'ee tr'iinin ihkhwaa. Googàa vigìn oodhiinjìk ts'ą' t'ee ch'iinìn chii tee neehadhałchįį akhài' googàa zhyąą jyàa dìi'in ts'ą' oozhee chii chan vijìh chii deetak aatil. Aiits'ą' t'ee zhat zhyąą dhindii văihnyàa. Aiits'ą' aii tr'iinin ihkhwaa aii t'ee oondìt naałchįį. Aiitł'ęę t'ee oondàa vits'eehòoshizhìi, shyaaghan gąįh nilįį k'it t'inch'yaa googàa gwintł'òo nidìi t'aihnyàa.

37.07 Aiits'ą' t'ee gał oodhiinjìk ts'ą' t'ee gał nèekwąįį jyàa dàłthan aiits'ą' t'ee ihkhwaa. Ch'iinìn chii tee něiighwąąįį. Oozhee gał nihts'įį gihtthak jyàa dàł'in ts'ą' t'ee chii kat gwinzįį naal'aa ts'ą' chii deetàa hìdhiighwąįį. Akwàt chii deetak gwik'yăaltil jì'jii vatth'àn chan łèehàanaii, nàhąą. Aii tthak gitr'îih'ee ts'ą' t'ee izhìk chan chii deetàa neiighwąįį. Neeshrâahch'yaa.

SF34.07 It happened afterwards. We were living at the *Koness River* after that, you see?

MR Mmm hmm.

SF34.07 Before that, she was left alone again one time. She was lying in her raggedy little tent, so we took her back with us and took care of her for one year.

MR34.36 Was this in *Arctic Village*?

SF Yes.

SF34.53 *Chief Christian* had no children, you see? But he still left his mother alone all the time.

MR35.06 How did you take her over there? With a toboggan?

SF35.08 It was a hot summer, so we traveled very slowly with her during the fall time. We traveled short distances with her.

36.03 We were traveling back over with her, you see? We were on the mountain when we were passing down a rocky slope, and I was packing a child on my back, but I held on to her hands to walk her across. But her legs were weak and wobbly and almost slipped between the rocks, so I told her to just sit down there and wait while I took the child across first. I came back over for her. She looked like a very thin old woman, but she was very heavy.

37.07 So I packed her over the rocky slope on my back using two canes for support. I went across there using the canes among the rocks. If she stepped between those rocks and fell, she would break her leg, you see. I didn't want to see her get hurt like that. That's why I packed her across that rocky slope. She was too old and weak. Poor thing.

50.34 Aii ch'adąįį' oonjìt tr'igwich'įį dąįį' tr'iinin nąįį shàh lęįį. Izhìk t'ee *surveyòr* ch'ìhłak *Fitz* òozhii.[7]

MR50.54 Aii tr'iinin dąąch'yaa ni'įį gwiizhìk?

SF50.58 It'ee tr'iinin lęįį shi'įį gwiizhìk t'agwaihnyàa. Aii oondee dąįį' *Arctìc Villàge surveyòr* nąįį gwigwinch'į', tth'aih nakwaa dàį' hee. Izhìk dąįį' aii *Fitz,* aii t'ee łyâa sheiinyą' tr'iinin nąįį jyàa dìnch'ii *canvàs* zhrąįh tr'oondak. Aii t'ee thał givee'ałtsìi. Aiits'ą' łeeheech'aa gwits'į' chan dzaa vidreek'įį k'iizhąą chan ch'adhàh, aadzii kwat geekâałkak.

51.47 Aiits'ą' t'ee khan łach'aa kwaa, izhìk t'ee aii *surveyor* t'aihnyaa t'ee oondee *Arctic Villàge* digwigwìlgǫ'. Izhìk dąįį' aii *Fitz* òozhii aii shik gweedhaa diihàadhìdìi. Aii t'ee t'ashàhnyàa, shik vànàldàii.

52.13 "Łyâa oo'òk dinjii veegach'agwadhan k'ìt t'inch'yaa nąįį gǫǫlįį googàa nakhwan neeshrôohch'yaa googàa tr'iinin tthąįį' ìgweech'in kwaa goh'įį łyâa geenjit shòo ihłįį," shàhnyàa. Izhìk t'ee shiinyą' iłtsąįį. Aiits'ą' kwaiitryah ehdan shigii nąįį neehiidàl kwàa.

52.29 Jidii yaaghà' gwà'àn *rubbèr shoe pàc,* aii dį' nilįį. Aii chan kwaiitryah givee'ałtsii. Tł'il hàa k'âałkaii ts'ą'. Aiits'ą' kwaiitryah ehdan chan neegihiidàl kwàa. Jii givehłì' kak chan dzaa aadzii geekâałkak rǫh. Aiits'ą' gootthài' ìgweech'in kwaa, izhìk geenjit shòh nìlįį. Aii t'ee shiinyą' iłtsąįį.

53.42 Aiits'ą' chan aii jyàa dàgavał'in kwàt zhat gwanaa dąįį' chan *rubbèr* kwaa, nàhąą? *Rubbèrs* chan kwàa. Aiits'ą' chan ch'adhàh khăiht'ii? Ch'adhah dril khăiht'ii aii chan jii? Jii gookwài' nìyuaałdak ts'ą' t'ee łooch'yaa kwaa ts'ą' gookwai' nìyuaałdak jyàa dąhnjyaa ałtsìk. Aii k'aa chan kwaiitryah zhìt gaa'yùu, nàhąą? Aiits'ą' jii gootthąįį' nahtraa kwàa. Aii tthak jyàa dàgavał'yà'.

55.00 Nitì' chan *gumboot* veedhałtsąįį.

7. Fitz was the nickname for Gerald Fitzgerald of the U.S. Geological Survey, who visited the *Arctic Village* area in the summer of 1927. For details and early photos, see Mishler 2018. —CM

50.34 Once when we were living over there, I had too many children. There was a surveyor there by the name of *Fitz*.

MR50.54 How many children did you have at that time?

SF50.58 What I'm saying is I had lots of kids at that time. Some surveyors once stayed at *Arctic Village*, which was before you were born. At that time, *Fitz* told me something I was really proud of. I used to make black canvas pants for my children, and I sewed a piece of white caribou skin on the knee so it wouldn't tear.

51.47 The surveyors spent the whole spring in *Arctic Village* that time. The one called *Fitz* always visited us, and he told me something I always remember.

52.13 He told me, "There are lots of really rich people and even though you are poor, your children are not raggedy and their skin doesn't show through their clothing, and I'm proud of you." He made me proud of myself. They never went barefoot either.

52.29 I also made boots out of rubbers. I sewed skin boots onto the upper part of shoe pacs using babiche. So they never went barefoot. I also patched caribou skin to their pants. That's why their skin didn't show through their clothing, and he was happy for that. He was the one who made me feel proud of myself.

53.42 So I also did that for my kids in those days. There was no such thing as rubber in those days, you see? And there were no boot rubbers. You know those thin skins I use after I cut off the hair? I also used a thin clean caribou skin which I wrapped around their feet inside their boots. The skin was waterproof and their feet didn't even get wet. I did lots for them.

55.00 I also made waterproof hip boots for your father.

MR55.03 Aii jidii hàa t'inlìk?

SF55.04 Aii ch'adhàh. Da'anlee khaiits'ą'. . .

MR55.49 Aii děiinlìk?

SF55.53 Aii da'anlee gwihiłtsąįį, gwîink'òo. Ootthàn dehłì' zhĭin'yùu teeneekhandidik gàa idluu ts'ą' khan teenidìk.

56.09 Aiits'ą' t'ee yaaghà' vadzaih dhàh vaghài' ninjyàa kwaa dhidlìi. Aii reh needhałtràa. Aiits'ą' t'ee tthahtsal òolaii hàa k'eedhăałkąį' chan videetak chan ch'adhàh dril niikhyuu, aiits'ą' k'eedhăałkąį', jyàa dąhnjyaa reh.

56.32 Dhałtsąįį ts'ą' vakwài' chan. Jyàa dihłik aii tthak tthahtsal òolaii hàa k'âalkaii, ch'ih hàa. Aiits'ą' t'ee chan hee idluu ts'ą' teeneedhizhìi. Yeendaa ch'iitsii ts'ą' nĭinzhii gwiizhìk reh aii jii k'eedhăałkąį' aii vintł'ĕiilìi.

56.52 "Jii *try* ąhtsii lèe," vàihnyàa. Aiits'ą' nihts'įį yizhĭin'yùu. Yizhĭin'yùu ts'ą' kwaiitryah yiyèhdak ił'yùu.

57.07 Aii yizhĭin'yùu ts'ą' chan hee teeneehan'inzhii. Akhài' jù' oondòk chųų zhìt hèe neehidik (adlaa).

59.34 Aiitł'ęę nįįzhùk hèe chųų zhit neehidik rǫh. Gohch'it oochyaa neezhìi. "Nik'ee vizhìt chųų?" văihnyaa, akhài' "Akwaa," shàhnyàa.

59.45 Kwàt chan zhik gwà'àn gwilii tr'igwee'aa kwàt chan jyàanch'ii *washtùb* chan kwàa. Daatłih ch'ik gàa kwaa izhìk gwanaa t'ishi'in roh. Izhìk hèe chan vadzaih dhàh tįį hee khan ch'adhàh agàa ałshii. Ch'adhàh veelin dachan.

<sfws105Cb>

MR2.56 Da'anlee gwìltsąįį dąį' łuk łęįį oodhoojìk?

SF3.00 Ąąhą', shriijaa reh. Łuk lęįį tr'òonjik.

MR3.08 Łuk daagąįį aii kwaa?

SF3.11 Ąąhą', shriijaa zhrįh. Chehlùk gàa reh.

MR3.23 Aii nijùk t'akhwa'ìn?

SF3.25 Oonjìt *Ch'at'oonjik* gwinyąą izhìk reh. Izhìk tr'igwich'įį, shriijaa gǫǫlįį ch'yąą.

MR4.10 *Ch'at'oonjik* gooch'ì' tł'ęę gwats'an, khaiits'ą' zhat gooch'ì' hęę?

MR55.03 What did you use for them?

SF55.04 Skin. The fish trap. . .

MR55.49 How did you do it?

SF55.53 He (*Johnny*) was building a fish trap while it was cold and went out into the water with his pants on, but he had to get out often because he got cold.

56.09 And there was this caribou skin lying around. I soaked it and sewed it using a plain sewing needle. I also used a strip of thin skin between my stitching. It was this long.

56.32 I sewed the pants with the boots attached to them using sinew in a plain sewing needle. He came back ashore again because he was too cold and was standing next to the stove when I showed him the pants.

56.52 I told him, “Try this,” and handed them to him. He put them on and put his boots on over them.

57.07 He put them on and went back out into the water. He was out there in the water for the longest time (laughs).

59.34 He was out there for a long time and finally came back up. I asked him, “Do they leak?” and he told me, “No.”

59.45 We tried lots of things like that too. There were no washtubs either. It was the time when there wasn’t even a bar of soap available. I even tanned a skin inside a caribou skin. I put wood around it.

<sfws105Cb>

MR2.56 When he made a fish trap, did you two get lots of fish?

SF3.00 Yes, grayling. We caught lots of fish.

MR3.08 Weren’t there any whitefish?

SF3.11 Yes, only grayling. And some loche.

MR3.23 Where were you doing it?

SF3.25 Over at the *Koness River*. We were living there. I remember there were lots of grayling.

MR4.10 Did you stay at the *Koness River* that fall?

SF4.18 Ą̀ąhą’, khaii tthak zhat *twenty-five year* tr’igwinch’ì’ naihnyàa!

4.35 Aiits’ą̀’ nilįį aii tr’ahgą̀įį, vadzaih gǫ̀ǫlįį ts’ą̀’ nilįį chan tr’ahgą̀įį. Tł’ęę khaii gwintł’òo.

6.07 Łyâa shih ehdan tr’agwąąh’yà’, nàhąą? Izhìk gwats’an it’ee jidìi zhyą̀ą tr’ehee’àa kwàa k’it t’inch’yaa googàa tthak gwinzįį ałgą̀įį. Ch’akwai’ gàa duuyeh akhŏiihnyàa.

7.44 Nahgwan dą̀į’ gwats’an łì’hàa ts’ik gòodlìt. Jii tr’iinin nąįį chan shandàh ehłìk. Aii gwats’an chan *flu* hàa dinjii niinjìk. Aii gwats’an jidìi ts’ik tr’iinin kat khàgwadantłii, jidii tthak gòodlit, nàhąą? Diidzìi gwìłts’ik datthak, diighò’ iłts’ik tthak. Aii t’ee shigii nąįį dink’ĭinjìk tł’ęęngwats’an t’igwìizhìk.

MR8.25 Vàanòodlit shìi gòodlit ts’an reh hęę?

SF8.30 Ą̀ąhą’. Jidìi *candy*, soongàii aii eh’àn t’igii’ìn. Shįį jyàanch’ii ih’àa kwaa ts’ą̀’ jii shaghò’ zhrįh tth’aii nizįį, nàhąą?

9.31 Tth’aii hee łyâa nizįį, googàa yee’òk tr’iinin nąįį tthak googhò’ khajyàa nàhąą? Aii t’ee zhik jidìi *candy*, soongàii, andàii ga’àa aii eh’àn googhò’ tthak kwaa gwilìi.

SF4.18 Yes, I'm telling you again that we lived there for twenty-five years!

4.35 There were lots of caribou, so we were drying meat there. It was cold that winter.

6.07 You see? We went through bad times having no food. So from then on, I even dried inedible parts from the caribou just in case. I didn't even throw away the caribou or moose hooves.

7.44 Sickness and disease came around not too long ago. I was around when all the children died off. People also died with the flu after that, and then from sores and other kinds of sickness, you see? There were also earaches, toothaches, and lots more. All kinds of sickness came around after my children grew up.

MR8.25 It happened when the white man's food came around, right?

SF8.30 Yes. It happened because of candy and sugar. I never ate those kinds of food. That's why my ugly teeth are still good, you see?

9.31 They're still really good, but all the children are losing their teeth, you see? They're losing all their teeth because of the candy and sugar.

Sarah Frank

Vashrąįį K'ǫǫ

<sfrf2b>

RF23.04 *Vashrąįį K'ǫǫ* kwaiik'ìt gokwàa?

SF23.06 Ą̀ąhą', kwaiik'ìt gokwaa gàa zhat dąįį hee dagogwaagǫ̀'. Dagogwaagǫ̀' ts'ą' łineegaadàl. Łuk eenjit. Aii jyàa dìgii'in t'agooràhnyàa.

23.25 Aiits'ą' łuk eenjit zhat tr'igwich'įį. Akhài' it'ee yaaghà' *Christian Choh.* Zhat gwànaa dąį' łyâa vit'èegwąąhch'yą' į'. Veenjit gwįįzįį aiits'ą' vigii nąįį chan gǫ̀ǫlįį kwàa. Aiits'ą' łì'hàa dinjii yit'ą̆ąhch'yą' t'inch'yàa.

24.06 Izhìk gwats'an it'ee gehchìt *Tryahtł'it* gwà'àn it'ee shoondee *Eziàs*[1] nąįį hàa khaiits'ą' tr'igwich'įį izhìk it shoondee *Eziàs* vigii nèekwąįį nąįį reh. Aii nąįį it'ee *tr'àł* zhìt dinjii gîilkhwąįį gwinyàa, zhyąą tr'igwîitth'àk. Akhài' aii geenjit t'ee *Tryahtł'it* tr'igwich'įį izhìk hee shoondee *Eziàs* nitsii hàa khàats'ą' hee nihts'ą' nihdèegii'òo ts'ą' nats'àhts'ą' gwich'ìighai' dèe k'eegwiich'yaa t'igwii'in jyàa dìgwehee'yàa k'ariheenjyàa t'ôonch'yaa ginyaa ts'ą' geenjit nihłàa gingiinjìi.

25.28 Gohch'it ree t'iginyàa, "Dinjii zhyąą khehłak tr'ohtsyàa. Khehłak tr'iłtsąįį ts'ą' dinjii chìt aii chan tr'iłtsąįį ts'ą'. Jyàa dìgwii'in hàa khehłak t'aih tr'agwàhįį jì' dèegwiheech'yàa lì'," ginyaa ts'ą' geegiginkhii.

26.03 Aiits'ą' it'ee *Vashrąįį K'ǫǫ* gwà'àn hee gwats'an ootthàn zheh nìneegiidàl. Izhìk chuuluh łii'ee gwinjik tr'igwich'įį. Aiits'ą' it'ee oonaa dinjii tr'ąąh'in jì' datthak hàh gwarahaandak ginyàa. Aiits'ą' it'ee gwik'ìt t'iginyàa. Dinjii tr'aah'in dąį' datthak hàa gogwaandak. Akhài' datthak giveechìi t'igwinyàa. Aiits'ą' it'ee datthak zhyąą łagòljik k'ìt t'igiizhìk. Ts'ą' it'ee izhìk

1. Sarah is talking about Eziàs Simon here. She calls him *"shoondee"* 'my older brother,' but he was apparently not her blood sibling. In the Gwich'in kinship system, first cousins are considered equivalent to brothers and sisters. —CM

Sarah Frank

Arctic Village

<sfrf2b>

RF23.04 There was no village in *Arctic Village* then?

SF23.06 Right, there was no village, but they used to gather there during spring break-up. So they all gathered there until break-up and also for fish. That's what they say they did.

23.25 We were living there, fishing. *Chief Christian* was there. We really depended on him. He was not having hard times and had no children. So he helped people a lot.

24.06 From there my older brother *Ezias Simon's* family and my family stayed at *Otter Creek* that fall. That was when my older brother *Ezias's* two children had shot a man in the brush, they said. That was why we stayed at *Otter Creek*. That's when my older brother *Ezias* and your grandfather used to visit together every night and used to talk about what they could do to prevent things like that from happening to them.

25.28 So finally they said, "Let's all live in one place and vote to have one leader, and we'll see what happens."

26.03 So from around *Arctic Village* we went down to where the trail meets from *Fort Yukon*. That's where we stayed. They say that so they can tell anyone coming along either trail about their plan. So they say that's what they did. They told everybody what they had planned. They say they all thought that was a good idea. So everybody got together. In those days there was hardly any money.

dą̀į' chan làraa chan àgwàntrìi. Zhyą̀ą ch'ara'àa gwizhrįh ree. Aiits'ą' it'ee *Vashrąįį K'ǫǫ Christian Choh* aii it'ee chìt giyìłtsąįį ts'ą' it'ee oo'òk dinjii gwich'įį datthak zhyą̀ą nihts'ìinyaa. Traa, shìh jidii k'aiichi'ii tsal tr'ii'įį kwaii hàa. Datthak nihts'ìgìinyàa. Ts'ą' jyàa dìgii'in ts'ą' t'ee gwitr'it gwigwìłtsą̀įį.

27.43 Aii gwich'ìighai' it'ee *Vashrą̀įį K'ǫǫ* kwaiik'ìt goodlìt. Tr'iinin chųų neegoondak. Traa chat gwik'ìt. Oo'òk zheh gwitee traa tsii dhidlii t'iihnyàa. Shrôonch'yaa gwigwìłtsąįį t'agwaihnyàa.

RF28.11 Izhìk shriit'agwąhkhyùk gooch'į'?

SF28.15 Nįįghyùk tr'igwinch'ì'.

RF28.17 Aiitł'ęę izhìk gwats'an nijìn hee gwats'ą' hoojìl?

SF28.24 Aiitł'ęę it'ee jyàa dìgwìizhìk ts'ą' aii duulèe *two years or three years* jyàa dahshùk *Vashrą̀įį K'ǫǫ* tr'igwįįch'ì'.

RF28.52 Geełèekhwajil dą̀į' kwaiik'ìt gòo'ąįį?

SF28.56 Kwaiik'ìt tr'igwiłtsąįį naihnyàa.

RF Ąąhą'.

SF29.00 Kwaiik'ìt tr'igwìłtsą̀įį. Âa, datthak gwįįzįį, Aiits'ą' it'ee ch'ìhłan nitsii aiits'ą' shòh gaadlìt kwàa. Zhyą̀ą reh. *Chief* chat inlį' į'. Izhìk jàghaii giit'ìnjyah'ee dhidlìt. *Peter* aii zhrįh diineeninidìk. Shaghwaii *Henrỳ John*[2] chan. Gohch'it ndàa ts'ą' t'ee zhyą̀ą gwintsàl tr'igwidìi dhidlìt į'. Dinjii danaah'in kwaa roh. Aiits'ą' it'ee zhyą̀ą vats'ą' gwigwìilchįį łee zhik dòoghai' jidìi geenjit ninzhùk ginìnji' rahthat dą̀į' gik'ìgwaandak k'ìt t'igwinjìk, nàhąą, aii gwik'ìt t'iizhìk. Aiits'ą' it'ee dhichįį akhài' oondee *Vashrą̀įį K'ǫǫ* ch'iinaa hee zhyą̀ą vàagwahàadhat łęę. Yee'àt *Gold Camp* izhìk gwà'àn it'ee vàh nàgoodhat łęę. Izhìk geh'àn it'ee yee'àt nìriinjil ǫ'. Aiits'ą' it'ee łyâa diidivęę gwįįzįį t'ôonch'yàa.

RF31.24 Aii lèe vah zhìt?

2. Henry John (1868-1962) was a Gwich'in medicine man who lived in *Venetie*. There are many stories told about his power.—CM

Our main thing was getting food to eat. So they elected *Chief Christian* for their leader at *Arctic Village*. People all helped one another. They helped one another with wood, food, and other things. They all worked hard to do this.

27.43 So that's how *Arctic Village* became a village. The kids used to pack water for each household. And I'm saying they did the same with wood. There used to be lots of wood piled up in front of the houses. I mean those were the happy times.

RF28.11 How long did you live there?

SF28.15 We lived there a long time.

RF28.17 From there where did you go?

SF28.24 So that's what happened, but maybe we lived there in *Arctic Village* two to three years longer.

RF28.52 When you lived there was the village there then?

SF28.56 I told you we made it into a village.

RF Yes.

SF29.00 We made it a village. Ah, everything was good. Until one time they got mad at your grandfather just for no reason. He was a chief one time up there, and I don't know why they turned against him. There were many people there, but nobody came to visit us. There was only this man named *Peter* who came by once in a while and also my brother-in-law, *Henry John*. So finally *Johnny* felt very hurt and upset. Nobody came to see us. When you think too much about something, then something happens, you see, and that's what happened to him, just like you knew what was going to happen. He was asleep when the vision appeared. He said he was flying in the air from *Arctic Village* until he flew over *Gold Camp* and then he returned. That's why we moved there ever since. We really had a good life there.

RF31.24 Was that in a dream?

SF31.28 Ąąhą’. Jyàa dìgwìizhìk ǫ’. Aiits’ą̀’ *Tryahtł’it* ts’ą̀’ oonjìt *Ch’at’oonjik* chan *Vashrąįį K’ǫǫ* aii gwats’an yee’àt.[3]

RF31.57 Yee’àt *Gold Camp* izhìk tr’ook’ìt dąį’ dzaa ts’ąįį zheh gòodlii hę̀ę?

SF32.07 Ąąhą’, dzaa ts’ąįį k’iitthàn gwik’ìraatąįį izhìk gwanank’įį gwà’àn t’ee tr’ohchìt zheh nèekok gwigwìłtsąįį. Aiitł’ęę, vijuu gwànaa izhìk it’ee dzaa kwaiik’ìt gogwahtsii, nàhąą. Izhìk chan dzaa tr’igwich’įį gàa dząą ninzhùk tr’igwich’įį kwàa.[4]

SF34.11 Izhìk zhat dąį’ it’ee *school* zheh tr’ohchìt gòodlit ǫ’. *School* gokwaa aiits’ą̀’ yee’àt gwizhrįh tr’igwich’įį.

RF34.44 Aii, aii gwitł’ee jì’ hee geegiriheekhyàa.

SF Ąąhą’.

RF34.47 Dzaa nijìn gwà’àn gooch’į’ geegirinkhii t’igwinyàa.

SF Ąąhą’.

RF34.52 Aii gwitł’ee jì’ gwàndaa noaałkat jì’ shàa gwandàk.

SF Ąąhą’.

RF34.55 Oondee *Gold Camp* hee gooch’ì’ izhìk 1930[5] gwànaa dąį’ lèe?

SF Ąąhą’.

RF35.05 1935 dąį’ gwànaa izhìk dąį’ it’ee k’eekhwadàl?

SF Ąąhą’.

RF35.12 *Vashrąįį K’ǫǫ* gwats’anh?

SF35.14 Ąąhą’, *Vashrąįį K’ǫǫ* gwats’an izhìk k’eeriidàl.

RF35.18 Tr’ihchoo hàa k’eekhwadàl?

SF35.23 Ch’adhàh tr’ihchoo hàa reh. Zhat dąį’ dachan tr’ihchoo kwàa. Ch’adhàh tr’ihchoo hàa t’ee yee’àt zhat k’eeriidàl ǫ’.

RF35.43 Izhìk it’ee ninghyùk gooch’į’ hę̀ę?

SF35.45 Ąąhą’, łyâa ninghyùk tr’igwįįch’į’ ǫ’.

RF35.49 Geełèekhwajil gàa kwaa hę̀ę?

3. She means *Gold Camp* here. —KP

4. She is referring to *Venetie*. —KP

5. Apparently this is an error. Nathaniel Frank remembered them arriving in *Gold Camp* in about 1934 or 1935. —CM

SF31.28 Yes. That's how it happened with us. We went from *Otter Creek* to the *Koness River* to *Arctic Village* to *Gold Camp*.

RF31.57 The houses over at *Gold Camp* used to be on this side [of the river], right?

SF32.07 Yes, there were three houses where the trail goes down. Maybe two. We lived there for a long time until we moved here.

SF34.11 The very first time they built two houses where the trail goes up the hill. That's when we lived here in *Venetie*. We didn't stay here very long. That was when they built the first school here.

RF34.44 Let's talk about that later.

SF Yes.

RF34.47 We were talking about where they say you lived around here.

SF Yes.

RF34.52 I'll ask you about it later and then you can tell me.

SF Yes.

RF34.55 Was it in 1930 when you lived in *Gold Camp*?

SF Yes.

RF35.05 Was it in 1935 you came here?

SF Yes.

RF35.12 From *Arctic Village*?

SF35.14 Yes, we came from *Arctic Village*.

RF35.18 Did you come by boat?

SF35.23 With a skin boat. At that time we didn't have a wooden boat. We went down there in a skin boat.

RF35.43 You lived there for a long time, huh?

SF35.45 Yes, we did live there for a long time.

RF35.49 You never left that place, right?

SF35.51 Ą̀ąhą’. Izhìk gwats’an geełèerahòojil kwàa. Gwiizhìk it’ee nitsii vakwàa. Aii yee’àt zhat tr’igwich’įį jìhnyàa. Izhì it’ee dzaa oo’ęę nàraajìl. Aii dęhtł’yaa aii giihàatr’agwąhdaii t’įįch’yaa, nàhąą.

RF36.32 Jidìi dęhtł’yaa?

SF36.34 Dzaa kwaiik’ìt tr’ohchìt shrigwigwilii izhìk aii gwidęhtł’yàa. *John Fredsòn book* jyàa dàantį’ aii kat datthak gwadâątł’oo į’. Aii łì’hàa gwandak nizįį iłtsąįį aii googàa hàa tr’igweendàii. Gàa oondùk yalàt gwats’ą’ nįįlii. Nijìn t’ii’in chan vàagwiindàii kwàa. Izhìk gwà’àn dhidlii gwìch’in t’inch’yaa nàhąą.

37.20 Aiits’ą’ yaaghà’ *book* t’aihnyaa, aii chan dzaa dèegwii’in datthak gwadâątł’oo. Aii t’ee dzaa kwaiik’ìt vit’èegwahaahch’yàa eenjit t’iyah’ìn. Akhài’ shachaa *John*[6] vakwaa ts’ą’ dèegiyinlìk googàa t’ee vàh gwiindàii kwàa. Aii łyâa gwandak nizįį t’aihnyàa.

RF37.54 Oondee *Aagamin (Ackerman) Lake* aii yù’? Izhìk chan zheh gwadhòhtsąįį hęę?

SF Ą̀ąhą’.

RF38.02 Izhìk *Gold Càmp* gwats’an zhyąą oondàk nìneekhwadàl?

SF38.05 Ą̀ąhą’, *Gold Camp* gwats’an oondàk zhat nan tr’oonjii ginyàa. Aii eenjit oondàk nineeriidàl shin hee łąįį ch’eeghwaa ts’ą’. Aiits’ą’ it’ee oondee zhat nan tr’òonjik ǫ’. Aiits’ą zheh tik zhat gòodlii. Aii ch’ìhłak it’ee *last summèr* dąį’ it’ee gwigwiłk’in łee į’. Tr’àł zhit hee. *Stanley* chan *Zheh Gwatsal* gwiłtsąįį. Aii hàa it’ee zheh *four* zhat gòodlii ǫ’.

39.17 Akhài’ jii łyâa dii*Zheh* aii it’ee tr’àł zhit t’ee zhat gwigwiłk’in łęę t’įįch’yaa, nàhąą. Jùu t’iizhìk gàhgwiindàii kwàa.

RF39.40 Shin hee zhat gohch’įį?

SF39.43 Ninghyùk zhat tr’igwich’įį. Shin hee oondàk nìneeriidàl.

RF39.52 Vadzaih eenjit lèe?

6. John Fredson was Sarah’s father’s sister’s son. As noted above, in Anglo-American terms he was her first cousin, but in Gwich’in classificatory kinship terms he was *shachaa*, ‘my younger brother.’ —CM

SF35.51 Yes. We left *Gold Camp* when your grandfather died. Like I said before, we were living there. That's when we came over here. They lost track of that book.

RF36.32 What book?

SF36.34 It was some kind of paper work they did when they were working with the community. *John Fredson* wrote lots of things down and it was very good. They lost all that. He sent some of it down to the states somewhere, and we don't know where. It's somewhere down there.

37.20 That book was all about what went on around here. We were going to use it for this village. Then my younger brother *John Fredson* died, and we don't know what happened to it. I'm saying it was really a good story.

RF37.54 What about *Ackerman Lake*? Did you build a house there too?

SF Yes.

KF38.02 You just traveled from *Gold Camp* to there, huh?

SF38.05 Yes, from *Gold Camp* they said we should get an allotment there. So we usually went there in the summer with dog packs. Then we did get an allotment there. There's three houses there. That one house burned down last summer. *Stanley Frank* built a small cabin there too. With that one, we had four houses there.

39.17 But our house was the one that burned down, you see. We don't know how it happened.

RF39.40 You lived there in the summer?

SF39.43 We lived there for a long time. We went there in the summer.

RF39.52 For caribou?

SF39.53 Shin hee zhyąą zhat gwà'àn garagwaahkii kwaii hàa t'igwii'in. Gàa zhik ch'ihłęę oondàk gwàts'an Vàanòodlit zhat oo'ęę nòozhii. Izhìk dąį' yee'àt *Gold Càmp* chan ts'ą' oondee *Aagàmin Lake* chan aii gwà'àn gwigwîiłkįį aii datthak googàa łyâa jùk zhat gwà'àn gògwàntii, nàhąą, àn giyinghan. Ch'iitsii tsal tak giłtsàk į'. Aii googàa jùk yaaghà' làfoo nąįį reh. Aii datthak àn gwigwiłtsąįį t'inch'yaa, nàhąą.

SF41.11 Jii *Vįįhtąįį* shrigwigwinlìk, nàhąą. *Reservation* chan giłtsąįį. Aii it'ee shachaa *John*, nitsii hàa t'igii'in reh. Nihts'ìgiinyaa ts'ą' datthak gwanzhįh deek'ìt datthak shrìgwigwinlik aii datthak gwabook t'aihnyàa. Izhìk dąį' it'ee dąįį shìh kwaa, nàhąą. Łùh kat googàa *shotgun* kì' nahtsìk. Aii googàa datthak dęhtł'yaa kat gòo'ąįį t'agwaihnyàa. Aii gwidęhtł'yàa dèezhik googàa vakwaa t'įįch'yaa, nàhąą. Dząą kwaiik'ìt vit'èegwahaach'yàa eenjit yìłtsąįį į'. Chat thok gwidęhtł'yàa ahtsii aii chan oondàk gwà'àn izhìk hee nìyinlii.

<sfws105Ba>

SF45.34 Oondee *Arctic Villàge* aii t'ee nijìi shreedrìn aii oohihshryàa gàa gàashandàii kwàa. Àkwàt aii izhìk tr'ohchìt *start* gwigwìltsąįį. Aiitł'ęę yaaghà' nitì', shoondee *Eziàs*[7], jii nąįį tr'ohchìt *start* gwìłtsąįį. Aii t'ee shoondee *Eziàs* aii vigii aii nąįį dinjii inghan gwinyàa. Izhìk geenjit t'ee dinjii khaihłak gòh'ì' nyąą ts'ą' t'ee.

46.47 Oonjit *Tryàhtł'it* tr'igwich'įį. Izhìk it'ee nitì' hàa t'ee shik nihłaa gigìinjii ts'ą' t'ee gèegìginkhii ts'ą' t'ee oondee *Arctic Villàge* dinjii nąįį datthak akòodagahnyaa ts'ą' hah gogwaandàk. Aiits'ą' aii gwik'iighai' t'ee *start* gwigwiłtsąįį ts'ą' *Arctic Villàge* chan kwaiik'ìt goodlìt.

MR47.50 *Why did they pick that spot?* Jaghaii oondee *Arctic Villàge* aii jaghaii zheh nìgwìgwiinlii t'inch'yaa? Zhat ch'atthąįį eenjit gwìnzįį eenjit *or*?

7. Apparently Sarah is talking about Ezias Simon here, but he does not appear to be her blood sibling according to our Frank Family Tree in Appendix A. —CM

SF39.53 During the summer we were just busy marking land. This white man came here to do a survey on the allotment at *Gold Camp* and also at *Ackerman Lake*. They marked all the land, you see, but too many young people came around and destroyed all the steel markers, you see.

SF41.11 They built up *Venetie* and then they got the Reservation. It was my younger brother *John Fredson* and your grandfather. They both helped each other and put in gardens. All this was in the book *John* wrote. That book would be a great help if we had it now. That spring there was no food. He even refilled shotgun shells. I'm saying all of that was written in that book. We don't know what happened to that book, you see. He kept a record of it for the future. He also kept a record of his own, but he left it up there somewhere.

<sfwsl05Ba>

SF45.34 I don't remember the month and year when *Arctic Village* was started. Your father and my older brother *Ezias* started the village. There was a rumor one time that my older brother *Ezias's* children got away with murdering some people, and he wanted people to settle down in one place.

46.47 We were living at *Otter Creek* when my older brother *Ezias* and your father talked about starting a village. They notified everybody about it; that's the reason they started *Arctic Village*.

MR47.50 Why did they pick that spot? Why did they build the houses there at *Arctic Village*? Was it because of large game animals or what?

SF48.05 Ą̀ąhą', ch'atthą̀įį eenjit t'igii'in, zhat łuk chan gǫ̀ǫlįį aii kwaii hàa tthak eenjit t'ee zhat kwaiik'ìt gòodlit t'ôonch'yàa.

<sfwsl05Bb>

SF26.05 Izhìk gwats'an t'ee aii jyàa dìgiinyą̀'? Aiits'ą̀' t'ee *Arctic Villàge* izhìk t'ee nìrìinjìl. At'ôohju' hee zheh gwigwiinghàn. Gwehchįį dą̀į' nahjyàa zheh gokwàa.

26.30 Zhyàą zhat łuk gǫ̀ǫlįį, dats'an chan, aii eenjit zhyą̀ą zhat gwak'àneegôiidal ts'ą̀' gwizhrįh. Zhat gwigwich'įį kwàa. Jyàa dìgii'in akhài' izhìk nitì', *Eziàs* hàa dèegiinyą̀' izhìk gwats'an t'ee zhat zheh gwigwiinghàn.

27.01 Izhìk gwats'an it'ee t'ôohju' hee t'ee *chief* gahtsìi.

MR27.11 Aii jùu *chief* giłtsą̀įį?

SF27.15 Shoondee *Eziàs* chan *chief* inlì'.

MR27.18 Aii lèe tr'ookìt *chief* dhidlìt?

SF27.25 *Christian Choh* aii t'ee gwehchįį dą̀į' gwats'an voozhrì' gǫ̀', googàa gwahàadhat tthak *chief* nihłigeeghàn.

MR27.36 *Eziàs* aii gwats'ąįį jùu *chief* inlì'? Aii jùu, aii dèe *first?*

SF *Christiàn.*

MR27.53 *Chief Christiàn* lèe?

SF Ą̀ąhą'.

MR27.55 Aii tr'ookìt lèe t'inch'yàa?

SF27.56 Aii t'ee tr'ohchìt.

MR27.57 Aii t'aràhnyàa.

SF27.58 Aii t'ee tr'oochìt t'ee *chief* nilįį.

MR27.59 Giyeenjit *vote* dhidlìt?

SF28.06 Nàkwàa, gwìch'in roh. Izhìk dą̀į' gwànaa *vote* gilìi kwàa.

29.12 Shoondee *Eziàs* t'iginyaa gwats'an *Arctìc Villàge* kwaiik'ìt nàgwaatth'at jìhnyaa? Izhìk gwats'an if ee *chief* gahtsìi. Khàiinjih tthak gootagwahàadhat *chief* nihłagaatsìk. Nitì' agàa *chief* inlì' t'inch'yàa.

MR30.07 Aii *chief* gahtsìk, aiits'ą̀' gwikįh tth'aii *chief* gahtsii kwan dą̀į', aii jidìi shrit ts'ąįį gwinzįį?

SF48.05 Yes, they did it because of the game animals and because there were plenty of fish there. The village was started there because of that.

<sfwsl05Bb>

SF26.05 And so they continued talking about it until we finally moved to *Arctic Village* because of it. They started building houses there for the first time. There were no houses there before.

26.30 There were plenty of fish and ducks there. That's why people always used it to make a stop over there. Nobody lived there until your father and *Ezias* kept talking about it, and that's how a village was started there.

27.01 They started having chiefs after that.

MR27.11 Who was elected chief?

SF27.15 My older brother *Ezias* was chief once too.

MR27.18 Was he elected chief in the beginning?

SF27.25 *Big Christian* was already a chief before. Every one of them was chief at one time or another.

MR27.36 Who was chief after *Ezias*? Who was the first chief?

SF *Christian.*

MR27.53 You mean *Chief Christian*?

SF Yes.

MR27.55 Was he the first chief in the beginning?

SF27.56 He was the first elected chief.

MR27.57 That's what I'm asking about.

SF27.58 He was chief in the beginning.

MR27.59 Did people vote for him?

SF28.06 I don't think so. I don't think they used votes at that time.

29.12 Remember I said that after my older brother *Ezias* and *Johnny* were always talking about it? From then on, *Arctic Village* started and then they started having chiefs. Every one of them was chief at one time or another. Your father was chief once too.

MR30.07 Which time was better, do you think? Having a chief or no chief?

SF30.20 Aii *chief* gahtsii kwaa dąį', izhìk gwànaa gwinzįį googàa *chief* gahtsìk, gwiizhìk chan zhik gwà'àn làraa, nàhąą? Aiits'ą' łi'hàa datthak gwìizųų gòodlìt.

30.56 Gwichįh làraa kwaa dąį', dinjii tthak gwinzįį nihts'ìinyàa. Akhài' aii *chief* tr'ahtsìk ts'ą' it'ee gwìizųų.

31.39 *First time* zhat zheh gwigwìłtsąįį dąį' t'ee. Aii dąį' shoondee *Eziàs* chan *chief* nilįį, *Elijah* chan aii jyàa dìgii'ìn.[8] Izhìk dąį' t'ee dinjii tthak nihts'ìinyaa ts'ą' zhik gwà'àn traa, chųų, shìh, jidìi datthak hàa nihts'ìgiinyaa. Àa, shrôonch'yaa gòodlìt.

<sfkflb>

CF20.23 Shitsii *Johnny* chan zhòh dink'yąhjik ch'ìhłan?

SF21.28 Shįį zhrįh aii zhòh dink'yàłthat į'.

CF Ôq.

SF21.35 Łąįį ąhtsii dhidlit.

CF21.37 Nijìn oodhoojìk?

SF21.39 Yaaghà' shin neerihiinjìk.

CF Ą̀ąhą'.

SF21.43 Izhìk gwànaa dąį' zhòh zhuu *sell* ilìi. Aiits'ą' zhòh zhuu gaghàn. Googàa yeendee shitseii *Jimmỳ* aii zhòh zhuu k'at deedhizhii łee. Akhài' yalàt inghan googàa zhòh zhuu gwandàii łee jyàa dąhtsii reh gwandàii ts'ą' oo'ęę nąąhchįį. Aiits'ą' reh t'avăihnyàa, "Yaaghan łąįį hal'yàa dik'yàhałthaa shantł'ăhchii." Akhài' "Âa, ts'an an'įį," shàhnyàa.

CF22.40 Neeshrâahch'yaa gwich'in hęę?

SF Ą̀ąhą'.

SF22.45 T'ąhtsal tr'òonjik, nàhąą, googàa zhòh nilįį geeèehàazhii kwaa t'aihnyàa.

CF Hah.

SF22.57 Gòhch'it reh jyàa dąhtsii dhidlìt roh. Vak'ăałtii ts'ą' gadhałchaa. Tł'yah ninjyàa hàa dadhałchaa ts'ą' vach'ał'àa. Vadrąįį hihshik ts'ą' it'ee jyàa dishilik.

8. She's talking here about Ezias Simon and Elijah John. —JE
Since they're talking about Arctic Village, it's more likely to be Elijah Henry. Elijah John lived in Venetie. —CM

SF30.20 It was better when there was no chief. Money was involved when they started having chiefs, you see? So people started having problems among themselves over money.

30.56 People used to help each other a lot before money came in. But it was no good after we started having chiefs.

31.39 After building houses there for the first time, my older brother *Ezias* was the chief and also *Elijah* and so forth. People used to help one another with wood, water, and food. Everybody helped each other. Gee, it was good.

<sfkflb>

CF20.23 Did my grandpa *Johnny* raise a wolf at one time?

SF21.28 I raised that wolf myself.

CF Ooh.

SF21.35 It got as big as the dogs.

CF21.37 Where did you get it?

SF21.39 While we were traveling from place to place in the summer.

CF Yes.

SF21.43 At that time they sold young wolves. They used to kill lots of young wolves. But my grandson *Jimmy* came across some young wolves. Although he killed some of them he brought one home alive and it was this big. So I told him, "Give it to me so I can raise it as a dog for myself." So he said to me, "You can have it."

CF22.40 He must have been a cute one, heh?

SF Yes.

SF22.45 He was just a pup, see, but he never stopped being a wolf.

CF Oh.

SF22.57 Finally he was this big. I took care of him and kept him tied. I had a long chain on him and fed him. Every time I got near him he did this (gesturing).

CF23.21 Geetèe chan tree tsai haahthàk dǫhłįį?

SF23.24 Aii nizįh kwàa chan shòh shìłts'ąįį kwàa. Gwilin shòh shìłtsąįį kwaa t'avăihnyàa. Àkwàt aii zhòh zhuu oondòk *survey* nąįį nan tąįį gogwaahkìi nàhąą. Aii ch'ìhłak chan aii zhòh zhuu injidĭindhàt. Googàa t'ǫhłįį gwintł'èerahahchyaa văihnyàa. Googàa shineetak aii zhòh zhuu gwintsìi kwaa danoiinkwàt t'aihnyàa. Aiitł'ęę aii Vàanòodlit chan yeh'àn *fine* dhildlìt t'aihnyàa. Oonìn neeyihìłchįį akhài' izhìk hęę vits'į' tr'iyùunjik łèe.

CF24.27 Hah! Shitsųų ch'adąį' gwànaa nich'it inlįį dąį' khaiits'ą' tǫǫ neegwaatth'ak hęę ijii. Yeedòk hee są' gwànlįį hęę? Tǫǫ oozhrii chan adrii łyâa shrôonch'yaa hęę? Izhìk gwà'àn nik'ee ganandàii? Oo'òk gohch'įį shrôonch'yaa gwìch'in.

SF25.00 Gwazhrąįį hee. Neerihiinjìk łyâa shrôonch'yaa zhat gwànaa.

CF Ąąhą'.

SF25.14 Izhìk hee oondôk neerihiinjìk hęę chan dàatłìh ch'ìk googàa kwaa ts'ą'. Shoh? Dhàh tsal jyàa dąhtsii ąįį chat ląįį kak gałtł'įį. Aii t'ee vakàt ch'àłshìi.

CF Hah!

SF25.45 Dachan veenjit łihts'ineiihtthàk ts'ą' reh. Aii kat dałchaa ts'ą' reh ch'adhàh vizhit nàłchàa. Aii kat it'ee ch'ałshii ǫ'. *Ganbuu*[9] chan dhałts'ąįį ǫ'. Izhìk dąį' *rubbèr* kwaa roh. Aiits'ą' chan shìh dhàh aii chan jèiinch'yaa chųų vizhìt dhałkąįį ts'ą' vaghài' tthak veełèehàajìl. Aii chan dąįį dzan keegehee'yàa łee chųų kwaiitryah givee'iighan į'. Ts'ą' duuyeh gookwąį' nahtraa. *Ambrose*[10] chan kwaiitryah veedhałts'ąįį, yaaghà' nitsii chan. Aii hàa oo'òk chųų gǫǫlįį neegihiidàl gàa ree gookwąį' nahtraa kwàa. Nitsii chan khaiits'ą' gwîink'oo

9. *Ganbuu* are handmade hip boots.—JE
These are not actually gumboots but more like what we call hip waders. —CM

10. Ambrose William, Sarah and Johnny's son-in-law, was the husband of their oldest daughter Lucy. He was living next door to them at *Gold Camp* when I visited there in 1972. —CM

CF23.21 Usually he cried?

SF23.24 He [*Johnny*] got me upset sometimes too. I'm saying he got me upset many times. The surveyors were up this way to survey the land. And one of surveyors really fell in love with the young wolf. I just went and told him that we were going to give it to someone else. But I mean *Johnny* went and sold it to him very cheaply without my permission. Later on that white man was caught and fined for it too. He took the wolf back down to the Lower 48, and that's when they took it away from him.

CF24.27 Hah! Grandma, when you were young, in the fall time do you remember how it gets pitch dark? Way up there the stars are so bright? The moonlight is bright and it's beautiful out. Do you ever remember it? It must have been lots of fun in those days.

SF25.00 I sure did. It was fun to travel around in those days.

CF Yes.

SF25.14 As we traveled up around there we didn't even have one bar of soap. But I had one little black bear skin tied to a dog pack. And that's the one I tanned skins on.

CF Hah!

SF25.45 I pounded some sticks into the ground. And then I hung the edges of this bear skin on the stick and shaped the skin into something like a pan. That's how I soaked my skins. I made hip boots too. At the time there were no rubber boots. So I used this bear skin for a tub to soak skins in so much that all of its fur came off. So come springtime I used that same bear hide and made boots for them, so they wouldn't get their feet wet. I made a pair for *Ambrose* (*William*) and also one pair for your grandfather. They even walked in the water with them and their feet never got wet. Your grandfather did it too in the fall when it was cold. And when he was going to roh. Ts'ą' chan da'anlee gwihìłtsąįį izhìk chan vadzaih dhàh kal vaghài' ninjyàa kwaa reh.

27.03 Jèiinch'ii gǫ̀ǫlįį. Aiits'ą' it'ee yeechìt thał zhùu'yuu ts'ą' teenidik gàa zhyàa teeneevatan'aadhàk. Aiits'ą' needaaghok, aiitł'ee chan teenidìk. Akhài' it'ee aii ch'adhàh zhyą̀ą *try* hałtsyàa nihthan ts'ą' chųų nàłkhyàa. Khan neevatràa'aadhàk roh. Aiits'ą' chųų zhǐilii tł'ęę t'ee gwiizhìk gwatrał eenjit yeendaa dachan kwaii gwanàn nahchìt ǫ'.

27.53 Da'anlee gwihìłts'ąįį t'ii'ìn. Aiits'ą' ree chųų zhit dizhàłjil ts'ą' ree tł'ęę ree dzaa nàa'ąį'. Jyàa dąhjyaa tthak dhałt'uu tł'ęę chan k'eedhaałkąį'. K'eedhaałkąį' vakwài' chan. Aiitł'ęę it'ee chan hee ookyàa neevahtan'àanàii. Aiits'ą' vats'ą' yahàdhałjil.

28.35 "Jii vizhǐin'yaa ts'ą' vàhteeniindìi lèe yaaghà' vizhìt chųų gwehèelyaa gwìch'in gàa," văihnyàa. Dazhoo t'inch'yaa ǫ'. Aiits'ą' vizhit chan dazhoo. Aiits'ą' ree dehłì' trah zhìt tr'iin'yùu ts'ą' ch'izhii dehłì' dąhshùu zhìnee'yùu ts'ą' it'ee yizhǐin'ùu ts'ą' t'ee yeendaa tèehan inzhii. Tineevatan'aadhak ch'yąą ree yeendaa chųų zhìt hee kagwìł'ąįį. Akhài' vizhit chųų kwàa. Gwįįzįį k'eedhăałkąį' ǫ'. Aiits'ą' it'ee jyàhts'ą' *ganbuut* dhałts'ąįį ǫ'.

29.34 Izhìk it'ee chan *rubbèr* kwaa roh. *Rubbèr* àgwàntrìi, aiits'ą' chan shigii nąįį, neegwahtraa roh. Aii chat vadzaih dhàh jyàa dąhthee nàa'ąį', kwaiitryah gwiyèhzhak givee'iighàn. Kwaiitryah giiyèhdak zhùu'yùu. Duuyeh gookwą̀į' nahtràa.

CF30.07 Jyàa dàkhwa'yą' neekhwanjik aiitl'ęę tôohju' hee *Gold Camp* nŏondii?

SF30.12 Ą̀ąhą'. Shigii nąįį tee gwintsìi gòodlit gwiizhìk yee'àt nìriinjil ǫ'.

CF Hah.

build a fish trap. At that time I had caribou hides with just the fur cleaned off of them.

27.03 I had lots of them. He went right down there into the water with just his pants on and then he got out for a while. But he was just too freezing cold. So right there I got that caribou skin. I just thought I would try it. So I heated water, and it soaked fast too. So I put it all in there. I soaked it in water while he was down there hammering the poles in for the fence.

27.53 He was building a fish trap. So after I soaked the skin in water, I cut it and reached up this far and this long and then I sewed it, even his foot. So when he came back up again freezing cold, I just threw it to him. I told him to try it on and go in the water with it.

28.35 "The water might get inside but try it," I told him. It had fur on it, and it had a fur lining too. So he took off his wet pants and put on dry pants and then he put on the skin pants and went back in the water. Before, he kept getting in and out of water from getting so cold. But this time he stayed in the water. The water didn't get inside the boots. So that's how I made hip boots.

29.34 Again there was no rubber. It was hard to get rubber. And then there were my kids and everything they had on was wet. So again I made long insulated boots for them and they wore their worn out skin boots over them. Their feet would not get wet.

CF30.07 After you had done all this traveling, then you all ended up at *Gold Camp*?

SF30.12 Yes. After all my children had grown up.

CF Hah.

Sarah Frank

Gold Càmp

<sfwsl05Bb>

MR33.21 Jàghaii *Gold Càmp* nŏojil t'ôonch'yàa?

SF33.31 Oondee nąįį tthak nitì' ts'ą' shòhgaadlit kwàa. Izhìk geh'àn geenjit *worry* nilįį nats'àhts'ą' dèeheech'yàa, tr'iinin lęįį chan tr'ii'įį, nàhąą?

33.47 Aiits'ą' tr'iinin lęįį chan tr'ii'įį gwiizhìk datthak diits'ą' gìizųų nàhąą? Aiits'ą' gwintł'òo *worry* dhidlìt, nitì', shant'eh gàa reh. Aiits'ą' gwintł'òo *worry* tr'iinlįį ts'ą' t'ee izhìk it'ee nitì' aii zhyąą gineihłyàa vats'ą' gwìgwìilkįį gwìch'in roh. Gineihłyàa ts'ą' t'ee yee'àt zhat it'ee sheenjit gìrìgwìiłchįį k'it t'igwìizhìk nyaa ts'ą' it'ee yee'àt nìriinjìl.

MR36.00 Aii gwikįh dąį' nik'èe yee'àt dee'àn zhat nìneekhwadàl? Nats'àhts'ą' gàandàii t'ii'ìn? Nats'àhts'ą' zhat gwinzįį ts'ą' gàandàii?

SF36.23 Gwik'èerįįłtįį k'ìt t'iizhìk, *show* vats'ą' tr'igwìłtsąįį k'ìt t'iizhìk ts'ą', it'ee zhat nìriinjìl.

MR36.59 Nats'àhts'ą' zhat gwats'ą' nŏojil? Nakhwatth'àn hàa or. . .?

SF37.05 Ąąhą', ch'adhàh tr'ihchoo hàa reh.

<sfwsl05Cb>

SF45.20 Izhìk gwiizhìk t'ee diikhwan aii tr'iinin lęįį tr'ii'įį ts'ą' oo'àt hee shìh tsal, shin chan nilįį tr'iłgąįį, aiits'ą' shìh tsal tr'aahkhwąįį kwaii hàa zhat khaihłan nìriinlii ts'ą' t'ee khaii t'ee zhat tr'igwich'įį, oo'àt *Gold Càmp.* Aii gwiizhìk dzaa hee tr'iinin school ahtsii roh.

46.07 *Jackfish,* aii chan oo'àt zhat khàneedàl. Aiits'ą' łyâa gwinzįį shìh vakwàn khaii tr'iheedàa tr'òonjik. Akhài' dzaa *Vįįhtąįį* shìh kwaa, nàhąą?

Sarah Frank

Gold Camp

<sfwsl05Bb>

MR33.21 Why did you move to *Gold Camp*?

SF33.31 Everybody in *Arctic Village* got mad at your father. Because of that, he was worried. He was worried because we had lots of children, you see?

33.47 They were treating us badly while we had lots of children, you see, and your father and I became worried. We worried about it, and then your father had a dream and a vision. That's what led us there.

MR36.00 Did you ever go there before? How did Father know about the place? How did he know it was good place for him to live?

SF36.23 He had a vision in his dream which showed us where to go, so then we moved there.

MR36.59 How did you travel there? By walking or . . .?

SF37.05 Yes, we also traveled with a skin boat.

<sfwsl05Cb>

SF45.20 We were living back at *Gold Camp* because we had lots of children, and we had dry meat from the summer before and were still living there that winter. They were having school here.

46.07 Jackfish (northern pike) come up the river to *Gold Camp* too so we really had plenty of food that winter. But nobody here in *Venetie* had anything to eat, you see?

SF46.33 Izhìk dąį' t'ee *first time airplàne* tr'ąąh'in. *Jim Dodson, first time* neech'ahąąht'ee.[1]

MR47.10 Njìn needaadhàk?

SF Vankat reh. Han gwinjik agàa neeneedąądhàk. Khaii t'ii'in roh.

MR47.42 Oo'àt gohch'įį gwiizhìk dzaa tr'iinin nąįį shìh kwaa lèe jiinyàa?

SF47.47 Dzaa shìh kwaa ts'ą' oo'àn dineenìneegiidàl.

MR47.52 Aii jùu nąįį oo'àn nìneedàl?

SF47.54 *Jùu* datthak reh. Yaaghà' *Elijàh John,* vigii nąįį chan. *Ned* vigii, shaghwaii *Henry* nąįį gàa tthak, oo'àn jyàa dìgii'in. Izhìk hee givintł'eech'arahchak akhài' diikhwan chan diishìi kwàa.

48.36 Aii *Jim Dodsòn* zhat neeneedąądhàk. Nihkhàn t'ii'in kwàa. Ch'ihłòk oochyąą nìdìilnąįį. *Eight hundred pounds* shìh oochyąą k'ilìk.

MR Aii lèe Vàanòodlit shìi?

SF Ą̀ąhą'.

MR48.59 Aii nats'àhts'ą' ookwàt?

SF49.18 Nin dhàh hàa reh. Izhìk gwànaa dąį' làrąą kwàa (adlaa).

MR Aii tsèe dhàh dąhkhài' ootthàn yahàadlii hęę?

SF Ą̀ąhą'. Aii tsèe dhàh yintł'ànaazhik ts'ą'.

MR49.44 *No*, nats'ąą, tr'ookìt oo'àt needaanaii vǎiinyàa.

SF Qǫh, ąąhą', izhìk it'ee ootthàn yàhnòozhìi.

MR49.55 Adahkhài' oo'àn dihìilnàii?

SF Ą̀ąhą', nǎihnyàa!

MR Aiits'ą' yizhǐnzhii ts'ą' ootthàn yàanòozhìi? Nats'àhts'ą' oondee gohch'įį ts'ą' nakhwàandàii?

1. Although Jim Dodson was probably the first pilot to land at *Gold Camp*, other planes had previously been in the area. The anthropologist Robert McKennan chartered a float plane flown by Joe Crosson to visit *Arctic Village* in 1933, about four years prior to Dodson's first flight (see Mishler and Simeone (2006:166-168). —CM

SF46.33 We saw an airplane for the first time that year. *Jim Dodson* was the first pilot.

MR47.10 Where did he land?

SF On the lakes and rivers during the winter.

MR47.42 Did you say the children here had no food here while you were living at *Gold Camp*?

SF47.47 There was no food here so they came over to us for food.

MR47.52 Who all came over there?

SF47.54 Everybody. *Elijah John's* children, *Ned's* children, and also my brother-in-law *Henry John* and them. We gave all of them food, and that's how we ran out of food ourselves.

48.36 *Jim Dodson* landed there, but not too often. He came one time and brought eight hundred pounds of food.

MR Was that white man's food?

SF Yes.

MR48.59 How did you buy it?

SF49.18 We used fur to buy it. There was no money at that time (laughs).

MR Did *Johnny* take the fur down himself?

SF Yes. He also gave *Dodson* the fur.

MR49.44 No, I mean, what made *Dodson* fly over there for the first time?

SF Oh, I see. Yes, he did go down with him when he first landed.

MR49.55 Did he just fly over there on his own?

SF I'm telling you, yes!

MR Did he board the plane and go down with him? How did he know you lived there?

SF50.17 (Adlaa) Gàandàii, oondaa ałts'ik zheh *Doctor Burke?*[2] Zhat dąį' *Gwichyaa* dąį' gàa jyàa dòonch'yàa. *Gwichyaa* ałts'ik zheh gòo'aii, aiits'ą' dinjii lęįį ałts'ik dilch'įį, nàhąą? Aii nąįį jyàanch'ii diishìi łyâa giindhàn. Izhìk *Dr. Burke* chan gàandàii. Aiits'ą' aii t'ee oochyąą shìh kadìilnąįį aii gwik'ìighai' jyàa dìgwii'in t'iihnyàa.

MR52.21 Aii nilįį gavantł'ŏolii dąį' nik'ee geedant'ee gwinjihkhaii nakhwantł'ęę gaanjìk?

SF52.29 Aii *Dr. Burke* łi'hàa diilàk t'aràhnyàa. Aiits'ą' aii ootthàn k'àiich'ii gwinyaa, nàhąą? Jyàa dĭi'in ts'ą' *Dr. Burke* chan nilįį t'ąąhch'yaa, nàhąą? Aiits'ą' zhyąą *Gwichyaa* diits'an tr'ehilii gàa tr'agookwàt kwàa. Aiits'ą' *Dr. Burke* aii nilįį aii gwit'ìį goots'ą' nìrìlìk. Aiits'ą' zhyąą *free* ts'ą' oochyąą k'àiich'ii dineenaazhik t'ii'ìn.

53.13 *Dr. Burke* łi'hàa zhyàa làk danàa'ìį , yaaghà' shitseii *Mike* dèe'ìn gǫ̀'? Gwik'ìt t'adanahthan.

MR53.38 Izhìk shìh kwaa jiinyaa dąį' izhìk dąį' t'igii'in?

SF53.41 Ą̀ąhą', izhìk dąį' t'ee dzaa naa, aii jyàa dìgwìizhìk, nàhąą? Aiits'ą' jii Vàanòodlit shìi łùh chan ts'ą' *rice,* soongàįį kwaii zhrįh. *Cornmeal* aii kwat reh. Khwaii aii hàa oo'àn gahàajil akhài' aii jidìi *cornmeal* t'aihnyaa nilįį kwaii hàa goolìk arah'àa akhài' diikhwan chan danàh shìh kwaa nàgwàanàii. Izhìk t'ee ndàk ts'ą' tr'ahàandìi.

MR55.24 Nijìn gwats'ą' *move* dhoodlìt izhìk dąį'?

SF55.27 Izhìk dąį' zhyąą nitì' gwee'ęę tr'ohoojyàa văihnyaa gàa gitr'ii'èe. Shaghwaii *Charlie Johnsòn* chan danàh gwich'įį va'at kwaa ts'ą'. Aiits'ą' ałts'ik gwats'an nehshrit oo'àt k'idik, aii danàh gwich'įį .

MR55.51 Aiitł'ęę oo'ęę neegohòojil, geedan hee?

SF55.53 Ą̀ąhą'. Łąįį datthak àn dhidlìt łąįį neegahaazhik. Diikhwant'ee diilìk chan. Aiits'ą' t'ee oo'àt diizheh ndàk ts'ą' tr'ahàandii, dishìi kwaa ts'ą'. Gęhdee *Ch'aghaihchànjik Łinits'igwaa'ee* gwinjik izhìk

2. Dr. Grafton Burke was a missionary doctor who arrived in *Fort Yukon* in 1910 and served faithfully there until his death in 1937. His life is recounted in Clara Heinz Burke's biography *Doctor Hap* (New York: Howard McCann, 1961).
—CM

SF50.17 (Laughs) He already knew. You know *Dr. Burke* at the hospital? There was a hospital in *Fort Yukon*, and the patients there wanted Indian food, which *Dr. Burke* knew, you see? So *Dodson* came up for Indian food, and I'm saying that's how he came.

MR52.21 When you gave them meat, did they give you anything in return?

SF52.29 *Dr. Burke* was a close friend and almost like a relative to us. He needed the meat, you see? *Jim Dodson* brought our things up from *Fort Yukon* free in return for the meat we sent to *Dr. Burke*.

53.13 *Dr. Burke* thought of us as relatives. Just like my grandchild here, *Mike Holloway*.

MR53.38 Was that at the same time the people had no food?

SF53.41 Yes. At that time, look here. We did that, you see? He brought flour, rice, sugar, lard, and cornmeal. After that those seven people I named earlier came over. We fed them and their dogs our meat and cornmeal, and we ran out of food, so we moved farther up north.

MR55.24 Where did you move to?

SF55.27 I asked your father if we should come here [to *Venetie*], but he refused. My brother-in-law *Charlie Johnson* lived with us too. That was after his wife died. He barely made it over to us after a long illness.

MR55.51 The others who went over came back here, right?

SF55.53 Yes. All of their dogs died. Our dogs died too. And so we went further up north because we had no food. We went up to *Łinits'igwaa'ee* on the North Fork of the East Fork of the *Chandalar River* and were living there tr'igwich'į̀į , izhìk t'ee diniłèegòhòojìl. *Elijàh* chan ts'ą̀' aii vigii nąįį hàa, *Ginnìs*, shaghwaii *Henrỳ*. *Rufùs* aii chan jii nąįį tthak zhat diihàa neegihiidàl. Aii łąįį tthak àn dhidlìt. Aiits'ą̀' izhìk it'ee drin tthak ch'aga'àa kwàa. Googàa nitì' noondee *Allah*[3] hàa dinjik gąąh'in łii, akhài' dinjik goots'ą̀' tr'ąąh'oo łìi. Aiits'ą̀' t'ee nitì *Allàh* hàa t'ee aii dinjik tąįį gahàa'oo łii, akhài' łyâa niinzhìt k'ìt t'ôonch'yaa googàa t'ee giyuaahk'ee łii. Izhìk dąį' gwiyeendaa gwaatr'àl kwàa.

58.15 Akhài' dinjik gîiłk'ee. *Łinits'igwaa'ee. Aldzàk Vakwaii* t'agwaihnyàa. Zhik ddhah aii jyàa dìnch'yaa, nàhąą? Dzaa gweenaa vatł'an han gwìin'ee t'aràhnyàa, jyàanch'yaa aii *Łinits'igwaa'ee.*

59.31 Aii niinzhìt dąį' gwànaa dinjii aii Aldzàk òozhìi. Ddhah jyàanch'yaa, gweenaa han gwìin'ee dzaa t'ee vakwàn deek'ìt gwąął'in.

MR60.59 Łąįį ch'ìhłak gàa *leftovèr* dhidlìt kwàa?

SF61.20 Ą̀ąhą', diikhwan aii łąįį tsal *four.* Aii nąįį t'ee ch'aga'àa kwaa googàa t'ee giłchįį kwàa. Kwàt zhik ànts'ą̀' neehiidàl nąįį t'aihnyàa datthak goolìk kwaa goodlìt.

MR61.32 Aiits'à deegiizhìk?

SF Aiits'ą̀' t'ee aii nitì' dinjik diłk'èe jihnyaa aii t'ee oo'ęę neegiyàahchįį aii t'ee yeenjì' Shoo yaaghà' *Maggie Ts'it Zhuu* vigii nąįį nèekwąįį nąįį chan zhat. Aii dinjik t'ee łąįį ehdan oo'ęę neegiyìinlii ts'ą̀' t'ee aii ga'àa akhài' aii chan t'ee vakwàa. Aiits'ą̀' t'ee łi'hàa gwìizųų.

<sfwsl05Da>

MR0.45 Aiitł'ee yù'? Aii vakwaa tł'ee?

SF0.50 Aii vakwaa ts'ą̀' it'ee, aiits'ą̀' t'ee yaaghà' *Elijah, Steven*[4] nąįį gàa tthak aii yaaghà' tthak zhat diinihłèegohòojìl. *Vįįhtaii* gwats'ą̀'.

MR0.57 Dèegą̀ąhch'yaa łèe? *Five* ginlii?

SF1.30 Ą̀ąhą'. Dagats'àt zhrįh geelil ts'ą̀' t'ee neegohòojìl.

---

3. Allàh Frank, Sarah and Johnny's son. —CM

4. Elijah John and Steven Peter. —JE

when the other people came back down. There was *Elijah* and his children, *Ginnis*, my brother-in-law *Henry*, and *Rufus*. They went up there with us, but all their dogs died. They hadn't eaten all that day, and your father and your older brother *Allah* saw a moose in the distance and shot at it. It was not that brushy there that time.

58.15 And they shot it. *Łinits'igwaa'ee* is where *Aldzak Vakwaii* is located. The mountain is here like this (gesturing), you see? There's a river running in between these mountains. That's the mountain called *Łinits'igwaa'ee.*

59.31 A long time ago, there was this man named *Aldzak.* The river runs between the two mountains and there's a den there that belongs to him. I've seen it.

MR60.59 Not even one dog was left over?

SF61.20 Yes, four of our dogs lived. They stopped eating from being so sick, but they didn't die. I mean those others who came with us, their dogs died.

MR61.32 What happened after that?

SF They brought back the moose your father shot. Two of *Maggie Ts'it Zhuu's* children who were from *Shoo* were with us too. They brought the moose back without using the dogs. We ate up all the meat, and we had hard times without food after that.

<sfwsl05Da>

MR0.45 Then what? After the meat was gone?

SF0.50 After the meat was gone, *Elijah John* and *Steven Peter* and others left us and went back to *Venetie.*

MR0.57 How many of them were there? Were there five of them?

SF1.30 Yes. They were pulling only their blankets when they left.

MR1.36 Aiitł'ee deegiizhìk tinch'yàa? Aii kii'ee neegeedàa dąį'?

SF1.56 Kii'ee neegohòojil, izhìk t'ee łyâa giveegògǫ̀ǫtrii łee ts'ą' *Elijah* vigii naįį hàa. . . [5] Aiits'ą' zhat gęhjųų gwankhyųų diizheh gǫ̀ǫ'ąįį ǫ'. Izhìk zhat gwà'àn dehtsii tsal chan doo'àii. Aii zhik gwà'àn tth'an kwat gwizhĭt rilìi'.

Aii kwaii chù̧' gahtsii. Aiits'ą' zhat gwintsal gwigwinch'į' tł'ee t'ee gwe'ęę dzaa *Vį̀įhtaii* gwits'eegohòojil łee.

MR2.41 Aii nijìn nakhwa*Zheh* goo'ą̀įį?

SF2.44 Oo'àt![6]

MR2.45 *This side* ts'ąįį .

SF Vijuhts'ąįį.

MR3.22 Qǫ. Izhìk dąį' *Charlie Johnson* hee?[7]

SF Ą̀ąhą'.

MH3.30 *Charlie Johnson* stayed with them?

MR *Charlie Johnson* t'ee *Sarah* vaghwaii t'inch'yaa?[8] Ą̀ąhą'.

SF3.34 It'ee gwintsal veenjit gwinzįį k'it t'inch'yaa ts'ą' diits'ą' hàazhii, danàa dhidii. Aii gwiizhìk t'igwii'in ts'ą' gwe'ęę dinihłeegohòojil. Aiits'ą' t'ee nitì' aii t'inyàa, "Oo'òk neegihiidàl łi'hàa chìgaajìl, aiits'ą' jùk drin zhyą̀ą tr'ahâak'yàa," nyąą. "Neerahàazhìi," nyąą. Akhài' chan yeezhee git kat k'iidì' k'aii tsal dhidlìi. Izhìk zhat daagǫǫ chan yeezhee deenàajil, aii zhat daagǫǫ teerîiłk'èe. Aiits'ą' chan *zhat.* Aiits'ą' t'ee lee zhyą̀ą *Vį̀įhtaii* gwits'ee gohòojil.

4.15-7.57[9]

---

5. Sarah is interrupted by Maggie's translation and loses the narrative thread. —CM

6. *Gold Càmp geeginkhii t'inyą̀ą.*—JE
Venetie is on the east side of East Fork of the *Chandalar River* and *Gold Camp* is upriver from *Venetie* on the west side. —CM

7. Charlie Johnson was Sarah's brother-in-law. —JE

8. Maggie is translating Mike Holloway's question for Sarah.—CM
Question is not clear. Which Sarah is Sarah talking about here? —JE

9. This section is mostly in English and therefore not transcribed. —CM

MR1.36 What happened after that? When they were coming over here?

SF1.56 They were coming over when they became really weak, and one of *Elijah John's* sons. . . Somewhere near where they were, we had a cabin up on the slope. And in one of those small caches we stored some old used-up bones.

They boiled those to drink the broth. They stayed there for a while and then went back to *Venetie*.

MR2.41 Where was your house located?

SF2.44 Over there!

MR2.45 You mean over on this side [the *Venetie* side]?

SF The other side.

MR3.22 Oh. Was it *Charlie Johnson* that time?

SF Yes.

MH3.30 *Charlie Johnson* stayed with them?

MR (Speaking to *Sarah*) Did *Charlie Johnson* stay with *Sarah's* brother-in-law? (Speaking to *Mike Holloway*) Yes.

SF3.34 He was feeling a little better, so he came to us and was staying with us while all this was going on. After they left us, your father said, "We're all very tired from hunting, so we'll rest today," he said. There's this glacier in front of our place with little willows here and there. Ptarmigan landed there, and he shot seven ptarmigan. And then they all left for *Venetie*.

4.15-7.57

SF7.57 Aiits'ą̀' t'ee łyâa zhyą̀ą oo'ęę *Vį̀ihtaii* gwits'ee gohòojil. Aii ts'ą̀' diikhwan aii nitì' aii t'avăihnyą̀ą. "Yaagha' łyâa noonlyàa gwiihèezųų gwich'in. Yeetthàn zhat ts'ąįį diikhwant'ee googàa zhyą̀ą tr'ahoojyàa," văihnyą̀ą.

Akhài' geet'iindhan kwàa. Aiits'ą̀' shaghwaii *Charlie* chan gwik'it t'inyąą. "Shicheii nąįį neeshrâahch'yaa, goodhaii nàgaanąįį ji' gitr'ìh'èe. Shant'ee goovihłèehihdyaa kwaa t'inch'yàa," nyąą. Aiits'ą̀' t'ee diihàa t'inch'yàa.

MR Aiitł'ee yù'?

SF9.28 Aiits'ą̀' t'ee izhìk zhat t'agwăihnyąą? Daagǫǫ *seven* chan gîiłkhwą̀įį. Aiits'ą̀' gehzhee k'aii tsal tee chan k'iidì' vats'ą̀' iizhìi. Nitì' akhài' chan geh, aii chan diłk'èe. Aii t'ee zhat drin tr'a'àa. Aiitł'ee nìhkaa t'ee. . .

9.54 Tł'ee nìhkaa t'ee yeedàk ts'ąįį zhyą̀ą kheehìi'àl, nyaa. Izhìk dą̀į' yeechìt shigii *Hamèl,*[10] aii t'ee shrįįt'ąhtsìi. Aii t'ee ditì' hàa hàazhii. Akhài' gwinzįį ch'a'àa kwaa, veenjit gwìizuu, nàhąą? Aiits'ą̀' t'ee yeedak khàgaà'oo łee. Izhìk it'ee zhik ddhah jèiinch'yaa, nàhąą? Ddhah deetak jyàa dòonch'yaa, izhìk it'ee "Dhindìi," yàhnyąą łee.

MR Aiitł'ee yù'?

SF11.09 Aiits'ą̀' gehchiitthàn k'àii jèiinch'yaa. Aii zhik gehchuk. Jyàa diizhìk łee akhaì' dzaa zhat k'àii tthàn nàa'ąį' chiichyąą t'ee dinjik k'įh łee. Aiits'ą̀' t'ee k'iidàk *k'aii* deetak hee t'ee jyàa dìi'in ts'ą̀' ahaa dahłįį.[11] Akhài' reh gehdee gwàdàk aii dinjik dhichįį łee. Aiits'ą̀' t'ee dinjik yâak'įį, nàhąą? Aiits'ą̀' izhìk t'ee aii dinjik yits'ìį tr'iinzhii łee, akhai' yaaghà' nihtak *Hamèl* dhidii gwîiłk'à, eegwîiłk'in izhìk *Hamèl* dhidii gwiizhìk t'ii'ìn. Aiits'ą̀' izhìk t'ee aii dinjik yits'ìį jyàa dìizhìk łee akhài' aii Hamèl gwîiłk'aa ts'ą̀' tr'iinzhii, nàhąą? Aiits'ą̀' t'ee yųąąhk'èe. Akhài' łyâa zhyàa yîiłk'èe.

10. Hamel Frank, Sarah *vigii tsyaa.* —JE

11. The meaning of *dahłįį* is 'must have been.' —JE

SF7.57 After everybody left for *Venetie*, I said to your father, "We really should leave too since it seems like it's going to get worse." But he said, "No."

Charlie Johnson said "No" also. He said, "I don't want to watch my grandchildren suffer. If I do, I won't leave them." So he stayed with us.

MR And then what?

SF9.28 And then, you see what I was talking about? Where they shot the seven ptarmigan? In that same place I drove a snowshoe hare across to him through the little willows, and he shot it. We ate that snowshoe hare all day that day. Then the next day we. . .

9.54 The next day *Johnny* said he and my son *Hamel* would look around to see if they can get anything up on the slope. So they left, but *Hamel* didn't feel good from not eating, you see? So he didn't go very far. So *Johnny* told him "Sit here!" on the side of a small hill and left him waiting there while he went on ahead.

MR And then what?

SF11.09 Then he went down a slope through some small willows and found fresh moose tracks. He followed them and the moose must have heard him coming, so it took off, you see? And it accidentally came to where *Hamel* was sitting and waiting and had a campfire going. The moose got away from *Johnny* and came to *Hamel*, who aimed at it and really shot it.

13.19 It'ee aii dinjik dìłk'ee ts'ą̀' t'ee aii dinjik dìłk'ee ts'ą̀' it'ee łyâa diineenjit gwinzįį. Aiits'ą̀' t'ee yaaghà' dinjii nąįį eh'àn t'ôonch'yaa gwich'in rǫh.

13.39 Izhìk dąį' t'ee *Nathaniel,* noondee *Allah,* nitì nąįį hàa łyâa zhyą̀ą ch'agaahk'ee kwaa, nàhąą? Drin gwiteegwą̀ąnch'yąą zhyą̀ą dinjik gâahk'ee. It'ee gwinzįį. Shìh gǫ̀ǫlįį t'ee, izhìk gwats'an it'ee aii łąįį tsal *Ghoo*, văihnyaa. Aii nąįį ch'ìhłę̨ę iłchįį kwaa. Tthak gògwandàii, aii nąįį łyâa t'èegwą̀ąhch'yaa.

MR Aii *nineteen* dąąnch'yąą khwa'in lì' hèe? Shįį dałtsìi?

SF Nan tth'aih ch'ahmà' ǫ'. Ch'ahmà' gàa nihkhàn ch'ahmà' kwàa. Ma' nits'ì' t'oiinyąą ts'ą̀', "Ne'ę̀ę. Ch'ihłòk gwizhrįh, ma'," shăiinyąą t'ihnyą̀ą. Neehiindik ǫ̀'.

15.59 Aii t'ee izhìk jyàa digwiizhìk ts'ą̀' t'ee oondee Łinits'igwaa'ee[12] jìhnyaa. Aii gęhdee gwandak agàa oondàk naraajil t'ihnyàa. Izhìk tthak dinjik gaghàn. Aiits'ą̀' t'ee gwanahjyàa t'ee tan kat gǫ̀ǫlįį . Gwanahjyàa t'ee shìh, diveeneegaazhìk. Jyàa dìgii'in yaaghà diizheh gwats'ą̀', jyàa dìgii'ìn. Noondee *Allàh* chan t'eełì' khalchį' ts'ą̀' ch'adhàh, dinjik dhàh zhit googàa ch'eelil t'aihnyą̀ą. Izhìk it'ee tr'eenjyàa gwiizhìk chan shiinghwaa văiinyąą ts'ą̀' vant'įį nineiindik neeghwaa gwiizhìk chan ch'eelil ijìi.

MR16.47 Ganaldàii, izhìk gwizhrįh ganaldàii.

SF16.50 Neeghwaa gwiizhìk chan ch'eelil ijii!

MR17.48 *Łinits'igwaa'ee* lèe diinyąą łee?

SF *Łinits'igwaa'ee* ch'iinaa izhìk gwinjik ch'iinaa neereedàa. Aiits'ą̀' izhìk yaaghà' *Łinits'igwaa'ee.*

MR Vàanòodlit k'yàa goozhrì' kwaa hę̨ę?

SF Aii goozhrì' hàashandàii kwàa. Vàanòodlit k'yą̀ą gàashandaii kwàa. Goozhrì' hàashandàii kwaa rǫ.

---

12. *Gold Camp gęhdak.* —JE
Łinits'igwaa'ee is a creek with two forks that empties into the *K'aii'eech'uunjik* (*East Fork* of the *Chandalar River*) from the west side, just below *Gold Camp.* —KF

13.19 From then on, we did pretty well. We even thought that maybe we had bad luck because of those men.

13.39 At that time *Nathaniel*, your older brother *Allah*, and your father were all sharpshooters, you see? They shot moose almost every day. We did well after that. We had a lot of food after that. I named one of my puppies *Chubby*. He was the only one who survived. We really used him.

MR Do you remember what year that was, nineteen something? How big was I?

SF You were still breast feeding but not that much. I was trying to wean you, but I remember one time you said, "Mom, let me have milk." You were walking at that time.

15.59 After all of this, we all went up past *Łinits'igwaa'ee.* We shot a lot of moose around there. We had so much to carry that the men had to carry meat up further ahead, come back, and repeat it again and again. And we slowly moved back down that way. Your older brother *Allah* was in such a hurry that he even pulled lots of the meat in a moose hide over the ice. At that time while we were traveling, you kept bugging *Allah* to pack you.

MR16.47 That's the only part I remember.

SF16.50 He pulled meat the same time he was packing you on his back!

MR17.48 Did you call that place *Łinits'igwaa'ee?*

SF Yes. We were traveling from there and then. . .

MR Is there a name for *Łinits'igwaa'ee* in English?

SF I wouldn't know an English name for that.

Łinits'igwaa'ee.[13] Aii geh'an *Aldzàk*[14] gizhàavakwaii văihnyąą reh, zhat shik ndàa, ahàa.

MR18.22 *Aldzàk,*[15] aii Dinjii Zhuh k'yàa voozhrì' kwaa hee? Vàanòodlit k'yàa?

SF18.43 Izhìk it'ee nàa, izhìk gęhdee gwats'an oondàk nàraajil ts'ą̀ t'ee k'ìinjik neerohòojìl. K'ìinjik neerohòojil ts'ą̀' yaaghà' *Łinits'igwaa'ee* vijųų ch'iinaa git dha'àii. Aii chan k'atneereejil ts'ą̀' izhìk vijųų gwànaa. Aii shìh lęįį nìgiinlìi. Izhìk nìriindii, izhìk it'ee nitì' reh, izhìk it'ee diilìdii chan kwàa, diits'eet'ìt chan kwàa. Aiits'ą̀' t'ee yaaghà' *Vįįhtaii* nìhihshyàa nyą̀ą. *Vįįhtaii* nìhihshyàa nyą̀ą ts'ą̀' t'ee ni*Zheh* gwizhìk nilįį gwintsàl k'at danrahgąįį. Nilįį nizįį kwaii.

MR19.34 Aii lèe shin khwa'in?

SF19.40 Khaii reh! Khaii t'igwii'in. Aiits'ą̀' izhìk it'ee nìriindii, *Aldzak Vakwaii* vijųų. Izhìk tr'igwich'įį ts'ą̀' t'ee diilìdii chàn kwaa. Aiits'ą̀' *Vįįhtaii* nìhihshyàa nyą̀ą, nitì. Aiits'ą̀' t'ee aii nilįį gwintsàl shririlii, datthak vàl iłchàa. Aiits'ą̀' hàazhii roo.

MR20.10 Aii lèe łąįį hàa?

SF20.12 Ą̀ąhą'! Hàazhii ts'ą̀' t'ee zhat diikhwan zhrįh tr'igwich'įį. Shaghwaii *Charlie Johnson* chan yàht'iizhìk. Aiits'ą̀' gwanaa gahàa'oo ts'ą̀' dząą *Vįįhtaii* k'ineegii'òo lèe. Akhài' łyaa zhyą̀ą shìh kwàa. Shìh kwaa łee ts'ą̀' t'ee, aii shìh gwanaa yahàaluu, aii chan gwats'ą̀' shin chan jidìi łuh, *rice*, sǫǫngaii kwaii hàa, tsal zhat dhidlìi. Tr'aadlii, aii kwaii hàa. Aii nilįį yeelil khwaii hàa datthak ch'ihłòk vikeegiłch'yàa łee. *Jean Fredsòn*[16] aii vakaiiyahch'yaa reh, aii t'ee zhat gwich'in, tr'iinin nąįį, tr'injàa nąįį hàa tthak ch'aga'àa kwaa łee.

MR22.20 Izhìk dat' *school* zheh shìh gǫǫlįį lee t'ôonch'yàa?

13. *Łinits'igwaa'ee* means 'where the point meets.' —KP

14. *Aldzàk — Gold Camp gęhdak gwà'an.* —JE

15. A man named *Aldzak* once lived in a cave along *Łinits'igwaa'ee* creek and built a moose fence nearby. —KF

16. Jean Fredson – John Fredson *zhat dą̀į' va'at t'aràhnyąą.* —JE

Łinits'igwaa'ee. That's why I also called it *Aldzak gizhàavakwaii* because *Aldzak* made his living there.

MR18.22 Was *Aldzak* his only name? He had no English name?

SF18.43 From there, we went up further and then came back down. We were on the way from *Łinits'igwaa'ee* to *Gold Camp*, traveling on the glacier. Then we stopped to camp and ran out of both tea and tobacco. So your father decided to go back to *Venetie* to pick up tea and tobacco while we were at camp drying meat inside your house for a little while. Only the good edible meat.

MR19.34 Was that during the summer?

SF19.40 Winter time! It was during the winter. We were near *Aldzak Vakwaii*, and we stopped there to camp for a while. That was when your father said he would go to *Venetie*. We packed all the dry meat in his toboggan, and he left.

MR20.10 Did he go with dogs?

SF20.12 Yes! He and my brother-in-law *Charlie Johnson* left for *Venetie* while we were camping there. And when they arrived in *Venetie*, they found out there was no food there. So they cooked up all that meat and the flour, rice, and sugar we left there earlier for everybody in the village. *Jean Fredson* cooked it up because the children and women had nothing to eat.

MR22.20 Was there food at the school at that time?

SF22.24 *No, school* zheh shìh kwàa, izhìk chan shìh kwàa.

MR22.34 Gaa *John* aii dats'an t'ah'in?

SF22.42 Adan aii jidìi shìh tsal yat'ą̀ąch'yaa zhrįh. Aii zhrįh di'įį. Aii ts'an t'ee *five gallon* tyąh zhìt khyų'.[17]

23.50 Aii t'ee jyàa diizhìk, aii shìh k'ilik tthak, zhat łùh dhidlii kwaii hàa tthak vikee'iłch'yaa łèe. Aii t'ee tthak giin'àl łee ts'ą' t'ee. Aii jyàa diizhìk ts'ą' it'ee nitì' *chief* oolį' ahnyą̀ą łee. *John Fred* aii.[18] Jyàa nyąą ts'ą' t'ee yeenjit ch'oo'ahkat akhài' reh, akhài' ą̀ąhą' ginyaa łèe. Ą̀ąhą' ginyąą łee ts'ą' zhat *chief* giiyiłtsąįį, izhìk t'ee aii shìh zhat dhidlii tthak vakeegiłch'yàa t'agavaihnyą̀ą.

MR23.57 Qǫ, zhyą̀ą zhat nihee akhài'?

SF23.58 *Ą̀ąhą',* zhyą̀ą ootthàn nehee akhài' jyàa digiiyinlik į'. Aiits'ą' tth'aii hee t'ee gwats'ą' gwaldak t'ihnyą̀ą.

25.30 Aiits'ą' t'ee, aiitł'ee *chief dhidlit,* nichaii *Henry,*[19] shaghwaii *Charlie Johnson,* aii hàa t'ee oondàk gahàa'oo łee. Aiits'ą' oondee tr'igwich'įį dihnyąą. Izhìk tr'igwich'įį t'ee sheek'ineegii'òo. Gwiizhìk nitì' aii hiljìi. Aiits'ą' k'eegii'òo ts'ą' izhìk it'ee shįį chan tr'iinin gwach'àa tsai shats'ą' nìgiinlii łee. Aiits'ą' chan *jidìi flag* ijìi! Aii chan sheek'eegahchàa ì' (adlaa).

26.36 Izhìk dąį' łyâa gàashandàii kwaa nàhąą? Gàashandàii chan kwàa, aii gwiizhìk jyàa digiizhìk. Ts'ą' nitì' chan eenjit *vote* gaadlìt łee. Shįį chan tr'ìnjàa eenjit chįh nàshagąąhchįį t'igii'in t'agavaihnyą̀ą. Aiits'ą', aii *flag* shats'ą' nagąątsùu.[20] Izhìk dąį' gàashandàii kwàa.

28.30 Aii tthak łyâa ch'idįįhtł'òo chan kwàa. Dęhtł'yaa chan hàashandàii kwaa. Aii gwiizhìk t'igiizhìk dąį' gwintł'oo, hagàa ihtree t'agwaihnyą̀ą.

17. *Khyų'* means 'fish eggs.' —JE

18. Sarah uses John Fredson's birth name throughout. Like many of his generation, Fredson took his father's first name, Fred, as his surname. —JE and CM

19. Henry John, Sophie Choh *vakai'.* —JE

20. This was probably the same tattered American flag I saw flying over the Franks' cabin at *Gold Camp* in November, 1972.—CM

SF22.24 No. There was hardly any food there either.

MR22.34 Was *John* [*Fredson*] using his food?

SF22.42 He only kept what he needed for himself. That's all he had. Then he had a five-gallon bucket for fish eggs.

23.50 Afterwards they had a potlatch, and all the food was eaten, including what we left there in our cache. *John Fredson* wanted your father *Johnny* to become chief of *Venetie*. He asked the people and they all agreed. So like I said, they voted yes and *Johnny* was elected chief.

MR23.57 Oh, really?

SF23.58 Yes. That's how it happened when he went down there. So I'm still only halfway through my story.

25.30 So then *Johnny* became chief. Just your grandfather *Henry John* and my brother-in-law *Charlie Johnson* came back to our camp. But your father was gone. They brought back children's clothing for me. And also a flag! They brought it with them (laughs).

26.36 I really didn't know anything about it, you see? Then I found out I was elected women's chief. And at the same time your father was elected by votes. So that was why the flag was sent to me. I didn't know anything about it.

28.30 At that time I didn't even know how to read or write. Meanwhile, I'm saying I was so worried that I even cried.

29.02 Aiits'ą' t'ee jyàa digiizhìk, ts'ą' k'eegii'òo ts'ą' t'ee neegohòo'oo. Neegohòo'oo ts'ą' t'ee, it'ee reh nitì'. Neegohòo'oo tł'ee nitì' ookyaa neezhìi. Aiits'ą' t'ee oondìt diizheh it'ee dagwarahaagǫ̀' eenjit izhìk shìh nìgìlìi. Izhìk shìh nìgilii ts'ą' t'ee jyàa digwii'ìn. Aii gwiizhìk t'ee gwahgǫ̀'. Jyàa dòonch'yaa reh. Jyàa dòonch'yaa, aiits'ą' t'ee yaaghà diizheh reh, izhìk shìh tthak nìneeriinlii, aiits'ą' t'ee zhat dagwarahaagǫ̀' eenjit. Akhai' gwiizhìk it'ee yaaghà *Sam Robèrt,*[21] aii t'ee *John Fred*[22] oo'àn dehtł'yaa iłtsąįį. Dehtł'yaa hàa òo'an nìnidìk.

MR30.52 Dèegwąąnch'yąą oo'àn nìneehozhii t'inch'yàa?

SF30.54 Aii t'ee *John Fred* aii t'inyąą, nàhąą? "Aii *four-five day* gwizhrįh jii tthak, jii zhìt gwiindhat jì' it'ee *school* gweheekwàa.[23] Aiits'ą' jii ts'ą', jii zhìt, dzaa gwats'à hohjyàa," danàhnyąą t'ii'ìn. Aii eenjit dehtł'yaa oo'àn *three time* oo'àn nidhìzhìi. Aiits'ą' *last time* chan gwiizhìk. . .

MR31.31 Aii tr'ookìt oo'àn nòozhii dąį' deevohnyąą gǫ̀'?

SF31.54 "Dząą dagwaraahgǫ̀', yaaghà' chan shìh lęįį dząą nìriinlii, nats'ąą zhyąą oo'tthàn tr'eheedàa," gwìnyàa. Gitr'igwîi'èe.

MR32.17 Aiitł'ee yù'? Izhìk chan gatr'ôoh'ee?

SF32.21 Ą̀ąhą, *two time.*

MR32.53 Izhìk t'ee vaa oo'ęę neehòokhwa'oo hęę?

SF32.56 Ą̀ąhą' *last time* chan t'ee izhìk vàh oo'àn tr'ahàajìl. Aiits'ą' t'ee *last time* chan dęhtł'yaa hàa oo'àt k'inidìk. Aiits'ą' t'ee, it'ee googàa gwinyąą ts'ą' t'ee gwe'ęę tr'ahàajìl. Gwe'ęę chaavał hàa tr'eedàa, chaavał tik, aii chaavał tik tr'eelyaa. *Sam* chan, aii chaavał tik tr'eelyaa ts'ą' aii

21. Sam Robert, James *chan ts'ą'* Myra *hàa goo'gii tsyaa.*—JE

22. John Fredson — John Fred *chan giyàhnyąą.* —JE

23. The reason why the school was going to close was due to insufficient enrollment. In 1937 only two families were living in *Venetie* and only two children initially enrolled in the school. Fredson's note was designed to persuade the Franks to come to *Venetie* and enroll all their children so that the minimum requirement of thirteen would be met. —CM

29.02 And then the two guys left and your father (*Johnny*) came back up not long afterwards. Then we decided to spend the spring at our other house across the river, so we moved all our food over there. We were busy moving. Meanwhile *Sam Roberts* arrived as a messenger for *John Fredson*, carrying letters. He did that often over there.

MR30.52 How many times did he come over there?

MR30.54 And this is what *John Fredson* said in his letter, you see? "The school will close in four or five days from this date." And he wanted all of us to come back to *Venetie* because of that. *Sam* came over three times. When he came over the last time . . .

MR31.31 What did you tell him the first time he came over?

SF31.54 We told him, "We plan to stay here all spring and don't want to leave all our meat here." We told him we didn't want to go.

MR32.17 Then what happened? Did you still refuse to go?

SF32.21 Yes. We refused twice.

MR32.53 Did you all come back with him when he went over?

SF32.56 Yes! We came over with him the last time he came up. We finally decided to come back when he came again for the third time. We had three toboggans full of things.

tthak vatł'at dàch'ahochaa. Oondàa chan nilįį nàgaaluu tł'ęę tr'ahàajìl. Akhài' oondee *Nihtak Van*[24] ijìi? *Nihtak Van* dha'ąįį, aii gęhdit k'iidaa jyàa dòonch'yaa ijìi? Izhìk k'ii'ęę tr'eedàa akhài' zhah tsal googàa kwàa. Zhyąą nankat hee.

MR35.06 Aii łąįį aii nijìn gwats'an tr'ineegavŏolìi?

SF35.16 Jidii dèe?

MR35.18 Łąįį dǫǫ zhrįh tr'ii'įį diinyąą ìjii?

SF35.20 Aii łąįį nąįį *Sam* vilìk nąįį t'aihnyąą. Aiits'ą' aii nàhaa? Aiits'ą' jyàa dìgwiizhìk. Jyàa digwiizhìk akhài' zhah kwàa. Aiits'ą' chan łąįį khąhthàa, łąįį yizhìt ch'eeghwaa, łąįį tł'yaa, datthak chan oodhiinjìk. Aiits'ą' it'ee zhah kwaa nìriinjil ts'ą' chan . . .

SF36.13 Aiits'ą' oodee. . .yeedee ddhah aii ndìh ch'iidąą tr'eedàa. Aii gwats'an ch'iidaa tr'eedàa chan niinląįį agàa gòodlii rǫh. Aii ch'iinìn chųų zhìt googàa dząą gwee'àn chųų nàa'ąį' ts'ą', *"Jeez, that's a cold water,"* taihnyąą. Aii ts'ą' yaaghà yeedee gwit'eh jii tł'oo dàk naà'ąį'. Izhìk ch'iidaa t'ee gwanyaa chųų gǫǫlįį. Dzaa gwee'àn hee diineetâą'ąį' ts'ą' khantr'eedàa t'iihnyąą.

MR36.51 Aii lee *Natł'at Van*[25] k'iidaa rǫh hee?

SF36.54 Yaaghà' vijųų gwadąą. Aiits'ą' jii zhìt nàhąą? Jii ts'ą' tr'agwąhąą'yàa t'igwii'ìn. Aiits'ą' jii zhìt chųų zhìt googàa tr'eedàa. *School* zheh aii *save* tr'agwahahtsyàa t'igwii'ìn aiits'ą' t'ee. . .

MR37.30 Aiitł'ee yeedee *Van Choh*[26] ee'lin aii yù'?

SF37.33 *Van Choh* jyàhts'ąįį ch'iinii, izhìk it'ee dząą hęę? Tsyaa nąįį, jùu nąįį t'ii'in lì'. Yaaghà' *Peter* chan gwìch'in. Aiits'ą' chan *Peter*. . .tsyaa tik nąįį oodàk diinanghàih giihił'è' łee. Akhài' aii yaaghà' gwàdak hee, ch'aga'àa kwaa ts'ą' goveenjit gwìizųų ts'ą' zhyąą giłchųų łee.

24. *Nihtak Van—Vįįhtaii gehdaa ddhah choh zhee t'in'ee, aii ohts'aii van dha'aii t'arahnyaa.* —JE

25. *Natł'at Van — Vįįhtaii gehdee', Van Choh ehdee van vivee natł'at gwanlii aii t'arahnyąą.* —JE

26. *Van Choh — Vįįhtaii ehdee van nitsii dha'aii aii t'arahnyąą.* —JE

They moved some over a little ways. Then we started to travel also. You know where that *Nihtak Lake* is at, right? We were around there when all of a sudden there was no more snow on the ground.

MR35.06 Where did those dogs come from?

SF35.16 What?

MR35.18 I thought you said you only had four dogs?

SF35.20 I'm talking about *Sam's* dogs. And so, you see? We stopped there because of lack of snow. But I had dog packs and skin ropes with me, and then. . .

SF36.13 We were traveling down the slope of that big mountain when there were streams of deep cold water here and there, and we were wading in it. "Jeez, that's cold water," I remember. When we got to the foot of the mountain where the big meadow ends there was water everywhere, and it was up to our knees as we waded through it.

MR36.51 Was that around *Low Bush Cranberry Lake*?

SF36.54 From here we walked down. On this day, you see? We had to be here before the deadline, so we kept on traveling, wading in the water. We were trying to save the school, and then. . .

MR37.30 What about around *Big Lake*?

SF37.33 While we were traveling on this side of *Big Lake*, people from the village sent three young men to meet us so they could help us. One of them was *Peter*. I don't remember the other two. They didn't feel good from

Aii gwiizhìk gàh gwiindàii kwaa ts'ą' zhik ts'ąįį tr'ahàajìl. Akhài' zhat chųų lęįį tr'ecdàa t'ihnyąą. Aiits'ą' yaaghà' diinanghàih hàajil nąįį gooraąh'ya' kwàa. Izhìk gwiizhìk it'ee *John Fred* aii daga'at hàa, aii hàa t'ee yaaghà' van jyàhts'aii.

MR38.28 Tik nąįį lèe vaiinyąą?

SF39.30 Tr'iinin chan tr'eeghwàa. *John Fred* daga'at hàa nitì' *chief* giłtsąįį, nàhąą? Aiits'ą' t'ee ch'iidaa heehaa eenjit. Yaaghà' van ee'lin dàk it'ee *John Fred* daga'at hàa t'ee ch'iidàk gahàa'oo łee. Izhìk dąį' t'ee ch'iidàk tąįį gwigwìłtsąįį. Izhìk dąį' t'ee *Njaa Tąįį*[27] gàgàhnyąą. Aii gogwahtsii łee, diidigiheedàa t'igii'in akhài' àkwàa. Aiits'ą' yaaghà ts'ąįį t'igwiizhìk ts'ą' diigwach'àa iłtraa rǫh. Aii neerahàachii tł'ee it'ee *one day* gwizhrįh. Aii zhìt dzaa tr'agwahąąh'yàa t'igwii'ìn. Aiits'ą' t'ee diigwach'àa neerahaahchii tł'ee dzaa gwats'ą' tr'eeheedàa gwiindhàn. Aiits'ą' chųų zhìt teeraajil ts'ą' diigwach'àa trah tthak neeraahchii rǫh.

42.11 Diigwach'àa neeraahchii gwiizhìk it'ee *school kids* nąįį tthak łàa yee'ęę tr'iinjil. Tr'ahahchųų gwinyąą ch'yąą gòhch'it chan tr'ąhchųų kwaa t'iihnyąą.

42.50 Aii *Sam* chan diihàa needyaa, aii t'ee zhat diinihłeehòozhìi. Aiits'ą' t'ee tr'iinin nąįį goozhìt gwìłts'ik t'ii'in t'iihnyąą. Aiits'ą' nilįį tee, tyąh nitsìi chan neeraha'ak, aii zhìt nilįį givęętr'iłvìr, *rice* chan. Aii tthak gooneech'arah'àl tł'ee tr'ìiłchųų. Akhài' gwiizhìk chan tr'iinjàa nąįį chan ch'ii'ęę tr'iinjìl.

43.57 Ts'ą' chan, chan giveenjit chan shìh vikeech'iriłch'yaa chan neech'igiin'àl. Chan neegohòojil. Neegohòojil. Aiitł'ee t'ee tth'aii garaandàii gwiizhìk chan *John Fred* daga'at hàa chan yee'ęę tr'igiin'òo.

MR44.38 Ijìn dąį' oo'àn neezhii? Ti'yąą aii?

SF44.41 Gwats'ą' dąį' hee *flag* k'eegahchaa năihnyąą, izhìk tł'ee hee. Aiits'ą' t'ee aii *John Fred* chan zhat k'eegii'òo. Aii chan jidìi tsal gin'àl. Aiitł'ee t'ee t'inyąą, "Oochìt

27. *Njaa Tąįį — Vįįhtaii gwats'an Van Choh ts'ą' taii goo'aiì t'agwarahnyąą.* —JE

not eating, so they stopped to rest and sleep. We could have met them too, but there was too much water, so we went the other way and didn't see them at all. Meanwhile, *John Fredson* and his wife also came on that side of the lake.

MR38.28 Did you say there were three of them?

SF39.30 We were packing our children too. *John Fredson* and his wife got your father elected as chief, you see? And they were expecting us that day, so they must have walked up to *Big Lake* to meet us also. At the same time, both of them were making the *Black Duck Trail*. That's how the trail got its name. So they planned to meet us but didn't. We had only one more day left to get to *Venetie*, so when we finally came out of the water we decided to stop and dry all our wet clothes. Then we would go down, we thought.

42.11 While we were drying our clothes all the school children came to where we were. What I'm saying is we were planning to sleep for a while but didn't because of them.

42.50 *Sam Roberts* left us there and went ahead to *Venetie*. Those kids were very hungry too, and so I made meat soup with rice in my big pot and fed all of them. Just when we were getting ready to sleep, the women came to our camp also.

43.57 And so we cooked for them too. They all left too as soon as they ate. Everyone left. While we were still awake, *John Fredson* and his wife arrived also.

MR44.38 When did Father go back over?

SF44.41 I told you, right after the two men brought the flag. Then *John Fredson* and his wife arrived and ate a little bit and told us, "Keep on going so you could have a better jì' hee gwinzįį hohchųų, googàa jùuhch'yaa ootthàn hohjyàa," danàhnyąą, aii *John Fred* reh. Aiits'ą̀' t'ee jèiinch'yaa tr'ąhchų̀ų kwaa ts'ą̀' t'ee oodaa tr'ahàajil ts'ą̀' dzaa k'eeriidàl t'ôohju' hee tr'ąhchųų.

46.00 *School* zheh gwiheekwàa. Łihàa dat'àii hàa geetr'itagwah'yà' į'. Aiits'ą̀' aa dzaa k'eeriidàl łìhàa shoo nilįį.

46.30 Aii t'ee dzaa k'eeriidàl ts'ą̀' hee, izhìk t'ôohju' hee gwinzįį tr'ąhchų̀ų. Aiits'ą̀' t'ee oo'òk tr'iinin nąįį tthak gwinzįį ch'a'àa kwaa roh. Izhìk t'ee yaaghà' *Agnes Choh* vigii nèekwaii nąįį? "Khaiinjih gookwaa," t'agwaihnyàa. Aiits'ą̀' khaiinjih gookwàa. Aii gwiizhìk k'eeriidàl ts'ą̀' t'ee nitì' aii. . .

47.05 Nitì' aii t'ee *chief* tr'iłtsąįį nàhąą? Aiits'ą̀' t'ee t'inyàa. Aii ts'ą̀' gwiizhìk zhik gookàįį' nąįį nàhąą? Datthak yeenjì' dzan keegahàajìl. Dzan keegii'in googàa digi zheh neegogwąą'in kwàa. Oo'ęę neegiijyàa kwàa. Gwiizhìk t'ee zhat k'eeriidàl t'agwaihnyą̀ą.

48.06 Izhìk dąį' t'ee, zhik nankat jidìi trih vàràhnyąą? Aii jèiinch'ii khagahshrì' łee, aii chan kwaii chan kwàa. Aii chan zhyą̀ą chųų ch'įh hàa giiyahvìr. Aii zhrįh t'ee ga'àa łee t'agavaihnyą̀ą.

MR49.16 Aii trih k'ìt t'inch'yaa vǎiinyąą. Aii nan zhìt khagiiyahshrì' vǎiinyaa. Aii ninghit dąį' gwanaa, gwats'an jyàa dòh'in lèe t'iinch'yàa?

SF49.32 Ąąhą'. Aii ch'adąį' gwanaa diikhwan diinehnaa tr'agwandàii, dinjii gwandàii nąįį giit'ąąch'yaa į'. Shìh kwaa dąį'.

MR Jak k'ìt t'inch'yaa aii yù'?

SF49.38 Jùk gàa reh, jak aii chan shin gwizhrįh ǫh.

MR49.44 Aii gàa khaii eenjit jyàh giiyaatsii lèe t'inch'yàa?

SF49.48 Ąąhą', gàa dandaih, natł'àt, aii zhrįh. Jak aii ìizųų į'. Aiits'ą̀' aii trih chan, *carrot* gwìch'in *just like carrot. Indian call it* "trih."[28]

28. *Trih* is commonly known in English as "Eskimo Potatoes." —KP

sleep down in the village," which we did. And we finally went to sleep when we got there.

46.00 He really worked hard to keep the school open. So he was really happy when we came back.

46.30 So we finally had a good sleep. There was no food for the children in the village. And those two boys of *Agnes Peter*? "Almost died," I'm saying. They almost died. We arrived while that was going on . . .

47.05 Your father was chief, you see? All the men in the village went across the river for muskrat, you see? They were harvesting muskrat but hadn't come home yet. I'm saying that's when we arrived there [in *Venetie*].

48.06 That time, this one in the ground they call *trih*? That kind, we root them up. Since there was no grease, we boiled them in plain water. I mean, that's really all we ate.

MR49.16 You mentioned that *trih* root looks like a carrot. So they must have eaten that. Has it been used for ages?

SF49.32 Yes. It's been used since way before I was born whenever there was no other food.

MR What about blueberries?

SF49.38 Blueberries too, but only in the summer.

MR49.44 Did they store blueberries for the winter too?

SF49.48 Yes, but they spoil easily, so they stored alpine berries and low bush cranberries and also that carrot-like plant. Indians call it *trih*.

51.40 Aiits'ą' it' ee dzaa k'eeriidàl. Akhài' tr'iinin nąįį tthak ch'a'àa kwàa. Gwiizhìk chan dink'ee chì' chan kwàa. *Shotgun* chì', .22 chì', jii tthak kwaa ǫ'.

52.19 *John Fred* aii *school* shii tsal di'įį, nahąą? Googàa shìh tthak di'įį kwàa. Jidìi *can* kwaii, nihłehjùk t'iich'yaa kwaii di'įį. Aii zhrįh zhrįį t'ąąhch'yaa di'įį ts'ą' t'ee *Gwichyaa*[29] oothàn tr'agwahąąh'yàa eenjit gwinzįį gwilii. Aiits'ą' t'ee nitì' yuuahkat į'. Tr'iinin nąįį ch'a'àa kwaa roh. Aii enjit t'ee *school* zheh nishįį. Dąįį', "Ootthàn *Gwichyaa* tr'agwahąąh'yàa gwats'ą' vat'ąąch'yaa tsal aii tthak vats'an tr'iinlii ts'ą' ànts'ą' tr'oonadhak k'ìt t'inch'yaa aii shintł'eiinlìi," àhnyąą. Aiits'ą' *John Fred* aii t'inyàa. "Łihàa *law* ìizųų t'aiinyąą," yàhnyàa. Nitì' àhnyàa, "Akhài' aii *law* ìįzųų vaiinyąą shįį veenjit nihihthat t'inch'yaa. Aiits'ą' jidii vats'an shìh t'ąąch'yaa aii tr'iinlìi. Ts'ą' ànts'ą' tr'oonadhak aii shintł'eiinlìi," yàhnyàa. Aiits'ą' adlàa, "Łyaa *law* ìizųų t'àihnyąą kwàt googàa nik'it t'ihishi'yàa," yàhnyąą.

54.54 Aiits'ą' t'ee aii shìh jidìi t'àihnyaa. Tthak yats'anyit'eehąąhch'yąą datthak tthòk nìinlii ts'ą' yats'an tr'oonadhak chan tthòk nǐinlii. Aii t'ee nitì' yùunjik t'ee tr'iinin nąįį datthak tèeyàadlìi. Aii jyàa diizhìk.

55.30 Aii t'ee zhik ch'iyèhghan nilįį nąįį? Zhik dzan keegìi'in, nàhąą? Izhìk dzan keegii'in jì' aii làraa giideek'ìt nìheelyaa eenjit t'iyah'ìn jyàa digiyinlik į'.

MR56.25 Dzan tthąį' gàa oo'ęę neeginlìi?

SF56.30 *Nò.* Dąhkhyùk gwahàadhat, gòhch'it t'ee oo'ęę neegiijyàa, chan dzan tthąį' gwinzįį k'ineegilik kwaa t'agavaihinyàa.

MR56.45 Aiitł'ee yù'?

29. *Gwichyaa — It'ee Fort Yukon t'agwarahnyąą.* —JE

51.40 And so when we arrived we found out that the children were not eating very well. Nobody had any shotgun shells, .22 shells, or other shells.

52.19 *John Fredson* had only a small amount of school food, you see? Not exactly everything, but different kinds of canned food. At the same time there were plans for a trip to *Fort Yukon*. So your father said to him, "Give us some school food for the hungry children at least until they make a trip down to *Fort Yukon*," and *John Fredson* said to your father "It's against the law to do that." So your father told him, "Go ahead and give it to me anyway. If I get caught, I'll take all the blame for it." He told *John* to get whatever he needed and to give him the leftovers. *John Fredson* laughed and said, "You're really breaking the law, but I'll give it to you because I trust you."

54.54 And so he took whatever he needed from the school food and set aside the leftovers, and your father took them and gave them out to those children who needed it. That's what he did.

55.30 Those parents? They trapped for muskrat, you see? The parents who were out trapping at that time were supposed to pay back something when they got back, which they did.

MR56.25 Did they bring back any muskrat meat?

SF56.30 No. They were gone a long time, but like I was saying, they didn't bring home that much good muskrat meat.

MR56.45 Then what happened?

SF57.04 Aiits'ą' t'ee tth'aii oo'ęę neegiijyàa kwaa ts'ą' t'ee aii shìh *John* vats'an shìh jyàa dìnlìk. Aiitł'ee chan *Myrà* chan, *Saràh, Sophie.*[30] Jii tik nąįį, dehtsii zhìt gwà'àn nagantii akhài' dink'ee kwàn, dink'ee tsal, vihtr'ii kwaii hàa ineegogwàh'àk. Ineegogwàh'ak aii t'ee, aii hàa t'ee *John Fred* hàa òodak *Van Choh* ghat nineegii'òo, izhìk t'ee aii *shotgun* chan vich'ì' neerahtsii reh. Aii chan vichì' vahtsii kwaa. Aii t'ee nitì' t'igwihee'yàa kwaa t'ii'in t'avaihnyàa, Aii t'ee oozhee łuhkat ch'iizhàk yideek'ìt gwìłtsàii. Ch'iizhak t'ee yichì' gwik'yà'ak ts'ą' t'ee yichì' nahtsìk. Aii hàa t'ee oodàk dats'an kaneegii'òo. *John Fred,* nitì' hàa.

MR58.28 Dèegwąąch'yąą *time* t'iizhìk?

SF59.16 Gwilin t'iizhìk t'aihnyąą, lee gwiihchyàa gǫ̀'? Gwilin oodàk nineegihee'àl datthak jyàa dìgiiyah'in.

MR59.30 Adan *John Fred* hàa t'igii'in?

SF Ą̀ąha'.

<sfws105Db>

SF2.24 Izhìk it'ee dats'an. Geetàk dats'an *ten* àanch'yaa oodąą neegilìk, izhìk it'ee yee'àt tr'iinin nèekwąįį khaiinjii vakwaa văihnyàa. Aii ch'ìhłak oodàk adàh gihìlchįį. Adàh neegahaachìk.

2.46 Izhìk dąį' *Sophìe, Myrà, Saràh, Agnès* chan, aiits'ą' *Emmà*[31] vigii kwaa į', *Emmà* chan, aii tr'iinin, aii nąįį tr'iinjàa nąįį lęįį kwàa. Izhìk dąį' yaaghà' *Myrà* chan vigii nąįį lęįį, *Agnès* chan, *Sophìe* chan vitseii nąįį, yaaghà' *Elijah John* vigii nąįį, aiits'ą' izhìk dąį' ginlęįį į', aii tr'iinin nąįį lęįį. Aii zhrįh googii lęįį.

MR5.45 Izhìk dąį' lee ti'yąą nąįį dats'an oodaa neegaazhik dąį' ookìt gogwâahk'ik lèe ch'yąą?

SF5.50 Ą̀ąhą', dats'an tsal oodaa neegaazhik t'ee yee'àt jyàa dòonch'yaa giveenìgilik aiitł'ęę zhat giits'ą' nadàl ts'ą'

30. Myra Roberts, Sarah Roberts, and Sophie John. —JE

31. The women named here are Sophie John, Myra Roberts, Sarah Roberts, Agnes Roberts, and Emma Roberts. —JE

SF57.04 Before the men got back, the school food was given out. Then *Myra Roberts*, *Sarah Roberts*, and *Sophie John* — these three women, were looking in their cache and found gunpowder, pistols, and empty shells which *John Fredson* and your father used to reload and make new shotgun shells. Down in the ground he made a hole for it. So that way he made new shells. After doing that, *John Fredson* and your father went up to *Big Lake* and shot ducks.

MR58.28 How many times did they do that?

SF59.16 I'm saying they did it many times. Every time they went up they made shells.

MR59.30 Just he and *John Fredson* went up?

SF Yes.

<sfwsl05Db>

SF2.24 At that time, sometimes they shot ten ducks. Remember, I was telling you about those two children who almost starved? They took one of those children with them when they went up.

2.46 The following women were living in *Venetie* at that time: *Sophie John*, *Myra Roberts*, *Sarah Roberts*, *Agnes Roberts*, and *Emma Roberts*. *Myra* had lots of kids, and *Sophie* had grandchildren. *Elijah John* had kids, *Agnes* had kids, but *Emma* had no kids. So there were lots of kids. These were the only ones who had children.

MR5.45 At that time, when my father and them brought back ducks, did they build a fire for them down there?

SF5.50 Yes. After bringing the small ducks back down, they put them outside for the people. Then they sat down and tthak shrìgìyìlìk ts'ą' giits'ìk, giichų', datthak tr'iinjàa, tr'iinin nąįį hàa tthak ch'ihłòk neegiya'àl.

7.03 Giits'ìk, giithąį,' datthak hàa giyahvir, łyâa zhyąą zhat gwihiljii gogwahtsìk t'ee.

7.05-16.41[32]

SF16.42 Aiits'ą' izhìk *school* gwihèelyaa gwats'ą' it'ee, goolàt nąįį zhrįh. Jii shaghwaii *Henrỳ, Emmà, Saràh,* yaaghà' *Agnès* aii nąįį àkwàa. Aii nąįį chan jii nąįį oondàk hee neegihiidàl. *Carò*[33] ch'iindàk ts'ą' yee'àt diizheh, *Gold Camp* ch'iindàk chan.[34] Jyàa dìgii'in izhìk ch'iindàk neegihiidàl chan ch'atthąįį gaghan, aii chan giyąhgąįį. Giyąhgąįį ts'ą' ch'adhàh tr'ihchoo gahtsìk, aii chan ch'iinaa teeneegahłak, aiits'ą' khaii gwįįzįį. Khaii t'ee gwįįzįį. Aii vank'yąą chan vàanoodlit shìi, zhik jidìi łùh kwaii, aii kwaii goonjii.

MR17.42 Aii lèe *Henrỳ* nąįį chan ts'ą' *Jonàs* nąįį chan hee?[35] Aii ts'ą' *Emmà* nąįį chan, nakhwan t'eh? *Four* nąįį hęę? Izhìk dąį' *Vįįhtaii* gohch'įį hee?

SF19.18 Izhìk dąį' lèe? Izhìk dąį' t'ee *Vįįhtaii* tr'igwich'įį kwàa. Yee'àt chan tr'igwich'įį izhìk *last time* yaaghà' *school* zheh zhat neeragòonjik jihnyąą? Izhìk gwats'an t'ee oo'òk neerihiidàl ǫ'. Aii t'ee geetàk hee dzaa *school* gwihèelyaa izhìk dząą nineeriidàl ǫ' jyàa dìgwii'ìn.

MR19.53 Shin hee oondòk gohch'įį ts'ą' khaii hee dząą gohch'įį?

SF Ąąhą'. Izhìk dài' yeedee ddhah kat googàa łi'hàa vadzaih gǫǫlįį ǫ'. *Lots of caribou!* Tr'àł nìłshįį ts'ą', aiits'ą' ch'atthąįį hah'òo aii gwik'ìt t'igwii'in kwaa k'ìt t'ôonch'yàa.

MR Khaii aii dèekhwa'ìn?

SF21.34 Khaii aii googàa chan neerihiinjìk ǫ', neerihiidàl.

32. Section is not transcribed. Sarah talks about working on gardens here. I'm lost in the long conversation between Maggie and her mother. —KP

33. *Caro — Vìihtaii gęhdak han gwinjik* 60 miles *goo'aii. Caro* is a deserted gold mining camp on the *T'eedriinjik*, sixty miles upriver from *Venetie*. —JE & CM

34. *Gold Camp — Venetie gęhdee ddhah ǫhts'aii.* Johhny, Sarah Frank *hàa goonahkat.* —JE

35. Henry John and Jonas Roberts. —JE

worked on them. The women and children ate them all up, including the guts and the broth.

7.03 They ate up the guts and boiled the duck meat. When they finished, there was nothing left.

7.05-16.41

SF16.42 Before the school opened, people used to go up toward *Caro* and toward *Gold Camp*. My brother-in-law *Henry*, *Emma*, *Sarah*, and all them all went up, except for *Agnes*. That's how they did it then up that way, by traveling around and also harvesting big game animals and drying them. They dried meat and then came back down on the river using skin boats. So it was a good winter. A good winter. We had plenty of white man's food too, like flour and such things.

MR17.42 Was it *Henry* and his family, *Jonas* and his family, *Emma* and her family, and your family —four families? Were you living here at *Venetie* at that time?

SF19.18 At that time? We were not living here in *Venetie*. I'm saying we moved back and forth after the school was almost closed down. Then we moved here again just before school started.

MR19.53 Did you stay here [in *Venetie*] in the winter and go back up that way [to *Gold Camp*] in the summer?

SF Yes. At that time there were lots of caribou up here on the mountains. Lots of caribou! Now it looks like the caribou don't come by there anymore because of the brush that has grown up around there since then.

MR What did you do in the winter?

SF21.34 We traveled around from place to place even during the winter too.

MR21.45 Aii lèe jùu nąįį tthak? *School* gahtsii gàa lèe?

SF21.51 Kwa'! *School* gahtsii gwats'an it'ee oo'òk gwiizįį tr'agwąąh'in kwàa, *school* gwilii ts'ą' .

MR22.05 Ti'yąą aii yù'? Khaii hee dèe'ìn? Khyą̀h iłdlii?

SF Ą̀ąhą', khyą̀h iłdlii, datthak ts'ą' reh, dinjii tthak reh khyąh giłdlii. Yeendee ndàk chan.

22.44 Shìh chan oo'ęę neegaazhik, aiits'ą' t'ee gwįįtsàl gwįįzįį. Gwiizhìk chan oondee zhat dąį' *school* zheh traa dàaką', aiits'ą' shìh, traa hàa tr'ookwàt eenjit chan shìh dhidlii, aiits'ą' aii kwat tthak t'èegwąąhch'yaa ts'ą' gwįįzįį.

28.15 Jyàa dìgwiizhìk gwats'an t'ee gwįįzįį. Aiits'ą' zhik traa, shìh, *government* shìi. Aii chan dhidlii ts'ą' aii vit'įį traa tr'ich'yàa, nàhaa? Aiits'ą' shìh chan jyàa dàrah'in ts'ą' izhìk gwats'an gwįįzįį ǫ', izhìk nahnjyàa gògǫ̀ǫtrii jihnyąą izhìk dąį' łyâa gwìizųų ǫ'. Izhìk t'ee t'igwiheech'yàa t'igwii'ìn, aiits'ą' aii gwats'an it'ee nitì', nàhąą? Dząą tr'igwich'įį ts'ą' t'ee dachan zheh gǫ̀ǫlįį kwàa, dachan zheh gǫ̀ǫlįį kwaa ts'ą' t'ee datthak *meetìng* neegahtsìk ts'ą' oo'òk jyaa dòonch'yaa, zheh gogwaghan. Tthak chan nihts'ìgiinyąą ts'ą' zheh gogwahtsìi.

29.10 Aiits'ą' traa khał choh. Trah khał choh chan gahtsìk, aii kat t'ee dachan oo'ęę neegiilùu. Dinjii nąįį hàa tł'yah zhyą̀ą gǫǫtà' ts'ą' dachan oo'ęę neegaazhik hàa t'ee yeechùk zheh gǫ̀ǫdlìi.[36]

MR30.00 Gehjuu gwànaa dąhthee t'igii'in shrǫ̀ǫ yindhàn?

SF Gehjuu gwànaa gwiyeendaa nįįzhìt kwaa, izhìk it'ee khaii dachan goonjii, shin chan, aii chan khwą̀h hàa. Aii hàa t'ee yeechùk zheh gwigwįįghan, dehtsii kwaii hàa.

35.49 Izhìk nan *Resèrvatiòn* ginyąą, izhìk jyàa dìgwii'in tł'ęę t'ee gwats'an gwahàadhat kwaa, dąhshùk gwahàadhak lì'. . .

36. When I first arrived in *Venetie* in November, 1972, almost everyone was living down below the bank close to the river. After repeated flooding and federal grants for new housing, families started moving up onto the bluff above the river on both sides of the old air strip. This relocation took place in the 1980s and early 1990s. Today no one lives down below. –CM

MR21.45 You mean everybody did that? Even when there was school?

SF21.51 No! We hardly went out after the children started school.

MR22.05 What about Father? What did he do in the winter? Did he trap?

SF Yes, he trapped. So did everyone else. Everybody trapped up that way.

22.44 It was good after they started bringing in food. At that time, the school burned wood too, so they traded their firewood for food, and it was all useful and good.

28.15 Everything was good for us after that, trading firewood for government food. But before that time, it was really bad, so we had to go along with it and try our best to live, you see? There were no log houses here, no log houses, so your father and everyone held a meeting and decided to work together to build them.

29.10 They also built a big wood sled to haul logs in. All the men and young girls hauled logs in the big wood sled on a long rope and pulled it into the village. That's how those cabins down in the old village were built.

MR30.00 How long ago was that, do you think?

SF Not too long after that. They got house logs during the winter and brought down logs using river rafts during the summer. They built houses using those logs, and caches.

35.49 From the time they talked about getting the Reservation, I don't know how long after that they. . .

MR36.02 Dąąch'yaa *years* shrǫǫ yindhàn?

SF36.05 Aii khan nihkat dagàho'ąįį ts'ą' t'igiizhìk į'. Aii chan shachaa *John,* aii nitì' aii shik nihłàa gogwaandak, nàhąą? Izhìk t'inyąą "Oondùk hee *Resèrvatiòn* gǫǫlįį" gwinyąą. Izhìk "Gwik'ìt t'agoonjii jàghaii" nyąą. Nitì' aii jyàanyaa akhài' aii *John Fred* chan łyâa veechìi t'igwinyaa. Aiits'ą' t'ee gee gwitr'it t'agogwah'in, nàhąą. Izhìk dąį' *chief* nilįį. Tth'aii hee *chief* nilįį gwiizhìk tthak shrìgwįįlìk. Aii izhìk t'ee *resèrvatiòn* gòoli' nyąą. *Tr'ootsyaa* ginyąą, aiits'ą' t'ee dinjii oozhrì' goonjii, nàhąą? Dinjii oozhrì' goonjii ts'ą' aiitł'ęę t'ee dzaa tr'igwich'įį gwats'an yeendàk hee oondee *Ahtr'aii Kwànjik* ginyąą, izhìk gwànaa chan dinjii làt gwich'įį.

38.37 Izhìk oondàk nòozhìi, izhìk dinjii oozhrì' òonjik izhìk t'ee łyâa doozhrì' nizįį. Iłtsąįį giyàhnyąą. Vàaneerihii'òo į', vigii ch'ìhłak.

42.15 Aii shachaa *John Fred* izhìk jyàa dìgii'in, oozhee łùhkat dink'ee chì', nahtsik văihnyàa dèegwii'in datthak gwadâąatł'oo į'. *Book* jyàa dąąti' kat aii dèegįįlìk, aii t'ee vàashandàii kwaa, aii kat tthak gòodlìi. Shįį zhyąą gwik'ìits'ik hee geegwaldak t'ihnyąą.

43.15 *Book* jyàa dąąhti' reh, aii kat dèegwii'in datthak gwadâąatł'oo į'. Aii *book* dèeginlìk gavàashandàii kwàa.

MR Aii gwats'an yù'? Aii ch'oozhrì' òonjik t'ee?

SF43.44 Aii ch'oozhrì' òonjik tł'ee t'ee jii t'ee *resèrvatiòn* gòodlit ǫ'.

45.05-46.37[37]

MR46.37 Izhìk dąį' *Arctic Villàge school* gǫǫlįį lèe t'ôonch'yaa nyąą. Kwàa?

SF46.49 Aii dzaa tr'ohchìt *school* gǫǫlįį ǫ' aii t'ee t'ôohju' hee oondee chan *school* gòodlit ǫ'.

MR Dąąch'yaa *years* tł'ęę t'igiizhìk lì' hęę? Izhìk dąį' *school* gahtsii kwaa ts'ą', zhyąą jyàa dìginch'yaa hęę?

SF Ąąhą'.

37. This section is in English and was not transcribed. —CM

MR36.02 How many years do you think?

SF36.05 It happened a few years later. Also my younger brother *John Fredson* and your father always talked about the Reservation, you see? John mentioned, "There are lots of reservations down in the Lower 48." Your father wanted to do that and they say John was really glad about it. "Let's do it," he said. Your father was still chief at that time and they both went to work on it, and they collected signatures, you see? After doing that, they say there were also some people living up at *Wind River*.

38.37 *Johnny* went up there and collected names and signatures, and that's when he became well-known and admired by people for doing it. One of his sons went with him.

42.15 My younger brother *John Fredson* wrote down everything in his diary like the time they made shells and so on. He had a thick book on which he wrote down everything we did. I don't know what they did with that diary. I'm only telling about what I remember.

43.15 That book is about this thick (gesturing), and he had everything we did all written down in that book. I don't know what happened to that book.

MR What happened next, after he got the signatures?

SF43.44 After he collected the signatures, this land became a reservation.

45.05-46.37

MR46.37 He [*Mike Holloway*] is asking if there was a school in *Arctic Village* at that time. Was there?

SF46.49 We had a school here [in *Venetie*] first and then later on there was one in *Arctic Village*.

MR I wonder how many years later that was. At that time, there was no school up there, and they didn't do anything about it, right?

SF Yes.

Johnny Frank

Geech'aroąąhtan Zheh Tr'ookit

<jfka406>

JF14.34 Aiits'ą' *Vįįhtąįį* ootthàn nineihdìk, *school* gokwaa aii chan, dąąch'yąą *year* zhyąą gweedhaa.

Niti'izhii oothàn nineihdik gwiizhìk *chief* niłi'izhii gaghan.

Ts'ą' *council* nąįį googàa, *nothing.*

14.55 Aiits'ą' reh, gohch'it reh, ootthàn zhat shats'an khaii dhiilii, oochìt eenìneihdìi.

Akhài' reh *Elijah Figure* aii reh zhat dhidii łèe.

Aii videhtsì zhìt dhidlii rǫh.

Thirteen hundred pound *shìh reh.*

Aii zhyąą datthak k'èegwiich'yaa gigii'įį kwaa gwiizhìk chan *Tsyaa T'oo* va'at chan nìnghit łee ts'ą' reh izhìk k'eihdìk.

15.34 *Elijah* vành khàchee aiits'ą' reh shàa ginkhìi,

"Tr'agwazhrąįį *school* eenjit oonìn dęhtł'yaa neerahtsìk, *chief council* hàa khaihłan neegiidàl. Googàa diik'èegwarahthat kwaa," nyaa ts'ą' "Dôonch'yaa jyàa reh?" shàhnyàa.

15.53 "Àkwat dinjii nizįį ohłįį kwaa geh'an t'ôonch'yaa," gavăihnyàa.

Aiits'ą' chan kheedeegwii'àk.

"School yindhan eenjit lèe t'iinyaa?" gohch'it văihnyàa.

"School nihthan kwàt geh'at nĭinjinìhshit kwaa gàa deegwihihłyàa łàa gàashandàii kwaa, t'ihnyàa," jyąą nyàa.

16.25 "Kwàt łì'hàa *school* gòo'e' nihthan," jyàa reh nyàa.

"Kwàt *school* gòo'e' niindhan jì', łąhch'yâa khan ts'ą' *school* shrigwìhihłyàa t'ôonch'yaa," vaihnyàa.

16.41 *Yes or no,* łyâa zhyąą "*no*" gwinyąą "*hell*" t'agwaràhnyaa, kwàt "*yes*" gwinyaa "gwandaii" t'agwaràhnyaa văihnyàa.

Łì'hàa akòodinizhìk jì' łyâa tsee'in haanjyàa.

Johnny Frank

The First School

<jfka406>

JFI4.34 I continued going to *Venetie* now and then, but there was no school for years and years.

There were different chiefs and councils every year.

But still there was no school, nothing.

14.55 And then I went down there once to pick up 1,300 pounds of food I left in *Elijah Figure's* (*Elijah John's*) cache.

When I arrived in *Venetie*, *Tsyaa T'oo's* wife was dying, and hardly anyone had anything to eat.

15.34 *Elijah* woke up one morning telling me:

"We put a lot of effort into writing a letter. The chief and council had a meeting about it. But they don't write back," he said, "and people ask me, 'What's wrong?'"

15.53 "You people are no good; that's why it's that way," I told him. He still brought up that subject every time I went down.

So I finally asked him, "Do you want the school that bad?"

He said "Yes, I want a school, but I don't know how to start one, since there are no answers when we send out letters."

16.25 "I want the school to be there," he said.

And I told him "If you want a school, I'll arrange it right away."

16.41 So I really told him about what yes and no meant. I told him "no" meant "hell," and "yes" meant "life."

He was really curious as to what I had in mind.

"Dĕiinyaa t'iinyàa łyâa gàa'ooshandàii nihthan," jyàa reh nyàa.

17.09 Aiitł'ee *two day* gwiindhat ts'ą̀' t'ee yee'àt *school* zheh gòo'ąįį gwàdhałtsąįį.

School books tsal chan oochùk gwats'an reh, *first gradèr, fifth gradèr* aii vitee gǫ̀ǫlįį kwàa.

17.28 *First gradèr* zhrįh.

Aii tsal chan reh dehtł'yaa tyąh zhit jyàa dą̀ąch'yąą reh dhidlìi.

Aiits'ą̀' reh, *pencil* chan kwàa.

17.45 Gwiizhìk *Ned K'aa Chief* nilįį ts'ą̀' reh łyâa *smart* adâa'įį reh.

Łyâa akòo diindhan jì' eenjit dzaa jùk yeedì' kwantee hìi'al ts'ą̀' t'ee *school* zheh tr'agwahahtsyàa văihnyàa.

Jàghaii *government* vàa deegwadǫǫh'àii gwąął'in kwaa văihnyàa.

18.13 Dzaa gwich'in naii *government* k'it'iinch'yaa ts'ą̀' kwaiik'ìt shrigweheelyaa geenjit gwitr'itagwah'in kwaa geh'an t'ôonch'yaa văihnyàa.

18.20 Aiits'ą̀' *ten minute* tł'ęę, gwiizhìk *Ned Chief* nilįį veenihdee hihshyaa ts'ą̀' *ten minute* tł'ęę shik'įh hinhaii văihnyàa.

Aii ch'oohaałkat tł'ęę k'iidì' gwich'įį nąįį tthak tee k'eeriheedàl tł'ęę t'ee oodee zheh shreerigwiheełyàa văihnyàa.

18.44 Aiits'ą̀' aii *Ned K'aa* veenihdĕiizhìi.

Neech'aga'àa gigiinjii łèe, daga'at hàa gwiizhìk nehdĕiizhii.

"Dhindii," shàhnyàa.

Nŏiidii tł'ęę t'ee reh, k'eegwiich'yaa t'anakhwahaihjyàa, *Chief* inlįį t'ôonch'yaa văihnyàa.

19.06 Łyâa k'èegwaadhat choh jii kwaiik'ìt gwizhìt inlįį.

Gàa nikì' neeshrâahch'yaa t'ôonch'yàa văihnyàa.

Yes or no, aii zhrįh anoohaałkat văihnyàa.

No jiinyaa jì' haałchyaa kwaa ts'ą̀' cheehihdyaa văihnyàa.

Kwàt *yes* jiinyaa jì' gàanandàii kwaa gwinlęįį gwihîintth'ak t'ôonchya'aa văihnyàa.

"I really want to know what you mean," he said.

17.09 Two days later, a school building was up and ready for use.
Just first graders' books were available.
There were hardly any fifth graders' books.

17.28 Just first graders' books were in a small cardboard box.
But there were no pencils.

17.45 *Ned Roberts*, thinking he was pretty smart, was the chief at that time.
I told *Elijah* we would go from door to door to tell everyone.
I told him there was no reason for them to bother the government when they could make a school themselves.

18.13 I also told him that they themselves, the Gwich'in, were the government and could do something to build up this village and that the reason nothing was happening in the village was because the residents weren't doing anything about it.

18.20 I told him to follow me in ten minutes while I talked to *Chief Ned*.
I told *Elijah* that after I talked with *Ned*, he and I would go to people's homes and then we would fix up the house which was already there.

18.44 I went to *Ned Roberts'* house.
I walked in just when they had started to eat.
"Sit down," they told me.
And then I told him why I was there.

19.06 I told him about how important a chief is at making decisions.
I even told him about how ignorant he was.
I told him it was a yes or no question.
I told him if he said no, I would say nothing and walk out.
But if he said yes, he would hear a lot of things from me that he didn't expect.

19.33 Jyàa vǎihnyàa ts'ą' t'ee reh daga'at hàa dlòk hàa neenałagąą'ìk.

Gàa reh *"No,"* goonyą' giindhan gàa gwiizų̀ų.

No reh *"Go to hell"* t'iinch'yaa vǎihnyàa (adlaa).

Kwàt *yes* gwinyaa łyâa zhyąą zheekat gwik'èegwaadhàt gwizhìt nihdèe gweedįį t'aragwàhnyaa vǎihnyàa.

19.57 Aiits'ą' gohch'it reh, *"Yes,"* nyàa.

Va'at chan vadâazhìk.

It'ee gavàa gwaldak.

Zhik gwà'àn *handsaw*, dachan vàa'ìighwąą, *hammer,* gwatsàk ni'įį jį' aii chan teegwąhjìi vǎihnyàa.

Jidìi geenjit t'ihnyaa, aii dàa nagwahąhdal gwats'ą' *chief* inlįį gàa *one word* gąą hąąhchyaa kwaa vǎihnyàa.

20.26 *Council* chan *one word* gàa haahchyaa kwaa, nah shįį zhrįh děiihnyaa zhrįh tr'ooheendal vǎihnyàa.

Jyàhts'ą' t'ee kwaiik'it nirigwichii t'ôonch'yàa.

20.38 Jyàa vǎihnyàa ts'ą' t'ee reh, aii teegwąhjii vǎihnyàa.

20.54 Aiits'ą' t'ee reh, zhyąą dlòk hàa zhyąą dats'an teegwąhjii ts'ą' chan nihdêiinzhii ts'ą' adan chan *ditòol* nihdèe t'oon'ąįį.

Yuudì' datthak dagats'an teegogwąhjii ts'ą' t'ee reh yeendee hèedąį' reh yaaghà' tsyaa vizheh, zheh zhyąą nìgwigwiintthaii łèe.

Kwàt t'ee k'eegwiich'yaa gwizheh tr'agohtsyaa giindhan gàa chan dèegihee'yàa gàagiindàii kwàa.

21.25 Aii reh gòo'ąįį, dachan chyàh aii chan ęhjyàa dǎadlii, vinjyâa'yaa, gindêeenvyaa agàa.

Aii t'ee yaaghà' *Ginnìs Tsal*, *Andìroo Ch'àa* nąįį hàa t'igii'in reh.

Aiits'ą' reh goots'ą' nihděiizhìi.

21.42 Gooveevan nihděiizhii ts'ą' akǫ' jyàa daghwa'in gavǎihnyàa.

Dachan vàa'ìighwąą hàa, nijùk vinjyâa'yaa k'it ch'ìhłęę, ginděiinvyaa chan ch'ìhłęę.

Dachan chan tr'aghwąą.

19.33 I told him about it, and they just sat there glancing at each other.

They wanted to say no, but I didn't give them a chance.

I said they would all go to hell if they said no (laughs).

And if he said yes, then they say it meant they would go to heaven.

19.57 Finally, they both said "Yes."

So then I told them about my plans.

And I told him to pick up whatever tools he had — handsaw, plane, and hammer.

I told him not to say a word until we finished whatever we planned to do.

20.26 I told him even the council should not say one word about it.

I would be the only boss on this project and this is the way to start a village, I told him.

20.38 And so I told him that, and he picked up his tools.

20.54 He gladly went on his way and picked up his tools when *Elijah John* came around with his tools too.

And so did everyone else.

There was this empty house which some of the younger guys built a few years back but left unfinished, and I don't know why.

21.25 There was this house standing there with the windows, lumber, and door still sitting outside of it.

I guess it was *Little Ginnis* (*Ginnis Golen*) and *Andrew* (*Roberts*) who left it unfinished so I went to talk with those two.

21.42 We all went to the house, and I told them to get to work.

I put one person at the window with a tool, one at the door, and told the rest to make lumber for the floor.

Khàa ts'ą̀' t'ee tǫǫ nigwìhìltth'at gwiizhìk t'ee chanchyàh kat gwizų̀' hee reh.

22.07 Aii kwaii googàa aii jidìi gwizhìt gwįhdaii izhìk K'eegwaadhat zhrįh shichì' zhyą̀ą'ą̀įį.

Aiits'ą̀' t'ee tthak gile'ràadlii ts'ą̀' it'ee oo'àn neekhwajyaa, nìhkèe vành, nakhwazheh tr'iinin hàa tthak, dzaa nihdǫǫhjyaa.

Datthak gwik'èe nakhwahaałtyàa t'iihnyaa gavăihnyàa.

Aiits'ą̀' reh, akǫ̀ǫ digwìizhìk.

"Nakhwagii, nakhwa'at tthak khaihłan *one place* jyàa dohch'yaa," gavăihnyàa.

22.49 Shįį oondaa chanchyàh tł'an *chair* nĭi'ą̀įį.

"Jùk gwats'an yeedàa njii kwaiik'ìt gwiheezyàa.

K'eegwaadhat vàagwahaldak t'ôonch'yàa, nats'àa dèevăihnyaa aii shiginjìk anoondàii."

Nankak gwidinjì', gwanzhįį, nint'aii ts'ą̀' riginkhii k'ìt t'inch'yaa t'aràhnyaa gavăihnyàa.

23.12 Goondàh akòo diinyà'.

Tł'ęę gwintl'oo "Màhsi'," ginyàa.[1]

Dèeginyaa lì'.

Àkwàt jùk nakhwàa *meeting* hałtsyàa gàa ginjih ìhłak zhrįh anakhoohaałkàt, datthak zhyą̀ą jùu goihshįį nindhan gooheezhryàa gavăihnyàa.

23.45 Gàa zhik jùk *school* zheh gwadhòhtsąįį t'ôonch'yaa ts'ą̀' oothàn geedoondak shrǫ̀' goovaihnyàa.

Geegoondak jì' ohłęįį ts'ą̀' nihłehts'į' geegohoondak ts'ą̀' gwiihèezųų t'ôonch'yaa gavâihnyąą.

24.06 *Hannah Steven, Charlie Steven* hàa nįįzhùk *school* gindì' t'inch'yaa văihnyàa.

Andìroo chan gwintsìh kwaa *school* indì' gàa *fifth gradèr* gàa gwinzįį hàandaii kwaa gavăihnyą̀ą.

24.55 "Nats'ąą ninjich'ohthat k'ìt nakhwagweech'in nats'ą̀ą dòhch'yaa t'ohch'yàa," gavàihnyą̀ą (adlaa).

1. The Gwich'in word *màhsi'* ('thank you') is derived from the French *merci*. It was introduced by French Canadian fur traders in the mid-19th century. —CM

The floor was in just when it was getting dark outside, and it was a nice good floor too.

22.07 I have faith in God all my life, no matter what I do.

After finishing, we swept the floor, and I told the guys to go home.

Then I told them, "Bring the whole village to the new schoolhouse in the morning, children and all."

They did this very thing the next morning.

"Your kids and your wives just stay in one place," I said to them.

22.49 I put a chair in the middle of the room and told them:

"I will now pray and tell God about this, and everyone should remember my prayer about it," I said.

I also lectured them for a while about faith in God.

23.12 I gave a prayer.

Then everyone said, "Thank you."

And then we had a meeting and I gave them a chance to pick out a person.

23.45 I reminded them not to tell anyone outside the village about the new school.

Because there would be rumors and everything would be ruined for us, I said.

24.06 I told them about how educated *Hannah* and *Charlie Stevens* were.

I also told them that *Andrew* himself is educated a little but is not yet a fifth grader.

24.55 I told them, "You all seem to have good sense but don't put it to very good use" (laughs).

Kwàt jùk khyąh t'arah'in k'ìighai' shìh tr'aahkhwąįį k'ìighai' gwizhrįh ch'ara'àa tr'îilk'ìi.

Dinjii Zhuh tr'inlįį ts'ą' reh.

25.09 "Łyâa *early days* gwats'an tr'agwandàii t'ôonch'yaa gàa it'ee tr'iheedàa nìgwiindhàt.

"Googàa *chief* dòhnyaa googàa ch'ihłòk tr'ahaah'yàa agàa gwahtsii kwaa łyâa gwiizųų," gavàihnyàa.

25.22 Aiits'ą' t'ee reh, *Hannah Steven* aii zhik digii nąįį k'ąą zheh gwizhìt dhidii nilįį zhrįh gwats'an aii reh *teachèr* heelyàa, aii googàa reh gwadrąįį niinji'òhthat kwaa t'oohnyaa gavàiiinyàa.

25.40 "Àkwat zhik *Charlie Steven* aii va'at *teachèr* nilįį gwiizhìk vigii yavaa, traa kwaii hàa datthak eenjit gwitr'it t'agwahah'yàa t'inch'yaa," gavàihnyąą.

26.04 Ndàa gwâą'ąį' reh, "Dèegwąhtsii dèe naragooheekwàt?

School zheh indì' kwat datthak gàanandàii t'ôonch'yaa," văihnyaa.

"Zhyąą shìh jidìi vini'įį kwaa, aii nihk'yaa chan khyąh tr'iheelyàa ts'ą' dèegwąhtsii jiinyaa łyâa zhyąą *evèn* tr'agwahahtsyàa gwats'ą' tthak naragooheekwàt," jyàa văihnyàa.

26.39 Akhài' reh, *$300,* nyàa.

It'ee sheenjit gwinzįį.

Aiits'ą' reh, *$50* zhrįh shi'įį aiits'ą' *$20* oondaa veenăałtsùu ts'ą' *Jimmy Roberts* chan *$7.*

Aii goolàt nąįį chan *$1,* aiits'ą' tuuvìt, hoovìt[2] hàa reh.

Gah gwinlęįį reh gwihiljìi.

27.10 Shįį reh gwìhiljii jyàa gìnyàa, nats'àa gwihiljìi, khyąh t'ahąh'yàa t'ôonch'yaa nats'àa gwihiljii.

"Nàhaazhrii agàa?" văihnyàa.

"Zhyàà dèegwàhtsii k'ehąhdraa jì' gwats'an *$5, $10* oondaa nâahtsùu ji' gàa laraa t'inch'yaa," văihnyàa.

27.27 Zhyąą dlòk hàa tthak gwik'ìt teegoot'oo'aanąįį reh.

It'ee łyâa giveenjit gwinzįį.

2. *Tuuvìt* and *hoovìt* are the Gwich'in equivalents of 'two bits' and 'four bits.' —CM

I also reminded them that we were Indians, and the only way we can make a living is by trapping in order to put food in our house.

25.09 "We've been around since the really early days, but we'll be gone soon," I said.

"You people say 'chief,' but the chief doesn't do anything for you and that's really bad," I said.

25.22 And then I told them about how *Hannah Stevens* could become our teacher.

25.40 "Even though she has a husband in *Charlie Stevens* and small children of her own, she still can come and be a teacher," I told them.

26.04 I finally asked, "How much should we pay you?

You should know all about school," I told her.

"Whatever food you don't have, we can go trapping and just make it even with you," I told her.

26.39 She agreed to $300.

I felt good now.

I donated $20 out of the $50 I had, and *Jimmy Roberts* also donated $7.

Some of them gave $1, others gave 25 cents, or 50 cents.

Lots of other people had nothing.

27.10 Some people complained that they had nothing to donate.

"What do you mean, nothing?" I said.

"You're going to be trapping or hunting and can donate meat," I said.

"And you could donate $5, $10, or any amount out of your trapping," I said.

27.27 They all laughed and decided to work together.

They really did what I asked them to do.

Aiits'ą̨' reh t'agavaihnyàa,
"Gwitł'ęę niizhùk kwaa jùu zheh nihee jì', *school bòoks, writìng papèr, pencìls.*
Zhyą̀ą giniinkhii kwaa gàanandàii t'ôonch'yaa," văihnyàa.
"Chan *school* zheh tr'igwìłtsąįį vàagwahandak kwaa ts'ą̨' zhyą̀ą tr'iinin goohąąłchyàa shats'an tr'igwìłtsąįį.
Pencil, writing papèr, school book extra nilii jì' aii shintł'ĕiinlìi.
Shats'ą̨' nĭinlii jyàa văiinyàa.
Tr'ookwàt oiinyąą jì' narooheekwat.
Aii zhrįh goots'an ąhtsii văihnyàa aiitł'ęęànts'ą̨' geedąhkhài' gik'ìgahaandal gwats'ą̨' geenjit nilįį dzaa niheehàa t'ôonch'yaa," văihnyàa.
28.31 Ànts'ą̨' zhyą̀ą geegoondak shrǫ̀' gavăihnyą̀ą.
"Kwàt yaaghà' ootthàn neheehàa aii chan dęhtł'yaa zhrįh k'eehahchaa ts'ą̨' *school* zheh eenjit geegwahaandak kwaa ts'ą̨' *teachèr* intł'èeyahahchàa," jyàa gavăihnyàa.
28.45 *Andìroo* aii ootthàn yàahàazhii łèe.
Gęhdaa khàa it'ee reh *school* tr'ahtsìi.
Gwintł'oo gavàa shrôonch'yaa t'iihnyàa.
Łyâa gagàa gwinzįį goovaa gwahałtsyàa gàa jùk it'ee akhàgàvòiihnyaa.
29.14 Jùk *Vįįhtąįį* khèedąį' dęhtł'yaa shats'ą̨' nìrìinlii yeendìt gwats'an.
B.I.A. reh.
Gwitr'it eenjit laraa dąąch'yąą niindhan.
$37,000 kwaiik'ìt vàa shreerigwiheelyàa.
Zheh tr'igwiheeghàa.
Jidìi gwit'èegwą̀ąhch'yaa tthak vàa gwitr'it t'agwahaa'yàa, tąįį tr'agwahahtsyàa kwaii hàa tthak reh.
Aii googàa shik'èe gwigwìłthat kwàa.
Gwiizhìk ootthàn *meeting* nineihdìk.
Second class ihłįį oochìt.
29.50 Aii googàa gaveh'àn akhàgòiihnyaa.
Oochìt gwitee dhiidii jùk it'ee shant'ee łyâa laraa lęįį shantł'èerahaazhik gàa reh akhàgòiihnyaa.

Then I said to them, "The next time someone goes to *Fort Yukon*, they should get school books, writing paper, and pencils from the school there.

"Don't talk for nothing," I said.

"Don't even say that we built a school. If they have extra pencils, writing paper, and school books, tell them to give those to you. If they want us to buy them, we'll buy them. From there on, they'll figure out that we're running our own school and will send a government person for this kind of matter," I said.

28.31 And so I told everyone not to say a word about it.

"And the next time someone goes to *Fort Yukon*, he should carry a list of school supplies with him to give to the teacher there." That's what I said.

28.45 *Andrew* (*Roberts*) must have gone to *Fort Yukon* later on with the list.

School was in session the very next night.

I'm saying the children were very happy.

I really could have done lots of other good things after that, but I quit.

29.14 Years later, I received a letter from the Bureau of Indian Affairs willing to help the village with money.

So I asked for a $37,000 grant which would go for improving the village, such as new houses and new roads, but they didn't approve it.

I continued to go to meetings in *Fort Yukon*.

I was even treated second class there.

29.50 I quit because of them too.

If I was still on that committee, I think I could get lots of money by now, but I just quit.

30.09 *Last time* t'ee, *president* ąhtsii shàgàhnyaa goonąhtan ts'ą' *president* heelyàa ts'ą' ginkhii chan goohąąhchyàa shàgàhnyaa.

Kwàt chan *council* chan nats'ąą geenjit *council* gwinyaa tthak geegavoohąąhchyàa.

30.32 Aiits'ą' *Chalkyitsik, Beaver,* oondee, dzaa datthak gwitee neehindik shàgàhnyàa.

Tr'agwazhrąįį yee'òk gootee neehihdik jyàa gavăihnyaa nakhwàh gwahaldak gavăihnyaa, googàa aii dinyaa ihłįį kwaa ts'ą' shidįį chan gahaahchìi kwàa.

33.00 Gàa dzaa jùk shįį zhrįh gàa kheenjit gwinzįį gwahaltsyàa.

Some wày ts'ą' laraa hałtsyàa.

Gwinkeegihihkhyàa aii shantł'èe tr'igwihee'aa t'ôonch'yaa roh.

33.16 Jyàh ts'ą' gwinzįį gòodlit.

Aii gwats'ą' *three year gwìindhat ts'ą'. . .*

No. . . two year gwìindhat ts'ą' aiitł'ęę khaii aii t'ee *John Fred* gwats'ą' hàazhii.

33.39 Oondùk nankat lęįį nąįį shįį *teacher* oihłi' nyaa.

Ch'iinii dęhtł'yaa jyàa dinlìk googàa *John Fred* aii N.C.[3] dhidii aii eedan aii shoąąhkat tł'ee t'ee reh, ąąhą' văihnyàa.

33.52 It'ee reh, *school* goodlit.

Aii three year tthak *chief* inlì' łąįį gàa ihdàndhàgąįį.

Ned dinjii gàa vijìh àn dhidlit.

Izhìk geh'an *chief* shìłtsąįį t'aihnyàa izhìk dąį' t'ee *Resèrvatiòn* oodhiijìk.

34.18 Aiitł'ee chan *homestèad* chan oodhiinjìk kwàt Dinjii Zhuh ch'ìhłęę gàa jyàa dii'in kwaa datthak t'ishi'ìn.

3. The N.C. was the Northern Commercial Company, a store and trading post in *Fort Yukon* and many other rural Alaskan villages. It was replaced in the 1970s by the A.C. or Alaska Commercial Company store. See Mishler, 1982. —CM

30.09 The last time I went, they told me to form a village council with a president and send for a preacher to be in charge here.

And to give the council training.

30.32 They also told me to travel to *Chalkyitsik* and *Beaver*.

I used to walk around to people's houses, trying to tell them about the meetings I went to, but nobody listened or said anything.

33.00 I could even start a community here (at *Gold Camp*) if I got to work on it.

Some way I think I would make big profits if I was given enough money to start something like that.

33.16 So that's what really happened in the past.

After that, three years passed. . .

No, two years passed, and then that winter *John Fredson* came.

33.39 Lots of teachers in the Lower 48 wrote letters and asked to become teachers up here, but *John Fredson* asked me, and I gave him permission.

He was working at the Northern Commercial Company store at that time.

33.52 We had a school after that.

Ned was chief for three years and even all the dogs starved to death.

Even the people almost didn't make it.

That's why *John Fredson* made me the chief, and that's when I got the Reservation.

34.18 I also got myself a homestead, and I did lots of things that one Indian person alone couldn't do.

Sarah Frank

<sfwsl05Cb>

SF14.32 Izhìk dąįį' *Ned,* aii *chief* nilįį, aii dąįį' *school* gwehèelyaa eenjit dęhtł'ee gahtsìi. Oonìn dęhtł'ee gahtsii gàa gook'èegwaadhat kwàa. Aii t'ee zhik yaaghà' *Stevèn* chan, *Rufùs* aiits'ą' yaaghà' *Ginnìs Tsal,* yaaghà' *five* giilįį. *Ginnìs Tsal, Abràhàm, five* giilįį aiits'ą' t'ee jùunch'yaa zheh zhyąą gwigwìłtsąįį.

15.23 Gàa zheh gwigwìłtsąįį ts'ą' t'ee k'èegwiich'yaa aii eenjit t'igii'in gàa jidii geenjit t'igii'in izhìk gàagiindàii kwaa ts'ą' zheh gwigwìłtsąįį. Gàa dachanchyàh kwàa, vinjyâa'yaa chan kwàa. Aii gwiizhìk it'ee *Ned chief* nilįį aii oonìn dęhtł'ee ahtsii, *school* eenjit. Googàa gwik'ìt t'igwii'in kwàa.

21.19 Izhìk gwànaa dąįį' nàhąą? Jii Vàanòodlit shìi chan kwaa ts'ą' zhyąą zhik gwà'àn nin gwandàii tr'ihee'àa eenjit gwizhrįh nijìn gwinzįį izhìk it'ee ninzhùk tr'igwich'įį. Diikhwan jyàa dìgwii'ìn. Aiits'ą' yee'àt t'ee gwinzįį *Vashràįį K'ǫǫ* giłèeràhàajil ts'ą' yee'àt nìriinjil ts'ą' t'ee zhat tr'iinin nąįį chan gwinzįį ch'a'àa, diilìk chan. Aii eenjit yee'àt giłèerehijyàa kwàa, aiits'ą' *three years* tr'igwinch'ì', aii gwiizhìk it'ee dzaa *school* eenjit giginkhii gàa àkwàa.[4] Aiits'ą' jii zhit t'ee nitì' aii. Nitì' aii dzaa oo'ęę nèhèe, akhài' aii t'ee jyàa àgàhnyaa hàa gogwaandak, *Elijah, Ned* hàa.[5] Aiits'ą'*school* gwehèelyaa eenjit shų' oonìn ch'aroaahkat ginyàa.

23.45 Nitì' hàa gogwaandak ts'ą' t'ee gwiizhìk aii zheh gwigwìłtsąįį gòo'ąįį. Vinjyâa'yaa chan kwaa, dachanchyàh chan kwàa. Aiits'ą' t'ee *Ned* t'àhnyàa, "Shįį jì' *opèn* gwahałtsyàa t'ôonch'yaa," jyàa yàhnyaa łìi.

---

4. The Franks moved to *Gold Camp* about 1934 or 1935, and the first *Venetie* school seems to have opened around 1938 or 1939. —CM

5. Sarah says *Nitì'* ('your father') because she's speaking directly to her daughter Maggie. —CM
Elijah and Ned are Elijah John and Ned Roberts. —JE

Sarah Frank

<sfwsl05Cb>

SF14.32 *Ned Roberts* was chief at that time, and he was writing letters asking for a school. He kept writing letters, but they wouldn't do anything. Counting *Ned*, there were five people: the others were *Steven Fredson, Rufus Roberts, Little Ginnis Golen*, and *Abraham Christian.* They built a cabin.

15.23 There was already an unfinished house there. All five of them worked on it, but they didn't know why they were working on it. There were no windows or floor in it. *Ned Roberts* was chief. He continued writing letters for a school but got no answer.

21.19 Back in those days, you see, there was no white man's food, so we stayed here and there, wherever there was plenty of game. Sometimes we stayed for a long time in one place. We moved away from *Arctic Village* to *Gold Camp* where it was good. We ate well there and so did the dogs. We were there for three years when people here asked for a school. And now this is your father (*Johnny*). Your father came over here once, and that's when they told him about it. That was *Ned Roberts* and *Elijah John.* So they told him they couldn't get a school going.

23.45 That unfinished house was still there when they talked to him about not getting any answer concerning the school. There were no windows or floor for the house. So *Johnny* must have told *Ned* this, "If it was me, I would start and open a school."

24.07 Aiits'ą' *Ned* aii veechìi t'igwinyàa. Veechìi t'igwinyaa ts'ą' t'ee, "Aii jì' *opèn* gwąhtsìi," yàhnyàa. *Elijah John* chan *secònd* nilįį, aii chan hàa gwaandak ts'ą' chan aii chan akoodìnyàa. Aiits'ą' t'ee, tł'ęę t'ee łyâa *opèn* gwahąhtsyàa t'iinyaa jì', jùk diineenjit *opèn* gwąhtsii giyàhnyàa łìi.

25.18 Aiits'ą' t'ee gàh *meeting* giłtsąįį ts'ą' t'ee, nitì' aii akòo dàgavàhnyaa łii roh. Jùk ch'ìhłęę zhyąą heedyàa kwaa ts'ą' datthak oo'àt zheh dachanchyàh vinjyâa'yaa hàa ǫhtsii gavàhnyaa łìi.

26.04 Datthak dzaa gwich'in ginlįį ts'ą', datthak *hammèr* tèegǫhjii gavàhnyaa łìi. Aiits'ą' t'ee datthak jyàa dìgiizhìk ts'ą' dachanchyàh, vinjyâa'yaa hàa tthak gwik'ìginlįį. Aiits'ą' gwizhit chan gwigwîiłk'ìn.

26.49 Aiits'ą' t'ee gwigwîiłk'in ts'ą' t'agavàhnyàa. Aiits'ą' chan gavàa *meeting* ìłtsąįį. Aiits'ą' gavàa *meeting* iłtsąįį ts'ą' t'ee tagavàhnyàa, "Jùk dzaa it'ee geenjit gwitr'it t'agwahaa'yàa. Aiits'ą' tthak dzaa khaihłan nǫ̀ǫhjyàa ts'ą' datthak geenjit khàrigiheejyàa," jyàa gavàhnyaa łìi.

27.31 Aiits'ą' datthak jyàa dìgiizhìk. Tr'iinin nąįį hàa tthak jyàa dìgiizhìk ts'ą' t'ee giveenjit khageedì' łìi. Giveenjit khageedì' tł'ęę t'ee t'agavàhnyàa, "Aiits'ą' jùk geenjit khagigeedì' ts'ą' it'ee shoh hàa datthak gwizhìt ch'oodzaa gavàhnyaa łìi. "Ch'ahoodzaa tł'ęę chan *teachèr* kàreheentyàa aii gooteekàreheentyàa, aii eenjit gwats'ą' ch'oodzaa," gavàhnyaa łìi. Aiits'ą' t'ee tthak gwik'ìt t'igii'ìn.

29.30 Aiits'ą' chan ch'agaadzyàa. Aiitł'ęę t'ee chan hee t'agavàhnyàa. Gootee jùu nąįį gwintsàl ch'adantł'òo, aii *Andrèw* chan ts'ą', shųų *Hannàh* chan, *Charlie Stevèn* chan, *three* nąįį. Jii ch'ìhłęę eenjit, ch'ìhłęę *try* gwahahtsyàa gavàhnyaa łìi. Aii jùu shrit nohthan aii ohshrìi gavàhnyaa łìi. Akhài' *Charlie Stevèn* ginyaa łìi. Akhài' nitì' aii t'agavàhnyàa, "Izhìk gwintsàl tr'idèegôiidhan t'ôohnyàa, jii *Charlie Stevèn* aii jii

24.07 *Ned* was happy when *Johnny* told him that. So *Ned* said to *Johnny*, "Open the school then." *Elijah John* was second chief. They also told him and he was happy for it too. They both told *Johnny* to go ahead and open it.

25.18 They held a meeting and *Johnny* told everyone his plans for the school. He gave orders for them to put in windows and doors.

26.04 He told everyone there to pick up their hammers, which they all did, and they put in the windows and doors. They even started a fire inside of it.

26.49 After they got the fire going inside, *Johnny* held another meeting with them. He said, "Everyone come to the meeting so we can pray for luck."

27.31 Everyone came, even the children, and he prayed with them. After praying for them, he told them, "Let's have a dance in here, and then we'll find a teacher after you dance." And that's exactly what they did.

29.30 Then too after the dance, he told them about some people who could write a little bit. They were *Andrew Roberts*, niece *Hannah Stevens*, and *Charlie Stevens*, those three. He wanted them to try and choose one of them. At first, they wanted *Charlie Stevens*, but your father (*Johnny*) told them, "*Charlie Stevens* is needed at home for dizheh tr'iinin yihee'àa traa datthak, aii eenjit gwitr'it t'agwah'in t'inchyàa."

30.52 Aii tr'idèegôiidhan t'ôohnyaa gavàhnyaa łii. Aiits'ą' chan *Andrèw* chan t'agàhnyaa gàa aii chan àkwàa. Aiits'ą' t'ee *Hannàh* aii t'ee *one year.* Aiits'ą' t'ee gwik'ìt t'iginyaa ts'ą' gwik'ìt t'igiizhìk. Aiits'ą' *one year* gweedhaa izhìk t'ee dzaa gwich'in nąįį.

MR32.25 Nats'àhts'ą' giigookwàt aii?

SF32.27 "Dzaa gwich'in nąįį akòo dǎiinyą'. Tsèe dhàh ohtsii gwats'an nakhwateegwąąch'yaa ts'ą' datthak làraa veenjit khaihłan nǫǫhłii," jyàa gavàhnyaa łii.

MR33.45 Aiitł'ęę nakhwan chan oo'ęę neekhwajil?

SF33.47 Izhìk t'ee gwats'ą' gwaldàk. Aiits'ą' t'ee *one year school* iłtsąįį *Hannàh.* Aii t'ee oochìt *Gwichyaa.*[6] Jidii *book* tsal kwaii ootthàn gòonjik łii, aii hàa t'ee tr'iinin nąįį ǫǫąhtàn.

MR35.08 Aii jùu ootthàn nòozhii lì', hęę?

SF35.17 Adan gwìch'in roh.

MR Aii juu?

SF *Hannàh.* Adan aii oochùk *book* tsal jyàanch'ii tsal jiinyaa yàhnyaa aii ootthàn kòozhii gwìch'in roh.

MR35.54 Aii nats'àhts'ą' ootthàn nòozhìi?

SF35.57 Ootthàn łąįį hàa reh. Izhìk dąį' *airplàne* kwàa. Ootthàn nìgìyìłchįį. Aiits'ą' izhìk jyàa dǐizhìk. Aiits'ą' *one year* tr'iinin nąįį *school* iłtsàįį. Aiits'ą' t'ee zhik datthak gogwandàk goodlit łii. Datthak gogwandàk gòodlit łii ts'ą' t'ee oondùk ànihłik hèe shįį zhat *teachèr* hihłyàa, gwats'ą' hihshyaa gwinyaa nyàa. Aii shachaa *John Fred,* aii geegwaandàk.

MR37.00 Aii nijìn gwich'įį t'inch'yàa, aii *John Fred* izhìk dąį'?

SF37.03 *Gwichyaa Zheh N.C.*[7] dhidii t'ii'ìn.

MR37.27 Aiitł'ęę dèegiizhìk?

6. *Gwichyaa* is the nickname for *Fort Yukon.* —JE

7. Again, the N.C. was an acronym for the Northern Commercial Company store. —CM

hunting and getting firewood for his family, so we can't hire him."

30.52 They also talked about *Andrew*, but then decided not to. But *Hannah* taught for a year. And they did what they promised. So they decided on *Hannah* and she taught here for a year.

MR32.25 How did they pay her?

SF32.27 "Tell all the people here. Bring in the fur, collect the money, and pay her," he told them.

MR33.45 Did you move back from *Gold Camp* after that?

SF33.47 I haven't got to that part yet. *Hannah* taught school for a year. One of them went to *Fort Yukon* to pick up a few books, and she used those to teach the children.

MR35.08 I wonder who went down to get them, do you know?

SF35.17 She herself did.

MR Who's that?

SF *Hannah*. I think Johnny told her to pick up the books, and she went down herself.

MR35.54 How did she go down?

SF35.57 Someone took her down with a dog team. Because there were no airplanes at that time. She taught school to those children for one year. Then word got around about the opening of the new school. Even teachers from the Lower 48 all wanted to come, they say. My younger brother *John Fredson* told us about it.

MR37.00 Where was *John Fredson* staying at that time?

SF37.03 He was working at the N.C. Company in *Fort Yukon*.

MR37.27 What happened after that?

SF37.29 Aiits'ą' t'ee adan aii. . .*next year* adan aii t'ee zhat gwats'ą' hàazhìi. Va'at chan gǫ̀ǫlįį ts'ą' vigii nèekwąįį nąįį chan gǫ̀ǫlìi.

MR38.14 Aii nats'àhts'ą' giyùunjìk? Adąhkhài' t'iizhìk?

SF38.18 *John Fred* lèe? Adąhkhai' t'iizhìk. Oondùk ànihłik jyàa gwinyaa gàa adan aii dzaa valàk nąįį gǫ̀ǫlįį, nàhąą? Aiits'ą' shįį aii giveenjit *teachèr* hihłyàa niindhan ts'ą' gwik'ìt t'iizhìk adąhkhài' łyâa zhyąą dzaa gwats'ą' hàazhìi.

MR39.25 *School* iłtsąįį t'inch'yàa hęę?

SF *John* lèe? *Thirty years* oonìn *school* iłtsąįį.

MR Dąhtsii gwiizhìk hàazhii văihnyaa łii?

SF39.42 Jyàa dąhtsii gwiizhìk it'ee *Mrs. Wood,* aii t'ee yùunjìk.[8]

MR Aii lèe Vàanòodlit?

SF39.59 Ąąhą', tr'ìnjàa. *Mrs. Wood, Mr. Father* hàa tr'ohchìt k'eegii'òo, *Gwichyaa*. Izhìk dąį' it'ee jii yaaghà' shachaa *John Fred* chan, aiits'ą' yaaghà' *Paul Needąąjal*[9] chan, *Alfrèd* chan, *three* nąįį. Aii nąįį goohan kwaa, nàhąą? Goohan kwaa aii nąįį, jii tik teegwìłjìk, oonìn neehàadlii. Aiits'ą' oondùk hee *school* giłtsąįį.

MR40.43 Aii nijùk gwà'àn hee *school* giłtsąįį lì' hęę?[10]

SF40.47 Oondìt *state* gwà'àn dǫhłįį. Aiits'ą' t'ee dzaa k'idìk. K'idik dzaa t'ee *Hannàh school* iłtsąįį gwats'ąįį, adan chan *anothèr year* adan chan *school* ahtsìi. Izhìk gwiizhìk t'ee dzaa *Vįįhtąįį*, nàhąą? Łì'hàa shìh kwàa.

42.19 Vàanòodlit shìi chan kwàa. Zhik gwà'àn diishìi tr'a'àa googàa kwàa. *John Fred* tr'oochìt *school* ahtsii dąį' tr'iinin nąįį gàa gwinzįį *school* iłtsąįį kwàa.

MR43.21 Aii jàghaii gooshìi kwàa?

8. Lizzie Woods was a school teacher in *Fort Yukon*, arriving there in 1905 and staying until 1910. She also served as the village nurse and postmaster. She had previously worked for three years at the hospital and Episcopal mission in *Circle*. —CM

9. Paul Needąąjal is possibly Paul Williams Sr.. —AR

10. Although first tutored by Lizzie Woods, John Fredson had his advanced schooling sponsored by Archdeacon Hudson Stuck. —CM

SF37.29 And then he. . . *John Fredson* came to teach the next year. He had a wife and also two children.

MR38.14 How did he get chosen? Did he do it himself?

SF38.18 You mean *John Fredson*? He did it himself. They say lots of other teachers wanted to come, you see? But *John* had lots of relatives here too, so he came on his own.

MR39.25 He went to school himself, did he?

SF You mean *John*? He went to school for thirty years in the Lower 48.

MR How big was he when he left?

SF39.42 He was this big (gesturing) when *Mrs. Woods* took him.

MR Was she white?

SF39.59 Yes, a woman. *Mrs. Woods* and *Mr. Woods* came to *Fort Yukon* for the first time and took in three children. At that time they were my younger brother *John Fredson, Paul Needaanjal,* and *Alfred*, those three. They were orphans, you see? They had no parents, so they took them back to the Lower 48. That's where they went to school.

MR40.43 I wonder where they went to school?

SF40.47 Maybe down in the states. *Hannah* taught school for one year. And then *John Fredson* came here and started teaching school the next year. He was teaching here for about a year, you see? Then people right here in *Venetie* ran out of food.

42.19 There was no white man's food or our kind of food. When *John Fredson* was first teaching, children hardly went to school because of no food.

MR43.21 How come they didn't have food?

SF It'ee gògwàntrii ts'ąįį t'ôonch'yàa. Shìh tr'aahkhwaii gògwàntrii roh.

MR43.33 Izhìk dąį' dinjii dąąch'yaa nąįį zhrįh dzaa gwich'įį t'ôonch'yàa? *Ned Robèrts, Jonàs.*

SF *Henry, Ned. . .*

MR Gootèech'ooanzhrį̀'.

SF43.58 *Andrèw, Jonàs, Jamès, Ginnìs* chan, *Elijàh John,* aii nąįį zhrįh.

<sfws105Ea>

MR2.23 Izhìk dąį' aii ti'yąą jyàa dìi'in dąį' tthak nan t'ee dèeni'ìn?

SF2.33 Izhìk hee t'ee shant'ee deehishi'yàa, aiits'ą' zhik tr'ohchìt shant'ee giveenjit *try* gwałtsii. Ts'ą' *flag* shantł'èerąhtsuu ts'ą' reh. Aiits'ą' t'ee oondàk shin neerihiinjìk.

MR Aiitł'ęę yù'?

SF3.10 Aiits'ą' t'ee jidìi zhat dąį' jidìi zhat gwà'àn ch'adhàh kwaii, ch'idree dhàh, dinjik dhah, vadzaih dhàh, *parka* heelyàa, jii tthak giveenjit oodhiinjìk.

MR Aii ijìn gwà'àn t'akhwa'in t'inch'yàa?

SF3.36 Oondee *Neetr'ee Ddhàa* kat ch'iindàk.[11]

MR4.25 Aii nan ąhkhii *or* geedan giyahkhii?

SF4.28 Oonaa neeriinlii, aiits'ą' dzaa k'ineeriidàl ts'ą' t'ee aii *Elijàh John* chan, *councìl* nilįį, aiits'ą' aii shachaa *John Fred*[12] chan, aii chan gwik'èech'igilìk t'ii'ìn, akǫ̀ǫ kwàt aiits'ą' t'ee aii ch'adhàh tthak oonaa neeriinlii ts'ą' t'ee tthak yeezhee nǐilìi. Nǐilii ts'ą' t'ee, jii jùk tr'ohchìt gǫ̀ǫlįį, *try* tr'agwahtsii t'igwii'in, aiits'ą' jii tthak veegwitr'it'agohoh'yàa ts'ą' aiitł'ęę *sell* tr'ahahtsyàa ts'ą' aii valàràa, tr'onkwàt jì' aii gwįįtsàl *save* tr'ahah'yàa. Aiits'ą' aiitł'ee nijìn gòodhaii nàgwaadhàk

---

11. *Neetr'ee Ddhàa*—above *Gold Camp gehdak t'agwarahnyąą.* —JE
This was the site of Johnny Frank's caribou hunting camp, located upriver from *Gold Camp* and *Arctic Village*. Lots of caribou migrate over this mountain. —JF

12. John Fred — *Dinjii Zhuh naii jyahts'ą' gwizhrįh giyuuzhrii.* This is the only way Indian people called John Fredson. —JE

SF Because people couldn't get any game at all.

MR43.33 How many people were living here besides *Ned Roberts* and *Jonas Roberts*?

SF *Henry John, Ned Roberts . . .*

MR Name them.

SF43.58 *Andrew Roberts, James Roberts, Jonas Roberts, Ginnis Golen*, and *Elijah John* — that's all.

<sfwsl05Ea>

MR2.23 At that time when my father was doing all this, what were you doing?

SF2.33 What I was doing at first was trying to improve everything for people. That's why the flag was given to me. And so we traveled around from place to place during the summer too.

MR What happened after that?

SF3.10 At that time I saved animal skins — like caribou leg skins, moose skins, and caribou skins, and some to make parkas with.

MR Where were you doing this?

SF3.36 Up at and around *Neetr'ee Mountain.*

MR4.25 Were you tanning it or were they tanning it?

SF4.28 We brought it back to *Venetie*. *Elijah John* and *John Fredson* were on the council, and my younger brother *John Fredson* was the one who had the idea about the skins. We brought back all the skins and showed them to everyone. We told them that this is going to be the first try and we didn't know if it would work out, but we told them to work on the skins and sell them and jì' chan vit'èegwahaadhàl. Gàa shik làraa vàh heelyàa tr'ahah'yàa. Aii eenjit jyàa dahoh'yàa eenjit nakhweenjit ch'adhàh kwaii oodhiinjìk gavàihnyaa oozhee nǐilìi. Googàa ch'įhłee gwik'ìt t'iizhìk kwàa. Zhyą̀ą gwigwîitth'ak gwizhrįh.

SF6.25 *Two time* jyàa shizhìk, aii gàa àkwàt dàgavaihnyaa gàa gwik'ìt t'igii'in kwàa. Aiits'ą̀' t'ee akhàgavoiihnyaa. Aiits'ą̀' yaaghà' dachan k'eedài' tr'oonjii jihnyaa. Izhìk gwizhrįh geenjit chan *school* ahtsii khàihkwaii oaałkat į'. Zhik zhyą̀ą gwitr'it gwaatsii, aiits'ą̀' dinjii ch'ihee'àa geenjit gwizhrįh nik'èe shìh tsal duulèe diits'an tr'ahahtsyàa jì'. Jyàa vǎihnyàa. Oaałkàt. Akhài' chan *"Sure,"* shàhnyàa. "Gwik'ìt t'anairahah'yaa t'ôonch'yaa," shàhnyàa. Aiits'ą̀' izhìk dachan goonjii, zheh gogwahtsii kwaii hàa tthak chan, shįį shik'ìighai' ch'iriin'àl ǫ'. Zhyą̀ą ch'aga'àa, laraa gahtsii kwaa gàa zhyą̀ą ch'aga'aa gwizhrįh giveenjit shìh gaayii dhaltsąįį į'.

MR9.00 Aii gwats'ąįį yù'? Aii gwats'an k'èegwiich'yaa t'ini'in nik'èe?

SF9.11 Izhìk gwats'an t'ee *one time* chan *teachèr* ch'ìhłak łi'hàa zhyą̀ą *boss* nilįį ts'ą̀' *Vįįhtaii* nǐinzhìi. Aii zhrįh chan voozhrì' ìizųų dhałtsąįį.

MR9.29 Aii chan lee *Ednà Hall* reh hèe?

SF *Ednà Hall* kwaa, *Mrs. Hall.*

MR9.33 Aii reh.

SF9.39 Aii, dzaa naa, jii *council* kwat *chief* nilįį naii datthak googàà ts'ą̀' k'èegwaadhat. Aii naii googàa tthak doł'yà' nįįdhan gwik'ìt t'ii'ìn. Chan vik'ìighai' chan ch'iriinii. Aiits'ą̀' t'ee *somebòdy* sheenjit ch'adâątł'oo ts'ą̀' t'ee oonjìt *Junèau* hee gwats'ą̀' veenjit dęhtł'yaa naałtsùu.[13] *Junèau* hee veenjit dęhtł'ee akhài' khan dęhtł'yaa giits'ą̀', niłtsaii łèe. Dęhtł'yaa giits'ą̀' niłtsaii.

13. *Juneau* was the headquarters for all Bureau of Indian Affairs village schools in Alaska during territorial days. Teachers such as Mrs. Hall, who taught in *Venetie* in 1952, were hired and supervised from *Juneau*. —CM

save the money for emergencies and put some in a savings account later on. So I brought my skins and laid them down right there. But not one person did anything about it. They just listened, that's all.

SF6.25 Two times I tried to get them to do it, but they didn't do it, so I just let them be. I also asked the teacher for food from the school so we could cook for the workers. This was at the time people were getting house logs and building cabins. The teacher told me, "Sure. We'll do it for you." So that's how they got free meals because of me. They weren't getting paid for working, so I got the food for free just by asking.

MR9.00 What happened after that? What else did you do?

SF9.11 One time too there was this teacher who was real bossy who came to *Venetie*. I got her into trouble.

MR9.29 Was that *Edna Hall*?

SF Not *Edna Hall*, *Mrs. Hall*.

MR9.33 That's her.

SF9.39 She was boss of the chiefs and the councils here. She made them do whatever she wanted them to. She even introduced drinking. So I had somebody write a letter for me complaining about her and sent it to her boss in *Juneau*. She must have gotten a letter back from her boss because when I went to see her she ignored me.

Khaltsùu. Aii gwiizhìk it'ee chan oaałkàt. Aii chan tr'iinin iłts'ik googàa nihk'ìt *school* ahtsii àhnyąą, nàhąą? Izhìk geh'àn, izhìk chan vats'ą' hìdhiizhii. Aiits'ą' nihdèiizhii akhài' gwįįzįį shràgwąąhch'yaa kwàa. Aiits'ą' reh, "Hâa, *Saràh,* jàghaii t'ini'ìn?" shàhnyąą. "Àkwàt k'èegwiich'yaa geenjit noołkat nihthan t'ishi'ìn," jyàa văihnyàa. Aii gwiizhìk t'ashàhnyàa, "*Saràh,* oonìn *Junèau* hee sheegįhè' łèe, yaaghà' gwidęhtł'yàa iłtsùu," shahnyàa. "*Next time* chan sheeneegįįjii jì' t'ee zhee gwaazhrąįį hiindyàa," shàhnyàa.

11.29 Aiits'ą', "*Sure,* zhee gwaazhrąįį hihdyàa sheenjit gwįįzįį," văihnyąą. "Gwiihèezųų năihnyaa kwàa," văihnyàa. "Aiits'ą' yaaghà' tr'iinin naii *school kids* naii gįįlįį kwàt jàghaii tr'iinin, iłts'ik googàa nihk'ìt *school* ahtsii t'ini'ìn *government* yits'ìheenjyàa eenjit jàghaii jyàa dini'ìn?" văihnyąą. "Kwàt jùk *David Henrỳ* vigii jyàa dàvaiinyąą tł'ęę jùk vakwàa. Gwik'ìt *Robèrt* chan jyàa dàvaiinyąą. Izhìk geenjit noohaałkat eenjit t'ishi'ìn," văihnyąą. Izhìk gwizhrįh chan *troublé* gwįįlì' ǫ'.

12.36 It'ee?

MR12.40 Aii lèe nan ti'yąą hàa *chief* dhoodlìt dąį' lèe?

SF12.46 Ąąhą'. Aiitł'ęę vijuu gwànaa.

MR12.52 Izhìk gwats'an t'agwaràhnyaa, nan ti'yąą hàa *chief* dhoodlìt, aii gwats'an deeni'yà' aii.

SF13.06 Izhìk it'ee k'eejìt dąį' geegwaldak gǫ̀'.

MR13.19 Aii gwats'an t'ee oo'àn neekhwajil hęę?

SF13.24 Ąąhą'. K'eegwiich'yaa t'igihee'yàa eenjit t'agavăihnyàa gàa gwik'èegogwahthat kwaa ts'ą' zhyąą akhàgoiihnyaa năihnyàa.[14] Aiitł'ęę vijuu gwànaa t'ee chan tr'injàa naii hàa nìneeshagąąhchįį, izhìk t'iihnyaa t'agwaihnyąą.

14. Sarah is referring to the skin tanning project here. —JE

I also asked her why she forced kids to attend school even when they were sick, you see. When I went to her, she said, "What do you want, *Sarah*?" And I said, "I came to ask you something." And she said to me, "*Sarah,* I have a copy of the letter you wrote to *Juneau* about me. Next time you write a letter about me like that, you're going to jail for it."

11.29 And I replied, "Sure. I'm willing to go to jail. I'm not afraid," I told her. "Why do you let the kids go to school even when they're sick? Just so the government will help them?" I said to her. "Right now, you did that to *David Henry's* son, and he died. You did the same thing to *Robert*. So I came here to ask you about it." That's the only time we had trouble.

12.36 Okay, now?

MR12.40 Is that the time you and my father became chiefs?

SF12.46 Yes, a little while after that.

MR12.52 We're talking about that time after you and father became chiefs, and about what you were doing as chief.

SF13.06 That's what I've been talking about.

MR13.19 You went back (to *Gold Camp*) after that?

SF13.24 Yes. I'm telling you, they didn't do what I wanted them to do. They didn't obey, so I just gave up. What I'm saying is I tried again later when I was on the women's council.

13.46 Aiits'ą' izhìk it'ee gwįįtł'òo gwitr'itagwarah'yà' t'ôonch'yàa. *School* zheh chan gashraròłjik zhyąą *free*. Aii jyàa dìgwee'yàa ǫ'. Aiits'ą' zhik tr'injàa naii chan, oo'àt zheh gwizhìt shreerigwilìk chan, aii chan it'ee akǫǫ dàgàvăihnyąą ts'ą' gwik'ìt t'igwii'in reh. Jyàa gwizhrįh shant'ee t'ishi'yà' t'ôonch'yàa.

MR14.26 Aii jidìi zheh?

SF14.28 Oo'òk dinjii zheh gòodlii, *school* zheh chan. Aii hàa t'ee gwitr'it t'agwarah'in izhìk. Aii t'ee *school* zheh łyâa goo'è' nihthan, aii hàa t'ee zhyąą *free* zhyąą geegwitr'it t'agwarah'in t'agwaihnyąą.

16.42 Izhìk dąį' chan làraa àgǫǫtrii. Aiits'ą' zhyąą dinjii tthak khaihłòk jyàa dìheech'yàa eenjit gwizhrįh nįįjich'ihthat aii hàa t'ee oo'òk tr'ìnjàa naii tee k'eejìt dąį' akǫǫ dàgàvăihnyaa ts'ą' t'ee jùu zhik gwà'àn neeshrâahch'yaa k'ìt t'įįch'yàa. Aii naii googàa tthak eenjit gwitr'it t'agwarah'ìn. Izhìk akǫǫ dàgàvăihnyaa ts'ą' gwik'ìt t'igwii'in t'agwaihnyąą.

MR18.28 Aii zhrįh dzaa gwee'àn gwigwich'įį roh hęę? *Henry* chan ts'ą' *Enòch*[15] naii hàa.

SF Ą̀ąhą'.

MR18.35 Izhìk gwà'àn kwàntee datthak gohtr'àt diinohnyaa ìjìi.

SF21.19 Ą̀ąhą'. K'eejàt dąį' geeragwaandak, nàhąą? Aii gwik'ìighai' jùk dzaa *town* jùk gwįįtsìi gòo'ąįį t'ôonch'yàa. Zheh gwįįzįį chan tr'agwaghàn. Àkwàt zhat dąį' gwik'ìt t'igwiizhìk kwaa jì' deegwiheech'yàa lì? Aii *Sam Robèrt* aii chan diikhwan, diik'ìighai' łyâa zhyąą *school* jyàa dìgwiizhìk ǫ'. Jùk yee'òk zheh gwizų' chan tr'agwaghan, nàhąą? Jùk t'ôohju' hee geenjit shòh ihłįį (adlaa). Jyàa dàgwąhtsii geenjit nankat tr'agwandàii gàa gwįįzįį ǫ'. Diik'ìighai' k'ìt t'ôonch'yaa, kwaiik'ìt gwįįzįį nàgwaatth'at lì'hàa geenjit shòo ihłįį ǫ'.

15. Henry John and Enoch John. —JE

13.46 We worked hard at that time. We kept the school clean for free, without any pay. That's how much we wanted the school here. I even told the women to clean other people's houses, and they did it. I did all this.

MR14.26 Which houses are you talking about?

SF14.28 Anybody's house. Also the schoolhouse. We worked for the school for free. I'm saying that's how bad we wanted to keep the school open.

16.42 Money was hard to get at that time. I only thought of people living together and getting along and taking care of one another. I told them that's why I wanted the women to help each other and to work for those who were poor and needed help.

SF18.28 Were *Henry John's* and *Enoch John's* families living here at that time?

SF Yes.

MR18.35 I remember you told us to rake people's yards at that time.

SF21.19 Yes. Compared to what I've told you about in the past, you see, this town is big now. We all have good houses. If we didn't do what we did for the village, I wonder what would have become of us? I think it was because of us and *Sam Robert* that the school stayed open. Right now there are good houses everywhere, right? I'm happy now when I think back (laughs). It's nice that we have done something good for once in our lives. I think it's because of us that this place became a good village, and I'm really happy about it.

22.35 Jii t'àgwaihnyaa chan aiits'ą̀' jùk dząą shichìit'ik gwintsàl nehkaii gǫ̀ǫlįį k'ìt t'ônch'yaa, nàhąą? Aii chan zhik kwànchų̀' heekwàa geenjit tr'agwarah'in aii gwikìighai' juk chan jii kwaiik'ìt chan dinjìi nahkhìi kwaa, nàhąą? Aii googàa jii shakat gwìłts'ik, aii googàa zhyą̀ą k'ìt sheenjit t'ôonch'yàa. Aiits'ą̀' jii gwìhìljii dinjii gwįįzįį gwandàii ts'ą̀' nahkhìi kwaa, nàhąą? Izhìk t'ee geenjit jùk shoo ihłįį t'ihch'yàa. Jyàa dàgwąhtsii gwatsal gwitr'it t'agwarąh'yà' googàa jùk geenjit màhsi' nihthan ǫ'. Izhìk t'agwăihnyaa vàa gwandàk.[16]

16. She's referring to interviewers William Schneider and Mike Holloway here. —CM

22.35 You see this scar I have on my head? I got that when we were working to stop drinking in the village, you see? Right now, nobody is staggering around here. I'm glad everybody has a good life because nobody drinks in the village, you see? Because of that, I don't mind this scar on my head. I'm really thankful for that work we did. Tell them about what I've just said.

Fig. 27. Bureau of Indian Affairs site visit to Old John's Cabin on Old John Lake, July, 1979. Left to right are James Gilbert (standing), Tony Day, Moses Sam, Martha James, Abraham John (standing), Leila Wise, Alice Peter, Caroline Tritt-Frank, Myra Kay, and Carol Varner. Photo by David Libbey.

Part III
Tribal History and Lifeways

The final section of this book, narrated entirely by Sarah, contains stories and conversation about the social, political, economic, and religious history of the Chandalar Gwich'in. While Part I should appeal strongly to folklorists and Part II to biographers and oral historians, the narratives and dialogues contained in Part III should attract students of anthropology, ethnogeography, tribal politics, and material culture.

Gwich'in contact with early missionaries and cultural exchanges with Iñupiat Eskimos from the Arctic Slope and the central Brooks Range are described here in substantial detail. There are still several Nunamiut elders in Anaktuvuk Pass who remember walking and sledding several hundred miles to visit the Gwich'in living in and around Arctic Village. These are apparently the same people Sarah Frank vividly and joyously recalls playing games with at Vitsyaa Ts'ik ('Red-Finned Grayling') during her youth. Sarah was careful not to stereotype the Iñupiat (local Inuit), for whom she had much respect. She confirms, for example, that they ate raw caribou meat but quickly denies that they did this because they were too lazy to cook.

For the Gwich'in of Arctic Village and Venetie, as well as the Nunamiut at Anaktuvuk Pass, caribou is the animal most depended on for subsistence. Sarah talks at length about the days when they used caribou fences and corrals to hunt the herds during spring and fall migrations. In addition to bows and arrows, the Gwich'in used a short-handled spear with a bone point, called a *toh,* for killing caribou and sheep From Johnny's stories in Part I we know this *toh* was also essential to Gwich' in warfare prior to the introduction of firearms. Examples of this highly important piece of Gwich'in hunting and fighting technology, to my knowledge, have never been collected by any museum, and the art of making them has apparently been lost by today's elders.

Fig. 28. Sarah Frank cutting chum salmon. Photo by Mike Holloway.

Subsistence forms the heart of the Gwich' in economic system and is the underpinning of Gwich'in social structure. Even though today hunting and gathering are mixed in with a western cash economy, they, along with fur trapping, were the basis of Johnny and Sarah's livelihood. As many Gwich'in will attest, subsistence or *t'eediraa'in* is not just an economic system. It is also spiritual in that it defines the relationship of the people with the land and the animals and with one another. Through the sharing of food and labor, subsistence helps define the tribe's unique culture and way of life.

In her speech on subsistence, Sarah makes an extremely important point about the Gwich'in approach to teaching and learning. She shows her impatience with non-Natives who ask her how to make dry meat, "Even if we tell you how," she says, "you'll still say, 'I don't know.'" She stresses the importance to Indians of learning by observing and participating hands on rather than by memorizing a complicated set of verbal instructions. She also suggests that women's and men's domains of knowledge and behavior are in many ways exclusive.

As a companion to Sarah's recollection of Chief Peter and of caribou (uniting, readers may be interested in an unpublished account of the way Gwich'in people living in the area of present-day Arctic Village organized caribou hunts in the mid-1870s. The Anglican missionary, Kenneth McDonald, brother to Archdeacon Robert McDonald, paid a winter visit to it band of Neets'it Gwich'in living at a place called Big Sake, "where they have built a barrière." At this caribou fence, he conferred with John Ch'ijinjaa, the Christian leader of the camp, and several days later penned this account:

> Provisions are scarce so that after morning prayers all set out to hunt. 1 accompanied them. About two miles from the camp we espied a herd of deer [caribou] feeding on the side of a mountain. There being another mountain opposite the one the deer were on, the Indians decided on trying to drive the deer in the valley, and if possible, to surround them. Accordingly, the young men set out, several to the right and several to the left, and by making a long detour succeeded in getting in the rear as well as on the sides of the herd.

> The elderly men then took up positions at one end of the valley about 100 yards distant from each other. Three or four pieces of crusted snow placed upright formed a place of concealment and as a mark of respect, I suppose, I was placed among the elderly men behind a bank of snow. When all was ready the young men behind the deer showed themselves on the mountains, and immediately the whole herd made a furious stampede down the side of the mountain and whenever the deer showed any inclination to take [to] the mountains, the men on the sides and rear commenced howling in imitation of wolves. It had the desired effect. The deer came straight for us and when they were about fifty yards off Peter, the chief, fired and missed. I then took up a flint lock gun lent me in the mom and snapped several times at them. The deer escaped unhurt as no one else was within shooting range. (McDonald, Kenneth 1874)

Readers interested in Sarah Frank's discussion of caribou fences may wish to consult the field survey completed by Roseneau et al. 1975), where fence construction methods and corral designs are illustrated in some detail.

While moose now add greatly to the protein-rich Gwich'in diet, it is a historic fact that *dinjik* arrived in the northern Yukon Territory and Alaskan subarctic only recently—in the late 19th and early 20th centuries (McClellan 1987:33; Huntington 1993:181). As Johnny Frank says above in *"Deenaa Dą̀į' Dinjii Zhuu,"* during the days when animals and fish could talk to humans, there were no moose, and people depended mostly on fish, small game, and caribou. In the prehistoric period, there seems to be little doubt that caribou was the primary subsistence food resource for both the Di'hąįį and the Neets'it Gwich'in, and for the majority of Venetie and Arctic Village families today *vadzaih* is still considered to be the most important of all the game animals.

The tribe's traditional focus on caribou was intensified when the Gwich'in organized a large international gathering at Arctic Village in 1988 to oppose oilfield development in the nearby Arctic National Wildlife Refuge, a critical habitat area which provides the summer calving grounds for the Porcupine caribou herd. Joining ranks with environmentalists, the Gwich'in Steering Committee waged an intense lobbying campaign in the U.S. Congress between 1988 and 1992 and, at least temporarily, successfully defeated the oil companies. In the process, caribou emerged as a conscious symbol of Chandalar Gwich'in social identity and cultural survival. Journalists started calling the Gwich'in "People of the Caribou" and strengthened the idea that subsistence hunting was the foundation of their culture. Sarah is careful to remind us, however, that when the caribou were scarce they were prepared to eat boiled *trih,* a small carrot-like plant, and other humble foods like dried ground squirrel intestines.

From a political perspective, the most important first step toward tribal sovereignty and self-determination for the Chandalar Gwich'in was the school they established in Venetie in 1937. (See Johnny and Sarah's accounts in Part II above.) Establishing that school resulted in the hiring of the young Gwich'in teacher and scholar John Fredson. And the hiring of Fredson led in turn to the second most important step, the creation of the Venetie Indian Reservation. Although others certainly had a hand in getting the Reservation, John Fredson and Johnny Frank working together provided much of the leadership. Without Fredson's understanding of the federal Indian Reorganization Act of 1934, as amended in 1936, the villagers might not have learned how to file their land claims for another thirty years.

The first task before them was to write and pass a corporate charter and a constitution and by-laws. These were all ratified on January 25, 1940, creating the IRA Council form of government. Then, as a result of Johnny Frank's work as chief going around to collect signatures and John Fredson's ability to process all of the necessary paperwork and survey the boundaries, the people filed for and received the 1.4 million acre Venetie Indian Reservation, proclaimed by the Secretary of the Interior on May 20, 1943. Given a choice following the Alaska Native Claims Settlement Act in 1971, the tribe opted to take fee simple title to the Reservation rather than share in the large cash settlements and much smaller quantities of land awarded to other Alaska Native villages.

Fig. 29. Building the first school in Venetie, circa 1937. Left to right are Daniel Roberts (on roof), unknown, Jimmy Roberts Sr., and Jim Roberts (holding rope). Photo courtesy of Dan Frank.

Even this title was a substantial compromise because the Reservation, large as it is, does not accurately reflect the amount of land used for subsistence by the Gwich'in of Arctic Village and Venetie during the early 20th century. Johnny and Sarah, for example, used the Middle Fork of the Chandalar and much of the land and waters between the Middle Fork and the East Fork, even though the East Fork defines the western boundary of the Reservation. Old Robert, the founder of Venetie, told John Fredson he was born near the old mining camp of Caro on the Middle Fork, and when Robert McKennan caught up with Chief Christian in 1933, his band was hunting caribou at the forks of Smoke Creek, another western tributary of the East Fork.

Lands to the north and the east of Arctic Village were also part of the tribe's historic use area. Johnny and Sarah and many other Arctic Village people once lived on the Koness River east and north of the eastern boundary of the Venetie Reservation. At one time in the early 20th century there was also a village on the Sheenjek

River. In 1950 and 1957 the tribe petitioned the Department of the Interior for rights to hunting, fishing, and trapping on lands now included within the Arctic National Wildlife Refuge. Residents of Arctic Village said they were not fully aware of the boundaries of the Venetie Reservation when it was established in 1943. Considering the infrequent communications between Venetie and Arctic Village before and during World War II, this statement would seem to have substantial merit. These claims were renewed once again in the spring of 1981 but were soon rejected by the Department of the Interior (Lonner and Beard 1982).

The study of Indigenous local knowledge and land use from primary sources such as Johnny and Sarah is absolutely critical for understanding Gwich'in traditional culture, but outsiders have also made a substantial contribution based on their fieldwork and living with the Gwich'in. For further detailed insights into Alaska Gwich'in tribal history, subsistence, and lifeways, readers are encouraged to consult not only the classic ethnographies written by Cornelius Osgood, *Contributions Towards an Ethnography of the Kutchin* (1936) and Robert McKennan, *The Chandalar Kutchin* (1965), but also more recent works such as Richard Nelson's look at hunting and trapping strategies in Chalkyitsik in *Hunters of the Northern Forest* (1973) and Richard Caulfield's *Subsistence Land Use in Upper Yukon Porcupine Communities* (1983), a general overview of subsistence use patterns and seasonal rounds in Venetie, Arctic Village, and other Gwich'in communities in the region.

Those interested in Gwich'in material culture should consult Fred Hadleigh West's doctoral dissertation on Arctic Village, "The Netsi Kutchin: An Essay in Human Ecology" (1963), where he describes the manufacture and use of snowshoes, toboggans, sleds, skin boats, muskrat canoes, aboriginal clothing, and house designs. In addition, both Kate Duncan and Eunice Carney's A *Special Gift: the Kutchin Beadwork Tradition* (1988) and Judy Thompson's *From the Land: Two Hundred Years of Dene Clothing* (1994) offer richly illustrated documentation of Gwich'in visual and decorative arts.

A comprehensive ethnographic overview of many topics covering Gwich'in communities on both sides of the Alaska-Canada border has been compiled by Richard Slobodin (1981: 514-

532). Published fourteen years ago in the Smithsonian Institution's *Handbook of North American Indians,* Slobodin's essay cites a wealth of other sources, including unpublished dissertations, and no recent bibliography has superseded it. Students of Gwich' in history and social organization on the Canadian side will also want to look at Slobodin's earlier study of the Peel River Gwich'in (1962).

For Gwich'in religious history since historic contact, Slobodin's essay on Gwich'in beliefs in reincarnation, called *nahdlii* or *nehdlii* (1970), and my own paper (Mishler 1990; also in Mishler and Frank 2023) on the conflict between Anglican and Oblate missionaries provide some context for the acceptance of Christianity and the strong faith witnessed by Sarah's stories.

During the early 1980s, Richard Caulfield, working for the Alaska Department of Fish and Game, Division of Subsistence, interviewed village elders and then worked with Katherine Peter to document hundreds of Gwich'in place names in the Venetie and Arctic Village areas. These interviews resulted in a pair of large blueline maps that are essential to future ethnohistoric research in the region (Caulfield 1981a; Caulfield 1981b). Kenneth Frank and I have collaborated on the importance of kinship to Gwich'in personal naming traditions (Mishler and Frank 1995, also 2023), drawing upon the Frank family tree and elaborating on Katherine Peter's earlier work (1978). Our book *Dinjii Vadzaih Dhidlit: The Man Who Became a Caribou* (Mishler and Frank 2020) offers bilingual oral accounts of twelve Alaskan and Yukon elders well versed in the traditional knowledge and anatomy of caribou.

Fig. 30. Johnny Frank at Venetie with pack dogs, getting ready to walk to Gold Camp, circa 1960. Dogs left to right are Vat'aii, Granger, and Leader. Photo courtesy of Richard Birchell.

Sarah Frank

Petèr Khaìhkwaii

<sfalBIA>

TG0.41 Shitsųų, ą̀ą?

SF Hą̀ą?

TG Aii *Petèr* Khaìhkwaii,[1] nijìn gwats'an nilįį chan ts'ą̀' aii kwaiik'ìt, oo'àt kwaiik'ìt gwihìłtsąįį văiinyaa nàhąą?

SF Ą̀ąhą'.

TG Aiits'ą̀' izhìk dąį' dąhtsìi, izhìk kwaii hàa danàa gwandak nàhnyaa t'inyàa, shitsųų. Aiits'ą̀' t'ee chan hee oonjìt gwats'an hee geeneegwahandàk.

SF1.06 Aii t'ee izhìk dąį' teetł'an ts'ą̀' gwalàt tthak ganaldàii. Gàa teetł'an ts'ą̀' gwalàt ganaldàii kwaa gàa *Petèr* Han Gwich'in[2] nilįį.

TG Ą̀ąhą'.

SF *Petèr* Khaìhkwaii Han Gwich'in nilįį ts'ą̀' yeendòk hee *chief* giiyìłtsąįį.

TG Ôq.

SF Aiits'ą̀' *chief nilįį* ts'ą̀' t'ee oo'àt t'agwaihnyąą izhìk it'ee nìgiinjil, aii khaiits'ą̀'. Nìgiinjil ts'ą̀' t'ee dinjii vaghàih łiiljìl. Aiits'ą̀' zheh ch'ìhłak gwizhrįh giiyeenjit gwìłtsàįį. Aiits'ą̀' gàh zheh gokwàa. Aiits'ą̀' ch'adhàh zheh gwizhrįh gwizhìt gwigwich'įį. Aiits'ą̀' izhìk gwats'an jyàa digiizhìk, akhài' zhyą̀ą nijin gwats'an ts'ik t'ii'in gàagwiindàii kwaa, aii gooteiinzhii ts'ą̀' zhyą̀ą dinjii tanh nilyaanaii t'igwinyàa. Aiits'ą̀' gwiizhìk zhat dąį' Vaanòodlit shìi kwaa nàhąą?

TG Ą̀ąhą'.

1. *Peter* is pronounced as *Veter* by the Gwich'in. —JE

2. The Han speak a different language than the Gwich'in. Their traditional homeland is along the upper *Yukon River* roughly between *Dawson City, Yukon* and *Circle, Alaska*. A few speakers of Han can still be found in *Eagle, Alaska* and *Dawson City, Yukon* (see Osgood 1971; Mishler and Simeone 2004). —CM

Sarah Frank

Chief Peter

<sfalBIA>

TG0.41 Do you hear me, Grandma?

SF What?

TG Remember you talked about *Chief Peter* — where he came from and how he once started a village?

SF Yes.

TG We would like to know how big you were at that time, Grandma. Tell us again from the beginning.

SF1.06 I only remember half, and I don't recall the other half, but Peter was a Han Gwich'in.

TG Yes.

SF *Chief Peter* was a Han Gwich'in and people up north made him a chief once.

TG I see.

SF He was the chief and was camping out at this one place during fall time when people came and gathered there for him. They built him a house there. The rest of the people lived in skin huts. They were all staying there when an unknown sickness went through them and they all just froze and died in an instant. There was also no white man's food at that time, you see?

TG Yes.

SF2.28 Aiits'ą̀' zhyą̀ą zhik ch'atthaii kwàt nintsal hàa zhrįh t'èegąąhch'yaa aii gwiizhìk it'ee łyâa zhyą̀ą gooshìi kwaa gwiizhìk it'ee lęįį nąįį niinjìk. Ts'ą̀' aiitł'ęę t'ee gwintsal givèenjit gwinzįį neegwìdhìdlìt ts'ą̀' t'ee shrahtèegaajìl.

2.51 Izhìk dą̀į' t'ee yaaghà' aii shitsųų t'aihnyaa aii t'ee dinjii aii yit'ïinzhii gwich'in giiyàhnyàa. Aii dinjii lęįį niinjik ts'ą̀' dinjii ch'ìhłak aii ts'an łyâa kwàntee gàanìgwìi'aii ginyaa aii gwiizhìk it'ee tthak gwintsàl gwinzįį gòodlit ts'ą̀' t'ee gehdiidì' tr'ahàandìi.

3.32 Ti'yąą aii shee'ii *John Fred Vitì'*,[3] aii nąįį hàa chiidì' gahàandìi. Izhìk gehdì' tan kak tr'eedàa gwiizhìk it'ee aii shitsųų vakwàa.

TG3.46 Izhìk geh'àn gehdìt vanaanjik łii hee?

SF Ą̀ąhą'. Aiits'ą̀' oodit zhat gehdit giinąąhjìk.

TG3.55 Ànts'ą̀' *Henry John* vijùu nèekwąįį nąįį chan jiinyaa hęę.

SF3.58 Ą̀ąhą'. Lęįį nąįį niinjik. Googàa gwinzįį goonaldàii kwàa.

TG4.04 Ànts'ą̀' yaaghà' *Mil* văiinyaa aii vigii chan lèe văiinyàa?[4]

SF Ą̀ąhą'.

TG4.08 Aii nijìn gwats'an t'inch'yàa?

SF4.10 Aii yeendòk gwìch'in į.

TG Ôq.

SF4.12 *Mil Vitì'* gwinyaa aii vichi' reh aii t'ee yaaghà' *Jonas Choh* tr'oochìt yùunjik į'.[5] Tr'oochìt yùunjik izhìk it'ee adant'ee vakwàa.

TG4.30 Aii k'eejit dą̀į' *Stevèn Fredsòn* danàh gwaandak, jyàa nyaa it'ee łyâa t'inyaa łee hee? Aii gàh aii goonandàii kwaa hęę?

SF4.39 Ą̀ąhą'. Gàh aii gwinzįį gòonaldàii kwàa. Gàa lęįį nąįį niinjìk gàa dą̀ąch'yaa niinjìk googàa gàashandàii kwàa.

3. Sarah is referring here to Old Fred Oozhrii Kaii, her mother's brother. —CM

4. Mil was considered to be one of Sarah's grandmothers, although she doesn't appear on the John family tree. This is because it's common for the Gwich'in to call any woman of their grandmother's generation *shitsųų*. —CM

5. This was apparently Mil's stepdaughter. —CM

SF2.28 They only depended on large game and smaller game, but they couldn't get any so a lot of them died. The ones who survived got a little better, and that's when they all went their separate ways.

2.51 They think that one of the dead person's spirits took my grandmother that time because they heard it among the houses. Everything got a little better so we traveled downriver.

3.32 My father and uncle, who is *John Fredson*'s father, all traveled on downriver, and we were on the river when Grandma died.

TG3.46 So that's the reason why she's buried there, huh?

SF Yes. That's where they buried her.

TG3.55 Did you say two of *Henry John's* sisters too?

SF3.58 Yes. Lots of them died, but I hardly remember who.

TG4.04 Did you say one of *Mil's* children too?

SF Yes.

TG4.08 Where was she from?

SF4.10 From up north.

TG Oh, I see.

SF4.12 They say she was the daughter of *Mil's* father. *Big Jonas* married her as his first wife but she died.

TG4.30 *Steven Fredson* was just telling us that too, so it must be true. Do you remember the rest of them?

SF4.39 Yes, but I don't remember some of them. A lot of them died, but I don't remember how many.

TG4.54 Aii gwat'san t'ee *Chief Petèr* yeenjì' ts'ąįį neehòozhii hęę?

SF4.58 Izhìk jyàa dìgwiizhìk tł'ęę duulèe gęhdaa khaii izhìk duulèe t'igwiizhìk gwìch'in nihthàn.

5.14 Izhìk it'ee yeendòk zhat dinjii t'inch'yaa nàhąą? Aiits'ą̀' dinjii datthak shìh kwaa goodlìt. Nintsal gàa kwàa. Aiits'ą̀' t'ee oondee *Old John Lake,* izhìk gwà'àn gwàndàk t'iginch'yaa. Łyâa shìh kwaa gòodlit ts'ą̀' t'ee zhat gwich'in nąįį. Ch'anjàa nilįį nąįį tthak reh. Aii nąįį datthak yeenjì' shìh kwaa dąį' yeenjì' *Old Crow* ch'iinjì' gahàajìl.

5.53 Izhìk t'ee aii *Petèr Khàihkwaii* chan oonjì' neehòozhii. Aii t'ee oonjìt *Circlè* geeghaih gwà'àn nijìn gwà'àn vatth'ank'ìt gòo'ąįį giiyàhnyàa. Jyàa gwinyaa veegwîihtth'àk.

6.18 Aiitł'ęę izhìk zhat t'ee ti'yąą. nąįį zhrįh, zhat *Old John Lake* gwà'àn gwigwich'įį. Akhài' dinjii kwaa yeenjì' tthak gahàajil łìi.

TG6.32 Yeenjì' Indlis nąhkak k'iinjì' hee gàa gahàajil hęę?

SF6.38 Oonjì' *Old Crow, Vantee* ginyaa, gwats'ą̀' ch'iinjì' jyàa dìgiizhìk.[6]

TG13.10 Ginkhii gàa kwàa. Shitsųų, zhat dąį' hęę?

SF13.18 Ą̀ąhą'. Ginkhii gàa kwàa. Izhìk tth'aii hee shigwilìi kwaa gwiizhìk t'ee troochìt *first time* Indlis ginkhìi nąįį yeendòk k'eedhijìl.

TG Hąh.

SF13.37 *Bishop Bompàs* chan nyaa, aiits'ą̀' *Mr. Rowdlỳ* aii nąįį gwìch'in roh.[7] Aii nąįį t'ee tr'oochìt yeendòk k'eegidhijìl.

TG14.01 Aii nehnaa dąį' reh hęę?

SF14.25 Ą̀ąhą'. Tth'aii shigwilìi kwaa gwiizhìk. Googàa Indlis ginkhìi aii duulèe chųų shats'an iłtsąįį gwìch'in. Aii chan tr'iinin nitsìi nąįį gwiizhìk t'ôohju' hee chųų ts'an gahtsii reh.

6. A section here has not been transcribed. —CM

7. William Bompas was an Episcopal missionary who spent some time in *Fort Yukon* starting as early as 1869. See *William Carpenter Bompas*, *Diocese of Mackenzie River* (1888). —CM

TG4.54 Is it from them that *Chief Peter* went back over?

SF4.58 I think maybe it happened that following winter.

5.14 At that time, some people lived up north, you see? And they all ran out of food. There was no small game. They were somewhere near *Old John Lake*. Those people there were out of food so they all moved to the *Old Crow* area. Even the elders went.

5.53 *Chief Peter* went back with them. They say that his grave is located around *Circle*. I've heard what they say about him over that way.

6.18 Only my parents stayed and lived at *Old John Lake*. Everybody else moved away.

TG6.32 Did they go as far as the land of the English (to *Canada*)?

SF6.38 They all went to the *Old Crow* area.

TG13.10 There was no priest those days. Is that right, Grandma?

SF13.18 Yes, there was no priest. The English priests first came up north before my birth.

TG Hąh.

SF13.37 They said one of them was *Bishop Bompas* and I think *Mr. Rowdly*. They were the ones who traveled north.

TG14.01 Was that before you were born?

SF14.25 Yes, before my birth. But I think maybe one of the English priests baptized me. They also baptized lots of children who were already big.

<sflg2b>

SF23.39 Ąąhą', aii it'ee *Petèr Khaìhkwaii* giyàhnyaa ąįį it'ee dinjii ik'ee ch'igilìk hàa dinjii t'eedaa'in ts'ą' vik'ìighai' dinjii gwįįzįį gwiindàii vàràhnyaa t'aihnyàa.

LG23.54 Izhìk gwànaa khaìhkwaii gii'įį hee jyàa dagoogah'in gwìch'in rǫh hęę? Gook'eech'igilìk ts'ą'. Łyâa zhyąą dèegihee'yàa datthak eenjit datthak akǫǫ dàgàvàhnyaa gwìch'in ǫ'.

SF24.04 Ąąhą', gwiizįį dinjii ik'èe ch'igilìk aįį it'ee t'èegąąhch'yaa ts'ą' ąįį dèenyaa aii gwik'ìt gwizhrįh t'igii'in t'agoogàhnyàa. Aii it'ee yaaghà' ni'ęę it'ee chan giveegwaandak t'aihnyàa. Łyâa dinjii vit'èegwąąhch'yà' łyâa diichįh įįdì' ginyàa.

24.42 Aįįtł'ęę chan ni'ęę chan yąąh'yą'. Yàandaii t'aihnyàa. Ąįįts'ą' it'ee geetàk shìh gaahkhòk ǫ'.

25.06 Shìh gaahkhòk dąį' łàgwàntsii łąa shìh tsal hàa nihk'èegaantii. Aįį gwiizhìk ąįį łì'hàa giik'ą̀ąhtìi. Drin datthak ch'ara'àa kwaa t'agwaihnyàa. Ganaldàii.

LG25.25 Ąąhą'.

SF25.38 Jyàa dìgii'in ts'ą' ąįį dinjii łyâa giit'âąhch'yaa łì'hàa gwinzįį k'èegaahtìi. Izhìk hee ni'ęę t'inyaa vànhdąį' dazhoo gwàahch'yaa zhrįh gii'įį ǫ'. Aįįts'ą' it'ee vànhdąį' hee tth'aih hee tǫǫ gǫ̀ǫlįį gwiizhìk it'ee zhik nijìn ch'atthą̀įį t'įįch'yaa jì' izhìk ts'ąįį gahadàl gavàhnyàa.

LG Ąąhą'.

SF26.22 Aiitł'ęę it'ee zhik ch'atthàįį gwats'ą' nàgoolii izhìk ch'atthą̀įį ik'ìgaandak ts'ą' it'ee nihk'yąą jyàa dìginjìk. Ch'atthą̀įį nàdagoondàl zhik t'agwą̀htsii gaahkhwąįį gavàhnyàa.

26.46 Izhìk hee vadzaih giits'an k'èiich'ii akhòonyaa kwaa į'. Giidàa zhik vidreedhàh googàa. Ch'akwài', tth'an jii datthak łì'hàa t'èegąąhch'yaa. Tth'an chan łyâa giichų̀' dinįį. Lìdii chan kwaa ǫ'. Aįįts'ą' tth'an chan łyâa t'èegąąhch'yaa. Aiits'ą' łì'hàa zhyąą gwįįzįį nihk'èegąątii googàhnyaa t'agwaihnyàa.

<sflg2b>

SF23.39 Yes, they say *Chief Peter* was a leader who gave directions on how they would hunt, and I mean this is how many people lived well.

LG23.54 In those days that's how the chief treated them, ok? He gives them orders. He really tells them all exactly what they're supposed to do.

SF24.04 Yes, he really gives them directions, and they follow them. They only do what he tells them to. As I said, my mother told me about it. They say he was the most needed person who had been our chief.

24.42 My mother saw him. I'm saying she remembered him. She said if he thought there was food was in a certain area, then he gave orders to go there, and that's just what they did. Sometimes they ended up with food.

25.06 And when they got food they all shared it evenly. I'm saying they really shared their food. I recall that we often didn't eat all day. It was hard. I remember.

LG25.25 Yes.

SF25.38 So this is what they did, and he was very useful for people, and they took good care of him. That's when my mother said it was still dawn when hunters went out toward the areas where they thought the game would be.

LG Yes.

SF26.22 After they found out where the big game was, then everybody would ambush it. That's how they got enough food.

26.46 They never left anything behind from a caribou. The skin, leg skin, and the hooves—they used all of it. From the bones they drank the broth. There was no tea then. They also used the bones. So what I'm saying is they said they really took care of each other.

27.41 Izhìk gwànaa geegwaandak văihnyaa gwànaa dink'ee kwàa. K'į' zhrįh.

LG Ą̀ąhą'.

SF27.56 Jidìi tth'an tòh ginyaa. Ąįį tsį̀į chan tth'an ch'ok gàngahtł'įį. Ąįį it'ee kheeghan giyàa'įį.

LG28.11 Ą̀ąhą'.

SF28.21 Zhik ganaldaìi jìhnyaa, izhìk gwànaa it'ee shin ch'ìh gyàh zhrįh t'èegąąhch'yaa, nàhąą. Ch'ìh gyàh zhrįh t'èegąąch'yaa ts'ą̀' tthaa zhik gwà'àn geh daagǫǫ ąįį zhrįh jii ch'ìh gyàh gahtsii ąįį zhrįh t'èegąąch'yaa. Aįį zhrįh hàa nin gaghan.

29.13 Izhìk it'ee ąįį yaagha' shitsųh naii it'ee gogwaandak, izhìk geegwaldak t'iihnyàa.

LG29.23 Ą̀ąhą'.

SF29.26 Aiitł'ęę vijuu gwànaa it'ee anihłik datthak ganaldàii. Ganaldàii k'ìt t'ôonch'yaa izhìk chan geegwahaldàk.

29.47 Izhìk dąį' łyâa dząą k'ǫǫ yeedee *Van Choo* ąįį kwaii łyâa dinjii yat'ą̌ąhch'yą' į'.

30.04 Aii it'ee łuk eenjit. Tthaa chan łi'hàa dinjii yit'ą̌ąhch'yaa. Aiits'ą̀' izhìk gwànaa dąį' gwįįzįį geh ąįį gwįįzįį gwiyeendaa vagǫ̀ǫlįį į'. Aiits'ą̀' zhik daagǫǫ chan. Daagǫǫ zhat gwànaa dąį' jii nankak gwiyeendaa gwaatr'àl kwàa, nàhąą.

LG30.42 Mmm hmm.

SF30.43 Aiits'ą̀' nijìn k'àii dòk k'àii dhidlii izhìk dąį' it'ee gwaghàih daagǫǫ nèenàdàl. Aii chat t'ee zhik k'àii dòk t'įįch'yaa ǫ', goghoo tee k'àii hàa tthal gahtsii izhìk hee daagǫǫ gaghan. Ąįį jyàa dìgii'in k'ìighai' it'ee dinjii gwiindàii t'igwinyàa.

LG Ą̀ąhą'.

SF31.23 Hmm. Aiits'ą̀' it'ee gehjųų gwànaa izhìk it'ee shrìit'agwą̀htsii ganaldàii. Izhìk dąį' ch'eedąįh zhrįh t'èegąąhch'yaa ǫ'. Ąįį hàa gwizhrįh łuk googit. Aįįts'ą̀' ah chan.[8] Ah chan gahtsii, da'anlee chan.

8. The *ah* is a fish trap made from willows, and the *da'anlee* is another kind of fish trap. —KF

27.41 When she talked about that time, it was back when they didn't have any guns. Only bows and arrows.

LG Yes.

SF27.56 They say they had this bone cane or short spear called a *toh.* That also has a long shaft, and on the tip of it they tied a real sharp bone. They used that for a weapon.

LG28.11 Yes.

SF28.21 As I said before, what I remember was that they used only snares during the summers, you see. The ground squirrels came out, also the snowshoe hares and ptarmigan. They used only the snares they made for them. That's what they caught them with.

29.13 I'm telling you the stories my grandmothers used to tell.

LG29.23 Yes.

SF29.26 Then years later I can still remember lots. What I think I remember I will tell about.

29.47 During that time people really lived off the slough down there and *Old John Lake* up there.

30.04 It was for fish. People survived off of ground squirrels. So at that time there were hardly any snowshoe hares around. The same is true for ptarmigan. Around this country there was hardly any willow brush. So wherever there were willows, the ptarmigan landed there, you see.

LG30.42 Mmm hmm.

SF30.43 Only where there were willows. So among the willows the people made a fence-like structure out of willows. And then they set snares for ptarmigan. That's how they caught them. They say that's how people lived.

LG Yes.

SF31.23 Then later on I remember well the time when we were down at the slough. They only things they used were spears. That's what they got fish with. And the *ah,* they made this also, and another kind of fish trap called a *da'anlee.*

LG31.55 Mmm hmm.

SF31.56 Ąįį hàa chat gwit'èegąąhch'yaa. Izhìk hee łuk tsal gwilìk dąį' ree, aii kwat t'èegąąhch'yaa ǫ'.

<sfwsl05Aa>

MR41.24 Aii *Chief Viidàr Khàihkwaii*[9] vǎihnyaa aii nats'àhts'ą', nats'àhts'ą' dèe'ìn? Jyàa dàkhwa'yàa dinjii nąįį àhnyàa?

SF41.41 Ąąhą', aii t'ee ch'iindàa dinjii adagwaandàii, nàhąą? Ch'iindàa gwandàii zhrįh ga'àa ts'ą' t'ee dagogwaandàii nàhąą? Aiits'ą' zhik gwà'àn traa, jidìi t'eegąąhch'yaa, traa gwigwîiłk'ą' k'ìighai' gwinzįį izhìk chan gàandàii. Aiits'ą' aii kwaii geenjit t'ee, nìivyaa zheh tr'igwich'įį ts'ą' jùunch'yaa kwàntee ch'ii'àn chahak gwats'an oo'àn zheh gwitee khàginjihdatràk.

42.14 Aii jùk drin jyàa dìgwehee'yàa t'ôonch'yaa jyàa nyàa. Aiits'ą' anihłik hee gwats'ą' ree, "Ąąhą' jyàa dìgwehee'yàa," ginyàa, duuyee akhàgogoonyàa.

MR43.22 Aii *Chief Peter,* nalàk nilįį lèe t'inch'yàa?

SF Diilàk, it'ee zhat dąį' gwinzįį diilàk k'ìt gwizhrįh tthak nihteegwaraatą' gwànaa t'agwaihnyąą. Aiits'ą' diilàk nilįį t'inch'yaa ǫ'. Łyâa zhyąą jyàhts'ą' gwizhrįh dinjii diinch'yà' ǫ'.

MR44.46 Datthak nihła'adan gwìch'in k'yąą nihłagòozhrįį, nàhąą? Aii, ti'yąą aii chan jii gwìch'in nyaa, nyaa yàhnyàa. Ti'yąą, ti'yąą goohàa gwaandak łèe. Aii zhik gwich'in nąįį *like* Dì'hąįį Gwich'in *like* . . .

SF Dì'hąįį Gwich'in, aii t'ee yeedì' gwich'in t'aràhnyàa. Dì'haįį Gwich'in ts'ą' Teets'ii Gwich'in, oo'àt Tanan ginyàa.

MR Aii t'ee *Fairbanks.*

SF Jyàa dòonch'yaa, yeenjì' chan. *Gwichyaa*, nàhąą. Gwichyaa Gwich'in. Aiits'ą' oonjìt Old Crow Gwich'in. Itłyaavik *(Aklavik)* Gwich'in. Aiits'ą' dzaa gwee'àn chan Neets'it Gwich'in. Jyàhts'ą' gwitôolzhrì' t'agogwàhnyàa. Aii googàa dinjii. . .

9. This is redundant because *khàihkwaii* means 'the chief' or head of the community. –AR

LG31.55 Mmm hmm.

SF31.56 They used all of these. If they caught a few fish, that's what they lived on.

<sfwsl05Aa>

MR41.24 That *Chief Peter* I mentioned, what did he do? Did he tell the people what to do?

SF41.41 Yes, you see how people made a living, right? They only ate animals and made a living that way, right? So whatever they need, like wood, they only use wood for a fire, and he knows about that, so when we lived in a skin house, right outside the door. . .

42.14 He goes out and yells out and says what will be done today. So from other skin tents people answer "Yes, we'll do that," they say, and they won't put him down.

MR43.22 Was *Chief Peter* related to you?

SF What I'm saying is, in those days everybody considered everyone else their relative. I'm talking about him so he's related. That's really how every person was.

MR44.46 There is a name for every tribe from different places, right? My father said there was a name for each tribe from different places. My father told them. Like the Di'hąįį Gwich'in, like. . .

SF The Di'hąįį Gwich'in are from downriver. Di'hąįį Gwich'in, Teetsii Gwich'in, and Tanan, they say.

MR From *Fairbanks*.

SF From across too. Gwichyaa Gwich'in, you see, are from *Fort Yukon*, and *Old Crow* people, *Aklavik* people, and around here are the Neets'it Gwich'in. That is how they name tribes. But people. . .

SF46.07 Teets'ii Gwich'in. Dì'hąįį Gwich'in chan ginyàa. Yeedì', Dì'hąįį Gwich'in. Neets'it Gwich'in. Neets'ąįį Gwich'in. Dzaa gwee'àn t'ee, Neets'it Gwich'in, Vantee Gwich'in. . .

MR46.56 Nik'èe ch'izhii *chief* chan gii'įį gavàhnyàa?

SF47.01 *Chief* gii'įį, *chief* gi'įį nihdeek'ìt nìneegiidàl. Dzaa gwee'àn, yi'èenaa dąį' aii shichì' ti'yąą chan vehnaa dąį' hee gwee'àn chan dinjii, dinjii chìt gǫǫlįį.

47.21 Gaa aii gàvàhshandàii kwaa į'. Aiits'ą' yaaghąt *Viidàr Khàihkwaii* gwinyàa? Aii gwats'an it'ee tł'ęę chan nihdeek'ìt nineegiidàl k'ìt t'igwii'in ts'ą' chan Viidàr òozhìi. Aii chan Han Gwich'in. Aii t'ee chan yideek'ìt dzaa gwee'àn *chief* inlì' į'. Ts'ą' *Gwichyaa* chan yaaghà' *Shàhnyaa Tì'* ginyaa aii chan. Aii chan *Gwichyaa.*

MR Gàa niłeenjit *vote* gilìi kwaa hęę?

SF47.57 Ąąhą'. Zhyąą dinjii, nàhąą. Aiits'ą' zhat dąį' lèe. . .

MR48.23 Aiitł'ęę gwats'ąįį aii yù'? Aii chizhii *Petèr* yideek'ìt nìneezhii văiinyàa.

SF48.50 Ąąhą'. Aii khaiinkǫǫ. Aii khaiinkǫǫ yaaghàt *Petèr Chief* neelį'? Aiitł'ęę, aiitł'ęę izhìk it'ee yaaghà' ti'yąą nąįį gogwandàii, ti'yąą nąįį gogwandàii gwànaa it'ee, it'ee dinjii zhyąą *chief* ginyaa kwàa, gahtsìk kwàa. Jùu dinjii gwinzįį dalàk nąįį ts'êheenjyàa k'ìt'inch'yaa, aii t'ee *boss* gahtsìk. Aii t'ee gook'èech'igilìk ts'ą'. K'iindàa gwizhìt t'ee dagogwaandàii t'agooràhnyàa. Aiitł'ęę yaaghà' nitì' nąįį gogwandàii. Izhìk gwànaa at'ôohju' it'ee dinjii eenjit *vote* gilìk t'igii'ìn.

MR50.05 Aii dinjii, tr'ìnjàa kwaii hàa tthak gigikhìk lèe t'inch'yàa nyàa?

SF50.10 Ąąhą', aii t'ee jyàa dìgii'in k'ìighai' it'ee ch'iinaa łyâa gògwàntrii gwiniindhàt. Aii googàa dzaa ch'iindàa nìdiigiinlìi. Goots'an tr'agwandàii nąįį t'aihnyàa. *Hard time* gwinyaa, *hard time* t'agogwahnyàa. *Meat. That's all they ate.*

SF46.07 Downriver is Teetsii Gwich'in. Dì'hąįį Gwich'in also, way down the river. Neets'it Gwich'in is Neetsąįį Gwich'in. Neets'it Gwich'in are from this area, Vantee Gwich'in . . .

MR46.56 Were there any other chiefs?

SF47.01 They had chiefs, and they changed chiefs one after another. Way before me or my father they had leaders.

47.21 They had a leader, but I didn't know him, but that *Chief Peter*, after him they had a replacement. So another *Peter* who was a Han Gwich'in was chief here. In *Fort Yukon* it was *Shahnyaa Ti'.*

MR But they didn't vote for each other did they?

SF47.57 Yes, they didn't, you see. So there when. . .

MR48.23 Who was next? After the other *Peter* you said took over.

SF48.50 Yes. The last *Chief Peter* was around when your father was still living. That was when they picked a person they think will take care of his people. He's the boss and tells them what to do and that's how they take care of each other. Then in your father's time they started using votes to elect chiefs.

MR50.05 Do all the men and women talk about it first?

SF50.10 Yes, that's what they do, and those were hard times, but today we're still living because of them. That's what I'm talking about. When they said hard times, they meant hard times. Meat, that's all they ate.

MR51.31 Geetàk shìh kwaa dązį' łyâa ninzhyùk ch'aga'àa kwaa gwìch'in ǫ '.

SF51.41 Izhìk it'ee, izhìk aii t'ee yaaghà' ti'yąą aii vichįh dązį' vichįh dązį' gwandàii. Jii chan gwichįh dązį'. Jii aii it'ee chan gwichįh dązį' gootì' nąįį. Izhìk gwats'anh jii nąįį, jii nąįį t'ee it'ee łyâa gògwàntrii gwinyaa ǫ'.

MR Aii jùu vitì' nąįį, văiinyàa?

SF52.18 Aii yaaghà' vats'anh tr'agwandàii nąįį t'aihnyàa, diichìt nilįį nąįį. Gavoozhrì' lèe hàashandàii.

MR Aii, aii nèekwąįį nąįį jùu voozhrì' nąįį t'avaiinyàa?

SF Jii lèe, jii it'ee, goots'an tr'agwandàii nąįį gavoozhrì'.

MR Nakhwatsii reh hèę? Nakhwatsii nąįį.

SF52.28 Ą̀ąhą', diitsii nąįį, zhat ti'yąą nàhąą. Ti'yąą vitì', aii t'ee *Kǫ̀'dah T'yaa* oozhii į'.

MR Aii, aii dèegwinyaa t'igwinyàa?

SF *Kǫ'dah T'yaa* gwinyaa aii t'ee zhik oondaa gał vitsįį kǫ̀', nahąą, kǫ̀' vitsįį kǫ̀' ddha'aįį neeraha'ak izhìk geenjit garòłshrii t'inch'yàa.

52.50 Izhìk gwànaa dązį' jidìi, tł'yahk'it giiyàhnyàa zhrįh hàa gwigwîiłk'a', nàhąą. Aii zhrįh hàa neegwagwâahk'ik ts'ą̀' t'ee aii eenjit t'ee. Aii eenjit t'ee łi'hàa zhyą̀ą gwik'èegeegadąąhtii gooràhnyaa t'agavaihnyàa. "Nakhwakǫ̀' nakhwàa noochyaa shrǫ̀'," ginyàa. Aiits'ą̀' oondaa gwagwâahk'ik, nàhąą. Aiits'ą̀' jidii dąhshyaa aii chan oondaa chik gîiłtin, jyàhts'ą̀' tthak gwiniindhàt t'ôonch'yaa.

MR51.31 Sometimes when there was no meat, I guess they didn't eat for a long time?

SF51.41 I mean the people who lived before my father's time and also the people who lived before that. Their fathers really had a hard time, they say.

MR Whose fathers, did you say?

SF52.18 The people we came from, our first people. I don't know their names.

MR Those two you're talking about, who are they?

SF You mean these?

MR Yes.

SF These are the ones we're descended from.

MR Your grandfather? Your grandfathers.

SF52.28 Yes. These are just our grandfathers and my father, you see. My father's father's name was *Kǫ̀'dah T'yaa.*

MR What do they say that means?

SF They say *Kǫ̀'dah T'yaa* means 'the stick with fire at the end of it that we carried,' you see, so they called him that. At that time all they used is what they call flint.

52.50 In those days they said they carried a torch, which they used to start fires, you see. That's all they used. I mean they say they guarded it very closely. So they would say to each other, "Don't let your fire go out." Once they started a fire, they left an old piece of rotten wood in it to keep it going because it held the heat.

Sarah Frank

Ginkhii Nąįį

<sfws105Ab>

MR2.26 Aii gwikįh, aii ginkhii gwahąąh'yàa gwikįh dąį' lèe dinjii làt nąįį, dinjii làt nąįį nik'èe K'eegwaadhat hàagiindàii shrǫ̀ǫ? nyàa. Nik'èe k'eegwiich'yaa goots'ą̀' t'igwii'in?

SF2.49 Aii t'ee yaaghà', jii shitsųh *Mil Vahan*. Aii chan ti'yąą chįh dąį' gwats'an gwandàii į'. Aii t'ee nałyà' į', shàhgwaandak. Shàhgwaandak t'inyàa. K'eegwaadhat gǫ̀ǫlįį ts'ą̀' chan gàagwiindàii kwaa ginyàa, googàa. . .

3.12 Googàa zhik, shree, shree chan ts'ą̀' oodee Yahdii gwinyaa ijìi. Aii, aii zhrįh k'eegąąht'ii gavàhnyàa. Dèegwìłdaii zheekak gwizhrįh gwik'èegąąhtii t'agavàhnyaa gǫ̀?

MR4.30 Aii zhat dąį' shan k'ìt t'inch'yaa zhrįh t'eegąąhch'yàa?

SF4.33 Ą̀ąhą', shan aii t'eegąąhch'yaa. Aiits'ą̀' zhik K'eegwaadhat gǫ̀ǫlįį gàagiindàii kwaa, nàhąą. Aiits'ą̀' zhik shan, giizhan aii k'ìighai' gineeginlyàa. Chan aii k'ìighai' zhree dèegwehee'yàa gwintsàl gàhgiindàii k'ìt t'iginyàa. K'ìt t'igwinch'yaa ts'ą̀' gwigwiindàii gooràhnyàa.

5.00 Aiits'ą̀', jii zhik shree, nàhąą, shree chan jyah zhik gaha'ak, nàhąą. Jyàhts'ą̀' jyàa dinjìk dzaa vaghàn igweech'in kwaa, nàhąą. Aii dąį' t'ee shìh heekwàa ghat t'ii'in giiyàhnyàa.[1]

MR Dak a'ee dąį' lèe?

SF Jyàa dinjìk dąį'.

MR Oh, zhak t'injìk.

SF5.33 Aiits'ą̀' kiitł'įį ts'ąįį jyàa dinjìk dąį' t'ee, aii dąį' t'ee gweheezyàa. Shìh eenjit gwiheezyàa eenjit t'ii'in giiyàhnyàa. Jyàh dinjìk izhìk it'ee jidìi tsal jyàa dąhtsii,

1. The late Myra Robert of *Venetie* once sang a song for me about The Boy in the Moon which ties in closely with Sarah's account of famine forecasting (see Mishler 1974; also Paul Solomon's story in McKennan 1965:146-147; also Kenneth Frank's story in Mishler and Frank 2020:378-383). —CM

Sarah Frank

The Missionaries

<sfws105Ab>

MR2.26 Before people saw preachers, did you know of anyone who knew about God? Did any miraculous things happen to them?

SF2.49 My great-grandmother *Mil Vahan.* She was older than my father and lived before him. I saw her too. She told me stories. She told me that they didn't know about God, but. . .

3.12 But they merely kept watch of the sun and the Big Dipper, she said. What else could they have been watching the skies for?

MR4.30 Did they only use a medicine man then?

SF4.33 Yes, they used a medicine man. And they didn't know about God, you see. So they say they used a medicine man. As in a dream, it seems like they knew what would happen in the future. That's what they say about them.

5.00 When the moon rises and sets upside down, you see, that means there will be no food. But when it sets right side up, you see, they say that means there will be plenty of food.

MR Is that when it's upside down?

SF When it's like this (hand gesturing).

MR Oh, when it's down.

SF5.33 And when it turns this way (hand gesturing), we would have good luck. That meant they would get food. When it moves this way (gesturing), they would pack a little tr'ehee'àa tsal jyàh dąhtsii khwaagaachaa ts'ą̀' kwàntee toh gii'įį ts'ą̀', aii gwich'ilìk aii vàashandàii kwàa.[2]

MR Aii t'ee, aii t'ee k'eekhwaa yahchik reh?

SF6.22 Ą̀ąhą'. Gwich'ilìk chan igidlii gàa vanaldàii kwaa.

MR7.14 Aiitł'ęę dèegii'ìn? Aiitł'ęę.

SF7.18 Aii kwàntee tthak giihàa khwaahahdàl kwàntee giihàa khwaahahdàl.

MR7.27 Aiitł'ęę nagaazhrii?

SF7.30 Ą̀ąhą', aii jyàa dìgii'in it'ee shìh dìt t'ii'in ginyaa ts'ą̀' shòh hàa t'igii'ìn. Aiitł'ęę gwich'ilìk aii analdàii kwàa.

MR8.00 Drin gwiteegwąąch'yąą nagaazhrìi t'inch'yaa hę̀ę?

SF Ą̀ąhą'.

<sfwsl05Aa>

MR55.01 Aii *Peter, Chief Petèr* gwandàii dąį'. Aii nitì' aii nik'èe khèhkwaii inlì' łèe?

SF55.23 Khèhkwaii inlì' kwaa t'inch'yàa ti'yąą. Hęę? Ginkhii zhrįį. Dinjii eenjit khagiinjii izhìk it'ee, aii ti'yąą aii. Dinjii eenjit khagiinjii eenjit t'ee dzat gwee'àn ts'ą̀'. Ch'eekwaii t'ee chan ts'ą̀'. Oochùk, kwaii hàa izhìk gwà'àn neehidik izhìk it'ee dinjii eenjit khagiinjii gwizhrįh t'iinyą̀' vanaldàii.

MR56.13 Izhìk dąį' nakhwan gàa vàaneekhwadàl?

SF Ti'yąą lèe?

MR Ą̀ąhą'.

SF56.22 Khainkǫǫ t'ee vàh dinjii tee neerihiidàl izhìk diindàh dinjii eenjit khagiinjìi.

MR Gwikįh dąį' adąhzhrįh t'ii'in?

SF56.33 Aiitł'ęę adąhzhrįh tii'in į'.

MR56.41 Izhìk dąį' jùu, jùu aii nakhwak'ą̌ąhtìi, jyàa dìi'in gwiizhìk?

2. Sarah's discussion is permeated with hand gestures showing various phases of the moon, but these gestures were not recorded. Marie-Francoise Guédon (1974: 201-202) has documented a similar traditional winter game played by the Upper Tanana and Tanacross people. The game was played in December, when people went house to house holding a stick with several hooks and using nonverbal signals to request gifts of food and other items. —CM

food and go to each other's houses with a stick and sing. But I don't know their song for it.

MR Were they packing and singing?

SF6.22 Yes. They also sang while doing that, but I don't remember their song.

MR7.14 And then, then what did they do?

SF7.18 They would go packing from house to house.

MR7.27 And then did they hunt?

SF7.30 Yes, when they went from house to house, they did it thinking they will be lucky to get food. I don't remember the song that went with it.

MR8.00 They hunted every day, right?

SF Yes.

<sfwsl05Aa>

MR55.01 When *Chief Peter* was living, was your father chief too?

SF55.23 No, my father was not a chief. Ok? He was only a preacher. He just prayed for the people. My father prayed for people here and also for the Inuit, and he would go downriver. All he did was pray for people, I remember.

MR56.13 Did your family go with him?

SF You mean my father?

MR Yes.

SF56.22 The last time we traveled with people I saw him pray for people.

MR Before that he went by himself?

SF56.33 Yes, he did go by himself.

MR56.41 Who took care of you all while he was away doing that?

SF56.51 Aii it'ee tthak tr'intsìi gwiizhìk t'ii'in ts'ą̀' ne'ęę vakwàa. Aiitł'ęę t'ee, aii t'ee zhik gwà'àn neehidik ts'ą̀' izhìk hee dinjii eenjit khagiinjii t'aihnyàa shįį chan.

MR57.09 Àkwàt nahan yàagwandàii dąį' yù'?

SF Izhìk dąį' gàa dinjii eenjit khagiinjii.

MR Aiitł'ęę ne'ęę vakwaa tł'ęę at'ôohju' hee zhik gwà'àn tthak neehidìk?

SF Ą̀ąhą'.

MR57.35 Izhìk dąį' ginkhii gǫ̀ǫlįį gàagiindàii lèe, nyàa?

SF Ą̀ąhą'. Aii jàghaii?

MR58.04 Nijìn dąį' tr'ookìt ginkhii noh'yà'? Nitì' jyàa dìhee'yàa gwats'ą̀'?

SF Yeendôk reh. Izhìk dąį'.

MR Aii gwikįh dąį' gàa t'ii'in *or*...

SF Aii gwichįh dąį', izhìk jyàa dìi'in kwàa. Indlis[3] ginkhii nąįį yeendòk tr'ohchìt Indlis ginkhii nąįį neehiidàl. Aii tr'ąąh'in izhìk gwats'an it'ee t'iginyaa t'agwaìhnyàa. Gwintł'òo ch'anjàa lęįį nąįį tr'igwidìi hàa khageedì' t'agwaihnyàa.

MR58.55 Aii ginkhii nats'àhts'ą̀' voozhrì'?

SF59.05 Ginkhii *Archdeacon Stuck.*[4]

MR *Archdeacon Stuck.*

SF59.11 *Archdeacon Stuck* aii chan yeechìt *last time* yeechìt *Gwichyaa* ginkhii nilįį. Aii gwichįh dąį' *Bishop Bompàs* ginyàa. Aii chan ginkhii, aiits'ą̀' ch'ìhłak chan aii chan nats'ąą oozhrii ch'yąą. *Mr. Bompàs,* ginkhii aii nèekwąįį nąįį *first time* yeendòk dinjii tee gwagwąąh'yà' t'agavaihnyàa. Izhìk dąį'.

MR Nats'àhts'ą̀' onzhrìi?

SF59.49 *Bishòp Bompàs.* Canadiàn.

MR60.12 Nats'àhts'ą̀' giiyuuzhrii Dinjii Zhuh k'yàa?

3. *Indlis* is the old fashioned Gwich'in pronunciation of "English." —MRG

4. Archdeacon Hudson Stuck was an Episcopal missionary and intrepid explorer who was based in *Fort Yukon* from 1905 until his death from pneumonia in 1920. Bishop William Bompas was the Anglican bishop of *Selkirk* in the *Yukon* starting in 1891 and lasting until 1905. —CM

SF56.51 We were all grown up when my mother died. I'm saying he prayed for people all over the area.

MR57.09 What about when your mother was still living?

SF Even then he still prayed for people.

MR So after your mother died he started to travel?

SF Yes.

MR57.35 At that time did they know anything about preachers?

SF Yes. Why?

MR58.04 When's the first time you saw a preacher? Before your father prayed for people?

SF Up in the mountains.

MR Did he pray for people before the preacher came or . . . ?

SF No, he didn't do it before English preachers came. They were the first ones that we saw up in the mountains, and then they started the praying. What I'm saying is lots of elders prayed with worry and fear.

MR58.55 What was that preacher's name?

SF59.05 The preacher was *Archdeacon* (*Hudson*) *Stuck*.

MR *Archdeacon Stuck*.

SF59.11 *Archdeacon Stuck* was a preacher in *Fort Yukon* the last time. Before that they say *Bishop Bompas* was a preacher too. Like I said, *Mr. Bompas* and another preacher were up in the mountains for the first time. Back then.

MR What was his name?

SF59.49 *Bishop Bompas*. He was a Canadian.

MR60.12 Did they call him by any Indian name?

SF60.17 Jyàhts'ą̧' gwizhrį̧h reh giiyuuzhrìi. *Ginkhii Choo* zhrį̧h giiyàhnyàa.

<sfwsl05Ab>

MR23.45 Nan aii, tr'ookìt nagòodlìt dą̧į̧', *Saràh* nàgàhnyaa lèe t'inch'yàa? Nagòodlìt dą̧į̧' reh hę̧ę̧?

SF23.54 Ą̀ąhą'. Izhìk dą̧į̧' t'ee Indlis ginkhii nąįį oondàk neehiidàl jihnyaa. Izhìk dą̧į̧' aii nąįį chuu shats'an iłtsąįį gwich'in ǫ'.

MR25.39 Tr'ookìt ginkhii gàa neekwąįį gąąh'in dą̧į̧', aii gîiłkhwąįį gwinyaa łyâa lèe t'igwinyàa nyàa.

SF Deenyaa văiinyaa?

MR Tr'ookìt ginkhii gąą'in dą̧į̧', aii Vàanòodlit ginlįį ts'ą̧' zhik Dinjii Zhuh nèekwąįį nąįį chan goohàa neegihii'òo akhài'nijìn dinjii ts'ą̧' tr'agoogahahchyaa izhìk gagąąhjat ts'ą̧' aii ginkhii, ginkhii gîiłkhwąįį ginyaa łyâa lee t'igwinyaa nyaa.

SF26.17 Izhìk ree gàashandàii kwaa t'agwaihnyaa. Dinjii giiłkhwaii, tr'aahkhwąįį kwàa. Aii gwats'ą̧' dą̧į̧' googwandàk gǫǫlįį, nàhąą. Googwandàk gòodlìt aii ti'yąą chan *two time* ginkhii keedhizhìi aii *Canadian side* ts'ąįį.

26.40 Aiits'ą̧' aii dinjii tee neegavahchik. *Mr. Gaaman*[5] chan nyaa *Mr. Bompàs* chan. Jii nèekwąįį nąįį aii t'ee oondòk dinjii tee neegihii'òo dą̧į̧', aii nąįį hàa chan neehidìk. Ti'yąą.

MR Oonjì' gavankànidik?

SF27.01 Ą̀ąhą'.

MR27.50 Izhìk dą̧į̧' nats'àhts'ą̧' nitì' aii nats'àhts'ą̧' ginkhii k'ìt t'inch'yaa dhidlìt yàhnyàa? Gwigwil'èe *or*. . .

SF28.02 Aii ginkhii jyàa dàh'in izhìk gàh it'ee, gah it'ee zhyą̧ą̧ zhat dą̧į̧' ginkhii chan tr'ahtsii kwàa. Aiits'ą̧' ginkhii òonjìk nèekwat ginkhii keedhizhìi. Aii t'ee tr'iinin jyàa dąhtsii nąįį gàa chųų goots'an nilįį kwaa eenjit t'ii'in.

5. This was most likely Thomas Henry Canham, the English Anglican missionary who was based at *Tanana* from 1888-1892 and also preached to the Gwich'in. He then became Archdeacon of the Yukon from 1892 to 1924. —CM

SF60.17 That's his name, but people called him *Big Preacher*.

<sfwsl05Ab>

MR23.45 Did they name you *Sarah* when you were first born? Were you named that when you were born?

SF23.54 Yes. That was when the English preachers were coming around. I think they baptized me.

MR25.39 The first time when they saw the two bishops, is it really true that they were killed? They (*Mike Holloway* and *William Schneider*) want to know.

SF What did they ask?

MR The first two preachers were white men, and there were two Natives with them. They were scared to take them to the other people, so they killed them. They want to know if it's really true that they killed these white preachers?

SF26.17 What I'm saying is I don't know anything about that. They didn't kill them. The story about them was that my father went to get the bishop two times, you see. On the Canadian side.

26.40 So he took them out among the people. *Mr. Gaaman, Mr. Bompas*, he said, those two. Whenever they traveled among the people, my father went with them.

MR Did he go to *Canada* to get them?

SF27.01 Yes.

MR27.50 How did your father say he became a preacher? Did he learn or what?

SF28.02 By going around with the preachers, that's how. At that time they didn't ordain them. So he went to *Canada* two times and brought back preachers for the kids that were not baptized.

Aiits'ą̀' it'ee, zhyą̀ą dinjii tee neehidik ts'ą̀' dinjii eenjit khàgidiinjii t'aihnyàa, aii ti'yąą.

29.27 Izhìk gwats'ą̀' nahjyàa izhìk it'ee jii lęįį nąįį ti'yąą chan,
jùu dinjii tthak ts'ą̀' ginkhii tr'ahtsii gàagiindàii kwaa
gwìch'in. Aiits'ą̀' jùu dinjii tthak tr'aah'in datthak
K'eegwaadhat gǫ̀ǫlįį ts'ą̀' gàagiindàii kwaa, nàhąą.
Nahjyàa. Aiits'ą̀' izhìk K'eegwaaadhat gǫ̀ǫlįį jyàa
gwinyàa. Googwandàk gòodlit ts'ą̀' t'ee dinjii nąįį
khaiinjih datthak nihkheenjit khàgigiinjii į'. Izhìk
gwizhrįh ganaldàii. Ginkhii tr'ahtsii kwàa. Gàa
nikheenjit khàgigiinjii hàa jyàa dìginyàa.

30.38 Datthak gitree ts'ą̀' t'ee nihkheenjit khàgigiinjii
t'agavaihnyàa. Tr'injàa nąįį googàa jyàa diinyą̀' ǫ'.
K'eegwaadhat gǫ̀ǫlįį ts'ą̀' gàagiindàii kwaa roh. Aiits'ą̀'
tthak gwigwîitth'ak dą̀į' tr'ìnjàa nąįį googàa tthak jyàa
dìginyaa. Goonaldàii datthak gitree ts'ą̀' khàgigiinjii.
Aii nąįį datthak jùk kwaa roh. Ch'ìhłęę gàa gwandàii
kwàa.

So my father went around to people and prayed for them.

29.27 Later on, lots of people preached, including my father. They must not have known about ordaining preachers. None of the people they met knew about God, you see. That was later on. So they say there was a God. The news spread quickly and people started praying for each other. That's all I remember. They didn't ordain them at that time yet. But they say people prayed for each other.

30.38 I'm saying they all cried and prayed for each other. Even the women were praying. They didn't know there was God. So when they heard about it, even the women were crying and praying. I remember them all crying and praying. None of them are alive now.

Sarah Frank

Ch’eekwaii

<sfrf2a>

RF0.35 Ch’eekwaii nąįį gwintsàl givee goinkhyaa jaghaii?

SF Haa?

RF Ch’eekwaii.

SF0.39 Haa?

RF0.40 Tr’ookìt dàį’ oondee nangàa gavąąh’yą’ gavăiinyaa hę̀ę? Oondee *Arctic Villàge* gę̀hdee.

SF Ą̀ąhą’.

RF0.50 Izhìk gwintsàl geegwandàk, dèekhwa’in reh.

SF1.19 Zhyą̀ą ch’aga’àa izhìk łyâa gavàashrôonch’yaa eenjit gwizhrįh jyàa dàgoorah’in roh. Gàa Ch’eekwaii ch’ìhłak khèhkwaii gaa’ìį. Aii dèegoo’yà’ gavàhnyaa łyâa duuyee akhàgogoonyàa. Dyąhch’į̀’ àkwàt *old* nilįį nąįį googàa datthak it’ee yiginjìk k’ìt t’ii’ìn.

2.06 Izhìk oo’ęę neegiidàl hee vadzaih gaghan nàhąą, aii oo’ęę neegaazhik ts’ą̀’, âa, shrôonch’yaa gah k’èegwiich’yaa t’igii’in kwàa. Ch’aga’àa eenjit gwizhrįh goohàa shrôonch’yàa. Gwintł’òo gwilin lidii dhałtsąįį t’agwaihnyàa.

RF2.38 Ginlęįį?

SF2.39 Ą̀ąhą’, ginlęįį. Aiits’ą̀’ izhìk it’ee jyàa dìgii’in agàa ch’agaadzaa t’agavaihnyàa. Oodee *Old John Lake* vęę gwà’àn chan khaii hee chat k’eegiidàl. Ts’ą̀’ t’iyąą nąįį zhrįh zhat gwigwich’įį roh. Aiits’ą̀’ it’ee Drintsal chan giveeniłtsą̀įį. Zhik gwà’àn shìh gǫ̀ǫlįį roh. Aii shìh zhrįh tr’aghan ts’ą̀’ vàanòodlit shìi gǫ̀ǫlįį kwàa. Aiits’ą̀’ izhìk hee ch’agaadzaa t’agwaihnyàa. Gavàa shrôonch’yàa. Aiitł’ęę it’ee Drinchoh chan zhìt, chan zhat gâak’į’. Izhìk datthak, âa, shrôonch’yaa t’iihnyàa.

RF4.05 Ginlęįį ts’ą̀’ neegihiidàl? Ch’eekwaii.

SF Ą̀ąhą’.

RF4.08 Goo’at nąįį gàa lèe? Googii nąįį gàa lèe?

SF Ą̀ąhą’.

Sarah Frank

The Inuit

<sfrf2a>

RF0.35 Could you talk a little bit about the Inuit?

SF What?

RF The Inuit.

SF0.39 What?

RF0.40 You said you've seen them too, huh? Up around *Arctic Village*.

SF Yes.

RF0.50 So talk a little bit about what you all did.

SF1.19 We did all this with them and also they enjoyed our food very much. But they had one Inuit for their leader. Whatever he said, it had to be done. Even the elders took orders from him.

2.06 When they came here they killed many caribou, you see, and brought them back and had a good time and ate well, and they did nothing besides that. They were just happy that they ate well. I'm saying I sure made lots of tea then.

RF2.38 Were there lots of them?

SF2.39 Yes, lots. So that's all they did, and they even had dances. They came to visit around *Old John Lake* during the winter time. There was only my father and them living there then. So he also celebrated Christmas with them. There was lots of food. We had lots to eat, but we didn't have white man's food. That was when they danced. They had good times. They stayed for New Year's. What I'm saying is all that time they had fun.

RF4.05 Were there many of them traveling? Those Inuit.

SF Yes.

RF4.08 Their wives too? And their children?

SF Yes.

RF4.15 Zhyą̀ą neegihiinjik lèe t'igii'ìn?

SF4.16 Neegihiinjik t'igii'ìn. Zhat k'eegiidàl ts'ą̀' Drintsal, Drinchoh hàa zhit zhat gwigwinch'į̀'. Aiitł'ęę it'ee ti'yąą chan khaiits'ą̀' shih tsal shriit'agwąhtsii goonjik ǫ'. Yaaghà' nitsii nąįį hàa. Aii datthak gwigwin'àl tł'ęę t'ee ree shìh kwaa nàgwàanàii. Gwiizhìk it'ee yeezhee *Van Choo* dha'ąįį, nàhąą. Aii oodìt di'nàa'ąį' izhìk *Vìtsyàa Tsik* ginyàa. *Vìtsyàa Tsik* ginyaa izhìk gwà'àn łyâa vadzaih gǫ̀ǫlį̀į.

5.11 Izhìk chat gwats'ą̀' gahàajìl zhat chat ninzhùk tr'igwinch'ì' t'agwaihnyàa. Âa! Vadzaih oo'ęę neevalgaadàl. Tr'ìnjàa nąįį chat thòk ch'a'àa gogwą̀h'įį, geedan. Dinjii nąįį chat thòk.[1] Jyàhts'ą̀' tìgii'ìn.

RF5.41 Nakhwàhzhrįį gàa gavàa gohch'įį?

SF Ą̀ąhą'.

RF5.47 K'èegwiich'yaa t'anakhwagah'in kwaa?

SF5.49 Duuyeh, diihàa shràgogwąąhch'yaa t'agoovaihnyą̀ą. Izhìk it'ee *Willìam Ginkhii* văihnyaa, aii it'ee ookyąą nòozhii į'. Aii it'ee chųų goots'an inghàn. Aii dyąhch'į' nąįį gàa datthak chųų ts'an inghan ree. Chųų nats'an tr'iłtsąįį gwinyaa gàanandàii?

RF Ą̀ąhą'.

SF6.37 Aiits'ą̀' datthak chan gavoozhrį' inghàn. Dagoozhrį' ineegahàandee gwits'į' datthak shik niłagoozhrįį roh. Izhìk it'ee Ch'eekwaii dyąhch'į' ch'ìhłak aii *Davìd* yàhnyàa. Aii eegildee łèe. Aiits'ą̀' giyuaahkat, "Nan aii nats'àhts'ą̀' dee ginkhii nòozhrii łèe?" giyàhnyàa. Akhài' gwats'ą̀' kwaa, *"Deevil,"* nyàa (adlaa).

7.33 *David* aii anaandàii kwaa aiits'ą̀' *"Deevil,"* nyàa (adlaa).

7.45 Aiitł'ęę, âa, tsèegii'in hee geenjit ginzįį kwaa t'agavaihnyàa. Izhìk hee Dinjii Zhuh ree tr'inlįį ts'ą̀' diikwan aii gwintł'òo tr'inlęįį kwàa. Aiits'ą̀' yeezhee tan kat tsèerii'in ǫ'. Nèhkak hàa reh. Nèhkak

1. The Gwich'in tradition was for men to eat separately from the women and before the women. This was still the custom I witnessed through the 1970s at village potlatches, but it's not observed much today. —CM

RF4.15 Were they just traveling around?

SF4.I6 They just moved around. So after they came they stayed for Christmas and New Year's. My father had lots of food from that past fall. Your grandfather was there too. After a while they ate up everything, so there was no food. *Old John Lake*, at the very end of *Old John Lake* is where the creek came out, you see. They say there were really lots of caribou around that *Red-Finned Grayling* area. That's why we all went there.

5.11 What I'm saying is we stayed there a long time. Ooh, they hauled lots of caribou. The women ate together but separate from the men. The men ate together separately from the women. That's what they did.

RF5.41 You stayed with them by yourselves?

SF Yes.

RF5.47 Did they do anything to you?

SF5.49 They wouldn't. They were very friendly. That was when the preacher named *William Loola* came there. He baptized everybody. He even baptized elders. Do you know what baptized means?

RF Yes.

SF6.37 He named everybody too. They kept calling out each other's names so they wouldn't forget them. So one of the old Inuits was named *David.* They must have forgotten him. So he asked, "What was the name that the priest gave you?" they said to him. Very unexpectedly he said, "Devil" (laughs).

7.33 He forgot he was named *David* and he said "Devil" (laughs).

7.45 As I said, they were crazy about playing games. We were Indians, but there were just a few of us there. We were playing on the ice below from where we're at with a ball. We were passing the ball. They were stronger than giveekheerii'àk. Datthak diindaa t'agâąht'aii roh. Zhyąą nèhkak neegàhchàk, akhài' jii dazhoo ik nagàazhii nàhąą. Jùu nèhkak oontà' aii kat jyàa dìginjìk. Aiits'ą̀' jii goots'èe tr'ahchak ts'ą̀' goozhèech'arahchàa (adlaa).

8.44 Geetàk chan jii dazhoo ik nihk'èhdàk nàgaazhìi. Jii gwiyèhzhak chan dazhoo ik tsal. Chan diindaat'agâąht'aii ǫ'. Aiits'ą̀' gwiizhìk diijyàa k'àa jyàa diginjìk. Izhìk hee dzaa goot'įį ndàk gwik'ìraatrak. Dzaa hee gwats'an k'iidąą jyàa dàgòorah'ìn. Tsèerii'in gwigwiindak hee łyâa dlòk nitsìi tr'ahtsii t'agwaihnyàa.

9.35 "Yeekwal nąįį łyâa tsingwąhch'yaa tsèe'in," ginyaa nee gahahkàk.

RF9.44 Jidii ginyàa, *Yukon?*

SF9.48 Yeekwal nąįį. Aiit'ee Dinjii Zhuh nąįį. Nidàhval chan Ch'eekwaii. "Yeekwal nąįį łyâa tsingwąhch'yaa tsèe'ìn," ginyaa. Geeneedlòk gahahkak.

RF10.07 Gwintsàl gavôohtth'ak nik'èe?

SF10.09 Ą̀ąhą'. Needlòk gahahkàk, aiits'ą̀' t'iginyaa, jyàa dàgoorilìk gwiizhìk, "Aazhraa!" ginyaa ts'ą̀' geełeech'agahaaghàa. Oo'òk kwàntee traa kwaa dąį' chan diikwàntee googàa datthak traa k'èech'ìgìichyaa t'agavaihnyàa. Âa, gavàh shrôonch'yàa.

RF11.19 Gootee nik'èe jyàa dhantsąįį?

SF11.27 Âa, diijyàa gǫ̀ǫlįį t'ôonch'yàa. *Four* nąįį shijyàa nilįį t'agwaihnyàa. Izhìk gwitee chan Ch'eekwaii gòonjìk. Aii chat diigii tr'iłtsąįį reh. *Williàm Ginkhii* aii chųų goots'an ahtsii roh. Aiits'ą̀' nikhèegavąhchįį. Aii chat diigii gooriłtsą̀įį. Àa, gwinzįį diik'ą̂ąhtii t'iihnyàa.

RF12.14 Izhìk dąį' tr'iinin lęįį ni'įį?

SF Ą̀ąhą'.

RF12.25 Jùu nąįį?

SF12.33 Shigii *Lucy, Nathanièl,* vachaa *Allàh, Dinàh. . .*[2] Shiigii nąįį lęįį ǫ'.

RF12.51 Aii nąįį gogwandàii lèe?

SF12.53 Ą̀ąhą'.

2. She said one more name, but I cannot hear it. —LG

we were. They always took the ball from us, but then they wore fur coats. They just all fell on top of whoever held the ball. Then we grabbed his hood and wrapped it around his neck (laughs).

8.44 Sometimes they wore two fur coats on top of each other. They wore a smaller fur coat underneath. They were stronger than we were. They jumped on top of our friends. That's when we put our hands down their backs and tickled them. After we finished playing we just laughed lots.

9.35 "The *Yeekwal* play funny," they said. They just laughed lots.

RF9.44 What did they say? Yukon?

SF9.48 *Yeekwal* means 'Indian' and *Nidahval* means 'Inuit' in Gwich'in. "Those *Yeekwal* sure play funny," they said. And then they would just bust up laughing.

RF10.07 Do you understand them a little?

SF10.09 Yes, they laughed and they would say, *"Aazhraa!"* and then run away. I'm saying they even cut wood for us when we had no wood in front of our house. Oh, it was fun with them.

RF11.19 Did you make any friends among them?

SF11.27 Oh, we had many friends. I had four friends. One Inuit got married among them too and we were their sponsor. That preacher *William Loola*, who baptized everyone, did the ceremony. So we were their sponsor. Like I said they really treated us well.

RF12.14 At that time did you have many kids?

SF Yes.

RF12.25 Who were they?

SF12.33 My daughter *Lucy, Nathaniel*, his younger brother *Allah, Dinah*. . . I had many kids.

RF12.51 Were they all living?

SF12.53 Yes.

UN12.55 Izhìk Ch’eekwaii hàa tsèeni’in diinyaa dą̀į’ nigii nąįį dą̀ąch’yą̀ą?[3]

SF13.02 *Five* ą̀ąhch’yaa nąįį.

RF13.06 Gooteegwintsàl dòhłįį?

SF13.08 Ą̀ąhą’, goolàt nąįį. Gwintsàl shriit’agą̀htsìi.

UN13.19 *Young* inlįį, shitsųų, izhìk dą̀į’ hę̀ę?

SF13.24 Ą̀ąhą’. Âa, shigii zhuu *Frank* chan òozhii, ch’ìhłęę chan *Joseph.* Gwintł’òo dinjii giveet’iindhàn. Jùu datthak giveet’iindhàn.

RF14.04 Aii Ch’eekwaii nąįį ninyùk gâak’į̀’ zhat?

SF14.07 Ą̀ąhą’, aiitł’ęę izhìk ninzhùk hee tr’igwiinch’į̀’. Aiitł’ęę t’ôohju’ hee it’ee yeenjì’ neegohòojìl. Izhìk gwats’an gwànaa it’ee Ch’eekwaii oo’ęę neegwąą’in kwaa ǫ’.

14.31 Izhìk it’ee tr’ikhit gwìizųų t’igii’ìn. Shin hee googàa neegihiidàl aii t’ee ch’adhàh eenjit t’igii’ìn. Ch’adhàh tèegogwąhjìi. Aiits’ą̀’ shin hee chan vadzaih gaghan nàhąą. Aii chat akhàgòonjìk giitthą̀į’ gàa ch’adhàh zhrįh goonjii. Aiits’ą̀’ giveegogwaandak akhài’ giveenjit *law* gòodlit ts’ą̀’ gwats’an oo’ęę neegogwąąh’yą̀’ kwaa į’.

15.43 Diijyàa gilìk nàhąą, aii dą̀į’ geedant’ee chan jidìi tsal diinan eet’igiindhan, zhyą̀ą goondak į’. Diikhwant’ee chan jyàa dìdiigah’ìn. Jyàa dìgwii’ìn.

RF16.03 Ch’agwaahkat kwaa?

SF16.04 Ą̀ąhą’. Jii ts’an hal’yàa ginyaa ts’ą̀’ gwizhrįh. Aiits’ą̀’ geedant’ee chan dagats’an aii chan, “Jii veet’indhan jì’ ts’an an’į̀į,” ginyaa. Jyàa dàgwą̀hsų’ nihk’èerąąht’ii t’iihnyàa.

16.33 Shin hèe gwinìndhaa nàhąą. Giihee’àa oo’ęę neegaazhik chan yaaghà’ gwà’àn zhyą̀ą dhidlìi. Ąhjat gàa ree. Jèiinch’yaa googàa giits’an chat ch’a’àa reh.

UN16.55 Ach’įį chan ga’àa, hę̀ę, shitsųų?

SF16.57 Ą̀ąhą’, gwazhrąįį hee.

3. Someone unidentified asks Sarah this question. —LG
Sarah’s fifth child, Allah, was born in 1918, and her sixth, Hamel, was born in 1920. This helps date the events. —CM

UN12.55 When you said you were playing with the Inuit, how many children did you have?

SF13.02 About five.

RF13.06 They must have been small then?

SF13.08 Yes, some of them, but some were a little older.

UN13.19 Grandma, were you young at that time?

SF13.24 Yes. Ooh, my son's name was *Frank* and another one was *Joseph*. Many people liked them. Everybody liked them.

RF14.04 Did those Inuit stay for long then?

SF14.07 Yes, we all stayed there for a long time. After that they all went back home. After that we never saw them again.

14.31 At that time they were bad for traveling around. They even traveled around just so they could get skins. They took skins. They killed caribou in the summer and they even left the meat behind. They only took the skins. So they reported them to the law, and they warned them. After that they never returned.

15.43 Once you become friends with them, you see, they believe that what's yours is theirs. So any time if you have something they like they will take it, and it's all right for you to do the same.

RF16.03 They don't ask?

SF16.04 Yes, they just say, "I'll have this," and that's all. And they say if you would like to have this, then they say you can have it. I'm saying that's how nice we treated each other.

16.33 It was in the hot summer, you see. They just left the food they brought home lie around. It spoiled. But they ate it even though it was like that.

UN16.55 Grandma, do they eat raw food?

SF16.57 Yes, they sure do.

UN17.00 Vadzaih gaahk'ee dąį' zhat vadzaih tth'ąį' nindhaa nàhąą, aii gwiizhìk gàa ga'àa lèe t'inch'yàa?

SF17.07 Ą̀ąhą', jyàa dìgii'in į'. Ąhjat googàa reh.

RF17.29 Shitsii aii gavàhnyaa, vikeech'agaach'yàa tr'agoogidiinjìk gavàhnyàa.

SF17.34 Tr'agoogidiinjìk kwaa, gàa. . .

RF17.48 Zhyą̀ą dlòo didlii t'inyaa gwìch'in roh.

SF18.00 Izhìk khaiinkǫǫ oo'ęę nìneegiijyàa googàhnyàa. Izhìk it'ee *Vashrąįį K'ǫǫ* hee oo'ęę nìneegidhijil łèe. Gàa diikhwan goorąąh'yą' kwàa.

18.14 Diikhwan aii *Tryahtł'it* tr'igwich'įį. Geedan zhrįh oo'ęę nàgaajil łee, izhìk dąį' t'ee Dinjii Zhuh nihteeroojyàa ginyaa googàhnyàa. Ch'agwaahkat googahnyąą gàa *Christian* aii àkwaa gavàhnyaa łèe. Gwik'ìt t'igiizhìk jì' Ch'eekwaii nąįį gwihèelyaa ǫ'.

RF18.44 Duulèe *half breed* tr'iheelyàa jùk.

18.49-19.13[4]

SF19.14 Ch'eekwaii nąįį diiteiinjil jì' łąhch'yaa zhyą̀ą, âa, shràgogwaąhch'yaa t'agooràhnyàa.

<sfkfla>

CF5.29 Shitsųų, ch'adąį' gwànaa oondee *Van Choo Vęę* gwà'àn Ch'eekwaii nąįį hàa *trade* gilìi ganandàii izhìk?

SF5.43 Ch'eekwaii nąįį oo'ęę nìneedàl lèe?

CF Ą̀ąhą'.

SF5.46 Ą̀ąhą', geetàk niinzhyùk diihàa gwigwich'įį į'. Izhìk dąį' hee it'ee oondee *Old John Lake* ginyaa, izhìk it'ee khaii, aii vęę. Ti'yąą vizheh gòo'aįį izhìk it'ee khaii Drinchoh Zhìt tr'âak'į'. Ch'eekwaii nąįį agàa. *Christmàs* chan zhat gâak'į'. Âa, gwintł'oo gavàh shrôonch'yàa. Aii Drinchoh tł'ęę t'ee shìh gǫǫlįį kwàa.

4. I can't hear all of what all they said here. —LG

UN17.00 Did they eat raw caribou meat when it was freshly cut?

SF17.07 Yes, that's what they did. Even if it was spoiled.

RF17.29 My grandfather said they were too lazy to cook, that's why.

SF17.34 They were not lazy, but. . .

RF17.48 He must have just been joking about it.

SF18.00 The last time they were here they were in *Arctic Village*, but we never saw them.

18.14 We were living at *Otter Creek* when they came back. That's when they say they asked both Indian and Inuit to join together. But *Chief Christian* and them said no. If that happened we would have many Inuit.

RF18.44 We could have been half breeds.

18.49-19.13

SF19.14 If the Inuit joined us, oh, I'd say they were very kind people.

<sfkf1a>

CF5.29 Grandma, do you remember when those Inuit used to come to the shorelines of *Old John Lake* to trade with you?

SF5.43 You mean when those Inuit used to come?

CF Yes.

SF5.46 Yes, sometimes they lived with us for a long time. At that time we stayed by what they called *Old John Lake*. That was when we celebrated New Year's at my father's house. The Inuit as well. They stayed with us during Christmas too. Oh, they really enjoyed themselves.

Aiits'ą' t'ee yeedìt *Van Choh* ch'iidi' nàa'ąį' izhìk *Vitsyàa Tsik*[5] gàgàhnyaa į'. Izhìk gwà'àn ree vadzaih gǫ̀ǫlįį. Izhìk it'ee ch'iidì' goots'ą' gahàandii Ch'eekwaii nąįį hàa datthak ts'ą'. Ti'yąą nąįį yaaghà' shoondee *Esiàs*[6] nąįį gàa datthak izhìk hee gwats'ą' rahàandìi. Izhìk chyǎadląįį tr'igwich'įį gwiizhìk, it'ee *Williàm Loolà* ginkhii nilįį į'. Aii it'ee oondàk nòozhìi.

7.54 Aiitł'ęę Ch'eekwaii dyaahch'į' nąįį agàa datthak chųų ts'an iłtsąįį. Datthak chųų goots'an iłtsąįį ts'ą' gavoozhrį' chan inghàn. Aiits'ą', âa, vadzaih gǫ̀ǫlįį shrôonch'yaa t'iihnyàa. Tr'igwich'įį hee zhat tan kat gòo'ąįį. *Van Choh* ts'an hàhdląįį yeezhòk tan kat gòo'ąįį. Izhìk hee chan, âa, tsèegii'in hàa jyàa dìgii'ìn.

8.29 Izhìk ree Ch'eekwaii nąįį, Dinjii Zhuh tr'inlįį ts'ą' ree it'ee datthak tsèerii'ìn. Izhìk hee Ch'eekwaii nąįį jii dazhoo ik nagaatsùu, nàhąą. Jyàa dąhjyàa ąįį gwiyehzhak chan dazhoo ik aii vaghài' ts'ąįį goots'ąįį goo'ąįį ts'ą' gwiyèhdak chan.

9.00 Nihk'èhdak hee dazhoo ik nàgaazhìi. Izhìk hee tsèerii'in datthak ts'ą'. Tsèerii'in izhìk hee oozhee jidìi *Nehkak* ree, aii hàa tsèerii'ìn. Aii zhyąą googit dineekheegidiitrak, aiitł'ęę giveegwàrah'aii. Aiits'ą' yeezhee ch'ìhłęę nèhkak oondak, aii k'ąą jyàa diginjìk roh. Gwiizhìk jii dazhoo ik nàgaazhii aii jii goonàn ìgwèech'in t'agavaihnyàa. Aii goo'ìk teet'įh k'iidàk gwik'ìraatrak ts'ą' goot'įį ch'iidąą jyàa dìgwinjìk. Izhìk hee it'ee gwik'iighai' gwintsàl gogwahahthàk. Aiitł'ęę tsèerii'in gwigwiindak tł'ęę, âa, geeneedlòk gahakàk. "Lyâa *Yukon* nąįį tsingwąhch'yaa tsèe'in łee," ginyaa.

5. *Vitsyàa Tsik* literally means 'red-finned grayling' and refers to the outlet or mouth of a creek several miles south of *Old John Lake* near the headwaters of the *Christian River*. There's also a mountain and a lake with that name. See Caulfield 1981b. —CM

6. This is apparently a reference to Esias Simon. *Shoondee* 'my older brother' in this case is not her blood sibling but an affectionate term for the member of a cohort of her own generation. —CM

They played games after the New Year. Then after New Year's they got low on food. There were lots of caribou down at the south end of the lake at a place they call *Red-Finned Grayling*. The Inuit and everybody traveled toward the place where there were lots of caribou. Even my father and my older brother *Esias*, all of them went there. There is a creek that comes down from *Old John Lake*. That's where we were living. That's when the preacher *William Loola* came and visited.

7.54 Even the old Inuit were baptized. They were all baptized and given names. There were lots of caribou and it was fun. There were ice ponds all over where we stayed. The creek from *Old John Lake* was right below us and the ice was on there. They just played lots on there.

8.29 That was when the Indians and Inuit played together. The Inuit wore long fur coats with fur linings inside.

9.00 They wore double fur coats. That's when we all played ball, and they kept pushing it away from us. Finally we found a way to take the ball away from them. When someone got the ball everybody got on top of him. As I said they were wearing fur coats and you could see their bare backs. Somehow we put our hands inside their coats and that's how we slowed them down. They all laughed about it after we got through playing. "Those Yukon people really play funny," they said.

10.50 Jii goots'èe ts'eh aii nàgaazhii kwàa, aii chan tr'ahchak ts'ą̀', aii hàa chan gooyèech'irizhųų. Izhìk ree gwintsàl gogwahahthàk.

<sfdlBIA338a>

CF6.59 Dzaa gweedi' łyâa kwą̀nk'ìt gǫ̀ǫlįį nyaa, nik'ee jùu t'ii'in gàakhwandàii? Nakhwahnyàa.[7]

SF7.16 Tii zheh gwà'àn geendii lèe? Ch'eekwaii nąįį dzaa Drinchoh zhìt dzaa nàgàajìl. Izhìk dąį' diilàt lęįį nąįį chan dzaa nàgàajìl. Aii nąįį tthak yee'òk gwigwįįch'į' į'. Aiits'ą̀' izhìk Drinchoh neegiłtsàįį.

CF7.45 Hę̀ę'.

SF8.05 Zheh goghoo zhyą̀ą gogwàhtsii.

CF Ôq.

SF8.10 Ch'adhàh hàa. Ch'adhàh gwanagôołjìk aii hàa. Zheh goghoo gogwahtsii ts'ą̀' yee'àt gwà'àn jùunch'yaa ts'ą̀' lęįį nąįį gwįįchį' į'.

CF8.21 Aii lèe k'àii hàa zheh goghoo gogwahtsìi? Gwadachàn hàa?

SF8.25 Ą̀ąhą'.

CF9.28 Aii Ch'eekwaii nats'àhts'ą̀' dzaa gwà'àn gîilk'įį?

SF9.31 Ch'eekwaii nąįį lèe? Oo'ęę neegiidàl. Ch'adhàh eenjit. Vadzaih dhàa zhreh.

CF9.56 Aii Ch'eekwaii nąįį nijìn gwats'an k'iinaa neegihiidàl yàhnyàa? Oonjìt *Chųų Choh Vęę* reh hę̀ę?

SF10.04 Chųų vęę gwats'anh. *Point Barrow* gwats'an chat ts'ą̀' geh'àt gehndee gwàndàk chat ts'ą̀' *Bartèr Islànd.* Izhìk gwats'an Ch'eekwaii nąįį gǫ̀ǫlįį ts'ą̀' aii nąįį oo'ęę goonànhkat ch'atthą̀įį kwaa ts'ą̀' dzaa gwee'àn ch'atthą̀įį gǫ̀ǫlįį aii eenjit ch'atthą̀įį dhàh. Aii eenjit oo'ęę neegiidàl t'igii'ìn.

11.10 Tr'ohchìt shandàh geegogwaandak reh. Zhat gwànaa dąį' jèiinch'ii chųų tyąh jèiinch'ii googàa datthak kwaa, nàhąą? Akwàt jidìi dèe t'eegwąąhch'yàa? Aiits'ą̀' chųų tyąh googàa kwàa, ch'ìk chan kwàa. Aii dąį' it'ee *Russiàn* ts'an tr'ohchìt tyąh jèiinch'įį kwat gòodlit

7. This interview with Sarah was done at Old John's cabin on *Old John Lake.* —CM

10.50 They didn't wear their hoods up, so we grabbed their hoods and wrapped them around their necks. That's when they really slowed down.

<sfdlBIA338a>

CF6.59 He (*David Libbey*) said there are a lot of old camp sites around here (at *Old John*'s cabin), and he wants to ask you who the people were.

SF7.16 Around this house? One time during New Year's a bunch of Inuit came here. At the same time people from around this area came too. All those people lived here. And they all celebrated together at New Year's.

CF Huh.

SF8.05 They built a round hut.

CF Oh.

SF8.10 With skin. They covered it with skin. A lot of them lived in that round hut made out of skin.

CF8.21 Is this the kind where they use willows to make it round? I mean the poles they used.

SF8.25 Yes.

CF9.28 How did the Inuit come to visit here?

SF9.31 You mean the Inuit? They used to travel here to trade for skins. Only for caribou skins.

CF9.56 He (*David Libbey*) asked where these Inuit came from. They're from the *Arctic Coast* area, huh?

SF10.04 They're from coastal areas. They're from *Point Barrow* and also another village around there and from *Barter Island*. Lots of Inuit came here. There was no food at their home so they came here for food and skins.

11.10 The first time I heard about this. In those days we didn't even have this kind of cup, you see? We didn't have cups or plates. This is when they first got cooking pots ginyàa. Aii kwaii chan nitsìi ree. Izhìk gwats'an tr'ohchìt tyąh gòodlìt.

12.01 Aiitł'ęę vijųų gwànaa izhìk at'ôohju' hee Ch'eekwaii nąįį zhik chųų vęę dee'àn *ship* neehii'òl, nàhąą? Aii it'ee oo'àt teenee'òl ts'ą̀' geetàk *ship* tik gàa zhat gwà'àn dhidlii ginyàa. Izhìk gwats'an t'ee dzaa gwats'an ch'ii'àn oonjìt hę̀ę. Nijìn *Dizhèenjik* ginyaa izhìk gwitł'it ch'ii'àn, aiits'ą̀' yaaghà' *Njuu Njik* gwitł'it ch'ii'àn hàa t'ee oo'àn chųų vęę nìneegiidàl. Izhìk gwats'an it'ee lìdii tsal kwat tr'ąąh'ìn. Nąhjyàa łyâa àkwàa, gògǫǫtrii t'ôonch'yàa.

CF Hę̀ę.

SF Gògǫǫtrii t'ôonch'yàa.

CF13.08 Hę̀ę. Aii nats'àhts'ą̀' aii lìdii kwaii oodhoojìk? K'iinaa nìneegiidàl? Ch'eekwaii nąįį?

SF13.16 Dzaa gwee'àn gwich'in nąįį oo'àn chan nìneedàl. Aii it'ee ch'adhàh, jidìi nilįį kwaii hàa t'agah'ìn. Aii oo'àn neegahaazhik t'ìį geedant'ee k'aiich'ii goots'an gàhtsii.

CF13.35 Aii t'ee nihłach'agookwàt googàhnyaa dąį' reh hę̀ę?

SF Ą̀ąhą'.

from the Russians. They were all large pots. So that's where they first got the pots and pans from.

12.01 Then years later, the Inuit started to travel to where all the ships docked, somewhere in the coastal area, you see? Sometimes even three ships came at the same time. Since then the people from here traveled over there. They followed either the *Coleen River* or the *Juunjik* up to the headwaters and from there they traveled over the mountains to the coast. That was when we were beginning to get more things like tea and such. Before then it was very hard to get things like that.

CF Huh.

SF It was a very hard time back then.

CF13.08 Huh. How did you and other people get your tea? Did they come over? Those Inuit?

SF13.16 People from here traveled over there too. They took meat and skins to them. They took all this with them and traded with them for store items.

CF13.35 Is that what they called trading or bartering with each other?

SF Yes.

Sarah Frank

Vaa Tseerii'in

<sflg2a>

SF4.29 Âa, googàa t'agwą̀htsii łyâa gavàh shrôonch'yaa t'agavaihnyaa (adlàa). Izhìk dą̀į' chan gwaatr'àl kwaa, nàhąą. Gwaatr'àl kwaa ts'ą' zhyą̀ą nan làii dha'ąįį k'ìt t'ôonch'yaa ts'ą' ree. Âa, gwįįzįį ch'aga'àa ts'ą' ree aiitł'ęę yee'àt gwà'àn chat tsèegii'in ree.

4.55 Goonaldàii į' izhìk. Aiits'ą' ch'atah chat gahaatłàk. Ch'atah gahaatłak chan jyàa dìgii'in izhìk chat gaayii nałagaatsìi. Jùu ch'atah aatłak aii gaayii ch'ahtsii, nàhąą.

5.17 Jyàa digii'in į'. Aiits'ą' chan han gwatsal gwįį'ee dą̀į' chan jìdii Neehîilak[1] giyàhnyaa, aii chan hàa tsèegii'in, âa, shrôonch'yaa gogwahtsii t'agavaihnyàa. Aiits'ą' ąįį shìh it'ee. . .[2]

LG5.52 Aii Neehîilak aii gwįįzįį nats'àhts'ą' giyàa tsèehee'yàa goo'ąįį t'inch'yàa?

SF5.57 Aii jidìi k'àii. . .

LG6.00 Ą̀ąhą'. Nah'in į' nats'àhts'ą' vìgwèech'in ch'ìhłan *Isaac* jyàiinch'ii iłtsą̀įį.

SF6.04 Ą̀ąhą'. Aii k'àii jyàa dą̀hujyaa reh aii vathoochàn gǫ̀ǫlįį aii giithoochàn k'eech'it'ìi ts'ą' vakat k'àii shrah gwìch'in dhidlii, nàhąą, Aii oondaa vitł'yàa gǫ̀ǫlįį, aii oondaa jyàa dìgiyah'in ch'iidì teeyaahthàl gwiizhìk jùu yuuheendàl jì' eenjit t'igii'ìn.

6.35 Teeghàih nihts'įį jyàa dìgii'in ts'ą' oondàa jyàa dìgiyah'in ch'ìhłęę khàyavyaa'aahthàk. Neehîilak giyàhnyaa aii.

1. *Neehîilak* is described by McKennan (1965:49) as a boys' game. —CM

2. Sarah didn't finish her sentence. I interrupted and asked another question.—LG It's not clear from the context whether she was talking about food or a brown bear. Both meanings of *shih* are possible here. —JE

Sarah Frank

Games

<sflg2a>

SF4.29 Ah, but I sure recall how they enjoyed it (laughs). At the time it was not brushy in the area, you see. The land looked so bare becausc it wasn't brushy back then. So they ate well and then they played games.

4.55 Yes, I remember them. They did the high jump too. What they did was compete among one another. Whoever did the high jump would compete, you see.

5.17 This is what they did. They also played this game called Neehîilak. If there was a small river or slough where they were at, they really enjoyed that game. And then this food (or this bear). . .

LG5.52 How were they supposed to play that game called Neehîilak?

SF5.57 It's like willows . . .

LG6.00 Yes. I saw the one *Isaac* (*Tritt*) made one time.

SF6.04 Yes. Then they all got long willows but chopped off all the branches on them. At the very end of the pole they tied a string. And at the other end of the string they attached a willow hook, so when the willow ball or Neehîilak is floating downriver, everybody would try to catch it with their hook and run ahead of one another.

6.35 They all tried to beat each other running along the bank, until finally one of them caught it. They called it Neehîilak.

<sfkfl a>

CF11.19 Izhìk oondee gwà'àn *Van Choh* vęę neerihiidàl ch'ìhłan ganandàii? Ch'anjàa nąįį lęįį oondee gwà'àn neehiidàl, ch'ìhłan shin?[3]

SF Ą̀ąhą'.

CF11.33 Izhìk nakhwàa neehihdik. Izhìk dąį' aii zheh nihdèeriin'oo akhài', "Dzaa łyâa zhyą̀ą chaavał kat gwint'aii ch'agaadzaa ch'yąą reh t'ôonch'yàa." Nihłàgaanyaa goonaldàii t'agwaihnyaa aii ch'anjàa nąįį.

SF Ą̀ąhą'.

CF11.50 Izhìk zheh nihdèeriin'oo, dèegwinyaa t'igwinyaa nihthàn. "Nats'ą̀ą chan zhyą̀ą chaavał kat ch'agaahaadzaa?" nihthan t'iihnyàa.

12.02 Akhài' chaavał nèekwąįį nihts'ąįį' nìgìchìk. Aii kat ch'agaadzaa t'agogwàhnyaa łee hęę?

SF Ą̀ąhą'.

KF12.19 Shitsųų nįįdąį' gwànaa ch'igidlii, aii k'ìt t'inch'yaa gwich'ilìk kwaii anandàii?i

SF12.30 Łą̀hch'yâa ch'igiilii goonaldàii kwàa. Jyàa dìginyaa kwaa į'. Goonaldàii kwàa.

KF12.52 Geetàk hee nàgahaazhrii k'ìt t'ôonch'yaa dąį' gàa geenjit ch'ilik gii'įį gavoiihnyaa lèe.

SF13.02 Łyâa gwik'ìt t'iginyaa kwaa į'. Izhìk gwichįh nąhjyàa izhìk dąį' it'ee jidii ch'ilik googàa gii'įį gwinyaa gàa jyàa digee'yą' kwaa t'iginch'yàa. Aii yaaghà' ti'yąą nąįį zhat gwànaa khehłòk dinjii gogwandàii gwanaa reh, łąą gwilìi gąhdal kwaa t'iginch'yàa.

13.43 Zhyàa shin neegihiinjik dąį' gwizhrįh ch'atah naatłak gwizhrįh, tł'eeval k'ìt chan. Aiits'ą' chan yaaghà' Nèhkak hàa tsèe'in hàa chan gwizhrįh. Izhìk gwizhrįh ganaldii į'. Shandàh łą̀ą ch'agaadzyàa kwaa į'.

3. See the above photo of this group at Old John's cabin in July 1979, p. 598. —CM

<sfkf1a>

CF11.19 Do you remember once we were by the shores of *Old John Lake*? That one summer we took lots of elders there?

SF Yes.

CF11.33 I was with you people. That was when we went inside this house. While we were in there some of the elder women said to one another, "This is where they used to dance on a toboggan."

SF Yes.

CF11.50 When we were inside the house I was wondering why they said that. I thought, "How can they dance on a toboggan?"

12.02 Then they meant that they laid two toboggans side by side with the bottoms up. That's what they danced on, right?

SF Yes.

KF12.19 Grandma, do you remember what kind of songs they sang a long time ago?

SF12.30 I really can't remember what they sang. They didn't do that. I don't remember.

KF12.52 I thought sometimes they had songs like that to go out hunting.

SF13.02 They really didn't say that. Before that they said they had songs, but it was not like that. During my father's time they didn't bother with that.

13.43 During the summer when they traveled they did high jumps and swings. And also they played ball games. That's all I remember. I never did see them dance.

14.16 Ch'ìhłan gwànaa ree aii nijìn gwà'àn t'igwii'in izhìk ree ganaldàii Dinjii Zhuh k'yą̀ą ch'agaadzàa. Jidìi ch'ilik igidlii t'iginyaa googàa goonaldàii kwaa į'. Aii t'ee ihtsìi kwaa gwànaa. Izhìk it'ee jidìi zhik gwà'àn dazhoo ts'àt.[4] Gwach'aa tsal giits'ąą ts'ą̀' reh zhyą̀ą reh nihghooteegijyaa k'ìt t'igii'in, tsingwahch'yaa ch'agaadzaa t'agoovaihnyą̀ą. Izhìk gwizhrįh shandaa jyaa digeeyą'.

KF15.23 Yaaghà' jidii tr'oaahkhaa ch'yąą gwik'ìt t'agah'in?

SF15.28 Ą̀ąhą', shùh ree.

KF15.33 Aii chan gwahkhaa ts'ą̀' lèe?

SF15.39 Ch'eekwaii nąįį ts'an tr'idiinjìk į'. Aii shųh.

KF15.51 Aii jì' goots'an k'ìt t'inch'yaa gii'įį łii hę̀ę?

SF15.54 Ą̀ąhą'.

CF15.56 Aii shitì' shàagwaandak chan Ch'eekwaii nąįį ts'at kat neegahaatłak ǫ' hę̀ę?

SF Ą̀ąhą'.

CF16.06 Aii chan diits'an tr'igwigwìin'ąįį t'iginch'yaa chan gavàhnyàa. It'ee łyâa t'inyaa dǫ̀hłįį hę̀ę?

SF16.10 Ą̀ąhą', it'ee łyâa t'iinyàa. Izhìk kwanh zhit nihdèegadàl, nàhąą? Izhìk it'ee datthak jyàa dìginch'yaa į'. Łihts'eegîilzhìi. Jidìi dinjii ts'an goondak dzaa diitth'àn deetak nihtsįį jyàa dìgiyah'ìn. Gwiizhìk diitth'àn deetak giyàheendàl gàa goochįh t'igii'in ǫ'. Googàa it'ee geetàk giyàhchàk. Aii dinjii vats'an tr'oondak, aii it'ee jyàa dǒo'yà' ginyàa. Izhìk gwizhrįh chan gàashandàii.

CF17.42 Khǎiinjih Neevee Deegoo'yą̀' k'ìt t'inch'yaa hę̀ę?

SF17.51 Ą̀ąhą'. Izhìk hee it'ee *Dinjii Choh* nąįį agàa *Anàazhrii Tsal* giyàhnyàa aii oondee dinjii tèegiłthat ts'ą̀' zhyą̀ą aii tr'iiniin haah'yàa, aii tr'iinin nahshų' aii tr'iinin ooghwaa ts'ą̀' niyuhshų̀' ginyaa dǫ̀hłįį. Gwiizhìk aii *Dinjii Choh* chan tr'iinin k'ìt itrèe. Aii gwiizhìk *Anàazhrii* aii nahshyų̀' ts'ą̀' diineeghwaa giyàhnyàa.

4. It's hard for me to understand the tape here. —LG

14.16 One time I don't know where we were at, but I remembered they danced a Gwich'in-style dance. I could never remember what songs they sang. It was while I was very young. That's when they had the fur blanket dance. They wore special clothing over their bodies and danced back and forth. I remember that was a funny dance. That's the only time I saw them doing that.

KF15.23 Did they do the one they beat on?

SF15.28 Yes, it was a drum.

KF15.33 Were they beating on that too?

SF15.39 That drum came from the Inuit.

KF15.51 So that's why they used the same thing huh?

SF15.54 Yes.

CF15.56 My father told me those Inuit did the blanket toss, huh?

SF Yes.

CFI6.06 He said that they got that idea from us. I wonder if it's really true?

SF16.10 Yes, it's true. When they all get inside the skin hut they go like this (gesturing), right? Sometimes they all sat in a circle. They took an item from someone, while sitting closely in a circle, and they had their legs folded up underneath them. They passed that item over to another person real fast, but he still grabbed it. Whoever has his item grabbed is told to do something. That's another game I know about.

CF17.42 It's almost like the game named Neevee Deegoo'yą' huh?

SF17.51 Yes. At this one game, they said they got something of *Dinjii Choh's,* and they told him to get *Anaazhrii Tsal* and act like he's a baby and rock him to sleep. So he packed him around and at the same time he tried to calm him to sleep. *Dinjii Choh* even cried like a baby.

Nàhtryàh tr'ahahtłaa chan.[5] Duuyeh akhagwàroonyaa giyàhnyàa reh. Aiits'ą̀' aii dinjii vats'an tr'oondak, aii jyàa doo'yą̀' ginyaa ǫ'. Aii it'ee gwik'ìt t'igii'ìn.

19.03 Izhìk it'ee yaaghà' *Drit* chan it'ee vats'an tr'ą̀htsìt dǫ̀hłįį akhài' zheh gwizhìt datthak dinjii gwànlįį. *Drit* aii chan vats'an tr'ą̀htsìt, yeedit kwàntee ch'iidįį ootryą̀' giyàhnyàa. Zhat nach'aa kaii yeedìt kwàntee ch'iidįį dazhoo thał zhàk ąąhtrat ts'ą̀' ch'iidįį neetł'įnzhaa giyàhnyàa. Zhat nitryą̀' aanaii giyàhnyàa. Jyàa dìgii'in aii chan duuyee akhagògoonyaa ginyaa t'aihnyàa.

19.57 Izhìk it'ee yaaghà' *Treenahtsyàh*[6] aii chan vats'an tr'ą̀htsìt. Aiits'ą̀' it'ee kweeghaih ndàk nàhtryàh ohtłaa giyàhnyàa. Aii ch'iindàk zhat nilghàa ts'ą̀' nàhtryàh hìłtłaa gàa tr'agwâadąįį giyàhnyàa. Vanàn njyah khaneetak giyàhnyàa. Khaiinjih dlòk hàa ch'inghan giyàhnyàa.

KF20.29 Shitsųų, aii tr'iinin nohshų' haadhàk lèe vǎiinyàa?[7]

SF Hąą?

KF20.42 Zhik geelin neediyęęghwaa ts'ą̀' geelin needęęhaa?

SF20.47 Ą̀ąhą', niyąhshų̀'. "Ą̀ąha'. Lee, lee," yàhnyàa.

KF20.52 Ǫ̂ǫ, khaniyaa'yu' ree hę̀ę?

SF20.55 Ą̀ąhą'. Gwiizhìk adant'ee, "Aghwąą! Aghwąą!" nyaa giyàhnyàa.

CF20.57 Itree adaa'įį yàhnyàa.

SF21.09 Jyàa dìgii'in hàa dlòk nitsìi neegahtsìk t'ig'inch'yàa.

KF21.15 Aii nats'àhts'ą̀' voozhrį̀' aii giyàa tsèe'ìn?

SF21.22 Jii Vęę Dèegoo'yą̀'.

KF21.25 Aii dagatth'àn t'eh k'àiich'ii neegaahthak, aii, aii yù'?

SF21.28 Aii reh.

5. The wolverine hop was an Indian game similar to the Inuit seal hop, in which a person must lean down and jump forward on his or her knuckles. —KF

6. *Treenahtsyàh* was one of the old women Sarah looked after in her early married years. See the story above, "Sarah Ts'à' Shyaaghan Nąįį Hàa."

7. The meaning of this is to get a crying child's attention by singing to the child. —JE

They said meanwhile he was packing *Anaazhrii* around and acted like he was getting him to go to sleep. The wolverine hop also. They have to do whatever they're told to do by the person who grabs their item. They have to do it.

19.03 At that time they also grabbed something of *Drit's* too. There were lots of people in there. So they grabbed something of *Drit's.* He was told to go to the toilet by the doorway. He just quickly got up and went to the doorway and pulled his fur pants down and actually did it. I mean they didn't hesitate to do what they were told to do.

19.57 They also grabbed something of *Treenahtsyàh's* too.
So she was told to do what a wolverine does as he's bounding along. So she lay down to do it, but it was hard for her, they say. All you could see was her back raising up high and going down, they say. She made everybody laugh so hard.

KF20.29 Grandma, did you say *Dinjii Choh* tried to rock and calm the baby?

SF What?

KF20.42 Was he packing him on his back and walking around and around with him?

SF20.47 Yes, and while he was doing that he was calming him, singing, *"Yes. Lee, lee."*

KF20.52 Oh, by lullabying him?

SF20.55 Yes. Meanwhile they say he was crying, "Waa! Waa!"

CF20.57 She said he pretended like he was crying.

SF21.09 Everybody had a good laugh by doing silly things.

KF21.15 What's the name of the game they played?

SF21.22 Jii Vęę Dèegoo'yą'.

KF21.25 What about that game where they passed something under their legs?

SF21.28 That's the same one.

Sarah Frank

T'eediraa'in

<sflgla>

SF0.22 Ch'atthàįį tr'oonilį'?

LG Ą̀ąhą'.

SF0.24 Juu ch'atthàįį gwinzįį oonil]', aii nats'ahts'ą̀' ch'atthàįį eenàhak. Nàts'àhts'ą̀' vats'ą̀' ahtr'aii. Duuyeh vats'ą̀' ahtr'aii gwiizhìk izhìk ts'ąįį duuyeh giits'ą̀' ha'òo. Izhìk chat giyeenjit gwak'ą̌ąhtii į'. Vats'ą̀' ahtr'aii k'ii'àn vats'ą̀' rehee'al kwaa į'. Izhìk ahtr'aii jyàa dìi'in nàhąą, jyàhts'ą̀' ahtr'aii eetsįh t'eh k'ìt'ôonch'yaa izhìk t'ee gwandàii eenàgo'oo t'igii'ìn. Vats'ą̀' ahtr'aii t'igwiizhìk jį', ninyìt vats'ą̀' tr'ee'àl gwiizhìk t'igwiizhìk jì', diik'yąhaandal?

LG Mmm hmm.

SF1.26 Aiits'ą̀' t'ee reh jyàa dìheenjyàa, àkwàt vats'ą̀' ahtr'aii kwaa izhìk ts'ąįį, ts'ąįį giyeenahkhaiich'iichik t'ii'ìn. Aii k'ìighai' it'ee jùu gàandaii nąįį t'ee ch'atthàįį gavee gach'agwadhan į'. Gwik'ìt t'inch'yaa kwaa nąįį it'ee shik ch'atthàįį giveezhìi jyàa gwinyàa. Aii it'ee zhik vats'ą̀' ahtr'aii ts'ąįį gweechyaa kwaa ts'ą̀' izhìk ts'ąįį yats'ą̀' hahak geh'àn khan yik'yǎandak į', ts'ą̀' jyàa dinjìk t'ii'ìn.

2.19 Zhik tthaa ghat di' ritł'ùk jìhnyaa, khyąh chat kwaa jį'. Aii chat łyâa goondàh t'igwii'in ts'ą̀' jyàa dàrah'in jį' gwik'ìighai' giyàaheendàii. Zhyą̀ą goohàa gwaraandak jį' chan dęę zhrįh giheelyâa į'.

LG Ą̀ąhą'.

SF2.44 Izhìk gwanaa khyą̀h kwaa ts'ą̀' ch'ìhgyąh zhrįh hàa nin goonilį', nàhąą?

LG Ą̀ąhą'.

Sarah Frank

Subsistence

<sflgla>

SF0.22 You want to know how we harvested large game?

LG Yes.

SF0.24 Anyone who knew how to hunt would have to know how to get close to game animals without distracting them. It all depends on how the wind blows. You cannot go directly toward them if the wind is blowing toward them. They're very cautious about that too. You're not supposed to walk toward animals if the wind is blowing toward them. So you see if the wind is blowing like that, then you have to stay downwind to get near enough without the animal sensing you. If you do go toward them with the wind blowing toward them, no matter how far away you are, you'll distract them, you see.

LG Mmm hmm.

SF1.26 That's what will happen. But if you go downwind, the way wind is not blowing toward them, that's how you get within shooting range. If the hunter knows all this, it makes it a lot easier for him to hunt for big game. They say that if they don't follow this advice, then they are very unlucky for hunting. The animals sense you and take off if you don't pay attention to how the wind blows.

2.19 I said that when there were no traps, we snared for ground squirrels. If kids really see us doing it, then they'll know how to do it. But if we just tell them about it, they won't know what to do.

LG Yes.

SF2.44 At that time we didn't have traps, so we only used sinew to snare small game, you see?

LG Yes.

SF2.53 Aii chan dachan, geh aii reh geetàk dachan łagahtł'ùk į', aii kat dachan jyàa dìgilìk aii t'ee oozhee digitł'uk. Izhik k'àii ch'ii t'įįn'ee giyahtsìk, aiits'ą' geh ìilok dąį' it'ee jii jyàa dinjìk ts'ą' t'ee geh zhee t'avyaa aadhàk, nàhąą.[1]

LG Ą̀ąhą'.

SF3.21 Ą̀ąhą'. Aii it'ee ch'ih gyą̀h kwaii reh.

LG3.26 Tthaa chan jyàa dagah'in?

SF3.28 Ą̀ąhą', aii tthaa chan reh. Tthaa, geh kwaii hàa. Aiits'ą' daagǫǫ chan. Aii chan ch'aka' zhrįh.

3.56 Łyâa gògwàntrii nàgwaanaii jì', yaaghà' ęę vàanòodlit tr'ìk t'aihnyàa. Aii t'ee valàt vandàh t'ihłìk į' t'aihnyàa.

LG Ą̀ąhą'.

SF4.11 Ch'adąį' gwanaa gògwàntrii gwìindhat dąį', "Dinjii Zhuh nąįį łì'hàa googàa gwats'an gwinzįį gwiindàii, aii gwitr'it[2] łyâa hàagoondàii gwiindhan gàa łyâa gògwàntrii," nyaa ǫ̀. Aiits'ą' t'ee yaaghà' tthaa gyàh t'aihnyą̀ą, chan geh gyàh chan. Aii ch'įh gyàh reh. Aii t'ee vandàh chat didhiitł'įį. Ch'įh gyàa dhałtsąįį chan vintł'ĕiilii t'aihnyàa. Aiits'ą' zhik naraazhrìi. Nàraazhrìi chan ts'ą' zhik nintsàl khat di' ritł'uk chan, khyą̀h nara'ak chan. Aii nąįį juudìn gwinzįį nin oonilį', jùu gwinzįį nin oonilį' nąįį tr'iinin jyàa dĭi'in gwąąhtan jì' gwiheezhyàa ǫ̂ǫch'yàa. Àkwàt zhyą̀ą goohàa gwaraandak jì' gàa dęę zhrįh goohàa gwihèelyaa į'.

LG Ą̀ąhą'.

SF5.44 Aiits'ą' goondàh t'igwii'in ji' gwizhrįh khan gik'ìgahaandal į'. Nitii hàa reh, zhik gwà'àn tsuk k'įh gǫ̀ǫlįį, ts'ą' "Jùu shrit tsuk iihìilok li'," nyą̀ą. Aiits'ą' khaihłęę ts'ą' nihghàih ree tsuk eenjit di' răatł'įį. Vizheh gwatsàl tr'igwiłtsąįį izhìk ch'iizhàk nihdèegweedįį izhìk ree gyàh didhiitł'įį. Adan t'ee chan gwik'ìt t'iizhìk.

1. Sarah describes here what is called a spring pole or tossing pole snare, widely used by northern Dene. See McKennan (1965:33) and (1959:61). —CM

2. *Gwitr'it* here means the old ways of how Indians lived. —LG
Gwitr'it normally means 'work'. —CM

SF2.53 Also pieces of stick, sometimes they tie the sticks together, and then they go over them with another stick, and then under that they put the snare. Then they put a willow branch a certain way, and when that snare catches a snowshoe hare, it pulls the hare up in the air, you see.

LG Yes.

SF3.21 Yes. That's how they used sinew snares for snowshoe hares.

LG3.26 Do they do the same with ground squirrels?

SF3.28 Yes, they do the same with ground squirrels. Ground squirrels and also hares. And ptarmigan too. But they only use toggle sticks to hang snares on.

3.56 Some day we might have really hard times again. I mean there was this one white woman. I told her and showed her how it was done.

LG Yes.

SF4.11 She said, "Indian people sure lived well long ago, even though they had a hard time of it. That's why we want to learn more of the old ways about how Indians lived." As I said, I had ground squirrel snares and snowshoe hare snares. I used sinew for snares. I set the snares for her. After that I gave her the sinew snares that I made. So that's how we hunted and how we set snares for small game and how we set traps. It would be really good to teach children about how to hunt and trap for game by people who are experts at it. But if you just tell them about how to do it they'll be lost and won't know what to do.

LG Yes.

SF5.44 So if you actually do it with them, they'll learn faster. There was only your grandfather and me. And there were lots of marten tracks, so we said, "Let's both set snares and see who'll catch one first." So we each set snares. We made a little house-like for them, and in the doorway I set the snares. He did the same.

LG6.48 Oonjìt chan shih tsal nàgahchak, aii chan dòozhį̨į̨ łèe? Nilį̨į̨ k'ìt t'inch'yaa gwizhìt nàgahchak aį̨į̨ zheh gwatsàl gogwahtsìk?

SF7.03 Ą̨į̨ lèe tsuk eenjit?

LG Ą̨ąhą'.

SF7.06 Tsuk eenjit t'igii'in dą̀į̨' geetàk chan nilį̨į̨ tsal t'agah'in į̨'. Geetàk chan geh dhàh.

LG Oh, ą̨ąhą'.

SF Aiits'ą̨' nihdèehahak t'ii'ìn. Ninjii chan ree. Ninjii chan gwik'ìt t'ii'ìn.

LG Aii chan jidìi reh giyàhnyąą ch'yą̨ą?

SF7.44 Łuk. Łuk łyâa veenjit nizį̨į̨ giyàhnyąą į̨'. Geh dhàh kwaii chan t'irilìk gàa nizį̨į̨ ninjii. Aii t'ee ch'adą̀į̨' gwanaa Gwichyaa Gwich'in nąį̨į̨ shandàh giyeegwaandàk. Aii jidìi oonjìt veenjit jyàa dìrilìk aii łeefaa vakat neeraahtl'àk giyàhnyàa. Aii łyâa eet'iindhan giyàhnyàa. Ninyìt gwats'an yahtsan, nàhąą?

LG Ą̨ąhą'.

SF8.22 Aiits'ą̨' yitsį̨į̨ hahak ree. Jidìi k'àiich'ii vagwaatsan aii łyâa veenjit nizį̨̀į. Aii tsuk t'aihnyaa chan. Aii yaaghà' gwà'àn ch'idin gwat'an reh, jèiinch'į̨į̨ aii oonjìt veenjit jyàa dirilìk łyâa nizį̨į̨ giyàhnyaa į̨'.[3]

LG8.52 Àkwàt nikhyą̀ą in'ąį̨ ch'yąh yų̀'?

SF9.31 Jyàa gwinyaa ts'ą̨' veenjit khyą̀h hàa t'iriinlìk t'aihnyàa. Adan t'ee khyą̀h nǐn'ąį̨ shant'ee chan geh'àt. Jùu shrit yiihàhdroo lì' gwinyàa. Aiits'ą̨' jyàa dìriinlìk akhài' shį̨į̨ aii tsuk ałdròo. Adan aii nàkwàa.

10.00 Nintsàl tr'oonilį̀, jii t'agwǎihnyaa khyą̀h dhidlii jii aii dinjii gàandaii, jùu veegàch'agwadhan, aii tr'iinin nąį̨ gwą̌ąhtan jì' heezyàa.

LG10.15 Ą̨ąhą'. It'ee łyâa t'avąį̨nyàa.

3. Part of this section is inaudible. —LG

LG6.48 Didn't they put bait inside the little house and whatever you call that? Didn't they put a little meat way back inside the little house they made for it?

SF7.03 You mean for marten?

LG Yes.

SF7.06 If it was for marten then sometimes they used a small piece of meat and sometimes snowshoe hare fur, so the animals will go inside of it.

LG Oh, yes.

SF They did the same thing for lynx.

LG What did they say they used for bait?

SF7.44 Fish. They say fish is really good for it. Sometimes snowshoe hare fur is good for lynx. That too I remember. A long time ago the people from the *Yukon Flats* said they splashed perfume on the hare fur. They say the lynx really like that. They smell it from far away, you see?

LG Yes.

SF8.22 So you see the animal follows the smell. Anything with a strong smell is good for it. The same way for marten too. They say you snare the same way for camp robbers and put a piece of bait way back inside the little house.

LG8.52 What happened to the traps you set?

SF9.31 So we set the traps. I'm saying we did it with traps. Johnny set his traps and I set mine. We both wondered who would catch something first. So that's what we did. Then I caught a marten. And he didn't.

10.00 Like I was saying before about trapping for small game, it must be a man who is good at trapping and finds trapping easy who should teach children. That will be good then.

LG10.15 Yes. You're quite right.

SF10.20 Duuyeh geegoorąąhtan kwaa gwiizhìk duuyeh gwinzįį t'igwii'in t'ôonch'yaa. Ch'adąį' *Ch'at'oonjik* oonjį' neeshagahchìk. Izhìk hee nilįį tr'ahgąįį dąį' vizhìt rilìi. Aii eenjit jèiinch'įį gąąh'in. Aiits'ą' chan nats'ąhts'ą' geenjit t'inch'yàa, ginyàa.

Shagwaahkat aiits'ą' ree t'agavaihnyàa, "Nilįį tr'ahgąįį dąį' nilįį tr'ahgąįį tł'ęę gwinzii *dry* ilìk tł'ęę aii vizhìt rilii t'inchyaa?" gavaihnyàa. "Aii nilįį nats'ąhts'ą' ohgąįį," shàhnyàa. Nats'ą' doh'in, nyàa. Izhìk chat t'avaihnyàa, "Akwàt zhyąą geeragwaandak jì' ree, googàa *'I don't know.'*" Zhrįh gwihèelyaa t'ôonch'yaa văihnyàa.

11.25 Googàa nilįį tr'ahgąįį, "Dinjii Zhuh dèe'in geenaroohîiłtyą' jì' ree oozhee dzaa gǫǫh'ìn gwiizhìk nakhweenjit jyàa dìgwii'in jì' gwizhrįh khan gàakhwahandàii văihnyàa.

Gàh duuyeh nakhwàa gwaraandak gǫǫh'in kwaa deegwii'in aii gooh'in kwàa. Nakhwàa gwaraandak jì' gàa reh dęę zhrįh nadhwàa gwihèelyàa. Aii ree gach'oohkat t'oohnyaa vaihnyàa.

12.05 Jidìi Dinjii Zhuh gwitr'ìt jyàa dǐnch'yaa aii łyâa oozhee tr'agwąąh'in ts'ą' gwik'ìt t'igwii'in jì' it'ee khan gàahakhwandàii. Gàa ree gooh'in kwaa gwiizhìk nashwàh gwaraandak jì' ree. Gàa dęę zhrįh nakhwàa gwihèelyaa t'ôonch'yaa," gavaihnyàa (adlaa).

13.48 Dinjii nąįį chan nin keegii'in nàgaazhrìi zhik gwà'àn nin gǫǫnilį'. Aii tthak gàhgiindàii į'. Aiits'ą' tr'ìnjàa nąįį chan geech'agoohîiłtyą' jì' dęę zhrįh gavàagwihèelyaa į'. Nats'ąhts'ą' nintsàl deegah'in aii giveeiach'agwadhan, nàhąą, dinjii nąįį. Tr'ìnjàa naii gwik'ìt t'ii'in kwaa, nàhąą. Aiits'ą' dęę zhrįh gǫǫlįį.

LG Ą̀ąhą'.

SF14.00 Ch'adąį' gwànaa Dinjii Zhuh gwandàii gwanaa łyâa *hard time* gǫǫlįį gwànaa. Zhik nankat neegihiidàl, nàhąą. Chadąį' *survey* chan nan *survey* gogwahtsii dąį' chan

SF10.20 They will not do good work if they're not taught how to do it. A long time ago they took me along to way over to the *Koness River*. There they found a meat cache. We dried meat after we stored the meat inside that cache, so that's why they looked at it and also asked why it was there.

They asked me, "When you dry that meat, what do you do to it?" So I told them, "When we dry meat, after the meat has completely dried, then we store it in there." That's what I said to them. Then he asked me how we dry that meat. That's when I said to him, "Even if we tell you how, you'll still say, 'I don't know.'"

11.25 Then I said to them, "If an Indian is going to teach you how to dry meat, you actually have to see how it's done.

That's the only way you'll learn fast. You cannot learn from me just telling you about it, without seeing it done. You still cannot understand the whole process that you're asking about.

12.05 Any kind of Indian activity has to be learned by observing how it's done. Then you'll learn quickly. But if you're simply told how it was done without actually seeing it done, you're lost." That's what I told them (laughs).

13.48 The men knew all about how to hunt and how to use traps and snares for all the game. But if women were to try and teach all these activities, they wouldn't know what to do. You see it's much simpler for men to hunt and trap small game. But the women don't do that, you see, so they simply don't know. If we actually do it in front of them, then they'll catch on fast.

LG Yes.

SF14.00 It was really a hard life for Indians a long time ago, especially when they had to move from one place to another across the land, you see. A long time nitsii chan geegavaahtan į'.[4] Jidìi nankat gwanzhįh tr'a'àa jì' kwaii. Izhìk dąį' it'ee chan nankat jidìi nahshįį tr'a'àa nàhąą, zhik gwà'àn jak, trih, aii tthak khàrahshrį' jyàa dìgwii'in ts'ą' tr'a'àa, nàhąą? Aii datthak googàa gogwadâątł'òo. Aii *survey* nąįį chat trih khahshrį' t'aihnyàa (adlaa). Danleedrìl k'al hàa trih khahshrį'. Nankat jidìi tr'a'àa jì' łyâa hàagoondàii giindhan į'.

LG15.27 Àkwàt aii ęę *Drit*, aiits'ą' *Drit Zhuu* nąįį gavaah'yą' lèe t'iginch'yàa?

SF15.39 *Drit Zhuu* lèe?

LG Ą̀ąha'.

SF15.41 Gavaał'yà' kwaa į'.

LG15.44 Ǫ̂ǫ, gavąąh'yą' kwaa?

SF15.46 *Shyaaghan Ndik*[5] aii it'ee gwandàii. Gwandàii gàa aii chan niła'adan hee tr'igwich'įį ts'ą' nał'yą' kwaa į' aii *Shyaaghan Ndik.* Aii it'ee yaaghà' shakàį' it'ee łyâa yàandaii į'.

LG16.11 Aii łyâa yagwandàk lęįį di'įį giyàhnyąą, hęę?

SFI6.16 Ą̀ąha'. Yagwandàk lęįį di'įį. Vandàh chan *three times* tr'igwiinghan giyàhnyàa. Izhìk gàa gwidiinzhìi. Ch'ihłan *last time* it'ee chan, chan hee vandàh dinjii tr'ahàaghan. Izhìk chan tsyaa nąįį. Tsyaa tsal nąįį tik gwit'ee ąhjil giyàhnyaa į'. Aii nąįį ts'an, aii ch'ìhłak it'ee yaaghàt ti'yąą voondee aii chat t'inlìk giyàhnyàa į'.

16.56 Aii it'ee oonìn *English* nąhkat hee izhìk hee vanàch'aatan. Izhìk it'ee vakwaa gwìch'in rǫh. Vats'an dinjii gwandàii giyàhnyą̀ą. Jii tik vandàh tr'igwiinghan gàa gwandahak giyàhnyą̀ą. Jii vachaa vęhdaa tr'aahkhwąįį googàa tr'iinin nąįį gwizhyą̌hjil, nàhąą. Aii nąįį hàa gwizhǐinzhii ts'ą' oodąą vęhdaa vachaa tr'aahkhwaii

4. These surveyors were Gerald Fitzgerald and John Mertie Jr. of the U.S. Geological Survey, who spent time in *Arctic Village* during the summer of 1927. Sarah refers elsewhere to her liking for Fitz. —CM

5. Shyaaghan Ndik was the mother of both Drit and Drit Zhuu. —LG

ago surveyors were surveying the land. And your grandfather (*Johnny Frank*) was teaching them about the plants and berries that we eat. You see, it was the time of year when we could eat them. There were berries and a carrot-like root called *trih.* They dug it out of the ground and ate it. The surveyor wrote all of this down. He actually dug for this plant (laughs) with his bare hands. So they really wanted to know which plants were edible.

LG15.27 Have you ever seen *Drit* or *Drit Zhuu*?

SF15.39 You mean *Drit Zhuu?*

LG Yes.

SF15.41 I never saw them.

LG15.44 Oh, you didn't see them?

SF15.46 But *Old Woman Ndik* was still alive. She was living at the time, but we never stayed in one place so I didn't get to see *Old Woman Ndik.* But my husband knew her really well.

LG16.11 They say he learned a lot of stories from her, huh?

SFI6.16 Yes. He did have a lot of stories from her. What they say about her is that she went through three wars. She survived them all. The last time when she was there they were attacked. There were some young boys. They say she hid these boys. One of the boys was my father's older brother.

16.56 That's where he came from. He went to the Canadian side and never returned home. That's where he died, I guess. They say the people survived because of her. They say she survived three different wars. You see, she saw her younger brother get killed, so she had to stay hidden with the boys. Meanwhile, it's said that she watched her younger brother getting killed. If it wasn't for the boys, you see, she would have challenged them. She would gàa zhyąą gwąąh'yą' giyàhnyaa į'. Aii tr'iinin nąįį kwaa jì' goots'ą' khàheehaa į'. Tth'an tòh kwat chan di'įį.

LG Ąąha'.

SF17.58 Aii hàa duulèe gootèech'iheegìt reh. Tr'ìnjàa łyâa zhyąą duulèe inlį' gwìch'in t'aràhnyàa. Aii t'ee yaaghà' *Drit* ts'ą' *Drit Zhuu* hàa aii hàa it'ee duulèe tr'iinin ihłįį gwànaa gogwandàii gwìch'in į'.[6]

19.06 Googàa gavaashandàii kwàa. Izhìk gwiizhìk it'ee yaaghà' nitsii aii reh gavàandaii ǫ'. *Drit* giyàhnyaa dlòo a'in eenjit tr'aanduu giyàhnyàa t'aihnyàa.

LG19.35 Hę̂ę, jyàa giyàhnyàa. Aii geh'àn łyâa dlôo goonàa'yą' łii hèę goots'an deedhaa nąįį?

SF19.40 Ąąhą'. Jyàa t'iginch'yaa į'.

LG Ooh.

SF20.07 Jii nintsàl tr'oonilį' t'agwăihnyaa łì'hàa tr'iinin nąįį tr'iits'ąhts'ą' geerǫąąhtan nihthan.

LG20.20 Ch'ii'àn neegoorahaazhik jì' gwizhrįh.

SF20.24 Ąąha' neegoorahaazhik ts'ą' ree.

<sfwsl05fa>

SF23.10 Jii t'ee ch'adąį' gwànaa shìh kwaa dinjii tèech'ìdlį' gwinyąą

Aiits'ą' dinjii ch'ìhłęę, dinjii ch'ìhłęę ąįį t'ee nehshrit gwandàii ts'ą' gwats'at tr'įįzhìi.

Nehshrit gwandàii ts'ą' gwats'an tr'įįzhìi, aiits'ą' jyàa dòonch'yàa.

Dąįį gwintsàl gwahgǫ' aii gwiizhìk t'ee oondee *Arctic Village* ch'iinaa, izhìk gwà'àn ch'iinaa it'ee neehidik giyàhnyąą.

6. *Drit* refers to the metatarsal bone of a caribou in its lower hind leg. It was the Gwich'in name of Edward Tritt, the father of Albert Tritt. Drit Zhuu ('little metatarsal') was the Gwich'in name for Drit's younger brother Frank, who was Johnny Frank's father. See the Frank family descendancy chart below and the anatomical caribou bone diagrams in Mishler and Frank (2020:142-143). —LG, CM, and KF

have come out. She also had her own short-handled bone-tipped spears, which we call *toh.*

LG Yes.

SF17.58 She probably could have speared them with those. They say she was a very brave woman. Maybe *Drit* and *Drit Zhuu* were still living when I was just a child.

19.06 But I never knew them. Yet your grandfather (*Johnny Frank*) knew them both. I mean they say *Drit* was a very comical person.

LG19.35 So that's what they say about him. Is that why a lot of his descendants are really comical?

SF19.40 Yes. That's how they are.

LG Oh.

SF20.07 Like I mentioned before about hunting and trapping for small game, I really hope there's a way we can teach these things to the children.

LG20.20 We can only do it by taking them outdoors.

SF20.24 Yes, you have to take them along with you.

<sfwsl05fa>

SF23.10 They say people used to freeze and die of starvation.
From among them, just one person barely survived.
That one man barely survived, and that's what happened.
It was during the springtime when the snow was melting that they say this man came down from around *Arctic Village*.

Aii shitsųų giyeegwaandak aii t'ee ch'iinaa ahàa, akhài' gwiizhìk t'ee oondee zhat *Ch'ootsik Tłòk*[7] giyàhnyąą.

Aii ndàk nàa'ąį' izhìk gwà'àn t'ee nanghoo jyàa dąhtsii dhidlii.

DF Hmm.

SF24.20 Nanghoo jyàa dąhthee dhidlii, aii vakat, vitrii trih[8] t'àn dòk choh zhyąą dhidlii reh.

Łyâa trih gǫǫlįį t'agwaihnyąą.

Izhìk it'ee ch'iinaa gwà'àn nihidik akhài' t'ee aii jèiinch'yaa vakat gwìłgǫ', nàhąą? Vakat gwintsàl gwìłgǫ' ts'ą' t'ee yakat łùh jyàa dah'in dǫhłįį, akhài' jeìinch'ii reh, jii k'ìt tįįch'yaa reh.

24.38 Aii t'ee khǎiintin vàràhnyàa.

Aiits'ą' jii t'ee yįį'àl ts'ą' t'ee chan oozhee aii gwiizhìk gwahkwaii, nàhąą?

Aiits'ą' jyàa diyah'ìn ts'ą', aiits'ą' t'ee yats'an trih tsal oondak a'àa, aii k'ìighai' it'ee gwandàii dhidlìt vàràhnyàa.

25.28 Aii gwiizhìk jyàa dìi'in gwiizhìk it'ee aii *Ch'ootsik Tłòk* aii ts'an łuk khǎiinlii, nàhąą?

Aii chan vitee ch'iidì' vats'an hàhdląįį zhyąą tł'ookat gòo'ąįį t'agwaihnyąą .

Aii ch'iidì' tł'ootee zhyąą àn nihłik hee jyàa dii'in, nàhąą?

Aii vandàh jyàa dìłyâa ts'ą' aii łuk chan ch'ìhłak dìłkhwąįį aiits'ą' t'ee veenjit gwįįzįį, gwandàii dhidlìt vàràhnyàa.

Aii gwats'ą' t'ee ch'a'àa kwaa jeìinch'ii reh.

Aii chan įį'àl ts'ą' aii t'ee łyâa gwįįtsàl shat'àii niłtsąįį yàhnyaa vàràhnyaa į.'

SF26.26 Jii łyâa shìh kwaa, oondaa dinehnaa shìh kwaa, dąį' łyâa giit'ąąhch'yà' į'. Jii t'ee goolàt naii trih khagahshrì', nàhąą?

---

7. *Ch'ootsik Tłòk Arctic Village* geeghaii gwa'an van oozhri' t'arahnyąą. This is a lake near *Arctic Village*. —JE
Ch'ootsik is our name for a small young whitefish. Today this lake is all dried up due to permafrost melting. —KF

8. *Trih* is good when dug out in the springtime. It's a root that can be eaten raw, boiled, or fried in grease. It comes in all kinds of sizes and is also eaten by bears. —KP

My grandmother told about this person who was somewhere between here and *Arctic Village* at a place called *Ch'ootsik Tłòk.*

At the end of this lake there's this high round ball-like mound.

DF Hmm.

SF24.20 On the tip of this high ball-like mound, there's a carrot-like plant called *trih* growing.

I'm saying there's really lots of these *trih* there.

He was somewhere near this area when he found them in a place where the snow had melted, you see?

The snow melted off of them, and he took them out of the ground like this (gesturing with her hands).

24.38 They say he took them out.

So he dug them out and ate them, you see?

He did that and took the plants and ate them.

Because of that, he survived, they say.

25.28 While trying to survive by eating plants, he took some fish coming out of *Ch'ootsik Tłòk* lake into a small stream that ran through a swampy place, you see?

I'm saying he was just looking around over there in the wet grass.

They say he killed the fish, ate them, and got his strength back.

Before that, he said he didn't have anything to eat.

He ate that and got his strength back, they say.

SF26.26 When there's really no food to eat, this *trih* that I'm talking about is a good eating plant, you see?

26.40 Aiits’ą̨’ jèiinch’yaa ts’ą̨’ zhik gwà’àn ch’adhàh zhìt jyàa dìgiyahthan ts’ą̨’ aiitł’ee khaii gwį̂įk’ǫǫ. Shìh kwaa dą̨į’ t’ee łyâa giit’ą̨ąhch’yaa, gooràhnyą̨ą.

26.58 Aii t’ee yaaghà’ *Shitsųų Mil Vahan*, aii łyâa shriit’agwą̨ąch’yąą shàh gwaandak aii t’ee vik’ìighai’ jyàa nyąą kwaii ganaldàii t’iihnyą̨ą.

<sflg2a>

SF0.32 Aii t’ee jyàa dìgii’in izhìk nagadàl da’anlee chan gogwahtsìk ah chan. Ąįį ah ąįį t’ee han gwatsal k’ǫǫ gwįįtsìi kwaa zhyą̨ą chigiyah’ak į’. Aiits’ą̨’ it’ee łuk vizhyàdàl, nàhąą. Kheegiya’ak ts’ą̨’ ąįį łuk neegidiinjàl tł’ęę t’ee datthak dèegwą̨ąch’yaa datthak łagwantsii nihtèegiyaandàk į’.

1.09 Ch’ìighai’ it’ee ch’aga’àa reh. Aiits’ą̨’ tthaa googàa tthaa chan jyàa dàgàh’ìn. Łyâa nihk’èegìiltįį t’agooràhnyàa. Izhìk it’ee jyàa dìgii’in it’ee łyâa ganaldàii. Ąįį łuk tsal gahgąįį ąįįtł’ęę it’ee yeendàk gahadàl. It’ee łuk kwaa gwilìk ts’ą̨’ ree.

1.52 Yeendàk gahadàl ts’ą̨’ ree. Yeendàk geenjyaa izhìk ree âa, zhik gwà’àn jidìi *anything,* jak, natł’àt, deenich’ų̀h’, jii kwat datthak gwiizhìk gaajyàa aii gà’aa.

2.17 Jyàa dìgii’in ts’ą̨’ geedàa ąįį gwiizhìk it’ee oondàk ddhah zhìt izhìk gwàndàk zhik *Jùunjik*[9] gwà’àn yeendàk han gwahàa’ee izhìk gwik’ìt gadàl ts’ą̨’ ree it’ee ree divii gahdròo.

2.45 Izhìk dą̨į’ chii nan googàa neegihiidàl t’igii’ìn. Izhìk hee geetàk divii gaghan dą̨į’ aii shìh oo’ęę neegaazhik shìh oo’ęę neegaazhik ts’ą̨’ shin hee jidìi vadzaih dhàh kal vadzaih akal aii k’ìt t’įįch’ii shin hee hàa zheh goghoo gogwahtsii t’avaihnyàa.

9. The *Juunjik* is a western tributary to the East Fork of the *Chandalar River* near its headwaters. —CM

26.40 And they keep it in a moose or caribou skin all winter and use it when there's no other food. That's what they say about them.

26.58 I'm saying that I really remember all these stories from my great-grandmother, *Mil Vahan.*

<sflg2a>

SF0.32 When they settled in one place, they set a fish trap with spruce boughs. They set it in a very small slough. After it had filled up with fish, they lifted it up and dumped the fish out. Then they divided the fish among one another.

1.09 That's how everybody got something to eat. They did the same thing with ground squirrels. What we say about them is they really took good care of each other. I sure remember all of this. After they dried some fish they traveled north, because there were no more fish.

1.52 So they went north. Boy, along the way they ate all these different berries — blueberries, low bush cranberries, and blackberries.

2.17 They did all this along the way until they reached the mountains. Sometimes they went up the *Jùunjik* or they went up the main river (the *K'aii'eechų'njik*) and caught sheep in snares.

2.45 At that time they went up among the really rocky mountains. And sometimes when they killed sheep, they took all the meat back to camp. I heard in the summertime when they traveled they used shaved caribou skins to make a round willow hut, and they used these skins to cover it.

3.22 Aii gwiizhìk t'ee neegihįįjik âa, izhìk hee ąįį shìh gaahkhòk ǫǫ'ęę neegaazhìk, aiits'ą' khehłòk zhyąą khaiinjih nàgadàl, aiits'ą' oondaa teetł'an ch'ìhłak gwizhrih gwigwîiłk'ą'.

3.44 Ch'ìhłak gwizhrih gwiiłk'a' ts'ą' izhìk hee aii shìh kwat vikeegaach'yàa. Ch'eekąįh chat duuyee akhagòonyaa. Aii giichų' zhit chat ch'eekąįh tìnjyàa.

4.02 Aiits'ą' zheh gwatł'an t'igii'in jyàa dàgwàhtsii łąą geetàk k'àii khàgadant'àa, izhìk t'ee łyâa ganaldàii khàgadant'àa ts'ą' ąįį kat hee oondaa shìh vikeegach'yàa nigilik ǫ'. Ąįįts'ą' juu datthak ch'aga'àa gwizhrįh.

<sflg2a>

SF24.38 Neegàholit ts'ą' it'ee âa, neeshreegwâahch'yaa adagogwaandàii t'agavaihnyàa. Ch'iitsii googàa chat kwàa. Zheh gwadhàh chat kwàa. Zhik gwà'àn ts'àt googàa kwaa ǫ'. Gwach'àa nàraazhii googàa.

Dazhoo gwach'àa zhrįh. Izhìk it'ee Dinjii Zhuh naii adagwaandàii, nàhąą. Èe, gook'ìt t'igwee'yą' t'įįch'yàa. Ąįįts'ą' vyàh hàa gwizhrįh ch'atthąįį gǫǫnilì', k'i' chan ąįį zhrįh.

25.23 Izhìk ts'ą' it'ee nin tsal jyàa dàgah'in. Ąįį k'ìighai' dinjii gwandàii. Izhìk hee dinjii t'eedaa'in, t'eedagaa'in nats'àhts'ą' nin goonilį' aii łì'hàa jùk tr'iinin *school* ahtsii naii gàandaii jì' nihthan ǫ'.

LG25.59 Ąąhą', it'ee łyâa t'iinyàa.

SF26.02 Aii geh'àn it'ee zhik tthaa gyàh, tthaa gyàh kwaii jùk dąį' hee giveenjit tr'ahtsii k'èerąąhtii jì' ąįį hàa chat goondàh t'igwii'in jì' gàh giheendàii į'. Ąįįts'ą' aii ch'ìh gyàh łyâa t'eegąąhch'yàa. Vyàh chan. Ąįįts'ą' chii ddhah kat dąį' chan chii khyąh chan. Ąįį chan aii kwat łyâa eegoorǫǫhtyą gavoiihnyaa gwiizhìk.

LG26.43 Aiit'ee *Isàac* gwik'ìt t'agavah'in geetàk hee.

SF Ąąhą'.

3.22 Along their journey when they killed game they all camped in one place and built one campfire in the middle of their camp.

3.44 They all cooked food on one campfire. They wouldn't even throw away the blood. They cooked the blood with the meat broth.

4.02 And so there in the middle of everything, as I remember, they would cut up willow branches and lay them down in one area and put all the food they cooked on there. That way everybody could eat.

<sflg2a>

SF24.38 What I said was that people were really poor. There were no stoves. There were no skin tents either. There weren't even any woven blankets or clothes. We only had fur and skin clothes.

Now that's how Indians made their living, you see. Gee, today nobody could ever do what they did. They used skin snares for taking big game and also bows and arrows.

25.23 They did the same thing for small game. That's how people survived. I wish we could teach the skills they used in those days to our children who are in school today.

LG25.59 Yes, you're right.

SF26.02 In the meantime, we should show them how to make and set snares for ground squirrels and snowshoe hares so they'll know what to do. They really need sinew snares and babiche snares too. And when you're in the mountains, you need the deadfall rock trap as well. I wish we could teach all this to them.

LG26.43 *Isaac Tritt* has done some work with them.

SF Yes.

LG26.47 Gàa kii khyą̀h văiinyaa ąįį łyâa vàashandàii kwaa t'àiinyaa, nàhąą.

SF26.56 Chii khyą̀h aii oondòk ddhah kat neerihiidàl hee geetàk zhik tthaa kwàn kat chii dril jyàa dinìłtsii kwat gǫ̀ǫlįį, nàhąą?

LG27.09 Ą̀ąhą' nał'in į'.

SF27.10 Ąįį it'ee zhik tthaa an ch'iinjì' nihkak deegiya'ak, nàhąą. Nihkak deegiya'ak ts'ą̀'. Aiits'ą̀', ęę, gwįįtsal tthaa ąįį ndàa t'ą̀hdii t'irilìk į'. Aii ch'iinjì' tthaa an jyàa dìgiyilìk ts'ą̀' nihkak doo'ą̀įį. . .

LG27.41 Nihkat doo'ąįį nats'àhts'ą̀'?

SF27.43 Ą̀ąhą', nihkak deegiya'ak ts'ą̀' dząą vit'eh deenìn chan chii tsal jyàa dìgilìk aii kak deegiya'àk. Jyàa dìgìyìlìk.

Ąįįts'ą̀' t'ee ch'iinjì' tthaa an ch'iinjìh jèiinch'yaa ts'ą̀' dzat giyeelin, nàhąą. Ch'iinii khàgweedii geelin tł'oo, tł'oo dilù' kwaa aii jèiinch'yaa giyeelin jyàa dìlìk. Ąįįts'ą̀' it'ee ch'iizhąą haatłak, nàhąą. Haatłak ts'ą̀' dząą vadzą̀įį ree jyàa dįįch'yaa ree dząą chii ts'ik tsal aii chat nihk'yą̀ą giyatthak aii kak doo'ą̀įį.

28.41 Ąįįts'ą̀' it'ee ree jii ch'iinjì' chii dril chan jyàa dìgilìk, nàhąą, aii kak goiin'ee jii chii ch'ok tsal. Aii kak goiin'ee ts'ą̀' ree ch'iinii tthaa kheehaatłak dą̀į' jii chii ts'ik kak daatàl, nàhąą, aii gwiizhìk it'ee jii chii jyàa dìnjìk. Nats'àh ts'ą̀' kheeheedyàa gǫ̀'.

29.23 Jyàhts'ą̀' t'ee chat tthaa goonilì' į'. Aii chat deegwiindhan gwik'ìt ch'a'àa kwaa t'agooràhnyàa. Jidìi tsal zhrih. Aii łyâa jùu, jùu gwįįzįį t'ii'in naii, łì'hàa aii naii it'ee googàa geh'òk dinjii aii chat gook'ìighai' gwandàii į'.

29.56 Jidìi tsal hàa nihk'èegąątii ąįį k'iighai' dinjii gwįįzįį gwandàii t'iginyàa. Aiits'ą̀' aii tthaa t'àihnyaa aii tthak t'ee khaii geenjit t'ee njyah giyahtsii. Tthaa ts'ìk, tthaa ts'ik googàa gahgąįį į'. Tthaa vàt chan, aii chan vitseezhù' tsal giizhìnilii ts'ą̀'.

LG30.37 Ą̀ąhą'. Aii t'ee niizhit dą̀į' tr'iinin ihłįį jyàa dàrah'in vanaldàii.

LG26.47 I mean I really don't know about that deadfall rock trap, you see.

SF26.56 When we're up in the mountains, there are lots of rocky areas, and there are a lot of flat rocks, right?

LG27.09 Yes. I've seen those.

SF27.10 They set two rocks on top of each other in the doorway of a ground squirrel's den, you see. That rock has to be heavier than the ground squirrel. After they set two rocks on top of each other . . .

LG27.41 How do they set them on top of each other?

SF27.43 Yes, after they set them on top of each other, they put a little rock in between the flat rocks so there's an open way through.

That's how it is when they set it in the doorway of the den, you see. They cover the rocks with light dried grass where there are open spaces. So there is his pathway, you see. In the very front of his pathway they open the two flat rocks with a long narrow rock so that one rock is set up high.

28.41 So you see, everything is set so that narrow rock is the main trip to make the flat rock fall. The narrow rock just barely supports it in the doorway, so that when the ground squirrel jumps on it, you see, it makes the high rock fall. That's how they used the deadfall rock trap.

29.23 They just barely got by to survive. What we say about them is that they never had much to eat. Only a small amount. The people with good skills to do all this saved the lives of many people.

29.56 They say that they shared what little they had. That's how many people survived. They were always busy with ground squirrels like that, and they dried them for the winter. They even preserved the ground squirrels' intestines. They also saved the ground squirrel stomachs and stuffed them with fat.

LG30.37 Yes. I remember we did the same thing when I was a kid.

SF30.40 Ą̀ąhą’, aii chat jyàa dàgah’in, ąįį goohàa jyàa dìgii’in k’iighai’ it’ee dinjii gwandàii t’iginyàa. Nihłehts’i’ ts’ą̀’ gwandàii tsal gahaahkhwàa geenjit t’igii’ìn.

LG Ą̀ąhą’.

SF31.26 Ąįįts’ą̀’ zhik ddhah tee neegihiidal, nàhąą, izhìk ddhah tee neegihiinjik dą̀į’ chan zhik chii tth’ah chì khàdeenjaa, nàhąą.

Aii t’ee chat tthaa gwik’yaatłak į’ aii chat khàgahchik giikak chii geełèehilii ts’ą̀’. Aii jyàhts’ą̀’ gwik’ìighai’ it’ee dinjii adagwaandàii t’igwinyàa. Ąįįts’ą̀’ zhik geetàk ddhah kak chii geetàk hee jyàiinch’yaa, nàhąą. Viteet’įh nàngohdįį k’ìt t’inch’yaa izhìk chan googàa chat tthaa khàgilii į’.

LG32.17 Shahan łyâa gwįlęįį jyàhts’ą̀’ tthaa hàłchįį nyaa.

SF Ą̀ąhą’.

<sfkf2b>

SF0.07 Jyàa dìgii’in ts’ą̀’ aii łuk tsal goonjii. Aiitł’ęę it’ee yeendàk ddhah tee gahadàl. Izhìk dą̀į’ gwaatr’àl kwaa ǫ’. Oondàk ddhah tee łyâa zhyą̀ą gwaatr’àl kwàa. Izhìk hee ch’iindàa geenjyaa, geedàa gwiizhìk geetàk chat tthaa eenjit gyàh dagaatł’ìį.

0.47 Aii t’ee geetàk gwik’ìighai’ ch’igehee’àa eenjit. Aiitł’ęę it’ee oondee ddhah łą̀įį gadàl ts’ą̀’ it’ee ree divii chat aghan nàhąą? Izhìk hee khehłok zhyą̀ą nìgìnjìk. Ch’adhàh kal zheh goghoo gwigwii’įį ts’ą̀’ reh. Izhìk nìginjik ts’ą̀’ it’ee yee’àt dagatł’an hee gwigwîiłk’ą’.

1.29 Aiits’ą̀’ dagatł’an hee gwigwîiłk’ą’, ts’ą̀’ it’ee divii gaahkhòk ts’ą̀’ aii oo’ęę neegaazhik aii khehłòk ga’àa ti’gii’ìn. Aiits’ą̀’ yee’àt zheh gwatł’an gwigwîiłk’ą’ ts’ą̀’. Geeghaii chan k’àii jidìi łuu’ah[10] reh aii gìgìitthàl.

10. *Łuu’ah* is a kind of brush known in English as dwarf birch. It’s known to burn fast and hot and is very handy for cooking in open areas where firewood is scarce. See Mishler and Frank (2021:6). —KF and CM

SF30.40 Yes, they're saying this is what they did with them too. That's part of how people made their living. They hunted in various ways to survive.

LG Yes.

SF31.26 When they traveled in the mountains, they spotted ground squirrels crawling under a bunch of rocks, you see.

Then they dug up the rocks, and that's also how they caught ground squirrels. It's said that that's still another way to find food. Sometimes the squirrel just runs behind one big rock, you see. So that when you move the rock, there it is.

LG32.17 My mother said many times she caught ground squirrels like that.

SF Yes.

<sfkf2b>

SF0.07 They caught fish and that's what they did. After that they went up into the mountains. It wasn't brushy back then. Up in the mountains there was hardly any brush. When they traveled like that along the way they sometimes snared for ground squirrels.

0.47 Sometimes that's how they got something to eat. After they reached the mountains, then they killed Dall sheep, you see? They all stayed in one place together. They used hairless skin huts then. After they all settled in, they built a campfire in the center of the camp.

1.29 While they had a campfire going in the center, they brought back the sheep they had killed, and they ate together. Right near there they chopped some dwarf birch.

Łuu’ah nizįį aii kat hee shìh vikeegahch’yàa deegilìk. Aii gwiizhìk zhyą̀ą zhik gwà’àn ch’ik chan drąįį kwaa ts’ą̀’ łigiidàa ts’ą̀’ oozhee shìh dhidlii it’ee ch’aga’àa ts’ą̀’ neegoondàk.

2.19 Jyàhts’ą̀’ dìgii’in izhìk it’ee łyâa ganaldàii t’agwaihnyàa. Aiits’ą̀’ shìh shriit’agwą̀htsii gaahkhòk ts’ą̀’ giilàt tsal chan oodàk dahchàk. Aii t’ee chan zhik gwitł’ęę geheenjyaa chan giihee’àa tsal chan gahahchàk.

<sfrf2b>

SF13.03 Vàanòodlit ts’an jĕiinch’ii tsal googàa tr’ąą’in gàa kwàa. Izhìk dąį’ it’ee *Vashrąįį K’ǫǫ* dagogwaagǫ̀’. Aiits’ą̀’ ch’eedąįh hàa gwizhrįh łuk hadàl, nàhąą. Łuk hadàl ts’ą̀’ it’ee. Chihvyàa chan kwàa. Khyą̀h gàa chan kwàa. It’ee dąįį gwahgǫ’ gwiizhìk it’ee Vantee chųų gwilìk ts’ą̀’ it’ee gǫ̀ǫlįį nàgwaadhàk. Zhik k’ǫǫ gòodlii hee.

13.52 Izhìk it’ee ch’eedąįh hàa gwizhrįh łuk googìt. Nihts’įį łuk gwihdàhàdàl hee nihts’įį teeghaii ch’eedąįh hàa neegihiidàl ts’ą̀’ gwizhìt łuk gǫ̀ǫlįį. Jyàa dìgii’ìn. Aiits’ą̀’ łuk tsal teech’igigìt. Aiits’ą̀’ it’ee łuk tsal gahgą̀įį.

14.24 Łuk zhrįh ga’àa roh. Łuk nitsìi kwaa goondak. Aiitł’ęę *July* nan it’ee łuk kwaa nàgwaadhàk. Aiits’ą̀’ it’ee yeendàk ddhah tee gihinjìk. Izhìk hee chan zhik gwà’àn ch’ih gyàh gaghan aii k’àii jyàa dą̀hjyaa kat jyàa dą̀htsii aii it’ee gyàh.

15.05 Vadzaih ch’ii vadzaih nan kak ch’ìh vàràhnyaa aii tthaa gyàh gahtsìi. Oozhee digiyitł’ùk, nàhąą. Tthaa an gwinzįį izhìk ch’iinìn. Datthak gihdàn gogwahtsii aiits’ą̀’ ch’ìhłak gwizhrįh khàgweedįį. Izhìk it’ee gał jyàa dą̀hjyaa nitsìi kwaa, nihzhrįį tthaa àn gwadą̀įį deenin nìgìyiichìk. Aii deetàk it’ee ch’ìh gyàh geenįįt’aii.

On the very fresh-cut dwarf birch is where they put all the food that they cooked, and everybody helped themselves as they were busy doing things.

2.19 I'm saying I really remember that they did things that way. They would get lots of food and some of it they hung to dry. Before they continued their journey they took enough food with them.

<sfrf2b>

SF13.03 We hardly saw any white men's things. That time when we stayed in *Arctic Village* at break-up, we fished only with spears, you see. We didn't have fish nets then. There were no traps. After break-up the water raised up in all the lakes so the fish started to run. There were lots of fish in all the sloughs.

13.52 They only speared fish back then. When the fish started to run, people would all be standing on both sides of the slough spearing them. That's how they did it. They got some fish and dried some of them.

14.24 They ate nothing but fish. After they saved some fish, then in July there were no more fish. So then they all went up into the mountains. And there they made snares out of sinew on these little sticks, and that's how they made snares.

15.05 They say they would get the tendons from the caribou backbone, and that's where the sinews came from, you see. That's what they used for ground squirrel snares. They set the snare in the doorway of the den hole. And they blocked all the other holes around the den. They only left one hole open, and that's where they set this with two sticks this long but not too long.

Aiits'ą̀' dzaa vakat chan gał tak tsal chat vakak dhitìn. Aii it'ee oozhee tthaa an digiyitł'ùk, nàhąą. Aiits'ą̀' jii gał tsal aii dzaa gweedąą gyàh nįįt'aii, aii t'ìt jyàa dìgiyilìk.

16.29 Aiits'ą̀' it'ee khaghàa kwaa, nàhąą. Tł'oo tsal chan neegąąhkhwat aii zhìt dee'àn gyàh nįįt'aii. Aiits'ą̀' it'ee tthaa ìilòk nàhąą. Tthaa ìilok dąį' it'ee jii gał jĕiinch'yaa aii deetàk gyàh geenįįt'aii ts'ą̀' aii deetak gwit'it jii vichì' jyàa dinjìk, nàhąą. Aiits'ą̀' it'ee vazhànch'iichaa. Zhik gał aii jyàa dinjìk ts'ą̀' reh.

They put the two sticks up in front of the den hole. And between the sticks they set the snare, and in between the sticks they set up the trip stick. And somehow they set the snares and when the ground squirrel bit the short stick then it got hung and died.

16.29 They covered the snares with thin dried grass so the ground squirrel would get caught in them, you see. When the ground squirrel gets caught in snares like this (gesturing), it gets hung because of how the sticks fall. This is the reason why it chokes itself.

Sarah Frank

Khyąh T'ah'in

<sfwsl05Ba>

SF3.46 Izhìk dąį' tsuk łì'hàa gǫ̀ǫlįį. Aii t'ee yaaghà' ti'yąą nąįį gwandàii gwànaa it'ee nin keegii'ìn. Izhìk t'ee nin keegii'in gàa zhik nin dhàh jyàa dǒonch'yaa tsèe dhàh ginyaa, goolàt nąįį tsèe dhàh lèe hàhgwiindàii gǫ̀. Gwintsìi kwaa gwizhrįh giyuukwàt gwìch'in roh.

7.34 Ch'ìh gyąh nał'yą', ch'ìh gyąh chan giyandoo ts'ą' reh zhik nin vichį' dąhtsii aii gąhtsii giyahtsik ts'ą' dzaa chat dachan tak tsal jyàa dąhjyaa, dzaa nihts'įį vagwâanlok ts'ą' reh, zhik oodee geetàk dèetin giyee'ahtsìk. Akwàt shin dąį' chan zhik k'àii gwanàgathak aii jyàa dìgilìk tthaa àn. Jyàa dìgilìk ts'ą' reh t'ee oozhee digiyitł'uu tł'ęę tthaa ìilok ts'ą' reh jii dachan nèekwąįį chan gweenìn neegiitthak aii t'ìt t'ee vichi' naadhàk ts'ą' reh viyèech'iichaa. Aii t'ee tthaa gyàh nał'in. Shandàa chan dìgìyàatł'įį yaaghà' *Myra Ch'ataii Gwatràt*[1] vǎihnyaa vitsųh gyàh tak chih neehichìk. Gwintł'òo tthaa kee'in ìizųų t'aihnyàa.

9.22 Jidìi dizhuu dhàh jyàa dǒonch'yaa gwats'an chadhàh reh. Ch'ìhłan dąį' gyàh, vyah reh, vyah *twenty* dhałtsąįį.

10.55 Làraa gǫ̀ǫlįį ts'ą' gàagiindàii kwàa. Yeenjìt *Canadiàn side* gwats'an, izhìk ts'aii łyâa nin dhàh gwintł'oo gòonjik googahnyàa.

13.15 *Russian* ts'an tyąh gòodlit ginyąą aii t'ee izhìk gwànaa gwintł'òo ihtsìi kwaa gwiizhìk t'igwii'in t'igwinyàa. Izhìk gwats'an it'ee tyąh jidìi *alumìnùm* chųų tyąh ts'ik njyàa dąhnjyaa reh. Aii *alumìnùm* nilįį.

Aii chan dzaa gwee'àn chan veegàngwîilchįį. Aii zhrįh chan chųųntyah nał'in t'agwaihnyàa.

---

1. This was the Indian name of Myra Kay of *Old Crow*. —CM

Sarah Frank

Fur Trapping

<sfwsl05Ba>

SF3.46 There were lots of marten at that time. My father was living at that time when they trapped for animals. They trapped for animals but we didn't know much about the value of them. I don't think they sold their furs for very much.

7.34 I've seen sinew snares. The sinew was braided, and the diameter depended on the size of the animal's head. The sinew was tied on both sides of the diameter to a little stick so that it stayed put. Sometimes they put an extra stick on top which the sinew was tied to. In the summer, they used a stick which was poked into the ground on the side of a ground squirrel's den. A snare was put on a willow and when a ground squirrel got caught, the two sticks which held down the willow fell. Then the willow would spring up in the air and the ground squirrel would get choked when its tail hit the two sticks that held down the willow. I've seen it myself. I've seen *Myra Chataii Gwatràt's* grandmother carry one like that. I mean she was "bad" for hunting ground squirrel like that.

9.22 A cow moose skin from about this time was also good for snares. One time I made twenty moose skin snares.

10.55 Nobody knew that money existed back then. They say that on the Canadian side they took a lot of animal furs.

13.15 When they talked about the Russian pots which came around for the first time, they meant the time when I was still small. A long aluminum measuring cup came in around the same time.

I'm saying that was the only kind of cup I ever saw at that time.

13.57 Izhìk t'ee yeenjìt *Fish Hòok Town* gwìnji' reh, izhìk t'ee *Ch'eeghwał Tì'* chan ginyaa aii vàhshandàii kwàa. *Ch'eeghwał Tì'* ginyaa. Aii t'ee tsèe dhàh gwintsàl ookwàt dǫhłįį.

MR14.18 Aii lèe Dinjii Zhuh?

SF Ą̀ąhą'.

MR14.21 *Ch'eeghwał Tì'* gwinyaa aii dèegwinyaa t'igwinyàa?

SF14.25 Tr'iinin nehshrit neehidik, nàhąą? Nehshrit neehidik aii t'ee ch'eeghwał, aii t'ee nehshrit neehidik ginyaa t'iginyàa. Nehshrit ahaa, nàhąą?

MR15.24 Aii lèe tsèe dhàh ookwàt?

SF15.25 Ą̀ąhą', tsèe dhàh ookwàt.

MR15.39 Dinjii Zhuh nilįį?

SF15.41 Ą̀ąhą'. Dinjii Zhuh gwandàii nąįį chit t'aihnyàa.

MR16.01 Jidìi hàa yuukwàt aii?

SF16.04 Jidìi lìdii chan, dink'ee chì', dink'ee kwàn, jii kwaii ànts'ą̀' izhìk it'ee oo'òk neehidik dǫhłįį. Gwiizhìk it'ee va'at t'ee eenàrà'òo dǫhłįį, lìdii eenjit. Aiits'ą̀' tsèe dhàh nitsìi reh. Zhat gwantł'ǎhtsùu dǫhłįį, akhài' reh jyàanch'ii chuuntyąh t'aihnyaa, aii zhìt dzaa veegwìgwìilchįį k'ìt'inch'yaa izhìk ną̀'ąį' it'ee zhrįh t'ee tsèe dhàh t'ii yintł'ěiinjaa dǫhłįį. Izhìk hee aiitł'ęę oo'ęę neezhii va'at yàhgwaandak giyàhnyàa.

16.51 Yaaghà' lìdįį kàraa'oo, yaaghà' tsèe dhàh gwintł'èerąhtsùu aii nąh'ìn. "Lìdįį tah dànaach'in ch'yąą gwiijii dèe tr'ijiinùu," nyaa vàràhnyàa. Gwalaii Han Gwich'in nilįį, Vantee Gwich'in.[2]

18.00 Vantee Gwich'in nilįį dǫhłįį, ghài' shrii, "Lìdii tàh dànaach'in ch'yąą gweejìi dèe tr'ijiinùu." Àkwàt nijìn nàa'ai' t'inlìk chan nyàa.

MR18.58 Aii dèenyaa t'inyàa, "Lìdii tah dànaach'in" nyàa?

2. Sarah is showing her amusement over Gwich'in dialect differences here. —CM

13.57 At that time, they talked about a man called *Ch'eeghwał Ti'* up around *Fish Hook Town* (*Chalkyitsik*). I didn't know him, but he must have bought animal fur.

MR14.18 An Indian?

SF Yes.

MR14.21 What does *Ch'eeghwał Ti'* mean?

SF14.25 What they mean by *ch'eeghwał* is a baby barely starting to walk, you see?

MR15.24 Was he buying fur?

SF15.25 Yes, he bought fur.

MR15.39 Was he an Indian?

SF15.41 Yes. He was one of the richest Indians around.

MR16.01 What did he buy with it?

SF16.04 Tea, shells, and gun powder. One day he was away and someone came around for tea and only his wife was there. He must have come around with a big beaver skin, and she gave him only a certain amount of tea using the measuring cup I mentioned earlier. They say after he came back, his wife told him.

16.51 He looked at the beaver skin and said, *"Lidįį tah dànaach'in ch'yąą gwiijii dee tr'ijiinùu?"* They say what he meant was, "Show me how much you gave him in the measuring cup." He was a Han Gwich'in but he spoke Vantee Gwich'in.

18.00 I think he was Vantee Gwich'in. That's why he said, *"Lidii tah dànaach'in ch'yąą gwiijii dèe tr'ijiinùu."* What he meant was, "How much did you give him?"

MR18.58 What did he mean when he said, *"Lidii tah dànaach'in?"*

SF19.02 "Lìdii tah dànaach'in," nyaa t'ee lìdii vichų̀' oondaa lìdii geetàk nint'aii tr'ahtsìk, nàhąą? Aii t'ahnyàa. Aii t'ee vichų̀' tr'ahtsii oozhee gwinzįį vìgweech'in aii gwik'yą̀ą yuuzhrii t'inyàa (adlaa). Oozhee geetàk hee chųų drinh, nàhąą? Lìdii tr'ahtsii dą̀į', geetèe gwintsàl nint'aii k'ìt t'inch'yaa, nàhąą? Aii t'ahnyàa.

MR20.42 Aii oo'ęę neezhii tł'ęę va'at yàagwaandak dèenyaa văiinyaa łii?

SF20.56 "Lìdii tah dànaach'in ch'yąą gweejìi dèe tr'ijiinùu" àkwàt daanch'yąą dèe vintł'ĕiinjàa nyaa vàràhnyàa.

21.07 "Nijìn dzaa vigweech'in izhìk gwintł'ĕiin'ak gwik'ìt reh t'ihłìk," yàhnyaa vàràhnyàa.

MR21.42 Ijùk gwich'įį văiinyaa łèe?

SF21.47 Oonjìt *Fish Hòok Town,* izhìk aii han gwinjik gwìnji' reh gwich'įį giyàhnyàa. *Jałk'iitsik,*[3] aii han gwinjik izhìk dą̀į' izhìk ch'iindàk łyâa dinjii gǫ̀ǫlį̀į.

MR22.08 Aii lèe *Black River* gwinjik reh hę̀ę?

SF22.10 Ą̀ąhą', izhìk gwinjik gwich'įį giyàhnyą̀ą.

MR22.31 Aii oonjì' *Old Crow* k'iinjì' chan nìneegiidàl hę̀ę? Izhìk t'ee tsèe dhàh *sell* gahtsii hę̀ę, aii t'ee ch'andaa t'agwą̀htsii t'igii'in t'inch'yaa hę̀ę?

SF22.40 Ą̀ąhą'. *Old Crow* gwìnji' ch'adą̀į' kwaiik'ìt gòodlii gogoozhrii gàa, *Zheh Gwatsal*[4] han ginyaa oonjì' *Łineeraadal* chan ginyàa, ts'ą̀' *Old Crow* gwìnji' izhìk gwinji' it'ee ch'igeeghwaa ts'ą̀', t'ee oonji' dink'ee chì' kàneegiidàl t'agooràhnyàa. Dink'ee chì' ghoo, jidìi *muzzlè loadèr* aii zhat gwànaa gòodlit dą̀į', aii chan dinjii tthak yii'įį kwàa.

3. *Jałk'iitsik,* meaning "the mouth of Fish Hook Creek," is the original name for *Chalkyitsik*. White people had a hard time pronouncing the word so they changed the spelling. —JE

4. *Zheh Gwatsal* was a small village near *Old Crow*. —JE
This is also the name used for *Christian Village* on the Alaska side. —CM

SF19.02 What he meant by saying, *"Lidii tah dànaach'in"* is "strong tea," you see? A strong tea looked good to him, so that's the way he always called it (laughs). Sometimes you can see clear water turning into strong tea, you see? He meant that kind.

MR20.42 After he came back, what did you say she said to him?

SF20.56 *"Lidii tah dànaach'in ch'yąą gwiijîi dèe tr'ijiinùu."* They say he meant to say, "How much did you give him?"

21.07 They say she told him, "I gave him the same amount you usually give out."

MR21.42 Where did you say he lived?

SF21.47 They say he lived on the river somewhere by *Chalkyitsik.* At that time, there were lots of people living along the river by *Chalkyitsik.*

MR22.08 Is that along the *Black River*?

SF22.10 Yes, that's where he lived, they say.

MR22.31 Did people used to go over to *Old Crow*? Is that where they sold their fur? Did they buy it at a higher price than anybody else?

SF22.40 Yes, I remember them calling the names of villages around *Old Crow*, but I remember them saying that people usually have gatherings at a village named *Zheh Gwatsal.* They say people used to walk over to *Old Crow* to buy shells. They would go over for round shells. That's the time muzzle loaders came around, but only a few people owned them.

25.58 Zhik ch'atthą̀įį tr'aghan dą̀į', nàhąą? Dą̀į' ch'itsìk, ch'ichyàa jii kwaii gahgąįį aii zhat *store* gwintł'èegàazhìk. Aii shìh aii łyâa geedant'eh gwit'èegąąhch'yaa t'agooràhnyàa. Vàanòodlit shìh gǫ̀ǫlįį kwaa, nàhąą?

MR26.22 Aii lèe Vàanòodlit nąįį lèe?

SF33.53 Ą̀ąhą'. Tr'ohchìt dą̀į' chan jidìi khał dachàn khal tsal gwìch'in gahtsìk, aii zhrįh gii'įį googàhnyàa. Aii zhìt giyàa neech'ihiiluu t'inch'yaa, łąįį kwaa ts'ą̀'.

34.21 Izhìk it'ee khaiits'ą̀' it'ee ąhshuu, aiits'ą̀' khaiits'ą̀' t'ee tr'iheenjyaa eenjit t'ee dachan gîili' khał tsal gaghan dǫhłįį. Khał tsal gaghan, izhìk it'ee dinjii ch'ìhłak reh, *Sheht'oo* chan giyàhnyaa, giyùuzhrìi.

35.29 "*Sheht'oo*, aii nijìn zhyą̀ą gwankhyųų gwizhrįh hiinlil eenjit dèe vìtł'ęę yàadlii nak'ąh nagwàn ąhtsìi?" Giyàhnyaa akhài', "Gwankhyųų tr'eenjyaa jì' yù'," nyaa giyàhnyàa.

37.56 Łì'hàa gogwàntrii ganaldàii. Aiits'ą̀' zhik vadzaih gaahkhòk, nàhąą? Vadzaih gaahkhòk dą̀į' ch'angwàl, ch'akwài' jii vatth'àn datthak googàa giit'ą̆ąhch'yaa.

Tth'an giichų̀' ahtsii ts'ą̀' giichų̀' dinìi. Aiits'ą̀' jii vadzaih vitrìk, vitrìk nilįį aii chan jùu vigii lęįį nąįį, vigii lęįį nąįį yùundak ts'ą̀' t'ee zhik gwà'àn gwinĭindhaa gwakak gwà'àn digiyìł'ą̀įį. Aiitł'ęę tr'iijii ga'àa dą̀į' aii vavàt zhìt ch'itrìk roh, aii googàa oozhee jyàa digiyah'in ts'ą̀' giya'àa googàa tthak ganaldàii. Izhìk t'ee łyâa gògwàntrii reh. Aiits'ą̀' ch'atthą̀įį gaahkhòk aii giits'an k'èiich'ii tsal akhŏonjìk kwàa. Izhìk gwànaa łyâa gogwàntrìi.

40.06 Izhìk shyaaghan nąįį, shyaaghan, dyąąhch'ì' nąįį hàa jidìi tsal hàa goozhèeraandàk. Aii nąįį chan ch'adą̀į' gwànaa łi'hàa ch'anjàa nąįį gǫ̀ǫlįį.

25.58 When we killed lots of moose or caribou, you see, they dried all the meat and traded with the store over there. They say they needed it too because there was no white man's food at all, you see?

MR26.22 You mean the white people?

SF33.53 Yes. In the beginning, people used to make a little wooden sled. That was the only kind of sled they used. They hauled their belongings in it because there were no dogs.

34.21 At one time just before winter, it snowed, and they were making a few little sleds like that, and there was a man they call *Sheht'oo.*

35.29 They said to him, *"Sheht'oo,* why did you make one side runner shorter? Do you think we can only travel on the side of a slope?" And they say he said to them, "We should only travel on a slope."

37.56 I remember the hard times. Whenever they killed a caribou, you see, they used every bone in it, including the cannon bones and the hooves.

They boiled the bones and drank the broth. Some big families with lots of kids even saved the caribou's rumen stomach and its contents. They put it in a warm place and ate it when there was nothing else to eat. I remember that. That's when times were really hard. Nothing was left behind whenever they killed something. In those days, times were very hard.

40.06 At that time, we were barely feeding the old women and old men with a little food. At that time, there were really lots of elders too.

Sarah Frank

Vadzaih

<sfkf2b>

CF15.02 Shitsųų, aii vadzaih tthał t'èegą̀ąhch'yaa nik'ee ganandàii?

SF15.11 Tthał lèe?

CF15.15 Izhìk gwànaa nik'èe ganandàii?

SF15.23 Izhìk dą̀į' yeendee ch'iinjì' tthak tthaì gǫ̀ǫlįį. Dachan àgwàntrii aiits'ą̀' ninzhìt hee gwats'an dachan goonjìi. Aii hàa tthał gahtsik. Aiits'ą̀' it'ee yeenihjyàa vadzaih hah'òo dą̀į' chan ch'iinjì' vadzaih hah'òo dą̀į' chan. Izhìk ts'ąįį giidą̀įį kheegwatthàk. Aiits'ą̀' ndàk jyàa dìnch'yaa àkwàt jii dzaa dee'àn dachan kwàa. Izhìk chan gał tàk jyàa dą̀hjyaa gwanàngatthàii. Aii kat chan nyą'shril, nan ghoo zhrąįh deegahtłii, aii it'ee vik'iighai' tthał zhìt ch'ah'òo t'igiyah'ìn. Tthał zhìt ch'ah'òo dą̀į' gwintł'òo gwìizųų gwìch'in roh. Aiits'ą̀' zhik nihk'yą̀ą hee jyàa dìnch'yàa. Jyàa dìnch'yaa ts'ą̀' oondàa dachan chat jèiinch'yàa. Aii dząą teetł'an izhìk it'ee gwintsàl nihts'ą jyàa dòonch'yàa. Oondaa tthał tsįį giyàhnyaa aii zhìt ch'ah'òo dą̀į' it'ee vadzaih tèech'àlą̀į'.

CF17.14 Aii vitèech'alą̀į' dą̀į' aii jidìi hàa giyàgwat ijìi, aii shyą'[1] òozhii lèe t'inch'yaa?

SF17.25 Tòh giyàhnyaa į'. Aii hàa t'ee geetàk hee tth'an tòh reh.

CF Ą̀ąhą'.

SF17.41 Izhìk hee tthał zhìt ch'ąh'oo gwinyaa.[2] Aii zhyą̀ą gogwandàk dìhtth'àk. Âa! Tthał ghàih tr'igwich'įį. Gwintł'òo, gwintł'òo shìh gǫ̀ǫlįį nàgwaadhàk t'igwinyàa.

---

1. The meaning of *shyą'* is uncertain; maybe it's *shyąh* 'entrance of caribou corral.' —KP

2. *Ch'ah'oo* and *ch'ąh'oo* have different tones. —JE

Sarah Frank

Caribou

<sfkf2b>

CF15.02 Grandma, do you remember when they used caribou fences?

SF15.11 You mean fence?

CF15.15 Do you remember back then?

SF15.23 At that time there were lots of fences up that way. It was hard to get logs. They got their logs from a long ways. That's what they built their fences with. If the caribou were coming this way or going the other way, that was the direction which they opened the entrance of the fence to. If there was no fence, in some places they stuck a pole up with some moss on the tip of it. It's pretty bad when it gets inside the fences. The fence goes in all directions, but at the very end is what you call a corral. Once the caribou get inside the corral they get caught in snares.

CF17.14 After they get caught in the snares, what do you call the weapon they used to spear them with?

SF17.25 They call it a *toh.* It was a short bone-tipped spear.

CF Yes.

SF17.41 They say that one time a herd of caribou got caught in the fence. It was just a story I heard. Ah, when the herd gets inside the fence, they say, everybody suddenly has lots of food.

Aiits'ą' ch'ìhłan tthał jèiinch'yaa, izhìk dzaa t'ee ch'iindàa vadzaih gwizhyah'oo, nàhąą? Zhik it'ee dinjii ch'ìhłak reh. Aa! K'iidąą vadzaih teech'alą̀į', nàhąą? Aiits'ą' vadzaih zhyą̀ą ch'iinjik jyàa dïizhik. Zhat zhyą̀ą vadzaih vak'altł'įį. Zhat gwà'àn chan nàdhadǫǫ ts'ą' k'ilt'aii giyàhnyaa reh. Tr'agwazhrąįį àn geełèehindii vàràhnyàa googàa t'inch'yaa tł'ęę vadzaih jyàa dìyinlik giyàhnyaa į'.

CF19.14 Gwint'aii neehaa'òo googàhnyaa hęę? Gwiizhìk. . .

SF Ą̀ąhą'.

SF19.19 Gwint'aii neehaa'òo. Zhik khèedą̀į' gwànaa łì'hàa vadzaih gòodlit ǫ'. Izhìk dą̀į' it'ee geetèe vadzaih nihłahaandik k'ìt t'ii'in ǫ'. Aii dą̀į' chigiijyaa dąhtsii googàa zhat vatąįį dhidlii į'. Aii it'ee vak'at ch'aatł'įk reh. Ch'ìhłan łyâa ch'igii lęįį àn dhidlìt t'ôonch'yaa. Izhìk hee ch'igii nitsìi t'aihnyaa aii it'ee vadzaih ch'iinjik geetàk iłchįį aragwah'ak t'aihnyàa.

20.13 Geetàk vadzaih digii òondak vàanòodlit ts'an ch'atthą̀įį aii vatąąh'oo giyàhnyàa. Vagwandàk tr'îitth'ak. Vatąąh'oo izhìk dą̀į' it'ee łyâa ch'igii tsal lęįį àn dhidlìt ǫ'. Vigwilìk googàa zhyą̀ą ah'àl nàhąą. Aiits'ą' aii ch'igii vatąįį gwinjik hee dhidlii ree. Ch'ìhłan jyàa dìgwìizhìk gwintł'òo ch'igii lęįį àn dhidlìt ǫ'.

21.15 Izhìk it'ee shaghwaii *Albèrt*[3] reh. Ch'atthą̀įį tr'ooheendal nyaa eenjit it'ee oondee *Dik'ii Tsal* giyàhnyàa. Aii it'ee neetthałhàatthaii akhài' gòhch'it gwik'ìt t'igwìizhìk kwaa ǫ'.

"Ch'atthą̀įį tr'ehee'yàa," nyaa eenjit t'ii'in akhài'. Gòhch'it gwik'ìt gòodlit kwàa.

<sfrfla>

SF29.25 Aii it'ee zhik shìh gaahkhok, nàhąą? Aii hineenjyàa gwats'ą' gwigwich'įį t'igii'ìn. Aiits'ą' aii shìh it'ee ninjìk ts'ą' it'ee chan gehinjik. Izhìk gwà'àn hee tthaa chan gòonilì'. Aii kwat hàa ga'àa t'igii'ìn.

3. This is Albert Tritt, the Gwich'in Episcopal priest in *Arctic Village*. For more about him, see McKennan (1965:22, also 86-88). —CM

One time the caribou were going into the fence, you see. Now there was this one man who went inside the fence just as the caribou were getting caught in the snares. Ah! The rest of the herd just turned around and ran, you see. So once the caribou did that, they ran over the man who was inside the fence. He was trampled over and just lay there. They told him to stay out of the way, but he stayed in there, and that's when the caribou ran him over, they say.

CF19.14 They say they really moved fast, right? Meanwhile . . .

SF Yes.

SF19.19 They moved so fast. When this happened sometimes we had lots of caribou then. It was like a stampede, and when this happened even their calves would be lying there dead afterward. The herd just ran right over the calves. At one time a lot of calves died. Like I said, we found lots of dead calves.

20.13 We once heard that white people mixed in other caribou with the caribou around *Arctic Village*. That's when most of the calves died. All the calves were lying dead behind the herd. Yes, one time lots of calves died.

21.15 They say my brother-in-law *Albert Tritt* wanted to build a caribou fence up on *Dik'ii Tsal* mountain. So he started to build a fence around it. But he never finished it.

He was saying, "We'll have our own big game meat to eat." But it never worked out.

<sfrfla>

SF29.25 Usually if they killed big game, you see, they stayed around until the food was low and then continued on their journey. Somewhere along the way they trapped ground squirrels and lived on that until they killed some other game.

30.05 Êee! Shrôonch'yaa gogwahtsii. Łyâa goonaldàii t'agavaihnyàa. Datthak ch'ìhłęę łąą nihłitr'ìi'ee kwaa, ts'ą' datthak khehłòk zhyąą jyàa dìgii'in.

30.34 Duuyèe chan nihkhehdan ch'aga'àa t'agavaihnyaa, khehłòk gwizhrįh. Âaa! Shrôonch'yaa neegogwaha'àk. Łyâa goonaldàii t'agwaihnyàa.

31.03 Izhìk geetàk hee shrii gǫǫlįį kwàa. Jidìi gwatsal, jyàa gwatsal jyàa dąhtsii aii nijìn gwats'an t'agah'in lì', aii tsal t'ee gooteegąąch'yąą. Googàa àn ts'ą' ch'ara'àa shrii kwàa. Izhìk hee geetàk tr'iinin nąįį ch'aga'àa dąį', ch'itsee gwatth'àn, vadzaih tsìk aii vatth'àn aii googàa hàa ch'ara'àa t'iihnyàa. Aii shrii giyàa'įį reh.

32.04 Àkwàt ts'ą' khaii chan nįįvyaa zhìt gwigwich'įį, nàhąą. Izhìk chan oondaa zhyąą gwâak'à'. Aiits'ą' vikeech'agaach'yàa dąį' geetàk chan shrąh giyàhnyàa. Tik ch'ìidąą nàndats'àii.[4] Aii kak geetàk ch'igìn, vadzaih gìn, ch'ak'oh, ch'ichì' aii nàngiłt'aii t'agavaihnyàa.

32.46 Gwiizhìk łi'hàa shrôonch'yaa ree. Izhìk dąį' tr'iinin nąįį, jùk yaaghà' tr'iinin nąįį, dats'ą' k'èegogwaajìi, nàhąą, gwik'ìt tr'iinin t'inch'yaa kwàa. Oo'òk tr'iinin nąįį geetàk jyàa dìginch'yaa gàa yee'àn zheh nihdèega'òo, nàhąą? Izhìk oondàk zheh gwizhìt oondàk nigihee'àl googàa gatr'agwaanyaa.

SF33.32 Duuyeh nihdèera'òo, dùuyeh ndàk ts'ą' gwarąąh'in. Izhìk hee geetàk hee nilįį tsal gavantł'èegiitràk. Aii dąį' łyâa shòh ginlįį.

33.56 Geetàk hee vadzaih, jidìi vadzaih tseezhų' giyàhnyaa ijìi, aii chan tsal igiigàa, chat tr'iinin intł'èegahchàk. Aii it'ee yeendaa kǫ' kak giyaach'yàa ts'ą' giya'àa reh.

4. Sarah is describing hooks hanging from a wooden tripod erected over the campfire. —CM

30.05 Wow! As I said, I remember how much fun they had. They all did these things together, and I don't even think there was one enemy among them.

30.34 They would never eat alone either. They always ate together. Ahh! As I said, they sure had a good time together. I remember it very well.

31.03 Sometimes there were no knives. They all had some kind of a small tool. But a few of them didn't own one. I'm saying the children and the people who didn't have knives used caribou rib bones to eat with. They used those bones for knives.

32.04 In the winter we lived in a skin house, you see. They had an open fireplace in the middle of the house. And when they cooked sometimes they used what you call a hook at the end of a stick that hangs with string. Sometimes they had three of these hung down over the open fireplace. I'm saying on that hook they sometimes hung a caribou leg, neck, and head to roast.

32.46 While doing that they really had so much fun. You see today how the kids are on their own a lot. In those days the kids were not like that at all, you see. The kids were like that, but whenever they went inside their neighbor's house they would stop at the doorway, you see? That's as far they could go unless they were invited to do otherwise.

SF33.32 I was like that too. When we went inside we weren't supposed to go any farther. At times they were given a little something to eat. Boy, they were happy then.

33.56 Sometimes they gave us children a small piece of what I think they called boiled caribou caul fat, or sometimes it was cooked over a fire.

34.16 Aii googàa łi'hàa gwinzįį t'igwii'in t'agwaihnyàa. Tr'iinin nąįį dats'ą' k'èegwaajìi kwaa t'agwaihnyàa. Yee'an zheh nihdèega'òo dąį' zhyàa reh gatr'agwaanyaa k'ìt t'ôonch'yaa ts'ą', zhik kwàntee ch'iidįį zhik chat nàradhat chan ganaldàii t'agwaihnyàa.

34.46 Izhìk it'ee jidìi tsal gavantł'èegiitrak googàa łi'hàa shòh ginlįį. Jùk zhyąą gwik'ìt t'ôonch'yaa kwaa, tr'iinin nąįį. Yee'an zheh nihdèegadal gàa zhyàa zhik gwà'àn k'èegogwaadhàt.

35.18 Izhìk gwànaa dąį' gàhgwiindàii kwaa gwànaa łi'hàa tr'iinin nąįį gwinzįį t'inch'yaa ganaldàii t'iihnyàa. Aii yee'an ts'an chan geetàk chiitąįį agogwàh'ak hee aii googàa gwinzįį gwintł'èega'àk. Jii yee'àt chiitąįį vagwàł'ąįį ginyaa ts'ą' reh.

36.04 Aii datthak gooyèhghan nąįį akòǫ dàgàvàhnyaa ts'ą' ree t'iginch'yàa. Yee'àn ts'an chiitąįį èenjik jì' oiinjii shrǫ̀' digigii àgàhnyàa. Gwik'ìt t'iginch'yaa t'agavaihnyàa.

34.16 That was one of the wonderful things they did. The kids were very shy and disciplined then. What I'm saying is I remember how much respect we showed when we went inside someone else's house.

34.46 When we were given a little something to eat we appreciated that very much. The kids are not like that anymore. They just do whatever they want when they walk into someone else's house.

35.18 I was just saying that I remembered how well the kids behaved in those days. If they found something, they always returned it to the owners. They would tell how it was found.

36.04 Their parents let them know all about it. They would tell their kids not to take someone else's things. Like I was saying, that's how they were.

Sarah Frank

Vį̀įhtąįį Resèrvatiòn

<sfwsl05Eb>

MR2.42 Jàghaii nan chan ts'ą̀' ti'yąą hàa, jàghaii *Resèrvatiòn* oodhoojìk, jàghaii *Resèrvatiòn* aii nizįį nohthan t'ôonch'yàa?

SF3.00 (Adlàa.) Gwiizhìk zhik nin nįįzhìt dąį' gwànaa *hard time* gǫǫlįį dąį' vàanòodlit shìi chan tr'ąąh'in kwàa, aiits'ą̀' jii gwandaii, vadzaih àkwàt dinjik, divii. Aii zhrįh tr'a'àa aiits'ą̀' jii *Resèrvatiòn* zhìt, aii zhìt nin gwandaii kwaii zhyąą *free* t'èegwąąhch'yaa izhìk geenjit gwizhrįh. Jyąhts'ą̀' diihthan t'ôonch'yàa. Izhìk geenjit shòo ihłįį.

MR4.31 "Izhìk dąį' gwànaa dąį' aii nan ǫhjii dąį' nan, aii nan ǫhjii dąį'. Nakhwak'èegwahaadhat kwàa, nakhwak'èegwìldhat kwaa jì' izhìk geenjit noojat?" Nakhwàhnyąą.[1]

SF5.04 Ą̀ąhą'. Dinjii gòodlit jì', nàhąą? Dinjii gòodlit jì', nats'àhts'ą̀' yaaghà' gwà'àn k'eerihee'òo googàa gògǫǫtrii, izhìk tthak ginìnjich'arahthat hàa, t'igwii'in t'ôonch'yàa.

MR6.03 Aii nats'àhts'ą̀' gàakhwandàii? nyàa. Jùk gweendàa hee dinjii gwihèelyàa?

SF6.10 Aii zhik *Indiàn Biblè. Indiàn Biblè* kat jyàa gwinyąą. *Indiàn Biblè* jyàa dąątį' į'. *First time* tr'ohchìt gwandak. Genèsis, aii zhìt gwaandak. Gwats'an oondaa, dzaa ch'iindàa gwandak niłehts'ì' t'inch'yaa dhidlii. Aiits'ą̀' *last time* gwik'èenaatii. Gwik'èenaatii ch'iindaa jii. . .

MR7.45 Aii *Biblè read* gahtsii dąį' nats'àhts'ą̀' giyîitth'ak t'inch'yàa yàhnyàa?

SF7.54 Kwàt dzaa jùk nihts'ą̀' giriinjii, nàhąą? Nihts'ą̀' rigiinjii dèegwinyàa gǫ̀'? Geetàk geenihłàa eenihłàa gwaraandak, nàhąą? Jyàa dįįch'yaa į'.

1. Maggie is translating a question in English from William Schneider that was not transcribed. —CM

Sarah Frank

The Venetie Reservation

<sfwsl05Eb>

MR2.42 Why did you and Father get the Reservation? Why did you think the Reservation was good?

SF3.00 (Laughs.) During all the hard times long ago, before we ever saw any white man's food, we lived only on caribou, moose, and Dall sheep. We got the Reservation because we just wanted free animals. That's what I think, and I'm happy for it.

MR4.31 "At that time, when you were trying to get the land, were you afraid that the land would not be given to you?" he (*William Schneider*) asked.

SF5.04 Yes. We were afraid this place would be swarming with people, you see, that it would be hard to get around. We got the Reservation because we were thinking that would happen.

MR6.03 How did you know back then that there would be lots of people trying to move here?

SF6.10 It says that in the Indian Bible. The Indian Bible is a very thick book. The first part is Genesis on through to Revelations. There's all kinds of news from the first part to the last part.

MR7.45 How did they understand what it meant when they read the Bible?

SF7.54 It's the same as you and I speaking together right now, you see what we're saying? Sometimes we talk and tell stories, you see? It's the same as that.

MR8.40 Dinjii gwihèelyaa aii nats'àhts'ą' *Biblè* zhìt gàakhwandàii nakhwàhnyàa?

SF8.48 It'ee *Biblè* zhìt jyàa gwìnyaa t'ôonch'yàa, tr'ohchìt, nàhąą? Tr'ohchìt vizhìt gwandak. Khàrigikhìk, nàhąą? Aiits'ą' gwandak ch'iindàa dàazhii ts'ą' niłi'izhii gwandak khànêelghan k'ìt t'inch'yaa. Aiits'ą' aii zhìt tthak geerigįįkhii dąį' jii zhik gwà'àn chųųtyąh, nàhąą? *Tablè, chair,* ch'iitsii, jidìi datthak yeendàa jì' gwihèelyàa gwinyąą, jyàa vàràhnyąą aii jùk datthak gòodlìt. Aiits'ą' *airplàne* chan, *car* aii datthak yeendàa jì' vigwihèelyaa vàràhnyąą gwinyąą, jyàa nyaa į', Dęhtł'yaa kat. Yeendàa jì' vigwihèelyàa vàràhnyąą. Aii jùk datthak zhik gwà'àn nał'in rǫh.

10.39 Aiits'ą' jùk, nàhąą? Zhik ch'igęę'ąįįdik gwandak t'aihnyąą chan ndàa dàazhii. Oondaa khąįįkǫǫ *last* gwik'èenaatii danàhòtł'òo. Gwats'ą' *Jesus* vigwihèelyàa gwinyaa *Matthew.* Aii ts'an ndàa ts'ą' *John,* gehndaa gwik'èenaatii, aii zhik ch'iindàa t'ee *last. Last* it'ee gwandak ndàa nàa'ąį' į'. Aii zhik dzaa ch'iindàa chan tr'eedàa k'ìt gwich'ìn zhyąą nihthan ǫ'. Aiits'ą' jùk dèegwihee'yàa gwinyàa? Aii datthak jùk gwik'ìt t'igwii'in gwąął'in. Aiits'ą' łyâa zhyąą *it's true.*

11.52 Aiits'ą' zhik, nàhąą? Jidìi kwànchų' aii chan vigwihèelyàa gwinyàa. Dęhtł'yaa kat aiits'ą' dinjii lęįį yàa àn adahaatsyàa gwinyaa jyàa agàh vàràhnyąą. Aii tthak, jùk gwik'ìt t'igwii'in gwaał'in.

MR13.20 Aiits'ą' aii *Resèrvatiòn* aii oodhoojìk aii gwik'ìighai' aii. Jyàhts'ą' nakhwadivee gwiheezyàa aii eenjit t'oolìk lèe t'inch'yàa?

SF13.40 Ąąhą'! Jyàhts'ą' diidivee gwiheezyàa jì' jyàa gwiindhan eenjit t'ee t'igwiizhìk ǫ'. Kwàt shin dąį' gàa oonjìt, ch'adąį' tr'igwiindàii oonjì' nìdhiizhii, nàhąą? Oonjì' nìneeshagahchìk. Izhìk dąį' *last time,* aii dinjii *boss* nilįį oaałkat. Akhài' t'inyąą. Jii *Jesus…*[2] gwee'àn

2. Sarah accidentally said the word Jesus here. I think she was still thinking about the Bible. —JE

MR8.40 How do you know from the Bible that there will be lots of people?

SF8.48 It actually says that in the Bible, you see? It talks about it here and there from the beginning through to the end. They say it even talks about or predicts that there will be material items such as cups, tables, chairs, stoves, airplanes, cars, and so on. It says that in the Bible. I see all these things right now.

10.39 The time is here, you see? I mean the Bible is divided into sections. The last part talks about the last days. It talks about the birth of *Jesus* in Matthew. From that section is John. Then it talks about faith and the last days in the last section. The Good News is all in the Bible. I think we're in that period now. Whatever it says in the Bible is happening right now. It's just really true.

11.52 Look here, you see? It also says in the Bible that there will be lots of liquor and people will die from it. I see it happening right now.

MR13.20 Is that why you got the Reservation? So you could have a good life without all this stuff?

SF13.40 Yes! We got the Reservation thinking that we would have a better life. I used to be taken down there. When I went down for the last time I asked the boss there. I nan ch'adąį' vit'èegwąąhch'yà' jùk vineeragwaahchìi t'igwii'in. "Aii lèe yeendàa jì' shigii, shitseii naii chan gǫ̀ǫlįį, aii naii gàa zhyą̀ą *free* gwit'èehaahch'yàa lee t'ôonch'yaa," văihnyaa.

14.57 Akhài' *"Sure,"* shàhnyą̀ą. "Aiits'ą' jii zhik gwineegòo'ee ts'ą' *survey* gwagwahtsii, aii t'ee dinjii gòodlit jì' gwįįzįį gàanigwigwihee'aa kwaa eenjit t'igwii'in," jyąą shàgàhnyą̀ą.

15.20 Aii gwik'ìt jii *Resèrvatiòn* zhìt tr'agwandàii, nàhąą? Aiits'ą' izhìk gwà'àn dèegwįįdhan gwik'ìt t'igwii'ìn. Jyàa dìgwii'in izhìk łyâa sheenjit gwįįzįį. Shitseii naii tr'iits'àa gwahahkhit, oo'àt *Fairbànks* gwąął'in, nàhąą? *Fairbanks* gwąął'in dąį' reh yaaghà' oo'àn nìrihee'àl googàa gogǫ̀ǫtrii hę̀ę? Aii gwik'iighai' jii *Resèrvatiòn* tr'ii'įį jì' aii zhìt zhyą̀ą *free* k'ìt t'ôonch'yaa ts'ą' adats'ą' k'èeragwaadhat k'ìt t'ôonch'yaa. Izhìk dąį' gwats'an jyàhts'ą' ginįįjich'arahthat geh'àn t'igwiizhìk ǫ'.

MR17.19 *Fairbànks* gǫǫh'in kwaa t'ôonch'yaa hę̀ę? Jii nan oohǫhdal gwats'ą' reh hę̀ę?

SF17.26 Gwats'ą' zhat tr'agwąąh'yà' ǫ'.

MR17.30 Nan oohǫhdal gwats'ą' lèe?

SF Ą̀ąhą'.

MR17.34 *Fairbanks* gǫǫh'yà'? Aii nijìn dąį'?

SF17.36 Aii gwats'ą' dąį' hee. Ch'ìhłan *Junèau* iłts'ik zheh iidì' ganandàii?

MR18.03 Izhìk dąį' nan tr'oonheendal gwats'ą' dąį' nizhìk lèe t'ôonch'yàa?

SF18.07 *No.* Aiitł'ęę tishi'in ǫ'.

MR18.09 Aii t'agwarahnyąą, ti'yąą nan ooheendal gwats'ą', nan ineetł'yaa hęękhil gwats'ą'.

SF18.19 Izhìk dąį' zhat tr'agwąąh'in kwàa. *No,* tr'agwąąh'in kwàa. Izhìk gwats'ą' niizhìt tth'aii hee sharoonjii kwaa dąį' it'ee.

MR18.42 Aii ch'adąį' hee vàagwandàk.

asked the boss this question: "Are we claiming the land that we've used in the past so my children and grandchildren can use it for free in the future?"

14.57 And he said, "Sure. The land is being surveyed to prevent other people from trying to move in." That's what they told me.

15.20 So we can do whatever we want to do inside the Reservation, you see, which I'm really happy for. I see my own grandchildren and other people have a hard time getting around in *Fairbanks* because it's so overcrowded, right? So we thought if we had a reservation, we wouldn't be like *Fairbanks*. At that time, we thought about it this way. That's the reason we wanted the Reservation.

MR17.19 Had both of you been to *Fairbanks*? Before you got the land?

SF17.26 We saw it before that.

MR17.30 Before you got the land?

SF Yes.

MR17.34 You went to *Fairbanks*? When?

SF17.36 Before that. Do you remember once when I went to the hospital in *Juneau*?

MR18.03 Were you in the hospital before we got the land?

SF18.07 No. It happened after that.

MR18.09 That's when we were talking about—before Father got the land. Before the boundary was drawn.

SF18.19 We had never been to *Fairbanks* at that time. Before I got married.

MR18.42 You already told us the story about that part.

19.04 Aii nats'àhts'ą̀' gàakhwandàii izhìk gwànaa dą̀į' hę̀ę? Jùk gweendàa jyàa dìgwihee'yàa.

SF19.14 Aii t'ee nitì' aii? Nitì' aii t'ee t'inyąą, gwats'ą̀' dą̀į' googàa, jyàa nyàa. Jùk oo'àt *Fairbànks* gideech'arâahtth'ak[3] nàhąą? Kwaiik'ìt gòodlii ts'ą̀'. Izhìk gideech'arâahtth'ak k'ìighai' it'ee łyâa zhyą̀ą thok nan tr'įį'įį k'ìt t'ôonch'yaa jì' łyâa gwiheezyàa jyàa nyaa į'.

MR19.53 Aii nats'àhts'ą̀' gôohtth'ak, *radiò* zhìt *or*. . . ?

SF19.57 *Radio* zhìt, zhyą̀ą tr'igwîitth'ak gwandak jyàa dìi'in, nàhąą? Gwandak geetèe tr'îihtth'ak, nàhąą? Aii k'ìighai' oondìt gwà'àn ch'ìhłan *resèrvatiòn* zhìt dinjii gwandàii eeragwaandak, aii gwik'ìighai' t'igwiizhìk ǫ'.

22.07 Geetàk hee zhik gwà'àn vàanòodlit diik'at dahak ǫ'. Than t'ôonch'yàa vàanòodlit geetàk tr'ąąh'ìn. Aii geetàk diinàa dhidii dą̀į' geetàk diihàa gwaandak, nàhąą? Aii kwaii hàa tthak gwik'ìighai' jii *resèrvatiòn* gǫ̀ǫlįį gwinyaa tr'igwîitth'ak ǫ'.

MR24.12 *Gwichyaa Zheh* gwà'àn gwigwinch'į' lèe t'inch'yàa aii ti'yąą naii? Izhìk gwà'àn nik'èe *school* iłtsąįį?

SF24.20 *School* iłtsąįį kwàa. *Nevèr school.*

MR24.26 Nats'àhts'ą̀' gik'yǎanjik lì' hę̀ę?

SF24.31 *School* iłtsąįį kwàa. Shant'eh chan *school* dhałtsąįį kwàa, nah! Aii jidìi oondòk vàanòodlit diik'at dahak jìhnyaa? Izhìk aii vàanòodlit chan ts'an geetàk gwandak tr'îitth'àk. Aiits'ą̀' aii gwik'ìighai' it'ee jii Dinjii Zhuh dę̀htł'yàa aii t'ee hàandàii, Dinjii Zhuh dę̀htł'yàa hàandàii, aiits'ą̀' aii t'ee chan adąhkhài' yeedoodîiltin reh. *ABC* reh giyeek'ìteegijìk gwìch'in roh akhài' aiitł'ęę. . .

3. The meaning of *gideech'arâahtth'ak* is: 'To hear news now and then.' —JE

19.04 How did you know back then what would be happening now?

SF19.14 Your father, you see? Even your father said we should own our own land. After what we heard from *Fairbanks* now and then, you see? He talked that way before we got the land, after hearing about land claims.

MR19.53 How did you hear about them? From the radio or. . . ?

SF19.57 News traveled even at that time, even on the radio, see. We got the idea after hearing about people claiming reservations in the Lower 48.

22.07 Sometimes we met white men out in the woods. Sometimes they told us about land claims, you see? That's how we heard about getting a reservation.

MR24.12 Did Father and our family live in *Fort Yukon* once? Did he go to school at that time?

SF24.20 He never went to school.

MR24.26 How did he teach himself then?

SF24.31 He never went to school, and neither did I. He taught himself by learning to read the Indian Bible. Lots of times we met white men too. Sometimes they gave us some news. He could understand what they were telling him from reading the Indian Bible. He taught himself how to read using the ABC's. . .

25.23 Aii *ABC* aii k'ìighai' it'ee zhik ginjih nilįį nihchìitsįį k'ìt t'įįch'yàa. Aii diidęhtł'yàa. Aiits'ą' aii diidęhtł'yàa. Aii k'ìteech'igikhii, nàhąą? Akhài' vàanòodlit *Biblè* chan yaaghà' Mrs. . . Mr. . . Chiitąįį Gwigiinkhìi[4] nats'àa oozhrii łèe? Oochìt ch'adąį' khik neenjit khagiinjii. . . *Bardwèll.*[5]

MR *Mr. Bardwèll?*

SF *Mr. Bardwèll,* aii t'ee *Bible* giyintł'ìn'ąįį.

<sfwsl05Ab>

MR59.53 Aii į'. Ninghìt dąį' gwànaa oondee. *Njuunjik* gwats'an k'iindàk *Ackèrmàn Lake* dee'àn hee nineegiidàl gavaiinyaa dąį'. Aii nijùk dee'àn neegihiidàl tł'ęę nijùk neegihiidàl?

SF Jùu nąįį?

MR Aii dinjii t'agavàiinyaa nąįį.

SF Ôo, aii jyàa dìgii'in tł'ęę t'ee it'ee zhyąą.

MR Zhyąą needigęędàa gwizhrįį t'igii'in?

SF Ą̀ąhą'. Oondòk ddhah nįį'ee, tee' èhnjit *Shiinjik Ga'àltąįį* ginyàa. *Zhik Ddhah Njaa* ginyàa. Aii t'ee vijųų gwà'an gwats'an yeendòk ddhah nįį'ee.

SF60.40 Aiits'ą' oondee *Ch'idrìi,*[6] aii deedì' hee aii chan ghootee hee neegihiidàl ts'ą' it'ee chan gwandàii eenjit t'igii'ìn. Izhìk gwats'an t'ee geetàk hee yeendòk *Old John Lake* gwà'àn geetàk hee kwanh gahtsìk.

MR *No,* zhik *Ch'idrìi* dee'àn neegihiidàl dąį' gwats'an nijùk neegihiidàl, nijùk ts'ąįį?

SF Izhìk gwats'an reh. Izhìk gwats'an yeendòk gwanahjyàa jyàa dzaa gweetthàn gogwgąąh'in kwaa į'.

MR61.12 *Ackèrman Lake* k'iinaa neegihiidàl?

SF Ą̀ąhą'.

4. *Chiitaii Gwigiinkhìi* is an Assembly of God minister. —JE
The name means 'outdoor preacher.' —KP

5. Mr. Bardwell first came to *Fort Yukon* in the 1940s. —KP

6. *Ch'idrìi* ('Heart Mountain') is located on the *Ch'idriinjik* or *Middle Fork* of the *Chandalar River* just north of *Ackerman Lake.* Johnny and Sarah's daughter Maggie Roberts had an allotment there. —CM

25.23 And that's how he learned the pronunciation of our words. That's how he learned to read the Indian Bible too. Remember that *Mr. and Mrs. Bardwèll*? The Assembly of God people who used to pray for you?

MR *Mr. Bardwèll*?

SF *Mr. Bardwèll* gave him a Bible.

<sfwsl05Ab>

MR59.53 A long time ago. You said you traveled up the *Juunjik* and over to *Ackerman Lake*. Which way did you go?

SF Who?

MR These people you mentioned.

SF Oh, they traveled around here, then . . .

MR Did they only travel around?

SF Yes. They traveled along the mountains up to *Shiinjik Ga'àltaii*. They went from down below somewhere through another long series of mountains. From there is where the *Dhah Njaa Mountain* is.

SF60.40 Then they went zigzagging through *Ch'idrii Mountain*. They did that just to get food. From there they went up to *Old John Lake* where they sometimes stayed in huts.

MR No. Which way did they go from *Ch'idrii Mountain*? Which way?

SF From there, they passed through the mountains. They never came down this way.

MR61.12 Did they travel by *Ackerman Lake*?

SF Yes.

MR Zhik *Git Tsal Vęę*[7] aii yù'?

SF Izhìk gwà'àn hagàa reh. Izhìk t'ee gwik'ìighai' nitì' it'ee dinjii gaayii dìltsąįį vàràhnyaa ijìi. *Washington, D. C.* gwats'an hee dinjii oo'àt nihee. Aii t'ęę jii *Reservatìon* òonjik, nàhąą, nitì'. Aii t'ęę tł'yah nįįt'aii dųhts'aii chan zheh gwiltsąįį, nàhąą. Izhìk tr'igwiich'ìį. Izhìk it'ee *Washington, D. C.* gwats'an dinjii oo'àt zhat nòozhii į'.

61.55 Izhìk dąį' t'ee łì'hàa nitì' sheetsin'a'in yaaghà' reh. Aii t'ee kwàt. tr'ochìt nihdĕinzhii ts'ą' t'ee dęhtł'yaa yaaghà' chan nįįlìi. Aiits'ą' ch'ideheehtł'òo eenjit izhìk. Aiits'ą' t'iyàhnyàa, "Yeenjìt reh *Reservatìon* oodhiinjìk kwàt jàghaii jii tł'yah dųhts'ąįį chan jàghaii zheh gwadhantsąįį t'ini'ìn?" yàhnyàa.

62.28 Jyàa yàhnyaa akhài' yats'ą' tth'eehàatthaii, "Jii nan yeendòk nįį'ee, shits'ì' oohindal kwaa t'ôonch'yàa." Jyàa yàhnyaa ǫ' (adlaa).

7. *Git Tsal Vęę* is a local place name that means 'the edge of the little glacier'. This glacier is located between Gold Camp and Ackerman Lake. Johnny Frank had a pole cache there. It was also his moose and caribou hunting camp. In the winter time the glacier has a lot of ice and overflow, but in the summer it turns into a little creek that's very good for catching grayling. —RF

MR What about through *Git Tsal Vęę?*

SF Yes, even there. Because of that we think your father Johnny outspoke a man. A man from *Washington, D. C.* came to *Gold Camp* for this *Venetie Reservation*. Your father worked to get the *Reservation* and then he built a house outside the *Reservation* boundary, you see. And we lived there. So a man came from *Washington, D. C.*

61.55 That was when your father really made me laugh. When the man first came in the house, he set his papers down and shook hands with us. Then he said, "Why did you make a *Reservation* and then build outside the border of the *Reservation*?"

62.28 Your father pointed to him and said, "So you will not take away all this land that surrounds me." That's what he told him (laughs).

Fig. 31. Crystal Frank Welker and Kenneth Frank at the World Eskimo-Indian Olympic games in Fairbanks, 2013. Photo courtesy of Sean Topkok.

Appendix A
Frank Family Tree Descendancy Chart

compiled by Kenneth Frank, Craig Mishler, and Crystal Frank Welker
August 8, 2024

This family tree was compiled from a wide variety of sources, both oral and written. Written sources include the 1900, 1910, and 1920 U.S. Census and the Venetie school census records from the Bureau of Indian Affairs covering the years 1938-1966 (RG 75). These records are all on file with the National Archives in Seattle. Oral sources were many, but the primary ones who gave us many hours of their time are Johnny and Sarah Frank, Hamel and Mary Frank, Isaac Tritt, Katherine Peter and Stephen Peter Sr., Caroline Tritt-Frank, Abraham Christian, Elliott Johnson Sr., Hannah P. Solomon, Steve Frank, and Hannah Bundschuh. We also consulted Albert Tritt's journals at the University of Alaska Rasmuson Library, in Fairbanks.

Alternate names are shown in parentheses or quotation marks, and birth years are also shown in parentheses when known. All 19th century birthdates are approximate. Living spouses are not shown unless formally married. Multiple spouses are indicated by "Sp1," Sp2," etc. Numbers to the left of names show the generation, starting with Diitsii Giitł'uu and his wives as the first (1). New names have been added since the 2nd edition (2001) to reflect children born since then, and some names have been corrected for spelling. We are now up to eight generations.

Johnny Frank's Father's Side

1 — Diitsii Giitł'uu

**Diitsii Giitł'uu had six wives, but only four are still remembered, and it's not known which wife bore him the following daughter.*

2 — Ch'aadzaa Vahan (Bella, Drit Tr'ik)

3 — Enoch John (1882)

3 — Gabriel John

Sp1 — Shijyaa Tr'oonyaa (Lucy, Shoot'oo Vahan)

2 — Old Robert (Shoot'oo Gaamin, Shree Neevah) (1845)

Sp — Annie Daazhyah (1855)

**Old Robert Shoot'oo and Annie Daazhyah have many descendants with the surname of Roberts which are not listed here. Old Robert and his wife are generally considered to be the first residents of Venetie.*

Sp2 — Jaandii (Diitsii Ahdii)

Sp3 — Deedzii

Sp4 — Shyaaghan Ndik Sarah

**Shyaaghan Ndik Sarah, a Di'hąįį Gwich'in woman, was previously married to another Di'hąįį man named Vatroogwiłtsii before she married Diitsii Giitł'uu. From this earlier marriage, she gave birth to John, the father of Peter John and Henry John. From Peter John came Stephen Peter and the Arctic Village family with the surname of Peter.*

2 — Drit (Edward)

Sp — Vitsii'ahaa (Anna, Joseph Vahan)

**The Descendants of Edward Drit and Anna Vitsii'ahaa, especially through their son Albert Edward Tritt and his two wives, have not been listed here because they lead to a separate and equally large family tree as the Franks. Anna was the sister of Old John Vandeegwiizhii, an important link with the family of Sarah Frank.*

3 — Joseph Tritt

3 — George Tritt

3 — Rachel Tritt (1885)

Sp — Chief Christian (Christian Choh) (1880)

3 — Albert Edward Tritt (1880)

Sp1 — Leera (Laura)

Sp2 — Sarah Ghoo (1874)

3 — Mary Tritt

Sp — Elijah Henry

2 — Dritzhuu (Frank, From, Drizhuu) (1857)

Sp — Lucy Ch'igwihch'in (1863)

3 — Maggie Divi' (1879)
Sp1 — Natr'aadhat (Jozhur)
4 — Myra Kay (Ch'atąįį Gwatrat)
**Myra Kay was Maggie Divi's stepdaughter.*
Sp2 — Gilbert Joseph (1876)
4 — James Gilbert (1909)
Sp — Maggie
**James and Maggie Gilbert have many descendants which are not listed here, and Maggie has children by another spouse.*
4 — Alice Gilbert (1902)
Sp — Gabriel Peter
3 — Johnny "Zhrąįį" Frank (1884-1977)
Sp — Sarah "Tł'at" John (circa 1892-1988)
4 — Lucy Frank (1909)
Sp — Ambrose William (1899)
5 — William "Oolim" William
5 — Hannah J. William
Sp — Jonathon P. Solomon
6 — Raymond C. Solomon (1954)
7 — Raymond Solomon Jr.
7 — Jenna Solomon
8 — Kelsey Solomon (1997)
6 — Mary Beth Solomon (1956)
7 — Diana Dee Solomon (1973)
8 — Micala Peter (1994)
7 — Noah Ambrose Jonathon Solomon
6 — David Solomon (1957)
7 — Shawnda Mae Solomon
7 — Felicia Solomon
7 — Kaylynn Solomon (1997)
7 — Terrence Lee Solomon
6 — Bobby Solomon (1958)
7 — Ritchie Solomon
7 — "Neezhuu" Solomon
8 — William Jonathon Solomon (1999)
7 — Shawn Solomon

6 — Sandra Ann Solomon (1959)
Sp1 — Ben Phyfe
7 — Elizabeth "Ben Vigii"
Sp2 — Ron
7 — Vanessa
Sp3 — Jeff Plourde
6 — Teddy "Nekodh" Solomon (1976) (adopted)
6 — Georgina Marie Solomon (1980) (adopted)
6 — Jonathon Solomon Jr. (1963)
Sp — Arlene Joseph
7 — Vanessa Solomon
7 — Roland Solomon
7 — Miranda Solomon
6 — Duane Allen Solomon (1965)
Sp — Sue
7 — Juan Vetta
7 — Simeon
5 — Mary Hadeh'an
5 — Hugh William
5 — Ruth William
4 — Nathaniel Frank (1911)
Sp1 — Martha John (1916)
5 — Stanley Frank
Sp2 — Annie Roberts (1922)
5 — Dinah Frank (1945)
Sp — John Denning
6 — Gail Denning
7 — Christy Lynn Denning
7 — Faith Denning
5 — Caroline Frank (1947)
Sp — Andy Haley
6 — Michelle Haley
Sp — Michael Garnett
7 — Raenne Garnett
7 — Anthony Garnett
8 — Sean Wolf Garnett (2020)

5 — Clifton Frank (1948)
5 — Amos Frank (1949)
Sp — Lucy James
6 — Amos Frank Jr.
7 — Laticia Whitwell (2006)
Sp — Angelica Horace
7 — Maddison Frank (2008)
7 — Ladainian Frank (2012)
7 — Aziah Frank (2016)
6 — Sarah Ann Frank
Sp — Gerald Joe Sr.
7 — Nevaiya Lynn Joe (2011)
7 — Leiah Annie Joe (2014)
7 — Annie Frank Joe (2016)
6 — Danny Frank
5 — Jimmy Frank (1951)
Sp — Karen Johnson
6 — Jamie Frank
6 — Nena Frank
7 — Conrad Frank
6 — Nathaniel Frank
5 — Albert Frank (1952)
5 — Jeanie Frank (1954)
Sp — Calvin Tritt
6 — Fabian "Diitsii Giitł'uu" Frank
6 — Lisa Frank
7 — Lynnea Jean Annie Frank (2009)
5 — Orin Seybert Frank (1957)
5 — Johnny Carter Frank (1959)
5 — Nancy Jessie Frank (1960)
6 — Clint
6 — Clyde
5 — Marilyn Darlene Frank (1962)
6 — Christina Frank
Sp — John Mayfield
6 — Cynthia Mayfield
6 — Jessica Ann Mayfield (1994)

4 — Frank Frank
4 — Joseph "Nahnaa" Frank (1915)
4 — Allah Frank (1918)
Sp — Annie Roberts (1922)
5 — Hannah "Tsuk Zhrak" Frank (1940)
Sp — Gregory Bundschuh (1940)
6 — Michael Bundschuh (1963)
Sp — Marina Dick
6 — Paul Bundschuh (1965)
6 — Monica Bundschuh(1966)
Sp — Greg Taylor
7 — Marina Rose Taylor
7 — Alexander Paul Taylor
7 — Hanna Ruth "Baby Banana" Taylor
6 — Julie Bundschuh (1967)
Sp — Troy Borge
7 — Troy Borge Jr.
7 — Monica Lily Borge
6 — Jimmy Nathaniel Bundschuh (1976)
5 — Dorothy Frank
5 — Robert (Raavat) "Tsuk Khyaa" Frank (1944)
6 — Danny Lee Gemmill (1979-2017)
7 — Duran Coty Gemmill (1996)
7 — Triston Koyte Peter Gemmill (2000)
Sp — Bertha Erick
6 — Robert Frank Jr. (1969)
6 — Salina Frank (1967)
7 — Curtis "Vitsii Toh" Frank
7 — Clarence "Vitsii Ghwaa" Frank
7 — Sloan Natalie Frank
6 — Paula "Vichųų Kwaa" Frank
7 — Swan Healy Saylor
4 — Hamel "Vi'iidzee Ndee" Frank (1920-1998)
Sp — Mary Johnson (1931-2023)
5 — Louise Frank (1949-2021)
6 — Gerald Wayne Frank (1969-2023)
6 — Terry Frank (1970) – twin of Sherry

7 — Raymond
6 — Sherry Frank (1970) – twin of Terry
6 — Michael Frank (1971)
6 — Melinda "Shyaaghan Ndik" Frank (1976)
7 — Nikeeta Frank (1997) – twin of Natasha
7 — Natasha Frank (1997) – twin of Nikeeta
8 — Shanata Judy Louise Frank (2013)
7 — Jaden James Paul (2007)
5 — Lawrence Dale Frank (1951)
5 — Kenneth Everett "Drizhuu" Frank (1953)
6 — Brandi B. Barber (1978)
7 — Sayana Barber
6 — Charla A. Alexander (1979)
7 — Macayla Evea Jade Alexander (1999)
7 — Roman Alexander (2010)
7 — Cache Alexander (2019)
Sp — Caroline "Maagii Gwat" Tritt
6 — Crystal Annette "Dzehgak" Frank (1982)
Sp — Gabriel Welker
6 — Tisheena Katie "Divi'" Frank (1986)
5 — Jerry Gregory Frank (1955)
6 — Bernice "Sheegwal Tsal" Frank
7 — Marcus Hamel Jerry Frank (1998)
8 — Lyla Mae Love Kious (2019)
7 — Timothy John "Ch'iji' Nah'in" Isaac (2002)
6 — Sonya Villagecenter
5 — Burns Jones "Ben Zhuu" Frank (1957)
5 — Ronald Dean (Ronnie) Frank (1958)
Sp — Eveline Neely
6 — Benjamin Hamel Frank
6 — Samson "K'aiiheenjik" Frank (1989)
5 — Ricky Lee "Vi'iidzee Zhuu" Frank (1960)
6 — Amanda Dawn "Ch'ahk'ii" Tritt (1988)
7 — Myrcediz Tritt (2011)
7 — Rhainnan Roberts (2012)
7 — Kali Roberts (2014)

6 — Corrinne "Ch'ahk'ii Zhuu" Tritt (1991)
7 — Maliyah Helene Rashae Tritt (2009)
7 — Cody Travis Kendrick McCarty Jr. (2012)
7 — Hamel Ricky Cruz McCarty (2014)
7 — Treyvon Donald Lee Tritt (2020)
6 — Dustin Lee "Ko'nii'ak" Frank (1996)
7 — Caiden Lee Frank (2019)
5 — Marky Ray Frank (1962)
6 — Marky Frank Jr. "Khiitł'uu" Frank
5 — Connie Joyce Frank (1963)
6 — Gareth "Gwidee'ii" Frank
Sp — Nicole Williams
7 — Dalen Frank (2007)
7 — Brooke Frank (2014)
7 — Gareth Frank Jr. (2017)
7 — Gunner Paul Frank (2018)
Sp — Earl Henry
6 — Kyle Henry
6 — Jonas Benjamin Henry
6 — Earl "Ch'atł'at" Elliot Henry
7 — Abraham Henry
4 — Dan Frank (1924)
Sp — Jean Ribaloff (1914)
**Jean Ribaloff also has children from another spouse. See below on Sarah John's father's side.*
5 — Buddy Frank
5 — Tommy Frank
6 — Thomas Jason Frank
6 — Everett Wayne Frank
5 — Danny Frank
5 — Eddie Frank (1949-2025)
Sp — Sarah Jane Howarth
6 — Jethro Frank
6 — Danielle "Somik" Frank
7 — Melissa Frank
7 — Amber Frank
7 — Chad Everett Frank

6 — Jean Nan Frank
7 — Makala Frank
6 — Freda Frank
7 — Lezzlie Sarah Marie Rustad (2002)
7 — Karilee Emelia Firmin (2010)
5 — Steve Frank
Sp — Beth Frank
6 — Rachel Dumps
Sp — Jeffrey John Dumps Jr.
7 — Sophia Danielle Dumps (2009)
7 — Jeffrey John Dumps III (2011)
6 — Jennifer Frank
5 — John Frank
5 — Donna Frank
6 — Steve Graham
Sp — Mary John
7 — Zachary Graham
6 — Sonja Yatlin
Sp — Solomon Kent Yatlin
7 — Stephanie Nadine Williams (1998)
7 — Lydia Rose Yatlin (2005)
7 — Sasha Satina Yatlin (2008)
7 — Dan Brett Yatlin (2009)
7 — Kobe Evander Yatlin (2011)
7 — Jeremy Avory Lee Yatlin (2013)
7 — Tatiana Aliyah Roxanne Yatlin (2018)
6 — Lee Graham
4 — Dinah Frank (1925)
Sp — Thomas Robert
5 — William Robert
4 — Agnes Frank (1931)
4 — Joshua Frank (1932)
4 — Kias "Giiyaa" Frank
4 — Maggie "Tsal" Frank (1935-2013)
Sp — Jimmy "Gwat" Roberts (1932)
5 — Lawrence Dale ("Daazhuu" or "Daadhuu") Roberts (1953)

6 — Tony James "Anaazhrii" Roberts (1993)
6 — Timothy James Roberts
6 — Megan Emily Roberts (1997)
Sp — Mary Rose Tritt
6 — Julian Roberts (1975)
Sp — Christina Hamkin
7 — Elaina Haley Nicole Roberts (1995)
7 — Kayla Rose Roberts (1998)
7 — Bethany Roberts (2000)
6 — Julius Roberts (1976)
7 — Ryan Ginnis Roberts
6 — Allah Roberts
5 — Rita Rose Roberts (1955-2011)
6 — Joshua Lee Roberts (1975)
6 — Daniel Johnny Roberts (1979)
6 — John Fred Roberts (1982)
6 — Maggie Jamie Roberts (1983)
5 — Sylvia Salina "Vyaavyaa" Roberts (1957)
6 — Keith Allen Roberts (1976)
Sp — Grafton Biederman
5 — Melody Jean Roberts (1959)
6 — James Donald Martin (1979)
6 — Susan Maggie Martin (1981)
7 — Alicia (2000)
6 — Vincent Lawrence Roberts (1984)
6 — Jessica Elaine Roberts (1989)
6 — Antonia Maggie Marie Roberts (1990)
6 — Jerome Linus Roberts
6 — Kimberly Conkle (1991)
5 — James Jr. "Anaazhrii" Roberts
5 — Susan Elizabeth Roberts (1961)
5 — Lucy Roberts (1965)
5 — Tony Gene Roberts (1970)
5 — Laurie Roberts
6 — Donald Jimmy Adams (1997)
6 — Caitlin Nena Charlotte Adams (2000)
5 — Sarah Roberts

6 — Christopher Henry Strickland
3 — Francis Frank (1887)
3 — Elisha Frank (1890)
3 — Jenny Frank (1875) – twin of Julia
Sp — Jumbo Bill
4 — Margaret
Sp — Isaac John Sr.
4 — Mabel
Sp — Jim Christian
3 — Julia "Naach'in" Frank (1875) – twin of Jenny
Sp — William Loola
4 — Mary Loola
4 — Annie Loola
4 — Hudson Loola
4 — Nina Loola
Sp — Emil Bergman
5 — Grafton Bergman
Sp — Hannah (1957)
5 — Adeline Bergman
4 — Esais Loola (adopted)
Sp — Myra
**William Loola had two sons by his first wife, Mary Sheegwal. They were Charlie Loola and Esais Loola (a different child than the one adopted).*
3 — David "Neerahadhak" Frank (1899)
Sp — Sarah Jin Peter
4 — Myra Francis
3 — Harry "Tłok" Frank (1903)
3 — Nishuk Frank
3 — Annie Frank (1873)
3 — Jimmy Frank
3 — Mary Frank (1878)
Sp — John Kiolet (1869)

Johnny Frank's Mother's Side

1 — Diitsii Geh Ik Ti'
Sp — Diitsųų Geh Ik Vinh
2 — Ch'igwihch'in (Lucy) (1863)
Sp — Dritzhuu (Frank, From) (1857)
3 — Maggie Divi' (1879)
Sp1 — Natr'aadhat (Jozhur)
4 — Myra Kay (Ch'atąįį Gwatrat)
**Myra Kay was Maggie Divi's stepdaughter.*
Sp2 — Gilbert Joseph (1876)
**Maggie Divi' and Gilbert Joseph have many descendants with the surname of Gilbert which are not listed here.*
3 — Johnny "Zhrąįį" Frank (1884)
Sp — Sarah "Tł'at" John (circa 1892)
**Johnny Frank's and Sarah John's descendants are shown under Johnny Frank's father's side.*
3 — Julia "Naach'in" Frank (1875)
Sp — William Loola (1854)
3 — Francis Frank (1887)
3 — Elisha Frank (1890)
3 — Jenny Frank
3 — David "Neerahadhak" Frank (1899)
Sp — Sarah Jin Peter
4 — Myra Francis
3 — Harry "Tłok" Frank (1903)
3 — Nihshuk Frank
3 — Annie Frank (1873)
3 — Jimmy Frank
3 — Mary Frank (1878)
Sp — John Kiolet (1869)

Sarah John's Father's Side

**Ko'nịi'ak's father was named Tuuł and Tuuł's father was named Vit'eh Viti'. We have not assigned generation numbers to them, however, in order to keep all the other generations historically parallel.*

1 — Ko'nii'ak
 Sp — Nich'itr'oonii
  2 — Vats'a' Ch'araathan
  2 — Vitsii Deeyuunyaa
  2 — Old John Vandeegwiizhii (1840)
   Sp1 — Toh Val'i'
    3 — Philip
    3 — Lucy
     Sp — Gaalin Tsal
      4 — Ginnis Golen (1894)
       5 — Mary Golen
        Sp — Trimble Gilbert
        **Mary Golen and Trimble Gilbert have many descendants who are not listed here.*
       5 — Annie Golen
        Sp — Abraham Christian
        **Annie Golen and Abraham Christian have many descendants who are not listed here.*
   Sp2 — Mary Ch'idįį
    3 — James "Jimmy" John
     Sp — Bella
      4 — Abraham "Dihdoh" John
      4 — Arthur "Tsoo" James
    3 — Sarah "Tł'at" John (circa 1892)
     Sp — Johnny "Zhrąįį" Frank (1884)
     **For the many descendants of Sarah John and Johnny Frank, see Johnny Frank's Father's Side.*
    3 — Peter John
    3 — Charlie "Jyaalii" John
    3 — Christian John
    3 — Ellen John
     Sp — Jonas Henry
    3 — Charley John

2 — Vitsii'ahaa (Anna, Joseph Vahan)
Sp — Drit (Edward)
3 — Joseph Tritt
3 — George Tritt
3 — Rachel Tritt
3 — Albert Edward Tritt
Sp1 — Leera (Laura)
Sp2 — Sarah Ghoo
3 — Mary

**The children of Anna Vitsii'ahaa and Edward Drit have many descendants with the surname Tritt who are not listed here.*

2 — Nitsihghaih (Louisa)
Sp — Oozhrii Kaii (Old Fred, "Anaazhrak") (1850)
3 — Daniel (Donald, "Ch'itril Dzak") Fredson (1874)
Sp — Ann
3 — Enoch Fredson (1876)
Sp — Emma
4 — Steven Fredson (adopted) (1912)
4 — Helen (adopted)
4 — Elizabeth (adopted)
Sp — Abraham Christian

**Abraham Christian has children by another spouse, Annie Golen.*

3 — Ellen Fredson (1885)
3 — Mary "Dzan" Fredson (1887)
Sp — Charlie Johnson
4 — Lena Albert
Sp — Robert Albert
5 — Albert "Side" Albert
5 — Johnson Albert
5 — Pauline Albert
5 — Virginia Albert
5 — David Albert
4 — Fred Johnson
3 — Lucy Fredson (1890)
3 — Jimmy Fredson (1891)
3 — John Fredson ("Zhoh Gwatsan") (1896)
Sp — Jean Ribaloff

**Jean Ribaloff has children by another spouse, Dan Frank. See Johnny Frank's Father's Side.*

4 — Bill Burke Fredson (1933)

4 — Virginia Fredson (1937)

5 — Dennis

5 — Michael

5 — Richard

5 — Diana

4 — Lula Fredson (1942)

Sp — Don Young

5 — Dawn Young

5 — Joni Young

Sarah John's Mother's Side

1 — Ts'it'ee Ts'ik
Sp — Kǫ'dah T'yaa
  2 — Walsun Viiyehtr'ik
    3 — Andrew Choh
  2 — Robert "Raavat" Deetreezhuu
  Sp — Sarah Chiichyaa
  2 — Oozhrii Kaii (Old Fred, "Anaazhrak")
  Sp — Nitsihghaih (Louisa)
  **Old Fred's and Louisa's descendants are shown under Sarah John's Father's Side.*
  2 — Mary Ch'idįį
  Sp1 — Nidik
    3 — Leera (Laura)
    Sp — Albert Edward Tritt
    3 — Mary
    3 — Albert
  Sp2 — Old John Vandeegwiizhii (1840)
    3 — James "Jimmy" John ("Ch'ik'ih")
    Sp — Bella
    3 — Sarah "Tł'at" John (circa 1892)
    Sp — Johnny "Zhrąįį" Frank (1884)
    **Sarah John's and Johnny Frank's descendants are shown under the Johnny Frank's Father's Side.*
    3 — Peter John
    3 — Charlie "Jyaalii" John
    3 — Christian John
    3 — Ellen John
    Sp — Jonas Henry
    3 — Charley John

Appendix B
Audiotape References

All of the texts in this volume are based on cassette tape field recordings. The tapes exhibit a wide range of sound quality and listenability due to the different levels of experience among those persons making the recordings as well as the technical quality of the recorders and microphones available to them. A few tapes could not be transcribed because of audio problems.

The source identifiers for each transcribed tape segment are given at the beginning of each transcription in a shorthand coded form. These code times were devised as a consistent way of identifying the person interviewed — either jf for Johnny Frank or sf for Sarah Frank, followed by the initials of the interviewer, a sequential number (usually assigned by the interviewer), and finally, an "a" or "b" to indicate which side of the tape was transcribed. For example, <sflg2a> is Sarah Frank interviewed by Lillian Garnett, tape #2 side a. Tapes made by staff members of the Bureau of Indian Affairs are identified by the letters "BIA."

As a result of many individual efforts, there are now about thirty-five hours of folklore, oral history, and ethnographic observations from Johnny and Sarah scattered about in public and private tape collections. All of this taped material along with several iterations of our working manuscripts, numerous photographs, and the videotape of Sarah have now been gathered and deposited in the Oral History Collection of the Rasmuson Library at the University of Alaska Fairbanks. A closely related digital collection may be found online at the Alaska Native Language Archive. See the search engine at: https://www.uaf.edu/anla/. Some of the original tape recordings listed below may be found among the Craig Mishler Papers at the University of Alaska Anchorage Consortium Library archives. A finding aid to these papers is available at https://archives.consortiumlibrary.org/.

The Johnny Frank Collection

<jfcmla> and <jfcmlb>
<jfcm2a> and <jfcm2b>
<jfcm3a>

Johnny Frank interviewed by Craig Mishler at Gold Camp on November 16-17, 1972. Transcribed and translated by Judy Erick. Tape <jfcm2a> is almost entirely in English and was not transcribed, except for several of Johnny's songs. Tape <jfcm3a> contains three short Eskimo songs but is mostly in English and was not transcribed. The original tapes are located among the Craig Mishler Papers at the University of Alaska Consortium Library Archives in Anchorage.

<jfka401> and <jfka403>
<jfka405> and <jfka402>
<jfka404>
<jfka406>

Johnny Frank interviewed by Kathy Alexander at Gold Camp, April, 1973. Transcribed and translated by Judy Erick. Circulating copies of these tapes are archived in the Oral History Collection of the Rasmuson Library, University of Alaska Fairbanks under the numbers H91-12-295 through H91-12-300. The original 400-series numbers used here were assigned by the Alaska State Library, the agency which sponsored the field recording of these and many other tapes in the statewide Songs and Legends collection: Tape 401 is the same as H91-12-295; 405 corresponds with H91-12-296; 402 is the same as H91 -12-297; 403 is the same as H91-12-298; 404 is the same as H91-12-299; and 406 is the same as H91-12-300. It is impossible to tell in what order these tapes were originally recorded except that 401 continues on 403 and 405 continues on 402. All tapes are single-sided.

<jfmh1a>

Johnny Frank interviewed by Mike Holloway in Gold Camp, September.

The Sarah Frank Collection

<sfcm>

Sarah Frank interviewed by Craig Mishler in Venetie, May 14, 1979. Transcribed and translated by Lillian Garnett except for the story of the Old Woman and the Brown Bear, First Version, which was done by Judy Erick. The original tape is located among the Craig Mishler Papers at the University of Alaska Consortium Library Archives in Anchorage.

<sfwsl05Aa> and <sfws105Ab>
<sfwsl05Ba> and <sfwsl05Bb>
<sfws105Ca> and <sfwsl05Cb>
<sfwsl05Da> and <sfwsl05Db>
<sfwsl05Ea> and <sfwsl05Eb>
<sfws105Fa> and <sfws105Fb>

Sarah Frank interviewed by William Schneider and Mike Holloway, with Maggie Roberts interpreting in Venetie, April, 1980. Mixed English and Gwich'in. <sfwsl05Aa> and <sfwsl05Ab> were transcribed and translated by Mary Rose Roberts. All of the others were transcribed and translated by Judy Erick. The original tapes and circulating copies are archived in the Oral History Collection of the Rasmuson Library, University of Alaska Fairbanks under different numbers: <sfwsl05A> is tape #H87-105A, <sfws 105B> is #H87-105B, <sfws105C> is #H87-105C, <sfws 105D> is #H87-105D, <sfws105E> is #H87-105E, and <sfws105F> is #H87-105F.

<sfdlBIA337a>
<sfdlBIA338a> and <sfdlBIA338b>

Sarah Frank interviewed by David Libbey of the Bureau of Indian Affairs and Caroline Frank at the site of Old John's cabin and Sarah's mother's grave at Old John Lake, July 17, 1979. Transcribed and translated by Lillian Garnett. The original tapes are on file at the Bureau of Indian Affairs ANCSA Office in Anchorage. Circulating copies are archived in the Oral History Collection of the Rasmuson Library, University of Alaska Fairbanks under different numbers: <sfdlBIA337> is tape #H83-337 and <sfdlBIA338> is #H83-338.

<sfalBIA>

Sarah Frank interviewed by Alice Lynch of the Bureau of Indian Affairs and Trimble Gilbert in Venetie on August 3,1983. Transcribed and translated by Lillian Garnett. The original tape is on file at the U.S. Bureau of Indian Affairs, ANCSA Program Office, Anchorage.

<sfrf1a> and <sfrf1b>

<sfrf2a> and <sfrf2b>

Sarah Frank interviewed by Ron Frank in Venetie, June, 1982. Transcribed and translated by Lillian Garnett. The original tapes were in the private collection of Ron Frank of Gulkana.

<sflgla> and <sflglb>

<sflg2a> and <sflg2b>

Sarah Frank interviewed by Lillian Garnett in Arctic Village, June,1984. Transcribed and translated by Lillian Garnett. The original tapes are in the Arctic Village school collection.

<sfkf1a> and <sfkf1b>

<sfkf2a> and <sflf2b>

Sarah Frank interviewed by Kenneth Frank and Caroline Tritt-Frank in Venetie, Fall, 1985. Transcribed and translated by Lillian Garnett. The original tapes are in the private collection of Kenneth Frank and Caroline Tritt-Frank of Arctic Village.

<sfvala> and <sfvalb>

Sarah Frank interviewed by Virginia Alexander in Fort Yukon, June 6, 1986. Not transcribed because of poor audio quality. The topic is plant lore and folk medicine. Original tape is in the collection of Virginia Alexander, Fort Yukon.

The Frank Family Collection

<ffla> and <fflb>
<ff2a> and <ff2b>
Nathaniel Frank, Hamel Frank, Dan Frank, and Maggie Roberts interviewed by Craig Mishler in Venetie on October 5, 1989. In Gwich'in. Transcribed and translated by Judy Erick, but not marked for tones. The original tapes are with the Craig Mishler Papers at the UAA Consortium Library Archives in Anchorage.

<ff3a>
Hamel Frank, Dan Frank, Maggie Roberts, Kenneth Frank, and Caroline Tritt-Frank interviewed by Craig Mishler in Venetie on June 19, 1990. Mixed Gwich'in and English. Not transcribed.

Contributors Tape Legend

SF — Sarah Frank
JF — Johnny Frank
WS — William Schneider
MH — Mike Holloway
M — Maggie Roberts
DF — Dan Frank
CF — Caroline Tritt-Frank
KF — Kenneth Frank
RF — Ron Frank
TG — Trimble Gilbert
KA — Kathy Alexander
AL — Alice Lynch
LG — Lillian Garnett
AR — Adeline Raboff
MRG — Mary Rose Gamboa

References Cited

Alaska Library Association. 1977. *Stories of Native Alaskans* (broadside posters). Fairbanks: University of Alaska Press.

Attla, Catherine. 1990. *K'etetaalkkaanee: The One Who Paddled Among the People and Animals.* Fairbanks: Yukon Koyukuk School District and Alaska Native Language Center.

Bloomfield, Leonard. 1934. *Plains Cree Texts.* Publications of the American Ethnological Society, Vol. 16. New York: G.E. Stechert.

Bompas, William Carpenter. 1888. *Diocese of Mackenzie River*. New York: E. and J.B. Young Co.

Burch, Ernest S. Jr. and Craig Mishler. 1995. "The Di'hąįį Gwich'in: Mystery People of the Brooks Range." *Arctic Anthropology* 32(1): 147-172.

Bureau of the Census, U.S. 1900. *Twelfth Census of the United States.* Microfilm copy on file at the National Archives, Alaska Region, Anchorage.

——. 1910. *Thirteenth Census of the United States*. Microfilm copy on file at the National Archives, Alaska Region, Anchorage.

——. 1920. *Fourteenth Census of the United States*. Microfilm copy on file at the National Archives, Alaska Region, Anchorage.

Bureau of Indian Affairs. 1980. Report of Investigation for Old John's Cabin, Site No. F-22590. Anchorage: BIA ANCSA Office.

——. 1983. Report of Investigation for Johnny Frank's (Gold) Camp, Site No. F 22654. Anchorage: BIA ANCSA Office.

Camsell, Charles. 1915. "Loucheux Myths." Edited by C.M. Barbeau. *Journal of American Folklore* 28:248-257.

Cannon, Chris M. 2021. Northern Dene Astronomical and Sky-Related Knowledge: A Comparative Anthropological Study. Ph.D. dissertation. University of Alaska, Fairbanks.

Caulfield, R.A. 1981a. *Venetie Nan Gwik'it Teedanahotł'oo: Gwich'in Athabaskan Place Names for Venetie, Alaska.* Fairbanks: Alaska Department of Fish and Game, Division of Subsistence.

——. 1981b. *Vashrąįį K'oo Gwik'it Teedanahotł'oo: Gwich'in Athabaskan Place Names for Arctic Village, Alaska.* Fairbanks: Alaska Department of Fish and Game, Division of Subsistence.

——. *1983. Subsistence Land Use in Upper Yukon-Porcupine Communities, Alaska: Dinjii Nats'aa Nan Kak Adagwaandaii.* Technical Paper No. 16. Fairbanks: Alaska Department of Fish and Game, Division of Subsistence.

Cooperative Parks Studies Unit. 1979. National Register Nomination: Johnny Frank's Stone-lined Meat Caches. Site No. F22591. CPSU Collection, Box Al 979, Folder F-22591, Alaska and Polar Regions Dept., Rasumuson Library, University of Alaska, Fairbanks.

Cruikshank, Moses. 1986. *The Life I've Been Living.* Fairbanks: University of Alaska Press.

Duncan, Kate and Eunice Carney. 1988. *A Special Gift: The Kutchin Beadwork Tradition.* Seattle: University of Washington Press.

Fitzgerald, Gerald. 1927. U.S. Geological Survey Field Journal for 1927. Unpublished notebook in the possession of Mrs. Patricia Aubin, Gaithersburg, Maryland.

Frank, Kenneth Drizhuu. 2014. *Vadzaih Nilii Gaih Tr'ahtsii: Making Caribou Dry Meat*. Video narrated in Gwich'in with English subtitles. Edited by Craig Mishler. 20 minutes. Unreleased 2014.

Guédon, Marie Françoise. 1974. *People of Tetlin, Why Are You Singing?* National Museums of Canada.

Hall, Edwin S., Jr. 1969. "Speculations on the Late Prehistory of the Kutchin Athapaskans." *Ethnohistory* 16(4):317-333.

——. 1975. "Kutchin Athapaskan-Nunamiut Eskimo Conflict." *The Alaska Journal* 5(4):248-252.

Holloway, J. Michael. 2014. *Dreaming Bears: A Gwich'in Indian Storyteller, a Southern Doctor, a Wild Corner of Alaska.* Seattle: Epicenter Press.

Huntington, Sidney. 1993. *Shadows on the Koyukuk.* Anchorage: Alaska Northwest Books.

Hymes, Dell. 1981. *"In Vain I Tried to Tell You." Essays in Native American Ethnopoetics.* Philadelphia: University of Pennsylvania Press.

Keim, Charles, ed. 1964. "Kutchin Legends from Old Crow, Yukon Territory." *Anthropological Papers of the University of Alaska,* XI(2):97-108. Fairbanks.

Kitchener, L.D. 1954. *Flag Over the North.* Seattle: Superior Publishing Co.

Leechman, Douglas. 1950. "Loucheux Tales." *Journal of American Folklore* 63:158-162.

——. 1952. *Folk-lore of the Vanta-Kutchin.* National Museum of Canada Bulletin 126:76-93.

Lonner, Thomas and S.W. Beard. 1982. Arctic Village. In *Sociocultural Assessment of Proposed National Wildlife Refuge Oil and Gas Exploration,* Final Report. Part IL Anchorage: University of Alaska, Arctic Environmental Information and Data Center.

Mackenzie, Clara. 1986. *Zhoh Gwatsan: A Life History of John Fredson.* Anchorage: Alaska Pacific University Press.

Marshall, Robert. *Arctic Village: A 1930s Portrait of Wiseman, Alaska.* Orig. 1933. Fairbanks: University of Alaska Press, 1991.

Martin, Richard. 1993. *K'aiiroondak: Behind the Willows.* Edited by Bill Pfisterer. Fairbanks: Center for Cross-Cultural Studies, University of Alaska Fairbanks.

McClellan, Catharine. 1987. *Part of the Land, Part of the Water: A History of the Yukon Indians.* Vancouver: Douglas & Mclntyre.

McDonald, Kenneth. 1874. Journal entry for December 4. Included in Robert McDonald's Journal, Mss 4001. Microfilm. Winnipeg: Archives of the Ecclesiastical Province of Rupert's Land.

McDonald, Robert. 1876. "Legends of the Tukudhs." *The Church Missionary Intelligencer and Record,* Vol. I. pp. 411-416; 461-467. London: [Anglican] Church Missionary House.

McGary, Mary Jane, ed. 1982. *John Fredson Edward Sapir Hàa Googwandak: Stories Told by John Fredson to Edward Sapir.* Fairbanks: Alaska Native Language Center.

McKennan, Robert. 1933. Ethnographie field notes: Chandalar River, Dihai. McKennan Collection, Series 2. Alaska and Polar Regions Dept., Rasmuson Library, University of Alaska Fairbanks.

——. 1935. "Anent the Kutchin Tribes." *American Anthropologist* 37(2):369.

——. 1959. *The Upper Tanana Indians*. Yale University Publications in Anthropology Number 55. Yale University Department of Anthropology. New Haven.

——. 1965. *The Chandalar Kutchin.* Montreal: Arctic Institute of North America.

Mertie, Evelyn. 1982. *Thirty Summers and a Winter.* Fairbanks: University of Alaska Mineral Industry Research Laboratory.

Mertie, J.B. 1927a. Mertie photograph collection. U.S. Geological Survey Field Records Library, Denver.

——. 1927b. The Chandalar-Sheenjek District, Alaska. U.S. Geological Survey Bulletin 810. Washington, D.C.

Mishler, Craig, ed. 1973. *Kutchin Tales.* Anchorage: Alaska Learning Laboratory.

——, ed. 1974. *Music of the Alaskan Kutchin [Gwich'in] Indians*. FE 4070. Lp and cassette recording with liner notes. Smithsonian/Folkways Recordings. Washington: Smithsonian Institution.

——. 1981a. *Gwich'in Athapaskan Music and Dance: An Ethnography and Ethnohistory.* Ph.D. dissertation. University of Texas at Austin.

——. 1981b. '"He Said, They Say': The Uses of Reporting Speech in Native American Folk Narrative." *Fabula* 3 /4: 239-249.

——. 1982. John Fredson: A Biographical Sketch. In *John Fredson Edward Sapir Hàa Googwandak: Stories Told by John Fredson to Edward Sapir*, edited by Mary Jane McGary. Fairbanks: Alaska Native Language Center.

——. 1983a. Review of *"In Vain I Tried to Tell You": Essays in Native American Ethnopoetics,* by Dell Hymes. *Journal of American Folklore* 96(382):481-483.

——. 1983b. Mizhur, Monsieur: A Gwich'in Athabaskan Card Game. Paper presented at the American Folklore Society Annual Meeting, Nashville, Tennessee. Published in Mishler and Frank, 2023: 251-265).

——. 1984. "Telling About Bear: A Northern Athapaskan Men's Riddle Tradition." *Journal of American Folklore* 97(383):61-68.

——. 1990. "Missionaries in Collision: Anglicans and Oblates Among the Gwich'in, 1861-1865." *Arctic* 43(2): 121-126.

——. 1993. *The Crooked Stovepipe: Athapaskan Fiddle Music and Square Dancing in Northeast Alaska and Northwest Canada.* Urbana and Chicago: University of Illinois Press.

——. 2013. *The Blind Man and the Loon: The Story of a Tale*. Lincoln: University of Nebraska Press.

——. 2018. "Anthropology on the Rocks: Portraits of the Gwich'in by American Field Geologists, 1898-1927." *Alaska Journal of Anthropology* 16(1):1-20.

Mishler, Craig and Kenneth Frank ('Drizhuu'). 1995. Oaazhrii: Gwich'in Personal Names and Kinship Ties. Paper presented at the Second International Congress of Arctic Social Sciences, Rovaniemi, Finland.

——. 2020. *Dinjii Vadzaih Dhidlit: The Man Who Became a Caribou.* 2nd ed. rev. Hanover: IPI Press.

——. 2021. Shriniinlii 'Fix It': the Grease Mechanics of Translating Gwich'in. *In Indigenous Languages and the Promise of Archives*. Pp. 461-478. Ed. by Patrick Spero, Abigail Shelton, and Adrianna Link. University of Nebraska Press, Lincoln.

——. 2023. *Crooked on the Stretcher Board: Ch'ats'ą Vizhit Teech'iriikii: Collected Essays on Gwich'in History, Language, and Folk Culture*. Hanover: IPI Press.

Mishler, Craig and William Simeone. 2004. *Han, People of the River: An Ethnography and Ethnohistory.* Fairbanks: University of Alaska Press.

——. 2006. *Tanana and Chandalar. The Alaskan Field Journals of Robert A. McKennan*. Fairbanks: University of Alaska Press.

Morlan, Richard. 1973. *The Later Prehistory of the Middle Porcupine Drainage, Northern Yukon Territory, Canada.* National Museum of Man. Mercury Series Archaeological Survey Paper 11 Ottawa.

Nelson, Richard K. 1973. *Hunters of the Northern Forest: Designs for Survival among the Alaskan Kutchin.* Chicago: University of Chicago Press.

Osgood, Cornelius. 1936. *Contributions to the Ethnography of the Kutchin.* Yale University Publications in Anthropology No. 14. Reprinted by the Human Relations Area Files Press. New Haven, 1970.

——. 1971. *The Han Indians*. Yale University Publications in Anthropology No. 74. New Haven.

Peter, Katherine, trans. 1975a. *Deenaadai' Gwich'in Gwandak: Traditional Gwich'in Stories.* Told by Natalie Erick. Fairbanks: Alaska Native Language Center.

——. 1975b. *Vasaagihdzak; Shoh Deetrya' Hàa Gwandak; Tr'injaa*. Fairbanks: Alaska Native Language Center.

——. 1975c. *Olti' Daga'at Dik Hàa: Olti' and His Wife Dik.* Fairbanks: Alaska Native Language Center.

——. 1976. *Alaskan Folktales: Dinjii Zhuu Gwandak: Gwich'in Stories.* Austin, Texas: Dissemination and Assessment Center for Bilingual Education.

——. 1978. *Deenaadai' Gwich'in Oozhri': Traditional Gwich'in Names*. Fairbanks: Alaska Native Language Center.

——. 1979. *Dinjii Zhuu Ginjik Nagwan Tr'iłtsaii: Gwich'in Junior Dictionary*. Fairbanks: Alaska Native Language Center and the National Bilingual Materials Development Center.

——. 1992. *Neets'ąįį Gwindaii: Living in the Chandalar Country*. Revised edition. Fairbanks: Alaska Native Language Center.

Peter, Katherine and Mary L. Pope. 1981. *Dinjii Zhuu Gwandak: Gwich'in Stories*. Anchorage: National Bilingual Materials Development Center.

Petitot, Émile. 1886. *Traditions Indiennes du Canada nord-ouest*. Paris: Maisonneuve frères et C. Leclerc.

——. 1970. "The Amerindians of the Canadian North-West in the 19th Century, as seen by Émile Petitot." In *The Loucheux Indians*, Vol. II, edited by Donat Savoie. Ottawa: Department of Indian Affairs and Northern Development.

Petrone, Penny. 1990. *Native Literature in Canada: From the Oral Tradition to the Present.* Toronto: Oxford University Press.

Pfisterer, William, ed. 1982. *Shandaa: In My Lifetime*. Fairbanks: Alaska Native Language Center.

Ray, Patrick Henry and W.R. Richardson. 1900. "Suffering and Destitute Miners in Alaska and What was Done for Their Relief." In *Narratives of Explorations in Alaska 1898*. Washington, D.C.: U.S. Government Printing Office.

Rooth, Anna Birgitta. 1971. "The Alaska Expedition 1966: Myths, Customs and Beliefs among the Athabascan Indians and the Eskimos of Northern Alaska." *Acta Universitatis Lundensis*. Sectio I, Theologica Juridica Humaniora 14.

——. 1980. "The Wolverine's Trap." In *The Alaska Seminar*. Uppsala and Stockholm: Almqvist & Wiksell International.

Roseneau, D.G., P. Stern, and C. Warbelow. 1975. "The Kutchin Caribou Fences of Northeastern Alaska and the Northern Yukon." In *Arctic Gas Biological Report Series,* Vol. 32. Canadian Arctic Gas Study, Limited and Alaskan Arctic Gas Study Company.

Russell, Frank. 1898. Myths of the Wood Crees. In *Explorations in the Far North*. Iowa City: University of Iowa.

——. 1900. "Athabaskan Myths: Loucheux Tribe." *Journal of American Folklore* 13:11-16.

Schrader, F.C. 1899. Chandalar and Koyukuk River Expedition field notes. Notebook 106. Technical Data Unit, U.S. Geological Survey, Anchorage.

Slobodin, Richard. 1962. *Band Organization of the Peel River Kutchin*. National Museum of Canada Bulletin 179. Ottawa.

——. 1970. "Kutchin Concepts of Reincarnation." *Western Canadian Journal of Anthropology* 2(1):67-79.

——. 1975. "Without Fire: A Kutchin Tale of Warfare, Survival, and Vengeance." In *Proceedings: Northern Athapaskan Conference, 1971,* Vol. 1:295-301, edited by A. McFayden Clark. National Museum of Man. Mercury Series Ethnology Service Paper 27. Ottawa.

——. 1981. "Kutchin." In *Handbook of North American Indians.* Vol. 6: 514-532, edited by J. Helm. Washington, D.C.: Smithsonian Institution.

Tedlock, Dennis. 1972. "On the Translation of Style in Oral Narrative." In *Toward New Perspectives in Folklore.* Austin: University of Texas Press.

Thomas, Kenny Sr. *Crow Is My Boss: The Oral Life History of a Tanacross Athabaskan Elder*. Ed. By Craig Mishler. Norman: University of Oklahoma Press, 2005.

Thompson, Judy. 1994. *From the Land: Two Hundred Years of Dene Clothing.* Ottawa: Canadian Museum of Civilization.

Tritt, Albert, n.d. Chronicle Given by Albert E. Tritt of Arctic Village. Taken down by Miss Winifred Dalziel. Box 7, Frederick B. Drane Collection, Alaska and Polar Regions Dept., Rasmuson Library, University of Alaska Fairbanks.

——. 1992. *The Tritt Journal.* Translated by Lincoln Tritt. Unpublished manuscript based on the diaries of Albert Tritt and Isaac Tritt. Private collection of Caroline Tritt-Frank.

Voudrach, Paul. 1965. *Good Hope Tales.* National Museum of Canada Bulletin 204, Contributions to Anthropology, 1963-64, Part II, edited by R. Cohen and H. Osterreich. Ottawa.

Wallis, Velma. 1993. *Two Old Women: An Alaska Legend of Betrayal, Courage, and Survival.* Fairbanks: Epicenter Press.

West, Frederick Hadleigh. 1959. "On the Distribution and Territories of the Western Kutchin Tribes." *Anthropological Papers of the University of Alaska* 7(2): 113-116. Fairbanks.

——. 1963. "The Netsi Kutchin: An Essay in Human Ecology." Ph.D. dissertation, Louisiana State University. University Microfilms.

Whymper, Frederick. 1868. *Travel and Adventure in the Territory of Alaska.* London: John Murray.

Williams, Henry. 1976. *Vasaagihdzak.* Transcribed and translated by Moses P. Gabriel. Fairbanks: Alaska Native Language Center.